The David Lennox and William Murdoch
Family Histories

The David Lennox and William Murdoch Family Histories

Compiled and edited by Bette Ann Murdoch Christensen

*With assistance from Janet Romney Hull
and Janet Lennox Murdoch Wilson*

TEMPLE HILL BOOKS

ISBN 978-1-4341-0334-5

Copyright © 2011 by the James and Mary Murray Murdoch Family Organization. All rights reserved.

Printed in the United States of America. Published by Temple Hill Books, an imprint of The Editorium, LLC.

The content of this book does not necessarily represent the position or opinions of the publisher. The author (or authors) alone are responsible for its content. The reader alone is responsible for any use of its content.

The Editorium
West Valley City, Utah 84128-3917
www.templehillbooks.com
Editorium™ and Temple Hill Books™ are trademarks of the Editorium, LLC.

Contents

Contents	v
About the painting "The Passing of Mary Murray Murdoch"	vii
Introduction	xiii
Acknowledgments	xv
My Thoughts	xvii
1 James and Mary Murray Murdoch	1
2 Children of James and Mary Murray Murdoch	13
3 William and Janet Lennox Murdoch	47
4 David Lennox and Elizabeth Pinkerton Thyne Murdoch	59
5 William and Jeannette Cousins Smith Murdoch	161
6 David Lennox Murdoch and Ora Maurine Clark	215
7 Mary Smith Murdoch and Gordon L. Weggeland	361
8 John Thyne Murdoch and Ruth Streeper	369
9 Elizabeth Murdoch, George John Ross, and LeMoyne L. Hatch	379

10 Jeannette Murdoch and Wendell Bitner Romney	389
11 William Murdoch, Jr. and Lucy Deanne Parkinson Nibley	495
12 Ellen Jean Murdoch and David Jesse Buckwalter	513
13 Robert Gail Murdoch and Betty Lue Clark	521
14 LaVonne Bonnie Murdoch and John Granville Leonard, Jr.	623
Conclusion	639

About the painting "The Passing of Mary Murray Murdoch"

Comments by Clark Kelley Price on His Painting of Wee Granny

I have known about Wee Granny for a long time. I knew that my great great grandfather, James Steele and his wife, Elizabeth Wylie, visited with John Murray Murdoch and his wife, Ann Steele, who was James's sister, and introduced the gospel to them. I have always felt very close to James and Elizabeth and with their missionary connection to the Murdochs, I have likewise felt a closeness to them. Since Wee Granny came with James and Elizabeth and their family from Scotland and was part of their party in crossing the plains with the Martin Handcart Company, I have especially admired her.

I had a lot of help as I attempted to portray her in the painting. I examined very closely the pictures of her daughters that were in your Murdoch books. I had several pictures sent to me that portrayed family members. They were helpful, especially one that portrayed a daughter of John Murray Murdoch. I felt a great strength from the fasting and prayers of the Murdochs as well as the fasting and prayers that my wife, Irene, and I offered. We asked the Lord to bless me that I would know how best to portray her.

As I started to draw her, she came together very easily. I generally have a hard time portraying women but when she came so easily, I felt I was on the right track and had a very good feeling about her. I can't say I had a vision or actual knowledge of her appearance, but I felt I was blessed by the Lord because of everyone's fasting and prayers.

A few years ago, our stake had a three-day handcart experience. We built one and pushed and pulled it over difficult terrain. To make the trek more realistic, we went with minimal food. Although it was very difficult going, and I had to use crutches part of the way because of my bad hip, I gained some important spiritual insights through that experience and I think they helped me in doing the painting.

I prayed about who should be in the scene and I felt good about who I portrayed. I felt impressed that I should show the other handcarts in the distance, and that because of Wee Granny's difficulties, her group was left behind and were the last of her company. I also attempted to show that the weather was hot and dry and that it was late in the fall. I took great pains to show the struggle of those who were with her, both in their faces and in the clothing they wore. I took some liberty with the placement of Chimney Rock and also the bluffs, but I wanted them to be prominent landmarks in the scene. The trail was on the north side of Chimney Rock and she died some miles east of it, about 4:00 in the afternoon, facing toward Zion or toward the west. That is why James is shading her face from the late afternoon sun. That is also why she could say, "Tell John I died with my face toward Zion". The scene is portrayed as I came to know about the circumstances of her death and it received a confirmation of the Spirit.

"I have been asked repeatedly to write something about our ancestors, where they hailed from – what were their avocations, where they resided, etc. I fully realize unless this is at least attempted soon, the generation of people to which I belong will soon all have passed away and the succeeding generation will be left without much information pertaining to those times, circumstances, and events."

David Lennox Murdoch

To our wonderful grandparents, James and Mary Murray Murdoch. James, who gave his life in trying to save another, and Mary (also known as Wee Granny) who gave her life is trying to fulfill her dream of living in Zion. To them we will be forever grateful for their examples of service, dedication, and testimony of Christ-like love.

Introduction

This book is a collaboration of journals, pictures, and stories of James and Mary Murray Murdoch, William and Janet Lennox Murdoch, David Lennox and Elizabeth Pinkerton Thyne Murdoch and William and Jeannette Cousins Smith Murdoch. In 1982, the Murdoch Family Organization published a book titled "The James and Mary Murray Murdoch Family History." This book contains a very complete and organized compilation of the family histories of the descendants of James and Mary, also known as Wee Granny. Our great, great, great grandmother, Mary, was the first in the Murdoch family to join The Church of Jesus Christ of Latter-day Saints, and after having lived several years after her baptism in Scotland, was determined to join her son, John, already in Utah. Wee Granny, at the age of 74, is an example of someone willing to sacrifice all she had to join the Saints in Utah and fulfill her dream of going to Zion. As she lay dying on the plains of western Nebraska from exhaustion and age, her last words, "Tell John I died with my face toward Zion" are a testimony of her determination and an instruction to us, her descendants, to always focus on correct principles. Her story is also included in this book as we take our ancestors, Mary (Wee Granny), William, her son, and David Lennox, her grandson, from Scotland to America and onto Heber City, Utah. Our grandfather, William, is the son of David Lennox and is the first generation to be born in America.

We have asked the descendants of William and Jeannette to write their personal histories and include pictures. We decided to focus much of this book on our great grandfather, David Lennox Murdoch, because of a suitcase that his daughter, Afton, kept which contained his journals, letters and pictures. David Lennox was a very prolific writer and kept wonderful journals that included his "Writings of David Lennox Murdoch Journal" and his "Missionary Journal", both of which have his thoughts, experiences and much of his poetry. He was very much a thinker and had strong opinions about how life should be lived. David Lennox joined the Church or Jesus Christ of Latter-day Saints in Scotland and came to America with his wife, Elizabeth, and his father, William, in 1878 and settled in Heber City, Utah. He had a strong testimony of the Gospel of Jesus Christ and was called to serve a Church mission to Great Britian and was assigned to the Scottish Conference in 1905. He later became the President of the Scottish Conference in the latter part of his mission. His journals and poetry will enlighten you with an understanding into the life and thoughts of this very intelligent, yet humble servant of the Lord. We hope as you read and ponder this book, you will gain insight into the character and personality of David Lennox. As his descendants, hopefully we can glean from his experiences, integrity, and attributes and apply them to us, as we are sure, he would want us to. How fortunate we are to have as our ancestor, David Lennox Murdoch!

As cousins, we hope this book will tie us together as a family as we get to know each other through the personal histories that are shared. We hope you will gain an appreciation for the efforts and sacrifices that our ancestors have made. As we learn their histories, we can better get to know them and make our lives fuller in the process.

"THE JAMES AND MARY MURRAY MURDOCH FAMILY HISTORY" CONTAINS MANY FAMILY GROUP SHEETS OF OUR ANCESTORS. IN THE INTEREST OF SAVING SPACE IN THIS BOOK, I WOULD REFER YOU TO THAT BOOK FOR THOSE RESOURCES. IT IS AVAILABLE IN A SOFT COVER EDITION AT WWW.MURDOCHBOOKS.ORG. A CD-ROM OF THE BOOK IS AVAILABLE AT MURDOCHFAMILY.NET.

Acknowledgments

We so much appreciate all the support and help we have received in the process of putting this book together for the preservation of our heritage. The Murdoch family has a great history and as generations continue to come to pass, we felt a need to update and continue on with the family histories. In 1982, the Murdoch Organization published a book entitled, "The James and Mary Murray Murdoch Family History". This wonderful book gave a history of the Murdochs beginning with James and Mary Murray and continued down through their posterity and contained many wonderful pictures, stories, and the genealogy necessary to know our ancestors. Because of this book, we feel it necessary to continue on with more histories that will be of great value to generations yet to come. We would like to especially thank Dallas Murdoch for his hard work and constantly helping us with articles and information to make this book unique. We would also like to thank Jack Lyon for his wonderful expertise in the art of writing a book. We had no idea how that would happen, but because of his talents and gifts, we have been blessed to know what to do and how to do it. Thank you to all who have contributed their family histories to make this book as complete as we could get it. We have attempted to include the family histories of the children of William and Jeannette Cousins Smith Murdoch and their descendants but were unable to obtain some of the histories. We have tried to make this book as complete as we possibly could. Thank you one and all for what you have done and for catching the vision of the importance of the Murdoch family history

My Thoughts

By Bette Ann Murdoch Christensen

When I was asked to gather the family histories of my Murdoch cousins and their children, I was happy to do it and as a result became the editor of this book, gathering and compiling information on the David Lennox Murdoch family and the William Murdoch family and their descendants. There have been many trials and blessings associated with putting the book together; however, the miracles that have occurred along the way have been humbling, indeed.

Trials include: an old computer (finally blessed with a new one), finding the right program for a novice to use to put a book like this together, a major program crash, learning how to use different programs with *author styles* to make the book uniform, putting in all the pictures, who knows how many hours sitting at the computer, a sore back and tired eyes. Well, let's just say it has been challenging but well worth the effort.

Blessings include: talking to cousins I haven't heard from in years, gathering stories and pictures of our ancestors, learning about their struggles and successes and how I can apply them to my life, answers to prayers that make me aware of the importance of a book like this, a very patient and understanding husband, Wynn, whose constant help and encouragement has made this more possible than anyone can imagine, and too many others to list.

Many miracles have happened: finding an article on the death of James Murdoch from 1831, transcribing histories of David Lennox Murdoch from his actual journals because of the acquisition of the suitcase his daughter had used to gather all of his writings into one place, having questions answered through prayer and personal revelation, finding stories and articles to enhance the information on our ancestors, and having the actual funeral notes of William and Jeannette Murdoch.

Many times I have knelt down by my chair to offer up a prayer asking for help to put my thoughts into words when I seem stuck and can't go on. When I am at the computer again, the thoughts flow and I know I my humble prayer was answered. Too many times to count, a thought came to my mind about what I should be working on next to put into the book. Usually I was not at the computer, but when I did get there, I still remembered with detail what I needed to do.

Many of the journals and stories have taken me many long hours to transcribe. I have tried to make this book accurate and without assumption. History can tell its own story and thus, this book has done just that. The transcriptions of the many journals and poems of David Lennox have been done as accurately as possible. He was truly an amazing man and I have grown to love and appreciate him, his many talents, and his firm testimony of the gospel of Jesus Christ.

This book would have been impossible without the help of my dear cousins, Janet Murdoch Wilson and Janet Romney Hull. Dallas Murdoch has constantly encouraged and given me information to make it as accurate and informative as possible. Jack Lyon, who has been blessed with the patience of Job, has guided me through many a rough time as we worked to get this book ready for publication. My daughter, Jennifer Christensen Johnson, who through the miracle of email attachments, has helped me fix many pictures that were beyond my ability.

I pray that you will read this book with the intent of learning more about your Murdoch ancestors, their testimonies of Jesus Christ, their dedication to their families, and their examples of love and sacrifice. How blessed we are to be the descendants of James and Mary Murray Murdoch, William and Janet Lennox Murdoch, David Lennox and Elizabeth Pinkerton Thyne Murdoch, and William and Jeannette Cousins Smith Murdoch! May the lessons learned from them be carried on through our own lives as we pass this onto the next generation.

Chapter 1

James and Mary Murray Murdoch

Their Stories and Their Children

James Murdoch was born about 1786 at Commondyke, Ayrshire, Scotland to James Murdoch and Janet Osborne. The village of Commondyke was between Auchinleck (pronounced Affleck) and Lugar. We don't know much about James' childhood but because of where he lived and the laws at the time, there is a good possibility that he began working in the mines at an early age. This area was covered with mines, called collieries, and many young men started working in them at an early age, some eight years and younger. Prior to 1799 and for over 200 years, colliers, (the working men) with their women and young children, were all slaves to the mines by order of Parliament. They were forced to sign contracts by mine owners which committed them to work in a particular mine for life and it was considered slavery. The colliers had no voice or rights and the deplorable conditions continued until 1799, when the law was repealed and their servitude was changed by an act of Parliament from one of slavery to the mines by the strict contracts, to freedom to work where they pleased.[1] There were many coal mines in the area of Commondyke and we don't know if James worked in the coal mines as well as the limestone mines, but the likelihood is great. Miners were paid according to the going rate of the price of coal, or limestone, in James' case. The going wages in 1836 (just after James' death) for a coal miner was 5 schillings per day.[2] Much of the money earned went to the rent toward the row housing provided by the mine owners where the miners and their families lived. Men received a higher wage than the women and children workers. According to several journals written by the Murdochs, James worked in the Lime Work Mine in Gaswater, or Grasswater, at the time of his death. Limestone

---

1. http://www.scottish-history.com, accessed 8 March 2010
2. www.scottishmining.co.uk, accessed 17 March 2010.

1

quarries were common in this region of Ayrshire, Scotland and lime kilns were built to process the limestone into a product to improve the soil for farming. Later, it was determined that the quality of the limestone was not as good as other places and the depth of the quarries was more shallow than expected. As time went on, the process became more industrialized and the kilns and the quarries were abandoned. The small villages and towns that depended on the mines were also abandoned which is why Gaswater (Grasswater) and Commondyke are no longer in existence.

Mary Murray was born October 13, 1782 in Glencairn, Dumfries, Scotland. Glencairn is located in Dumfriesshire County and is south of Ayrshire County, where she lived with James and her children. We don't know what her father did to provide for the family, but the likelyhood of him being a farmer, as were most of the people in that area, is pretty great and considering the resourcefulness of Mary, it is a good possibility. Her parents were John Murray and Margaret McCall. We don't have much information on Mary, her parents, her childhood or even how she met James. From an old book with a description of the area, written in the very early 1800s, a description of the life of the people in Glencairn is depicted as one of comfort.

> "The land in general is good. The homes and meadows upon the sides of the rivers, are fertile. Next to these, on the rising grounds, there is a light, warm, kindly, arable soil; and, in the highest parts, there is fine pasture for all sorts of cattle, particularly sheep. The rivers are very rapid, and often overflow their banks, to the great damage of the land adjacent.
>
> "The people are, in general, healthy; and several now alive, as well as others lately dead, have arrived at 80 years of age, and upwards. Their houses and dress, of late, have been much improved; and, in the latter of these respects, people of every class seem to be running into an extreme. The manners of the people, in general, are very agreeable, mild, courteous, and obliging; and they are distinguished for hospitality, and natural civility to strangers. . . . . . The diseases, which prevail most, are rheumatisms, and pains in the stomach and bowels; owing, perhaps to the low and damp situation of their houses, most of which are placed too near the rivers. — The water is of an excellent quality; light, clear, and soft. The streams abound with trout, as the hills do with game."[3]

We don't know how these two met because Mary was from Dumfriesshire, a southern county, and James was from Ayrshire County. They were married on 10 January 1811 in Auchinleck, Ayrshire, Scotland. The first child, Janet, was born on 8 December 1811 in Boghead, Ayrshire. This little town is located east of Auchinleck and still exists today. Their second child, Mary, was born on 16 June 1813, also in Boghead and sadly, died as an infant or child. We don't have any information on her death. The third child was James. He was born on 29 July 1814 in Gaswater. Sometime

---

3. The Statistical Account of Scotland 1791-99 vol.2 p.343 : Glencairn, County of Dumfries, accessed on 17 March 2010.

between the births of Mary and James, they moved to Gaswater. Veronica was born on 16 June 1816 also in Gaswater. Mary was the fifth child to be born to this growing family on 3 October 1818. (It was very common when a child died earlier to the family, that they used the name again, which is the case with this Mary.) John Murray was born on 28 December 1820 in Gaswater. Their seventh child was Margaret who was born on 30 December 1822. Margaret died as a child or infant and we have no records of her death. Their eighth child, William, was born 3 July 1825 in Gaswater.

James and Mary lived in the housing provided by the mines which were called *miners rows*. It was by far the most convenient because of the location close to the mines but the living conditions were not necessarily the best. They were very small and with six children, it must have been very crowded. James was employed as a miner at the Lime Works in Gaswater, Ayrshire and died, sadly, trying to save another. He was about 45 years old. The following account is from a journal of David Lennox Murdoch, his grandson.

> *The son of a farmer at a place called Dalfad, happened around and his curiosity, or something of that nature, produced a desire within him to be lowered into a new shaft which had been lately sunk. The pits at this early date in this neighborhood were all sunk on the out-croppings of the mineral field – not deep, but on the contrary, very shallow and operated by a windlass. The Boy went down and was overcome by foul air or choke damp which had accumulated at the bottom and he fell helplessly out of the bucket and whatever it was [he was in]. The alarm was given and Grandfather was lowered down to his rescue, but he also was overcome in a similar manner. By the time the efforts were made to disperse the damp and foul air and bring the bodies to the surface, life in both instances was gone – and thus the lives of two had been snuffed out in a few minutes. The father, that provided [for] this little family was thus taken and we can imagine what a sad and sorrowful little home it was.* [4]

The following article was published in the *Scotsman Newspaper* on 2 November 1831 and tells of the accident. It provides valuable information, that was previously unknown, as to the details of this tragedy.

> *21 October 1831*
> Two Men Suffocated – On Friday last, the 21st ult., at Grasswater Limeworks, in the parish of Auchinleck, two young men of the name of Baird, sons of a farmer in the neighbourhood, came to a coalpit, five fathoms deep, that was sinking. One prevailed on the other to let him down the pit to see it; but, when near the bottom, he fell down, from the effects of the chokedamp. The brother gave the alarm, when a man of the name of Murdoch came to his assistance, and went down the pit, but he shared the same fate. David M'Leod, another man now went down, and he also shared the same fate. James Davidson, a third person, next went down but before reaching the bottom, he called out to be taken up. He got a rope fixed round his body and attempted it again, but did not succeed. A fire was got and let down into the pit and one of them was heard to

---

4. From the David Lennox Murdoch Journal, "Murdoch History"

moan. The smoke was quite close in the pit and nothing could be seen. However, when the windlass was turned it was found some of the three persons below were attached to the rope, and when the windlass was hoisted to a certain height, there appeared but one of the men, David M'Leod, hanging by one hand to the rope. He was immediately rescued by the people at the pit mouth. The other two men were dead before they could be got out. We understand Murdoch has left a wife and young family to lament his loss. M'Leod recovered so far as to be able to walk home to Auchinleck in the evening. [Scotsman 2 November 1831] [5]

This newspaper article states that James died on Friday, October 21, 1831. David Lennox's journals (and other journals) state the death date as October 20, 1831. We will never know for sure, but if James did die on a Friday, then the October 21 date is the correct date according to the 1831 calendar. None of the journals state the day of the week of his death. The term *chokedamp*, as used in this article, refers to the fact that the mine atmosphere is low in oxygen and high in carbon dioxide and other toxic gasses which causes choking.

Mary was left alone to care for her family. None of her children were married yet, so the burden of being the provider fell on her shoulders. William was just six years old at the time of his father's death and the family had taken in Margaret Murray, Mary's niece, who became an orphan with her parents' deaths. As mentioned before, the family was renting a row house from the Lime Works, James' employer, and the family needed to move. We learn from journals that James and his younger brother, John, helped to build a thatched roof, stone cottage for the family a few years after James' death. It is also mentioned that through the kindness of neighbors, this little house was completed.

In 1907, William Lindsay (husband of Mary Mair, daughter of Mary Murdoch Mair) visited Ayrshire and saw the ruins of Wee Granny's cottage. He also saw the spot where James Murdoch lost his life. The shaft in which he died was just a new one and was about twenty-five feet deep, but after the tragedy it was never sunk any deeper, but was allowed to cave in and fill up. The depression was about five feet deep and had wild daisies growing in it. [6]

In order to survive and provide for the family, most of the Murdoch children had to be sent out of the home to work. This area of Ayrshire had farms as well as mines. Times were very difficult, but they managed to survive with many meals consisting only of potatoes and salt.

Mary was about four feet seven inches tall and is described by Janet Lennox Murdoch (wife of William) in David Lennox's journal as "strongly built". She had blue-gray eyes, a medium complexion and weighed a little over 90 pounds. Being a very poor family, she did her best and was hard

---

5. http://www.scottishmining.co.uk/320.html, accessed June 2010
6. The James and Mary Murray Murdoch Family History, p. 52

working, frugal and thrifty. The sudden death of her husband caused Mary much grief and sorrow.

In 1850, missionaries from the Church of Jesus Christ of Latter-day Saints came to Scotland preaching the restored gospel. John, who was married to Ann Steele, readily accepted it and shared it with Wee Granny and Mary, her daughter, who were also convinced of its truth. They were baptized into the church when Wee Granny was sixty-seven years old. Later Veronica and William were baptized. These four children, John, Mary, Veronica and William all immigrated to Utah.

In 1852, John and his wife, Ann Steele, took their two young children and immigrated to Utah.[7] In 1856, he sent Wee Granny the money she needed to come to Zion. She was 73 years of age when she started on the long 6,000-mile journey. She traveled with her daughter-in-law's brother, James Steele, his wife Elizabeth, their two young sons, James Ephraim and William George, and Mary Ann Wylie, Elizabeth's mother. They left Liverpool, England on 25 May 1856 and sailed on the ship *Horizon*. Mary was very determined to accomplish what she deemed was right. She loved the gospel, and her desire was to be with her son and the saints in Zion was her driving force. In 1856, the Mormon immigrants began arriving in Boston, Massachusetts and were transported by railroad to Iowa City, Iowa. They no longer had to make the long journey to New Orleans, up the Mississippi River to St. Louis, then onto Council Bluffs on the Missouri River, which is the route John Murray Murdoch took when he immigrated in 1852.

When the Steeles and Wee Granny arrived at Iowa City, they were assigned to the Martin Handcart Company. Edward Martin was on the ship just returning from a three year mission to Great Britain and had also been a member of the Mormon Battalion. He was asked to be the leader of a company of saints. There were five companies to leave in the summer of 1856. The first three arrived safely in Salt Lake City with little difficulty, but the Martin and Willie Handcart Companies met with tragedy. Because wagons and oxen were slow moving and very expensive, these groups used handcarts they could pull themselves with the idea that they could walk faster than slow oxen. Because the handcarts and tents were not ready, the Martin and Willie companies were forced to wait until late July. They were advised not to make the trek so late in the season, but it was their desire to go.

The Martin Company was the last to leave and was made up on 575 people, 145 handcarts and eight wagons.[8] This group was made up largely of immigrants from England and Scotland and had the largest number of old, young and handicapped of any of the handcart companies that left that

---

7. See John Murray Murdoch History
8. www.lds.org/church history/pioneercompany, accessed 18 March 2010.

year. Of course, there were many ages represented, but our Wee Granny was one of the oldest at 73 years of age with two others 75. There were also many who had large and young families. They left Iowa City on July 28, 1856 and it was a month later that they left Florence, Nebraska, the last settlement for hundreds of miles. Their hastily constructed handcarts were made of unseasoned wood and they fell to pieces in the hot prairie sun. Repairing them on the trail meant losing valuable travel time. Their food became scarce and they were weakened by the lack of nourishment. They were improperly clad for the inclement weather. An early and severe winter had set in. By September, there were heavy frosts. Of the 575 members of the company, almost one fourth of them died before they reached Utah. They were buried in shallow graves, usually wrapped only in a sheet, or many times without anything. Sometimes a common grave was dug and all who died that day were buried together. Some poor souls were buried in a bank of snow. Much has been written of the handcart pioneers and their history is Wee Granny's history.

Our Wee Granny died on October 2, 1856. Thankfully she did not have to endure the early snow storm that hit the company less than a month later. James Steele, with whom she traveled, died November 10, 1856, on the cold Wyoming trail. The rest of his family finally made it Salt Lake City.

In a journal written by John Jacques, also a member of the Martin Handcart Company, he notes the following:

> "Oct. 2 - Mary Murdock, age 72, Scotland, died of diarrhea at 4 p.m., buried 10 miles east of Chimney Rock". (On page 140 of this same journal, he makes the following entry), "Thurs. 2: Hot day. Fri. 3: Hot day. Left camp about 7 a.m. . . . Baited opposite Chimney Rock, east of a low bluff, close to the river. Traveled about 17 miles".[9]

From this journal entry, we know that Mary died about 4:00 P.M. on October 2, 1856 about 10 miles east of Chimney Rock, Nebraska on a hot and dry day. She was just eleven day's shy of her 74th birthday. She had walked nearly 700 miles before her exhausted and weak body gave out. Her last words to the Steele family were, "Tell John I died with my face toward Zion." As depicted in the Clark Kelley Price picture of her death, we can visualize the types of conditions that existed at her passing. Our Wee Granny was buried next to the trail in a shallow, probably unmarked grave.

We can only imagine the kind of person who would leave their beloved homeland and with all she was familiar, to travel to a far-away place to be with her son, his family, and the saints in Zion. She is a true example of someone who was determined to do what she knew to be right and gave her life in the process.

What can we learn from her story? Perhaps she wants us to all know of her love of the Gospel of Jesus Christ; that she was willing to do whatever

---

9. "Life History and Writings of John Jacques", p. 306, p. 140.

necessary to go to the land of Zion because she had a vision of what she wanted to achieve. Perhaps she wants us to know that determination was an important characteristic to her and that by following her example, we can be on the right path to our goals. Perhaps she wants us to have hope and faith in ourselves and the Lord will provide the rest. Even though she died before living in Zion, as her descendants, we find her story to be one of inspiration. We can all look up to our wonderful Wee Granny for the many lessons she has taught us.

JAMES AND MARY WERE THE PARENTS OF EIGHT CHILDREN:
Janet, born 8 December 1811, died 28 June 1866
Mary, born 16 June 1813, died as a child
James, born 29 July 1814, died 12 September 1884
Veronica, born 16 June 1816, died 4 October 1908
Mary, born 3 October 1818, died 5 December 1900
John Murray, born 28 December 1820, died 6 May 1910
Margaret, born 30 December 1822, died as a child
William, born 3 July 1825, died 12 March 1913

Sunrise at Chimney Rock

What solemn thoughts pervade the soul
As on this scene we meditate,
This resting place for wearied Saints
Tired, travel stained, and desolate.
This scene portrays in vivid ways
A spot made dear on journey drear
By handcart means in early days,
A halfway place on journey here.
Impelled by faith and filled with hope
That soon they'd reach the appointed place
Inured to toil, with trials cope,
To Utah's vales they set their face.
But some along this dreary road
Worn out and faint, oft fell asleep
Ere they could reach the cherished spot
The Valley dear and friends to greet.
Brave honest souls at early morn
As pilgrims in a holy cause
Who dared to face a world of scorn
To obey God's call and keep his laws.
Somewhere around the stopping place
As years go by—'tis fifty-seven—
Wee Granny died. There is no trace
Of earth's abode; her soul's in Heaven.
"Tell John," she said as she lay down
Her worn-out frame in this lone place,
"That I died here, but with my face
Turned Zionwards, the cherished place."
Blest be their names with fondest love.
We'll cherish aye their mem'ries dear,
Soon we may meet with them above
And greet them in their higher sphere.

David L. Murdoch December 24, 1913

The James Steele Story

EDITOR'S NOTE - *James Steele played a major roll in Mary Murray Murdoch's (Wee Granny) life as she traveled to Utah. He is the brother of Ann Steele, who was married to John Murray Murdoch (Wee Granny's son). John and Ann were already in Utah when Mary left with the Steeles' on their journey to Utah. James, Elizabeth, their two sons, James Ephriaim and William George, and Elizabeth's mother, Mary Ann Wylie, were Wee Granny's traveling companions for the journey. Because of this, we felt it important to include a part of his history in this book.*

James Steele was born on 25 June 1826 in Kirkconnell, Dumfries, Scotland to Elizabeth Kerr and James Steele. Elizabeth Wylie was born on 27 February 1827 in Johnston, Ayrshire, Scotland to Mary Ann George and Oliver Wylie. James and Elizabeth married on 24 August 1851 in Manchester, Lancashire, England. They had three children: James Ephraim Steele was born 22 June 1852 in Manchester, Lancashire, England, a daughter born about 1853 in Manchester, Lancashire, England and died as an infant, and William George Steele who was born 19 January 1855 in Manchester, Lancashire, England.

James Steele, his parents and their family were living in England in the early 1850s, although all had been born in Scotland. James met Elizabeth Wylie, who had joined the Church of Jesus Christ of Latter-day Saints in 1844. She introduced the gospel to James and he readily accepted it and was baptized in 1849.

> "At an ourdoor meeting in Glasgow, Scotland, Robert Kirkwood, a Mormon Elder, had just finished speaking and Ralph Rolly, another Elder, was bearing testimony about Joseph Smith and the restoration of the gospel. The crowd threatened to throw the Elders into the river. Rovert Patrick stepped forward and said, "You shall not harm these men." A man named James Steele joined with him in protecting the missionaries until they could retire from the scene." This occurred about December 24, 1851.[10]

James' sister, Ann, married John Murray Murdoch on February 25, 1848 at Auchinleck, Ayrshire, Scotland. It is speculated that the Murdochs knew the Steele and Wylie families well, possibly because of the marriage connections.

James had returned to Scotland to tell his sister, Ann, and brother-in-law, John Murray Murdoch, about the gospel of Jesus Christ being restored to the earth and that a young man by the name of Joseph Smith had seen God and Jesus Christ and talked with them face to face. God called Joseph as the prophet of this dispensation, to prepare the world for the second coming of the Savior, Jesus Christ. Joseph Smith had translated a sacred record and the Book of Mormon was carried by missionaries as they preached the gospel.

---

10. *The LDS Biographical Encyclopedia*, Vol. 1, page 665

Members of the church were beginning to gather in America and settle in Utah, away from the persecutions in Illinois and Missouri. John Murray Murdoch and his wife, Ann Steele, knew they needed to migrate to Utah and John answered the call that Brigham Young, President of the Church, wanted a Scottish shepherd to care for his sheep. John and Ann promised James, Elizabeth and Mary Murray Murdoch, that they would save their money and send it to them for their journey to Utah. After a long and difficult journey, John and Ann arrived in Salt Lake on September 3, 1852.

In 1856, John and Ann sent the money James, Elizabeth, their two sons, Mary Ann and Mary Murray Murdoch needed for their trip to Utah. They left England on May 25, 1856 on the ship *Horizon* and arrived in New York on July 8, 1856. After taking a train to Iowa City, they were assigned to be in the Martin Handcart Company, which left late in the season to be walking all the way to Utah. They encountered many challenges along the way including food becoming low and people becoming very tired. A few miles above Grand Island, Nebraska, they encountered a large herd of buffalo. One evening, the buffalo scattered the cattle. It took three days to round up the cattle. Some of the people lost their milk cows as well as some of their beef cattle. Some lost their oxen. This created a hardship in the way of food they needed for their daily well being, as well as making a hardship on the oxen that were left. The supplies they were expecting hadn't arrived. They were traveling along the Platte River and the nights were getting cold. They could see snow on the mountains ahead of them and they knew they needed to pick up their pace. They left many of their belongings along the side of the trail to lighten their load.

The lack of food and difficult walk made the journey unbearable to some and they began to die along the trail. Mary Murray Murdoch (Wee Granny) was one who passed away just a few miles from Chimney Rock, Nebraska. Her journey complete in life, she told James, Elizabeth, Mary Ann and the children, "Tell John I died with my face toward Zion"

On 8 October 1856, they reached Laramie, Wyoming. They rested but worried a great deal because their provisions were very low. Feeding the company enough to give them the energy to walk became a great concern. Many in the group went to the Fort and sold their watches and jewelry for the provisions they needed.

An early storm came up, which was unusual for early October and the travelers were unprepared for this type of weather. They had lightened their load to enable them to move faster pulling the handcarts but in the process threw out valuable clothing that could protect them from the cold weather. Around the 19th of October, they reached the last crossing of the Platte River, near the Red Buttes and a little west of what is now Casper, Wyoming. Here two wagon trains caught up with the Martin Handcart Company and helped the weary travelers cross the river. The river was wide and the current was strong. The water was exceedingly cold and as they crossed, the snow and wind made for treacherous conditions.

About twelve miles above the last crossing of the Platte River, the company was snowed in and came to a standstill. Deaths continued in the camp. James Steele worked hard to keep his family alive and as warm as he could. It must have so difficult to see your little family suffer as his did. After arriving at Devil's Gate on 3 November, James and his family were really feeling the effects of the conditions and on 10 November 1856, James Steele died at Bitter Creek, Wyoming.

Clark Kelly Price, great, great grandson of James Steele, relates that in the summer of 1997, he visited Martin's Cove in Wyoming. This is where the handcart company took refuge and is now an LDS historic site and has the Martin's Cove Visitor's Center. While there, he spent considerable time trying to locate the actual spot where James Steele died. He found that the nearest creek on the map named Bitter Creek was too far away to be considered. There was a creek near Martin's Cove named Cottonwood Creek that seemed to be in a reasonable location. In speaking to the resident citizens of the area, they related that the creek used to be referred to as Cottonwood Bitter Creek. He felt this creek was most likely the place where James Steele died. He also related that according to the family tradition, Ephraim Hanks, one of the rescuers from Salt Lake City, came into camp with buffalo meat on his horse for the stricken Saints the night that James Steele died. James had been giving his portion of food to his wife and children and, in spite of the arrival of buffalo meat, he was unable to survive and died.

Elizabeth Wylie Steele and her two sons, James Ephraim and William George, survived and traveled on to Salt Lake City. Elizabeth remarried David Wood and died in American Fork, Utah in 1901. James Ephraim grew up, married, and moved to Iona, Idaho. He died in 1829 and is buried in Iona. William George grew up in American Fork, married and also moved to Idaho. He died in 1917 in Idaho Falls and is buried in Iona, Idaho.

Chapter 2

Children of James and Mary Murray Murdoch

EDITOR'S NOTE: As you read through these histories of the children of James and Mary, you will probably notice they had two daughters that they named Mary. It was very common that if a child died, especially very young, the parents used the name again on another child. Mary was born June 16, 1813 and died. They later named another daughter Mary who was born October 3, 1818.

JANET MURDOCH SMITH

Janet Murdoch Smith was the first child of James and Mary Murray Murdoch and was born December 8, 1811, in Boghead, Ayrshire, Scotland. She was probably named after her grandmother Janet Osborne Murdoch, the wife of James Murdoch, her father's father.

Being the oldest, much was expected of Janet in helping the family live in such meager times. She helped in the care of seven other children born to the family. She was probably sent out to work on nearby farms as soon as she was old enough to do so, as were her younger brothers and sisters James, Veronica, Mary, John Murray Murdoch, and William.

Her father, James, being a miner, died in a mine shaft on October 20, 1831, when trying to rescue a young man who had gone down into the pit and was overcome by the foul gas called "black damp."

Two years later, on December 20, 1833, Janet, at about the age of twenty-two, married an Alexander Smith, who is listed as a coal miner in the 1851 and 1861 Scottish census. Janet was listed as a handsewer. Our present records say they were the parents of twelve children. Two children died under age eight and five more under the age of thirty-one. Janet died on June 28, 1866, of heart disease at only fifty-four years of age. Her youngest child would have been ten at this time. Alexander, her husband, died in about 1876 in Glasgow, Lanark, Scotland.[1]

David Lennox Murdoch, son of William Murdoch, wrote in his missionary journal in 1906, the following concerning the family:

> "Aunt Jennie, the oldest, married Alex Smith, lived in Birnieknowe about three miles from Grasswater. She had quite a family and was in rather poor circumstances the most of her life. Her husband—a good man,—but rather delicate and asthmatical. A son, William, whom I knew in Glasgow, imigrated to the state of Washington some number of years after we came. He and his wife are now gone, but they have left up there several sons and at least one daughter." (From his Writings about Murdochs.)

MARY MURDOCH

Mary was born June 16, 1813 in Boghead, Ayrshire, Scotland. She died as a child in Ayrshire, Scotland. We don't have any records or information of her cause of death or the death date.

JAMES MURDOCH

James Murdoch was the third of eight children born to James and Mary Murray Murdoch. He was born on July 29, 1814, in Gaswater, Ayrshire, Scotland. He no doubt was named after his father and grandfather, being the first son in the family. He was seventeen years old when his father lost his life in the mining accident. Being the eldest son, he probably had been working for several years to earn his own keep and assist the family in those meager times.

John Murray Murdoch, in his own history, mentions James helping build a cottage for Mary Murray Murdoch (Wee Granny) and the rest of her family in the years following their father's death. He also said that he worked for his brother James doing repairs on a mine at Lugar in 1851.

James married when he was twenty seven.. He married Margaret McCall on November 24, 1841, at Leadhills, Dumfrewshire, Scotland. Margaret is said also to have been born there about 1820.

Before November 7, 1853, James moved his family to Glasgow, Lanark, Scotland. This was the date of his son Thomas's birth in Glasgow. Here on August 26, 1854, he and Margaret were to experience the death of their six-year old son, William. This was only the beginning of sorrow for them,

---

1. FROM GENEALOGICAL SOCIETY LIBRARY FILM #103–651 A-B AND FILM #103–799 A DATED 1851 AND 1862 RESPECTIVELY, WE HAVE A RECORD OF THE CHILDREN OF ALEXANDER SMITH AND JANET SMITH LISTED AS ROBERT—SON 10, JAMES—SON 8, JOHN—SON 6, MARY—DAUGHTER 4, AND ON THE 1861 CENSUS WE FIND LISTED BESIDES ALEXANDER SMITH AND WIFE JANET, MARY—DAUGHTER 14, STEWART—SON 10, AND ALEXANDER—SON 5.

as four other sons died, all of which were under the age of twenty-seven and they preceded James in death, as did his wife. They were the parents of nine sons.

David Lennox Murdoch said about James:

"James married Margaret McCall. They had a large family and lived in Glasgow. I think they all must be gone now as I could get no trace of any of them while over there 1905–06–07 altho I even advertised in the paper for them. A son William (second) came here and lived for a time in Heber City and Park City. He died in this city and was burried in the City Cemetery."

Margaret McCall is said to have died about 1880 in Scotland, and James on 12 September 1884, at seventy years of age in Glasgow, Lanarkshire, Scotland. From the letter printed from James to his nephew David Lennox Murdoch written on December 16, 1878 we sense a loneliness.

"I hope you are all in good health and that it is not trouble or want of time that some of you are not minding old Jamie that you have left behind with a bit letter at a time to cheer up his cast down spirits, you don't know how glad I am in a morning when my Laird comes up to my door with a letter in his hand saying its an American."

James was now alone except for nieces and nephews from the Smith family and his sons, perhaps James, John, Thomas, William, and George, who we do not have death dates. His mother and his only living sisters and brothers and their families had all gone to America.

Neither James nor any of his sons ever joined the Church as his mother, two sisters, and two brothers did.

VERONICA MURDOCH CALDOW GILES

Excerpt from a history written by Veronica's niece, Lizziebell Murdoch Davis

Veronica Murdoch, daughter of James and Mary Murray Murdoch, was born 16 June 1816, at Gaswater, Ayrshire, Scotland, the fourth child in a family of eight. She was christened 30 June 1816, at Auchinleck Parish Church.

When her father, James, died in a mining accident, the children who were old enough to work had to help in every way possible to assist their widowed mother. Veronica adapted herself to all kinds of hard work. She was not able to attend school regularly but took advantage of every opportunity to learn. She was a constant reader and retained well what she read.

She married George Caldow on February 15, 1839. She was the mother of eleven children: Mary, George, James, John, Alexander, William, Thomas, Joseph, David, Brigham, and Nephi. She was left a widow and worked diligently to raise her family and provide for their needs.

Her brother, John Murray, was the first of her family to join the Church of Jesus Christ of Latter-day Saints and was soon followed by his mother, Mary Murray Murdoch, his sisters, Mary and Veronica, and sister-in-law Janet Lennox Murdoch, who was married to her brother, William.

John Murray Murdoch and his family were the first to come to Utah in January 1852. Veronica's sister, Mary Mair, came next in 1866. In 1878, her brother William and his family made plans to come to Utah, and arrangements were made for her to come with him, he being responsible for her and paying her way. Her family was agreeable to her coming, thinking it best for her to be with her brothers and sister in Utah and with the body of the church she had joined. She was in straitened circumstances and at the age of sixty two, suitable work was hard to find in Scotland. I am sure that she had thought that at some future time at least part of her family would join her, but this was not to be.   In 1878, Veronica traveled with her brother, William, his daughters, Margaret and Janet, William's son and daughter-in-law, David Lennox and Elizabeth Pinkerton Thyne Murdoch and John Adamson.

Veronica married Thomas Giles on July 3, 1879 and her life with him was a pleasant one. When he died several years later, he left moderate means to take care of her needs. She had a pleasant disposition and with her bit of humor and Scotch brogue, fit in to all occasions. After she was again left a widow, she lived alone for several years.

Aunt Vachey did some knitting but her main pastime was sewing carpet rags for people. She always kept busy. Auntie liked to tell jokes on herself. I remember her telling of going to the doctor. She had been bothered with a chest pain and went to have an examination. She told the doctor how miserable the pain was and also said, "I feel like there is something living about me." When she unbuttoned the tight quilted basque she was wearing, a poor little mouse jumped out. She and the doctor had a good laugh. He said, "'Sure enough Auntie, there was something living about you."

The dear old soul must have had many hours of loneliness thinking of the family in Scotland. I am sure that in the beginning she had hopes that they too would come to Zion. Now her only hope was to meet them in their eternal home. She was not one to burden others with her heartaches and woes. She went on about each day's duties keeping silent on any unpleasant thought.

To know her was to love her. Her last days were with her nephew, Andrew Mair, and his good wife, Mary Ann. She passed away at their home October 4, 1908. Her funeral service was held in the Wasatch Stake House. Burial was in the Heber City Cemetery.

She was baptized September, 1852, and was rebaptized July 28, 1878.

She was endowed July 3, 1879, in the Endowment House. She was sealed to Thomas Giles July 3, 1879.

EDITORS NOTE: *Veronica was supposedly the mother of eleven children, namely Mary, George, James, John, Alexander, William, Thomas, Joseph, David, Brigham and Nephi. (Genealogical sheets done by Ruby Hooper) David Lennox Murdoch said the following about her family in his writings about Murdochs in his* Missionary Journal 1905–6-7, *in Scotland. "Aunt Veronica was another member of that family from Grasswater and the Mother of a large family by her husband George Caldow in Scotland. She saw hard times, trials, and difficulties and poverty being a widow alone, her family having all married but one. He was old enough to be almost a Grandfather, she was immigrated and came with us in 1878." "Sept. 10, 1906: While in Cumnock, I hunted up where Cousin Mary Caldow Baird used to live and found a daughter, a Mrs. Nichol, living not far from there. I had a talk with her. Her father is living, her Uncle George, unmarried, lives with him. Her Uncle John lives at Burubank, a widower with a family. Her Uncle James lives at Mauchline. She promised to write to her Grannie, Aunt Vachey, in Heber City and to let her know all about her relatives."*

MARY MURDOCH MAIR MCMILLAN

Excerpts from Family histories by Phil Rasmussen and others

Mary Murdoch Mair McMillan was the fourth daughter and fifth child of James and Mary Murray Murdoch. She was born at Gaswater, Ayrshire, Scotland, 3 October 1818. Because her father died when she was only 12 years old, she was compelled to go out to work for other people to help support the struggling family. The Murdochs lived in a farming area and this is where Mary was employed. She learned much about farming and was a very hard worker.

Mary helped knit the family's stockings, most likely learning from her mother. During the winter, she attended school but did not attend for very many years. She did learn to read, write, spell, and she learned to count. Thus she grew to be a strong and healthy young woman, quite efficient in all kinds of women's work and as such, with a cheerful disposition, she attracted the attention of the young men in that neighborhood. When she was about twenty-two years of age, she married a very steady young man, Allan Mair, who grew up with her in the little village.

Allan and Mary were soon comfortably settled down in a little cottage and were happy and contented with their lot in life. This was about 1840. In 1841 their oldest child, John, was born and in a very few years they had quite a little family to provide for. They had a total of nine children. They were both hardworking and saved what means came into their hands, and of course got along very well and seemed to be prospering nicely.

This was a strictly religious community where practically everybody attended church, and the Sabbath day was very strictly observed by all. In 1850, the Mormon elders came preaching the restored gospel of Jesus Christ in their vicinity, and not long after, Mary's brother, John Murray, and his wife, Ann Steele, became interested in their doctrines and after due consideration were baptized. Mary, having recently lost two of her children, Matthew and William, in infancy, readily accepted their doctrine of the Plan of Salvation and life after death. She tried hard to convince her husband of the truth of Mormonism too, but he could not see the need of making a change in his religion. Mary went ahead and was baptized on June 4, 1851, by William Aird, and was confirmed by John Drennan on the same date. Her mother, Mary Murray, her sister, Veronica, and brother William's wife, Janet Lennox, also joined the Church within the next two years.

Because of Mary's affiliation with this new religion, some contention began to develop that disrupted the harmony in their home. She could not convince her husband and children of the truthfulness of the restored gospel, much to her great sorrow. There also arose a spirit of persecution by former friends and neighbors against those who had joined the Mormon Church. Mary felt quite alone and could not discuss anything about the gospel with her family; however, in David Lennox Murdoch's journal, he recorded that she had many long talks with his mother, Janet Lennox Murdoch.

About 1865, Mary's two oldest sons left home and went to Maryland, in the United States, hoping to better their conditions financially, and her third son was making preparations to be married. She still had three children at home, Mary, thirteen; Andrew, ten; and Alexander, six; three children having by now died in infancy. She grieved that her children were growing up in ignorance of the truths of the gospel, which she could not even teach in her own home. She finally made up her mind if Mary, who was thirteen, would help her carry out her plan, she would leave her husband and home and go to Utah, where her younger children could be taught the gospel and live among the saints in Zion.

Daughter Mary readily took hold of the proposition and together they began to make preparation for leaving as soon as all arrangements could be made for their trip to Liverpool. John Aird, a member of the Church, acted as agent for them. They sent him money to secure their passage across the ocean. He notified them just when the ship would sail from Liverpool so they could leave home at the right time. She gave her husband to understand they were just going on a short visit and in this way left him and started for Utah. Andrew, not knowing that he would not be back home in a few days, asked his father to feed his rabbits till he came back. This was in the month of May 1866. They boarded the *Saint Mark,* a sailing ship bound for New York with a company of Mormon emigrants. They sailed from Liverpool, England, June 6, 1866, with a Mr. A. Stevens in charge. They arrived in New York City on the twenty-sixth of June.

Allan Mair learned of this and had a cablegram sent to his sons in Maryland asking them to go to New York and at least prevent the children from going to Utah to live among the Mormons. His sons got the message and came to New York City, but they were too late, the company having left just a few days before. They then gave up the chase and returned to Maryland.

Mary and her little family arrived at Uncle John Murray Murdoch's in Heber City, Utah the end of September 1866. It had been fourteen years since Mary had last seen her brother, John, and the reunion was one of great rejoicing.

Not long after their arrival Thomas Todd, who had known Mary in Scotland, came to visit her, and after a few visits he asked her to become his plural wife. She accepted his offer, and they went to the Endowment House in Salt Lake City and were married. Their marriage did not prove entirely satisfactory, and in less than four years, they separated and were legally divorced.

About 1871, Daniel McMillan, the village blacksmith and a widower with a grown family, asked Mary to marry him and she accepted his offer. Mary's son, Andrew, married Mary Ann Thompson in 1879, and Alexander married Eliza Thompson in 1883. Andrew later had eleven children and Alexander had ten.

One day, a woman with three children came along and asked Mary if they could stay in the old house that Mary and Daniel had lived in. She said she would only be there for a few weeks and of course she was given permission. After being there a few days she asked if Mary would take care of her two little girls, four and six years of age, as she had to make a short visit to Park City. This was also granted and the woman left and never came back. Mary cared for them just as if they had been her own and supplied all their wants and sent them to school. In later years, Mary had an attack of rheumatism in her back and was unable to walk. The girls by this time were old enough to attend to the housework and wait on her when necessary. They both proved true and faithful to Mary and waited on her just as if she had been their real mother. The girls' names were Elva and Nettie Olsen. They both married well and raised good families. Elva married Joseph Howarth and Nettie married James Reid Lindsay. So, the little girls left in her care actually proved a blessing to her in her later years.

In March 1869, Mary's oldest son, John Mair, came and had a few days visit. He seemed to be quite favorably impressed with what he saw. In fact, he said that perhaps it was better for the younger children that they came to Utah. He had come west with a group of bridge builders for the Union Pacific Railway, from Omaha, Nebraska. They were paying good wages and he wanted to come west to see his mother, brothers, and sister. He could only stay two days as he had to go back to his work. When the railroad was completed he went to his home in North Lawrence, Kansas, and died there in 1872, leaving a wife and two children, Allan and Mary. (These two grandchildren never married or had children.)

In 1898 Mary's other son, James Mair, came to Heber and stayed two or three weeks, visiting his mother and all the relatives. He too seemed to enjoy his visit very much and formed a very good opinion of the Mormon people and their way of living. He admitted before he returned home that the Mormons were a much better people than he had had any idea of. He had some long talks with his dear mother and felt to forgive her for leaving her husband in the way she did. He also felt that the children were much better off in every way than they would have been with their father in Scotland. He married in Maryland in October, 1868, to a very good woman named Mary Ann Pengelly from Cornwall, England. Some three years later he and his wife came and spent a month visiting all the relations in their homes and attending various Church services. They were taken to see all the sights of interest in the valley as well as Park City and Salt Lake City, where a few of the Murdoch families were. They had long talks with John Murray and William, Mary's brothers, on religion and other topics, and also with William Lindsay, with whom they stayed most of the time. James and his wife returned in 1912 and had another four weeks visit, which they thoroughly enjoyed. They returned to Eckhart, Maryland, where James Mair died in April, 1915; his wife died there in October, 1922. They were good, honest, and kind-hearted people and very much respected in their community. Mary, James's sister, visited them in Eckhart in 1907 and was royally treated by them for some three weeks.

Mary Murdoch Mair McMillan died on December 5, 1900, at the age of eighty-one years. She was loved and respected by all who knew her, and never lost her faith in God or in the gospel for which she had suffered so much. She was generous and kind to the poor, sick and afflicted. She set a worthy example for children and friends to follow of faith, patience and loyalty to God. She was indeed a humble and faithful member of The Church of Jesus Christ of Latter-day Saints.

JOHN MURRAY MURDOCH

Written by himself at Heber, Utah, Sept. 5, 1898

John Murray Murdoch, son of James Murdoch and Mary Murray, was born at Gaswater, Auchinleck, Scotland Dec. 28, 1820. I was born of good parents and reared among the wild heathery hills of Scotland, being in my youthful days, a shepherd. Living quite a distance from any schools, my chances for education were very limited. My father lost his life trying to rescue a young man who had fallen victim to foul air in the bottom of a new shaft they were sinking. Both died together. I was then ten years of age. My mother was left a poor widow with seven children, two of them younger than myself. We were then living in a rented house belonging to the lime works where my father had been working before his death.

My mother remained a widow and by her industry supported herself and the two small children, one of them being her niece, an orphan girl about four years of age. Her name was Margaret Murray. My brother, William, was then about five years old. My brother, James, and sisters Janet, Veronica, and Mary, were all at service and quite able to do for themselves.

I had been herding before this time, but came home that winter and went to school. The most of our living consisted of potatoes and salt. Mother earning our living. In the spring I went herding again and by the blessing of the Lord, I have been able since that time to keep myself and many others that have not been so fortunate. I kept on herding until I was about nineteen years old. By this time, mother had built a home of her own with a little help from her family and a few kind neighbors. I then went to work in the coal mines and boarded with my mother until I was about 27 years of age. Wages were good and I was able to save a little money.

On the 24 of Feb. 1848, I married Ann Steele and went to Kirkconnell where her parents lived on a small farm. I remained there, but still working in the mines. On the 21 of Nov. 1848, our eldest child, Elizabeth, was born. Our first son, James, was born at Kirkconnell in June 1850, but I have not the exact date.

It was about this time, I first heard of the people called Latter-day Saints. A young man named James Steele, my wife's brother and dear companion, had been in England for some time and had become a convert to that faith by a young woman, Elizabeth Wylie, whom he afterwards married. He made us a visit at Kirkconnell and preached the gospel to us. I found to my surprise that he had something far in advance of the religious teachings of the day and I marveled to think that he had come so far ahead of me in his knowledge of the scriptures in such a short time he had been gone. The only fault I had with him before was that he did not care about religion. In a few days he went back to England having borne his testimony to us which never left me up to this present moment.

I had at this time been a member of the different churches and was acquainted more or less with the creeds of the Catholic and Protestant churches; but all were so different from the religion of Jesus and the Apostles that I could read of in the Testament, that I had become disgusted with the whole lot and would have become infidel to all religion if not for the testimony of that young man, my brother-in-law, who plucked me out as a brand from the fire. I do not think that the testimony of anyone else on earth could have had the same weight with me—good honest soul. He died at Bitter Creek in Wyoming while traveling with the belated Martin

Handcart Company, leaving his faithful wife and two small boys, James E. and George, to mourn their loss.

A DREAM

I felt quite lonely after he had gone back to England and night and day, I was pondering over the things he had told us—the first we had heard of the true gospel, as there were no saints in that part of the country. In my dream I thought I went out into a garden and saw a very pretty little tree that my brother-in law had planted, but two or three days before. It looked green and thrifty, I caught hold of it and to my surprise found that it already had taken root and was fast in the ground.

On the 29th of Nov. 1850, my wife and I were baptized by Thomas Hittley. A branch of the church was organized and met at our home until the time we left for Utah. During that time, I had ample proof of the interpretation of my dream. The gospel had taken root and I was the first fruits in that part of the country to come to Zion. Being young in the church, I was very anxious for a testimony from God to myself of the truth of the work. I had heard some speak in tongues and others interpret and some prophesy. But I did not get an outward testimony nor any of those gifts that I could read of the ancient saints enjoying. I also knew of some young girls who had the gifts of poetry and who could write some very nice pieces and hymns which they could sing very beautifully. Thinking that perhaps I was not worthy of any of those greater gifts, I besought the Lord very earnestly that he would give me the gift of poetry so that I could compose a piece, though ever so simple, I would receive it as a testimony from Him until I might, through faithfulness, be worthy of a greater testimony. What I got was the following. The meetings were being held at our home and what I received came in the form of an invitation to a dear friend whom I was anxious to convert to the gospel.

Dear Thomas, my friend, these few lines I send,
I truly abhor strife and schism,
But I humbly pray that you make no delay
Till you taste the sweet fruits of baptism.
We know from the word that three bear record
'Mongst the glorious armies of Heaven,
So likewise on earth we receive the new birth
And the same three fold record is given.
So next Sunday noon I invite you to come
Where the truth it will shine bright as day,
And the laws of the Lord as revealed in His word
Shall be open for you to obey.
Dear Thomas, my friend, to these few lines attend
And the truth for yourself you shall know,
Like the eunuch of old, as we plainly are told,
On your way you rejoicing will go.

About this time I moved away to another coal mine where there were a few saints. My former employer had become very bitter against me because of my religion. The few saints who lived there gathered around and we held meetings in our new home as we had done at our former home but to better advantage. We baptized some more converts. I was ordained a priest and two traveling elders were sent to that part of the country and we soon raised up a nice branch of good faithful saints, although many of them were very poor on account of the hard times. In fact it was hard for some of them to live at all. I had a chance to get work some six miles distant where work was more steady and wages better. But now came a great trial. If I should go away what would become of the little branch that I had been partly feeding and clothing through those hard times? Some of them came quite a distance on the Saturday to meet with us on Sunday and had to be taken care of. If I stayed where I was this state of things would soon make me the poorest of the poor and I was not far from it now. When I inquired of the traveling elders what I should do their answer was "The Lord will direct you, we cannot advise you." I was very much troubled under these conditions. Want and poverty was staring us in the face with no prospect of things being any better. The elders all said, "Trust in the Lord and he will direct you." I was driven to do this as I had no place else to go.

I was working for my brother James at that time. He had a contract and favored me with a day's work when others were idle. I was doing repairs that could not be done when the other men were at work. One day while in this anxious condition of mind I was all alone away down in the bowels of the earth hundreds of feet from the light of day. I felt impressed to ask the Lord for wisdom to do the right thing. I had prayed several times before for the gift of tongues but had not had sufficient faith to exercise it. I reflected seriously and queried in my mind as to why the Lord had not given me that gift as I thought it would be a great blessing to me in my sore perplexity. The elders always said trust in the Lord and they had also said if I would open my mouth having full faith in God's promise, He would give me words to say. Acting upon this advice, I immediately spoke in tongues. But although I had spoken in tongues I did not understand a word of what I had said, but I reasoned this way. Now that the Lord had given me that gift he would also give me the interpretation and to my astonishment it came thus: "Get up and leave this place for in less than six months there will not be a blowing furnace in Lugar." This seemed almost impossible and very unlikely as it would cost the company so much money to close down and start up again some other time.

It also meant the closing down of nearly all the coal mines in that vicinity except such as I had the promise of work in. Immediately I left that place acting entirely on what I felt sure was the word of the Lord to me as given through the gift and interpretation of tongues. Not knowing what would become of the little branch we left that place with hearts full of sorrow. However, it turned out all right. Although we were 6 or 7 miles from the former place, some of the brethren and sisters still came to our home to attend meetings, some coming 12 to 15 miles and of course had to be provided for at our expense. This however, was not so hard as it had been before as I had constant work and better wages. We baptized a few in this place and in addition elders were sent to us from Glasgow to travel and preach. We now had three traveling elders, their names being William Baird, John Drennan, and Andrew Gerguson, all very faithful brethren. We had good meetings and rejoiced very much in each others society. The spirit of brotherly love and good feeling prevailed among us.

I had now been a little over a year in the church although the gospel had been preached in the British Isles 12 years before ever I heard of it and thousands had been baptized and hundreds of them had emigrated to America. It was about this time that the Perpetual Emigration Fund was started and thousands of the poor saints were looking to it for their deliverance who had been faithful members of the church many years before I had. This of course made me think that the time of my deliverance was a long way off; that many years of hard labor and poverty were yet to be my lot. But the Lord thought very differently and inspired his servant Brigham Young to think that he needed two Scotch shepherds with their dogs to take care of some sheep that he had bought from some California emigrants that were passing through Utah. They were glad to get rid of the few the wolves and coyotes had left. President Young had instructed Franklin D. Richards, President of the British Mission, to send him two Scotch shepherds with their dogs. I happened to about the only one that had been raised to that business who belonged to the church at that time, and I was selected as one of the two and instructed to prepare to go to Utah.

I was to sell off all of my effects and put what money I could spare into the Emigration Fund and if it proved enough to take me through after buying two good dogs as well. If not, I would be assisted to what I needed to take me and my family to Utah. I went to work gladly to carry out the instructions but after sending what money I thought I could spare to Liverpool, I received a letter from brother Colvin, the other man selected, saying he had bargained for the dogs but had no money to pay for them. They cost three sovereigns ($14.67), and he ask me to send him the money to pay for them which I did and this left me very short for my own needs. There was very little time given to get ready. A party was given us at New Cumnock, six miles from where we lived, in honor of our departure at the home of brother Fallacher, a baker, and one of my converts. It was a very pleasant time to gather, very many hearty handshakes, farewells, and heartfelt blessings were showered upon us. It was expected that each one present would do or say or sing something, and my wife sang very beautifully: (EDITOR'S NOTE: This song was taken from the LDS hymnbook.)

> *Yes, my native land I love thee*
> *All thy scenes I love them well.*
> *Friends, connections, happy country,*
> *Can I bid you all farewell.*
> *Can I leave thee,*
> *Far in distant lands to dwell.*

I sang the following song, composed by myself for the occasion:

(EDITORS NOTE: *This was sung to the tune of* Flow Gently, Sweet Afton.)

> *Oh, Scotland, My country my dear native home*
> *Thou land of the brave and the theme of my song.*
> *Oh why should I leave thee, and cross the deep sea*
> *To a strange land far distant, lovely Scotland, from thee.*
>
> *How pleasant to view are thy mountains and hills,*
> *Thy sweet blooming heather and far famed blue bells,*
> *The scenes of my childhood where in youth I have strayed*
> *With my faithful companions, my dog, crook, and plaid.*
>
> *Oh Scotland, my country and land of my birth*
> *In fondness I'll ever remember thy worth.*
> *For wrapped in thy bosom my forefathers sleep*
> *Why then should I leave thee and cross the wild deep.*
>
> *But why should I linger or wish for to stay*
> *The voice of the Prophet is "Hast flee away.*
> *Lest judgments o'er take you and lay Scotland low."*
> *To the Prophets in Zion, O, then let me go.*
>
> *Farewell, then my kindred, my home and my all*
> *When duty requires it we bow to the call.*
> *We brave every danger and conquer each foe*
> *To the words of the Prophet, O, then let me bow.*
>
> *Farewell, then dear Scotland, one last fond adieu*
> *Farewell my dear brethren so faithful and true.*
> *May angels watch o'er you till warfares are o'er*
> *And in safety we'll all meet on Zion's fair shore.*

I then bade adieu to my kindred and friends in Gaswater and neighborhood where I was born and raised, and took my wife and two children back to Kirkconnell where her mother, stepfather, brothers and sisters, and her youthful companions still lived, to bid them all a last fond farewell. Her mother and stepfather were the only ones belonging to the church. Brother and Sister Thomas Todd were there living in the same house I had left about one year before. These four were the only Latter Day Saints that the town of Kirkconnell could boast of.

At that time many were very bitterly opposed to our church and were full of spite and a spirit of persecution. I will here relate one little incident: Many of the people were so bitterly opposed that they gathered at times to discuss the best plans to put us down and this damnable delusion, that if let alone would surely spread and destroy the morals of the people. Some of the farmers from the country came to town in the evening to help put down this damnable hearsay. One of them on his way home after dark in some way lay down or fell into a small gutter and was found there the next morning dead. It was known he and others had been drinking while making their plans to stamp out these terrible Latter Day Saints. Although most of the people were prejudiced and bitter still we had a few good friends. And they prepared a grand entertainment for us at the home of my wife's parents and many kind friends met to bid us a last fond adieu. Some of our well meaning friends however, had thought of a plan that would prevent us from going. It was to take our children and hide them as they were sure we would not go without them. But, however this plan was not carried out. This party was held on the evening of December 31, 1851. Next morning, being New Years Day, January 1, 1852, we boarded the train, tearing ourselves away from our heart broken friends, from country, and from home. Though our all was at stake, we started for Utah.

Five months of the six given by the interpretation of the tongues were now past and we would soon be on the ocean and probably would never know whether the tongues proved true or not. However, I did learn a year later that it proved true to the exact time. This I learned from William Aird who came to Utah the year after I did, and gave me the much desired information in Salt Lake City. "Yes," he said, "Shortly after you left the furnaces were all blown out." I said in my heart, "Thank God for His mindfulness of me, His poor servant." I had kept this whole matter to myself lest by any means it might fail. My brother, William, came to Utah many years afterwards and testified to the same fact. He became underground manager to the same company at Muirkirk.

The same day we left Kirkconnell we landed in Glasgow. It was there that I first saw and met my companion with the dogs. Being New Years night, there was a large gathering of the saints at their usual meeting place. They welcomed us very kindly, we being strangers to them all. Many kind words were spoken to us and many blessings and heartfelt prayers for our safe arrival in Salt Lake City were offered and showered upon us. Many said to us they wished they had been shepherds. We stayed that night and the next day with a very dear old friend. He had had much sickness in his family and lost his wife and was in rather poor circumstances yet treated us very kindly. I got one sovereign ($4.89) out of nine ($44.01) I had loaned him some years before. But to his credit, be it said that before his death, he instructed his son to send the money as soon as the estate was settled and came into his possession which he did, but without interest some years later, after I was in Utah.

That same evening we boarded a steamer bound for Liverpool. It was a very stormy night and the smokestack was blown down by the heavy wind and altogether things were very disagreeable. We were detained in Liverpool some ten days and being disappointed in not getting that money in Glasgow and having paid all my surplus to the office in Liverpool some weeks before, I was now rather short of means to start on this long and perilous journey. The ship *Kenebeck*, on which we were to cross the sea, being all ready the gang plank was lifted and we started on our voyage across the stormy sea with its motley crew of saints and sinners on board. There were about a hundred Irish emigrants of the lowest grade on board. They were partitioned off by themselves in the fore part of the ship. But we were all on deck and all had to cook on the same big stove or Galley, as it was called. We had a rather rough passage being nine weeks from Liverpool to New Orleans. Just before reaching land a terrific wind storm came up and the mighty waves reached and tossed our ship till many of the passengers were panic stricken and feared the ship would sink. Whether the captain and crew were alarmed, I know not, but one purporting to be an officer went among passengers and warned them that unless the load was make lighter we would sink, and asked all to prepare parts of their belongings to be thrown overboard. We, with others, complied with the request. Then we were stuck on a sand bar at the mouth of the Mississippi River some ten days. It was here where our worst troubles began.

Our captain had only furnished oatmeal for his Irish emigrants but had supplied them with other things from our stores, being longer on the sea than was expected. Many of the storage passengers suffered for lack of food and water. There were small boats come with provisions to sell to those who had money to buy with. As for myself, I got along very well with the oatmeal and the brackish river water which was all we had. But such food was not good for our dear little children, and on this fare both were taken ill and it was finally the cause of their death. I believe our ship was supplied with ample stores, if proper care had been used in the handling. We finally got on board a steamboat and started up the Mississippi River bound for St. Louis and without any food except what we could beg from the man who had charge of us crossing the sea, John M. Higbee, who was a returning missionary and was not perhaps as thoughtful of others as he might have been, in my opinion.

The steamboat being crowded, it was some time before we all got berths or even places where we could be sheltered from the sun and the rain. Sometimes it was quite cold, so I got permission and with pieces of boards rigged up a bed under a steam pipe where my wife and the sick children could be comfortable and out of the rain. But they were not allowed to stay there. I was told that place was wanted for the sick. I made no reply but thought it was already occupied by the sick. The kind engine man made this person believe there was danger of the pipe bursting so we got the place as long as we needed it.

As we went up the river, we came to a little clearing and to our astonishment we saw hanging on a clothes line, many of the articles we had supposed were thrown overboard at sea, among them some beautiful Scotch plaids which were among our treasures and we wondered if the nice dishes we had given away to help lighten the ships load had not also found their way to land.

Our children were getting worse and weaker and we had no food to give them, only oatmeal that was left from the *Kenebeck* and though it was all right for my wife and me, and we were thankful for it, it was bad for our poor sick children and had a bad effect on their bowels. We begged our president for nourishing food for the children but he said he had no money given him to provide for us. My wife once begged of him with tears in her eyes for a small piece of pie for her sick boy. He said if he is sick it is medicine he needs and [he would] get him some. But neither the medicine nor the pie ever came. I am sorry to say this of my president but in writing history the truth must be told. Some three or four years later in Salt Lake City, I met him and he was then in poor circumstances.

To me it was heart rending to look on the wasted body of my little boy crying for bread and none to give him. I had always had an independent mind from my boyhood and rather than cringe to anyone I would rather die. But now my proud heart was humbled and I went to a single man not belonging to the church but he had crossed the sea with us. I said to him in the bitterness of my heart which was aching like to burst, "Sir, I believe my little boy is dying for the want of food." He hastily replied, "I don't believe it." I ran from his presence and hid myself behind the paddle wheels of the boat. I was then about thirty years of age and had never shed a single tear to my knowledge since I was a boy of 12 or 13 years of age. I had concluded that my days of crying were past. But not so. If I had not given vent to my feelings in a flood of tears, my heart would have burst. I had to unbutton my vest and the head band of my pants to make room for the surging of my wounded heart. As soon as I could compose myself, I hurried back to the place where I had left my little boy with his grief stricken mother. She was calm and had a pleasant smile on her care worn face to think he had got bread and his life would be saved. That bread was the last he ever ate. He got it from a strange man that we had never seen before nor since.

May that all-seeing eye that sees and knows all and hears the raven's cry bless the kind heart of that man for he administered to us in our distress. Our little boy died on the 20th of March only a short time after our eating the bread and he was buried in a wood yard on the banks of the Mississippi River, 12 miles from Columbia. I met the man who hurt my feelings so bad by disbelieving my word when begging bread for my dying boy. He said to me, "I have a little sage in the hold of the boat. If you will help me hunt it up you can have some of it for your little boy." I said, "Kind sir, he has no need of it now." He seemed astonished and said, "Is he dead?" I answered, "Yes sir, and buried too." I could speak to him now that my bleeding heart had spoken to me and excused himself by saying that the people had run on him so much for food he had scarcely any left for himself. I believe he told the truth. For I think we were as hungry a set as ever went up that river.

We landed at St. Louis. We were now in the charge of A. O. Smoot from Utah who had charge of the emigration that year. Our little girl was still very weak and although we and others did everything that kind hearts and willing hands could do for her, she too passed and was buried in a strange land among strangers. This past statement has stood as true in our family until now though I have known to the contrary. After the little girl's body was prepared for burial and placed in a substantial box, a strange man came along and apparently sympathized with us in our bereavement. He told us that a short distance away was a cemetery and said he would send a wagon to convey the casket to the place of burial free of charge. We gladly accepted the offer. When all was ready he said, "Now, the wagon road goes around that large building you see but there is a trail leading direct to the cemetery which you and I can take and we will be at the burial place when the wagon comes." The wagon came and we deposited the box in the grave and I carefully covered it over with the earth. Again I was very sad and lonely and instead of going back to camp the way I came I decided to go by the wagon road. Going into the building, I saw a large vat of boiling water and as I watched it, a human form came to the surface. Surprised, I stood gazing and to my horror saw the head of my own little girl with her yellow curly hair rise to the surface and disappear. It is impossible for me to express my feelings, but went to camp and kept this sorrow to myself until the present time. We learned that this was a dissecting establishment.

The people at St. Louis were very kind to us. We remained there one month waiting for a shipload of saints that left Liverpool after we did. We then went up the Missouri River to what is now Kansas City, (then only a wood yard) where we got our outfit for crossing the plains. Cholera broke out in camp and we moved nine miles out on the plains. Quite a number died there and were buried with split rails for coffins. I was appointed one of the nurses to care for the sick and see to burying them, being relieved from all other camp duties.

Our little boy was aged one year and eight months old when he died. Our little girl died on the 4th of April three years and eight months old leaving us childless in a strange land without money but not without friends. However, on the 20th day of May 1852, a girl baby was born to us in a tent in the midst of the most terrific thunder storms I have ever seen. We blessed her and gave her the name of Mary Murray. She has since added Duke to her name and is the mother of eight Dukes, but not any Earls or Lords.

In a few days we started our long and wearisome journey under Captain Smoot, with Christopher Layton as his assistant. We also had a captain of every ten wagons. Two yokes of oxen and a yoke of cows on each wagon. Each person was allowed one hundred pounds of luggage including bedding and cooking utensils. Everything above the weight was made a burnt sacrifice. The health of the company was very good and from that time on we had no cholera.

Captain Smoot warned us to be careful not to eat too much. My wife was able to walk and carry her baby almost every step of the way. We started when the baby was about 8 days old. Nothing occurred worthy of note till we were a few days on the way. We killed a new born calf belonging to a cow that made part of one of the teams and then drove on with the train some twenty miles to where we camped. The cow of course went back as soon as she was turned out to the place where she last saw her calf. Next morning I mounted on a mule and was sent back to get the cow while the train was moving on. Before starting, Captain Smoot told me not to follow the road the wagons had used the day before, but that when I came to a certain place to take another road as the distance would be shorter to overtake the train. I remembered where there was a fork in the road the day before and thought sure that was the place for me to turn off. So when I came there returning with the cow I took the other road thinking they would come together at some distant point. I drove on with the cow as fast as she could travel knowing that the camp would likely move about 20 miles that day.

After traveling most of the day and seeing no sign of a camp I felt surely I was on the wrong road, but still thought they might come together. So I hurried on till near sundown. Here the road took a turn and I saw the smoke of campfires and I felt sure I would soon be in camp with my wife and baby again and all would be right, having accomplished my errand and I was then tired and hungry as also was the mule and cow. But I found this was not our train but men hauling merchandise to Oregon. The captain asked me where I was going with the cow and where I had come from. He said I just be 80 or 90 miles from the place where I had started from in the morning. He said the only safe way for me was to go back to the forks of the road where I had taken in the wrong road. He offered to buy the cow and give me a good price for her and said, "You will not get her back to your camp anyway." But I said, "No, the cow is not mine and I'll get her back to camp or die trying." He smiled and said you're a brave but foolish Scot. However, he said, "Supper will soon be ready and you better eat with us and stay tonight and get rested and go back in the morning." I thanked him but said supper was the least of my thoughts, although I had not eaten since I left camp in the morning. I started back determined to get the cow back to camp if possible and thinking it was better for me to try to reach camp before they traveled on another day. I had passed an Indian horse ranch some miles back and though very tired, I thought I would try to get back that far and put the cow in that corral and get a little milk from her for my supper, so I managed to get there and put the cow in all right, got some milk and fastened the bars good and larieted the mule and lay down to rest being very tired.

At daybreak next morning, I went to saddle my mule but he kicked at me with both feet hitting the saddle and knocking me down, but unhurt. I finally got him saddled and went to the corral to get the cow but to my surprise she was gone. I followed her tracks some distance but soon lost them. It was rainy and a thick fog settled down and hid every object from my view. I wandered around not knowing one direction from another. I finally found my way to the house and asked the Indian lady where her husband was. She said, "He is out hunting for your cow." I felt impressed right then that he was driving the cow where I would never find her. The fog began to clear away and I went to the wood where I could watch unobserved thinking maybe I might get sight of the cow or the Indian. But after watching for hours I could see neither. I decided that if the cow was loose she would sure go back to her calf, and if the Indian was hiding her, I would never get her. So I started back to the place where the calf was killed but it was dark when I got there. In fact, it was about midnight and I staked the mule and lay down to rest. There was no cow there nor any signs of her having been there. At daybreak again I was up and got the mule, which was very stiff and tender footed.

I realized that three days were gone and also my prospect of ever getting the cow. I knew my wife and all the people in the camp would be thinking something terrible had overtaken me. I was hungry and worn out and the mule also and I made a desperate attempt to reach the camp and finally succeeded. Captain Smoot had taken suddenly ill the day I left the camp and they had not traveled only the one day, which was lucky for me.

Even as it was I had all I could do to reach the camp worn and weary and nearly starved but thankful that I was spared to see my dear wife and friends who had almost given up hopes of ever seeing me again. I was now appointed as nurse for Captain Smoot and after a few days rest we began to travel again and I acted as his nurse during the day as we moved slowly along. He had a sort of carriage to ride in. Being very weak he was always very anxious to be taken from the carriage when we stopped and laid on a bed on the ground. Once in my hurry to get him on a bed without noticing it, I spread the quilts on an ant bed and got him laid down and then saw the ants and told him, and he said, "Brother John, never mind. I am glad to get laid down and if the ants will let me alone, I will let them alone." This noble saying from him relieved my anxiety. We got to be very close friends and he called me his little Scotch Johnnie and was always grateful to me for ministering to his wants and under my care, he soon got well. When we got along into the Black Hills, I was taken ill with mountain fever and became very sick and Captain Smoot insisted on being my nurse, and in this way he paid me back with interest. He could not have treated me better if I had been his own son. So I have always had a great love for Captain Smoot.

On the 3rd of September, 1852, he landed his large company of weary pilgrims safe in Salt Lake City. This was the first company that came aided by the Perpetual Emigrating Company. We camped on the public square, President Young came to the camp and gave us a hearty welcome and gave us many kind words of encouragement. Captain Smoot introduced us to President Young as his two shepherds with our dogs and gave us a very good recommend. President Young informed us that he had no sheep now as most of them had been lost and the few that were left were now rented out to his brother, Lorenzo, for five years. So he would not need us at present. But he said, "You need to rest a few days anyway. You just stay here in camp and the brethren will bring you something to eat and the way will open up for you so you will get work to do."

Before the close of the second day, there was not a soul left in camp except us two shepherds, our wives, our children, and our dogs. Then a man named Dalton from Farmington came and hired us to work one month for him. He took us home with him and was very kind to us. My companion was troubled with a sore foot and came back to Salt Lake City. I stayed for the month, got my pay, and felt rich enough to divide with my poor lame companion. Then President Young hired me to dig his potatoes, one acre and a quarter. I dug them all with a spade and had much joy in my labors to think that I now had the privilege of working for the Prophet of the Lord and now the greatest man on earth. While working hard digging the potatoes, a few dissatisfied men came around, one of them from my own country, which made their tale of woe the more plausible, and told me they had done some work for Brigham and that he had not paid them as he ought to have done, and that I would not get my pay either. They asked what share I was to get for digging such a hard lot as this. I replied

I had not made any bargain but I was sure the President would do right by me. Then they would turn away with derisive laughter saying I would soon learn better. I paid no attention to them whatever but kept right on with my work and I want to say that my dealings with President Young were entirely satisfactory to me in every way and that I love and honored him as a Prophet of the Lord.

Not long after our arrival while we were having quite a struggle to get food and shelter, President Young blessed me and told me I would live to have houses and lands and would prosper in the land. In the year 1854, my wife and I were endowed and sealed together as husband and wife. By this time I had got a yoke of oxen and used them at all kinds of work. We also had got a cow and I worked hard mowing hay to feed them through the coming winter and got up quite a nice stack of hay. In the fall, I turned my oxen in the big field thinking they could get food there until the winter came on. Then I would bring them home and feed them the hay. But to my dismay when winter came, I hunted for days but could not find them nor hear of anybody who knew anything about them and of course, I felt very bad after working so hard to get the hay to feed them and after using every other means without any encouragement, I prayed earnestly to the Lord that he would in some way assist me to find my oxen and I testify that an audible voice said, "You will find your oxen."

However, the time went on and no word of my finding them. Feed was scarce and I was offered a good price for my hay and sold it. But I still had faith in the voice that said that I would get my oxen. Next spring, I was notified by Apostle F. D. Richards that a large herd of cattle was being brought to a certain corral in the city and he thought I could buy a yoke of oxen from that herd, so I went up to look at the cattle and lo and behold I saw my own oxen in that herd. I informed the men in charge that two of those oxen belonged to me but they said that was impossible. I immediately went to Apostle Richards and together we returned to the corral. The man in charge was not satisfied as there were no marks nor brands on them. He said, "Are there any besides you who can identify them." "Yes," I said, "Every man, woman, and child in the third ward, but we will not need them. If I call the oxen they will come to me, and if they will not own me I will not own them." "Alright, try it," they said. I got off the fence and went where the off ox could see and hear me and held out my hat and said, "Come Bob." He came right up to me. I put my right arm over his neck and called, "Come under, Bright" and the other ox came up and stood as if under the yoke. The men clamped their hands and said, "These are his oxen, no one can dispute that kind of evidence." I selected a well matched yoke of young oxen and bought them, this making me two yoke.

In the year of 1854, the grasshoppers destroyed most of the crops and many of the people had very little bread to eat for months. My wife along with others went to the hills and dug sego and thistle roots to help appease our hunger, but with it all we got along wonderfully well. I got a city lot in the third ward and built a small house where we lived some years. I was ordained a High Priest by Presiding Bishop Hunter and set apart as a counselor to Jacob Weiler who was Bishop of the third ward in Salt Lake City, and held this position as long as I lived there. On the 14th of September 1854, my wife gave birth to another baby girl and we named her Ann after her mother.

After we were well settled down and began to get a little property together we turned our thoughts to our dear friends back in the old country whom we knew were very anxious to get to Zion. I, of course, was very desirous to help my dear old mother out here where I could care for her in her old age and my wife was equally anxious to help her brother and his family to get here. To accomplish this we both agreed to save every cent possible. However, it was the year 1856 before we could save enough for this purpose. The money was sent and they gladly accepted the chance to come to Zion. My mother though 74 years of age bravely started out hoping that she could stand the journey knowing that practically all the saints were to cross the plains with handcarts that year.

They sailed from Liverpool May 25th, 1856, on the sailing ship *Horizon*, with Edward Martin in charge of the company which landed at Boston and reached Iowa City, Iowa by rail July 8th. They were detained waiting for their handcarts to be made so that it was the 25th of August when they left Florence, Nebraska to cross the dreary thousand miles of plains and mountains that lay between them and Salt Lake City. However, they started out bravely on that fateful journey.

Knowing they were so late in getting started they naturally traveled as far as possible each day. And of course all had to walk. My dear old mother was not equal to the strain and when about 400 miles on the way near Chimney Rock in Wyoming and on the 3rd day of October she weakened and died without a murmur of complaint. Just before she passed away she said these words to those around her, "Tell John I died with my face turned towards Zion." She died from fatigue and exposure, a martyr for the gospel's sake. There is a crown of glory awaiting all such I am sure. James Steele and family came on and suffered very much from cold and hunger and fatigue being caught in the snow soon after leaving the Platte River. Their provisions practically all gone, it was no wonder that so many perished by the way and James Steele among the rest. His wife and two little boys survived and came to us to relate the terrible experiences they had gone through on that dreadful journey. Had not relief been sent from Utah to help them through they would all have perished back on the Sweetwater.

This was a dreadful shock to us who had stinted ourselves for years to save means to bring our dear friends here and for them to perish on the way. But even with all our sore trials we did not feel to complain, but rather to acknowledge the hand of the Lord even in our sad bereavement. Our sister-in-law and the two little boys stayed at our home until they found a place of their own.

On the 20th of December 1856, my wife gave birth to another baby girl and we named Janet Osborne and as usual all went well with mother and the baby.

In the fall of 1857, I was one of that noble band who went to Echo Canyon to prevent Johnston's army from coming into Utah with hostile intentions. I was made a captain of fifty under Major Daniel McArthur. We were there some 8 weeks and prevented the army from coming into Utah. They were forced to make their winter quarters at Fort Bridger and actually had to live on mule meat without salt part of the winter, and when they did come into Utah the next spring, they were under orders not to make a permanent camp within 35 miles of Salt Lake City. The army, when it did get in, really proved a blessing financially to the people of Utah. It was not so intended by those that sent it. When arrangements had been made to allow the army to come in to Utah in the spring of 1858, President Brigham Young advised all our people to move south at least as far as Provo and to make preparations to burn up their homes in case the army showed signs of hostility. So of course we followed his advice. I had two yoke of oxen by this time and a wagon. So we loaded our belongings in the wagon and went south as far as Goshen and spent that summer there. In the fall everybody was advised to go back to their homes for winter which we did and lived in Salt Lake City till the spring of 1860.

I had heard that a few families had gone into Provo Valley, (Heber) a new settlement in 1859 and had proved that wheat could be matured there. That land could be got by merely paying the surveyors fees and water was plentiful for irrigation purposes. I decided to go there and get some land and make a permanent home where I could settle down and raise my family and help to build up a new town as the original Pioneers did. However, we had still another baby girl born on January 15, 1859 in Salt Lake City and we named her Sarah Jane and as usual all went well. So early in the spring of 1860, I disposed of my property in Salt Lake City and in company with William Foreman and others, loaded all our belongings into our wagon and started for Provo Valley. It took us about three days drive with our ox teams.

Soon after our arrival we secured land and also a place in the Fort where I made a dugout for my family to live in till I could put in my crops and get time to haul logs to build a home for winter. I succeeded in getting a small crop of wheat, oats, and potatoes and began to make preparations for building a log house to live in through the winter. There was then plenty of green cottonwood trees over on the river that were straight and alright for building houses and stables or sheds for our cattle. We brought a cow, a pig, a few sheep, and a few chickens in our move from Salt Lake City to our new home.

EDITORS NOTE: *This is the end of John Murray Murdoch's personal narrative. The following is a continuation written by his nephew.*

In August 1862, he married Isabella Crawford as a plural wife. She was born at Blantyre, Lanarkshire, Scotland, had joined the Mormon Church there, and had emigrated to Utah a few years before. She proved a good true loving wife to Uncle John as long as he lived. She became the mother of seven children, so that in time, was the father of twenty two sons and daughters. Soon after marrying Aunt Bella, as she came to be called, he built quite a large frame house of six or seven rooms to accommodate his growing family and where they all lived together under one roof for years in peace and harmony. Later he took up a ranch some six miles north of Heber where he could keep his sheep during the summer months and he built a home there where part of his family lived some years.

In 1866 when the Blackhawk Indian War broke out, he was made captain of a company of Infantry in the Utah Militia and had fifty men under his jurisdiction. This lasted most of two years and he did his share in bringing peace again in the land.

One winter about this time, he went south with his herd of sheep intending to winter there as usual, but it became an extra hard winter and his health was not good so he leased his sheep to a man who lived near by as he was not in condition to care for them himself and came on home where he could be better cared for. This leasee in some way lost or sold the sheep so Uncle John never got any return from them. The fine herd of sheep that he had spent years in building were all lost and gone. He found that the man had no other property so he let the matter go entirely and said very little about it.

In the year 1878, his brother William and his family, that is, David L. and his wife Elizabeth, Janet and Margaret and his sister Aunt Veronica came to Utah from Scotland. Uncle John, Wm. H. Giles and Wm. Lindsay met them in Salt Lake City with two horse teams prepared to haul them and their luggage to Heber. It was a happy meeting of the two brothers after a separation of some 26 years. Next day they were landed safe at Uncle John's ranch and the day after in Heber where Auntie Ann was overjoyed to meet them.

About the years 1887, the government officials in Utah under orders from Washington started a crusade against the polygamists. They sent deputy marshals into all parts of the State to make arrests and in April

1891, Uncle John was arrested and taken before Judge Blackburn at Provo and sentenced to one month in the penitentiary. Uncle John very politely told the judge his home was in Heber and he had not expected he would have to go to prison, and he hadn't brought a change of clothing and he did not like to be in the penitentiary for a month without a change of under clothes. He said, "If you will give me the privilege to go home and get my clothing I will promise to go right to the penitentiary without any officer or any extra expense." The Judge said, "All right, you can go." So according to his promise Uncle John went home, got his clothing and promptly presented himself at the penitentiary for admittance. The warden asked for his commitment papers and Uncle John had none. For a time he refused to take him in, but Uncle John insisted and was finally taken in and served his time among all kinds of criminals, although many of the inmates, like himself, were serving time for what was called unlawful cohabitation.

In 1890, Uncle John was ordained a Patriarch by Apostle F. M. Lyman and he gave many patriarchal blessings to the people of this Stake of Zion. He was well suited to this office and as he took much real joy and satisfaction in blessing his brethren and sisters, and in telling them what the Lord had in store for them.

Finally Auntie Ann became very feeble and ill and finally passed away on the 15th of December 1909. She had been a faithful and true wife to Uncle John for over sixty years, always ready to do her part in all the trials and troubles of their eventful married life. For years she was Stake President of the Primary Association and traveled by wagon and carriage to visit with the children in the different towns in this Wasatch Stake and using her best endeavors to instill faith in the hearts of the children.

Uncle John's health also had been failing for sometime and he missed the kind words and loving actions of his beloved Ann who had shared in all his joys and sore trials that they had been called to pass through in their married life. Although Uncle John still had Aunt Bella to attend to his wants he failed rapidly and on the 6th day of May, 1910, he too passed away honored and respected by all who knew him. He gave over 200 patriarchal blessings. He was a wise counselor and many came to him for counsel and advice when in trouble. He was buried by the side of his dear wife, Ann, only about six months after her death.

After Uncle John's death, Aunt Bella gave up the home and went to live with her daughter, Katie Hicken, where she could have company and be more comfortable as she too was getting well along in years. Aunt Bella has been heard to say after Uncle John's death, "That if she could have her choice of all the men in the world she would choose John Murdoch who had been so faithful and true to her." On the 10th of April, 1916, Aunt Bella passed from this stage of existence, surrounded by her family and kind friends. Thus was ended a truly eventful life. Her remains were placed in the Heber cemetery by the side of her husband and his wife Ann. Altogether, they were a noble trio.

EDITORS NOTE: *The previous material was copied by Dallas E. Murdoch from a typewritten manuscript that that came from his aunt, Tressa Garrett. It was apparently initially taken from the personal writings of John Murray Murdoch and towards the end were the recollections of his nephew, since John Murray Murdoch is referred to as "Uncle John". The identity of this writer is unknown but it may have been David Lennox Murdoch. Minor editing changes were made from the original manuscript.*

MARGARET MURDOCH

Margaret Murdoch was born on December 30, 1822 in Gaswater, Ayrshire, Scotland. She died as a child. We don't have any records or information of her cause of death or the death date.

WILLIAM MURDOCH

William was born in Gaswater, Ayrshire, Scotland, 3 July 1825. His full history is in the following chapter of this book.

EDITOR'S NOTE: *The following two accounts are included because they are from fairly recent visits to the area of Scotland where our ancestors once resided. These accounts tell of what they were able to find with the little clues they had. The town of Gaswater, where James and Mary lived, no longer exists. The Lime Works Mine, mentioned as his employer, also no longer exists. The land is now farmland and open grass lands with little evidence of the abandoned town of Gaswater, or Grasswater, that David Lennox Murdoch refers to in his journal.*

In Quest of Mary Murray Murdoch

By Joanne B. Doxey

Joanne B. Doxey, her husband, David, their daughter, Cindy, and grand daughter, Betsy, journeyed to Scotland. Here is their story.

Many journeys have been made to Scotland where Mary Murray Murdoch lived and raised her children, but this year we decided to actually go to the area of her birth, Dumfrieshire. The town of Dumfries was a typical town; with all the charm and accent of a Scottish village (some say it hasn't changed in centuries). We went to the Ewart Library to check the census (1841-1851), the OPR (Old Parish Records) and the Kirk Sessions; the Dumfries Family History Society, and the LDS Family History Center at the Stake Center, but found nothing profound. It would be well to follow-up on some of the publications of local information at the "Society". At first they didn't know where Glencairn was (where Wee Granny was born), but then decided the parish was near Moniaive, north and west of Dumfries.

On closer inspection of the Family Group Sheet, we noted that the John Murray family moved from Glencairn when Mary was in her second year, so there were few traces of that family at the Parish of Glencairn, but we had to go see and "feel" the area. The sun was low in the sky (about 8:00 p.m.) as we drove down the winding roads, through the green fields, the rolling hills, and saw tiny villages nestled in along the way; we couldn't help but feel a peace and belonging to such a setting. We saw no evidence of mines in this area, mostly farming, but it appears that the family was indeed engaged in mining (in the mountains just beyond the village), and as the mines closed the family moved on. Only the first two babies, twins who died, and Mary were born when they lived there.

We stopped at the Glencairn Parish Church outside of Moniaive and walked among the tombstones, very old and hard to read, but saw few Murrays that were early enough. There was a row house in the village that said it had been "restored by John Murray," but the dates did not coincide with Mary's family. We were glad to see where the villages of Thornhill, Penpoint, Trynron, Keir, and Kirkland were located as they always seem to crop up when studying about the area. Returning to Dumfries town we felt well-rewarded having seen the countryside.

Moving on, the next day, we drove along the A76, passed Thorn hill to Sanquhar. The terrain changed somewhat to a dryer, hilly landscape with slag piles visible on the larger hills. Wanlockhead was off to the right where one of the children was born. It was noted for its lead and gold mines; perhaps that is why this son was named Adam Goldie. Life would have been very hard here with severe winters; the miners barely eked out an existence. This was in 1786, however, in a pamphlet I purchased it said there was a "famous" Miners Library established there in 1756, so it's possible there was some culture.

Sanquhar was a modest-size town, established as a Royal Burgh since 1672. Coal mining and its attendant industries took center stage in the area. This is the major city referred to in this area when researching family history, for example "Kirkconnel near Sanquhar." Another son, John, was born to the Murray's in Sanquhar.

Kirkconnel, an important city for finding the Murrays, the Steeles, and the Kerrs, literally means "The Church of the Connel." The parish church had been a scene of our research 10 years ago, finding additional information on Elizabeth Kerr (Steele) Campbell. We stopped for pictures, and then discovered we were right near the Heritage Center on the main street. Going in we told them of our desire to find ancestry and they were most responsive, especially Jackie Wilson, an antiquarian and former miner in the area. He said he was now "preserving heritage by gathering history." The younger man at the computer said they had just completed the Churchyard Project which had all of the monumental inscriptions in the church cemetery on CD. It was a delightful hour discussing history as Jackie sees it and tells it in his Scottish way.

During the visit, the Reverend at the church popped in. He wasn't quite so happy to see us, our being Mormons from Salt Lake City, but he quietly listened to our perspective, including an explanation of the Tabernacle Choir. Jackie happily accepted a CD of the Choir because he "loves gospel songs." We accepted their CD - free, for a donation to their Heritage Center, and then continued down the road to the churchyard. There was nothing new, but we had the hope of being able to read their transcriptions even better off of the CD when we got home. Fun place - Kirkconnel!

Up passed New Cumnock, we continued on to Old Cumnock, then to Auchenleck where James Murdoch and Mary Murray were married, 10 January 1811. At the Parish Church we saw lots of Murdoch graves and took pictures to decipher them later, but none seem to be the right family and right time. A large prominent obelisk contained a memorial to William Murdoch (James' cousin) who invented the gaslight, along with Watts. There were two churches in the yard, one old and one newer. The many head stones were mostly of old sand stone and had weathered so the inscriptions were hard to read. On the hill adjacent to the churchyard there was a mine entrance of white metal built above ground. This was truly coal mining country from here to Muirkirk where the Murrays had moved by 1790 (and had three children there). The next four children were born in Wilsontown, Lanark, and the last one in Muirkirk again, tracing the whereabouts of their family living (all according to the opportunities for work in the mines).

We were now traveling through Ayrshire, where James and Mary raised their children, two who were born in Boghead and six in Gaswater. The countryside between Auchinleck and Muirkirk is sparse with rolling hills, little foliage (except in heather season) and was somewhat sad, knowing the trials this family endured there. However, they rose above their problems and accepted the gospel and raised a righteous family. If we hadn't been in Gaswater before, we never would have found the mine where James Murdoch lost his life.

We turned off A70 onto the little road that we had gone down years before on instruction from the librarian in Lugar who had looked up where Gaswater was. We never would have found the spot because now it is completely filled in. There was only an indentation on the berm. There were pieces of coal here and there which I picked up. Nearby there was an open cast mine, Pow Harnal, which is like an open pit mine where they excavate and do strip mining. To the south on the hills there were slag heaps, and to the north there were sheep on semi-cultivated land with ancient rock walls separating the properties. At Muirkirk there were open pit coal mines, also, which may have been among the mines that closed down just after the Murdoch's left.

This wonderful experience in Scotland made us realize again the strong, dedicated, and faithful ancestry we have in the Murdoch family. Dear Wee Granny did not find relief from her tests until she was almost to Utah to join John's family, but was released from this life to be with her other loved ones. She endured to the end and gave us the privilege of a legacy remembered. We owe it to her to continue to find more information on her ancestors, as we search every source, turn over every stone, and seek for more inspiration about those we do not yet know who came to earth before she did, and who have blessed our lives with a legacy renewed.

From the May 2006 Edition of the Murdoch Messenger

Our Great Scotland Heritage

By Gary M. Lloyd

In the summer of 1990, my wife Donna and I set out to not only go to the country of my ancestors, but to use specific maps to identify the general locations where much of the Murdoch early history took place. We also wished to, where possible, research some of the sites and speak with some of the people who lived there, hoping for added information about home sites of our Murdoch ancestors.

While in what used to be Gaswater, the Lime Works mine that James Murdoch worked, we were informed by some of the older generation that the mine had been closed since the middle 1850's. That time agrees with the experience that James had while trying to save the life of a [young boy] who "had fallen a victim of foul air in the bottom of a new mine shaft they were sinking". Both were overcome by gas and died on October 20, 1831.

Even though the map in the Red Murdoch Book shows where the community of Gaswater, Ayrshire, Scotland, was located, it took us three hours of asking local residents to find the former location. Current maps do not have most of the check points as shown on the Murdoch book map.

We also knew that the James and Mary Murray Murdoch family lived within a short distance of the mine. After another three hours of going door to door, asking local residents if they might know the location of the Murdoch home, I happened onto a very old farmer (perhaps 93 years of age) about eight blocks away from the mine. At first he did not want to even say hello and after telling him of our purpose, he said he knew where the Murdochs and two or three other families lived. His directions were as follows: "Go back out to the main road, turn left, go about four blocks, just before coming to the old road on the right that leads to the mine, you will find that the land is level with the road back about 100 feet and then the land jets up about three feet where there is a lot of grass. Below that grassy area you will find the foundations of three homes. As far as I know the Murdoch home was in the middle. There is also some loose red brick that formed the home laying around."

Coming south from Glasgow on highway M77, travel about 23 miles until you reach highway A77 and pass the city of Kilmarnock. Proceed another 6 miles until you see highway A76. Proceed 15 miles until you pass Auchinleck, where James and Mary were married at the old Auchinleck parish church. This church, found in the Red Book, was a great experience to see, along with the many headstones around, many of them with the Murdoch name. Turn on highway A70 to the left and before reaching Cumnock, travel about four miles on a two lane road. At this point I believe it would be good to stop and ask around to see if someone could direct you to what used to be the Lime Works in Gaswater Again the farmer's direction on getting to the Murdoch home foundation is about as good as I can offer. Six of the children of James and Mary were born in Gaswater.

Another site worth locating is on highway A76, continuing on past Cumnock to the township of Kirkconnel

We are very happy to have found the foundation area and brought back some of the soft red brick that we have since placed in a block of cement and placed near the front door of our home in Midway, Utah.

Donna and I both commented as we drove in this choice area of Scotland, how much we felt the spirit of the area. We greatly enjoyed traveling in the specific areas where our ancestors spent many difficult years trying to raise families and eventually, after joining the Church, heading West to the United States to find the seat of the gospel.

Well, there you have it. At best it will be difficult to find the place. When we return one day, I believe we will have some difficulty reaching that special Murdoch foundation, not far from where the Lime Works mine once offered work for the hungry Scotsman.

Donna and I felt a clear spirit of the great country of Scotland, as we walked on some of the same paths taken by our great Murdoch relatives. Thanks for tuning in.

from a 2004 Murdoch Messenger

With My Face Toward Zion

With my face toward Zion
And the Gospel in my heart,
I started from the land of Scotland
Bent to do my part
With my face toward Zion,
I left from England's shore,
And bid farewell to kids and kin
To see them nevermore
I traveled on by rail,
Then joined the handcart trail
In longing for my dear son, John,
My courage never failed,
As my faith in Zion
Grew stronger on the way,
My strength to move along the trek
Grew weaker day by day,
With my face toward Zion,
On God I did depend.
He led my trail beyond the veil,
Where I found my journey's end.

by Joanne Doxey and Betsy Stevens. Sung at Wee Granny Memorial Service, 24 June 2001, Scottsbluff, Nebraska

Editor's Note: Even though we don't know the exact location of Mary Murray Murdoch's burial, we do know that it was close to Chimney Rock, Nebraska. The Murdoch Organization held a memorial service honoring her on June 24, 2001 (see *Wee Granny Memorial Service* at www.murdochfamily.net) where a headstone was placed in the small pioneer "Chimney Rock Cemetery" close to Chimney Rock, Nebraska. The following are the directions the editor received from Dallas Murdoch, former Murdoch Family Organization President:

You could go first to Bayard, which is a few miles east of Scottsbluff on Highway 26. Go through Bayard and continue on south about 3 miles where you will come to the junction of Highway 92 coming in from the west and Highway 26 coming in from the east. This is the location of the original Oregon Trail. Continue on south for about 1/2 of a mile and you will pass the Chimney Rock Visitors Center. Then go about 1/4 mile further south and you will access a dirt road that goes to the west. Go another 1/4 mile on this dirt road and you will see the "Chimney Rock cemetery" on the left and Chimney Rock to the right about 1/2 mile away. Wee Granny's grave site is the first one accessed as you enter the cemetery.

Headstone of Mary Murray Murdoch near Chimney Rock, Nebraska

Back of headstone

Chapter 3

William and Janet Lennox Murdoch

Their Stories and Their Children

EDITOR'S NOTE: *Much of the following history of William and his wives is from the writings of William Lyndsay, husband of Mary Mair, niece of William.*

William Murdoch was the eighth child and youngest son of James and Mary Murray Murdoch. He was born at Gaswater, Ayrshire, Scotland, 3 July 1825. He was christened 24 July 1825, in the Parish Church at Auchinleck, Ayrshire. His parents were Presbyterians, or the Church of Scotland. His early history is one of hardship and trial. He was only six years old when his father, James, lost his life on 20 October 1831 in a mining accident trying to save a young boy, George Baird of Dalford, who went into the mine and was overcome with choke damp. [Choke damp is a mixture of unbreathable gases formed when oxygen is removed from an enclosed area.] This left their family in very dire circumstances and the children in the family had to look to others for work.

Just as soon as he was old enough to herd a few sheep on the bonnie heathered hills close by, William was hired out to be a shepherd. The sheep in this part of Scotland were most likely the black-faced sheep. The breeding and skill of the shepherds in this part of Scotland produced the finest black-faced sheep. This helped him earn a little to provide for himself and assist his widowed mother, Mary. She saw to it that he had a little schooling during the winter months. He was provided with yarn by his mother, and he learned to knit stockings for himself and others. Very shortly before his death, he knitted a pair of stockings for each of his children.

William met Janet Lennox, born 24 September 1821 in Old Cumnock. She was the daughter of Elisabeth Templeton and David Lennox. William called her "Jessie" and they were married on 23 June 1846 in Auchinleck, Ayrshire. They lived for several years in the Gaswater and Cronberry area of Ayrshire where they had five of their six children. William, Janet and the family later moved to the Muirkirk area, where their sixth child was born. William went to work in the coal mines as a overseer of the coal pits.

Janet Lennox and William Murdoch's first child was a girl who they named Elizabeth, born 18 April 1847, and was named after her grandmother. She was born while they were living in Gaswater, Ayrshire, Scotland. Next to be born were two sons. James D., born 3 January 1850, and was named after William's father, and David Lennox, born 13 January 1852, and was named after Janet's father. Both boys were born in Cronberry, Ayrshire, Scotland. Mary was born 9 September 1854 and named after her grandmother, Mary Murray Murdoch. Mary died 11 days after her birth on 20 September 1854 and is buried in the Auchinleck Churchyard.[1] Janet was born 18 October 1855 and was named Janet after her mother. Both Mary and Janet had been born in Gaswater also. The sixth and last child, Margaret, was born 27 August 1858 in Ponesk, Ayrshire, Scotland. They again had cause to sorrow when their oldest daughter, Elizabeth, passed away in her seventeenth year on 24 March 1864. She was buried in Muirkirk, Ayrshire, Scotland where they were living at the time.

According to an 1851 Scotland Census Record, William was 25 years old and Janet was 29 years old. They lived in Auchinleck, Ayrshire and their address is listed as Cronberry. His occupation is listed as "Ag Lab", which is an agricultural laborer. They had two children listed on the census, Elizabeth was four years old and James was one year old. On the 1861 Scotland Census Record, William was 35 years old and Janet was 39 years old. They lived in Muirkirk with their address listed as "Linkey Burnhouse" and his occupation as "Overseer of Coal Pits". They had five children at the time, Elizabeth was 14, James was 11, David was nine, Janet was five and Margaret was two.

---

1. Information on Mary's death is on the headstone erected at the Muirkirk Churchyard Cemetery for Elizabeth Murdoch and Janet Lennox Murdoch.

Uncle Willie, as he was usually called, was a very steady, sober man, very dependable, trustworthy, and a willing worker. He did well in a temporal way and in time became underground manager in one of the coal pits owned by the Eglinton Coal and Iron Company. He lived in the village of Muirkirk, Ayrshire, Scotland where he was considered one of the most prominent men in the village. Getting better pay than the common miners, he was able to send his two sons, James D. and David Lennox, to some of the best schools in the country after they graduated from the village school. They both received very good educations and became prominent young men in the community where they lived.

The village of Muirkirk began growing after the establishment of the iron works in 1787. According to an 1834-1845 Statistical Account of Muirkirk,[2] these iron works consisted of three large blast furnaces for making pic-iron, an extensive forge for making bar-iron, and a foundry which employed 400 workers. Muirkirk was known for its iron mining and manufacturing but coal was an important part of the process. Coal and lime were used extensively to make a superior quality of iron bars which could be beat out instead of rolled, which is the conventional way of processing it.

The church of Muirkirk got its name from the Muir Kirk - "a puir wee kirk, theeked wi' heather" - erected here about 1650 to accommodate the scattered inhabitants of "the moorlands of mist where the martyrs lay."[3] When Elizabeth and her mother, Janet, died in Muirkirk, they were buried in the churchyard of the parish church. The "Moor Kirk", according to the 1834-1845 Statistical Account, "is situated near the centre of the parish, and is as convenient as it possibly can be for the greater part of the inhabitants. It will be between four and five miles from the extremities. It was built about twenty years ago, and has lately undergone a thorough repair, and is capable of accommodating 1000 sitters. The manse[4] has been repaired within the last four years, and is at present comfortable. The glebe[5] extends to about 14 acres, has been greatly improved, and is now capable of raising almost any crop."[6] The discrepancy in the construction years of the church lies in the fact that although it was built in 1650 (some sources say 1631), when the population grew because of the iron mines bringing in more inhabitants to the town, a new church was required and the one completed in 1814 replaced the old church, or kirk.

---

2. The Statistical Account of 1834-45 vol.5 p.155 : Muirkirk, Ayrshire; accessed 20 March 2010.
3. www.ayrshireroots.com, accessed 2 April 2010
4. The house and land occupied by the minister, especially in the Presbyterian faith.
5. An area of land consisting of farm area or open fields gifted to a church.
6. The Statistical Account of 1834-45 vol.5 p.155 : Muirkirk, Ayrshire; accessed 20 March 2010.

A few years after William's marriage, his brother John, sister Mary, and his mother, Mary Murray Murdoch, joined The Church of Jesus Christ of Latter-day Saints, and shortly afterwards his wife, Janet, became convinced that it was the true church and was baptized 8 October 1853 by James Gallacher. Their daughter, Elizabeth, also joined the church. William at this time could see no need of his making a change. He was a member of the Church of Scotland, or Presbyterian Church, as were his forebearers. He was highly respected in the community and it was considered a disgrace to join the despised Mormons. Janet though, fully convinced of the truth, went about her daily tasks quietly so as to keep peace and love in the home. She cherished the hope that at some future time her husband would come to see the truth and beauty of the gospel. She wanted also to teach it to her children and ultimately go to Zion to make her home among the saints in Utah. Uncle Willie, seeing that Janet's health was failing, realized that her membership in the the Church of Jesus Christ of Latter-day Saints was something that he should take more seriously and began investigating its principles himself. He soon realized and gained a testimony of what she already knew and he and his daughters, Janet and Margaret, were baptized 8 October 1877, by Elder David Elilne, just two months before his dear Jessie passed away. Before she died, Janet had the blessed assurance that as soon as convenient, her husband and the family would make their home among the Saints in Utah. She died in Kilmarnock, Ayrshire, Scotland on 20 December 1877. She was an exceptional woman in

Janet Lennox Murdoch with her children: James "D" and David Lennox in the back, Janet and Margaret in front. The other two daughters had already died when this picture was taken. Mary died in 1854 as a child and Elizabeth died in 1864 at the age of 17.

more ways than one. In death she rejoiced in seeing her fond hopes realized and could lay her weary, wasted body calmly down to rest in peace in the Kirkyard at Muirkirk, where their daughter, Elizabeth, had been buried some years before. Having performed the sad task of laying the body of his dear Jessie in the silent grave, William and his daughters continued to live on Gilmour Street, Kilmarnock until they had all arrangements made for going to Utah..

About the first of May 1878, they left Kilmarnock and went by train to Glasgow, where they joined David Lennox and his young wife, Elizabeth Pinkerton Thyne Murdoch. John Adamson, a young man who was engaged to marry William's daughter, Margaret, was with them. From Glasgow they went to Liverpool where they joined a company of Mormon emigrants on board a steamship in which they crossed the Atlantic Ocean in about ten days. They left May 24, 1878, on the steamship *Nevada*. Accommodations on the steamship were very good and the food good and plentiful. The journey by train from New York was finished in three days, so that it was only two weeks from Kilmarnock to Salt Lake City. Letters had been received stating the date of their leaving Liverpool and their probable arrival in Utah. Uncle John, William M. Giles, and William Lindsay met them in Salt Lake City with two teams of horses and wagons. They prepared to take them to Uncle John's home in Heber. The trip from Salt Lake to Heber took just one long day. They all arrived safely in Heber the next day and the brothers and sisters met, having been separated many years. It was a joyful meeting. At last they were all reunited in this blessed land and all were now members of the true church. They had left their homes and native land to cast their lot with the Saints in Utah's peaceful valleys. Much credit is due to Uncle Willie. After he did become convinced of the truth, he gave up a good position where he was respected in his community, and in his old age came to a new country, among strangers, to make a new home. However, they all seemed contented and went to work at any little job they could find.

On June 29, 1882, in the Endowment House in Salt Lake City, Utah, William married Christina Graham. She was also born in Scotland and had been baptized earlier when about twelve years old. This marriage wasn't entirely satisfactory and they later divorced. They had no children. Uncle Willie bought a land claim up on Lake Creek, four miles east of Heber, and also a team of horses. With the help of his son-in-law, John Adamson, they built houses, stables, sheds, and fences. Soon they had one of the best farms on Lake Creek. Of course they had to hire help until they learned how to irrigate the crops and many other things, but they had the money to do so. Uncle Willie's experience on the farm as a young boy with cattle and sheep and horses was a valuable asset to him now. In order to irrigate part of his land it was necessary to make a new irrigation ditch in which about twelve other farmers were interested further down the ditch. They all agreed to help put the ditch clear through so all could get the use of the water. Some of them seemed to have no further interest in it after it reached their land, but Uncle Willie, although his land was at the head of the ditch, helped through to the lower end, so all could benefit. John Adamson, Margaret's husband, helped him considerably the first five or six years. He stayed with him until the farm was fenced and under cultivation.

About 1887, nine years after coming to Utah, William married Mary Reid Lindsay, the widow of Samuel Lindsay, who had four children, the oldest being fourteen at the time of their marriage. William and Mary had three children: William Louis, born 4 April 1888, Mary Murray, born 26 February 1891, and Lizziebell, born 25 January 1894. Mary Reid was born 23 October 1851 in Glasgow, Ayrshire, Scotland to James and Elizabeth Cummings Reid. She came to Utah with her family and traveled as a young child, not yet five years old, in the Martin Handcart Company, the same as Mary Murray Murdoch. After 1915, she moved to Lorenzo, Idaho to be near her children and died there 22 June 1929. She was brought back to Heber City and buried by her first husband, Samuel Lindsay.

As time went on, the farm became too much for William. He sold it when he was 75 years old and he and Mary moved to Heber City where he built a house and lived comfortably for many years before his death.

William received his temple endowment on 29 June 1882s. He became an American citizen March 18, 1884.

Uncle Willie was quite robust, even in his old age and a very industrious man. He was sixty nine years old at the birth of his last child. He was cautious in making transactions, but once made, he would stand by them regardless of the consequences. He was honest and honorable in his dealings with his fellow men. Being very industrious himself, he despised laziness and shiftlessness in others. He held the office of a High Priest in The Church of Jesus Christ of Latter-day Saints for some years before his death, which took place on 12 March 1913. Uncle Willie was a highly respected member of the community and left a splendid record behind him as a true friend, a good neighbor, and a respectable citizen. He set a good example in every way for his children and grandchildren to follow. He had a total of nine children and thirty-eight grandchildren. Many good things were said of him at his funeral services. He had filled a long life of usefulness, being eighty eight years of age at the time of his death. He was buried in the Heber City Cemetery.

August 18, 1907 - David Lennox Murdoch at the Muirkirk Cemetery at the grave of his mother, Janet Lennox Murdoch, and his sisters, Elizabeth and Mary

Muirkirk Church from the back

Janet Lennox Murdoch's headstone as it appears today.

Muirkirk Church

Countryside at Muirkirk

EDITOR'S NOTE: *William was also married to Mary Reid Lindsay and they had three children together. The following is her story.*

Mary Reid Lindsay

Mary Reid was born 23 October 1851 in Glasgow, Ayrshire, Scotland to James and Elizabeth Cummings Reid. She was the third child in a family of nine. Her parents and four children left Scotland for America in 1856, enduring many hardships and suffering from exposure. Mary, a child of almost five years, walked all the way. She and her family began their journey to Utah in the Daniel D. McArthur Handcart Company.[7] James was shot[8] and the family was detained in Florence, Nebraska while he recovered. They then joined the Willie Handcart Company for the rest of their journey to Utah.[9]

The family eventually moved to Heber Valley in the fall of 1862 and then to Cache Valley in Smithfield, Utah. Mary returned to Heber and worked for various people, doing general housework. Samuel Lindsay and Mary Reid were married 31 December 1871 in Heber. Samuel Lindsay was born 4 March 1851 in Lanarkshire, Scotland to William and Christina Howie Lindsay.

Samuel and Mary had four children: William C., James Reid, Margaret, and Georgiana. They homesteaded a plot in Center Creek. Samuel worked part-time in the mines in Park City, Utah, to provide for his family. While in Park City in 1880, he contracted an illness and died suddenly on 27 July 1880.

With the help of her children, she made a brave struggle to support her family. In 1887, she married William Murdoch whose children were all married. William and Mary had three children: William Louis, Mary Murray, and Lizziebell. They lived in Lake Creek area and eventually sold that property and moved to Heber, where they lived for many more years. William passed away on 12 March 1913 and was buried in the Heber City Cemetery.

On 9 January 1917, Margaret Lindsay Burt, her daughter from her marriage with Samuel Lindsay, died in Heber and was buried in the Heber City Cemetery. Margaret was married to Peter Burt. On 9 November 1918, her daughter, Mary Murray Murdoch, died in Heber of influenza at the age of 27. Mary sold her home in Heber and moved to Lorenzo, Idaho living close to her children, two sisters and a brother. She died on 22 June 1929 and was brought back to Heber City to be buried by her husband, Samuel.

---

7. HANDCART COMPANY, D. [DANIEL] D. McARTHUR, CAPTAIN. LEFT IOWA CITY CAMP, JUNE 11, 1856, http://lds.org/churchhistory/library/source/1,18016,4976-8788,00.html, accessed 10 March 2011.

8. "16TH JULY: Brother [James] Reid shot in the leg by a 'Gentile.'", from Bermingham, Twiss, "To Utah–By Hand," American Legion Magazine, July 1937, 27, 58-61, http://lds.org/churchhistory/library/source/1,18016,4976-2836,00.html, accessed 10 March 2011.

9. http://lds.org/churchhistory/library/pioneerdetails/1,15791,4018-1-18305,00.html, accessed 10 March 2011.

EDITOR'S NOTE: *The following was written after the death of William by his Priesthood Quorum to honor him. The spelling of Murdoch to Murdock will be left as printed and spelling and punctuation are as printed.*

RESOLUTION OF RESPECT

TO THE MEMORY OF WILLIAM MURDOCK, who was a faithful member of the High Priests Quorum in the Wasatch Stake of Zion for many years.

William Murdock was born in Ayrshire, Scotland, July 3rd, 1825. Was baptized into the Church of Jesus Christ of Latter day Saints about 1877. Emigrated to Utah in June, 1878, coming direct to Heber to make his home, where he has resided ever since. He was ordained a High Priest about the year 1891, and attended his meetings regularly as long as his health would permit. His death occurred on the 12th of March, 1913.

WHEREAS, Brother Murdock left a position of honor and high standing among his fellowmen for the Gospel's sake; he being an honest, industrious capable citizen always willing to do unto others as he would have them do to him.

THEREFORE, BE IT RESOLVED by the High Priests of this quorum that in the death of Uncle Willie Murdock as he was familiarly called, we feel we have sustained a severe loss; that we console with the dear family and numerous friends he has left to mourn his loss; that these resolutions be spread upon the records of the Quorum, and that a copy be sent to the family of our departed friend and brother.

Adopted unanimously by the Quorum in their regular meeting, May 3rd, 1913.

Committee in behalf of Quorum
William Lindsay
Joseph A. Rasband
Robert S. Duke

PATRIARCHAL BLESSING OF WILLIAM MURDOCH

Patriarchal blessing given at Heber City. Dec. 12. 1899 by John M. Murdoch patriarch on the head of William Murdoch son of James and Mary Murdoch born in Scotland July 3, 1826. Brother William, I place my hands upon your head in the name of the Lord Jesus Christ to seal and confirm upon you a patriarchal blessing. Thou art of the seed of Joseph that was sold into Egypt through the lineage of Ephraim his son that have been scattered among the gentiles in the dark and cloudy day. Thy pure spirit has been permitted to come forth in this dispensation of the fullness of times when the holy gospel of the Lord Jesus Christ has been restored onto the earth. You have been inclined to receive the gospel with an honest heart choosing to leave the pleasures of the world and suffer for a season with the people of God. Therefore thou art blessed of the Lord because of the integrity of thy heart. Your greatest wish has not been for riches but that you might be a true friend for the good of thy fellow men. Therefore the Lord is pleased with the integrity of thy heart. His watchful eye and kind providence has brought you through safety from many dangers and accidents. Thy life has been preserved for a wise purpose in the Lord. You shall be an instrument in the hands of the Lord in assisting to bring salvation temporarily and spiritually of both the living and the dead. Thy name is written in the Lamb's book of life. A great work is before you therefore prepare thy heart to receive the revelation of the Lord that shall be given unto you from time to time. Brother William by authority of the holy priesthood given unto me to seal upon earth and to bind for heaven I seal you up unto eternal life to come forth in the morning of the first resurrection with many of your kindred and friends and be crowned with them in honor and glory in the presence of God and the holy angels. All which I seal upon you upon condition of your faithfulness. In the name of Jesus Christ. Amen

Isabella C. Murdock, clerk

Chapter 4

David Lennox and Elizabeth Pinkerton Thyne Murdoch

Their Stories and Their Children

(History written by Janet Murdoch Thompson, daughter of David Lennox and Elizabeth on June 5, 1938)

> *"A good heart, benevolent feelings and a balanced mind, lie at the foundation of character. Other things may be deemed fortuitous; they may come and go; but character is that which lives and abides and is admired long after its possessor has left the earth."—John Todd*

So it was that Father's life impressed family. He possessed a heart of gold, a goodly share of benevolent feelings, and certainly a well-ordered, balanced mind. He was kind, yet stern; generous, yet intolerant with extravagance and waste; very sympathetic, yet not given to over-indulgence. His life portrayed a keen intellect, an orderly mind and a disciplined soul.

How futile words seem in attempting to pay tribute to him. He lived so abundantly. His ever-thoughtful consideration for others, his sincerity of purpose, his dignity and poise, and his profound humility were shining examples of a true Christian citizen.

Father lived daily the pattern he wanted his children to follow, and that pattern daily directed us to no uncertain paths. He definitely impressed upon our minds our obligation to face life honorably, truthfully, and humbly. We were all healthy, mischievous youngsters, and I dare say Father's task was not an easy one—but thanks for all the "spankings" and corrections he saw fit to administer—they are greatly appreciated now.

We enjoyed a glorious privilege in having a Father who definitely defined a course he considered proper for us to follow. There was never a half-way point we might cling to—right was right and wrong was wrong. He pointed the way, led the way forcefully and clearly emphasized the requirements necessary for successful living. There were two requisites he particularly wanted his children to possess. He wanted them to acquire the true spirit of obedience, and to reap the fullness of honest endeavor. Early in life we were taught the maxim, "Obedience is Heaven's first law, and order is its result; this a lesson good to learn for child and for adult." Also, "Honesty is the best policy." These principles, so strongly implanted in our lives, are now priceless, and frequently we remind ourselves of the debt we owe our parents..

Their constant, fine tutelage taught us many of the deep things of life—faith, spirituality, duty, honor, truth, courage, love of home, love for one another, obedience, devotion, simplicity, patience, and perseverance, self-denial, kindness, and helpfulness—all those human elements that go into the building of substantial, worthwhile characters.

Father was the third child of William and Janet Lennox Murdoch, and was born in Cronberry, County of Ayr, Scotland on the thirteenth day of January, 1852.

William Murdoch had few opportunities for the type of education he was anxious to acquire; however, he obtained sufficient schooling and understanding to become socially prominent in the community in which he lived, He rose to be underground manager of the Muirkirk Iron and Coal Works, a position he held until coming to America. The home he occupied still stands. It was maintained for the use of the underground manager.

"Linkienburn Place. On its front wall is a plaque stating: Home of William Murdoch, Underground Manager of the Muirkirk Iron and Coal Works."

Grandmother Janet Lennox Murdoch was the first of her immediate family to join the Church. Father states in his diary that he often heard his mother singing:

"Redeemer of Israel our only delight,
On whom for a blessing we call
Our shadow by day and our pillar by night,
Our King, our Deliv'rer our all."

In his youth, he did not sense the impact of it, but in the intervening years it recurred to him many, many times, and he often wondered if his mother sang it purposely, in order to make an impression upon him. Father's education was quite limited. However, he was an apt student and eager to acquire all the schooling possible. When fourteen years of age, he left home to become associated with the Whitelaw family as office boy. Later, by constant study and application to his work, he became secretary to Mr. William Whitelaw, a member of Parliament for the City of Glasgow. He served in that capacity for over four years, and lived all during that period of time with the Whitelaw family, part-time in London and part-time in Glasgow. It was interesting to hear Father tell of the style and ceremony of such a position. He invariably dressed for breakfast, luncheon, and dinner, for evening affairs; and oftentimes strictly formally but that type of life appealed to him—it was fascinating, elevating, and held for him a particular charm. He became accustomed to and enjoyed it.

It is most amusing to read in his diary how upsetting it was to him when he decided to notify Mr. Whitelaw of his intention to marry and go to America. He says, "I always was a kind of tender-hearted chap and this occasion and occurrence could not take place without my shedding tears. However, I was greatly relieved when it was over."

Father married Mother in Glasgow and sailed early in May 1878 for the United States. They were eleven days on the Atlantic. Their party consisted of William Murdoch; Mother and Father; Father's sisters, Janet and Margaret; Aunt Veronica; and John Adamson from Muirkirk.

Upon arrival in Salt Lake City, they were sealed in the old Endowment House and then traveled to Heber City by four horse teams—there was not a railroad operating at that time between Salt Lake and Heber.

In view of the fact that Father had no particular work to go to, he spent the summer months working in the fields, haying and so on. This type of work was such a departure from the fine position he had occupied that his hands became very sore and many blisters formed. In the winter months he taught school in Heber City. His first son, William, was born there.

Later he moved to Salt Lake City and became an employee of ZCMI [Zion's Cooperative Mercantile Institution], where he remained for many years as chief accountant and credit man.

It was his great pleasure to return to his native land and have the opportunity of preaching the gospel that was so dear to his heart. The entire period of his mission was spent in Scotland, where he served as mission president, and where some of the happiest experiences of his life were

Taken early 1902. David Lennox Murdoch, Lennox Murdoch as a baby, William Murdoch, and William Murdoch, son of James and Mary Murray (Wee Granny) Murdoch

recorded. To be able to return to his native land, the place of his birth, and to renew his old friendships and live over again the simple, yet wholesome pleasures of his youth, brought indescribable joy to him, and as an outlet to his emotions, he penned on the fifteenth of September, 1906, the following verses:

The Place Where I Was Born

In the upland, near the moss, where grows the bonny heather,
'Twas yesterday, I hied away in lovely autumn weather
To Gaswater and old Cronberry, the place where I was born
Some fifty years and more ago, upon a January morn.
Ensconsed within a grove of trees, I found the little cot
Where first I saw the light of day, a pure and hallowed spot,
'Twas there a mother tenderly around me did entwine
Her arms of loving kindness about that little form of mine.
'Twas here I learned to creep and walk and play about the door,
And share the little ills of life which all mortals have in store,

No matter where I wander now or wherever I may be,
I'll cherish always fondly the dearest thoughts of thee.
Time's ravages so plainly show what changes you have seen
And from the bonny sheltered nook that looked upon the green
No sound of human life we hear, all, all is quiet and still
As we gaze upon the ruins of the house upon the hill.
That dear old place, I love it yet, tho' shattered are its walls,
And crumbling down to mother earth as rock and mortar falls,
I see its form as there I stand and gaze upon its face
A few more years and then, alas, no remnant we can trace.
In the upland, near the moorland, let me wander once again,
And hear the lark prolong its notes through the sunshine and the rain,
Let me see the cot beside the wood, the place where I was born
Which sheltered me in infancy upon that winter morn.

David L. Murdoch

[The folloiwing description is from a publication in the Cumnock News.] "9 Fairyhill RoadKilmarnock, Sept. 5, 1906 The above verses are the production of Mr. David L. Murdoch, a native of Muirkirk, on revisiting the place of his birth after an absence of thirty years."

Mother and I left Salt Lake early in June, 1907, to join Father in Scotland, tour about some, and then return home with him. What a delight to visit such interesting places with them—what a great opportunity to again live with them their experiences of the past, and what a privilege to have Father escort us to all the historic spots of England and Scotland that were so dear and familiar to him.

Upon his return home, he and his son, William, established the Murdoch Grocery, purchasing property and erecting a building to house such an establishment. By January 1, 1908, the store was completed, fully stocked, and ready for business. However, before the building was completed, Father joined the office staff at ZCMI and remained there until two and one half months before his death.

All his life, Father enjoyed excellent health. His robust constitution fortified him to weather any illness he might have developed. In his married life he never spent one day in bed because of illness. I remember upon one occasion remarking to my brother, "Well, I hope when I reach Father's age (he was then seventy-five), I'll have the mentality he has." My brother jokingly replied, "Well, I hope I'll have his stomach." He was never too old to go coasting or bobsleighing. He was a great lover of the outdoors and thoroughly enjoyed canyon picnics. He was particularly fond of hiking and could outdistance many of the younger boys and girls.

One day over twenty years ago, he chanced to meet an old friend on the street who had met with reverses. In the course of conversation this person persuaded Father to loan him two or three hundred dollars on some property in Lamb's Canyon. Father knew nothing of the place, had never seen it, but he did not question his friend's word, and immediately gave him the money. Eventually the property fell into Father's possession. Later on he decided to visit the property and investigate the situation. Certainly this small act of kindness richly rewarded Father—he discovered he owned one of the choicest lots on the Forest Home property in Lamb's Canyon. Negotiations were immediately made to construct a summer home, and since that time many, many happy summers have been spent there.

Father would roam all over the hills surrounding the Forest Home property. On reaching one of the highest peaks (probably 11,000 feet high) in that vicinity, he decided it would be a fine thing to make yearly excursions to it, and took pride in guiding visitors there. He made it a point to see that everyone who made the trip contributed to the "rock pile." This he called the Cairn. He christened this peak Mount Murdoch—today it has its place on geography maps and is known as Mount Murdoch.

Father's sister, Janet, married William Baird of Heber City. They and their family moved from Heber to Carey, Idaho, where they purchased extensive land interests and followed ranching and cattle raising as a vocation. They became quite independent and prospered in their ventures. Several members of the family are now located there,

Another sister, Margaret, married John Adamson, one of those who accompanied Grandfather William Murdoch's party to America. Uncle John and Aunt Maggie, as we called her, became very prominent in Church work, both in Park City and in Carey, Idaho. Uncle Billie and Uncle John (Father's brother-in-law) were splendid, energetic, reliable, dependable men, and accumulated considerable means in the ranching business, at one time owning extensive land interests and the Hot Springs near Carey. Uncle John's boys branched out into the mercantile business and at present are engaged in this business as well as the sheep industry.

Uncle James (Father's brother) came to America before his family, and located in the East. After the family came to Utah, Uncle Jimmie followed them and located in Park City, where he became very prominent and wealthy through his connections with the mining industry. He was very active in Masonry, having served as a past Grand Master of that order. Consequently, he did not join the Church until very late in life. He was greatly respected in the community for his honest dealings, yet he was considered a "close" Scotsman.

In reflecting upon the past, I am sure Father's family today would say, "How well Father used what money he had." Well do I remember one evening when he came home from business quite upset. He was a director in a certain building society, and in one of their meetings that particular day, it was decided that the stockholders were to be paid a certain amount for every meeting they attended. Father was much grieved over this decision. He had made a motion at that meeting that instead of the stockholders being paid for attendance at the director's meetings, the money be used for helping widows and other struggling women depositors to carry their load. His motion did not carry and for some days he was quite perturbed over the affair.

He enjoyed fine business connections, and although he did not acquire much of this world's goods, he did maintain a large home and was a splendid provider. There was an abundance of everything about the home. Father's independent nature saw to it that there was plenty for the family. There was plenty for those less fortunate and plenty to hold him secure in his declining years. He was always quite proud of the fact that it was his privilege to be one of the owners of the first paper mill erected in Utah. It was located at the mouth of Cottonwood canyon, and burned down before operations began.

Again, I hope I shall be pardoned for quoting some of the sentiments expressed when Father passed on, April 24, 1928. Brother Orson Romney said:

> "The home-life of Brother Murdoch was most admirable; his business life most honorable; his faithfulness to Church duties was untiring. We love to think of his home—we appreciate our long acquaintance with him."

Brother William Romney, a close business associate said,

> "It is in business where you come to know men and know their true worth. I was always inspired by his fidelity, his honesty, and his ability. He was one of the best office men I have ever had the pleasure of meeting. He was punctual and thorough, and during many years of close association I learned to love his many good qualities. He was a man to be trusted; his word was his bond. As a young man I used to look up to him as an exemplar along those lines, and as years advanced, that respect for him grew into ripened knowledge of his intrinsic value. As a member of the Church, Brother Murdoch was consistent and thorough. He was one of those who did not take everything for granted. When he was not quite sure of a thing, through study and research he endeavored to convince himself as to the truth or falsity of things, and having been convinced that he was right, stood up manfully for his convictions. He believed thoroughly to carry out in his every thought and conversation the principles of the meek and lowly Nazarene."

James H. Moyle said:

> "Brother Murdoch was the same solid, substantial, stalwart, courageous character always—independent, completely intelligent, but above all, courageous and true to his convictions. A true friend—there was no favor that he ever could do for one that he did not grant. He never asked anything much of anybody. He stands out as one of the outstanding and upstanding characters of my business life. He has lived a noble life and was ever an example well worthy of emulation."

An expression from Nephi L. Morris:

"In all his official acts I can certify to his unquestioned integrity and his honesty of purpose and his sound business judgment. David L. Murdoch was a trained businessman, technically trained. He had a principle in business, he knew what ought to be, and yet he had a heart. Often there was a conflict between his heart and his judgment as to what should be done, for there is nothing more pathetic than to see a human being in distress when he needs help, and I suppose nearly all of us have been that person at some time in life. I have often seen the exacting demands of business practice speak "NO," and then I have seen David L. Murdoch come and plead for a new decision, and when it could not be given I have seen him pledge his own name and his own credit to help a brother who was in need. David L. Murdoch was of a literary trend, in addition to his business training. He wrote poetry, he was highly spiritual minded, and a very intelligent man, always giving personal attention to the question of religion. I congratulate his family on having had so noble a sire, one of such assertive independence as to deny or defy the demands of conformity, for if you wish to succeed, just conform; but some stalwart people have succeeded in spite of their non-conformity, and he defied the traditions and the orthodoxes of his homeland, his native land, and the traditions of the time, and took his place manfully with the people of his adoption. He came to this country, has made a name—he has won distinction and honor."

George Albert Smith made this statement:

"It was a little difficult for me to get acquainted with Brother Murdoch when I was a child; in fact I rather felt that he was cold and distant, but as the years went by and I discovered his real worth and the tenderness of his heart, I learned to love him, and I am grateful to my Heavenly Father to have had the companionship of such a man. The only favors he ever asked of me that I can recall were in the interest of somebody else—a desire to please someone who needed encouragement."

Father passed away very suddenly—he had just picked up his pen to write a check when death called him. There has always been consolation in the words of Brother Nephi L. Morris; he said,

"You had better let the vibrating string of the violin snap while vibrating with sweet harmony, with vitality and life, than to die out gradually and see a decline of power and influence and ability to produce."

But in the living of such an honorable life, may I dare say, he was deserving of all the blessings he enjoyed. His whole life was dedicated to the service of others. His motto, *Service Before Self* and his favorite quotation, "0 why should the spirit of mortal be proud", gave impetus to a rich and noble life. In conferring gifts or favors, or in dispensing or sharing his material belongings, Father was very particular to see that his right hand knew not what his left hand did. His modesty in such matters was one of his charms. It has been my desire not to write so much of his business or occupations in life, but to give some idea as to how well he lived. If this short biography can inspire others to emulate his philosophy of life, I shall be happy indeed.

Baptism Account of David L. Murdoch

Transcribed as written

David Murdoch and his wife, Elizabeth Pinkerton Thyne Murdoch, were babtized by President Alexander F. Macdonald in the River Clyde on Thursday evening, 16th May 1878 about half past 9 or between that and 10 o'clock. Brother Macdonald was assisted by his sons Alexander F. Jr. and Aaron. The place of babtism was at the bend of the River past the upper Suspension Bridge, which is the usual place of babtism for the Saints in Glasgow. David Murdoch was confirmed a member of the Church of Jesus Christ of Latter Day Saints on the Sunday following by President Alexander F. Macdonald and Elizabeth was confirmed a member same time and place, Trongate Hall, by Brother John McKenzie. David Murdoch was rebabtized in Spring Creek, Heber Utah Territory on Sunday 20th September 1878 by his Uncle John M. Murdoch and reconfirmed same day by Bishop William Forman. D.L. Murdoch was ordained a Priest on Sunday Afternoon 30th March 1879 by Elder F [illegible word] Sr., Bishop Rasband and [Bishop] Foreman. Elder [illegible word] acting as month. Elizabeth P. was rebaptized on Saturday 17 May 1879 in Spring Creek by John M. Murdoch and reconfirmed same evening by John M. Murdoch. David Murdoch ordained an Elder by John M. Murdoch and Bishop Forman on Monday 19 May 1879. David L. and Elizabeth P. sealed thro the Endowment House and recorded that [illegible word] for time and eternity on Friday 22 May 1879.

William, first born of David L. and Elizabeth P. Murdoch, born 15th of Sept. 1878. Blessed and named as above by John M. Murdoch. Elizabeth Pinkerton Thyne, second born of David L. and Elizabeth P. Murdoch 17 March 1880. Janet Lennox, born August 7, 1884. Blessed by Brother T. B. Lewis when eight days old and again blessed and named at Fast meeting first Thursday in October by Brother James Hamilton. Veronica, born July 2/86, blessed by her Father when 3 days old also at Fast meeting first Thursday on Augt. (5th day) by Brother White. Friday 7 February 1890 at 8 ½ minutes past 5 p.m. was born a daughter unto us. Friday 21st February 1890 blessed and named her Norah Thyne. Mother and child get along so far very nicely. Thanks be to the Lord for all his mercy and blessings.

Journal of a Voyage – Liverpool to New York

By David Lennox Murdoch

EDITOR'S NOTE: *This journal is originally written in David Lennox's handwriting and has been fairly easy to transcribe. The spelling, punctuation, grammar, capitalization, etc. are as he wrote it. Words within [ ] are explanations and are added by the editor. David Lennox used "&" and "and" interchangeably. He seldom used commas and connected many sentences with a hyphen.*

ALSO NOTE: *The following is a list of the people referred to in this journal and with whom he traveled to Utah:* David Lennox *and his wife,* Elizabeth, *but referred to her as* Lizzie; *his father,* William; *sisters* Janet *and* Margaret, *referred to as* Maggie; *Margaret's future husband,* John Adamson; *and William's sister (David Lennox's aunt)* Veronica.

Friday – May 24, 1878
Busy getting luggage on board. "Nevada" steam tender lying at No. L Bridge landing stage for "Nevada". Goodly company (over 300) of Danes, Norwegians, English, Scotch, Irish, all busy looking after their luggage and beds. Great many strangers looking on and evidently wondering at so many going to "Utah", which was printed on most of the boxes. Left landing stage at 7:00 o'clock for Nevada barywell in mid river. Arrived at Neveda in a few minutes and commenced putting women, children on board, then the luggage which was strung on board in big bundles and pretty roughly handled some of it was. Only hope it may reach its destination in something like safety. Waited by to see all our luggage strung on. Afterwards went and had tea in Ladies Saloon—slept first night on board in cabin—our own bunk not being made up.

Saturday – 25th
Got up at 6:00 o'clock and visited Father, Aunt and the steerage. Some up and some getting up, some washing, etc. Men , women and children all huddled together and apparently quite happy. Father Aird not very well. Got a little better after breakfast. He told us that a number of those in steerage had never been in bed, but had been singing and dancing and playing musical instruments. Father Aird not feeling very well felt annoyed at the noise and said there was no fools like those of latter days. He also said the Scotch saints were the best. Got breakfast shortly after 8 o'clock which consisted of Irish stew and roasted steak and coffee. Between breakfast and dinner a number of Immigrants came on board. Dinner at 12:00 o'clock. Broth, roast beef and potatoes was our dinner. We all enjoyed dinner very well. 2:13 P.M. Steam tender which brought few other passengers has just left. Anchor being weighed we sailed at 2:20 from nearly opposite the Victoria Dock Liverpool. Weather very fine and warm slight and everyone seems in first rate spirits and quite glad to leave their native land. Have not seen anyone grieved like. Would almost have been impossible to have left

under more auspicious weather. 6:00 P.M. Sailing continues fine, have just had tea and cold meat to it. Feel first rate. Got on top coat and up to deck again. Meeting held at 9 P.M. when the arrangements were announced for the voyage as regards worship vz. ½ past 7 morning and 8:00 o'clock at night. Thos. Judd, President or Captain, with Elders Neve and Howell as Councellors. Elder Ball as Chaplain. Elder Clawson as Secretary & other Elders & Brethren to assist all in their power.

Sunday morning – 26th

Got up about 6:00 o'clock having slept well and passed a nice night. Got on deck and found a good many there already. Off the coast of Ireland a few drops of rain falling occasionally but think it will keep up and be fine throughout day. Prayers at 7:30 by Elder Neve. It was announced that for the future the hour of morning prayer would be 7 instead of 7:30. Signalled the Sister Ship Wyoming 7:45 which takes a number of elders to England. Breakfast at 8. Tea, Irish Stew & Steak. 10:45 A.M. entered Cork Harbour leading up to Queenstown where about 30 passengers were taken on board and 3 went ashore. The Harbour of Cork is very beautifully situated, has works and erections of defense placed at the mouth entering into Queenstown Bay. Much indebted to Brother John Allan for use of field glass which brings Queenstown and surrounding scenery quite near to us. 11:45 leave Queenstown Bay - shortly will have one last look of land for a few days. Dinner at 12 - Broth, Roast Beef, potatoes and plum pudding. Have just come on deck from our dinner. Sun shines bright and warm slight head wind, with the exception of part of coast of Ireland we now see nothing but the great expanse of the mighty deep as far as the eye can reach. Just visited the Steerage, they are coming up from their dinner and a number are busy washing their dishes. Brother Aird is busy washing his with cold water. He has never done the like of this all his days, he says and can't get on with the cold water. I advise him to rub them well but he says that cold water will not rub off "creesh". Went down to Steerage at 2:30 to meeting. Br. Ball spoke very plainly to the saints as to using their soap keeping themselves cleanly and I am sure his words were much needed. More Latter Day Saints than those on board the Nevada require the same preaching. Had tea at 5. Boat heaving a little - several had to rise from the tea table. Janet could not come to tea. Maggie had to rise from it. Good deal of sickness on board this Sunday afternoon. Janet gone to bed wishing she was landed. Maggie also in bed. Lizzie vomited and a little better afterwards. Just going out of sight of land 8:40 P.M. Very many of our company sick and vomiting sorely this afternoon and evening.

Monday – 27th

Got up shortly after six oclock—boat heaving a good deal - vomitis on [illegible word] up could not take breakfast. Got cup of tea and small piece of bread, threw it up sometime after. Could not go to dinner. Great amount of sickness on board. Vessel dipping at stem & shifting seas. Lizzie not up today. Janet & Maggie the same. Father & Aunt never been sick at all - two or three hail showers today, wind pretty high and cold - have seen nothing in the shape of vessel outward or home bound. Nothing would stay on my stomach at all today - got a little brandy at bedtime which made me sleep and feel better.

Tuesday – 28th May

Got up about 8 o'clock - got on deck and found it literally covered with passengers - morning beautiful and fine - wind slightly changed to Southwest - sea so smooth that no white seen at all. Most passengers great deal better this morn. 9 - could not go to breakfast but got some oat cakes, pickles and red herring and enjoyed it fine - made me thirsty and drink a great deal. Went down to dinner and got pea soup and corned beef and potatoes - feel nearly all right today. Lizzie went to breakfast and also to dinner today. Jenny and Maggie great deal better also and all on deck. Ladies all retired early except Lizzie and all feel sickly again. Sea little rougher. Retired shortly after 8 o'clock - slept very little, heaving considerably.

Wednesday – 29th May

Got up about 8 o'clock. Boat still rocking a good deal - had a little tea & bread to breakfast then went on deck - good number there already notwithstanding a drizzling rain accompanied by a mist which enshrouds everything at a distance of about 200 yards. Informed we passed the "Idaho" this morning about 4 o'clock on her homeward bound voyage. Ladies all in bed this morning and taking very little. Lizzie up laughing and vomiting alternately. Back to bed again. Went to dinner today had broth, currie rice & potatoes. 4 oclock - rained all day, up till now. Clearing up somewhat. Passed a Brigantine outward bound. Lizzie managed up to deck. Janet and Maggie still keep their bunks. Janet and Maggie managed on deck a short time had tea at usual time – weather rather unsettled like - wind pretty much ahead. Went to bed about 7 or little after - not feeling quite well,

Thursday—30th May

Awoke before 5 and found we were standing still - got up about 6 and got on deck - good many there - working away at engines - got a start made about 7 - strong head winds - was told by man in cabin that some of the brasses round one of the cylinders were getting too much heated and were melting.

Was told by 2nd mate that a rat had got its tail into the safety valve and so had stopped the engines and that the rat was so anxious to get its tail out as they were to have it out. Surly looking day - got breakfast of dry hash and cold water. Lizzie, Jenny and Maggie all in bed and getting some breakfast. They all seem pretty well but won't get up all that we can do. Lizzie got up a little before and went into dinner. I had for dinner today, soup, halicot & potatoes & plum pudding. Day keep dry but very gusty. Birth on board this morning - a boy—a dane, or rather an oceanic - born in the steerage of the Steam Ship Nevada on Thursday morning about 8 o'clock. The boy was blessed this afternoon and named Nevada Atlantic.

Friday morning—31st May 1878

Got up this morning before 6 o'clock not having rested very well and feeling as if I would like to vomit. Got on deck and very stormy morning and very few there - out of 342 Saints and about 100 of a crew. Vomited shortly after getting on deck and felt much better afterwards. Before going down to breakfast at 8 o'clock we sighted a Barque [sailing vessel with three masts] outward bound—she was battling with the strong breeze as well as she could, but was laboring good deal. Had salt fish and a little tea for breakfast. Felt better afterwards. Lizzie up this morning as also Jenny & Maggie for the first time for 3 days. Saw a bottle nosed whale this morning a short distance off blowing the water in the air. Strong head wind still blowing - keeping us back considerably. Had dinner of pea soup, hotch potch [thick stew made from meat and potatoes] & potatoes - did not enjoy it very much. Got disgusted this afternoon at so many dirty devils of Mormons - boys and men smoking & spitting all round - felt so bad that quite out of sorts and like to vomit. It is quite evident that a good number of people on board are carrying all their old practices and pernicious habits with them. Had tea with a little pie but still suffering from an ill temper caused by the selfishness of some dirty fellows smoking & blowing away like a furnace even beside women & young children. Took a little brandy and retired to bed about half past 6 - slept well at intervals.

Saturday—1st June 1878

Got up about 7 and got on deck. Few there - morning cold - strong North West wind blowing - went down to breakfast shortly after 8. None of our ladies up this morning except "Aunt". Was told we were on the Bank of Newfoundland. Water seems green this morning instead of blue as heretofore. Had curried beef & rice to dinner. Cold wind still blows - into last thousand miles now - passed two Barques today - one outward, other homeward bound. Had tea at usual hour - got on deck again - still blowing strong and very cold - sighted few more Newfoundland Fishing Boats passed one quite close by and waved to them they waved to us.

Sunday—2nd June 1878

Got up this morning about 7 o'clock and got on deck. Lovely morning - slight head wind. Nearly everybody on deck - even our ladies have all got dressed and got on deck. Had breakfast at 8–hot bacon and tea - enjoyed this meal better than any got on board - the bacon was really first rate. Sun shines bright this morning and everyone seems cheery and in good spirits. This is our second Sunday at Sea and the day is so fine and the ship going so steadily that one quite forgets all the sickness and unpleasantness of a sea voyage. Had dinner of Kidney soup, stewed rabbit & plum duff [stiff flour pudding that is steamed and contains currants, raisins and citron] - appetite gets keener and enjoyed it well. Present at meeting this morning about 11 o'clock in the cabin when the Captain went through the English church service form of worship - the cabin was quite filled. Was present also at meeting in the Steerage at 2 o'clock when Brothers Ball and Morton spoke. Had tea at 5 with some pie. Was at meeting for prayers in steerage at 8 o'clock and retired shortly after.

Monday—3rd June 1878

Got up on deck this morning about 5 o'clock - about half a dozen there. Sun just breaking through. Water calmer this morning than any day since beginning our voyage. Fog came on about 6 o'clock and has been very dense all day. Fog whistle blowing nearly all day and on to 10 at night. Had breakfast of Irish stew & tea. Dinner of soup, boiled pig, cabbage & potatoes - Tea at 5 again. Went down to meeting in the Steerage at half past 6 o'clock when directions were given as to how we were to proceed at New York with luggage, Ry tickets etc.

Tuesday—4th June

Got up at half past five got on deck and found a few there. Dense fog still prevails and we seem to steer very slowly. Sailors busy washing and cleaning so as to appear as clean as possible. Had breakfast of potato soup and tea. Some people think they smell land this morning: Had dinner at 12 of pea soup, stewed rabbit & potatoes. Shortly after noon the mist cleared quite away and the sun shone out bright and warm. Had tea at five with cold meat. Great preparations going on this afternoon for a concert which is to take place for the delectation of those invited in the cabin. Myself and wife were not invited and so did not attend. Mist still comes at intervals and goes off again. Passed quite close by an American Fishing Boat with a good number of hands on board - the men waved their hats and bonnets towards us and a number of our company did the same.

Wednesday—5th June

Got up at 5 o'clock and got on board. Few there - morning fine and mist quite cleared away - was told we took Pilot on Board at 1/2 past 12 at night. Sighting a good many Smacks [a fishing boat in various sizes often having a well used to transport the catch to market] etc. this morning. Went down to breakfast at 8 and had a red herring and some Irish Stew - Steerage passengers throwing their beds and meat utensils overboard. 10 A.M. Land not yet seen but all eager on the outlook for it. 11 A.M. approaching land. Sun gets warmer, everybody on deck and all seem glad our sea journey is at an end. Steaming up Hudson River and are waiting for Doctor. Doctor ultimately comes on board and we all pass before him. Being all in good health and no sickness. We then proceed to the Guron landing place where a few of Cabin passengers get ashore. Steam out again to the Guron Pier where Brother James met us. [James "D" Murdoch] We had a busy time getting baggage out of hold and putting it on to a tender. We got through it very smartly and well. Everything was in ship shape fashion and there was no trouble. Got into Castle Gardens [Predates Ellis Island and was a processing center for immigrants coming into New York. It was located on an island off the tip of Manhattan.] about half past five. Stayed over night at Stevens Hotel which is on the European plan - in Broadway. We were informed this morning that the "Idaho" one of the Guron lines which we passed on Wednesday 29 of May had struck on a rock off the Irish Coast and gone down in 20 minutes - all hands saved.

Thursday—6th June

Got up this morning had breakfast and took a walk up Broadway and then to the Central Park. Saw the menagerie there and were much pleased with the exhibition of so many animals, birds, etc. Had ice cream & some fancy bread - this treat was immensely thoughtful - we being all a little tired & hot, it was so cooling. Came back to hotel had dinner and then took ourselves off again to Castle Gardens - we got on to steam tender again and crossed over to the Jersey side where we got onto the Railroad cars. We got started on our Railway Journey about 7 P.M. We got away very slowly – with numerable stoppages.

Friday—7 June

We are all awake at daybreak - few of us slept much some none at all - but all seemed pretty well and before 6 o'clock we had a little singing. Morning beautiful. At about 6 o'clock we began to go along the "Banks of the Susquehanna" - we continue to run alongside a considerable way. It is a beautiful broad but shallow river. The scenery at some parts is very fine particularly at the Susquehanna. Quite a [illegible word] moving it up and down the river - proceeding on towards the Allegheney Mountains, which we do following a river most of the way - the scenery is very beautiful, perhaps a little sameness about it. The horseshoe bend was pointed out to us as being a very quick curve. Got into Pittsburgh about 9, where we had to change cars. This movement was encountered with the utmost confusion and disorder. It was understood by those in charge of companies that we should all take up the relative positions in the new cars as we held on the old. This was not carried out at all - the Scotch and a number of English got all muddled up together in the first carriage. The English would not move and the Scotch thinking they were in the right place stood firm, so we stood there for sometime in the utmost confusion. At length those of the Scotch and English who could not get accommodations in the first car had all to move themselves and their baggage through 7 or 8 cars right at the end of the train. In the center of the train as made up at Pittsburgh were placed the Russian Immigrants - 2 carloads so that in moving we had to leave through the Russian Ranks. The odors and smells arising from those people together with the wild ghastly appearances they had as they lay. Men, women and children separated up on the floors of the carriage on seats and every inch of vantage ground was sickening and when the journey had to be made more than worse it became doubly so. However as the darkest night has always its dawn so our little troubles will come to an end. At length we got arranged as well as we could and got to sleep. We all slept better this night than the previous one from the fact I suppose of being all more tired.

Saturday—8th June

Awoke about 4 o'clock - morning wet. People soon begin to stir, some to eat, some to wash - was told this morning that the cars with the Russians had been moved to the back of the train after leaving Pittsburgh - this rectified matters very much as our people were as before in continuous and succeeding cars. We had frequent stoppages today of short duration but long enough to permit of many of our company stepping out to pluck flowers. Arrived at Chicago about 9 o'clock - changed on to the Chicago & North Western Railway. At Chicago and for many miles around the ground soaked with wet - in some places flooded - the ground here abouts is as level as the floor of a house and of course this will account for the dampness.

Sunday—9 June

Did not sleep much during the past night - awoke at intervals - was hearing the rain falling heavily. Got up washed about 6 o'clock - morning continues dull till about noon when it cleared up fine and warm. Stopped at several places today a short time which gave us time to take runs out for water, flowers etc. At the larger of those stations at which we stopped today the residents thronged down to see us - I suppose they knew by wire about the time we would arrive because they were in considerable numbers. Some of them were very curious to see us all and forced their way down through the cars. Some of them were very forward and gave evidence of malicious feelings - others were quite pleasant to talk to and seemed very anxious to enter into conversation. Crossed over the Missouri by a very large bridge as we entered into Omaha. The darkness of the night prevented us from getting a very good view. Got into Omaha about 10 o'clock where we changed into Union Pacific Railroad cars. This change was for the worse as regards [to] the accommodations in the cars. The cars themselves were old and dirty and rattled as if we were riding over [illegible word] instead of upon rails. The luggage also had to be changed into U.P.R.R. Cars which took up a little time. This was the first change the luggage undergone since leaving New York. Got started somewhere about midnight - traveling very slowly our train load being pretty heavy - it consists of three baggage cars in front, followed by 3 car loads of emigrants (Americans) for California. They again were followed by 9 Car loads of our company.

Monday—10 June

Got properly awaked this morning about 6 o'clock having slept badly during the first night. Morning cold but soon got very warm - still traveling nicely but rather slowly along. Stopping today as yesterday at good many stations for water etc. - got out, sometimes for a run and to pull a flower or two. Grasshoppers this morning - first real natives we had seen. Got out - several of us - got out in the afternoon and amused ourselves by high leaping and running. There was a concert in our carriage in the evening when several fine songs were sung by members of our company.

Tuesday—11th June

Got up this morning at half past 5 having slept well. Dark morning cold but grew warm as it approached noon. Moving along at miserably slow pace with frequent stoppages - many taking runs out today to pluck flowers and to look at any object having any interest at all attached to it. Arrived at Cheyenne about 4 o'clock shortly before there was a thunderstorm passed over us - the rain which fell cooled the atmosphere nicely. At Cheyenne we saw several bars of silver for New York market. Reached summit of Rocky Mountains about 8 o'clock. Shortly after leaving here we passed through a good many snow sheds.

Wednesday—12th June

Got up about 6 o'clock - stopped a short time at Carbon where one or two of the old country people came in and talked a short time with some of our company with whom they were acquainted. Morning very warm. 377 miles to Ogden from this station. This is our 18th day from Liverpool. After breakfast my wife and self got bad with sickness vomitis and [illegible word] diarrhea. This illness was our worst during the whole journey. The vomiting and retching was very painful. Got some brandy [illegible word] and took it which helped us very much. One curious thing about this illness was that we both got bad at same time and both seemed to get better about same time.

Thursday—13th June

Got up about 6 o'clock feeling much better after yesterday's illness. Fine bright morning and much cooler and pleasanter than some mornings past. Traveling very slow - don't understand why - it seems as if the journey from Omaha to Ogden was more tiresome & wearisome than the rest of the whole journey put together. The cars still rock & vacilitate very much and when stopping or starting the shock is like to tear one in pieces. Stopped at Evanston a short time - a few people there recognized some amongst our company and chatted a little. Passing down the Echo Canyon the scenery becomes at once wild and grand - the rocks tower way above us many hundred feet. Arrived at Echo station - the greetings that some of our people received from friends & relations and acquaintances was quite enthusiastic & warm. Our car was quite besieged for a short time. Passing on from there we shortly passed the Devil's Slide - we next pass through Weber - the Valley seems rich & fertile, while the surrounding mountains are clad with snow. Passing along the Devil's Gate is pointed out to us which is a large projecting rock contracting the channel of the water to a narrow pass the water rushing down thro' at a very rapid pace - a road passes round the ledge of the rock just the breadth of the wheels and no more - this continues for a considerable distance and should two vehicles meet one or other must give way and turn back before they can pass. The scenery at the Devil's Gate is of that wild & grand character portrayed above. We reached Ogden about 6 P.M. Confusion prevailed here for a short time so soon as we had stopped - just so soon were our cars besieged by people looking for their friends and the talk and the changing of cars and personal luggage and the meeting of friends occupied about an hour. We then got off for Salt Lake City which we reached somewhere near 9 o'clock. Of course our first outlook was for Uncle John but no Uncle John was there we having arrived a day or two earlier than was expected. We shortly found H.G. Park who kindly took us to the Valley House where we remained over night. Went down at the station next morning I found Uncle John on horseback who then took charge of us and conveyed us to his home [in] Heber in waggons where we found many friends ready & willing to minister unto our wants. It was quite like returning home after a long absence - so many friends around us hardly left us time to think on the old Country. Our journey up to Salt Lake City was performed in 19 days, 11 days by sea 1 day & night in New York and 7 days by rail across the vast Continent of America - the distance was at sea 3100 miles and rail 2475. It is now past & gone as a dream - it returneth not anymore - at times it seemed wearisome and we felt like as if we never would undertake another such, but after a little rest and after so much kindness from friends we seem to quite forget our little hardships & troubles and think no more of them. Our luggage turned out all right and nothing so far as known lost. Our Captain of Company, Thomas Judd, deserves a word of praise for his kind and patient and impartial attention to all. Like a good Captain having a great responsibility upon him, he was always at hand late and early looking after the comfort and welfare of his charge. His mind must have been greatly relieved, of it was possible to have been embarrassed when he got released of his charge at Salt Lake City. His company did well under him and turned out one more on arrival at destination than what we commenced with. The cleverest man amongst our company and another man rumored says, got left at Chicago. I presume they would come on soon after.

EDITOR'S NOTE: *Once again, this journal entry is printed as David Lennox wrote it. You may find words capitalized that normally wouldn't be or no commas where we would put them, but it is transcribed as he wrote it and was most likely accepted as standard in his time. This journal does not have a date but it was after his mission to Scotland in 1905-1907.*

Murdoch History
Introductory

I have been asked repeatedly to write something about our ancestors, where they hailed from – what are their avocations, where they resided, etc. I fully realise that unless this is at least attempted soon, the generation of people to which I belong will soon all have passed away and the succeeding generation will be left without much information pertaining to the those times, circumstances and events. With these thoughts then, and with a desire to comply with the request so often made, I will attempt to put in writing what little I know of the past of our ancestors on the Murdoch side and others also, associated with them by marriage and otherwise.

In writing this narrative, I feel that from our point of view, on this far western land of America, the subject of the cause of our gathering here demands first consideration. – The primal consideration was the Restored Gospel, through the means of the Prophet, Seer and Revelator, Joseph Smith.

The Gospel was restored and I take it that everyone Latter Day Saint is familiar with this most wonderful event.

The Church of Jesus Christ of Latter Day Saints was organised on April 6, 1830 with some six members.

The Gospel was carried to England by Heber C. Kimball, Willard Richards, Joseph Fielding and John Goodson in the late Summer of 1837. These brethren arrived there, so Heber C. Kimball's life's story, by Orson F. Whitmer, advises us without any means to prosecute their labors in a strange land. Heber C. was absolutely pennyless. With wonderful humility and faith and reliance upon the Lord, they were led to go to Preston, Lancashire where the way was immediately opened up – friends were raised up and it seems that the people were eagerly waiting for and ready to receive the message then delivered to them. The wonderful, it might be truly said, the marvelous success these Elders met with is most interestingly narrated in Whitney's *Life of Heber C. Kimball*. The reader should own a copy of this Book and read it. Heber C. Kimball then with these other brethren were the Fathers and Founders of the British Mission. They spread out in the surrounding Country and established many Branches. This work was greatly augmented and further established over a large part of England in 1840. When Heber C. Kimball, Brigham Young, Wilford

Woodruff, Parley P. and Orson Pratt, John Taylor and others were over there at that time and added upon and developed that which had already been accomplished some two or three years previously.

The Introduction of the Gospel to Scotland

In 1839 Elders Samuel Mulliner and Alexander Wright carried the Gospel to Scotland, their native land and were instrumental in opening up and establishing branches at Paisley, Johnstone, Bridge of Weir and Thornleybank. In 1840 Scotland was visited by Apostle Orson Pratt who established the Edinburgh Branch. Thus was the Gospel carried to Scotland and shortly afterwards Glasgow was included with the above mentioned places and with the news filtering through from England where it was introduced some three years earlier, and its establishment in Scotland it spread out into Ayrshire and sometime before 1852 it had reached Grasswater, Kirkconnel etc. It was there that Uncle John received his first impressions at the hands of Aunt Ann's brother, James Steele, while on a visit from England where he was then located. James Steele received it from a young lady who had received it and been a member of the Church for some years. This young lady became Mrs. James Steele and these two with their children James E. & George emigrated in the year 1856 on the good ship "Horizon" and in that ship and in their company, was Mary Murdoch of Grasswater, about two miles from Lugar and about 6 or 7 from Muirkirk. Mary Murdoch was known in her day as "Wee Granny". Being, as I have heard it stated many times by my mother and others, quite short in stature but strongly and, I presume, stockily built. But of this we shall have more to say further on.

According to our Genealogical Records James Murdoch of Grasswater was born about 1786 and Mary Murray of Glencaurn 13 Oct 1782 were married January 10, 1811 at Glencairn. They had children -

Janet, born 8 Dec 1811 died 28 June 1866
Mary born 16 June 1813 died in infancy
James born 29 July 1814 died Sept 12, 1884
Veronica born 16 June 1816 died Oct. 4, 1908
Mary born 3 Oct 1818 died Dec 5, 1900
John M. born 28 Decr 1820 died May 6, 1910
Margaret born 30 Decr 1822 died in infancy
William born 3 July 1825 died Mar 12, 1913 in Heber City

Their family then consisted of 8 children two of whom died in infancy. The conditions then of life and existence were somewhat poor. The period was before the days of Railways. The iron and coal industry was in its infancy. Manufactures were few and about the only employment or work obtainable by these growing children was by hiring out to Farmers in the surrounding neighborhood. Grandfather and Grandmother could not afford to keep them at home because his wages would be very small and the great wonder is how they managed to get along at all. Frugal to a degree they must have been. The very strickest woman must have been of necessity their constant thought and care. Their home was Grasswater where the family was all raised. As has already been stated, Grasswater is some 6 or 7 miles west of Muirkirk – 2 miles from Lugar and about 4 miles from the town of Old Cumnock, all in the country of Ayr. Their pleasure and enjoyments were very few and were only such as are or were incidental to a farming life in that rural district at this early age.

A sorrowful event happened to this contented little family on the 20th of October 1831. The Father, James Murdoch, was employed at some of the pits sought to be established at this period not far from his happy little home and family.

The son of a farmer at a place called Dalfad, happened around and his curiosity, or something of that nature, produced a desire within him to be lowered into a new shaft which had been lately sunk. The pits at this early date in this neighborhood were all sunk on the out-croppings of the mineral field – not deep, but on the contrary, very shallow and operated by a windlass. The Boy went down and was overcome by foul air or choke damp which had accumulated at the bottom and he fell helplessly out of the bucket and whatever it was. The alarm was given and grandfather was lowered down to his rescue, but he also was overcome in a similar manner. By the time that efforts were made to disperse the damp and foul air and bring the bodies to the surface, life in both instances was gone – and thus the lives of two had been snuffed out in a few minutes. The father, the provider of this little family was thus taken and we can imagine what a sad and sorrowful little home it was.

My Father was but five years of age – Uncle John was 10 or 11. Granny was very brave – Her older children had to go out and work – Uncle John was almost old enough to herd cows at some nearby or neighboring farm. My Father before he was seven years of age was doing the same and from those early years in their lives they never knew anything else by work and then for a mere pittance, but they got some kind of board, chiefly oatmeal – Tea they got once a year at New Years day and that was then considered wonderful. Time went on, the opportunities for education were of the most meagre nature. Very, very little they got. And in thinking it all over and reflecting upon the times then, their impoverished condition the hardships they had to endure, and the struggles of life and existence, it appears really marvelous and wonderful that men like Uncle John and Father could ever come to maturity and keep level or on a par with others far more favorably raised and situated. It is almost unbelievable that Uncle John could ever be expected to attain to the learning and understanding that he acquired during his life and to the high social standing he held in the Community in which he so long resided. It is equally the same with my Father. He rose to be underground manager at the Muirkirk Iron and Coal works. A position he held for quite a number of years before emigrating to America.

I always loved Aunt Mary. She was always so good and kind and considerate. Aunt Veronica was another member of that family from Grasswater – The mother of a large family by her husband George Caldow in Scotland. They saw hard times, trails and difficulties and poverty. Being a widow and alone, her family having all married but one – and he was old enough to be almost a grandfather, she was emigrated and came with us in 1878. Thus five our of the six embraced the Gospel and left their native land for the Gospels sake. Aunt Jennie, the eldest married Alex Smith and lived at Birnicknowe, about three miles from Grasswater. They had quite a family and was in rather poor circumstances the most of her life. Her husband, a good man, but rather delicate and asmatical. A son, William whom I knew in Glasgow emigrated to the State of Washington some number of years after we came. He and his wife are now gone, but they have left up there several sons and at least one daughter. There remains but one more to mention and that was James. He married Margaret M. Call. They had a large family and lived in Glasgow. I think they must all be gone now, as I could get no trace of any of them while over there 1905-6-7 altho I even advertised in the paper for them. A son William, came here and lived for a time in Heber City and Park City. He died in this City and was buried in the City Cemetery.

I felt as if I need to take space enough to say what I have about the Grasswater Murdochs. Notwithstanding their humble station in life, they got along wonderfully well, overcame many obstacles that would have made the stoutest hearts quail. They succeeded admirably in life battle and came through as much respected and loved as the great majority of mankind.

Uncle John tells us in his journal of record, which he wrote with his own hand at a very advanced age, some rightly or thereabouts, that after attaining manhood he boarded with his mother at Grasswater. When about 28 years of age he married Ann Steele in 1848 where home was at Kirkconnel. They lived for a while there and here it was that he got his first impressions of Mormonism from James Steele, brother of Aunt Ann who was residing then somewhere in England. The Gospel has now been preached in England some eleven years. James Steele was keeping Company with a young lady there who had been a Mormon for years. And their close intimacy led to his conversion. Uncle John narrates that James Steele from being very indifferent about religious matters had now become thoroughly familiar with the Scriptures and could easily overcome any arguments or statements that Uncle John could put forth. This was a wonderful surprise to Uncle John. He felt that James Steele had acquired a wonderful knowledge of the Scriptures and things spiritual.

In 1850 James Steele visited them at Kirkconnel and it was at this time that Uncle John began to seriously investigate. He states that his business called him back to England and that Uncle John never saw him again. Very shortly after this Thomas Todd, for many years a resident of Heber City, and then a native of Sanquhar was baptised. Some two weeks later Sister Todd was baptised and also Uncle John and Aunt Ann. The first fruits of the Gospal in this dispensation in that part of Scotland "all from the planting of James Steele." His record preceeds – In the spring of 1851 I moved my family to Birnicknowe around there were a few scattered Saints and a little branch was established. "We soon baptised a few more. My mother and my sister Mary being among the number." By this time they were being visited by the Elders by whom they were encouraged and comforted. Meetings were held at Uncle Johns house – perhaps the only place where the little branch and the few Saints could meet – hold their little meetings and rejoice in each others Society. Meetings also were held at "Wee Grannies" house at Grasswater and here it was that my mother had the opportunity to attending them and becoming familiar with the Gospel. My Father then belonged to a church in Cumnock and I believe it was while he would be away there that the meetings were held at "Wee Grannies".

Shortly after this Uncle John moved to Garallan, near Cumnock which was the last place he lived at before emigrating to America. His home here was the meeting place also for the Saints & Elders, but not for long. President Brigham Young sent to Franklin D. Richards then presiding in Liverpool, for two Scotch Shepherds and their dogs. Uncle John was one of those selected. Preparations were made to depart. Farewell parties were held at Garallan and at Kirkconnel immediately prior to their departure and on the morning of January 1, 1852 they took the tram at Kirkconnel for Glasgow en route thus far. From Glasgow they proceeded to Liverpool by boat and had a very rough passage. In due time they got to Liverpool staying there right on ten days for the vessel to get her cargo in. At length on the 10 day of January 1852 the "Lennebee" [Kenebeck, according to John's personal history] sailed away for America.

Just before leaving his native land Uncle John composed and sang the following song to the tune of "Afton Water" The tune seems very appropriate for near there, Kirkconnel, where he and Aunt Ann spent their last night in Scotland the "Afton" flows quietly along amongst its green braes and joins the "Nich" lower down.

Oh Scotland, my Country, my dear native home
Thou land of the brave and the theme of my song.
Oh why should I leave thee and cross the deep sea
To far distant lands lovely Scotland from thee?
How pleasant to view are thy mountains and hills

> The sweet blooming heather and far famed bluebells
> The haunts of my childhood where oft I have strayed
> With my faithful companions – my dog, crook and plaid.
> Oh Scotland, my Country and land of my birth
> In fondness I'll ever remember thy worth
> For wrapt in thy bosom my forefathers sleep
> Oh why should I leave thee and cross the wide deep.
> But why should I linger or wish for to stay?
> The voice of the Prophet is haste, flee away
> Lest judgments o'ertake you and lay Scotland low
> To the faithful in Zion Oh then let me go.
> Farewell then loved Scotland, my home and my abode
> When duty requires it we bow to the call
> We brave every danger we conquer each foe
> To the voice of the Prophet oh then let me go.
> Farewell then dear Kindred, on last, fond adieu
> Farewell my dear brethren, so faithful and true;
> May Angels watch o'er you till warfares are o'er
> And in safety we all meet on Zion's fair shore

A very creditable composition and worthy of reproduction in his memoirs. It might here be mentioned that wherever the Gospel has been introduced, the spirit of poetry takes possession of the people affiliating as Latter Day Saints. In every number or volume of the "Millennial Star" poetic effusions are there found, expressive of joy, gratitude, affection and love. The same spirit prevailed in this land. Our Hymn Book is full of very choice pieces by early members and prominent members of the Church. It is needless to mention a few names, both male and female, of the authors. The Hymn book, I presume is in the home of every member of the Church and forms very interesting and instructive reading. I hope that some day, the history of every Composition in the Hymn Book will be published and the authors suitably mentioned and honored.

From the Millennial Star Vol. 14 The sailing of the Hennebee is noted as follows.

> "This large, new and commodious ship of ten hundred and seventy tons register, went out of the Bramleymore Dock on the morning of the tenth instant – 10 January 1852 having been detained two days by adverse winds, which blew a heavy gale outside. They had three hundred and thirty three souls of the Saints on board. We had chartered the Ship Devonshire, but being a little disappointed in her qualifications for sea, we also blew a head wind and secured the Hennebee, which is an unusual spacious and commodious vessel. After getting their luggage put to rights, the Saints seemed very cheerful, and gave out to their feelings in songs and praise as the noble ship passed out upon the bosom of the Mersey, and left the shore fading in the distance.
>
> Included in this company were Elders John T. Higbee, John Spiers, Thomas Smith and W.C. Dunbar, each Presidents of Conferences, faithful in their callings and going up to the Lion of the Lord having done a great and good work in this land. Many thousands, who will have obtained the gift of Eternal Life through the instrumentality of these faithful men, will rejoice with them in the Kingdome of God. We have pleasure also in

announcing the departure of Elder John Pack of the French mission with about a dozen Saints from the Channel Islands. How joyous to witness the departure of Saints of the different tongue and families of the earth from their native lands, to mingle with God's people in establishing his purposes on the earth. Elder Higbee was appointed president of the Company, and the several Elders above named were called to be his Councellors, under whose excellent superintendence, the Saints will doubtless enjoy much of the Spirit of God during their passage on the waters."

I have not been able to find much about the voyage of the "Hennebee" in Vol 14 of the Millennial Star. From Uncle John's record, we find they were some nine weeks at sea which was an unusually long time. It seems provisions were very scarce and water also for the steerage passengers and this caused much discomfort and sickness, especially amongst the children. Uncle John speaks of oatmeal, which was as I take it, their principal food. Having no money and no other means of subsistence, the children suffered and pined during this period and by the time they got on the Mississippi they were in a very reduced and sickened condition. It must have been distressing and heartbending to see their two little ones pine away and cry for bread, which could not be got for them. Nine weeks at sea would bring us to about March 15. They were detained at the mouth of the River eight or ten days on a sand bar. It would therefore be now about March 25. The River Boat was very crowded and with the sick children, we can well imagine what a terrible trying time it was for Uncle John and Aunt Ann and all the rest of them. The little boy, James by name, died on March 20, after 1 year 18 months and was buried in a wood yard on the banks of the Mississippi river twelve miles from Columbia. It will be seen that there was apparently some discrepancy about dates here. The Journal proceeds "we landed at St. Louis & were then in the care of A.O. Smoot from Salt Lake City, who was in charge of the emigration that year. Uncle John says "our little girl, Elisabeth by name, had now become very weak and although everything that willing hands and kind hearts could do for her, she passed away April 4, aged 3 yrs 8 mos. and was buried in a strange land amongst strangers. The people were very kind to us. We remained in St. Louis about one month waiting a ship load of Saints that left Liverpool after us. We then went up the Missouri River to Kansas City where we got our outfits for crossing the plains". Cholera now broke out and quite a few died and were buried there about nine miles out on the plains.

On May 20th a little girl was born to them in a small tent in the midst of a terrific thunder storm. They were pleased and named her Mary Murray Murdoch. This was Cousin Mary Duke and later Mary Ryan. Aunt Ann was able to walk and carry her baby almost every foot of the way from the time her baby was eight days old. On the way Captain Smoot was taken sick with the cholera and the team was held up some to allow him needed rest. Uncle John was his day nurse. Later on, while in the Black Hills Country, Uncle John was taken sick with the mountain fever and was in turn nursed by Captain Smoot. On September 3, Captain Smoot landed his large company of weary pilgrims in Salt Lake City after a long and tedious journey of seventeen weeks on the plains. This was the first company that came by the Perpetual Emigration Fund. Captain Smoot introduced Uncle John to President Young as one of his two Shepherds with their dogs and gave him a very good recommend. President Young informed them that he had routed what few sheep he had left to his Brother Lorenzo for five years and would not need them at present for that purpose. He said we needed rest and to remain at Camp and the brethren would find them something to eat and the way would be opened up for them to get work. Before the evening of the second day there was not a soul left in Camp but the two Shepherds, their wives, the two children and the two dogs. A man by the name of Dalton from Farmington came to Camp and hired us to work for him one month. He took us home and was very kind to us. My companions foot was still getting worse and became unable too work and was anxious to return to Salt Lake. Uncle John finished his month, got his pay and considered himself rich enough to divide with his companion. He then was hired to dig potatoes for President Young. He says he had much joy in his labors, although the work was hard, thinking that he was working for the Prophet of the Lord and the greatest man on earth.

Uncle John located in the Third Ward in Salt Lake City and became second Councillor to Bishop Jacob Weiller. On the removal from the ward of the first Councillor, he was made first Councillor in which capacity he acted until the time of the "move" caused by Johnson's Army coming here. With others he then moved to Provo Valley, now and far long known as Heber City. This was in 1860. Their first home was dug out and others had similar places to live in. This was a new start in life again. They all obtained land and proceded to subdue it, plant crops and do everything requisite and necessary in a new and virgin country. With industry, perseverance and faith that knew no battering they gradually grew up in their new settlement and with the blessings of the Lord they patiently toiled on and overcame all hindrances, obstacles, privations and suffering until life became more tolerable and prosperity and comparative comfort came to them in their little domicile there. None of the present generation, none but those who actually came through such times and days and years of toil and labor and striving can ever know how much they are indebted to the Pioneers, yes the grand and noble fathers, mothers, sons and daughters of the most worthy people that ever lived. Firm and undaunted in their faith, they pursued their course and kept right along in the way mapped out for the children of our Heavenly Father in these latter-days in building the Zion of our God in these valleys of the mountains.

The blessings of the Lord were with them, and chief amongst these, was the blessing of health and strength to enable them to overcome all hardships and privations incidental to the establishing themselves in this new country. Another great blessing they enjoyed was the gift of a large and helpful family. Many they brought with them, a babe in arms, Elizabeth and James, as has already been stated died on the way. Ann, Janet Osborne and Sarah Jane have the Third Ward, Salt Lake City, for their birthplace. Jacobina Wells Osborne was born in Heber City as were also John, Isabella Lovina, John William who died in infancy, Thomas Todd – Lucy Veronica also died in infancy, Joseph Al, David Steele and Millicent Sophia. Some fifteen in all. Glory- Hallelujah! Praise the Lord. Altho the first portion of the family were all girls, they were not only a comfort and blessing to their parents but were also a real aid and assistance to their Father and mother in the days of hardships and toil.

In those days Polygamy was practiced by the Latter Day Saints. Uncle John and Aunt Ann were just as much impressed with the importance and necessity of observing that principal of the Gospel then as any other, and, when the proper time and person should come along it was understood that Uncle John should observe it. In the course of events, Isabella Crawford from Blantyre, Scotland, emigrated to Holyoake, Massachusetts, in company with others and were engaged there in a Cotton Mill. Some five years passed – they saved their earnings and were enabled to purchase a yoke of oxen and a wagon in which they came to Utah. One of the Scotch lassies with whom Isabella Crawford emigrated was named Catherine Campbell who married William Foreman although was later one of the Bishops in Heber City. Isabella Crawford was visiting her friend there and in this way an acquaintance was formed which ripened into friendship and a little later led to a visit to the Salt Lake Temple[1] where Uncle John and Isabella Crawford were married the eighth day of August 1862. From this union the following were issue: - Margaret Ann, Catherine Campbell, James C., Brigham, Robert, John Murray Jr. and Isabella Crawford. Twenty two children altogether – 15 of whom lived to manhood and womanhood. At a Murdoch reunion held at Vivian Park 17, 18 &19 August 1921 commemorating the one hundredth anniversary of Uncle John's birth, the following statistics were given:

22 children

126 grandchildren

20 great grandchildren

317 total descendants from Uncle John and his two good faithful wives.

In the late eighties, the raid was on and it was hot, hateful, vindictive and in many cases bitterly, ruthlessly and heartlessly cruel and severe. Judge Charles T. Lane was on the Bench and tried many of the cases.

---

1. The Salt Lake Temple was finished and dedicated in 1894. David Lennox was probably referring to the Endowment House in Salt Lake City that was used for ordinance work while the Salt Lake Temple was being built.

Feelings were pretty high while it lasted. The leaders of the Church were in exile, hiding up from the officers of the law who were using every device and stratagem that the Devil could inspire them with to harass, annoy, and imprison. To the great credit of most of those arrested, tried and convicted for disobeying the Edmunds-Tucker Act, they paid the fine and went to the Penitentiary to suffer the term of imprisonment inflicted like men. Uncle John was getting along in life. He had lived in Heber city a long time everybody knew him, and he was one of those who were caught, tried and convicted and sentenced by Judge Lane to a term in the Penitentiary. He asked the judge for the privilege of going home to Heber City from Provo where the trial was held for the purpose of getting the necessary change of underwear while in the Pen. This was granted. He returned home, got the necessary clothing and left home of his own free will and option to go to Salt Lake to serve the time imposed upon him to satisfy the law demand. In due time he presented himself at the Penitentiary, told them his name, where he hailed from and that he had come to suffer imprisonment according to the sentence passed upon him. It appears that no commitment papers had been sent the Marshall or Warden – they knew nothing about him or the papers and could not receive him. Uncle left and came up to our place and told his tale. "They won't have me." he said. And he seemed very much put out about it. Any other ordinary man would have rejoiced at the reception he got and might have and most likely would have thought at least, if he had not said it, well you can go to the devil, I will go home and when you really want me bad enough, you can come for me. Not so with honest to goodness Uncle John. He explained the whole matter to them and they told him to come back again at a certain time when they would have the papers and receive him and he give him a zebra striped suit which all prisoners then wore. Can you imagine of a more honorable, honest, guileless soul than his. He returned to the Pen, was admitted and served his term. He might have gone to California, or Timbuctoo if he had wanted to.

This incident is a wonderful illustration of his honest, reliability and dependability and keep sense of right and trust. "They won't have me." I could occupy much more space in writing and commenting upon the lives of these good people, but I realise that Uncle John himself has made a history of his life, brief at that, also, Nettie, Sarah and Kate with the assistance of William Lindsay who has written much for them have also written many particulars and incidents in the lives of their parents and these all in greater detail which will be more interesting to the families directly concerned and affected and as considerable is aid and was printed in the papers at the time of their demise. I will copy that herein and finish this portion of my narrative and succeeding that, proceed to give a brief account of the gathering of Aunt Mary and her family of three, Mary, Andrew and Aleck in 1866. And following that a brief account of the gathering of Father, myself and wife and Sister Janet and Margaret and Aunt Veronica and John Adamson in 1878.

The following by Mrs. Janet McMullin written for the Daughters of the Pioneers is well worthy of a place here and quite appropriately follows what has preceded it.

Let us turn our memories back
Far along that dreary track
There's a band of Pilgrims filled with hopes and fears
They had left their home – their all,
Gathering here at Father's call,
And now are known as Utah's Pioneers.
Chorus
Then all honor to their name
Who have given us this fame
It was earned with love and toil and faith and prayers
As we meet from day to day
We feel it in our hearts to say
We are children of those grand old Pioneers
When they reached this promised land
Mid those mountain vales so grand
They were earnest serving God, who brought them through
Nice log houses they did build
With large families they were filled
Oh! – they truly builded better than they knew
They were united in their way
And their flocks and herds did raise
They did card and spin and weave and make our clothes
With their faithful honest toil
They did cultivate the soil
And made the desert blossom as the rose.
As their children when we meet
In those vales so calm and sweet
We prize their lives of service more than gold
And love them more and more
As we read their history o'er
Yet, the half of this grand story not's been told.

The Spirit of gathering very quickly takes possession of the Church members after baptism as a rule. Their associations with friends and neighbors, becomes often times strained and unpleasant. Those who are not impressed with the truth and will not join the Church are frequently somewhat hostile in their feelings and bitter in their denunciation of it. And it has not at all been unusually for the Saints to be ostracized and persecuted. This condition, no doubt increases their desire to gather and get away from amongst them.

Mary Murdoch at Grasswater (Wee Grannie) and Mary Murdoch Mair, at the Stables, about a mile or so distant, and another (Janet Lennox Murdoch) at the Grasswater Rows were left behind. Little meetings continued to the held at Grannies and with an occasional visit from the Elders in Ayrshire, the fire within kept flickering and burning and in the case of each one of them, it never dimmed nor became extinct as long as life lasted. Time went on. Some four years had now passed since the departure of Uncle John and Aunt Ann on the *Kennebec*.[2] Uncle John was by this time able to send for James Steele and wife and his two children and his mother, Mary Murdoch. I can just remember the day Wee Grannie came down to our house to bid us good bye on her way to Liverpool. My recollection is not clear however. I can just remember the occasion. Twelve days after Uncle John left his native land, I was born, so that by 1856 when Grannie and the others left, I was but four years of age.

In the eighteenth volume of the Millennial Star, we find that the ship Horizon,[3] sailed from Liverpool, for Boston May 25, 1856 with 856 souls of the Saints on board under the Presidency of Elders Edward Martin, Jessie Haven and Geo. P. Waugh. "The following Elders who have held responsible positions in this country, also sailed on this ship – Elder T.B. Broderick and John Toone from Utah – the latter retires from his labors on account of ill health. John Jaques, Robert Holt, Thomas Ord, James Stones, Henry Squires and Robert Evans were Presidents of Conferences. Elder Martin has labored in the ministry in Britain over three years, and during most of the present seasons emigration, has been engaged with us in the emigration department of the office. His labors have been of that faithful and efficient character which commend themselves.

The following piece is taken from the "Star" May 5, 1856, and is very fitting for this and every other company leaving Europe's shores:

> *I'm away, I'm away, o'er the wide spreading sea,*
> *To the land of the brave, to the land of the free,*
> *To the land of the light, to the land of the truth,*
> *To the land of our Joseph, a Prophet in youth*
> *To the land where the Gospel first dawned on our day*
> *Ship, spread out thy canvas and bear me away.*

---

2. From "Immigrant Ships Transcribers Guild, Kennebec, 259 MURDOCK, John M 31 Glasgow Shepherd 260 MURDOCK, Ann F 22 Glasgow 261 MURDOCK, Elizabeth F 3 Glasgow 262 MURDOCK, James M 1 Glasgow

3. http://www.eancestry.org/docs/histories/000150.pdf, accessed 12 March 2010 Voyage of the Horizon – Ship Journey Details Transcription by Chad G. Nichols Ship: Horizon Date of Departure: 25 May 1856 Port of Departure: Liverpool, England LDS Immigrants: 856 Church Leader: Edward Martin Date of Arrival: 30 Jun 1856 Port of Arrival: Boston, Massachusetts Source(s): BMR, pp. 151-188 (FHL #025,691)

I'm away, I'm away, for to see and to know
The things which our Prophets have told us below
To build up the Temple, that now is begun
High up in the mountain, for father and son
Who died without hearing the truth of the day
Ship spread out they canvas and bear me away.

I'm away, I'm away, where the husband and wife
Unite to be one for the regions of life
Where the love and the joy of the life giving pair
Can only be known by the just who are there
Where the Lord in his mercy, His wisdom displays
Ship, spread out thy canvas and bear me away.

I'm away, I'm away, where the sire and the son
In the cause of their God, have unitedly run
Where the Priest and the Prophet, the matron and maid
For the sake of Religion, the ransom have paid,
To where they departed from temples of clay
Ship, spread out they canvas and bear me away.

I'm away, I'm away and I bid you adieu
Oh Elders of Israel be faithful and true
And pluck not the daisies that grow o'er the green
Full fresh in my country and blossom unseen
And for years deliverance for ever I'll pray
Ship, spread out thy canvas and bring them away.

Crooked Stick from the mountains.

The eighteenth volume of the Millennial Star contains a number of choice poetical effusions from some on board the Horizon and others contemplating leaving their native land about this time. To my mind, they are full of beautiful sentiment and thoughts, and so much do I admire their poetic style and beauty that I now reproduce some of them nearly seventy years after their first publication.

The Hour of Prayer

List to that sound, soft, floating through the air
It is the hymn of praise, the voice of prayer.
From gathered hundreds upon yon proud ship
Where bursts the chorus from each joyous lip
In loved Hosannahs praising Him on high
Who rules o'er earth and heaven eternally
Now hushed the strains while silence still and deep
Reigns o'er all, e'en nature seems asleep
A meek petition follows – raised above
To seek the aid Divine, the ransom'd love
Of Him, the lofty one, to Israel dear
Whom Saints delight to praise, and sinners fear
To ask for blessings on that chosen land
Taking a farewell of their native land
To seek in mountain wilds repose and joy
Where sin is not and peace knows no alloy.
Blest of their God, confiding in his care
They know no sense of danger, fear or snare
They have obeyed his laws, fulfilled His will
And life or death for them can bring no ill.
Proud of their calling, chured with hopes of bliss
In other worlds – pain turns to joy in this
From every life repeated o'er again
The prayer concluded, comes the deep "Amen"
E'en strangers seem to feel the spells control
And simple prayer to steal away the soul
Its peaceful influence calms all minds to rest
And Gentiles feel midst Saints supremely blest.

K.J.R., London on the ship Horizon, May 23, 1856

The following piece is by Emily Hill, Liverpool, May 2, 1856. Miss Hill emigrated about this time from England. A very fine and highly gifted lady, afterwards became Mrs. Joseph Woodmancy and had a family.

Oh England, proud England, thou place of my birth
I bid the farewell for the land of the free
Yes my heart with peculiar emotion is swelling
As I turn from the scenes so familiar to me.
Oh once I esteemed thee and prized thee most dearly
And thought thee the cordrest spot on the earth
Till truth op'ed my vision and then I saw dearly
How much was thy value, how much was thy worth.
Then England thy beauties receded before me
I found thou wast burdened with malice and strife
Thou hatest the truth and I ceased to adore thee
As before I had done e're I found evil so rife.
I know thou art one of Old Babylon's daughters
And doomed to destruction by heavens high hand
Though mighty thou seemest as the sound of great waters
Yet the word of Jehovah, it surely will stand.
Oh stern is the vengeance and firm is His saying
His breathing can scatter thy prospects though bright
Thy strength and thy glory e'en now are decaying
And fast, yea with speed, thou art losing thy might.
And yet in thy midst are my kindred remaining
Regardless of danger – rejecting the truth
For its sake they have scorned me, all warning disdaining
And Oh, it is hard thus to sever in youth.
Yet why should the thought of the last adieu grieve one
Oh - I depart from my own native shore
Yea the voice of the spirit is bidding me leave thee
Farewell then forever, I'll view thee no more.

Emily Hill
(Taken in Martin's Hand Cart Company from my scrap book – by Josiah Rogerson)

From the foregoing we have traced the sailing of the "Horizon" from Liverpool which contained some 856 souls of the Saints. And from all accounts written by passengers, it was an excellent company in every respect – exceptionally well behaved and gave no trouble at all to the ship's captain and crew. In fact, it's related that so well behaved were they that when singing the well known song "I'll marry none but Mormons" as a pass time and for amusement while on the sea, the Captain said "And if I can have my way I'll carry none but Mormons." Their troubles began on their long, tedious and tiresome journey across the plains. Travel starved, weary, worn out, foot sore, faint, fatigued and ready to drop, they trudged along, day after day, week after week, month after month, suffering much from a most unfortunate late start and becoming very much belated on arriving at their journeys end on November 30, 1856 in considerable snow and severely cold weather during the last portion of the journey. Many fell by the way, over come by fatigue and the very severe trials and ordeals and exposure incident to such a prolonged journey. Young, middle aged and elderly people succumbed and were laid away by the roadside as well as they could under the circumstances, which at their best were poor, meagre and heart rendering to relatives and survivors accompanying. One by one at first they were "gathered in". Latterly they died in such numbers that decent internment was scarcely possible. What does the present generation know about the faith, endurance, hardships, privations, sufferings of the early Pioneers, who left all for the Gospel's sake? And who made this desert and wilderness a fit, habitable and delightful country to live in.

From people who have come over the trail or highway in these early days, yet living, it is learned that the road-way or high-way then was about three or four miles from Chimney Rock. To that as near as we know, or are ever likely to learn, Mary Murdoch, who would then be nearly seventy four years of age, died at or near chimney Rock, Oct. 3, 1856. This is the date that Martin's Hand Cart Company is said to have passed that historic spot. There, nature gave out. We believe she walked most of the way, waded streams, etc. Her heart was set on Zion, the Valley, her son John and his wife Aunt Ann who preceded her some four years. It is related of her, and we believe it is absolutely correct, thus, when she was stricken and realized that her most cherished hopes, desires and ambition could not be accomplished, she said to those in whose company she came, "Tell John that I died with my face to the Valley". Brave little woman! Wee Granny was truly a heroine, and her name will be remembered and spoken of as long as a Murdoch from her loins is found in the land. James Steele, in whose care she came, died at Bitter Creek, Wyoming, farther on the journey.

Some eleven years ago, the Z. C. M. I. calendar was Chimney Rock from a painting by Alfred Lambourne. It proved so popular amongst the Institution's friends and patrons, that a second supply had to be procured to meet the demands for it. This picture appealed also to many who had either come that way, or whose relatives had, myself amongst the number and I wrote the following lines, not claiming for them any merit whatever, but offering them merely as a token of love and appreciation to the memory of that true, devoted soul who gave her life for the Gospel's sake.

The picture was entitled – "Sunrise at Chimney Rock" and shows that well known landmark with an immense lot of caravans, or covered wagons, on the tract westward to the Valley.

What solemn thoughts pervade the soul
As on this scene we meditate
This resting place for wearied Saints
Tired, travel-stained and desolate.
This scene portrays in vivid ways
A spot made dear on journey drear
By Hand-Cart means in early days
A half-way place on journey here.
Impelled by faith and filled with hope
That soon they'd reach the appointed place
Inured to toil, with trials cope,
To Utah's vales they set their face.
But some along this dreary road
Worn out and faint, oft fell asleep
E're they could reach the cherished spot
The valley dear and friends to greet.
Brave, honest souls at early morn
As pilgrims in a holy cause
Who dared to face a world of scorn
T'obey Gods call and keep his laws.
Somewhere around this stopping place
As years go by – 'tis fifty seven
Wee Grannie died, there is no trace
Of earth's abode – Her soul's in Heaven.
Tell John she said as she laid down
Her worn out frame in this lone place
That I died here, but with my face
Turned Zionwards – the cherished place.
Blest be their names with fondest love
We'll cherish aye their mem'ries dear
Soon we may meet with them above
And greet them in their higher sphere.

Dec. 24, 1913, David L. Murdoch

With wonderful faith the early Saints – the first fruits of the Gospel in their native lands, embraced the Gospel giving a willing and ready ear to its glad sound and identifying themselves in small branches, studying, reading, seeking for truth and this too in neighborhoods, villages and towns that were exceedingly hostile and bitter in their attitude towards them. They kept on – faithful and true – hoping and praying that some day deliverance would come to them and that they too would be privileged to gather to the Valley, to Zion, and mingle and associate with their kindred, friends and acquaintances who had already gone there. Like a beacon light, these thoughts were ever uppermost in their minds – their hearts were fixed, their minds were firmly set and quickly they prepared for the time and the opportunity to get away. It took time – such patience, much care and anxiety to accomplish this object so dear to their hearts. The trials, tribulations and sorrowful and humble experiences of the past daunted them not. With marvelous faith, and relying upon the commands of the Lord, "Come out of her, O ye my people that ye be not partakers of her sins and calamities that shall come upon her." Their chief purpose was, ever prepare to get away. The Gospel light kept burning steadily in the bosoms of those left behind and who had identified themselves with the Church prior to Wee Grannie's departure in 1856. Aunt Mary, still residing at the Stables, Grasswater, as before mentioned and having raised a large and very fine family, was handicapped very seriously by her husband, Alan Mair, who could not see or accept the Gospel as had his wife. They did not see alike on this vital point and none but those who have had experience either personal, or by observation can fully comprehend what a serious thing it becomes in families. Aunt Mary was loving and kind and bore her cross for years without murmur or complaint. She had now no neighbors to confide in or talk to and give comfort and consolation to and receive same in return, as my Father and our family moved from the Grasswater Row to Cumnock where we were located for some two years or so and then again moving to Muirkirk for reason of Father's employment there. Thus Aunt Mary and my mother, who joined the Church, being baptised by James Gallacher in 1853, were separated by some eight miles or so, and as both were still having families, their opportunities for meeting and talking over matters were very, very few. I remember upon one occasion, my mother took me to Cumnock with her, ostensibly to visit some friends there and got some merchandise. I think we went by train, but walked all the way back. How it happened that we met Aunt Mary at Grasswater, I do not know, but Mother and Aunt Mary were engaged in a long conversation as we walked along. Neither do I know what they were talking about, but I do remember very distinctly and it has remained with me all my life, that Mother kept urging me to go on a little faster and not be in the way. I was then about 10 years of age or so. I did not know and I did not then think much about it, but from what has happened since then, I am firmly convinced they were having a real heart to heart talk about conditions as affecting them each in their different situations as pertaining to their positions as relating to the Gospel and the difficulties they had with husbands that could not then see as they did. They certainly did not want one to hear their conversation. Time went on – Often as I would come home from school or come into the house after being out for a while, especially if Mother was alone, I would find her attending to her household duties and humming away at something which then I did not know what, but as time went on I became familiar with the tune which alter I discovered to be "Redeemer of Israel, our only delight, on whom for a blessing we call, our shadow by day and our pillar by night, our King, our deliverer, our all."

Time and again I heard this. I can see now that when alone she was contemplating the things she had learned at Wee Grannie's in the little cottage meetings which they held previous to Grannies departure for the valley on the "Horizon" May 1856. This recurred to me all through the intervening years. I presume that most people have had similar experiences, there are things that happen in our youthful years that seem to make a lasting impression. I never heard her sing or hum it when other members of the family were present and I have wondered often times if it was purposely done for my benefit.

By the year 1866 in the month of January I got a job as cashier at the Lugar Iron Works Cooperative Store, about two and a half or three miles form the stables at Grasswater where Aunt Mary lived. When there I would walk home to Muirkirk on Sunday mornings to get my weekly change of clothing and walk back to Lugar again in the afternoon. The distance was about eight miles. One Saturday afternoon, I think it was in June or the last of May, cousin Mary came into the Lugar store and said her mother was outside the door and wished to see me a minute. I went out and had a short interview with them. I was but a boy fourteen years of age and I did not fully sense what was said or what it really meant. I understood however that they were off. They had very quickly slipped away making some excuse of their making to visit to some relatives a bit away from home. Aunt Mary had with her Mary, Andrew, and Aleck. The real facts were that after years of preparation, much thought and planning, they were saying goodbye to home and country and were going to Liverpool to sail for America. The Millennial Star Vol. 27 tells us that on the sixth day of June 1866 "the fine packed ship Saint Mark' cleared from Liverpool for New York carrying several hundred immigrants. The second cabin was occupied by 5 American adult passengers, members of the Church of Latter-Day-Saints. Elder Alfred Stevens, an English sea captain was appointed President and unanimously sustained by the vote of the saints. The saints were instructed in relation to the voyage and were promised a safe passage on condition of due diligence to all their duties. William Lindsay of Heber City writes on the date of December 13, 1924 as follows - "I find from Jensen's Chronology that the sailing ship Saint Mark, the one on which Aunt Mary and her family crossed the Atlantic sailed from Liverpool with 104 saints under the direction of A. Stevens on the sixth day of June, 1866. She came across the plains in Captain Scotts company. They left Iowa on the Missouri River August 8th with 49 wagons and about 300 immigrants and landed in Salt Lake City October 8th, 1866, and soon after arrived in Heber at Uncle John's. Now while you may think that Aunt Mary acted rather rashly in leaving her husband as she did, and it surely was a most unheard of undertaking, I perhaps received as great a benefit from it as any other person. If it had not been done, I never could have got the faithful, loving wife that I did get. I can hardly think that any other woman could have filled her place so completely to my joy and satisfaction, so kind, so loving and so unselfish through all our married life.

We had 11 children, 46 grandchildren and 16 great grandchildren. Two of our sons have filled missions and one grandson. All our children have been to the Temple and I do feel so thankful that I got such a wife as a Mother to my children. I do not deem it wise or necessary to enter into details or particulars of this occurrence. Those who know and understand all the reasons for it will I am sure not feel to concur Aunt Mary for her course. I may add that when Uncle Alan discovered that they had gone he was a very much worked up about it. I understand that he went to Liverpool to obtain his children at least but he was too late. The ship had sailed. His next step was to try and intercept them at New York and he had his two sons, John and James, who had previously emigrated to America, go to New York City to have them returned but nothing came of it and as we have already learned they came on and went to Heber City. It was a bold strategy and successfully carried out. Looking at it from our standpoint and view, it was not a matter for censure or even criticism. It was eminently successful and I believe better for all concerned. It created quite a commotion at the time and even forty years afterwards when on my mission in Scotland in 1906 and 1907 I encountered it at New Mills where a lady told me about it when tracting at her door.

I fully agree with what William Lindsay has said about his wife, my cousin. She was all that he says, she had a wonderful personality, was very kind and devoted to her husband and family and was a true Latter Day Saint, peace to her ashes. Her name and memory will no doubt be cherished and revered by generations yet unborn. She died in Heber City, date June 16, 1016. Aunt Mary's act was a great coup. It goes to show what can be done when there is the will and the determination to do it. The following taken from the *Millennial Star* Vol. 28, tersely puts it:

Where There's a Will There's a Way

There's an adage that no one should ever forget
as he travels through life's ragged road,
and encumbered with care, looks around him in vain
for a hand to help on with his load,
let him never despond, let him never despair,
for aside from the path never stray.
Let him buckle his armour and gird up his strength,
singing "Where there's a will there's a way".

If the world should look on with a cynical sneer
and the worldly efforts despise,
if a scoff or a jest from a friend that he loves
wrings a tear from his sorrowful eyes,
let him never be daunted, but still persevere.

And his strength shall suffice for his day,
to that cheer'd and refreshed he may still struggle on,
singing "Where there's a will there's a way".

There are foes to be counquered and feuds to be fought.
There are traitors without and within,
and the toll may be hard, and the battle be long,
but the one who endureth shall win,
for the good is at hand and the clouds shall disperse,
When he least looketh out for the day,
to that looking and hoping still let him press on,
singing, "Where there's a will there's a way".

My mother now was alone, the last left of the Grasswater saints. Uncle John and wife immigrated in 1852 – Grannie, Mary Murdoch in 1856. Aunt Mary and her children, Mary, Andrew, and Aleck came in 1866. Mother therefore was left. No other members of the Mrudoch family of Grasswater had up 'til now joined the church. My Father was under ground manager at the Muirkirk Iron Works. The fire kindled in Mother's bosom kept burning and patiently she kept on. Father was an Elder in the Free Church. Mother would never attend any church. The reason why, us youngsters did not know and understand then. But she had joined the Church of Jesus Christ of Latter-Day Saints in 1853 and had remained faithful ever afterwards. She is the only one of her family, the Lennox's of the Moor Farm, Old Cumnock, that has ever joined.

Patriarchal Blessing of David Lennox Murdoch

Salt Lake City, March 20, 1886. A Blessing given by John Smith, Patriarch upon the head of David Lennox Murdoch, son of William and Janet Murdoch born in Cronberry Parish of Auchinleck, Ayrshire, Scotland. January 13, 1952. Brother David, notwithstanding you were born in a foreign land, thou art numbered with the sons of Zion, of whom much is expected. Thou art of the house of Israel, and the Lord has yet a work for thee to do. Therefore, be prudent and seek to know His will and the vision of thine understanding shall be opened and thou shalt see things as they are and by the prophecy vision of thy mind that foretell future events. Thou shalt be called into council among thy brethren. It shall be thy duty to exhort the saints to faithfullness. It shall be thy privilege to travel much laboring in the ministry and if thy faith fail not, thy voice shall be heard among the nations of the Earth and on Islands of the sea. Truth and Virtue shall be thy motto, many shall seek thee for counsel and rejoice in thy teachings. Therefore be upon thy guard, for the Eye of the Lord has been upon thee from thy birth. The angel who has watched over thee in the past, shall direct thy course, guide thy mind and remove the stumbling blocks from thy pathway and give thee power over Evil and unclean spirits that thou shalt complete thy mission. Therefore, put thy trust in him whose right it is and all shall be well with thee. Thou are of the blood of Joseph, and shall receive thine inheritance with thy blessing in the tribe of Ephriam, which was the lineage of many of thy kindred who have gone behind the veil and look to thee for salvation, as thou are a legal heir to this privilege holding the Priesthood, and in as much as thou wilt follow the whisperings of the still small voice of the comforter, no power shall prevail against thee for the Lord knoweth the secrets of thy heart and will reward thee as thou shalt merit both spiritual and temporal. Thy posterity shall grow up around thee and bear thy name in honorable remembrance. Therefore, look forward to the future with pleasure. This blessing with also the blessings of Abraham, Isaac and Jacob, I seal upon thee in the name of Jesus Christ and I seal thee up unto Eternal life to come forth in the morning of the first resurrectioon, Even so. Amen.

EDITOR'S NOTE: *David Lennox was called to serve in the Great Britain Mission and was given a Missionary Blessing on August 15, 1905. He kept a very thorough journal of his mission, which was spent in the Scottish Conference, an area of the Great Britain Mission, beginning in 1905 and ending in 1907. Many entries were very much the same and repetitious and it was decided to omit them, which is why some of the dates are missing. The editors feel that the dates included in this book give the reader a great opportunity to read his experiences and gain an appreciation of his testimony, his dedication, and his character. David Lennox loved cultural events, art, and had a talent and love of talking to people. He loved to read and write poetry depending on the moment and his circumstances, which is why this journal has so many sprinkled in. He was very interested in genealogy and was always seeking opportunities to find a connection to any Murdochs he came across. He often mentions the Thynes and Gilmours as well as others, which are the relatives of his wife, Elizabeth. David Lennox and Elizabeth came to Utah in 1878. His mission was 27 years after their arrival.*

A Missionary Blessing

Pronounced upon the head of Elder David Lennox Murdoch, in the Salt Lake Temple Annex, August 15th, 1905, by Apostle George Albert Smith.

Brother David Lennox Murdoch, in the authority of the Holy Priesthood, we lay our hands upon your head and we set you apart for a mission to Great Britain, whither you have been called by the voice of revelation through the Prophet of the Lord in the day and age in which you live. We bless you and send you forth that you may be a tower of strength in the mission field for the promulgation of the Gospel of Jesus Christ. We bless you that you may have joy in this calling and ministry, that you may go forth by land and by sea in safety and arrive at your destination, having enjoyed your trip and feeling blessed and benefited thereby. We bless you that you may have a desire to listen to the counsels of those who preside over you in the mission field, and we promise you that if you will be humble and prayerful and will trust in the Lord and follow the advice and counsel of those who are placed there as presiding officers, your way shall be opened and you shall have no difficulty and every barrier shall be broken down, and you shall be able to go forth and accomplish much good. The Lord is mindful of your years of patience and faithfulness and has blessed you in many ways, and now this added honor has come to you and you shall go forth as one of the stalwart sons of God to proclaim the Gospel to the honest in heart, and you shall proclaim the truths of the Gospel in such a way that even those who are unworthy of them shall know indeed that you are a servant of God. We bless you with health and strength and with vigor of mind and body, and we bless you that your mind may be fruitful and your memory retentive, that you may retain the things you learn. We bless you that you may study the Bible, the Book of Mormon, the Book of Doctrine and Covenants and the Pearl of Great Price;

then put your trust in the Lord and in the hour that you need it. He will bring forth those truths with which you have stored [in] your mind.

Now, dear brother, we bless you with every desire of your heart in righteousness upon this mission, and we say unto you, thrust in your sickle and work while the day lasts, that you may have sheaves for your hire. We bless you with every blessing necessary for the discharge of this high calling to which you are called, and we set you apart to this ministry and dedicate you unto the Lord in the name of Jesus Christ, Amen.

Martin S. Lindsay, Reporter

Missionary Journal of David Lennox Murdoch
Diary of my Mission to Great Britain

August 16, 1905
August 16 – Left Oregon Short Line Depot at 7:10 A.M. There were there to see one off of my own family, with, Janet, Mary and Afton, Brother James and A. M. Olsen. My wife and Norah remained at home feeling too bad to come to the depot. There were in our company eleven souls of which I was in charge. They were as follows: N. P. Nielson, P. Johnsson, Thos. Emmett, Robert Price, A. T. Forsgren Wm. Selley, Kate Osborne, Gertrude Hanson, Marie T. Hanson, Anne Otte, and David L. Murdoch.

August 17 – Arrived in Omaha in evening.

August 18 – Arrived in Chicago in forenoon and were all transferred to the Nickle Plate depot. Stayed while in Chicago at the Majestic Hotel and had very good quarters.

August 19 – Left Chicago at 2:32 P.M. for Buffalo where we arrived next morning

August 20 – Took train to Niagara Falls. It is only a short ride to the falls. Arriving there we all took a ride around and over the bridge to the Canadian Side of the waters, which we thought were so much nicer than the American side. The Falls viewed from whatever side are indeed a sight, the like one may never see again. Left Niagara Falls in the evening, on Sunday for Boston and arrived there about 12:30.

August 21 – about 12:30. We had visited the 24th to look around and see the sights which we did taking in Bunker Hill Monument, The Common, the Navy Yard.

August 24 – Thursday, sailed on the "Arabie" at 5 P.M. Our voyage was very pleasant, the weather was good, it rained some, and was very cool considering how warm it had been before we came on board. The sea was never what you would call rough although there were some white caps. Was not sick at all and never missed a meal.

August 31 – Arrived in Queenstown about 5:30 oclock having been in sight of land from early afternoon.

Sept. 1 – Friday. Arrived in Liverpool at 10 A.M. and was met at Steamer by Elders Higgs and Rich. Was taken care of by them and escorted to headquarters, 10 Holley Road, Fairfield, Liverpool. Had a meeting with Pres. Heber J. Grant in his bedroom as he was sick with lumbago and could not get out of bed. After meeting, was assigned to Scotland and Elder Robert Price was sent to the London Conference.

Sept. 2 – Took Train for Glasgow, leaving Liverpool at 10:10 A.M. arriving at St. Enoch's Station at 4: o.c. same afternoon and drove up to 3 Holenhead Street..

Sept. 3 – Sunday. Held meeting at Green at 11 A.M. Brothers Brown and Tims spoke. Fast meeting at 2 oclock at Breadalbane Halls. Went to dinner at Sister McNeils and had a good meal and a pleasant time. Attended meeting in evening again at 6:30.

Sept 4 – Visited at Paisley with Pres. James Brown, this is the same James Brown who emigrated with us in 1878 on the Steamship "Nevada" to New York, and whom I had not seen from that time until my arrival at 3 Holenhead Street. 27 ½ years. Saw Wm. Naisbitts sister, Mrs. James McDonals at Elderslee. Took supper there. Saw Gleniffer Braes in the distance and the "bonnie wee well on the breast o' the brae". Saw the house where Fannahill was born and raised and on an inscription plate on the house it reads –

"He sang amid the shuttles din, the music of the Woods"

Also visited Brother and Sister Adams. She is a very pleasant, cheerful woman and enjoyed our visit. Also visited Bro. and Sister Hawthorne and enjoyed our visit there also. Got home about 11 o'clock.

Sept. 5 – Tracted in Henderson Street, Kinning Park. Delivered 100 tracts. Street meeting at Cathedral Square at 7:00. Distributed 20 tracts.

Sept. 6 – Did not go out tracting – wet all day. Brother Hugh McKay called in on his way home. Elders Moyes and James called in. Also Elder Lindsay from Ireland. All went to Bible class in Breadalbane Halls at night and had a fine meeting.

Sept. 7 – Tracting on St. James Street. Distributed 120 tracts and had 3 conversations. Was present at Baptism of David Brown, of Greenock, nephew of James D. Stirling of Salt Lake City, at Hulds Road Public Baths at 9 P.M. Elder Tims officiated. Afterwards came to 3 Holmhead Street and confirmed him. Pres. Brown acting as mouth with Elders Tims, Rich, and Moyes and myself.

Sept. 8 – Tracting in St. James Street, distributed 120 tracts. Attended Bible class at Brother Cambustang.

Sept. 9 – visited the Art Galleries in West end Park. Very extensive collections and galleries on this visited confined myself to statuary and paintings. Saw painting of "Woodside House on the Kelvin". This painting shows Woodside as it was in the beginning of the last Century and which now is all filled up and built up and could not be recognized. In the galleries, I also found a life sized painting of

> "Alexander Whitelaw"
> "Presented to the Corporation of Glasgow in recognition of is varied services to the citizens 1880"

EDITOR'S NOTE: *Alexander Whitelaw was a member of Parliament and David Lennox worked as an assistant to him. He wrote Alexander Whitelaw a long letter after his arrival in Utah, which is included later in this book.*

There were many other paintings of people I knew.

Sept 10 – Sunday. Meeting at Breadalbane Halls at 2 oclock. Administered the Sacrament. Spoke after Elder Rich and was followed by Brother Campbell. Attended meeting in evening also. Same place. Meeting addressed by Pres. Brown and Wim. Leggett. Sister Reed came up to dinner with us.

Sept. 11 – Tracting. Distributed 120 tracts.

Sept. 12 – Paid for suit (frock coat) at McCalls. L3.76 Called on Mr. George Patrick at 15 College Street, brother of Robert Patrick's of the 18th Ward, S. L. City, and had a talk with him very pleasantly. He said he would advise me of some evening when to call upon him at his home at Folleross. Called also at 168 West George Street and saw Mr. Brand and Mr. Taylor and had quite a talk with them. Mr. Taylor looks old and very grey and is all crippled up, nearly doubled up with Rheumatism and walks poorly with two sticks. Mr. Brand is the same old finical fellow he always was and gives you the impression that he has always just the same thing to do and the same thing to say at exactly the same hour of each day. He looks well and is not nearly as much changed as I anticipated. The grim reaper has certainly got in his work in this office. There are only three now there that were there when I was with them, viz Mr. Brand, Mr. Taylor, and Mr. Milue, the latter I did not see as he was away. His holidays. The following are all gone. Sir William Laird, Mr. Cottart, Mr. Raickin, Mr. Service, Mr. John Mitchell, Mr. Fraser, Mr. Mac Turk. Distributed 100 tracts and held street meeting at Cathedral Square. Distributed 25 tracts.

Sept. 13 – Paid for board to Mr. R. Reed for 10 days 14/6. Visited at Knightswood Rows. Saw Mrs. Nesbits and her husband, his uncle John died August 7, 1905. Called also upon his Uncle Archie. He is suffering a little bit from asthma. Called upon sister Reed at Maryhill, she is not in but saw her Father and mother, Brother and Sister Cook. Called also upon Andrew Faddies at Maryhill. He is blind. Has been in Utah several times. Attended Bible class at night.

Sept. 14 – Called at MacFarlane, Strang and Co. office 204 St. Vincent Street, which I found from the directory, and upon inquiry was surprised to be told that he [Strang] had not been there for about 14 years. I had quite a talk with a Mr. Morrison in the office who told me that Strang had flown high for a time. Lived at Prichhill house and drove into the office in the mornings. He speculated heavily and I suppose lost and I believe was indulging in liquor and eventually turned out. His wife, who was a daughter of the late Gen. Robertson's, a lawyer, and who inherited some L10,000. from her Father's Estate lives in London with her two boys, which I presume are young men now. So that he cannot be living with them, as he is burning around town trying to float companies and is pretty well down. I understood from Mr. Morrison that for a long time he was indulging and looked very bad. Poor Strang! How you have fallen! I also called on Mr. Alexander Park, but did not find him in. Will call again. I called also on Thynes' store in Hope Street and had quite a talk with the lady clerk, who is a very nice girl and whom I later learned is a Miss Fonall. Mr. McCallum is managing the business which failed about two years ago and I learned from Miss Fonall. Mr. McCallum was not in so I left my card and told her I would call again. Mamma's Uncle Robert died last April a year ago aged 85 years. Miss Fonall told me the firm of James and Robert Thyne was established in 1819 and that while they could not use the firm name at present they hoped to do so in the near future. (If the firm was established when she says it was, it must have been by their Father because Robert was only born at or about the time stated). Went tracting this afternoon and distributed 100 tracts. Had 3 conversations. Attended meeting at Bridgeton cross.

Sept. 15 – Wrote to James R. Smith and Willie Nisbit. Tracting this afternoon. Distributed 120 tracts. Bible class at Cawbuslang at W. Cook's. Visited Southern Nieropolis and after some searching found the burying place of Alex Gilmour. It is situated about half way along the high rock wall that separates the old from the new portion of the Cemetery. The stone is inscribed:-

The Burial Place of
Alexander Gilmour and Elizabeth Pinkerton, his wife
and their children
In memory of the six children of James Pinkerton Gilmour who died in
Infancy

Marion Alexander, his daughter, died 26 July 1861 aged 18 months.
Christine Hamilton Wright, his wife died 28 Oct. 1861 aged 32 years and 7 months
James Pinkerton Gilmour, died 10 May 1864 aged 37 years
Chas. R. Gilmour, their son died 6 Nov 1879 aged 20 ½ years.
In Memory of
James Service Thyne, Beloved Grandson of Alex Gilmour, who died 2 Febry 1853 aged 2 years and 11 months
Also:
James Thyne, their son in law died 10 March 1860 aged 44 years
Also the above:
Eliz. Pinkerton died 8th January 1864 aged 68 years
In Memory of
Marion Brown Wright wife of Alex Gilmour who died 23 Octob. 1857 aged 24 years
Also:
Alex Pinkerton Neil, his son, who died 28 January 1858 aged 2 years and 4 months
Also:
Jean Hutcheson, his daughter, who died 5th June 1864 aged 1 ¾ years
Also:
At Apswich, Queenland on 18th January 1869
Jessie Hutcheson, his wife aged 28 years.
"This lovely bud so young and fair
Called home by early doom
Just come to show how sweet a flower
In Paradise will bloom.
In centre of the ground, on marble base under glass is a wreath:-
"A token of respect from workers and Friends"

I learned from the gentleman in office at the Gate that Eliz. Thyne daughter of Alex Gilmour, died 7 March 1890 in Royal Infirmary aged 60 years. Alex Gilmour 10 Wilkie Street, son of Alex Gilmour died 21 Nov. 1895 aged 57 years. Christina died and buried there also.

Sept. 16 – Visited 145 Springburn Road. Saw Mrs. Langley, William Donald's daughter, who is living in the House her Father and mother lived and died in. She has 6 children – 3 boys and 3 girls, but as they were all out I did not see any of them. I learned from her that her Father, William Donald, died 25 May 1903 aged 77 years and that her mother Margaret Murray Donald, died 18 Sept. 1904 aged 78 years – buried in Tighthill Cemetery. Their children are James Donald, Parliamentary Road, William Donald, Saltcoats Margaret Donald, Langley, 145 Springburn Road, Glasgow, John, died aged 17.

Samuel Donald, Gasworks, Dundee. Jeanie Donald Moodie, 591 Alexander Parade. Aunt Mary Murray McLeod, Torrance of Cawpsie died about same time as Wm. Donald. She has a daughter from farm at Bishopbriggs –Mrs. Morrison. Aunt Rachel Murray Richmond, Torrance of Cawpsie died 5 or 6 years ago. John Murray, brother, died about a year ago about 80 years of age.

Called at Factory of Thomas Kay & Co. on Dundas Street and inquired if he was from Muirkirk. I learned from his Foreman that he was. So no doubt he is my School Companion. He had gone for the day, so I said I would call again and see him. His factory is just around the corner from here.

Attended City Hall Concert and enjoyed it. The Hall was crowded about 4000 there. There is a large organ in the Hall but I did not like the tone so well as the Tabernacle organ.

Sept. 17 – Sunday. Held meeting at Jail Square at 11:00. There was a good attendance who listened attentively. Spoke there. Attended meeting in Hall at 2 oclock and also at 6:30, same place. Elder James and myself spoke. Dist. 40 tracts at Green. Pres. Brown, Elder Tims, and myself visited Brother and Sister Hoggan and administered to their children.

Sept. 18 – Called upon Thomas Kay. He gave me a cordial welcome and said he recognized me but at first I could not him; however as I talked to him a while he gradually grew upon me and I believe I did begin to recognize him. I had a long conversation with him about Schoolboy days. He left Muirkirk at 13 years of age, April 1866. I left January 1866 so that next year, it will be 40 years. He is very well preserved and looks well. He kindly invited me to spend an evening with him at his home. I will see him again and have a further conversation with him.

I called on Mr. Alex Park, on Hope St., upstairs from Wm. Baird & Co., 168 West George St., Factory for Mr. Whitelaw's Estate and also for Mr. Weirs, and had a long talk with him. I learned that Mrs. Whitelaw is living at Bridge of Allan and that her daughter, Helen, Mrs. Fitzgerald, a widow stays with her. At present, Mrs. Whitelaw is sick, but Mr. Park is going out Saturday and will see how she is and will find out whether she would like to see me or not. Mrs. Blackburn, the eldest daughter, died some years ago. She had no children and her portion of her Father's Estate reverts to her brothers and sisters. Jeanie is unmarried and lives in London. She, it is who is estranged from her mother. Alexander lives mostly in the South of England. Graeme lives in Perthshire. William is chairman of the North of Scotland Rwy. and lives in Inverness. James Baird Whitelaw lives in Perthshire. Mrs. Francis (Mary) lives in England somewhere. Caroline lives near Carlisle and is a Mrs. Thompson, her husband, as I understand, being a Coalmaster. Mr. Park appears differently from what he did when I saw him last, has aged considerably and is getting grey and stout. I should never have known him. But as I talked to him, he gradually grows upon one, until you can recognize his voice and manner.

I also called on James McCallum at Thynes (This is the first time I ever saw him) to inquire about Sandy. He told me that he had a Mr. Kidd, a joiner, who had worked for the nursery for years and who knew all about them, looking him up, Mr. Kidd's place of business is Hyndland Road, Hillhead. He gave me unsolicited, quite an account of the Gilmour and Thyne families, and the one ones that got a good word were Alex Gilmour, James and Robert Thyne – all the rest, including Mrs. Alexander Gilmour, got a severe raking over, unnecessarily so I thought, as they have all passed over that "bourne from whence no traveler returns" and some of them so long ago that is grated on my feelings to hear him. From the information I received, I feel tolerably certain that Sandy will be located. I shall call upon Mr. Kidd as soon as I can. Mr. McCallum told me that Mrs. Bell is still living and that although both he and his sisters have called repeatedly, they are never shown in to see her and they have got tired calling. Mrs. Bell is the last of the family living. Mr. McCallum is older looking than I expected to find him. He looks puffy and getting grey as if he might be near to sixty. He told me that Robert Thyne died April 1904.

Tracting. Distributed 100. Attended baptism of Brother Joseph Leggett at Kinning Park Public baths by Pres. Brown. Afterwards we all went to his house and I confirmed him. Pres. Brown, Elder Tims assisting.

Sept. 19 – Writing up the foregoing all morning. Going down now to Plantation Quary to see Mrs. Price and daughter off on "Carthinginian" for America. Tracting. Distributed 100 tracts. In the evening went with Pres. Brown and Elder Tims to the Baths and saw Sister Bailey baptized. Elder Tims officiated.

Sept. 20 – Tracting. Distributed 100. Attended meeting at Cathedral Square and spoke. Those present seemed interested and remained to talk afterwards. From there we went to the Halls and had testimony meeting. Nearly all present bore testimony and we had a fine meeting. Sister Bailey was confirmed by Pres. Brown, Elders Tims, Rich, and myself assisting.

Sept. 21 – Tracting on Watt Street, off Shields Road. Distributed 100 tracts. Called on William Kidd, carpenter & c. on Hyndland Road Hillhead, recommended to me by Mr. McCallum as one who was acquainted with the Thyne family. I found him to be a very nice old gentleman. He knew Mr. James Thyne and Robert Thyne and all of them. He showed me an old album in which was a portrait of Mr. James Thyne taken from a brooch, also Mr. James Thyne. He knew all the children well as he worked around the nurseries a great deal. Mamma must know him. He told me that Sandy was working in some log dye work in Rutherglen Road and that I would not have any trouble in finding him he thought. Held meeting at Anderston.

Sept. 22 – Visited along with Pres. Brown by invitation at Mr. George Patrick's at Tallercross. I had supper with them and spent a very pleasant evening. Met Mr. and Mrs. Patrick, their daughter, Mrs. Speirs, and their youngest daughter at home, unmarried. They are very nice people and have entertained a great many Utah people sent there by Mr. Patrick's brother, Robert, in the 18th ward. Tracting today. Dist. 100.

Sept. 23 – At home all morning. Attended Saturday afternoon concert in the City Halls along with Elders Moyer and James.

Sept. 24 – Sunday. Held meeting at Glasgow green at 11:30. Pres. Brown occupied part of the time and William Leggett, the rest. Not a very large crowd. Held meeting in the Halls at 2 oclock. Afterwards all went to Sister McNeils for dinner and back again to evening meeting in the Halls at 6:30. Pres. Brown occupied all the time and we had a good meeting.

Sept. 25 – Holiday in Glasgow. Pres. Brown and I went out to Burnbank to visit Mrs. Andrew. Their (sister of Maggie Robertson Sneddon) before calling upon her we called at the Springwells boating works, but Mr. Peter Robertson was not at home and the book-keeper was away at dinner. We then proceeded Stonefield Blantyre to see Mrs. Kier. We found her out after some inquiry. She came to the door and we could see a man sitting in the house. She told us she could not ask us in as she had company. We told her we were from America and that I knew her mother well and Maggie also and that I called merely in a social way thinking she might be glad to see and talk with one from Salt Lake City, who knew her relatives. She seemed not to care to do so. Asked no questions in relation to relatives and talked disrespectfully of her mother and the Mormons to my utter astonishment. After talking further with her and giving her to understand that I was not looking for anything from her or any one else and telling her in answer to her reflection that there were no better people on earth than the Latter-day Saints. She then asked us to come in and she would ask her company to go out. We declined to do so and on my telling her that her sister, Maggie, had given me her sister's (Mrs. Moffatt) address at Canebuslang and that I thought of calling upon her, she was good enough to tell one that her sister Mrs. Moffatt, did not care to see or have anything to do with Mormons. I then told her that I should not call upon her and the most that I should do would be to send her my card. This was our visit to Mrs. Kier. Cold, indifferent, and inhospitable. We called on Brother and Sister Cook and were entertained kindly. Mrs. Cook told me how well she knew Mrs. Robertson and now well she liked her. Called back at the bottling works. Mr. Robertson not at home, presume he was away at Hamilton races, the book-keeper was quelling some disturbance and was bespattered with blood. He was very civil to us and told us it was his busiest time, otherwise he would have been glad to have shown us through the works. Called on Mrs. Sneddon. Pres. Brown had a picture for her that Prof. Paul had given her some years ago. Took train back home arriving about 9 oclock.

Sept. 26 – Tracting. Dist. 100. Held meeting at Cathedral Square. Good attendance. Rained some. Called at a South York Street. Log-dye work and inquired for Sandy Thyne. Sure enough he was working there and I saw him. He did not know me until I explained to him who I was. After looking at him a little, I could see that it was he. We talked a little while and I agreed to meet him Saturday afternoon, Sept. 30 at 2 oclock at Mrs. Thompson's 413 Rutherglen Road where he boards. He had aged and seemed to have lost all his teeth.

Sept. 27 – Saw "He was despised and rejected of men" by Sigismund Goetze in Sauchiehall Street. It is a great painting and was inspired by his attending services at St. Paul's Cathedral who heard the minister preaching from Isaiah 53 & 3. "He was despised and we esteemed him not." Mr. Goetze on leaving after services were over was surprised and astonished that the congregation were not thinking or talking about the sermon, but were talking about the affairs of life. This preyed upon him and as a result, he produced this picture – the labors of four years, showing the world as it is today in all their different avocations, the Ministers, discussing the scriptures, Society represented by a couple who think only of pleasure, the Scientist holding a measuring glass in his hand, the City sport reading the returns from the races or the exchange the little girl selling bouquets of violets, the working man on his way with pick upon his shoulder, the artist in the act of lighting a cigarette and the reflection lighting up her face and the socialist holding forth to a large audience in the background. The working man draining a big mug of beer. The newsboy, shouting out what his papers contain, the young mother and child sitting on the steps in front of the alter upon which is the Savior of the World, bound with cords and with a crown of thorns upon his head. On the alter are the Latin words, the English of which is "to the unknown God". Behind and above the Savior is the Angel of Gethsemane, holding aloft the cup which His Father had given him to drink. And above this and all around the top of the picture are angel faces rather dimly seen exemplifying the Savior saying "except ye become as little children, ye cannot enter into the Kingdom of Heaven". The scene is on the steps of St. Paul's Cathedral, London and is so modern as to be called up to date in contradistinction to Dores Christ leaving the practorium.

Sept. 28 – Went to 75 Hope Street to see Mr. Park but he was not in. I called then down stairs on George Street and saw Mr. Taylor and had a chat with him. From him I learned that Mrs. Wallace died some years ago of nervous trouble. I also learned that Mr. McSnellie died about two years ago [illegible word] man's home in Parliamentary Road. For years he had been pretty well down and owing from anybody and everyone that would lend to him. This Mr. McSnellie was at one time cashier at Muirkirk Ironworks and was discharged for neglect of business and ever since he has been bumming around gradually going down, down. I made the acquaintance of a Mr. Murdoch in Mr. Taylor's office and had an interview with him. He was in the Muirkirk Office at one time with Mr. Stewart and knows Father and our family. I talked to him about his ancestry and got him interested in genealogical work. He showed me what he had been doing in the Abingdon Baird case, where this young profligate after running through an immense fortune left what was remaining to first cousin's children, which of course includes Mr. Whitelaw's children. Mr. Murdoch's father's name is William and is from Cumnock. He thinks that Matthew McTurk who lived in Auchinleck must have left valuable information in relation to the Murdoch family as he had lectured about them in Auchinleck and also in Lugar. I believe this man was interested in Genealogical matters and he promised me to go out to Auchinleck some time and make inquiry into this most important matter. So, I must see him again. I saw Mr. Brand for a minute, he was going out today to see Mr. Fleming at 9 Woodside Crescent and as Mr. Fleming had expressed a desire to see me, he, Mr. Brand, would arrange with him for me to call out tomorrow between two and three oclock for this purpose. I gave Mr. Brand, Mr. Dunsmeier, Mr. Taylor, and Mr. Murdoch a copy each of "My Reasons" for leaving the Church of England, etc., etc. Tracting. Distributed 100. Held meeting at Cathedral Square.

Sept. 29 – Got a letter from Mamma this morning. Went out this afternoon to see Mr. Fleming and was shown up to his room and had nearly an hours talk with him. He was frank and cordial and communicative. We talked over all old offices and connections with the firm and Mr. Whitelaw and others. He told me how well they had succeeded in their business affairs. How that year after year they had done so well and made more really than they needed. He talked along in this strain and that he had no one very near to leave it too. He made me acquainted with his nurse and asked me to come again which I intend doing in about a weeks time. Went out to Cambuslang at night to Bible class meeting.

Sept. 30 –Went out to Botanic Gardens and walked through and around them, back thro Kelvingrove Park and Sanchichall Street. After dinner went out to 435 Rutherglen Road to see Alexander Thyne. He is staying with a Mrs. Thompson who seemed to be a very nice person. We took a walk through the Southern Necropolis and then walked out to Hampden Park and saw a football match between the 3 Lanark and Rangers. There was an immense concourse of people. I should think not less than 20,000 people. We then came back – had a fish supper and I told him I would come over some night through the week. Sandy has 5 children living. 4 boys and one girl. Two boys are in Glasgow working somewhere and his other is working with some Cooperative Society or store in Aberfeldy. The girl is staying with a women in Glasgow who wants to adopt her. Sandy does not know very much about the Gilmour's.

Oct. 1 – Fast-day. Fasted from Saturday night until 4:30 Sunday. Had meeting at Jail Square in morning. Spoke there. Then Fast meeting at 2:30 in the Halls. Meeting in Fullarton Hall. Tollcross at 7 oclock evening. (Rev. Donald MacLeod Stuart's) Pres. Tims and Elder Bachman spoke.

Oct. 2 – Tracting today. Distributed 100.

Oct. 3 – etc., etc. very wet all day

Oct. 4 – etc., etc. wet today. Attended testimony meeting at the Halls.

Oct. 5 – Tracting. Distributed 100. Went over and saw Sandy at night and spent some time with him.

Oct. 6 – Went out and called upon Mr. Fleming at 9 Woodside Crescent. The servant told me he was engaged at the time with some gentleman on business and that I might call back some other day. Took a walk out the Possilpark Road to see if I could recognize any of the old Landmarks. There are a few that have not changed very much.

Oct. 7 – Been wet all day. Did not go out at all. Friday evening the 6th, went out to Fullarton Hall. Tollcross with the brethren to a soiree there given by Rev. Donald McLeod Stewart, a Congregational minister who is trying to build up a branch.

Oct. 8 – Held meeting at Jail Square. Pres. Brown and Elder Tims occupied the time. Held meeting at the Halls at 2 oclock. Spoke there. Held meeting again at 6:30 and Priesthood meeting at close of that.

Oct. 9 – Went up to Townhead Baths in morning. Tracting in the afternoon, did 100. Had some nice conversations with Mrs. Carmichael 213 Watt Street – and Mrs. Raeburn 205 Watt Street, the latter is from Old Cumnock and the former from Kilmarnock. Went up to Brother John McCombis in company with Elder Tims and spent the evening there.

Oct. 10 – Tracting in afternoon. Dist. 100. Wrote to Mamma. Visited Brother and Sister Hoggan in evening with other Elders and had supper and spent a pleasant evening.

Oct. 11 – Tracting. Dist. 100 tracts. Held meeting at Cathedral Square. Elders Moyes and James speaking. Afterwards held meeting at the Halls.

Oct. 12 – Tracting. Dist. 100 tracts. Went out to Mr. & Mrs. Aithen's at Cambustang at night in company with Pres. Brown, Elders Tims, Rich, and Mrs. Reid and spent a very pleasant evening. The Aithens are old acquaintances of Pres. Brown's. Got home at midnight.

Oct. 13 – Visited Mrs. Wm. Shaw at 2 Princes Sq. Regents Park, Glasgow in company with Pres. Brown. Mrs. Shaw is John B. Cummook's sister. She received us very kindly. We saw her mother, who is 75 years of age and is well preserved and talked a way very freely and intelligently about times that are past. Mrs. Shaw took us a walk around the South Side Park and showed us the sights. We then came back to supper. She then took us to Mrs. McLaughlan's, her sister's and later she took us to her other sister's, Mrs. Ladler's. We enjoyed our visit and were invited to come again.

Oct. 14 – Went to Edinburgh with Pres. Brown. Were met at depot by Elders McCarty, King, Pendrey, and McQueen. Stayed with McCarty and King. Visited Brother Richardson's and spent the evening.

Oct. 15 – Sunday morning. Held Priesthood meeting in the morning. Sunday School at 12:30. Meeting at 2 oclock. Spoke then. Nice meeting of Saints in the Edinburgh Branch. Meeting again at 6:30 evening. Time was occupied by Elders McCarty and Pres. Brown. The Edinburgh Saints seem to be very united and have a very nice place to meet and it was a pleasure to meet with them. Visited Brother Robinson, who lives on High Street.

Oct. 16 – Visited Holyroad Palace and Abbey in company with Pres. Brown, Elders McCarty and Kin. Saw all the pictures of the ancient Kings and Queens of Scotland. The bed and bedroom of Mary, Queen of Scots. The bed and bedroom of the place where Rizzio was killed, etc. We walked from there up the High Street to the Castle, seeing many sights on the way as nearly every step was associated in some way with ancient history. The old Tolbooth Church and burying ground where Adam Smith, the author is buried. Also, Robert Ferguson, the poet, who died at the age of 23 years. Burns, when coming to Edinburgh visited the Poets resting place and sat down and wept. Burns at his own expense erected the stone to Commemorate the Poets life and death and composed the words upon the stone which read:-

> *"No sculptured marble here, nor pompous lay,*
> *No storied urn, nor animated bust!"*
> *This simple stone directs pale Scotia's way*
> *To pour her sorrows o'er her Poets dust"*

Novr. 13 – Had breakfast at Mrs. Love's and talked with her for some time afterwards. We then went down to Victoria Terrace and Elder Ritchie and us went over to Bellfielt House to see it and the grounds that have been left to the Poor of Kilmarnock and Riecarton. This place was owned by the Buchannan family. Their pictures in oil are hung around the rooms and also some of their needle work, writings, etc. It is a most interesting place. They had a splendid library, which is there and for use to be read only in the room. We went around by the Struther's steps – there is now an iron bridge across the brine, and back home by way of the River Bank. Had dinner and then called upon Mrs. Stephenson, who is sister to Mr. Stewart and youngest daughter of the late John Bird. We stayed & chatted a while with them and then took a walk up town to see the Laigh Kirk and other places of interest. Took train at 6:50 and reached home shortly before 8 oclock. Altogether, we had a very enjoyable time of Kilmarnock, having met with people who knew people that I knew and could talk about olden times. When at Bellfield, I learned that my old friend, Edward Andrew, with whom I used to associate with at Hurtford, died at a year ago. I was looking forward to an interview with him on this trip. One more has gone to the great beyond. On my return home found the photos of home and wife and children & Will & Cousie waiting for me. I am much pleased with them. They all look good to me. While at Kilmarnock, we called upon a Mrs. Barbara Black, who lives not far from Mrs. Loe, and will be 103 years old the 10th of next May. She was in bed and was feeble – her hearing is somewhat impaired, but could talk quite well – we all shook hands with her. This is the first person I have ever seen who has passed the Century mark.

Novbr. 20 – Thick, nasty fog still prevails. Can no more than see across the street. Got a letter from Janet this morning informing me that the American ticket had carried the election in Salt Lake City with the exception of Fuddenham & Harteustein elected on the Democratic Ticket, also that Anson had failed of election on the American ticket and that the Democrats in the Third had elected some on their tickets. The Elders all attended the silver wedding of Brother & Sister McNeil this evening and presented her with half a dozen spoons and a pickle fork and enjoyed a pleasant evening.

Novbr. 21 – Tracting. Dist. 160

Novbr. 22 – Wet & disagreeable – attended fast meeting in evening at Halls.

Novbr. 23 – Tracting – dist. 160. Wet still – went over to see Sandy in evening and showed them the pictures of the family and house.

Novbr. 24 – Called today at 168 West George Street. Saw Mr. Brand and had a talk with him. He took me into a room where Mr. Weir was and I had a conversation with him. When I left Scotland, Mr. Weir was very black in beard and whiskers, now he is very white and looks quite different. He used to be very gruff – now he is much mellowed and much milder in his manner. He asked for Father and how he was getting along and what he was doing, etc. He also asked me what I was doing and where I was located and I told him. I also told him what I was here for and about my mission and that about wound the conversation up. He did not say much more – only we talked about Muirkirk, the Willwood Pits, the iron works. Mr. Taylor had gone for the day.

Novbr. 25 – Pres. H. J. Grant arrived at the Central Station this afternoon about four oclock. Met him at depot with Pres. Brown. Held Priesthood meeting in evening at 3 Holmhead Street – all the Elders of the Scottish Conference being present. The Elders in turn reported their labors, then Pres. Grant spoke at some length and in the course of his remarks, explained the relationship of the Church and Moses Thatcher and the course the latter had pursued from some years before, until that time of the excommunication. He had neglected attending his meetings of his quorum – afterwards objecting to and finding fault with the Cusiness household in his absence.

Novbr. 26 – Sunday Conference morning. Assembled in Breadalbane Halls at 10 oclock. The attendance was only fair. Edinburgh turned out well – so did Ayrshire. Elders Lockhead and myself spoke and then Pres. Grant took up the remainder of the time. At 2 oclock Elders McCary and Packard spoke followed by Pres. H. J. Grant – the attendance was better at this session. At 6 oclock Elders Bachman and J. P. Anderson spoke followed by Pres. Grant. The attendance was very good and the attention was all that could be desired. It is usual to change the field of labor at this time and I have been moved to Edinburgh, 103 Easter Road, where I am now writing this record. I arrived here last night, the 27th.

Novbr. 27 – Spent the day at 3 Holmhead Street, Glasgow packing up and talking with the Elders who hung around there like bees around a sugar barrel. Took train at 6 oclcok for Edinburgh.

Novbr. 28 – First morning in Edinburgh. It is dry but cold. Will spend the day answering home correspondence.

Novbr. 29 – Writing Father.

Novbr. 30 – Bible class at Mrs. George White's. Large attendance and a fine class. Lesson 15 & 16 Ch. First Book of Nephi.

Dec. 4 – Tracting at Leigh. Visited Brother and Sister Hendry in evening. Took supper and spent evening with them.

Dec. 5 – Tracting at Leith. In the evening went to hear the boy preacher. His mother, who was with him, is a Negress and he is a half cast. It is strange that these people can come here and succeed in drawing such audiences, having nothing to offer the people but "come to Jesus right now and be saved this very minute, no matter what your condition may be."

The Rev. Dr. Archo Scott. I knew him before leaving for America and was anxious to hear him again. Has a fine fashionable church in the West End of Edinburgh. Afternoon meeting and evening meeting. Elder McCarty and myself occupied the time.

Dec. 24 – Sunday. Sunday School. Held Commemorative Services for Centennial Anniversary of birth of the Prophet Joseph Smith. Afternoon at 2 oclock my subject was "From the time of our Savior up to and including the time prior to the Birth of the Prophet." I occupied all the time although I hurried. In the evening services were continued. Elder John N. McQueen took the succeeding subject – The Birth of the Prophet, showing ancestral line & up to 1st vision. Elder King followed with period from 1st vision up to organization of the Church. Elder Packard went next with subject from Organization of the Church to expulsion from Nauvoo. Sister Mary McGill sang a solo and Miss Spence sang The Holy City. It was intended that Elder McCary should have wound up with period from Nauvoo up till present time, but time did not permit and he was thus shut out. Our Services were well attended at both sessions and everything passed off successfully. Went to Sister Craig's for supper.

Dec. 25 – Ate Christmas dinner at Brother & Sister Richardson's and spent evening there also.

Dec. 30 – Walked out to Portobello. When we came back Pres. Brown and Elder James were waiting for us. After dinner we went to the Carnival at Princes Street Gardens. Visited Pres. Richardson & family.

Dec. 31 – Sunday. Sunday School. Afternoon meeting & Evening meeting. Pres. Brown and Elder McQueen & Pres. Robinson spoke at afternoon meeting. At evening meeting, Elder James & Cook spoke also Pres. Brown. Went up to Pres. Robinson's about 11 p.m. and waited to see the ushering in of New Year's morning at the Tron Church. A vast concourse of people were there, that being the gathering place for the whole city to hear the Tron Church strike the hour. The crowd were mostly supplied with bottles and on the hour striking, the corks were drawn and treating and wishing the compts of the season began and from there spread all over the City.

January 1st, 1906 – Coming home about one oclock – we saw many broken bottles and many tipsy-people. We called on Brother and Sister White on our way home. In the evening we all spent the evening at Brother Richardsons, had supper & games till morning.

January 5 – Walked up to top of Arthurs seat and around Kings Carriage drive. Very foggy and could not see any distance.

January 13 – Visited Market Cross today immediately East of St. Giles Church on High Street to hear the Kings proclamation made announcing the dissolution of the Parliament and the calling of another Parliament to meet Febry. 13, 1906. Also calling upon the Scottish Lords to assemble at Holyrood in January 30 and select 16 Lords to sit in the House of Lords to represent Scotland. It was quite an imposing ceremony. The Band of the Pipers and a Brass Band accompanied the procession with troops, etc. This is the first time I ever saw this old and ancient custom carried out. This is my birthday and it is a long time since I was away from home on that occasion. It was now 40 years since I left home at Muirkirk to go to Lugar Co-op Store where I remained for about six months – going from there to the Portland Ironworks, Hereford, where I was for four years. From there I was transferred to the Gartsherrie Ironworks, Coatbridge, remaining there about two years. I was then moved into the Glasgow Office, 168 West George Street and was there until I left for Utah. For four years before this however, I was private Secretary to Mr. Whitelaw, who was M. P. for Glasgow 1874-1879.

January 14 – Sunday. Bible class. Meeting at two oclock and at six thirty. Blessed & named baby – "Henry Blake Miller" at close of meeting. I made a few remarks and prophesied that Elders, clothed upon with the power and authority of the Almighty would go forth in the performance of their duties and that many would be added unto the Church in the North, in Edinburgh and in Ayrshire. Visited Mr. William Murdoch and family at 2 a Parkside Terrace by invitation. Had a very pleasant interview with them from four oclock until 6:15 and enjoyed a very nice tea with them. The family consists of Mr. Murdoch, Mrs. Murdoch, and two daughters – one of whom is a school teacher at Portobello. Another daughter had married and immigrated to South Africa and had died there during confinement with her first baby. Talked much upon the Gospel in many of its different aspects and they received it all in a good spirit. I left with them "My Reasons" and bound "Rays" and was cordially invited to call again. After evening meeting Elder McCarty and I went up to Sister Craig's.

January 18 – Etc. Bible class in evening at White's. Received letter from Wm. Conald at Saltcoats which throws much light upon the Murdoch genealogy. Received others also from Mary and Afton, Calendar from Rasmussen.

January 26 – Visited the Art Gallery on Princess Street and although it is closed to the public, on explaining that I was from America and that I desired to see the painting of William Murdoch, I was admitted and got a good look at him. At the foot of the painting is a large plate containing the following –

"William Murdoch"
Applied Carburetted Hydrogen Gas to economic purposes at
Redruth in Cornwall. A.D. 1792
William Murdoch
1754 – 1839
Son of John Murdoch, Millwright, born at Bellow Mill, near Old Cumnock, 21st August 1754. His Father & Grandfather had been gunners in the Royal Artillery and pay sheets bearing their signatures are still preserved in the Royal Artillery Records at Woolwich. Died 15 Novr. 1839. Buried in Handsworth Church where there is a bust of him by Chantrey. Married Miss Paynter, daughter of a Mine Captain, residing at Pedruth and had two sons.William 1788–1831 John 1790–1862
Mr. Murdoch died in 1790 at the age of 24

May 1st – Went to Infirmary Street Baths with Elder King.

May 2 – Went up on top of Arthurs Seat in forenoon. Tracting in afternoon. Wet.

May 3 – Tracting in afternoon. Called on Mrs. John Bell, niece of Robert Michie of Heber City. They made me very welcome and had tea with them. Read to them his letter to me and they gave me one they had received from him in which he stated that he was on his 87th year. Bible class at Brother Whites.

May 4 – Went out to Gorbridge with Elder King and stayed overnight with Bro. & Sister Walkinshaw & took a walk in the Glen on Armiston Estate owned by Sir Robert Dundas and got some Primroses.

June 4 – Baird & Co. 168 West George Street. Saw Mr. Brand and had a talk with him also Mr. Weir, who was very pleasant. He is failing. Mr. Brand said it was a busy day so I did not stay. I then called out and saw Mr. Fleming who was quite feeble and in bed. I chatted a while with him. He was rather hard on the Latter day Saints. Talked away about Brigham Young and his many wives, etc. I gave him a few jolts. He then said we had better change the subject. I told him I had no desire to discuss with him. We talked away a while longer and he would still revert to that same subject. He has no conception whatever of what the Gospel is or the Plan of Salvation. With all his wealth, he will soon die – an old bachelor 82 years of age. In all the better sides of life an utter failure. Elder Condie & myself went to the Century Views in the Saint Andrew Halls. They were very fine. Left Glasgow at 8:20 and arrived home at 9:25.

June 18 – Went out to Dalhousie this afternoon – meeting Peter Hughes at Portobello to visit James Taylor and family and Robert Dean, read clerk at Newton, Grange Targe pit and works. This Pit is 350 fathoms deep, has an immerse round shaft, bricked up. The slides are four large round wire ropes set square in the shaft. The cage is a double decker – two compartment. There are six hutches or wagons on each deck, holding about 1000 lbs. Ea. or six tons of a lift. 48 men descent or ascend at one winding. They said it was the deepest pit in Gr. Britain. There are some seven seams being worked including the parrot seam, which is the tower. The works and pit are equipped by electricity. The Haulage is mostly arranged by wire ropes from the surface. The parties above mentioned are old friends of Martin Lindsay's who arranged through Peter Hughes for me to meet them. Returned by seven twenty train arriving at Waverley about 20 minutes at eight oclock.

June 26 – ditto. Elder Tolman & Anderson left.

June 27 – ditto in Leith.

June 28 – Arranged for Baths at Infirmary Street at 12 oclock Tuesday July 3.

June 29 – At home.

June 30 – Met Pres. Brown at Waverley Station at noon. After dinner and adjusting differences here in the Branch, walked out to Portobello in the evening.

July 1 – Sunday. Sunday School. Priesthood meeting held before Sunday School, however, at which the case of Alex. Scott was taken up and gone into thoroughly and unanimously voted upon by all present to excommunicate him from the church for appropriating to his own use church funds

– amounting to L4.14.0. Afternoon services were held at 2 oclock. Testimony meeting. Evening services at 6:30. Speakers, David L. Murdoch and Pres. James Brown. Good attendance.

July 2 – Sister White, Pres. Brown and myself went out to Roslin today. Walked through the glen to Loanhead. It is a beautiful and romantic glen. The scenery at this season of the year is lovely. The ferns and flowers enchanted us. We enjoyed it very much. Had tea with Sister White's sister at Loanhead and got back to Edinburgh at six oclock. Pres. Brown left on 9:15 train for Glasgow.

July 3 – Morning bright and sunny. Baptism of Marian & Susan Henry.

July 4 – Went to Waverley Station and met Elders Bachman & Condie. Called at Y.W.C.A. Rooms 122 George Street to see Miss Walker. She was out but an appointment was made at 3 oclock for me to see her. I called then and saw her and had a long interview with her. She is the sister to Mrs. Macdonald of the Blind Asylum at Dundee. I found out from her all about her Father today with Elders McMurrin and Broadbent who are here sight seeing from Bradford, England. They attended our Bible class meeting and left for home at 11 oclock.

July 14 - Met Thomas Murdoch at Crosshouse. He is a village Blacksmith and carries on quite a business. We all had tea with them. He has a nice family. We had a good talk with him about family affairs. He is well informed and very interesting.

July 18 – Tracting again. Went into the show shop of James Murdoch – old big round face and head. Mike Moran is working for him as a cobbler. Mike was at school with us. Mr. Murdoch remembered our family very well. I also called on Sarah Scott and Jean Mitchell, now Mrs. Urquhart and had a long chat with them. I also called on Robert Adamson and wife of the Smallburn and had a long talk with them. They are well. Mr. Adamson sent his love and kindest regards to Father. I also called on Mrs. Laidlaw and found her well and cheerful although somewhat bent with age. Our clock, which she bought, still stands and goes as well as ever. It looks quite natural.

July 20 – Called on Mr. Stewart at Springhill – did not see him. Very feeble. 84 years of age. Saw Miss Stewart. Walked out to Sanquhar Bridge. On way back called upon Andrew Murdoch in the Square. He is a little old man – stout and getting very white. His wife is a daughter of old Matthew Anderson's of the Square, Ann Andrew is now the only living one of his family. He was pleased to see me and we chatted away quite a while about old times. He is living in the self-same house that his father lived in when we lived in Linkieburn House. He showed me a "measure" which is prized very highly. It is a four gill stoup (pewter) which was well known in olden times as a "tapped hen". It belonged to John Lapraik the friend of Burns and has the initials "J.L." on the side of it. Called down at

Railway sheds upon James Hodge but he was away his holidays. Called on Robert Adamson & family on Main Street and talked with them a while. Also, on Thomas Weir and chatted with him. He was not very well. I also called on Jeanie Gibson who keeps a grocery store where her Father used to live and spent a little time very pleasantly with them. Her brother James is quite white and getting old like. Jeanie is still unmarried and looks well although getting gray.

> *Cauld blaws the win frae wast tae Eat*
> *The nights baith mirk and rainy O.*
> *The Hills are covered we wat and mist*
> *And the prospects ought but Cheerie O.*
> *We've seen the sights aboot the place*
> *Where aft – I've ran when auce a boy*
> *The Schule, the woods, the burns and glens*
> *That filled our hearts with youthful joy.*
> *Oor house is stanin just the same*
> *As when I left it years ago*
> *But nos it's a' made into one*
> *And rented by McCulloch's son.*
> *Cairntables tap I've hardly 'seen*
> *For clouds & mist have low oot oure*
> *Where many a time up there I've been*
> *We ither callants around the door.*
> *By Fibbies Brig awre Garpet's stream*
> *The Diel's back door on Glenmuir Shaw*
> *Where aft in fancy I hae been*
> *Since then we've wandered far awa.*
> *The Auld Sanquhar Road we its carpet a gleen*
> *Miahouse and Springhill are still to be seen*
> *Sae the tap o Wardlaw we its mantle o heather*
> *Come let us away and ascent it together.*
> *Auld Linkieburn – its memories dear*
> *Still cling to my heart at Earths fondest treasure*
> *The auld Quarry knowe at the back of the Square*
> *Remind me o days spent there with great pleasure.*
> *Auldhouseburn & Crossflat are changed not a shade*
> *With their fields and their plantains o green*
> *Nae mair may we walk thru their sweet scented glens*
> *Where in summer we often hae been.*
> *The Waulkmill still stands as if did in the fifties*
> *Ponesk is in ruins – now a thing of the past*
> *Reminding us always how fleeting this life is*
> *That youth flies away and old age cannot last.*
> *The Kirkgreen and the Garronhill*
> *Crafthead and Kirkburn falls*
> *Scenes that in youth's bright sunny days*
> *Sweet memories yet recalls.*
> *O dear to my heart are the scenes of my boyhood*

> *Revisited now after many long years.*
> *How fondly we meet those remaining that knew us*
> *Our greetings are mingled with joys and with tears.*

July 22 – Sunday. Attended meeting at Brother McKnight's – at 2 oclock. Meeting in evening at Hall at 6:30 and meeting at Cross afterwards.

July 23 – Went out to Kilmaurs with Elder Moench and called upon some people there. Called upon Miss Adamson on W. Netherton Street before going out there and had a long conversation with her.

> *There are dear hearts that knew me well*
> *When at the Schule we played together*
> *Why fate designed, I cannot tell*
> *That we should part from one another.*

July 27 – Were at McKnights this evening to supper. Had strawberries and cream afterwards.

July 28 – Left for Glasgow at 1:11 to attend Conference. Priesthood meeting at 3 Holenhead Street at 7:30. Pres. Grant was present and imparted instructions.

July 29 – Sunday. Conference at Gardon Halls, Paisley Road at 10 oclock. Elders Finlayson & Cook spoke. Meeting was then addressed by Pres. Grant. Meeting at two oclock. Elders Moench and myself spoke also Pres. Grant. Meeting again at 6:30. Elders Tolman & Condie & Pres. Grant occupied the time.

July 30 – Attended Social party this evening in the Halls. Had a very pleasant time.

July 31 – Went out to the Cathedral this forenoon with Pres. Grant, wife, daughter, Pres. Brown, and Elder Moench. Then took car down to the Trongate and went out to the Art Galleries. Pres. Grant & family left on 2 oclock train. Elder Pendrey and myself came to Kilmarnock on the 4:20 train.

August 5 – Sunday. Attended Irish Conference at 10. 1 & 6 oclock evening. Splendid turnout of people. About twice as many strangers present as Saints. Good spirit and I enjoyed it.

August 6 – Attended Priesthood meeting with the Elders which lasted about four hours. Went for a jaunting car ride with Elders Cassy, Thomion, Pres. Brown out to the Giants ring.

August 15 – Elder Pendrey and myself went out to Fenwick to see Matthew Fowlds, the centenarian. He was 100 years old last 22 May, on which occasion a grand dinner was given him in Kilmarnock. He has 3 sons in Minnesota and 1 in New Zealand. He is a hail old man. He can walk around a little, looks real well considering and can talk quite intelligently. He had on his old leather apron and a sleeved moleskin waistcoat on which garb he still occasionally does a little at his trade of weaving.

I gave him a bound "Ray" and "My Reasons" etc. An adopted daughter, Jeanie by name, had read of "Ann Elize" and "Escaped" wife of Brigham Young. Jeanie was kind enough to tell the old man that we were followers of Brigham Young. She seemed very much prejudiced.

Aug. 16th – At home all day. Wet.

Aug. 17th – ditto. At Bro. Breckenridge's at night.

Aug. 18th – went out to the Moss and got some heather.

Aug. 19th – Sunday. Meeting at Bro. McKnight's at two oclock. Evening meeting in Hall. Two strangers present. Gave them some literature. Held meeting at the Cross at eight oclock. Lines written on visiting Riccarton Mill after an absence of forty years.

> By Struthers steps o're Irvine's stream
> Lansyne when a boy I hae wandered
> In the sweet summer time, when natures so green
> How fendly the time we have squandered.
> Bright happy days, long long now gone
> How sweet is their memory still
> We often have met when the days work was done
> By the Brig, by the steps or the Mill.
> Some forty long years have passed now away
> Since first as boys we met each other
> I've longed to see your face again
> Alas thou'rt gone, and gone forever.
> I walk by the steps, by the brig and the Mill
> The Woods and the fields are a lonely and still
> I pass the auld house at the fir o' the brae
> But I canna see Edward, for he is away.
> Weil, wect dae I min, o, that happy time
> When cares lightly sat on us then
> When we romped and we played as fondly we strayed
> In the lang nights o summer thro woodland & glade.
> Far away in foreign lands my humble lot was cast
> I longed to see again the scenes where youth's bright days have passed
> I came, I saw, I was alone – no one there knew me
> Twas strange, twas sad, and yet it was to be.
> In lifes brief span upon this scene, congenial spirits meet
> Those that are alied to them, oh how they love to greet
> The Comrades of their boyish days, perhaps it was above
> They learned to know and understand and here renewed their love.
> If we were once, as yet perchance, we hope to yet become
> Comrades in another sphere, where death will cast no gloom
> Our present griefs and trials too will vanish from our view
> And we shall meet and greet them there, as we've been wont to do.
> Oh happy day, immortal time, we greet they welcome morn
> When we shall see as we are seen and know as we are known
> When truth's full era's ushered in and errors overthrown
> When love and peace o'er all mankind shall claim them as their own.

Aug.28th - While speaking at the Cross, I made known to my listeners that I was a native of Ayrshire and that I had lived in Utah a great many years and was familiar with conditions there and so on. One evening after meeting, a Mr. Brown engaged us in conversation about what we had been speaking about and as discussions are not allowed on the streets, an appointment was made at our lodgings. Accordingly, at the time stipulated, Mr. Brown appeared and after the usual salutations, the discussion of the principles of the Gospel proceeded. He seemed to be very prejudiced against us, in fact he made no effort to conceal it, and in the course of our conversation, he referred to so many newspaper reports concerning the Latter day Saints that were always of a character or nature to produce derision, contempt or abuse. And he specially emphasized those that portrayed the destruction of the system known to the world as Mormonism. The incident of the deportation of Susan Henry was an excellent theme to shoot off his loud mouth about in the midst of the crowd upon the Cross. And he propounded the wonderful conundrum "How are you going to get your converts into the United States now". I answered, the same way as we have always done. "Well but you can't." "The government has stopped it and you will have to take them in as stowaways." It was explained that Susan Henry was a child of about ten years of age and was lately taken out by one of our people having been given away by her parents, by both Father and Mother, with the object of adoption by a couple who desired a little girl, having none of their own. Everything was thoroughly understood and all was perfectly agreeable, but whether in the fault of drawing up the adoption papers, or whether there is not adoption law in Gr. Britain, the fact remains that the papers did not suit the Immigration officers at point of debarkation and she was returned. Another instance brought up was the fact that the Dundee News, some few months ago, published an article stating that Mr. R. P. Houston, M.P. declared that he had a conversation one day with the "principal son" of Brigham Young, who was to be seen the beginning of the summer on the streets of London. He was there so the report says with his seven wives having a suite of rooms in a well known Bayswater boarding house. The report goes on to say that when he sallies forth, his movements are interesting. He engages four hansoms, and off they drive in a sort of Indian file, two wives in three cabs and himself and seventh wife in the fourth cab. It is a sight to watch this gentleman conducting his wives, as if they were daughters, over the West End of London. It happened that I was ready for my friend, having previously communicated with Mr. Houston, asking him upon what authority he had made the statements attributed to him, as they were grossly untrue and calculated to do much mischief, etc. Mr. Houston replied immediately as follows –

43 Park Lane
   London, W.
   18 May 1906
   Dear Sir:
I am desired to Mr. R. P. Houston to acknowledge receipt of your letter of 17th enclosing newspaper cutting, and to inform you that he is in no way responsible for this. Presumably, it refers to a speech made by Mr. Houston in the House of Commons on Chinese Labour, and what Mr. Houston said can be seen in Hansard's Report, which in no way justifies the Construction which this newspaper puts upon it, or the introduction of his name into the article.

   Mr. Houston made no reference whatever to Polygamy but simply remarked that a son of Brigham Young had once informed him that they believed in educating people by the eye as well as by the ear, and this was the only reference made to either Mr. Brigham Young or Mormonism.

   It is apparent Mr. Houston can in no way be held responsible for remarks made in newspapers, and he certainly gave no grounds for his name being introduced into the article in question. I return the cutting as requested.
Yours faithfully,
   J. H. Cornford, Secretary

A copy of the correspondence was furnished the paper that printed the article but no notes whatever was taken of it. Our friend appeared not to be satisfied that all that appears about us in the public prints is not to be relied upon. He seemed now to take a new tack, however, for what purpose, I did not then comprehend, but the sequel will soon show. He seemed desirous of knowing when I emigrated to America, if I had lived in Hurlford, if my Father was a shoemaker there etc, etc. It appears now that a scheme was being hatched up by a number of persons to make me out the runaway husband of a Mrs. Murdoch who lived in the village of Hurlford and who was now on a bed of sickness from which she was not expected to recover. And this poor woman has been led to believe that her husband, who had deserted her a number of years ago and who had never communicated with his wife or family from the time of leaving them, had now returned from Utah, from the Mormons and was preaching upon the Cross at Kilmarnock. The word had got around amongst relatives and friends' curiosity, it seems was aroused, and a large delegation amongst whom was my (supposed) daughter, now a young lady, came in last Sunday evening to see the reported runaway Mormon Elder preach upon the streets and identify, if possible, the long lost Father and husband. Not the slightest inkling of their intentions [illegible word] ears with afterwards [illegible word] for Bigamy, Desertion and I don't know what. For I had shown Mr. Brown the photo of my wife and family in Salt Lake City, little thinking of what was being conjured up against us. Last Sunday afternoon, Mr. Brown called at our lodgings and asked for me. I was away at afternoon meeting and he was told where he would find me in the evening. When evening came, he intercepted me on my way to the Hall where we hold our meetings. He excused himself for appearing there but was very anxious to know if I did not belong to Hurlford. If my Father was not a shoemaker and how long it was since I emigrated and other questions of a like nature. Even yet, I never suspicioned anything. And although two large policemen hung around us in very close proximity at our meeting, to be ready for any emergency that might arise, I suppose, still I did not suspect that anything was in the wind. I told my friend, Mr. Brown, that I was a native of Muirkirk, that I lived in Hurlford for four years, that my Father was underground manager at Muirkirk, etc. I do not think Mr. Brown believed me and made an appointment with me to go out to Hurlford and see some folks there. We held our meeting, it was the largest I have seen there. We distributed two hundred tracts and did not have enough. Many were anxious to engage in conversation with us afterwards. According to appointment, I met Mr. Brown and before proceeding to Hurlford, I asked him what was the object of our visit there. Why, Mr. Murdoch to be candid with you, I will tell you that I was speaking to some of my friends about you and I told them that your name was Murdoch and that you had lived in Hurlford and that you were from Utah where the Mormon's come from and some of them asked me what you were like and I told them as best I could and in talking with one another, we came to the conclusion that you were probably the man who left there a number of years ago forgetting to say goodbye to his dear wife and family and so on and that he would like me to go out with him and see this lady, this deserted wife and family and satisfy them that I was not the man who had done this cruel thing. I was quite agreeable and off we started and in due time we reached our destination. Before proceeding however to Mrs. Murdoch's residence, my friend Brown, (not the President of the Glasgow Conference) thought it desirable to take along with us a Mr. Wallace, one of his associates in religious and templar circles as a witness perhaps of what might transpire at this identification. As it was however, we could not find Mr. Wallace, who was in the secret, and we proceeded to the Ladies House. When we arrived there it would be about eight oclock and was getting quite dark. We were ushered into the sick chamber where Mrs. Murdoch was laying. I quietly shook hands with her and inquired about her health. She answered me in a weak voice and asked something about Mrs. Cineron. I said who? She said, is this no oor minister? My friend, Brown then said, just a moment Mrs. Murdoch and I will make you acquainted with this gentleman as soon as the gas is lit. I was then introduced to Mrs. Murdoch as Mr. Murdoch about whom she had been told. I was also made acquainted with her daughter and her husband, Mr. Ramsay. A smile came over all present, except Mr. Brown, even Mrs. Murdoch laying there in an enfeebled emaciated condition, smiled and said, you are no him. I told Mr. Brown she said, that if you were him that you need no be feared to come home, for I would be glad to see you. There's his picture on the wall there and I'm sure you are no like him. I said I was sorry, for here was my daughter that I just felt like throwing my arms around her neck and she said she was sorry too for she expected to meet and have the pleasure of calling me father. The whole affair was not explained satisfactorily to all who were present. Mr. Brown was frank enough to say that he thought the best way was to bring me out to see them for if there was any doubt or dubiety about it and my possibility of me being the man he wanted to be the Sherlock Holmes. We engaged in general conversation which soon developed into genealogy and I gave them a copy of "My Reasons". I gave my daughter my card and I gave Mrs. Murdoch a blessing and when I returned home, I importuned the throne of grace in her behalf.

Mrs. Murdoch evinced a fine Christian spirit, she was pleasant indeed to see me and invited me to come again and see her. I learned from "my daughter" that her mother had had twins at one birth and triplets at another besides other children. "My daughter" being one of the triplets. I begin to see how near I was to imprisonment for desertion and bigamy. If my Father had only been a shoemaker and had hailed from Hurlford. If I had only been the husband of this lady, If I had only been the Father of those twins, and if I had only been the proud Father of those triplets. If I had not emigrated to Utah so soon as I did by some ten years nothing under heaven could have saved me from the felon's cell. Fortunately I did not desert this good lady and her family. Fortunately, Mr. Murdoch, the real husband never was a Mormon, never went to Utah, never even to America, but is said to have gone to Australia. Fortunately, another grand opportunity has absolutely failed to show how mean, despicable and vile the Mormons are. Oh what a disappointment to those who conceived this mare's nest. What a deadly blow could have been dealt out to the Mormons in Kilmarnock and Scotland. How the newspapers would have sounded our funeral knell. How it would have circumscribed the globe. But as it is only an everyday occurrence, let it pass.

Sept. 3 – Took 8:10 train for Cronberry. Walked up to High Gaswater to see Cousin Foulds Mair. He lives in a little below where Grannie [Mary Murray Murdoch] used to live. It is a link now running north & south with perhaps four or five houses on it. Foulds & his family use two of the places – the rest are used for store rooms or the like. All that remains now where Grannie lived is the gable and walls. It is evidently long roofless. Foulds is getting white and old looking and is much troubled with his breathing. He showed me around the place and pointed out the hole in the ground that represented the pit where Grandfather lost his life in attempting to save some others who had gone down and were overcome with fire damp or rather black damp. I pulled some heather not far from where Grannie lived and will send it home to friends. [illegible word] It is in ruins. The roofs are all gone. The walls and gables are crumbling away. The inside of the house is grown up with weeds and nettles. They were evidently good houses once upon a time. The situation is fine and would afford a splendid site for a home. I came on down past Morton Muir farm to Bronberry Rows to the School house and found there Mr. Hyslop, my old School Companion at Muirkirk. He received me with great warmth and satisfaction. He took me into his house, made me acquainted with his family and we were very shortly had tea. We recited in turn our lives to each other and talked over by-gone days as boys together and associated long, long ago. Mr. Hyslop looks pretty well, so do his wife and they have a fine family. His eldest son is principal of the Acadamy at Rothesay, an M.A. etc., etc. and I should judge a bright promising fellow. He convoyed me away down to within a stones throw of Bellomill and we were loathe to part. That was certainly a lovely walk through Bellapath. I called in at Bellomill for a moment as it was getting dusk. Went on down through Lugar and called upon Mr. John Clark, manager of the store and talked with him for a short time. He did not seem able to remember me, however in connection with the store, however he treated me very kindly and desired to be remembered to my Father, whom he knew in Muirkirk during the few months Mr. Clark was manager of the store at Muirkirk. He convoyed me nearly to Old Cumnock station where I got the train reaching Kilmarnock about 9:30. I forgot to mention that Foulds has Grannie's cupboard and sugar bowl. The cupboard has been a fancy article in its day. It has Chinese designs on the outside and inside are a number of little drawers and pigeon holes in one of which is kept the sugar bowl.

Sept. 10 – Went up to Auchinleck with 8:10 train. Called upon John Gervan, whose mother last held the Murdoch Stave, Staff or walking stick and he himself now holds it, although he is clearly not entitled to it. This was the first time I have even beheld it. It is, considering its age, in a good state of preservation, thanks to the substantial nature of the stave. I borrowed it and took it to Cumnrock with me and had my photo taken with it. It is a made or manufactured walking stick of some good foreign wood and well made with the head projecting about equally on either side, in other words, the handle is fastened somewhat in the relative portion that a handle is to a hammer. At the head of the handle is a brass containing the following inscription –

*THIS STAVE I LEAVE
IN LEGASIE TO THE
OLDEST MURDOCH
AFTER ME
IN AUCHNLECK 1743*

This inscription, I have endeavored to give just as it is upon the stave in the exact spelling put there by the donor, supposed to be John Murdoch of Bellomill, as the date 1743 is some eleven years prior to the date of the birth of his son, William, the inventor of gas.

*Present custodian of the stave, John Girvan, Auchinleck
who got it from his mother, Mrs. Girvan (Jean Murdoch)
who got it from Mrs. Terras, Dalsalloch, (Jean Murdoch)
who got it from David Murdoch, Gardener to the Marquis of Bute
who got it from John Murdoch, Coal road, Auchinleck, who is said to have [illegible word] to the ribs with it and bears evidence of having been used in this manner
who got it from Mrs. Rankins, Lugar*

While in Cumnrock, I called upon Mr. A.B. Tod, a well known character for many years in this locality, as writer and author. He is 84 years of age and does not look much more than 64 years. He is wonderfully preserved. I called specially thinking he might be able to give some information of a genealogical nature. He told me he was sorry he could not. I gave him a copy of "My Reasons" and my card. He told me he once owned a copy of the Book of Mormon and had read most of it but someone had borrowed it and had never returned it. He asked me if our Church split up and divided like the rest of them and I told him it did not. I bought some views of Cumnock. I hunted up where Cousin Mary Caldow Baird used to live and found a daughter, a Mrs. Nichol, living not far from there. I had a talk with her. Her Father is living, her uncle George, unmarried, lives with him. Her Uncle John lives at Burnbank, a widower, with a family, her uncle James lives at Mauchline. She promised me to write to her Grannie, Aunt [illegible word] in Heber City and to let her know all about her relatives. After looking around the town, seeing many familiar places that have not changed in forty or fifty years, such as the spout row, where we lived at one time, the Townhead, the Square, the Tanyard, the Graveyard, etc. I walked back to Auchinleck where I interviewed one Thomas Murdoch a carpenter there who is a direct relative of the Bellomill Murdoch. He could not give me any information such as I desired however. I found Matthew McTurk who would be lately or is even now perhaps designated as young Matthew. He will be between 50 and 60 years of age and is a son of old and very well known Matthew McTurk of Auchinleck. He got all of his father's papers, but has allowed a brother residing in England to get some of the more important ones and other to get others so that what might have afforded perhaps the best source of information, has been frittered away over the past five years. I got some information from him however and he took me all through a Cemetery where we saw the resting places of many of the Murdochs and others. I jotted down in my vest pocket book a copy of most of them which read as follows –

Here lies the body of David Murdoch in Highland of Auchinleck who died
Janry 10, 1789 aged 64 years.
Elizabeth Murdoch
Wife of
William Lamont, Farmer, died at
Stonepark, Cumnock, June 1831, aged 33 years
(Aunt of Thos. Murdoch, carpenter)

On a stone which Mr. McTurk told me was quarried at Gaswater, is recorded the following and nothing else

John Geddes
Gaswater

(He was neighbor to Grannie at High Gaswater)
 This stone was Erected by Andrew Templeton, farmer in Clockchuril his spouse

Elizabeth Murdoch and three of their children lay here 1797
Also in memory of Andrew Templeton, farmer. Auchalton, who died 30
November 1838, aged 54 years and
Robert Templeton, his son, started the divinity who died 3 June 1840,
aged 26.
Erected by
James Murdoch Lugar in memory of
his son William died 21 Novr. 1838 aged 4_ years
his daughter Margaret died 15 May 1849
his daughter Margaret 19 Sept. 1850
his daughter Isibella died 25 Dec. 1855
his daughter Prudence died June 24, 1865

The Murdochs are a very ancient old race in Scotland and so highly respected in the way of excellent behavior. Glasgow Cathedral was founded in 1123. At that time they were one of the Murdochs it appears was an architect the time Glasgow Cathedral was built and served others in Scotland besides the Iammas School of [illegible word].

Sept. 11 – Went over to the Moss at Riccarton. The heather bloom is just about all gone for another year. Were at Hawthorn's at night.

Sept. 12 – At home. Took a walk up by Dean Castle in the evening. Called at McKnights on way home.

Sept. 13 – Wet. At home. Book of Mormon Class in evening at Breckenridge's.

Sept. 14 – Saw Mrs. Ditty this morning before she left for Glasgow. Went tracting in Newmilus today.

Sept. 15 – Took a walk through Hay Park up to Burn's monument with Sister Ditty. Cousins Maggie Mair [illegible word] from West Kilbride to see me and was waiting at my lodgings when I returned. She is 22 years of age and is a fine looking big lassie. She had dinner with us then we went over to Rugby Park and saw the games and sports with the Scots Greys who came from Piershill Barran Edinburgh for the occasion. Cousin Maggie went out to Crosshouse and from there would take train back to West Kilbride.

October 21 – Meeting at McKnights in afternoon. Occupied all the time. Meeting at Hall in evening. Elder Pendery and myself were speakers. Held meeting at the Cross at 8 oclock. It turned out to be the best and largest meeting we have yet held there. Occupied all the time, about an hour. As we were distributing our literature, "Clark" came into the ring and commenced a harangue against the Latter-day Saints bragging that he would soon burst up Mormonism throwing out some of his nasty slurs and insinuations. When he got through I told him that I had known of many far bigger, brighter, and more able men than he ever dared to presume to be, attempt to accomplish this same thing, but as those who did so were mostly wicked men, failure marked their every effort, and they and he would be ground to powder. We left him then and after we were away down the street we could hear him shouting at the top of his voice.

October 25 – Kilmarnock Fair – went up town to see the sights. The streets were crowded. Saw Maggie Mair. In the afternoon went to the Cron Exchange to see them there where dancing is provided for them. Most of the boys and young men were the worse of [illegible word] drink and their behavior was very rough and uncouth. Bible class at Bro. Breckenridge's at night.

October 26 – Wet. Home all day.

October 27 – Pres. Brown came over from Glasgow to visit me and informed me that he would return home Novr. 23 and that I would succeed him as President of the Scottish Conference. [The Scottish Conference refers to the area of Scotland within the British Mission. David Lennox was called to the Great Britain Mission and the Scottish Conference was part of that mission.]

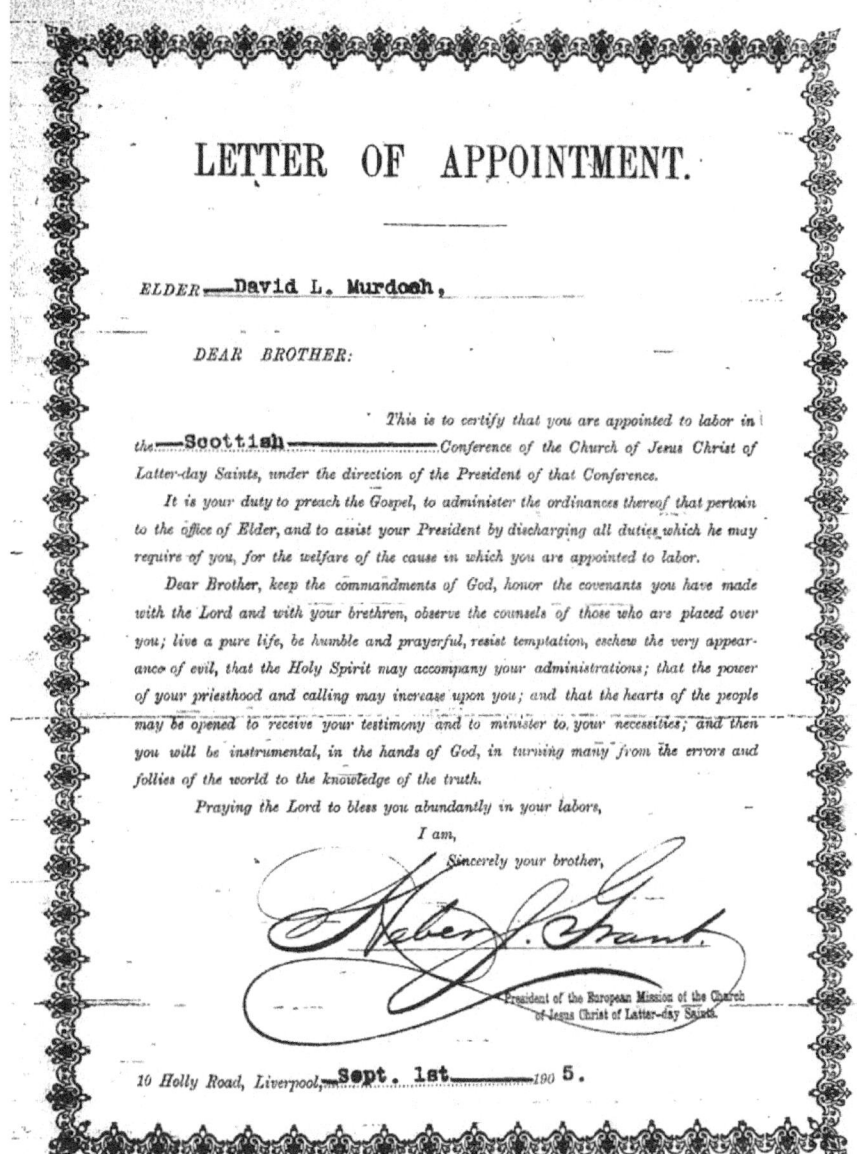

LETTER OF APPOINTMENT.

ELDER —David L. Murdoch,

DEAR BROTHER:

This is to certify that you are appointed to labor in the —Scottish— Conference of the Church of Jesus Christ of Latter-day Saints, under the direction of the President of that Conference.

It is your duty to preach the Gospel, to administer the ordinances thereof that pertain to the office of Elder, and to assist your President by discharging all duties which he may require of you, for the welfare of the cause in which you are appointed to labor.

Dear Brother, keep the commandments of God, honor the covenants you have made with the Lord and with your brethren, observe the counsels of those who are placed over you; live a pure life, be humble and prayerful, resist temptation, eschew the very appearance of evil, that the Holy Spirit may accompany your administrations; that the power of your priesthood and calling may increase upon you; and that the hearts of the people may be opened to receive your testimony and to minister to your necessities; and then you will be instrumental, in the hands of God, in turning many from the errors and follies of the world to the knowledge of the truth.

Praying the Lord to bless you abundantly in your labors,

I am,

Sincerely your brother,

Heber J. Grant

President of the European Mission of the Church of Jesus Christ of Latter-day Saints.

10 Holly Road, Liverpool, —Sept. 1st— 190 5.

Lines written by Elder David L. Murdoch in honor of President James Brown of the Scottish Conference at his farewell Social held at the Gordon Halls, Glasgow, November 16th, 1906.

Land of my Fathers again I bid thee farewell,
A last fond look and we may never meet again,
The wide, wild ocean on its Bosom's ceaseless swell
Shall carry me away from thee upon its billowy main.
Thy heather hills with purple tint and lovely fragrance sweet,
Thy mossy banks and flowered wooded glens,
They hills and dales, a summers safe retreat
Are cherished memories as of ever dearest friends.
Thy lochs and streams and woods with sylvan shade
Thy rugged steeps and crags with classic waterfalls
Immortalized by Burns and Scott, in song and story made
By them and others, by Ramsay and by Robert Tannahill.
The time draws near, when I must once more sever
Myself from thee and friends of olden time and kindred dear
To dear ones far away, who constantly are ever
Watching and waiting for the hour that brings me near.
And thus is life, we meet, we part, we live and love,
Our joys and sorrows are surely for some purpose great
That man may live and learn with wisdom from above
To fit him for a higher and a better state.
Accept my thanks, my highest aspirations are to live
And be remembered as your firm and faithful friend
May he who dwells on high still deign to grant and give
Us rich supply of all good things even unto the end.
O, Scotland!, on whose breast there still and peaceful lays
The ashes and the dust of ancestors of many by gone days
While far away in foreign lands my humble lot is cast
My heart responsively looks back to the memories of the past.
My fond desires, my dearest hopes, are still that thou mayest see
The truth, eternal, which has been revealed from heaven,
That we might know and understand God's purposes to be
For man's best welfare and his future glory given.

Lines written to Mr. Robert Donald on receiving from him 4 P.P.C of Muirkirk and his Xmas card. His Xmas card was entitled

"Keep Smiling."

Keep smiling, keep smiling, is a motto indeed
That Batchelors and Maidens should observe to succeed
Aye, and Benedicts too, for how much greater the bliss
To them who can smile, there is nothing amiss.
Like a sunbeam of light, thru the dense cloudy sky
It engenders a hope as the storm passeth by
It pierceth the gloom and the sorrows of life
And bids them disperse with their anguish and strife.
Keep smiling, not frowning, be cheerful, not sad.
For life is a mixture of the good and the bad
With its joys and its sorrows, its pleasures and pains
How pleased the sunshine, how dismal the rains.
As the Suns to the Earth, so be you to your friends
Warm smiling and happy on all that attends.
Diffusing your goodness wherever you go.
A friend unto many, whom to love is to know

January 2, 1907 David L. Murdoch

Decr. 24 – At home. Elder Wing went off with morning. Elders Pendrey & McQueen came in from Kilmarnock. Elder Budge came in from Perth.

Decr. 25 – Christmas Day. Elders Warner, Adamson, & Burt came through from Edinburgh. Called upon Mrs. Murray at 14 Oakbank Terrace and had tea with her. This is the Lady I met in tracting and who came to our meeting Sunday evening last. Got a number of Xmas cards and letters and with the letters from Will, Jeanie & Norah and John Adamson, I have indeed been well remembered and blessed for all of which I am very thankful. Amongst the many Xmas cards received was a very nice on from little Peggy Paton, daughter of Mrs. Paton at Kilmarnock. I sent her one in return, on which I wrote as follows:

My dear little P.P.
I am so pleased (you see) u.c.
That I send you this card
With my greatest regard
For your kindness in thinking of me P.P.

Decr. 31 – Went down to the Glasgow Cross to see the New Year ushered in there. Elders Nelson & Ritche went with me. There was an immense throng of people. When the hour of twelve arrived there was shouting and singing and dozens of bottles of whiskey were thrown at King William's statue and broken upon it. Some of the bottles missed the Statue altogether and it was a great wonder that the glass in passing street cars was not broken and that people were not hurt.

Janry 1st, 1907 – At home. Wrote to Pres. Penrose. Went down to the City Hall concert in the evening and enjoyed it very much.

Janry 2 – At home. Working on monthly reports as much as I could. Wrote a letter to Mr. Robert Donald who was so kind to us while at Muirkirk. He is now at West Kilbride.

Febry 10 – Conference convened in the Gordon Halls at 10:30 a.m. Pres. Penrose & wife all of the Elders and quite a number of Saints were present. The Statistical Report was read, the Authorities were presented and sustained. Elders Thand & Burt spoke briefly upon their labors and upon the principles of the Gospel. Pres. Penrose occupied the balance of the time in spirited remarks. 2 p.m. Elders Pendrey and Moench occupied a little time upon the principles of the Gospel and Pres. Penrose occupied the balance to the great satisfaction of all who were present. There was a good attendance. At the evening meeting the hall was pretty well filled up with Saints and strangers. Elder Rich and myself occupied a little time speaking on the Gospel. Pres. Penrose spoke at length upon a variety of subjects. The Saints all represent themselves as being greatly pleased and blessed with Conference. The Countenances of all were beaming and all seemed happy. The Elders were unanimous in their expressions of joy and happiness with Conference. Elder Peter T. Condie & William H. Russell rendered solos which helped out very much with our Conference.

Lines written on visiting Old Monkland Churchyard to see the resting place of Alex Whitelaw, late M.P. for the city of Glasgow in company with Alex Park.

> *Some thirty years have passed away since I left my native land*
> *And during all those many years while in a foreign strand*
> *My heart still longed to once more see the friends I knew in youth*
> *And grasp them warmly by the hand and leave with them the truth.*
>
> *I came and saw my Fatherland - the scenes are dear to me*
> *The woods, the glens, the burns and braes of happy memory*
> *Where oft in childhood's joyous days we've played from morn till night*
> *I think I see us in them yet and all our force and might.*
>
> *But where are all our Comrades gone, they are scattered far and wide*
> *And many have passed from our views - gone to the other side*
> *And those that are remaining here, how changed they seem to be*
> *I do not know one half of them and they cannot know me.*
>
> *There are some I love to think of yet, and why I cannot tell*
> *Unless perchance it was that before we came here to dwell*
> *We then were kindred spirits in a realm more pure than this*
> *Where they can all commingle in innocence and bliss.*

Some have grown great in workably things, while others have grown small
Some have pursued a selfish course, that's common to us all
Some have grown gray in honor's cause and justly may be said
To not have lived unworthily of this ancestral head.

There are some we loved that are not here, long since they passed away
And resting in their little home, they soon return to clay
Their spirit has gone up aloft, returned from whence it came
To stay here till the time shall come when they'll unite again.

I visit the silent cities - home of the great forgotten past
I see the little resting place that holds them safe at last
I leave a flower upon their grave, an offering of my love
That I have cherished long for one, whose kindness I have proved.

Only a spray of flowers placed on a little wire frame
Emblems of beauty and purity, they were lovely just the same
Only a little offering of an attached one's true regard
Only a kind remembrancer to you as a just reward.

Only a friend from a distant land thousands of miles away
Only here for a season and cannot much longer stay
And if never again I have the chance to show my true regard
I'll pleasantly think of the day we went to Old Monkland Parish Churchyard.

David L. Murdoch

July 1 – Tracting at Possilpark. Called on Mrs. Cofty.

July 2 – ditto. Called on Miss Fisher and Brother McQueen at Fordnenck Street.

July 3 – Tracting at Possilpark.

July 4 – Spent the 4th of July at Rothesay with the Elders. It was a very wet day. Took the "Lusitania" at the Tail of the Bank. Went to the Pavilion in the evening.

July 5 – The Elders left today for Edinburgh.

July 6 – Went down to the Green.

July 7 – At noon went to the Kinning Park Baths and had service there. Baptized the Sisters Cameron and one of Brother Laird's children, one of sister Grahanie's and one of Brother Gates – all boys. Held Fast meeting at hall at two oclock where they were all confirmed and Sister Gate's baby was blessed and named Mary Margaret. Held meeting at Halls in evening at six oclock. Elders Nelson, Budge & myself spoke. Held Street meeting on Queen Street later. Elder Budge spoke.

July 8 – Tracting today at Possilpark.

July 9 – ditto ditto

July 10 & 11 – At Home.

July 12 – got Telegram this morning shortly after midnight telling me that Mamma & Janet would arrive at 6:15. I went to the Central Station and waited for a couple of hours. Did not find them. Meantime they arrived at St. Enoch's and were at Barrington Drive when I got home. They were well but tired after traveling all night.

July 13 – Wet today. Took a walk in town. It is Fair Saturday and most of the shops are closed.

July 14 – Attended both meetings at Hall. Elder Morton who had just arrived from Liverpool and my nephew William W. Murdoch, who for the last three years has been laboring in Germany and who arrived in Glasgow this morning, spoke also Elder Budge. At the evening meeting, my nephew addressed the meeting in German. Elder McQueen gave his farewell address and I spoke afterwards. Later held street meeting on Queen Street and had a good meeting. Elder McQueen gave a very good address, followed by Elder Budge and myself. Sold 9 Books and distributed Rays 6 & 7.

July 15 & 16 – At Home.

July 17 – Visited Mrs. Fullay in Barrett Str. Mrs. Urie, Mrs. Irvine on James Street. Friends of Mrs. McKundrick and Mrs. Crawford.

July 18 – Went out to Tollercross Park and Museum and spend the afternoon there.

July 19 – Visited Ayr, Burus Monument, The Brig o'doon, Burus Cottage and Museum. Alloway's auld Kirk, came into Ayr and visited Aunt Agnes Lennox Callan – had tea there with cousin Mary Milloman & daughter. Called later on Mary Cameron and came back to Glasgow in the evening.

July 20 – At home.

July 21 – Attended two Hall meetings and one open air meeting on Queen Street.

July 22 – At home.

July 23 – Visited Mrs. Irvine on James Street, Bridgeton and had tea with them.

July 24 – Took a trip, Queen Street to Craigindoran, to Loch Gail and Loch Long to Arrochar, walked over to Tarbed, sailed down Loch Lomand to Balloch, train back to Charring Cross and had a most enjoyable day. Bishop Taylor and daughter, Ethel, and sister Bell were with us.

July 25 – Visited Patricks at Tollcross and spent a fine evening with them.

July 26 & 27 – At home.

July 28 – Attended Cambridge H. Church. Afternoon meeting at the Halls. Elder Nelson, Sister [illegible word]. Evening meeting at the Halls. Elder Budge and myself spoke. Street meeting on Queen Street. Elder Budge and myself spoke.

Augt. 1/6 – In Ireland. Saw Dublin Exhibition.

Augt. 7/14 – At home. Went to Rothesay on the 14th with Mrs. Liney and had a fine day.

Augt. 16 – Visiting James Gilmour.

Augt. 17/19 – At Muirkirk. Visiting places and at Glenbush.

Augt. 20 – Called upon David Gilmour at his office. In the evening spent the night at Mrs. Thaws and had supper.

Augt. 21 – Spent the evening at James Gilmour's. Had a nice time, supper, etc.

Augt. 22 – Left for London.

Augt. 23 – Arrived at London and went to 97 Farleigh Road & stayed there until evening of 26th. Saw many of the sights. The Bank of England, The Royal Exchanged, the Tower, the London Monument, London Bridge, The Thames Embankment, the Houses of Parliament, Westminster Abbey, Belgravia, the Kings Stables, the Zoo, Madam Tussaud's, Hyde Park, the Marble Arch, Epping Forrest, much of the principal streets of London. Attended Daby's Theatre and saw "The Merry Widow".

Augt. 24 – Arrived home from London. Visited Mrs. Kennedy's and saw Sandy and his boy.

Augt. 25 – At home working upon reports and Books.

END OF MISSIONARY JOURNAL

..

EDITOR'S NOTE: *The following is a letter written to Alexander Whitelaw, David Lennox's boss in Glasgow, Scotland. David Lennox was very fond of Mr. Whitelaw and wanted to tell him of his new life in Utah. This was written about a year after David Lennox arrived in Utah.*

Heber City
   Wasatch County
   Utah Territory
   America
   9 May 1879
   Alex. Whitelaw, Esq. M.P.
   Dear Sir,

You very kindly expressed a wish to hear from me when I had got fairly settled here. I have ever since I came to this country looked forward to the pleasure of writing you and giving you a little of my experience of the same; but I have to confess to a little diffidence on addressing you. I have not heard from Glasgow Office since Novr. last, but I have observed in the "Glasgow Weekly" two or three small notices since then concerning your health. The last was dated 5th April, reporting you to be able to take a daily airing and from this source I gather you have had sickness all winter more or less. I sincerely trust you continue to improve and gather strength and that you may be long spared to live and to do much good upon the earth.

   It is nearly a year now since I left Old Scotland and looked forward to the far west for my future home. The time occupied in performing the voyage and journey from Liverpool to Salt Lake City was 19 days. 11 days by sea. 1 day in New York and 7 on the cars. A very fair journey as regards time considering that the railway part of it was by an immigrant train. We had a pleasant and prosperous trip. I can say now, after a year's residence, and that truly that I like the country very much.

The climate is dry and very healthy. The soil once a sterile barren desert, is now most productive and with the blessing of the Lord and the labors of its husbandmen, blossoms like the rose. This Territory I believe is capable of raising anything in the fruit and grain lines. Sugar cane, etc., etc. Where I live (Heber City) it is more a grain raising and pasturing county, still fruit is being more gone into now. This is also a mineral county and the Territory is rich in minerals. Silver, Gold, Coal, Iron, etc. The celebrated Emma Silver mine is not far distant from here. And 12 miles from here there is a first class silver mine called the "Ontario" in operation employing a great many hands. So far as I am aware these mines are all mostly run by gentiles. The Mormons are not supposed to run after such things.

The settlements in Utah are all in valleys with high mountains running round. This is a pleasant little valley surrounded with very high mountains some of which retain a little of their winter garb all the year round. The extent of it will be about 10 miles North & South by about the same East & West, but it is widest East & West. It is about 40 miles from Salt Lake City. The people here are, with the exception of a Sawmill and Shingle mill men & tradesmen, [are] employees in Agriculture; And are a very independent class of citizens, i.e. they can raise all they require to eat and wear and export their surplus. As regards [to] myself, about the first work I did was assisting to build cattle sheds, a little in the carpentering line. Then I had haying & harvesting in their season. This I found to be very hard work, principally I think on account of the great heat, perhaps 110 degrees or more. I cannot exactly say. Then I had a little fall plowing, besides many other kinds of work entirely new to me. From the pen to the plough is certainly a change of occupation. After when I was in the field my mind would stray away back to the many pleasant days I have spent in your service, and one saying of yours repeatedly recurred to my mind. It was this "You'll find it hard work to grow corn." Many sayings of yours force themselves upon my mind from time to time. Another was one evening coming home Westminster to Eaton Sq. after riding nearly the whole way without a word being exchanged you remarked just as we were about to draw up to the door. "There will be no handsom cabs in Utah". A strange and true saying. The nearest approach I believe is called a "buggy".

You have been visited, as have most European Countries, with a most depressed season of trade, commercial calamities, Bank failures, etc., etc. What a contrast we present here. That wave of depression which so long has rolled over you is but little felt here. We are nearly all owners of the soil and are nearly and striving hard to be a self sustaining people. We are not rich in money, but as a rule our people here are rich in cattle, sheep, land, houses and everything that goes to make up the material wealth of a nation. I often thought when reading of the distress that prevailed in Glasgow last winter, that if these people could be planted out here, they would have a chance to make a comfortable living

I may say that I have not got fairly settled here yet, but hope soon to be a little better freed up. Still I have been desirous for a long time to send you a little of my experience of the new world. Last winter I taught school and was very successful I think. I am continuating at the same occupation for another term. I had no idea of turning domine, but a fellow is glad sometimes to submit to circumstances. As regards what brought & keeps me here. I think I gave you to understand that before I left. Allow one to here say that it was because I became convinced that all the different systems of religion of which I had any knowledge were a mass of truth and error – simply confusion – and that most of them had no idea of where they came from, what they were doing & whither they were going. And after I had heard the Gospel of Jesus Christ preached which I know has been revealed in these days, and had compared the same with the Bible & Testament, and had given the matter due consideration I yielded obedience to and was received into the Church by babtism which with them is immersion. It was a conviction, a knowledge that the system of religion called Mormonism was true that I joined myself to that body and gathered here to the valleys of the mountains to learn of the ways of the Lord. This to some people would appear arrant nonsense and I would be set down, as indeed I have been, as foolish and crazy. I say I am neither the one nor other, but simply and plainly declare that I know that God has once more set his Church & Kingdom upon the earth never more to be thrown down again. I know that this has been done by Revelation through Joseph Smith, who was a prophet of the most high God. And who sealed his testimony of the truth of this great work by his blood. I say I know this – all the knowledge and enlightenment of Divines etc. of the 19th Century to the contrary notwithstanding.-- If you will permit me, I will tell you how you will know whether there be anything in Mormonism or not. Try and confound it or controvert it. I tried it, unsuccessfully. And I never knew it to be done and believe it impossible to be successfully controverted. Mormonism has ever had these two bugbears to fight against, prejudice, & tradition. I would add another yet and that is the learning of men. I trust Mr. Whitelaw, I shall give no offense in touching upon this subject or any other. The being a first letter I should perhaps confine my remarks and as I am not aware whether you are willing and able to be inflicted with such a long letter. I feel as if I almost should make an apology. Nothing would give me greater pleasure than to write on the subject of Mormonism, if I only knew you wished it, except it would be to talk with you on it.

Hoping & trusting and praying that you are restored somewhat in health, and that I may at your convenience receive an acknowledgement of receipt of this. For I do really believe I would like to see you yet in the flesh.

With Much affection

I am Yours Sincerely

David L. Murdoch

ADDITIONAL POETRY OF DAVID LENNOX MURDOCH

EDITOR'S NOTE: *David Lennox was a prolific poet and much of his poetry has already been shared in this book. The following additional poems show his talent and tenderness toward the things he loved.*

An Appreciation

Lord, Keep us Leck, what's this you've sent
In Carton big, well tied wi' hemp
And stamps galore, tae bring it through
By parcel post, addressed by you.
Fish, Foul, or duck or deer, Na! Na!
'Tis something else as guid and braw
A great big cabbage new unfolds it's face
Solid and sweet, the biggest in the place.
Fair fa this jewel o' the Scotch broth pot
Man, Leck, I'll sup them when their hot
And smack my lips o'er ev'ry dish
Nae greater treat could I e'er wish.
Fit specimen fra the Hot Springs Ranch
Near Carey, up the Hailey Branch,
A great resort, too little known
But time it's greatness yet will own.
Friend Condie is the owner there
Of honest toil he has his share
The fruits of which are plainly seen
Hay stacks and stock on pastures green,
Long may he reap big bumper crops
Of hay and grain and horned stocks
That bring returns of honest gain
Filched from the soil by brawn and brain.
Carey, my dear, I love you well
There oft I think I'd like to dwell
Tis there I've spent some happy hours
Wood River's banks and shady bowers.
There yet I hope some time to bide
And wily tempt the finny tribe
Fresh caught and cooked, O' what a treat
On rivers banks so clean and neat.

David Lennox Murdoch
October 19, 1917

An Emblem for the Seventies

On a pinnacle of the Temple, with a trumpet in his hand,
Stands Moroni on a sphere like a sentinel o'er the land.
Every people, tongue and kindred shall hear the proclamation
Of the Gospel's joyous sound sent to each and every nation.
Hear all ye Isles and Continents, wherever there are found
Remnants of the Covenant people, let the angel's warning sounds,
Loud and long, let it resound throughout, each land and clime,
That Israel may be gathered in the Lord's appointed time.
Like an Ensign on a mountain, like a Standard just unfurled
Let the Angel's proclamation be heralded to the world.
By the Elders send the message, let the Seventies preach the word
And leave them then without excuse when the warning has been heard.
Glad tidings of great joy we bring to each true and honest heart,
Oh how our bosoms swelled with love when first we heard in part,
And how our faith has grown since then, as we the lesson learn
Of the Gospel's restoration with its power for fallen men.
And how the work is growing, growing larger year by year,
And how our Prophet would rejoice were he but with us here.
And how the Lord does magnify his servants in his cause,
As they show forth humility, keeping all His holy laws.

David L. Murdoch, 1908
Published in the Era

EDITOR'S NOTE: *In the back of the David Lennox Murdoch Missioanry Journal are many photographs put there by Afton Murdoch Warner. Because of the binding on the journal, she most likely thought this would be a the best place to put these photos. The following photos are taken from there. Some of the photos are from David Lennox's mission and some are taken in Salt Lake City. Quotation marks indicate the caption is from the original photo.*

LEFT: *David Lennox Murdoch standing on rocks at ruins.*
RIGHT: *Ruins in Scotland*

LEFT: *August 19, 1907 "The above is the Waukmill about a mile east of Muirkirk where we lived for a time just before moving to Linkieburn House Muirkirk."*
RIGHT: *In Scotland, Elizabeth and David Lennox, man unidentified*

LEFT: *Afton Murdoch, Alvera Jenkins, Norah Murdoch with Mary and Lennox Murdoch in front*
RIGHT: *Mary and Norah Murdoch with Lennox and Mary Murdoch on G Street.*

Headstones in the Salt Lake City Cemetery of
Elizabeth Pinkerton Thyne Murdoch and David Lennox Murdoch

ON FINDING THE DAVID LENNOX MURDOCH SUITCASE

By Janet Romney Hull

You can imagine the excitement we all felt when we heard from Dallas Murdoch, the President of the Murdoch Family Organization, that somewhere there were two suitcases belonging to our great grandfather, David Lennox Murdoch. Dallas stated in an email dated 2 September 2007:

"I was able to reach the widow of David Warner, Mildred. She is aware of the two suitcases and said they were either in her home or in the home of her son. She is coming to Salt Lake City around September 20th and will try to find them and bring their contents with her. I will contact her again as we approach that date and see what success she has had in finding them and where she will be staying so one of you can visit her and pick up their contents. I feel they will be rich with historical material."

Janet Hull and Janet Wilson acted quickly in finding out about this wonderful find. As was mentioned in the *Introduction* of this book, his daughter, Afton kept the suitcase, (there was only one, not two) and had given it to Frederick L. Warner, her grandson. Fred lives in Illinois. We contacted him and he said he was coming to Salt Lake City on a business trip. He was more than happy to bring the suitcase with him and we could meet him at his hotel. Janet Hull, Janet Wilson, and Nan Williams joined Fred and his sister-in-law at the hotel. It was like looking in an old treasure chest! The little white suitcase was filled journals poems and pictures - like they had just been neatly placed there. Janet Hull and Bette Ann Christensen went to Kinko's and copied pages from the writings of David Lennox. Bette Ann has transcribed these journals for this book. Great Grandfather David Lennox wrote stories and his feelings on everything he saw. Obviously, he had a great mind and a superb talent for writing poetry. He sheds a lot of information for us all to enjoy.

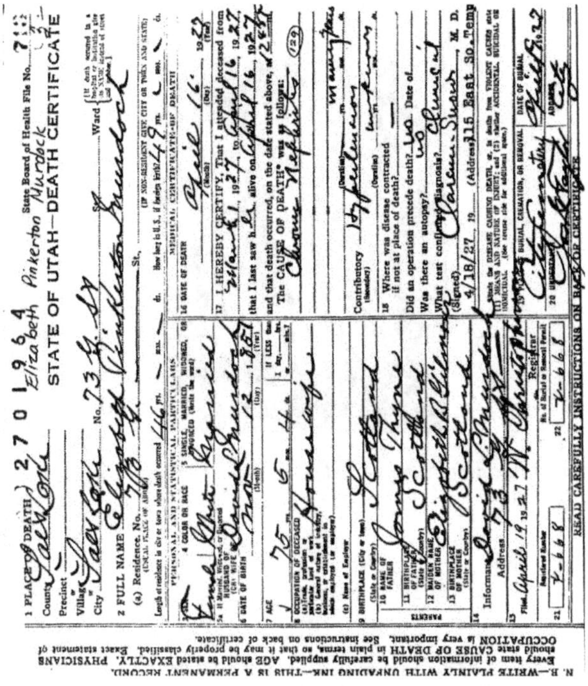
STATE OF UTAH—DEATH CERTIFICATE

State Board of Health File No. 712

1 PLACE OF DEATH 2 7 0 1 9 6 4

County Salt Lake

City Salt Lake No. 73 G St

2 FULL NAME Elizabeth Pinkerton Murdock

Elizabeth Pinkerton Murdock

3 SEX Female 4 COLOR OR RACE White 5 SINGLE, MARRIED, WIDOWED, OR DIVORCED Married

5a IF MARRIED, WIDOWED, OR DIVORCED HUSBAND OF David L Murdock

6 DATE OF BIRTH Mar 12 1851

7 AGE 76 yrs. 5 mos. 4 d.

8 OCCUPATION OF DECEASED Housewife

9 BIRTHPLACE Scotland

10 NAME OF FATHER James Thyne

11 BIRTHPLACE OF FATHER Scotland

12 MAIDEN NAME OF MOTHER Elizabeth Gilmour

13 BIRTHPLACE OF MOTHER Scotland

Informant David L Murdock

Address 73 G St

Filed April 19 1927 W. Christopherson Registrar

16 DATE OF DEATH April 16 1927

17 I HEREBY CERTIFY, That I attended deceased from March 1 1927 to April 16 1927

and that death occurred, on the date stated above, at 2:45 P.M.

The CAUSE OF DEATH was as follows: Chronic Nephritis

(Signed) Clarence Snow, M. D.

4/18/27 (Address) 115 East So. Temp

19 PLACE OF BURIAL, CREMATION, OR REMOVAL City Cemetery

DATE OF BURIAL April 19 1927

20 UNDERTAKER Larkin

READ CAREFULLY INSTRUCTIONS ON BACK OF CERTIFICATE

N. B.—WRITE PLAINLY WITH UNFADING INK—THIS IS A PERMANENT RECORD. Every item of information should be carefully supplied. AGE should be stated EXACTLY. PHYSICIANS should state CAUSE OF DEATH in plain terms, so that it may be properly classified. Exact statement of OCCUPATION is very important. See instructions on back of certificate.

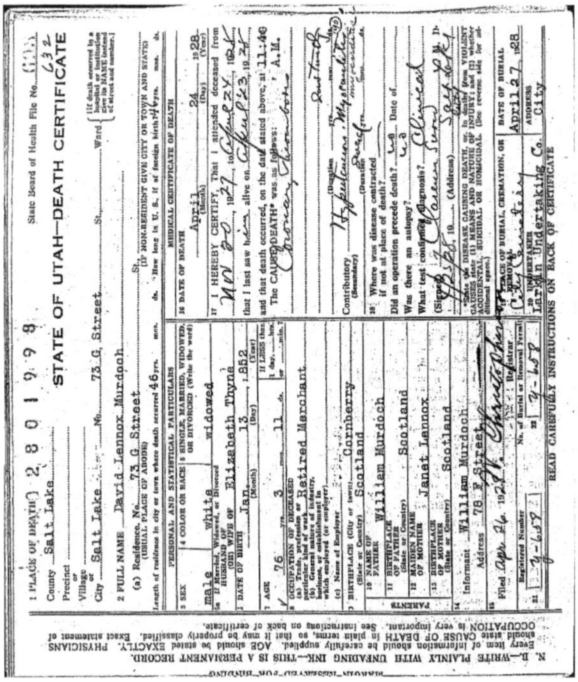
STATE OF UTAH—DEATH CERTIFICATE

State Board of Health File No. 632

1 PLACE OF DEATH 2 8 0 1 9 9 8

County Salt Lake

City Salt Lake No. 73 G Street

2 FULL NAME David Lennox Murdoch

(a) Residence. No. 73 G Street

Length of residence in city or town where death occurred 46 yrs.

3 SEX male 4 COLOR OR RACE white 5 SINGLE, MARRIED, WIDOWED, OR DIVORCED widowed

5a IF MARRIED, WIDOWED, OR DIVORCED HUSBAND OF Elizabeth Thyne

6 DATE OF BIRTH Jan. 13 1852

7 AGE 76 yrs. 3 mos. 11 d.

8 OCCUPATION OF DECEASED Retired Merchant

9 BIRTHPLACE Cornberry Scotland

10 NAME OF FATHER William Murdoch

11 BIRTHPLACE OF FATHER Scotland

12 MAIDEN NAME OF MOTHER Janet Lennox

13 BIRTHPLACE OF MOTHER Scotland

Informant William Murdoch

Address 78 F Street

Filed Apr 26 1928 W. Christopherson Registrar

16 DATE OF DEATH April 24 1928

17 I HEREBY CERTIFY, That I attended deceased from Nov 20 1927 to April 24 1928

and that death occurred, on the date stated above, at 11:40 A.M.

The CAUSE OF DEATH was as follows: Coronary thrombosis

Contributory Hypertension, Myocarditis

(Signed) Clarence Snow

19 PLACE OF BURIAL, CREMATION, OR REMOVAL City Cemetery

DATE OF BURIAL April 27 1928

20 UNDERTAKER Larkin Undertaking Co. ADDRESS City

READ CAREFULLY INSTRUCTIONS ON BACK OF CERTIFICATE

N. B.—WRITE PLAINLY WITH UNFADING INK—THIS IS A PERMANENT RECORD. Every item of information should be carefully supplied. AGE should be stated EXACTLY. PHYSICIANS should state CAUSE OF DEATH in plain terms, so that it may be properly classified. Exact statement of OCCUPATION is very important. See instructions on back of certificate.

Elizabeth Pinkerton Thyne

(Written by her daughter—Janet Murdoch Thompson, June 5, 1938)

My wish:

To keep a green point growing within myself
Whatever winds be blowing
To put out blossoms one or two
And when my leaves are thin and few
To have some fruit worth showing.

The above verse is so attuned to the life Mother lived, so typical of her ideals, ambitions, and desires, and so in harmony with her accomplishments, it seems most fitting and appropriate that I should commence this short biography by quoting it.

From my earliest recollections, Mother always kept a green point growing within herself, a green point growing within her home and garden, and a green point growing within her community. Countless blossoms she shared, bounteous fruits she harvested.

Mother's exemplary life, enriched by years of absolutely unselfish devotion and endeavor, has given to her posterity a heritage it should not fail to be worthy of.

At the present time Mother has only one surviving close relative—cousin James P. Gilmour of London, England. A short time ago I wrote to him asking for information regarding Mother's people. It has been quite a regrettable situation that we did not press Mother into telling us more of her early life and her family. She was most modest in relating any of her personal affairs and we, in our youthful and thoughtless years, neglected to learn more about her.

Cousin James has graciously sent the following, and I shall quote him before going into Mother's life as we have known her. Referring to Mother he says,

> "Cousin Elizabeth Thyne bore considerable resemblance to her mother, but on a smaller scale. As I knew her, she was a comely lass, high-spirited, with a vibrant, expressive personality. Self reliant and adaptable, she efficiently and faithfully performed the duty nearest at hand and earned the respect and affection of all in any circle in which she moved. Her interests and activities extended far beyond the limits of home and found scope in church work, especially as a Sunday School teacher. A pianist of more than average talent, I was touched when on her visit to us in Glasgow, over forty years ago, she played for me my mother's favorite air. Cousin Lizzie, attractive as she was in form and feature, and even in greater measure for her mental and moral merits, did not encourage philanderers, and altho she had not nearly reached the old-maidenish age, we had somehow come to think of her as vowed for the single life. It was therefore a great surprise when David Lennox Murdoch, then private secretary to William Whitelaw, a Scottish member of Parliament, who was a fine, upstanding handsome young man with charming manners, was introduced to us as her accepted lover. When he came courting her, and the parlor was "verboten" to us, we used to vie with one another as to who would carry in the cups of coffee which were served to the wooer and his "lady fair" towards the close of the long evenings of their foregathering. It was a still greater and more perturbing surprise when, leaving all to follow the man of her choice, Cousin Lizzie married David and they almost forthwith set sail for the United States.
>
> "It is difficult for us who have not lived through those narrower and harder times into the wider life and more liberal and humane thought and feeling of the present day, far as it still is from complete emancipation of the mind from the bonds of tradition and prejudice, to realize the virulence of the odium theologicum sixty years ago, when even the mildest heresy was looked upon with abhorrence, and its exponent treated almost as an outlaw. Mormonism in particular was held in evil repute, simply because of the gross misrepresentation of the doctrines of the Church of the Latter-day Saints, and the wicked fabrications as to the moral character of its members. I have sorrowfully to record that in our household, from Grandfather downwards, Cousin Lizzie was judged to have yoked herself to the ungodly and to have gone off to worship false gods. But none of us, and least of all we youngsters, could banish from our minds the thought of her goodness and kindness of heart, so that secretly we felt sure that, even were she astrayer from the fold, a place would be found for her at last in whatever heaven was reserved for us, and this mightily comforted us."

In speaking of religion, Cousin James writes,

> "Altho Grandfather, Uncle William, and my father were in substantial agreement theologically, there were minor points of doctrine upon which they did not see eye to eye and in discussing them more heat than light was apt to be generated. Once only did I venture to put in my oar. This was reproved as an act of presumption, but the head and front of my offending was the use of the word 'Sunday'. I think, even now, that I hear Uncle William thundering, "Never let me hear ye say that word again. I tell ye it's a pawgin word. Sawbath is God's word for the first day o' the week.""

I am, indeed, grateful to Cousin James for his consideration, thoughtfulness, and helpfulness in forwarding this material to me.

Mother was born November 12, 1851, in Glasgow, Scotland. Her parents were James Thyne and Elizabeth Barr Gilmour Thyne. Grandfather passed on during Mother's childhood days, and Grandmother Thyne moved to her father's estate in Kelvin Grove, Great Grandfather Gilmour being a prominent and influential nurseryman. Mother was reared in her grandfather's home and remained there until her marriage to Father.

As I have already intimated, Mother was not much given to speaking of herself or of her relatives, but from occasional conversations, we gathered a few facts we have always been grateful for. From facts obtained from Cousin James, we know Mother must have been a very clever individual in her younger days, and we children knew Mother as a real executive in the home—most original, ingenious in mind, and most active in body. In her enthusiasm to have her children amount to something, she occasionally would refer to the things she had accomplished in her younger years. When I was nine years of age Mother taught me to crochet, and one of the first things I made was a silk tie for my father. I remember taking it to school and showing it to my teacher. The teacher seemed to think it quite incredible that I could crochet as well as the tie indicated. When I returned home and told Mother the attitude the teacher had taken, she said, "Well, you just tell your teacher that I crocheted my grandfather one when I was six years of age." One can well believe that to be true, for Mother's indomitable will to succeed was predominantly conspicuous.

Grandmother Thyne and her father saw to it that Mother's education was carefully planned. Every opportunity was afforded her, and her alert, keen mind fashioned for her early in life abundant resources upon which she could draw.

Mother was educated at Dollar Academy near Glasgow, and was given the best schooling available at that time in music. Also, she was given practical training in sewing and homemaking,

Cousin James has often told us Mother was the life of the Gilmour household. Her cheerful, willing disposition to be of service and help seemed to ever prevail, and she achieved wide popularity because of her radiant personality and fine spirit of helpfulness.

Mother belonged to the Glasgow Choral Society for years. She was thoroughly acquainted with the music and words of the masters. She was also very familiar with the best of the operas and could without hesitation repeat phrase after phrase of the different oratorios and operas when the occasion presented itself.

Needless to say, immediately upon her arrival in Salt Lake, she sought affiliation with the different musical organizations, being a member of the old Salt Lake Oratorio Society, also the Tabernacle Choir. She was the first organist in Heber City, Utah, and after returning to Salt Lake to reside permanently, became organist in the Twentieth Ward

Ten children were born to Father and Mother, eight girls and two boys. However, only five lived to maturity, one boy and four girls, all of whom are at present living. They are William Murdoch, city commissioner of finance; Janet M. Thompson, a member of the General Board of the Relief Society; Norah T. Clark, at present hostess for the Twin States Light and Gas Company, Rochester, New Hampshire; Mary Murdoch, cashier of the Murdoch Grocery Company; and Afton M. Warner of Midvale, Utah.

If space would permit, many interesting stories might be told regarding Mother's active life.

She radiated life itself in every word and deed, and saw to it that all those with whom it was her good fortune to mingle radiated the best they possessed.

Mother was an expert with needlework and dressmaking, doing all of the sewing for her family, even to making coats and oftentimes hats. And oh, for the beautiful underwear she designed and made! It was not an uncommon thing for her daughters to wear panties and petticoats with yards and yards of insertion and lace or embroidery on them. Our wash days, always on Mondays, were quite an event, and seemed to consume most of the day. We all took turns at turning the handle of the washer. At the present time there are three old relics of washers painted up in our backyard. They are now used for flower stands and surely have considerable value.

Mother was not a very active Church worker. She maintained always that her first duty was to her home, and I guess her vociferous family pretty much saw to it that she magnified her first duty. However, she was most generous with her contributions, always willing to give of her time, talents, and money for the interest of the Church or the community. Well do I remember, when a certain bazaar was held in the ward, how determined she was on that occasion that the Relief Society should dispose of all the aprons Mother could make. If my recollection serves me correctly, she made approximately one hundred aprons. Although not an active member, she was imbued with the spirit of Relief Society, and her Scottish determination saw to it that that organization excelled in sales at that particular affair. Never once did she question Father's pocketbook, and never once did Father question her wisdom in spending. Both by nature were very generous.

Mother seemed to follow her father's inclinations for gardening, and her house plants and garden plants were always a thing of beauty. Everything seemed to bloom so prolifically—perhaps because she so generously shared the beauty of it all with those about her.

Every spring she and Father would spend hours searching the flower catalogs for rare and beautiful plants. How insistent Mother was that each plant purchased should be placed in a very definite spot in her garden—and Father invariably acceded to her wishes or decisions. How often have I heard Mother correct Father for the manner in which he watered the garden. In her garden, as with everything else, there was a systematic way of doing things, and the entire family was the victim of that system. But I dare say, we are deeply grateful for the system Mother attempted to inculcate in our lives.

In looking back on Mother's life, one is impressed with the splendid sense of balance she possessed. When we were small children we always had help in the home, but Mother and Father saw to it that no member of the family was slighted in having sufficient work to do to keep us "out of mischief" as Mother said. Each one was allotted a portion, and each one met his or her portion without question. None of our excuses ever worked. We usually enjoyed about two picnics a summer out to some resort. We were given a certain amount to spend—our parents never questioned what we spent it for—but we were never permitted to ask for more—it was definitely understood before leaving home what our obligations would be.

Another outstanding characteristic Mother possessed was her deep sympathy and understanding for animals. When horses were so popular, she delighted in seeing they were not abused. Often we children were embarrassed when Mother would severely reprimand some teamster for the manner in which he handled the "poor dumb brutes," as she called them.

Our home was one of genuine hospitality; our friends were always welcome. In fact, Mother insisted that we bring them to the home and entertain them; then she knew what we were up to. Frequently after school, half a dozen or more of our playmates would return with us, and we'd go into the laundry, where Mother had a stove for laundry work. We would light a fire, fry potatoes, bake apples, and devour the cookies concealed in the basement. It was Mother's delight to plan parties for us. Especially I remember one time when she planned a beautiful party for the entire eighth grade at school. This party was held on the second of December, and many of the mothers thought our mother extravagant for having such a party so close to the holiday season. Mother also saw to it that the larder was filled every Saturday with pies and cakes and fruit for the boys and girls who perchance might drop in. It is refreshing after all these years to hear some of these same boys and girls reminisce about the experiences they enjoyed at our house.

In reflecting over the happenings of past years, and analyzing the mission performed by Mother, we are not unmindful of the many sacrifices she made for the sake of the gospel and for the sake of her family. Mother left all that was dear to her in her native land, and embraced the gospel regardless of all protests of the family. She came to Utah, where she knew no one, and where few cultural things could be offered at that time and where few luxuries such as she had been accustomed to could be found. But Mother was fearless, she had implicit faith in the gospel. She knew that "in the way of righteousness is life; and in the pathway thereof there is no death." One of Mother's friends said,

> "When I think back upon the life and the association that we have had with Sister Murdoch, I can think of nothing but goodness in her life. She was a lover of all that was beautiful in the home and outside of the home. Pass their house anytime, and you will be impressed with the beautiful surroundings, beautiful flowers, and the well-kept garden—everything suggestive of that high nature."

We shall ever cherish Mother's devotion to her family—everyday in our home was children's day, and the spirit of friendliness, joy, and happiness that persistently radiated from the lives of our parents will ever endear them to their family and those they befriended. Surely, Mother was in every sense of the word a skilled homemaker. Her love for the gospel, for her family and friends, for flowers and music, confirms the fact that in every deed, thought, and action, she kept a green point growing - that the blooms she produced have born fruit, Such an exemplary life will ever serve as a beacon light to her family and will always be worthy of emulation,

Mother passed away on the sixteenth of April, 1927 - just one year to the month before Father's passing. We shall ever remember her independent spirit and her absolute determination that she should never be a burden to anyone. She succeeded nobly. She seemed to understand that her mission was completed and just slept peacefully on until the summons came.

Relief Society Talk about Elizabeth P. Murdoch

From a talk given by Mary Murray Murdoch in Relief Society of the 18th Ward in Salt Lake City on March 14, 1979

I might mention before I give my talk, our home was in 20th Ward and still stands at 73 "G" Street, Salt Lake City, Utah.

When Sister Grant asked me to give a talk on *Some One Person that Influenced Me in my Younger Years* – I could think of no one more wonderful than "my darling Mother."

She was indeed a marvelous inspiration all thru my life. She was not only an inspiration to me but to everyone. You never heard my Mother speak of her accomplishments, it was always on someone else she would help and praise the other person, or neighbor in need.

At an early age my parents moved the family of five into a large, newly built house – from then on the *"house became a home"*, where much love, happiness, tenderness, and care abounded.

Mother and Father were born in Scotland under the rigid discipline of the English rule, so naturally this discipline fell upon the teachings we received. How thankful and grateful we all were to have such a wonderful Mother and Father, a lovely home with such training.

Mother was indeed gifted – had many talents, expert Seamstress, made everything we wore. She would go to the ZCMI May Sale every year and purchase bolts of materials, so we all had dresses and shirts made of [the] same cloth. – She sang, played the piano, was an excellent cook – and had an outstanding flower garden known to everyone. [In] 1906 the Ward had a Bazaar – everyone making lovely things, also bringing cakes, pies, cookies, rolls – Mother made 50 aprons, all beautifully trimmed [with] lace and ric-rack braid.

Mother and Father knew the Gospel. Father read the Scriptures nightly, so the Spirit of the Lord was surely in our home. Father also was a great writer – wrote many poems, one I can remember was "Sunrise at Chimney Rock" where his Grandmother (Wee Granny) died. Father was President of the Elders Quorum and in 1905 to 1907 was on a Mission in Scotland. Many of the Converts stayed at our home until they found a place. I recall one morning seeing a pair of men's shoes at the base of the staircase. I said, "Mother, whose shoes are those there?" She said, "They belong to the English Minister for me to polish." I said, "Mother, you are not polishing shoes for anyone." Up the stairs I went and put them at his door.

Girls, I'll have to tell you about "tramps" and "Indians". They seemed to mark our home. Mother never turned them down. One day an old soul came, [it] was snowing and very cold. Mother asked him into our kitchen which was a large room. She told him to wash his hands then had him sit down at the table. He offered a prayer – as children we were so excited hearing his prayer. After his lunch Mother prepared a nice package for him to take.

We have with us here today our lovely Sister Carrie Patrick Hughes who was in our home many times. Twice a year we always invited our School teacher for lunch. Living so close to the Lowell School we could make it nicely.

Before I sit down I'll have to tell you about Grandpa, handsome old gentleman, Father's Father. His daughter came home from school and said, "Father, the teacher said I'll have to have some money to buy a dictionary." He said, "A dictionary? What do you think I am sending you to school for?"

These are just a few things about Mother and Father and our home. Yes our home was [a] haven of love and happiness. It is my wish that everyone have such a bounteous home life as we had.

[She signed this talk in her own handwriting thusly – Mary Murray Murdoch 3-2579 (her phone number)]

Patriarchal Blessing of Elizabeth Pinkerton Thyne Murdoch

Salt Lake City, March 23, 1886. A blessing given by John Smith, Patriarch, upon the head of Elizabeth Murdoch, daughter of James and Elizabeth Thyne born in Glasgow, Lanarkshire, Scotland November 12, 1851.

Sister Elizabeth, according to thy desire, I place my hands upon thy head and in the name of Jesus Christ, pronounce and seal a blessing upon thee that thy heart may be comforted and I say unto thee, be at rest in thy mind, suffer not thyself to be bowed down in spirit for the Lord has heard thy petitions and is pleased with thine integrity and will reward thee as thou shalt merit, be prudent and the blessings of the Lord shall attend thy labor and thou shalt have joy in thine offspring and thy name shall live in the memory of the Saints, and as a mother in Israel. Thou shalt be known among the people, thou shalt have a kind word for all and no one shall be turned from thy door hungry. It is the will of the Lord that you should live to a good old age. Therefore, be prudent and study the love of nature, and thou shalt be healthy and strong in body and mind. Thou shalt be enabled through prayer and faith to heal the sick of thy family and hold the adversary at bay that health and peace may reign in thy dwelling. Thou art of Ephraim and shall receive thine inheritance with thy blessings in connection with thy companion among those who have fought the good fight, kept the faith and won the prize. Therefore, be comforted for all shall be well with thee both here and hereafter, thou shalt complete thy mission and become a savior among thy kindred, for there are many honest in heart both among the living and the dead, who look to thee for salvation. It shall be thy lot also to counsel among thy sex, and to strengthen the meek. Therefore seek wisdom and as you gain knowledge thy faith shall increase and thou shalt better see and understand things as they are and all doubts shall be removed from thy mind. This blessing I seal upon thee and I seal thee up into Eternal life to come forth in the morning of the first resurrection with many of thy kindred and friends. Even so. Amen.

Children of David Lennox and Elizabeth Murdoch

Written by Mary Murray Murdoch, daughter of David L. and Elizabeth Murdoch, March 1975

EDITOR'S NOTE – *Included are the young children who were also born to David Lennox and Elizabeth that died as babies or children, and were not included in the original writings of Mary Murray Murdoch.*

WILLIAM MURDOCH

William was born 15 September 1878 in Heber City, Utah. He was married to Jeannette Cousins Smith and they are the parents of nine children. His history follows in the next chapter.

ELIZABETH PINKERTON THYNE MURDOCH

Elizabeth was born on 17 March 1880 in Heber City, Wasatch, Utah and died as a young child on 19 June 1882 in Salt Lake City, Salt Lake, Utah.

JAMES THYNE MURDOCH

James was born on 19 June 1881 in Heber City, Wasatch, Utah and died 11 August 1881 in Salt Lake City, Salt Lake, Utah

BABY GIRL MURDOCH AND BABY GIRL MURDOCH

These twin girls were apparently stillborn and the dates are unclear. According to the *James and Mary Murray Murdoch Family History*, they were born in Salt Lake City, Salt Lake, Utah and died before 18 October 1882.

JANET LENNOX MURDOCH THOMPSON

Janet Lennox Murdoch, nicknamed Jen, was born August 8, 1884, in Salt Lake City, daughter of David L. and Elizabeth Pinkerton Thyne Murdoch. She married Jerrold E. Thompson, known as Vie, in the Salt Lake Temple on September 29, 1909. She passed away April 24, 1953, at which time she was living in the home at 73 G Street with her sister, Mary.

Janet graduated from Lowell School, being an "A" student. She attended LDS Business College and was captain of the girl's basketball team. They won all games and led in school activities. Jen was an accomplished pianist and organist and was the organist for the 20th Ward on 2nd Avenue and D Street for years. Steve Wells was the custodian and would pump the organ for her. When Steve was not available, we sisters had to pump the organ. When the ward moved into the new building at G and 2nd Avenue, Janet was still the organist and pianist and Jen Romney Crawford assisted.

Norah, Afton, Elizabeth Pinkerton Thyne Murdoch, Jerrold E. Thompson (Uncle Vie, Janet's husband), David Lennox Murdoch, and Janet Lennox Murdoch Thompson (Aunt Jen)

Janet served thirteen years as President of Ensign Stake Primary Board and in April 1935 was called to the General Board of the Relief Society under Belle Spafford. She served on the Board eighteen years. She was Chairman of the Music Committee and under her direction, a Relief Society song book was prepared. Her days were spent in the selection of suitable songs and many hours and days were spent in transferring songs to fit the voices of the members of the Relief Society. The book was printed three months after she assumed her new responsibilities in the General Presidency of the Relief Society Association. She was also a member of the General Church Music Committee.

During her thirteen years in the General Presidency of the Primary, she decided a mural should be placed in a little chapel in Farmington, the birthplace of the Primary Association. Janet was chairman of that committee and executed the carrying out of the project. She went to the great artist, Lynn Faucett, to make sure that every detail of the painting would be just right. In 1938, she helped with the Singing Mothers, having 900 members at the time. When she passed away, President J. Reuben Clark said he was struck by her intellect, her judgment and her wisdom and that you never had to explain anything to her more than once. In 1938, a small percentage of the 900 Singing Mothers gave a concert over KSL and Janet helped with this concert. In October following the Relief Society Conference, the LDS General Conference heard the beautiful songs of the Singing mothers. Janet would be proud.

Janet also gave a talk to sound the Clarion Call – the first talk concerning the 100,000 members of the Relief Society wanted by 1942. At the Centennial in 1942, instead of the 74,000 members in 1937 they now had over 106,000 members of the Relief Society. Janet was appointed to the Membership Enlistment Committee.

Jerrold E. Thompson was born in Brigham City, Utah. He was a great musician and leading trombone player in the Salt Lake Theatre for years. He was also the leading trombonist at the Paramount Theatre under Edward P. Kimball. "Vie" Thompson was owner and operator of the Utah Cleaning and Dying Company at 1200 South State Street, Salt Lake City, Utah. This was a very flourishing company, which he operated until his death on March 30, 1942, of a heart attack. The services were held in the 20th Ward. They had no children much to their sorrow.

EDITOR'S NOTE: Aunt Jen, as she was known to her nieces and nephews, went to Lamb's Canyon each summer to help with the children of William and Jeannette. She was famous for making the children sweep the dirt road, a chore everyone hated but had to do. [See *Summers at Murdoch Cabin* later in this book] When the editor was going through the old pictures, she ran across this picture of Aunt Jen on her porch on G Street with her broom. It just had to be added to the book because of her famous chore.

VERONICA MURDOCH

Veronica was born 3 July 1886 in Salt Lake City, Salt Lake, Utah. She died on 5 April 1896 in Salt Lake City and is buried in the Salt Lake City Cemetery.

NORAH MURDOCH CLARK

Norah Murdoch was born 7 February 1890 in Salt Lake City, Utah. She married Herman E. Clark and one daughter, Betty, was born in Salt Lake City. After moving to Rochester, New Hampshire, they had four more children, Charles Everett, Janet, Georgia and Martha. She held a responsible position with the Metropolitan Life Insurance Company. She was so outstanding, taking care of missionaries and helping the poor. Norah had five grandchildren and all reside in New Hampshire and are reported to be very kind to the missionaries. Norah passed away 9 May 1959 in Concord, Merrimack, New Hampshire. She is buried in the Salt Lake City Cemetery.

MARY MURRAY MURDOCH

Mary was born in 1891. She resided [at] 69 G Street in Salt Lake City and moved to 73 G Street in 1893 where she lived for many years and was a member of the 20th Ward for 75 years. She sold the old home and subsequently moved to 19 A Street. She worked for 32 years in the Murdoch Grocery and 10 ½ years in the Salt Lake City Credit Bureau as head investigator and interviewer. She was Miss Hospitality from 1946 to 1966. She was a home teacher and active in the 18th Ward. Mary died in Salt Lake City in 1982 and is buried in the Salt Lake City Cemetery, next to her parents.

AFTON MURDOCH WARNER

1947 - Joe and Afton with their prize-winning Bantam chickens

Afton was born 2 June 1894 in Salt Lake City, Utah and was in the 20th Ward. She took part in plays until she married and moved to Midvale, Utah, where she lived 34 years. Her husband, Joseph M. Warner, was employed with the Utah Power and Light Company. They had three children, one son, Joseph, passed away; another son, David, lives in Vienna, Virginia, and has a fine position with the U.S. Government, Real Estate Division. David and his wife, Mildred, have two sons. All are active in the Church. David and Mildred were ushers at the new Temple in Washington, D.C. Mildred has a position in the Relief Society. Afton's daughter, Thyne, resided in California and her daughter has two sons. Afton has three grandchildren and two great grandchildren. Afton made her home in Salt Lake City and passed away there on 20 January 1985.

LEFT AND MIDDLE: *Mary Murray Murdoch* RIGHT: *Janet and Mary Murdoch.*
"*Mary's dress is dark blue grepe-de-chene trimmed in white & so is mine.
My hat is a varigated straw with a bright red silk crushed band.
Mary says this picture is 'awful' of her, but I did want you to see my hat.*"

LEFT: *Lennox and Aunt Norah. standing is James Adamson, cousin*
RIGHT: "*Sitting on our dining room window sill are Mary, Marian Obendorfer,
Norah, Claire Little and Jen*"

The David Lennox Murdoch Home at 73 G Street

LOCATION: *73 G Street.* STYLE: *Victorian Eclectic* ORIGINAL OWNER: *David Lennox Murdoch* ARCHITECT: *H. H. Anderson* BUILT: *1892-1894*

This 2-story house with its projecting towers, gabled bay and ornate front porch is an elaborate example of Victorian eclecticism. Fascia boards with rosettes and a triple window with an ornately carved sunburst pattern lintel fill the northwest gabled bay. The southeast tower includes arched windows with carved drip molding and a bracketed cornice. Its four-sided bell carved roof contains triangular dormer windows. Constructed of light brown brick and wood, the house uses contrasting red brick for decorative effect. In the interior much of the original oak woodwork remains.

Scottish immigrant David Lennox Murdoch was a prominent businessman on the Avenues. An active member of the LDS church, he managed the Twentieth Ward Co-op and worked as an accountant for ZCMI. The G Street house, which took more than two years to complete, remained in the Murdoch family until 1954.[4]

---

4. David Lennox Murdoch's home is listed on the Utah State Register of Historic Sites. It was nominated for that list on August 14, 1974.

Chapter 5

William and Jeannette Cousins Smith Murdoch

Their Stories and Their Children

Written by Mary Murray Murdoch, William's sister, March 1975

William Murdoch, was born September 15, 1878, Heber City, Utah, to David Lennox and Elizabeth Pinkerton Thyne Murdoch. He married Jeannette Cousins Smith, who was from a prominent, pioneer family of Sugarhouse, Utah, in the Salt Lake Temple, September 19, 1900. They became the parents of nine children; David Lennox II, Mary Smith, John Thyne, Elizabeth, Jeannette (twin), William Jr. (twin), Ellen Jean, Robert Gail, and Bonnie LaVonne.

William was Commissioner of Finance for the Salt Lake City Corporation and had served the City of Salt Lake in Public Affairs and Finance Dept. from Jan. 1, 1936, until his death on October 8, 1940.

The grocery store was closed in 1942. A plaque on the north side of the Salt Lake City Cemetery, with his name on it, commemorates the position which he held. Adam S. Bennion, in speaking at Will's funeral, said he succeeded wonderfully in his own home, had brought into the world honor and distinction, was successful in his business;

that he not only lived the 'Golden Rule" he also practiced it; and he was the absolute soul of integrity. President David O. McKay said his life was gentle of the elements so mixed in him that nature might stand up and say to all the world - "This was a man." First, character – what he really is; second, his family life; and third, his attitude toward his fellowmen.

Murdoch Grocery was the leading grocery and meat store in the area for many years; had the very best high grade goods, meats, fruits and vegetables. Customers were called each morning and orders were taken; deliveries were made twice daily. Wagons were used in those days and we had two wagons, one of them had a span of horses. Customers would receive a statement once a month and would send in their checks promptly. I, Mary, worked for my father until the store closed in 1942. Will was employed at ZCMI as Chief Accountant. William took over the store and every Thanksgiving and Christmas he made certain that all 'widows' and the 'poor' were remembered with chickens or turkeys. When customers paid their bill they always received a basket of fruit or a sack of candy. The store had a wonderful clientele, such people as David Keith, Thomas Kearns, J. E. Dooley, John C. Daly, the Cosgriffs, the Thomas Weirs, H.G. McMillans, James H. Collins, Senator Wm. King, Gilbert Williams, John Leonard, John Wallace and the Bambergers; all noted people in Salt Lake City.

William and Jeannette traveled to Europe in 1934. They left Los Angeles, California on April 30, 1934 on the SS California and arrived in New York City on May 14, 1934. They came back on the SS Europa sailing from Cherbourg, France on June 30, 1934 and arriving in New York City on July 5, 1934.

Back: William Murdoch, David Lennox Murdoch, Mary Huskinson Smith (mother of Jeannette), Jeannette Cousins Smith Murdoch. Front: William Murdoch, Lennox Murdoch (son of William and Jeannette), Jennett Cousins Huskinson (grandmother of Jeannette) and Mary Murdoch (daughter of William and Jeannette).

PATRIARCHAL BLESSING OF WILLIAM MURDOCH

Patriarchal Blessing given at Salt Lake City. October 4, 1901 by John M. Murdoch, Patriarch, on the head of William Murdoch, son of David L. and Elizabeth P.T. Murdoch born in Heber City, September 15, 1878.

Dear brother William in the name of the Lord Jesus Christ I place my hands upon your head to give unto you a Patriarchal Blessing which shall rest upon you from this time henceforth and for ever and be a comfort unto you and be a guide unto you by which you may walk. It shall be a lamp unto your path and a light into your feet in as much as you will listen to the still small voice of the spirit that shall rest upon you from this time forth. Thou art of the seed of Joseph that was sold into Egypt of the lineage of Ephraim, his son, therefore you are entitled to all the blessings of the Holy Gospel which you have received in the days of your youth with an honest heart trying to do right and to live the life of the righteous.

Therefore you shall receive in due time the fullness of the Priesthood and your mind shall become enlightened by the spirit and power of the Holy Ghost that shall rest upon you and as you grow in days and years, you will also grow in wisdom and knowledge and become useful in your day and generation. You shall be called upon by the voice of the spirit to go forth to the nations of the earth and lift up your warning voice in defense of the principles of the holy gospel. The power of God shall rest upon you and the wicked shall tremble before you, while the righteous shall rejoice at the sound of your voice. You may be thrown into perils by wicked men but in as much as you will be faithful, the power of God shall rest upon you and not a hair of your head shall fall to the ground without his notice. You shall be greatly blessed and the power of God shall rest upon you and make you fit and qualify you for every emergency. Therefore, be of good cheer, put your trust in the Lord, seek unto Him for wisdom, and you shall be guided by his spirit in all your undertakings. I bless you with health and strength and with ability to perform every responsibility that shall be placed upon you and you shall have great joy in your labors in as much as you will be faithful in keeping the commandments of God. And by the power and authority of the Holy Priesthood, placed upon me as a Patriarch, I seal you up unto eternal life to come forth in the morning of the first resurrection with many of your kindred and be crowned with them in glory in the presence of God and the Holy angels. All which I seal upon you on condition of your faithfulness in keeping the commandments of God, In the name of Jesus Christ. Amen.

Isabella C. Murdoch, clerk

THE PICTURES ON THE FOLLOWING PAGES ARE IDENTIFIED AS FOLLOWS:.
PICTURE 1: L TO R BACK: BILL, MARY, JACK, LENNOX AND BETH. FRONT: JEANNETTE, ROBERT, GRANDFATHER WILLIAM, JEAN, AND GRANDMOTHER JEANNETTE
PICTURE 2:: L TO R BACK: BETH, JEANNETTE, JACK, MARY, BILL, AND LENNOX. FRONT: BONNIE, GRANDMOTHER JEANNETTE, ROBERT, GRANDFATHER WILLIAM, AND JEAN
PICTURE 3: L TO R BACK: LENNOX, JEANNETTE, JACK, MARY, BILL, AND BETH. FRONT: BONNIE, GRANDMOTHER JEANNETTE, ROBERT, GRANDFATHER WILLIAM, AND JEAN.
PICTURE 4: L TO R BACK: LENNOX, MARY, JACK, JEANNETTE, BILL, AND ROBERT. FRONT: JEAN, GRANDFATHER WILLIAM, BONNIE, GRANDMOTHER JEANNETTE, AND BETH

Funeral Notes

EDITOR'S NOTE: *The following is taken from the funeral notes of William Murdoch on Friday, 11 October 1940 which was held at the Assembly Hall on Temple Square at 12:30 P.M. He died in Salt Lake City 8 October 1940 of pneumonia following a cold at the age of 62 years of age, according to his death certificate. He was buried in the Salt Lake City Cemetery.*

Bishop Edwin Q. Cannon of the Twentieth Ward officiated and after an opening prayer by President Harold B. Lee, Annette Richardson Dinwoodey sang "My Ain Folk" (a Scottish song), accompanied by Alexander Schrieiner. There was a "Presentation of Resolution" from the Salt Lake City Commission by Commissioner John B. Matheson, who pronounced the following:

"The passing of Commissioner Murdoch has taken from us one of the best respected and most loved associates and friends, and we, the City Commission, who have been permitted to know him best, have learned to love him most. With saddened hearts the employees of Salt Lake City join with the Board of Commissioners in expressing our sorrow at his passing, and our gratitude in the association we have had with him, and have caused to be passed the following resolution:

"WHEREAS, William Murdoch, Commissioner of Salt Lake City, Utah, departed this life October 8th, 1940,

"NOW, THEREFORE, BE IT RESOLVED by the Board of Commissioners of Salt Lake City, Utah, that, because of the outstanding character and public service of Commissioner William Murdoch, both as an official and as a citizen, working for the betterment of the State and of the City, an appreciation of his life and service should be incorporated in the public records of this City.

"Mr. Murdoch has served the City of Salt Lake as Commissioner of Public Affairs and Finance since January 1st, 1936, with honor and distinction to himself and to the City. He was a successful business man and his affable disposition, ability, and leadership called him into service for many high civic and national activities. He was a charter member of the Exchange Club and took part in its many branches of service.

"He enjoyed the love and respect of an unusually large host of friends and he was cherished by a loving wife and family. His passing is a great loss to the City and to his friends and associates.

"The Board of Commissioners of Salt Lake City, for and on behalf of the citizens of Salt Lake City, the members of said Board and the many friends of William Murdoch, does hereby express to Mrs. Murdoch and to the family, profound condolence and deepest sympathy upon the passing of their husband and father.

"BE IT FURTHER RESOLVED that this resolution be spread upon the minutes of the Board of Commissioners and that an engrossed copy be forwarded to Mrs. Murdoch and members of the family."

REMARKS BY DR. ADAM S. BENNION

My Brethren and Sisters and Friends, I sincerely trust that the few minutes I occupy here today I may enjoy the spirit of this occasion.

It is an honor to speak in the services of Will Murdoch. I wish I might have the genius to put into words what he so wonderfully well has done in his own living. His life shows us how effective the Golden Rule can be. His life is his own best tribute. If there could walk by this bier today the men and women and children who have come under his kindliness, what they would say in their hearts would transcend any words we shall put into speech.

Mine is but a tribute to him. It is as if he had caught the full meaning of that wonderful line of President Garfield's, "I mean to make of myself a man, and if I succeed in that, I shall succeed in all else." And I am sure President Garfield had in mind the word of the Lord as to what a man is expected to do and to be, in one of the finest passages of all scripture, old or new: "For the Lord hath shown thee, O Man, what is good, and what doth the Lord require of thee but to do justly, and to love mercy and to walk humbly with thy God." All the days of his life Will Murdoch squared with all three of those admonitions.

He succeeded, in my judgment, in the places where it is most important to succeed. In the absence of time to enlarge upon what he has done, may I bring this brief witness: He succeeded wonderfully in his own home – the most sacred spot to hallow in one's ministry. He and the woman who has been a helpmeet to him – and what a companion she has been – across these forty years have brought into the world and have reared in honor and distinction, nine children. If there were nothing else to be said here today, their accomplishments, their worthiness, the spirit of that home would be an eloquent tribute. Within this last two weeks it has been my privilege to join the family in a service which married one of the daughters. I know the spirit that is in that home. I know of its affection.

One of the children has been good enough to put into my hands what they think of their father. The tribute is too personal and close to read here. I shall keep it always [This tribute follows his talk.] and would that we might live so that when this event shall come into our lives, our own children might be good enough to say of us what these children have said of him. Out across forty years they bring a witness that he has been fair and honest and kindly disposed. We would like to have the witness, as have they, that out across those forty years no unkind word has ever scarred the affection of this good man and women. We include Sister Murdoch in our tribute today, extending the word of appreciation which she so richly deserves. This family today can be grateful that wherever they may go the door will always swing wide open to them because they bear the name of Will Murdoch.

While that song we being sung, "My Ain Folk" – it likewise is a favorite of mine – we realized that all the world stands at attention today at the greatness and the glory of Britain. The qualities of Britain are reflected in this, a son, who would honor any nation. It is unfortunate that time will not allow us to look into the home for the details which have made his life so rich.

He succeeded, in the second place, in his business. He not only lived the Golden Rule by way of preachment, he enacted it across the counter. His institution of F Street has been running now these thirty-two years. Mrs. Bennion's father was one of his first customers. I have a list of the families who have been doing business with him all those years. Could I bring you a sample of what they say? One of them puts it into words: "For thirty-two years we have been served by this man and his folk. The quality of his goods has been excellent and never in all those years have we found him anything other than the soul of integrity, and if any little difficulty ever arose he was so big in the transaction that he made us proud to do business with him."

There is one good friend here today – and I am sure he will not mind if I indulge in personalities – it is a great thing as to have lived that after fifty years of close association a man like David Afflect will give you this tribute: "Fifty years ago we began as cash boys, and ever since, he and I have been in the mercantile business. I have known him in that business, I have served with him on committees, I have been with him day in and day out, and I think I know his heart.

"Will Murdoch is the absolute soul of integrity. He based his whole career upon principles. He was a great champion of the right. Nobody ever took up an issue with Will Murdoch but knew that he would fight for what he knew to be right. But he was big enough to recognize and to correct the mistakes that are inevitable in the lives of men who do things."

The story will never be told of his baskets that have gone out of that store to folk in need, uncounted and unaccounted for. Children by the hundreds could pass by this afternoon who have been in his store to enjoy his generosity and kindliness and thoughtfulness. He so conducted his affairs that he helped all men to regard it an honor to have been in his kind of business.

It were enough to have succeeded in his home and to have succeeded in business, but he went beyond that, as the City Commission has just so well pointed out through its resolution. When the City Recorder, Miss McDonald, out of close association, is good enough to send the kind of tribute she has done, we know he has been one of Utah's outstanding citizens. May I quote:

"You have asked me to jot down a few of the outstanding qualities of Commissioner William Murdoch, knowing that I have been rather closely associated with him as Secretary to the Board of Commissioners.

"Mr. Murdoch was not only held in high personal regard and respect, but he was greatly loved by all who knew him, for his gentleness, his understanding, and his willingness to lend a helping hand. He was always ready to listen to our problems and aid in every possible way. He seemed to take a personal interest in each one of us, and it was a pleasure and a privilege to talk with him.

"Today there is a deep feeling of sorrow for a personal loss affecting all his associates. I have heard such remarks as: 'He was a real friend.' 'He was so understanding, tolerant and sympathetic.' 'Mr. Murdoch was always so kinds and thoughtful.' 'He was so affable and friendly.' "With all Mr. Murdoch's success and popularity, he expressed much humility and absolutely no personal aggrandizement. "We feel that we have lost a true friend and a valuable public official."

Your presence here today, the presence of those men in uniform, the presence of men of distinction in City and State, bear witness to his outstanding qualities. He served with honor and distinction in our State Legislature and his performance in the City Commission, charged with the responsibility of public affairs and finance, has constituted such a discharge of duty that every man, woman, and child who knows of his record has been taught to have confidence in his administration.

I have been with him a good bit of late. As we walked down the street the other day, a man out of the acquaintance of the early years walked up and with the kind of handshake that only a man like Will Murdoch can merit, passed this observation: "Will, it is always a pleasure to shake your hand, not because you are one of the City Commissioners of this City, but because as such you seem to be just as humble as in those first days when you operated the store up on F Street."

As long as this country has in the administration of its affairs men like Will Murdoch, democracy has its best safeguard. This distinction which he has brought to his office, I am sure wins the admiration of all this group gathered today to pay him homage.

His trust, his absolute faith in God, his service to his Church, will be given to you by one far more capable to discuss it. I would not indulge a preachment – I bring you but a tribute.

May I close with these lines.

The sadness of his going brings sorrow to his home, but the memory of his goodness will be their consolation and benediction, which, heightened by the power of God, will sustain them in this hour of grieving.

> *Sometimes, when day draws to its close,*
> *The departing sun will throw*
> *Back to the world, in fond farewell,*
> *A lovely afterglow.*
> *I wish that I might as live*
> *That when my sun of life sinks low,*
> *I may reflect to those I love*
> *A lovely afterglow.*

Until the end of time there will follow the trail of Will Murdoch, one of the finest afterglows that ever stretched across the horizon of life.

To the family, God bless and sustain you and preserve in your hearts the memory of one of the finest men it has ever been my privilege to know. May His peace attend you, I pray in the name of Jesus Christ. Amen.

CHARACTERISTICS OF WILLIAM MURDOCH

[Tribute referred to in the previous talk]

1. Three virtues that Father always tried to impress upon us were

Chastity

Honesty

Truthfulness

He always reminded us of the importance of keeping one's self-respect by being morally respectable. He never passed up an opportunity to point out the solid virtue of honesty. He was very emphatic about being truthful both to him, to Mother, and to ourselves.

2. He was so kind, considerate, and thoughtful. I have never heard a cross word spoken between Father and Mother. He loved his family more than words can express, and we have had such a deep respect for him, his home and his integrity.

3. He was helpful and unselfish. He always remembered the poor and needy – especially at Christmas and Thanksgiving. Many a basket of groceries I have delivered by horse and wagon and by truck to the needy at Christmas for Father.

4. He always seemed so patient. He was very slow to anger, and often said, "Now don't lose your head. Just bite your lip and take it."

5. He loved his children and made many a little tot smile with a cookie, a piece of candy, or fruit, when they came to the store.

6. He stood solidly for what he thought was right, regardless of the odds against him.

7. He loved the outdoors and spent every spare moment of every summer at his cabin in Lamb's Canyon. He loved fly-fishing and excelled as a good fisherman. He loved baseball and football and all outdoor sports.

8. He always worked hard, from early morning until late at night. He loved his work and he loved people. His policy was to always give a little more than you should. "Shoot square with everyone, and pay your bills on time." He was constantly reminding us of the value of a good credit rating and to live within our means.He did not abhor debt if it was honest debt to better yourself, your business, or your family.

Tenor Solo of "O My Father" sung by Richard P. Condie.
Accompanied on the organ by Elder Alexander Schreiner

REMARKS BY PRESIDENT DAVID O. MCKAY

In keeping with the impressive message of the song to which we have just listened, that of immortality of the soul, I wish to read the following: "Behold, I show you a mystery. We shall not all sleep, but we shall all be changed, in a moment, in the twinkling of an eye, at the last trump: for the trumpet shall sound, and the dead shall be raised incorruptible, and we shall be changed. For this corruptible must put on incorruption, and this mortal must put on immortality. So when this corruptible shall have put on incorruption, and this mortal shall have put on immortality, then shall be brought to pass the saying that is written, Death is swallowed up in victory. "O Death, where is thy sting? O Grave, where is thy victory?"

Before commenting further upon this principle, which I believe will bring us most comfort today, I desire, even at the risk of repetition, to pay my tribute of respect and honor to my departed friend, William Murdoch.

His life was gentle and the elements so mixed in him that Nature might stand up and say to all the world, "This was a man."

Those lines that were written in honor of a patriot who lived many years ago – also one esteemed as an honest man – were no more applicable to the one to whom they were addressed than they are to William Murdoch.

I last shook his hand Sunday afternoon, October 6th, in the hospital, and I blessed him. I felt at the time that he would recover. He seemed to have energy, he was active and responsive, so when the announcement came Wednesday morning that he had passed beyond, I was greatly shocked, as were the thousands of others of his friends. It seems difficult to be reconciled to the passing of one to whom we have been so near and whose services seemed so imperative. Parting from loved ones always brings sorrow, and when the parting is caused by death, the heartstrings are strained to the breaking point. There is comfort in this case, however, in the fact that we know that the departed has lived a long, useful and successful life.

A man's value to society may be measured by three standards: First, his character – what he really is; second, his family life; and third, his attitude towards his fellowmen.

It is said, "If a man obtain the fullest life for himself and be able to contribute most to the common good, he should cultivate certain cardinal virtues, among which are: honor, integrity, courage, temperance, justice, wisdom, loyalty, respect, and reverence." As I named those virtues, I am sure that you who knew our departed brother best said in his or her heart that Brother Murdoch exemplified them to a remarkable degree.

Every human being radiates what he really is, not what he pretends to be. The radiation from each individual comes from within. There is not a human being, there is not any form of life that does not give off that radiation. To live is to radiate. Some radiate cheerfulness, friendship, hope, faith; others radiate gloom, sarcasm, sadness, irritability.

When one came into the presence of William Murdoch, one sensed a soul as serene and stable as truth. It was the radiation of what Carlisle calls a "living-light fountain, which is good and pleasant to be near; a flowing light-fountain of native original insight of manhood, a heroic nobleness—in whose radiance all souls feel that it is well with them."

The fundamental virtue in Commissioner Murdoch's life as I knew him was sincerity, and the principal element in that virtue is honesty. I fancy that Brother Murdoch, who was a very honest man, has said in his heart that Washington one time wrote. "I hope", said the Father of our Country, "that I shall always possess firmness and virtue enough to maintain what I consider to be the most enviable of all titles – the character of an honest man." And today we crown his life with that most enviable of all titles, merely as a merit of that which he has won.

So with these two standards, his character, his home life, Brother Murdoch measures up to the full standard of useful men in society.

His fellow Commissioner and the previous speaker have paid tribute to his service in the community. I wish to pay tribute to him as a High Priest in Israel. He held the Melchizedek Priesthood, was Senior President of his Quorum of Seventy. Unostentatious, unobtrusive, he was ever willing to devote his time to the betterment of his fellows, and cherished the testimony that Jesus Christ is the Savior of the world and that man is more than a mere thing drifting here for a few years and then lost in the abyss of eternity. He cherished the ideals of the Christian religion and the revealed Gospel of Jesus Christ, and that included service: Service with the means with which God had blessed him; service with his talents; doing good to all men. That is the noble ideal, and so far as I know, Brother Murdoch achieved that to a remarkable degree. There is a third.

And now what about this conquering by death? "O Death, where is they sting: O Grave, where is thy victory?" It does seem that both have been victorious, for our hearts have been stung to the quick, our heartstrings, I repeat, strained to the breaking point, and unless there is something beyond, death is victorious.

But just a thought will convince all of us that death is not victorious. The very fact that these tributes are paid today to his character, that we think as we do of him, that his word was his bond – sacred, more sacred than his bond. As we think of his gentleness, as we think of his fearlessness in defense of right which he stood by, you and I know that death cannot touch those virtues, and those are the real things; those are the virtues which radiate. The body is lifeless. It is a house in which we live, but the virtues, which come from the soul, that make up the individual, transcend death. Death cannot touch them. "Our echoes roll from soul to soul and go on forever and forever." But living in deeds is not immortality. I grant you it is something which death cannot conquer.

Neither can prevent Brother Murdoch's character's being perpetuated from generation to generation through these choice sons and noble daughters. You hear him again in their voices. I saw it last night in their gestures. We live from generation to generation in our characters, our virtues. Isn't that true? Again I say, that is not immortality. Some day there will come a time when a grandchild does not live. It may be that we can conceive a time when those virtues will not be perpetuated.

Now we come to the third and last way in which Death is conquered. Here we enter the element of faith. Faith, which is real. It may not prove it. Science cannot answer definitely whether there is something which lives after the silencing of the body, the closing of the eyes, the stopping of the heartbeat, but there is a voice higher than science which says to everyone, Death is conquered. The grave cannot hold that which is of God – the spirit.

> *"Tell me not, in mournful numbers,*
> *Life is but an empty dream!*
> *For the soul is dead that slumbers,*
> *And things are not what they seem.*
> *Life is real, Life is earnest!*
> *And the grave is not its goal;*
> *Dust thou art, to dust returnest*
> *Was not spoken of the soul."*

Your friend, my friend, your beloved husband, your dear father passed from this world knowing that death is just as natural as birth, and that Yonder his personality will persist. If I knew him rightly, he could say as one of old, "I know that my Redeemer liveth and that He shall stand at the Latter day upon the earth; and though after my skin worms destroy this body, yet in my flesh (or out of my flesh, says the Revised Version) shall I see God."

> *Peace, Sister Murdoch! Peace, boys and girls!*
> *"Peace! He is not dead, he doth not sleep,*
> *He hath awakened from the dream of sleep,*
> *'Tis we who, wrapped in mortal vision,*
> *Keep phantoms an unprofitable strife."*

May I conclude, as I began with a tribute, with an admonition to these sons and these daughters. I believe he would have me say it to you, his associates in the City; to you fellow members in the Exchange Club; to you Seventies; and I am going to say it in the words of a Rotarian because Brother Murdoch could say more applicably and truly, I think, than most men can say:

> *"I have kept unsullied and untarnished*
> *That thing – a name – entrusted to my care;*
> *I have not let dishonor dim its luster,*
> *Nor have I let shame leave its black mark there.*
> *I have not let my name be classed with malice*
> *Nor fear, nor moral cowardice, nor greed,*
> *Nor bigoted intolerance toward others*
> *Nor lack of charity for those in need.*
> *But I have made, instead, my name synonymous,*
> *In all men's minds, with things the most worthwhile;*
> *With strength to do the right, though none might see me;*
> *With grit to meet disaster with a smile;*
> *With loyalty to those with claims upon me;*
> *With justice equally toward foe and friend;*
> *With honor, truth, integrity, square-dealing-*
> *'My word my bond,' now, as I reach the end,*
> *Too well I know that I have failed in efforts*
> *Where I have wanted greatly to succeed;*
> *Too oft I've seen my dreams, bright in the forming,*
> *Prove naught but vain imaginings, indeed.*
> *But this I do believe; when I have traveled*
> *Life's twisting road, and worked out Life's great plan –*
> *When I have gone beyond Life's praise or blaming,*
> *It will be said of me, "He was a man!"*
> *And so, because of this, I feel no shame,*

When I bequeath to you, my sons, my name. With that and his testimony, "I know that my Redeemer lives," I pray that the spirit of peace, and the spirit of righteous pride for your heritage, the spirit of testimony that you will meet your father again, may bring to your hearts consolation in this hour of parting, and may it bring that to all of us, I pray in the name of Jesus Christ. Amen.

REMARKS BY BISHOP EDWIN O. CANNON

On behalf of the membership of the Twentieth Ward, I wish to express to the family our deep grief in the loss of our fellow worker, Brother Murdoch, and assure you that we, with you, mourn his passing.

Brother Murdoch, as mentioned by President McKay, was the Senior President of the Thirteenth Quorum of Seventy. This was a position he has held for many years and a position which was held by his father before him for a great many more years. His father, I remember, took a great deal of pride in his activity in the Seventies' Quorum, and Will seemed to derive the same enjoyment from his association with this group of men. The family has requested that I extend their thanks and appreciation to all who have taken part today in any way whatsoever. I hesitate to mention any name or group for fear that in the doing I may overlook someone who has contributed to this occasion, so I am not naming anyone specifically. However, even though I encounter that danger, I cannot help but mention some of the groups who are here present today to do honor to Commissioner Murdoch. I mention the Exchange Club sitting in the choir seats; the Retail Grocers Association in the south wing of the choir seats; the members of the Thirteenth Quorum of Seventy who are wearing carnations, some of whom are acting as ushers and their main group sitting in the center section behind us; the Police Department on my right, and all those others of you who by your presence are showing your interest and your appreciation for our departed and beloved friend and brother, William Murdoch. The concluding number on our program today will be the contralto solo by Mrs. Dinwoodey, "I Know that My Redeemer Lives" and the benediction will be pronounced by Preston Nibley. Preston Nibley is young Will Murdoch's father-in-law. The dedication of the grave in the City Cemetery will be by former Mayor and former Bishop of the Twentieth Ward, C. Clarence Neslen.

BENEDICTION BY PRESIDENT PRESTON NIBLEY

At the conclusion of these services, our Heavenly Father, we again express our gratitude unto Thee for the life of this good man, our friend and our brother, William Murdoch. We express our gratitude for the character which he established in this community, for his public service, for his splendid family who have been left to carry on his good name. We express our gratitude for his loyalty, his fidelity to his church and people, and his belief that death does not end all. We pray, Heavenly Father, that Thy comforting influence may be with Sister Murdoch and the children and all of us who mourn, that we may realize and know that all is well with him and that he is safe in Thy hands. My we learn through our sorrow the great lesson that we shall have to pass through the same gate, the same door, and conduct our lives as he has conducted his, so that we may be able to render a full account. Again we express our gratitude for the comforting words that have been given us on this occasion and for Thy holy spirit that has been present to comfort us. We do this humbly and in the name of the Lord Jesus Christ. Amen.

"Solemn March" by Handel – Organ Postlude by Elder Alexander Schreiner

DEDICATORY PRAYER AT CITY CEMETERY BY BISHOP C. CLARENCE NESLEN

Our Heavenly Father, with bowed heads and sorrowing hearts we come before Thee at this time at this, the open grave of our husband, our father, our brother, our dear friend and Thy true servant, William Murdoch, and we dedicate unto Thee, our Heavenly Father, this spot of ground that has been selected as his last earthly resting place. We bless all that pertains unto this internment and we invoke thy blessings, O God, upon this hallowed spot. May thy peace here abide. May Thy spirit of comfort radiate here and may this be a hallowed spot in Thy presence and in the hearts of his dear family and friends. May they come here to receive inspiration and courage and renewed faith as they journey along through life. We thank Thee, O God, for this fine life that we have touched in our sojourn here. We thank Thee for his husbandhood, his fatherhood, for his friendship, for his devotion to Thy church, for his community service, and for all these fine attributes he has so beautifully manifested in his life here among us. Wilt Thou remember his family, his neighbors, and friends. We again invoke Thy comfort in their behalf. May peace ever be in their hearts, may love and unity be in their homes and may they realize as never before that the resurrection from the dead is a reality and not a myth. May they have renewed faith in Thee; may they in their hearts say that what Thou hast done and what has been done is for the best. May this family of boys and girls be blessed with fortitude and strength and with the faith of their father, and may they be a real monument to him and to the name that they bear.

Now, O Lord, we do consign to Mother Earth these remains and invoke Thy blessing upon this spot. May these remains rest in peace until the morning of the first resurrection, then may they come forth clothed upon with immortality and with eternal life, we humbly pray in Jesus Christ's name. Amen.

Active Pallbearers
Milton E. Lipman, Bert M. Olson, Frank K. Arnold, Herman H. Green, Alma H. Davis, Gerald Irvine
Honorary Pallbearers
Mayor Ab Jenkins, Commissioner John B. Matheson, Commissioner George D. Kayser, Commissioner P.H. Goggin, Governor Henry H. Blood, John M. Wallace, E.O. Howard, S.O. Bennion, J.F. Fitzpatrick, G.B. Heal, J. Reuben Clark, Jr., David O. McKay, Henry D. Moyle, Harold B. Lee, Police Chief Charles N. Olson, A.G. Schwartz, T. B. Burbidge, Herbert S. Auerbach, R.K. Hardy, Jerrold P. Beesley, Judge Oscar W. McConkie, Fire Chief LaVere M. Hanson, Earl J. Glade, Gordon Burt Afflect, Judge Wilford Moyle Burton, Marion G. Romney, D.A. Afflect, John D. Walsh

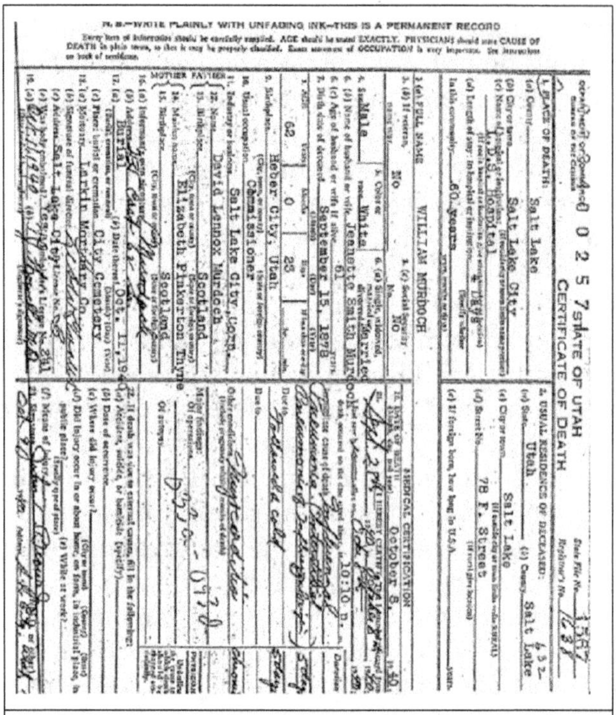
STATE OF UTAH
CERTIFICATE OF DEATH
Salt Lake
Salt Lake City
L.D.S. Hospital
60 years
Utah
Salt Lake
78 F. Street
WILLIAM MURDOCH
Male
White
Married
Jeanette Smith Murdoch
September 15, 1878
Heber City, Utah
Commissioner
Salt Lake City Corp.
David Lennox Murdoch
Scotland
Elizabeth Pinkerton Thyne
Scotland
October 8, 1940
10:10 p.
Burial
Oct. 11, 1940
City Cemetery
Larkin Mortuary Co.

STATE OF UTAH
CERTIFICATE OF DEATH
Salt Lake
Salt Lake City
Utah
78 - F. Street
JEANNETTE SMITH MURDOCH
Female
White
William Murdoch
Salt Lake City, Utah
John H. Smith
Scotland
Burial
Larkin Mortuary Co.

Newspaper Clipping from
THE SALT LAKE TRIBUNE
Wednesday, October 9, 1940

ILLNESS FATAL
MEMBER OF S.L. COMMISSION SUCCUMBS AT 62

William Murdoch, Commissioner in charge of the Salt Lake City Finance Department, one-time acting Mayor and prominent Democrat, died at 10:10 p.m. of pneumonia.

Mr. Murdoch, who in 1939 polled the largest popular vote ever accorded a commission candidate in the Salt Lake municipal primary, was taken ill a week ago. A Democrat, he had acted as Commissioner in charge of the City Finance Department since his election to that post in 1936. He first entered political life in 1934, when he was elected to the State House of Representatives for the 1935 session. Mr. Murdoch was slated to receive the mayoralty in 1938, when Mayor E.B. Erwin resigned as a result of the vice probe, but withdrew at the last moment and the post was awarded by the Commission to John M. Wallace. The Commissioner stated at the time that he wished to continue as Finance Commissioner, although his fellow commissioners signified that they wished to appoint him to the mayoralty.

SERVED BRIEFLY AS MAYOR

Commissioner Murdoch, however, acted as Mayor for a period in 1939, during the illness of Mayor Wallace, and assumed direction of the Public Safety Department in 1938 during the vice probe. Mr. Murdoch was born in Heber City September 15, 1878, a son of Mr. and Mrs. David Lennox Murdoch, and came to Salt Lake City with his parents while still a child. He studied in the Salt Lake Public Schools, graduating from the old Salt Lake High School. He began his business career at 12 as a cashboy for the Z.C.M.I., where his father had been employed for 47 years as a bookkeeper. The boy later worked as a machinist's helper at Park City and at 18 entered the Twentieth L.D.S. Ward Cooperative [a cooperative grocery store was owned by members of the Twentieth Ward which was started to supply groceries to its members. This was a common practice encouraged by Brigham Young who began forming cooperatives in 1868.], which he later managed. He established a grocery business at 78 F Street, the address of his present home, on January 1, 1908. The Murdoch Grocery Company, which grew from a small neighborhood store to a concern of city-wide reputation, is now conducted at 70 F Street. The Commissioner's business activities led to membership in the Utah Retail Grocers Association, in which he served as President for two terms, and the Salt Lake Retail Butchers and Grocers Association, in which he served as Director.

ACTIVE IN CIVIC AFFAIRS

Mr. Murdoch was also a charter member of the Exchange Club and a former President of the Utah State Cemetery and Memorial Park Association. In 1938 he served as General Chairman of the $50,000 advertising and promotional campaign of the Salt Lake Chamber of Commerce. He also acted as head of the State Food Code under the NRA.

Mr. Murdoch married Jeannette Smith in the Salt Lake L.D.S. Temple September 19, 1900. He had been a member of the Twentieth L.D.S. Ward since childhood. Surviving, in addition to Mrs. Murdoch, are the following sons and daughters: Jack Murdoch of Boise, Idaho, Mrs. Gordon Weggeland, Mrs. George J. Ross, Mrs. David J. Buckwalter, Mrs. Wendell B. Romney and D. Lennox, William Jr., Robert and Bonnie Murdoch, all of Salt Lake City; four sisters, Mrs. Jerrold E. Thompson of Salt Lake City, Mrs. Joseph M. Warner of Midvale, Mrs. Herman E. Clark of Rochester, N.H., and Miss Mary Murdoch of Salt Lake City, and eleven grandchildren.

Mary, Jeannette, Jack, Lennox, and William

Jeannette and William

LEFT: *William plead guilty to becoming the City Commissioner over Finance and Public Affairs in this prank by his peers.*
RIGHT: *William's name on the North Wall Entrance of the Salt Lake City Cemetery. The WPA (Work Progress Administration) provided jobs to put people to work during the Great Depression.*

Jeannette Cousins Smith Murdoch

Written by Janet Romney Hull, Granddaughter

On Valentine's Day, Feb. 14, 1879 an "elect Lady" was born to John Ross and Mary Huskinson Smith. Jeannette Cousins Smith grew up in Salt Lake City and was one of seven children. Unfortunately, not a lot is known about our dear grandmother. She was a very kind, gentle, and generous woman who was always doing for others. At some point, she met and married William Murdoch in the Salt Lake Temple on September 19, 1900. They became the parents of nine children which included twins—William Murdoch and Jeannette Murdoch Romney.

The family lived at 78 F Street. Next door to the home was the family grocery store—Murdoch Grocery. Most every day Grandmother cooked lunch for the employees, including those who drove the delivery trucks. Those were the days when everything was made from scratch. This sweet lady saw to it that the employees were fed, while taking care of nine children. My mother was one of the twins mentioned above. She always said that Grandmother served others unselfishly and never complained.

Jeannette was also an accomplished musician. She played the piano and organ for the Sugarhouse Ward. She was active in Relief Society and served as a counselor for eleven years. With her husband she was also active in educational and civic affairs. She lived a superb life in the community, not only among her own family, but across the fence to the neighbors or those who came to the store or those with whom she came in contact.

The day Grandfather took the office of Commissioner, he introduced our grandmother to Harold B. Lee, then an Apostle. He said, "I remember the day that he (Grandfather) took office. I saw this sweet mother of yours for the first time, and as he brought her to introduce her to me with his arm about her. He introduced her as his sweetheart. I think she was just that in every sense of the meaning of the word. I believe she was that to his dying day. I believe it was always so."

Grandmother worked hard all her life. In 1940, her husband of 40 years passed away. This was terribly hard on her. Not long after his death her health began to deteriorate and she became sad and lonely. Betty Lue Murdoch, wife of Robert, visited her after work each day and took her for walks and enjoyed the visits. She said she was a very sweet lady and even though suffered from dementia, was always appreciative and cooperative. She loved when Betty came so she could get outside and their long talks have become a favorite memory of hers. She said Jeannette had such a pretty, sweet face and one could tell what a beautiful woman she had been. On February 28, 1945, she died after being bedridden for a long time. At last she was free and had joined the love of her life for all eternity.

Jeannette Cousins Smith Murdoch, Mary Murdoch, Mary Huskinson Smith, Jennett Cousins Huskinson

LEFT: *Our grandmother Jeannette, John Ross Smith (her father), Mary Huskinson Smith*
(her mother), Mr. Huskinson, old sheepherder who lived with Cousie (Jeannette), Elizabeth
Murdoch, our grandfather William, and Mary Smith (Jeannette's sister)
RIGHT, BACK: *Norah Murdoch, Art Smith, Afton Murdoch, Mary Murdoch.*
FRONT: *Robert Smith, Ethel Smith, Lennox and Mary. Behind Mary is Wallace Smith.*
The Smith children are Jeannette's brothers and sisters.

TOP LEFT: BACK: *David Buckwalter, Beth, Lucy Murdoch, Bill, Ora Murdoch, Gordon Weggeland, and Jack, Lennox* FRONT: *Ruth Murdoch, Jeannette, Grandmother Jeannette, Jean, and Bonnie*
TOP RIGHT: *David Buckwalter, Lucy Murdoch, Ora Murdoch, Gordon Weggeland, Wendall Romney, and George Ross*
BOTTOM, BACK: *Lucy Murdoch, Jeannette, Jean, David Buckwalter, Ora Murdoch, Beth, George Ross, Gordon Weggeland, Jack, and Bonnie*
FRONT: *Bill, Grandmother Jeannette, and Lennox*

EDITOR'S NOTE: *This set of pictures was taken about 1943 when Bob was either on his mission or at war*

Patriarchal Blessing of Jeannette Cousins Smith Murdoch

Patriarchal Blessing given at Salt Lake City Oct. 4, 1901 by John M Murdoch, Patriarch on the head of Jeannette C. S. Murdoch, daughter of John R. and Mary H. Smith. Born in Sugar House Ward Feb. 15, 1879. Dear Sister Jeannette C. Smith by your request I place my hands upon your head and in the name of the Lord Jesus Christ and by the authority of the Holy Priesthood placed upon me as Patriarch give you a father's blessing. And I pray my Father in Heaven that he will let His Holy Spirit rest upon me, his Humble Servant, that the words I may say may be the words of the Lord into you in very deed. Thou art a daughter of Abraham of the seed of Joseph of the lineage of Ephriam the first born of Israel, therefore, you are entitled to all the blessings of the Holy Gospel which you have received in the days of your youth desiring to keep the commandments of God and to do good all the days of your life. Thy pure spirit dwelt in the presence of God your Father long before the foundations of this earth were laid and through your faithfulness you have been permitted to come here upon this earth by being born of goodly parents and having a name here among the people of God where you can be instructed in the ways of the Lord. You have been preserved by the power of God from sickness and disease and your life has been preserved for a wise purpose, that you might become a mother in Israel and bring forth the souls of men committed unto your care for which you will be accountable unto God, your Father, when the day of judgment shall come. Therefore dear sister, be of good cheer, the Lord Almighty is thy friend and protector and in so much as you will listen to the whispering of the Spirit that shall come unto you, you shall be guided and directed in the ways you should walk. You shall be greatly blessed of the Lord and in connection with your husband, through your faithfulness you shall be able to bring up your children in the ways of the Lord. They shall become a great blessing unto you and you shall have much joy in your labors and your children will rise up and bless you and hand down your honorable name to the latest generation. Therefore, seek unto the Lord for wisdom to guide you through the journey of life. And through the trials of life that come to the children of men while passing through this vale of tears. Be of good cheer and be comforted for the Lord will direct and guide you aright and you shall have power to accomplish all the good you desire and you shall have the desires of your heart in all things that shall be for your good. I seal you up into eternal life to come forth in the morning of the first Resurrection with many of your kindred and friends and with them be crowned with honor and glory in the presence of God and the Holy Angels. All which I seal upon you by the authority of the Holy sealing power that has been committed unto me as a Patriarch in the Church of Jesus Christ of Latter-day Saints upon conditions of your faithfulness in keeping the commandments of God. In the name of Jesus Christ. Amen.

Isabella C. Murdoch, clerk

Front: Lennox, Bonnie, Grandfather William, Grandmother Jeannette, Robert, Jean and Bill. Back: Ora, Mary, Gordon, Ruth, Jack, Beth, George, Jeannette, Wendell, and Lucy.

Jean, Jeannette, Mary, Beth, and Bonnie

Lennox, Jack, Bill and Robert

Jean, Jack, Mary, Lennox, Beth, Robert, Bonnie, Bill, and Jeannette

Robert, Jean, Bill, Jeannette, Beth, Jack, Mary, and Lennox

Bonnie's wedding: Back Wendall Romney, David Buckwalter, Ora, Bill, Lucy, Betty, Gordon Weggeland. Middle: Jack, Ruth, Jeannette, Bonnie, Jean, Beth, Mary. Front: Lennox, Robert, John Leonard.

Norah's memorial service held in Salt Lake City. L to R: Thyne Omo (Afton's daughter), Beth, Jeannette, Lemoyne Hatch, Martha (Norah's daughter), David Warner, Georgia, (Norah's daughter), David Buckwalter, Jean, Wendell, Betty Clark (Norah's daughter.) Joseph Warner (Afton's son), Aunt Mary Murdoch, Gordon Weggeland, Mary, Charles Clark, (Norah's son) Janet Clark, (Norah's daughter), Bob, Lucy, Bill, Ora, Jack, Lennox and Afton.

Funeral Notes

EDITOR'S NOTE - *The following is taken from the transcript of the funeral services for Jeannette Cousins Smith Murdoch held at the South Twentieth Ward Chapel in Salt Lake City, Utah on Saturday, March 3, 1945 at 1:00 P.M. She is buried in the Salt Lake City Cemetery.*

Born in Salt Lake City, Utah, February 14, 1879. Daughter of John R. and Mary Huskinson Smith. Married to William Murdoch, September 19, 1900 in [the] Salt Lake L.D.S. Temple. Died in Salt Lake City, Utah, February 28, 1945.

"Devotion" by Bossi – organ prelude by Virginia Freber

BISHOP WILLIAM E. STOKER (OFFICIATING)
My Brethren and Sisters and Friends, I am sure your presence is appreciated here today by this good family. Our service will be as follows: Sister Virginia Freber is the organist. The opening prayer will be offered by Stake President E. Q. Cannon, to be followed with a duet by Mr. and Mrs. J. Stuart McMaster, and the first speaker will be Bishop C. Clarence Neslen.

INVOCATION BY PRESIDENT EDWIN Q. CANNON
Our Father who are in heaven, we a few of Thy children, are met together this day to do honor to one of Thy handmaidens who has been called Home, and we pray Thee while we are thus assembled that Thy Holy Spirit may be here in rich abundance to direct and guide the things which shall be said and to direct and guide those who shall take part in any way in this service. We pray that Thou wilt pour out Thy spirit upon the family of Sister Murdoch that they may receive comfort thereby, that they may receive an assurance, through the instrumentality of Thy spirit, of the goodness and the kindness which was a part of her life, and of the reward which will come unto her as a result thereof. We pray that Thou wilt see fit to guide and inspire those who shall address us this day, that they may, under the influence of Thy spirit, give unto us words of comfort, consolation, and encouragement, that all of us, both those directly concerned as relatives as well as those of us who are friends, may derive much benefit therefrom. We pray these blessings of Thee, together with all others that will be for our good and benefit, through the worthy name of Jesus Christ, our Redeemer; even so, Amen.

"In the Garden" – vocal duet by Bishop and Mrs. J. Stuart McMaster.

Piano accompaniment by Mrs. J. Stuart McMaster

I come to the garden alone
While the dew is still on the roses,
And the voice I hear falling on my ear
The Son of God discloses.

> Refrain:
> And He walks with me and He talks with me
> And He tells me I am His own,
> And the joys we share as we tarry there
> None other has ever known.
> He speaks, and the sound of His voice
> Is so sweet the birds hush their singing,
> And the melody that He gave to me
> Within my heart is ringing.
> I'd stay in the garden with Him,
> Tho' the night around me be falling,
> But He bids me go; thro' the voice of wo
> His voice to me is calling.

Remarks by Bishop C. Clarence Neslen

My dear Brothers and Sisters and Friends, the honor the family have shown me today is duly appreciated. I feel it is a distinct honor to be asked to participate briefly here today. This honor is exceeded only by the weakness I feel in doing justice to the occasion.

I do so want to say that which will bring comfort to these sorrowing children and other relatives. I hope that my words will be inspired by our Heavenly Father, that they will reflect not only my own thoughts and my own sympathy, but that they will be expressive to these good people of your sympathy and the thoughts we all have for them in this, their hour of trial.

All of us who have had a similar experience as this, all of us who have had the Angel of Death come into our homes, know that it is never easy to part with those we love no matter how long they may have suffered, how old they may have been, or how deadly was the malady that took them hence. Although we may have implicit faith in the resurrection from the dead, still death does have its sting, and sadness comes into the hearts of all of us when our dear ones are separated from us, and although Sister Murdoch suffered long and painfully, while she had finished, perhaps, her mission here and the family may have been reconciled to a degree to her passing, I know they are mourning today, and justly so, because they are going to be deprived of that help, of that inspiration, of that courage and that example that she gave to them through the long years.

With that in mind, you and I have come here today to show to them by our presence or by our spoken word or by this music or by these floral emblems that we are with them in this, their hour of trial. I always feel on occasions like this that the sympathy that we have in our hearts for those mourning in some way seems to radiate, it seems to find lodgment, in due time, in the hearts of those who are mourning. I say we have come here today for that purpose, and we do sincerely and humbly pray for their comfort and assure them that we are willing to take upon ourselves, if possible, part of their grief. Indeed there is comfort in that, there is consolation to know that our friends are with us when trials come our way.

It is customary also, on occasions like this, at least among the people of this denomination, this Church, to have the services characteristic of the deceased; the formula so to speak, that permits of tributes being borne, and I think it is well that this is so. We are not here today to bear tributes with the thought in mind that the number or the beauty or the extent of the tributes are going to alter the status of Sister Murdoch in her Heavenly Father's presence. We realize that you are not her judges; we realize we are not character witnesses and that our Heavenly Father is not going to be influenced, perhaps, by what is said or done here today. She is not on trial; this is not a court martial, but we are here to bear tributes to her because we, ourselves, in so doing, get a fine picture of her life. We take our own inventory and are made better men and women because of inventory taking.

I am here today as an old member of this Ward, as an old friend of this family. I am here to bear a sincere tribute to this good woman and the family with which she was connected.

The eminent families are concerned here today, the Smiths and the Murdochs. I have known them both through the years, but especially the Murdoch family for over half a century. You know in life it is easy, perhaps, or not very difficult, at least, for a boy to rather pull the wool over the eyes of his teacher. He may deceive his parents. He may deceive some of the people with whom he does not come in close contact; but a boy never deceives his playmates. A boy does not deceive his playmates very long. Will Murdoch was my playmate. I have known him all my life.

I have known the Murdoch name from the beginning of my career here in this Ward. We have been neighbors for a long, long time. I have known them all. I have known their activities, I have known their integrity, I have known their industry, their devotion, their citizenship, their Christianity, if you please, and I am here today to say to those of you who do not know, that two excellent families are concerned today.

The Murdoch family was not a good, passive family. They were an active family. There are some people who are quiet, who keep the laws, but go around quietly and do nothing particularly for the benefit of the community; but not so with the Murdochs. While they attended their own affairs, were industrious, and went about their affairs in life, they found time to devote time and attention to the welfare of other people. They were fine, Christian people, upstanding citizens. There is no blemish on the Murdoch name. And Sister Murdoch came into our Ward shortly after her marriage and has been here all these years. She has lived a superb life here in this community, not only among her own family, but across the fence to the neighbors or those who came to the store or those with whom she came in contact as a Relief Society worker, as a Primary worker or in the Seminary institution.

I do not know, of course, what God's plans are, in detail, but I do think He has a standard of judgment that is going to be a little different than some of the standards we have in life. I often think as I go through this life, as I see people come and go, as I contact this thing called publicity and I see the things in life that are superficial, I see homage paid to those who are rich, I see the poor sometimes passed by, or I see the worthy unnoticed in life, that the Lord has different standards of judgment than some of us may have from time to time. Again I repeat, if I may, the words of a man whose name I do know, who said,

> "I know not how others view
> The prize which men seek after, called success,
> But unto me it seems a standard true
> By which to judge, is from the good we do,
> In giving unto others happiness.
> The man who loves his wife and family,
> (Or the women who loves her husband and family)
> Who does no other soul an injury,
> Whose life is filled with acts of charity
> Is a success, although he may die unknown."

In this case the deceased does not die unknown, her life was filled with acts of charity, she did no other soul an injury, she was true to her family, she was devoted, extremely devoted to a lovely husband, and I think that we can say of her today as a great orator said of his brother some years ago, "If everyone to whom she did some loving kindness were to bring a blossom to her grave, she would rest tonight beneath a wilderness of sweet flowers." I have often felt, and do today, that the Lord will have nearest to Him these fine Relief Society workers. There will be more devoted, humble people close to the Lord's throne than there will be millionaires or those whose names appeared so often in the public press, those who receive so much of the plaudits of this world. That is my view. I say, my friends, we are here today at the bier of a successful woman, a successful mother, a devoted wife, and a fine, good Christian lady. Peace be to her memory.

Now I think we are not concerned today particularly about any treatment of the subject of the resurrection, because we have that faith. No one that is here today questions but that there will be an afterlife, but I say to these good people that death is not a defeat. Death is not the end. Death is not a terminus. It is not the end of the line. It is just changing cars to go over the boundary into a more beautiful state. She has left this sphere of action, but her life has not ended. Life does not stop. Life goes on. It is not a question of how long life is, but how broad it is, and her life was broad as well as being fairly long, and while she has gone on today, her life has not stopped, and while she may have come to the end of this particular line, she has changed to another car and is still going on and on. Death is not a destination, death is just merely a change, as I have said, from one car to another.

The thought I want to give you now in conclusion is one that has been expressed thousands of times before. Benjamin Franklin, some two hundred years ago, put these words of record, and they seem to me very appropriate for this particular occasion. He said, "A man is not completely born until he is dead. Why, then, should we grieve the new child born among the immortals? We are spirits. That bodies should be lent us while they can afford us pleasure, assist us in acquiring knowledge and in doing good to our fellow creatures, is a kind and benevolent act of God, but when they become unfit for these purposes and afford us pain instead of pleasure, instead of an aid become an encumbrance, it is equally kind and benevolent that a way is provide by which we may get rid of them, and death is that way."

Isn't that true in this case? This good woman, the woman we knew, this personality, this character, was a spirit. Temporarily she was in a body which was loaned to her for a season, and that body for a time was strong, well and healthy, and afforded her an opportunity of rendering service, of enjoying life and doing good. Latterly, it became incapacitated, it became diseased, it became weakened and did not function as the spirit would have it, and it has now been taken away from the spirit that the spirit might go on and progress and still do things. That thing that separated her body from her spirit is what we call death, and death is not a defeat, death is a blessing; it is a promotion.

I have confidence that the all-wise Lord will be mindful of this life, that the things that she has done will not go unrewarded. The Lord will not have to take the case under advisement, will not have to summon up and call in character witnesses. Hers is a continuous record. Today it is an open book, and when it is tabulated it will show that she is very, very much on the credit side, and her reward will be very, very great.

To her children I say, be mindful of the great heritage that is yours. Remember that this name that you have received has come down through many generations. It is untarnished. Keep it untarnished and do as your good parents would have you do. Be Christians in every sense of the word. Be as your good father, my old pal, would have you be, and do that which your mother would have you do.

> "My son, do you know that your soul
> Is of my soul such a part,
> That you seem to be fiber and core of my heart?
> None other can pain me as you, dear, can do;
> None other can please me or praise me as you.

> *Remember the world will be quick with its blame*
> *If shadow or stain ever, darkens your name.*
> *'Like mother, like son' is a saying so true,*
> *That the world will judge largely of mother by you.*
> *Be this then your task, if task it shall be,*
> *To force this proud world to do homage to me.*
> *Be sure it will say, when its verdict you've won,*
> *'She reaped as she sowed. Lo, this is her son.'"*

May the spirit of comfort and peace be with this family, and especially with the absent one, the son who is in the far-off Pacific. When the word comes to him may it be tempered with consolation, with understanding, with faith from On High.

May this family be true and faithful, may the Lord be with them to bless and comfort and cheer them, I pray in the name of Jesus Christ's name. Amen.

BISHOP STOKER: Sister Virginia Barker will render for us a vocal solo, after which Apostle Harold B. Lee will speak to us.

Let Not Your Heart be Troubled

Soprano Solo by Virginia Freeze Barker

Organ Accompaniment by Virginia Freber

> *Let not your heart be troubled,*
> *Ye believe in God;*
> *Let not your heart be troubled,*
> *Ye believe in God,*
> *Believe also in me;*
> *Ye believe in God,*
> *Ye believe in God,*
> *Believe also in me.*
> *Peace I leave with you,*
> *My peace I give unto you,*
> *Not as the world giveth*
> *Give I unto you;*
> *Not as the world giveth*
> *Give I unto you.*
> *Let not your heart be troubled,*
> *Neither let it be afraid;*
> *Ye believe in God,*
> *Believe also in me.*
> *Peace I leave with you,*
> *My peace I give unto you,*
> *Not as the world giveth*
> *Give I unto you.*
> *Not as the world giveth*
> *Give I unto you.*

*Peace I leave with you,
My peace I give unto you,
Not as the world giveth
Give I unto you.*

REMARKS BY ELDER HAROLD B. LEE

The purpose of this service is not merely that we thus conform to custom, but more particularly because services of this character have a definite and important place in the religious worship of this people.

We have met here this afternoon and are blessed with a quiet, peaceful influence that I am sure we have all recognized as a benediction from the life of a sweet mother, and the spirit of the Lord has hallowed this service thus far with a benign benediction. This service, and others of its kind, have purpose in that they permit opportunity for friends of those who mourn most deeply to draw very close, and by their presence, by their words, by the music rendered, by the flowers, by expressions of sympathy may indicate to the mourners their love and their affection. This is for the purpose of mourning, for we are commanded to mourn for those whom we love who pass from this life, for the Lord has said, "We should live together in love so much so that we should weep for the loss of them that die, but more especially for them that have not hope of glorious resurrection." And so it is well that we shed tears for our loved ones today.

We are met here to speak words of light and truth, for you may say all the kind things that you will about those who pass, and as Brother Neslen has said, all our words will not add one whit to their records and will not detract one part therefrom, but the thing that will give us most comfort will be the comfort that Sister Barker's beautiful solo has sung of, a peace not given from the things of the world, but a peace which only God, Himself, can give in a knowledge and a faith that is not born of this world, and then we come here to speak in praise and to hold up the lives of those who pass for whom we mourn as an example to us who remain behind, for our course is not yet run; our record is not yet fully written; our lives are not yet complete. There remains behind the children of those who have passed, and the grandchildren and the friends and associates, who yet must spend years in mortality before they, too, shall come to the place of sweet music, the smell of lovely flowers, and where kind words are spoken. Many of those purposed have been already realized, and if this service should close now I think we might all go from here satisfied in the realization of the full purpose of our having met.

I cannot come to this responsibility, for which I feel greatly honored, without linking with her for whom we mourn the name of a dear friend, my own beloved Will Murdoch. My association intimately with the father and the husband began on election night in 1935, when he was the successful and winning candidate for the office of City Commissioner. Somehow what I seem to think and may be prompted to say about him could well be said about her, because their lives were as closely entwined that she was as much a part of him as he was a part of her, they lived so devotedly and so unitedly as one.

I remember some of the circumstances of our first associations together, and I recall them only for purposes of lessons to members of the family who know of these things.

I know you remember the political fight that ensured just after his election in contest for the vacancies that were to be filled in the City Commission. I saw the fibre of your father during those days, and I came to know how much his family meant to him. He knew that if he were to be placed in a spot where vice and crime and lawlessness abounded, which in all likelihood he may not be able to surmount or to direct or to solve to the satisfaction of many, and that in the event he should make a fatal misstep because of his unwisdom or lack of experience, he might bring upon his family something of disrepute. He had a feeling that not one thing that he should do in his public office should bring one stain upon the name of Murdoch; that no child of his should ever have to live with such feeling through their lives.

I remember the day that he took office. I saw this sweet mother of yours for the first time, and as he brought her to introduce her to me with his arm tenderly around her, he introduced her as his sweetheart. I think she was just that in every sense of the meaning of the word. I believe she was that to his dying day. I believe it was always so.

There was a fine faith in this family. Will Murdoch was not a man to wear his religion where it was paraded before men. As Bishop Neslen has said, this family lived a kind of religion that was too deep, ofttimes, for expression in words. I saw it portrayed in a little incident that to me is very sacred. I speak of it today only because I am among his friends and those who loved him and knew him best.

As is usually the case where there are political changes, "to the victor belong the spoils", and with the victor there come in ofttimes friends for public office, and in those days a job was a very precious thing. It meant the unseating of a number who had positions and the bringing in of new friends to occupy those positions. Always there were difficulties, and it was so in this case.

There lived in my Stake a very faithful, devoted, humble man. He had no political pull, he had no powerful friends, he had no money, but he worked as an inspector in the Public Health Department, and as this change took place I fancied that surely this man would lose his place. I spoke of my anxiety to him one day, and he said, to me, "President Lee," I then being his Stake President, "don't you worry. I have prayed to the Lord about this, and the Lord has given me the feeling that I am going to be all right."

I said, "You have more faith than I have. I know the power of politics. I am just afraid that you are going to be out."

Well, the days went past and finally one day there came down a list of the men who were to be replaced in the Public Health Department. This man's name was on the list, and I thought of the expression of faith that he had made, that he knew the Lord would answer his prayers, and I wondered what would happen to his faith after tomorrow when we voted and this man was replaced by someone else.

The next morning when the names were presented before the Commission, lo and behold, his was the only name left off the list! All the rest of them whom I had seen the day before were gone excepting this one man, and so concerned was I about it, so curious to know what had happened, I went into the office of Commissioner Murdoch. Now his was another office entirely. He was not directly associated with the Public Health Department.

"Can you explain to me," I asked, "why this man's name was left off this list of the changes?"

He smiled and said, "Well, I think I can."

I told him the story about why I asked and what this man's faith was, and he surprised me when tears filled his eyes and he said, "Well, I suppose I was the one the Lord chose to answer that humble man's prayer. I met the son of this man over in England filling a mission. He was a friend of my son." I don't know which one of the sons that would be here that knew this boy. He said, "I happened to meet him and he told me his father worked in the Public Health Department in Salt Lake City. At that time I had not the slightest notion that I would one day be in the City Commission."

He said, "The day came when this change was to take place, and as I ran down the list, something went through me as though almost by electric shock when I saw that man's name. I remembered what that boy had told me, and I knew he had not yet returned from his mission, and I thought to myself, 'Why, I can't let that man go. He is supporting this boy in the mission field. He has a responsibility. He hasn't much in the world. That job means everything in the world to him.' And I immediately began to do things to help that man keep his job, although I hadn't anything else but that impression upon me to save that man's job."

That is the kind of religion that this family expresses in their daily work.

I want to say this to you, not because I am talking to his family, but I want to say this with all the sincerity of my soul, I have seen many men in public office; I have watched and have known something of the intimate records of men who have lived much of their lives in public office, but I know of no man who served more devotedly, more honestly, more fearlessly for the welfare of a community than did Commissioner William

Murdoch, and I want you to know that he left his public office with the plaudits of his community upon him.

As I went to the hospital the night he died, and at his request put my hands on his head and gave him a blessing, I think perhaps I was the last one except the hospital attendants who spoke to him before his death, for shortly after he went into a coma from which he did not recover. I glory in those precious moments when I have drawn close to men like your father, whom I came to admire and to love with an affection almost beyond that of mortal ties.

As I come to this day and hold before you his record, I am linking it with that of your mother, who was tied and bound to him by cords stronger than the cords of death. To him she has gone this day, and in that union there must be happiness – there cannot be great sorrow – and so I fancy the tears you shed today will not be tears of anxiety about her welfare, because if you think of it from that side there would be nothing but happiness and cheer, for she has been released from the limitations of her earthly body which has grown frail and worn and racked by disease. From all that she is now released, and she has gone Home to that God who gave her life; she has gone Home to the bosom of her loving companion, in whose presence no doubt this day she is dwelling.

But today you and I who stay here have a responsibility which should cause us reflection. What have you to do before this time comes to you? May I ask. If tomorrow would be your last day on earth, what regrets would you have? What unfulfilled desire yet remains in you? For the Lord has said that life is a probationary period, and time for men to prepare to meet their God. Aren't you glad that this is not your last day, right down in your hearts now? Wouldn't you dislike to be called today before you have finished some of the things you have yet to do? Pause for a moment and reflect. You older folks who are on the sundown of life, do you have some temple work, some genealogical research that if you left would be neglected? If you got on the Other Side and saw some of your loved ones who have passed on before, who have hoped that you would rise to that responsibility which you have failed to do, and they accused you, "Why didn't you do it while you were in mortality?" wouldn't you wish that you could turn back the clock before you had that kind of reunion? This is the time to prepare to meet those folks and your God, and answer such questions.

Do you have some habits that you have formed here that are not very pleasing? Do you have habits that give you a feeling of unworthiness, that make you unsuited to dwell in the company of the righteous? If you do, today is the time to begin to uproot such habits, because that feeling of unworthiness that you have here will make you feel unworthy to dwell in the presence of the most righteous, for the same spirit that is in your bodies today will possess your bodies throughout eternity, and there will be within all who rise in the resurrection an awful remembrance of the misdeeds of mortality; the unrepentant acts that have been done; and this is the day for us to uproot those and thank God He has given us the time which is necessary to rectify our lives and to purge out from our souls that which is improper and unfits us for the company of the angels and the righteous in God's holy place. Perhaps there are wrongs that you have done that ought to be corrected. Perhaps you have done ill against a neighbor. Perhaps there are things that you would like to confess that you have not yet today quite had the courage. Let not the sundown of life go down upon your wrath; let no one go to his grave without having gone and corrected those things so that even your enemy may have a good word to say about you. Yes, there may be such that we would like to do before our time comes to go.

Then, too, are there feelings among you? Is there a wayward son or daughter that you have not yet been able to quite bring into the fold of truth? Perhaps you are the one with a kindly word, with a strong hand, who is the only one who can guide that one. Are you doing all you can while it is yet noonday, or are you walking in the darkness at noonday? Our Father says it is a condemnation when, in the brightness of opportunity, we fail to siege upon and do that which we had the opportunity and failed to do here in mortality.

Well, there are a lot of things that I wonder if you are thinking about. With the passing of both father and mother there is an estate, some personal effects, things to be done, and I wonder if when your time comes and your families have similar problems, you will have taken the steps to bring about a family solidarity that shall forbid the family squabbles that often result from family divisions of properties.

I believe that the kind of love that will forbid that sort of thing exists in this family, and I think that strength of family is in those who remain behind, that those things need not come to spoil and mar the name and memory of a lovely father and mother, but this thing now that brings hope and peace is the thing called the Gospel of the Lord Jesus Christ.

It was the promise of the Lord as he spoke through Isaiah, that "Thy dead men shall live; together with my dead body shall they arise. Awake and sing, ye that dwell in dust: for thy dew is as the dew of herbs, and the earth shall cast out the dead."

Hundreds of years passed before the fulfillment of that promise, and then we find written in the record after the crucifixion of the Savior, "The veil of the temple was rent in twain from the top to the bottom; and the earth did quake, and the rocks rent and the graves ere opened; and many bodies of the saints which slept arose, and came out of the graves after His resurrection, and went into the holy city and appeared unto many."

That is the same promise that after this day will mean most to you. It will be the promise that after you have finished this life, if you have lived worthy to associate in the presence of your father and mother, you shall come forth in that day from your graves and see them in the likeness of their physical bodies here, for they shall come forth in the perfectness of the physical body with which they have lived here in mortality. Thus the prophets since the beginning of time have taught and have promised.

Sister Murdoch has not gone to be immediately resurrected now. She has gone Home to that place that the Master spoke of as He hung on the cross between the two malefactors. You recall one said to Him, "Lord, remember Thou me when Thou comest into Thy kingdom."

And to this one the Master turned with compassion and said, "this day shall thou be with me in Paradise." Or, in the place of departed spirits. It was not a deathbed repentance and forgiveness, as some has unwisely and falsely thought, it is that place of departed spirits to which all may go, or do go when they die. To the righteous it is a state of paradise; it is a state of peace and happiness and rest from the toils and labors of this life; but to the unrighteous it is a state of anxiety, and fearful, awful looking for the fiery indignation of the wrath of God upon them. There they shall remain, the righteous in peace, the unrighteous in a state of unrest until the day when the trump shall sound that shall call them forth in the day of their resurrection. Those who shall come forth first in the resurrection will be those who are the most righteous, and those who are filthy and those who are unrighteous must be the last, in the day of the Lord's resurrection.

Where shall be that place where they shall dwell? The Lord has revealed, too, that this earth on which we dwell, after it has filled the measure of its purpose and its creation, shall become the abiding place for those who inherit the celestial glory of our Father, for for this purpose was it created and made, and until every spirit that lived with our Heavenly Father before this world was shall have come here into mortality and have taken upon them the bodies that were promised by our Father, until that time shall come, this earth shall stand, and when the last spirit shall have thus come and shall have this tabernacle in the flesh, then shall come the end of the earth, and then shall come the time when it will be cleansed and purified and become the celestial abode for those who are entitled to celestial glory. It shall be on that place where those like Brother and Sister Murdoch who, joined together in the bonds of love for eternity with their families, shall stand forth and be judged, such man according to the deeds done in the flesh. That is the promise and the hope of the scriptures and the teachings of the Gospel, that when all else fails will be that that will lift you through the veil of tears and shall point you to a beautiful tomorrow that can only be recompense for the things that could not be brought to us by a too short period in mortality.

What is the purpose of mortality then? It is to bring to pass immortality and eternal life. If a little child comes into mortality and lives but a few moments it shall be saved in that glory. Whether we live to be the age of a tree, then, or live but a moment in mortality, we have accomplished the first part of purpose in coming, that of immortality; but the question of whether we shall obtain that celestial place will be determined solely upon how we act and our deeds and our conduct here in mortality.

So to you, the family of Will Murdoch and his loved wife, your mother, your father, there are bequeathed yet a few days for you to prepare to meet your God.

In that place where they dwell they are blessed by another power, and that power is that their hearts shall be turned to their children. Whom on this earth do you think they will be most concerned about? It will be you, their children, their posterity. They will be just as anxious to surround you with influences and be concerned about your welfare as they were here in mortality, and I think even more so, and because they have thus been tied to you would you think it strange if God should appoint them a mission to be as a guardian angel to one of their loved ones here? A loved one who perhaps was in physical or moral danger, or where little children have to be shepherded through a treacherous period through life, or a son or a daughter faced with a tremendous problem that was almost beyond his own comprehension?

It was the Apostle Paul who spoke of a time when he stood out in the night when there was a furious storm on the Mediterranean and the tiny ship on which they rode was being tossed here and there. You remember that some of his mates were about to jump overboard; they thought the ship was sinking at times. He stopped them and said, "Gentlemen, not one of your lives will be lost if you will stay with the ship, for last night there stood with me an angel and told me these things."

In your night of storm and turmoil, if you have faith, maybe God will send a guardian angel to stand by you and comfort, and who knows but what in His plan, that guardian angel might by your own mother; it might be your own father privileged thus to associate with you children to whom their hearts have thus been turned, that might hear you children from various walks of life.

I see here Mayor Glade, representing the City, no doubt, in honor of Commissioner Murdoch's public service. I see the KSL representative, so no doubt to show to Lennox their love and affection. I see men and women of the armed services to draw near to their buddy, their sister in the service who mourns the passing of her loved one. I see members of the priesthood quorums and the Relief Society organizations, and just true friends. Well, we are all here just to sit with you through this hour in contemplation when your hearts are tender, and because of mourning are in tune as a fine, delicately tuned radio is in tune with the powers of our Father.

May into your souls, then, because of your mourning, come peace and the blessings of God to you, and a new resolve as you go from this service, to live better lives than you have ever lived before, strengthened by the memory of an illustrious father and a sweet, devoted mother.

These are the blessings I pray upon all in the name of the Lord Jesus Christ. Amen.

Remarks by Bishop William E. Stoker

This good family showed me the honor of listing me as one of the speakers on this occasion, but I feel it would be an error for me to take advantage of that invitation, and I should not go on to say anything that would detract from the things that have been said in honor of this good woman here today.

I knew Sister Murdoch as a sweet, patient sufferer in her last days. I am sure that her spirit, if it had the opportunity, would not wish to return to that emaciated body until it shall have been made new by the resurrection. I am sure that all that has been said of her and about her today can be testified to by all of us who knew her.

In behalf of the family I desire to extend to you their thanks and their gratitude for your presence here, for these beautiful floral offerings, for the words of sympathy, for the spoken word here today, the beautiful music, and all that has been done. I am sure that they truly appreciate it.

Sister Barker will sing for us again, after which the closing prayer will be offered by Gordon Weggeland, a son-in-law. The postlude will be offered by Virginia Freber, and this service will be concluded at the City Cemetery, where the grave will be dedicated by E. Wesley Smith.

The pall bearers are Joseph Warner, John Smith, George Smith, Wesley Smith, David Smith and Dewey Davis.

The Christian's Goodnight

Soprano Solo by Virginia Freeze Barker

Organ Accompaniment by Virginia Freber

> *Sleep on, beloved, sleep, and take thy rest;*
> *Lay down thy head upon thy Savior's breast;*
> *We love thee well, but Jesus loves thee best*
> *Goodnight! Goodnight! Goodnight!*
> *Calm is thy slumber as an infant's sleep;*
> *But thou shalt wake no more to toil and weep;*
> *Thine is a perfect rest, secure and deep –*
> *Goodnight! Goodnight!! Goodnight!!*

> *Until the shadows from this earth are cast,*
> *Until He gathers in His sheaves at last;*
> *Until the twilight gloom is ever-past –*
> *Goodnight! Goodnight! Goodnight!*
> *Until the Easter glory lights the skies;*
> *Until the dead in Jesus shall arise;*
> *And He shall come, but not in lowly guise –*
> *Goodnight! Goodnight! Goodnight!*
> *Only "Goodnight", beloved - not "Farewell",*
> *A little while, and all His saints shall dwell*
> *In hallowed union, indivisible –*
> *Goodnight! Goodnight! Goodnight!*
> *Until we meet again before His throne,*
> *Clothed in the spotless robe he gives His own,*
> *Until we know even as we are known,*
> *Goodnight! Goodnight! Goodnight!*

Benediction by Elder Gordon Weggeland

Our Father who art in Heaven, hallowed be Thy name. With gratitude and in humility we express our appreciation for the beauty of this sacred hour. We are grateful for the life of this, Thy daughter, Jeannette Smith Murdoch, for the life and memory of her husband, William Murdoch, and for their family that survives. Let Thy spirit and comforting influence be with each member of this family, and grant that the example of her life and her unselfish devotion may ever inspire them and us for good. In Thine own way, our Father, bless our absent brother, Robert Murdoch, who because of war is unable to attend these last rites of his mother. Comfort him and minister to him and sustain him through the dark hours ahead. Grant that he and all other sons might quickly return home, and that peace might prevail over the earth.

We are grateful for the music and the words of comfort that have been spoken during this hour. Help us to cherish them in our memory, and may we re-dedicate our lives to perfect the heritage of strength and devotion to God and country which our parents have given us.

For the life and character of Thy daughter, Jeannette Murdoch, again we thank Thee. May our lives, through dedication to Thee, exemplify this gratitude.

Let Thy blessings be with her dear mother, her brothers and sisters and all their family, and especially bless these sons and daughters as they leave here to go about their ways, remembering especially our sister Bonnie. Grant Thy choicest blessings upon her. Sustain her in every hour of her need. Grant her every blessing. Father, we realize that it is only Heaven that is given away, that Thou alone can be had for the asking. We know that reason alone cannot answer this hour. Let Thy faith come into our hearts to sustain us now as we journey toward the place of burial, and sanctify in our heart the beauty of this hour of this day and all that has transpired.

Bless us to this end, we humbly pray in deepest gratitude, in the name of our Father and of Thy Son, Jesus Christ. Amen.

Organ Postlude by Virginia Freber "Prelude" by Chopin

Dedicatory Prayer at Salt Lake City Cemetery by Elder E. Wesley Smith

NEWSPAPER CLIPPING FROM
The Salt Lake Tribune, THURSDAY, MARCH 1, 1945

EX-OFFICIAL'S WIDOW DIES

Mrs. Jeannette Smith Murdoch, 66, widow of former City commissioner William Murdoch, died at the family home 78 "F" Street, Wednesday at 8 P.M. after a lingering illness. She was born in Salt Lake City February 14, 1879, a daughter of John R. and Mary Huskinson Smith, and was married to Mr. Murdoch in the Salt Lake L.D.S. Temple September 19, 1900.

An accomplished musician, Mrs. Murdoch was organist for Sugarhouse L.D.S. Ward several years, where she became active in Relief Society and Church Welfare work. She was a counselor in the Relief Society eleven years. With her husband, she was active in educational and civic affairs. Mrs. Murdoch is survived by her mother, now 86, and nine sons and daughters, Jack Murdoch, Boise; D. Lennox and William Murdoch, Salt Lake City; Pvt. Robert G. Murdoch, Philippines; Mrs. Gordon Weggeland, Mrs. Wendell Romney, Mrs. George J. Ross, Mrs. David Buckwalter and Corp. Bonnie Murdoch, WAC, Salt Lake City, and 14 grandchildren, and the following brothers and sisters; Arthur J. Smith, Los Angeles; George W., John R. and Wallace R. Smith, Salt Lake City; Mrs. E. Wesley Smith and Mrs. C. L. Reynolds, also of Salt Lake City.

THE TINY OLD HOUSE ON F STREET

By Janet Romney Hull

EDITOR'S NOTE: *William and Jeannette Murdoch lived in this little home at 74 F Street in Salt Lake City. We assume they lived there until they built their larger home at 78 F Street, which is right next door. As time went on, Bill and Lucy Murdoch lived in this little house, where Bill was born, as they began their own family.*

On a lovely June day in 1994, the Murdoch cousins had a family reunion. We visited many family sites reminiscent of "Murdoch days" gone by. One such stop on our list was a tiny house on "F" Street, set way back from the street in between the larger Murdoch family home, where the William and Jeannette Murdoch children grew up and the Murdoch Grocery Store, which fed the family and provided a living for William Murdoch. On two cold days, January 14 and 15 in 1911, the twins, Jeannette and William, were born in that tiny house. Since several of the children of Jeannette and William were at the reunion and were greatly interested to see where their parents were born, it was decided to visit the little house.

A few days before the visit, the present owners were contacted and arrangements were made for a morning visit. We rang the doorbell and young girl carrying a baby under a year came to the door. We told her who we were and she gladly let us in. She was intrigued with the story of the house and said she had a surprise for us. She disappeared and shortly returned with a sack. She explained that they had not lived in the house very long and when they went into the attic, they found several items. We sat down and opened the sack and there were three very old-fashioned baby shoes, a tin can which once held pipe tobacco, a cap with an advertisement for Faultless Butter, a torn up postcard to someone named Ella, which never got mailed. Other things included a tiny ball, an old magazine which appeared to have been in a fire and where on the back was an advertisement for Gold Medal manufactured then by Washburn-Crosby Co.

Left to Right: Janet Hull, Sherri Porter, Anne McQueen, Nan Williams, and Jane Leonard

We talked to this girl for quite a while and thanked her for her hospitality. I was especially grateful as I ended up with the sack of treasures. As I look at them now, preparing to write this story, I can't help but think of the tiny feet that once wore the little shoes, and all the relics of a bygone time—a time when life was sweeter and simpler. It was a time unspoiled by the types of evil we have today. The Murdoch children could play in their yards unattended. They could roam the hills of Lambs Canyon without fear. It was a time of innocence, now gone forever. At least we have these reminders of the "good ole days"

SUMMERS AT CAMP MURDOCH

The Recollections of Jeannette Murdoch Romney

The Murdoch Cabin in Lamb's Canyon. Back L to R – Aunt Mary Murdoch, Aunt Jen Thompson, Grandmother Jeannette perhaps holding Bonnie. Lennox with hand on car, Grandfather William, Bill Murdoch perhaps by Grandfather William. People to the left are unknown.

For the children of our grandfather, William Murdoch and Jeannette Smith Murdoch, summer couldn't come fast enough! The beginning of vacation meant that Lambs Canyon adventures were about to begin!

Shortly after school closed, preparation was made for all the children to spend the entire summer at Camp Murdoch, the name given to the cabin that great grandfather, David Lennox Murdoch, had built. It was located way up into the canyon accessible only by a very narrow dirt road. Nestled in the pines on the hillside was the family cabin. The Murdoch car climbed slowly up the winding hill. Upon reaching the cabin, children jumped out and quickly ran for the cabin, excited that their wonderful summer was about to begin! Grandfather and the boys, Lennox, Jack and Bill would unload the groceries clothes, etc. Young Bob for a few years was too young to help with much.

The most important person to arrive at the cabin was Grandfather William's sister, Janet Lennox Murdoch Thompson. She would stay all summer and care for the nine active children, doing the cooking, cleaning and laundry. She would at times have other adult help from friends or other relatives. The cabin itself consisted of a large room with an old wood burning stove and a huge table that Great Grandfather and Great Grandmother had brought over from Scotland. Just beyond this room was a huge screened-in porch that went clear around the cabin. This was the sleeping area for the nine children and Janet M Thompson (Aunt Jen).

Front: Grandfather William and Heber Mary, who is the daughter of William and Mary Reid Lindsay, the half sister of David Lennox. She lived in Heber City and would come and help with the children at the cabin. David Lennox standing behind the car. Afton and Elizabeth P. Thyne Murdoch in seat. People in the back seat are not identified.

The boys would often go to bed with pellet guns and the girls would lie in their beds with great fear, waiting for the pack rats to climb up the screen. The boys would aim and fire and down would fall the rats. The rats that got away would often take an object such as a toy or something small and always leave in it's place an old piece of soap or part of a corn cob etc. No one could get rid of rats. They were simply a part of life at Camp Murdoch!

Another part of the family was their pet dog, Follie. She would go every summer and loved to roam the hills of Lambs Canyon. One day, poor Follie met up with a porcupine and came back to the cabin with a nose full of quills. After much loving care, the quills were pulled out. Follie withdrew to a corner of the porch to nurse her poor nose.

Trying to care for nine kids was no easy task for Aunt Jen! The boys especially would try her patience! Jack and Bill loved to climb up on the rafters just to tease her. She didn't seem to think this was very funny. She would plead and threaten them, but this only made the boys laugh harder. Even trying to swat them with a broom didn't work! When they finally did come down, Aunt Jen had had it!!! She would gather all the children, especially the boys, send them out with brooms and make them sweep the road!

The children loved every minute of summer life. You see, they didn't know what luxury was. Of course the cabin had no running water or inside plumbing. The outhouse was a ways away. Chamber pots provided relief for nighttime emergencies. All the Murdoch kids made their own fun. There was no radio or TV or cell phones, video games etc. which were decades away. Their fun was whatever they could think of. They provided fun for themselves.

On Fridays, Grandfather would load up the truck with groceries from Murdoch Grocery store and head for Lambs Canyon. The kids couldn't wait to see him. In late afternoon they would run to a cliff where they could see down to the road. After some waiting, finally they would spot their father coming up the road with the much needed supplies for the week.

Years passed, kids grew up and got married. The cabin was no longer a summer retreat. In 1942, the family decided to sell the cabin. Grandfather had died in 1940, and Grandmother was very frail. The decision to sell was later regretted by the family.

In June of 1994, The Murdoch cousins got together for a two-day reunion. One of the things we did was to go up Lambs Canyon and visit Camp Murdoch. It was still owned by the same owner who bought it from the Murdochs. His name was Bill Burrell. He was so kind in letting us see the place that had brought all our parents so much happiness in their childhood years.

LEFT TO RIGHT: *Jack, Beth, Mary, probably Mary Murdoch (Heber Mary), unknown girl, David Lennox, Jeannette (in back), unknown boy, and Lennox in front*

My Memories of Camp Murdoch

by William R. Murdoch

The Lamb's Canyon cabin was built from large pine trees on the lot purchased by David Lennox Murdoch, my great grandfather, in the early 1900's. The story goes back to my early teen years during World War II.

My father, Lennox Murdoch, and grandfather, Thomas Clark, used this remote facility on occasional annual deer hunts.

I vividly remember its rustic structure. It had a large living room with a rock fireplace, an attached kitchen with wash tub and wood burning stove. There was one bedroom with all rooms having exposed log beams and walls. Windows were placed on two walls. Surrounding the cabin was a walk-way, just wide enough to line up narrow beds on the cabin wall as to have room to pass by. The outside wall had rusty screens to keep insects at bay. Above, in the corners of the ceiling, small animals, field mice, rats, squirrels, chipmunks and bats made their home. It made for exciting sleeping companions.

I am sure in earlier days this situation was non-existent, since as as my father related to me, he and his eight brothers and sisters, with his mother, spent most of every summer at their mountain home.

My grandfather, William Murdoch, lived in Salt Lake City in the big house on the Avenues to work at his grocery store next to his home, and perform civic work as Finance Commissioner for Salt Lake City. He made the trip weekly to Camp Murdoch loaded with groceries for his hungry brood.

Plumbing in the cabin, from its conception to my visits, consisted of an outhouse and a 25 minute walk to a natural spring for water.

Our deer hunts were always productive, and during war times, with meat rationing, venison became one of our staple foods.

As a side note, it was this experience that prompted me to buy a 10-acre lot on a similar pine and quakie mountain, just up the street or freeway today. With a very understanding wife, I built our vacation cabin, which I am happy to report, has more up-to-date conveniences for our four children, 16 grandchildren and one great grandchild, who love this great get-away place. Camp Murdoch has been reborn to the Hearthstone.

The Murdoch Cabin

By Betty Lue Murdoch as told to Bette Ann Murdoch Christensen

My memories of the Murdoch cabin began in 1941 when I started dating Bob. He wanted me to see the cabin because he was so proud of it and it was such a big part of his life. We drove up and parked in front of the cabin. As we got out, Aunt Jen came out to meet us. Bob introduced me to her and then she quickly handed us each a broom, and told us to go sweep the dirt road leading to the cabin. I was astounded and couldn't believe I heard her right, but didn't say anything. When she left, I asked Bob about it and he said it was just something she always had the kids do – sweep the dirt road. I guess it hadn't been swept that day!

After that we went in and he showed me the cabin. I really liked it and it was a cute cabin. We went out on the porch and he showed me where I would be sleeping. We had chores we had to do the next morning. We swept the cabin and the porch. We made the beds and probably swept the road again.

Bob was really excited about showing me Mt. Murdoch, which was named by his great grandfather, David Lennox. He checked and that particular hill had never been named, so he claimed it and named it. It is on the records as Mt. Murdoch. We climbed up and it was a beautiful day. We got to the top and it was a beautiful view.

Bob told me many stories. One thing they all got a kick out of is that they had a lot of pack rats. They would come in the night and take a shoe and usually leave something that they had taken previously. I was always afraid they would take my shoes. One of the funniest stories is about Aunt Jen. The procedure in the summer time was for all the kids to go to the cabin for the summer to give their mother a rest from the nine children. Apparently, one day they were all pretty naughty. She threatened them and told them that if they didn't straighten up they would have to go back to Salt Lake and they would have to walk. She didn't have a car up there. They didn't believe her and she gathered them all together and told them to stick close. She *walked* them all the way back home to F Street in Salt Lake!

Bob liked to sit on the porch steps and shoot the prairie dogs when they stuck their heads up. He loved to shoot at the rats too. He became a pretty good shot.

Aunt Jen went to the outhouse one day and when she sat down, she got the ire of a porcupine. William, put her over the seat of the car and drove her to Salt Lake to get the quills removed.

July 1916. Jack, Grandfather William, Jeannette, Lennox, Bill, Beth, and Mary

VISIT TO THE MURDOCH CABIN IN 1994

A Murdoch reunion was held in June of 1994. We requested that the owner of the Murdoch Cabin in Lamb's Canyon let us visit. Bill Burrell was kind enough to oblige and we were treated to seeing the inside of the cabin we had all heard stories about. It is as if the Murdochs had just walked out the door. The beds were still lining the screen-covered porch where all the children slept and the cupboard or hutch still held many of the original dishes and plates the Murdochs used. The old wood cooking stove was still there. The huge table was in the main room with enough leaves ready to put in to make it fill up the room if needed. David Lennox brought the table from Scotland. Bill had a ledger on the table with original land documents ready for us to see. What a great experience for us all to see the legendary Murdoch cabin. We didn't bring any brooms to sweep the road as Aunt Jen would have liked, but that thought crossed all our minds.

LEFT: *Original wood cooking stove* MIDDLE: *Janet Hull on one of the beds*
RIGHT: *Table from Scotland*

*Picture taken at Bonnie's wedding on September 19, 1950 in Salt Lake City, Utah. Back: Lennox, Jack, Beth, Bill, Bob. Front: Jeannette, Bonnie, Jean, and Mary. (*Editor's Note*: Because it was difficult in some instances to get a picture of each sibling, the editor used this picture for the individual pictures in the chapter heads.)*

Chapter 6

David Lennox Murdoch and Ora Maurine Clark

Prepared by William R. Murdoch

David Lennox Murdoch was born June 29, 1901 in Salt Lake City, Utah. He was the first child of nine born to his parents, William and Jeannette Cousins Smith Murdoch. He married Ora Clark June 3, 1930 in the Salt Lake LDS Temple. They had three children: William Richard, Michael Clark, and Janet Lennox.

In his youth David soon lost his given name and took on his middle name, Lennox or Lennie. He attended Salt Lake City grade schools, graduating from East High, then attending and graduating from the University of Utah. He was head cheerleader and a member of the Sigma Kai Fraternity.

Lennox grew up working in his father's store, Murdoch Grocery, next door to the family's stately home on 'F' Street in

The Avenues north of the city. He told us stories of delivering groceries all the way to Sugarhouse, several miles south of the city. Summer was easy, but winter became an adventure.

His horse-drawn wagon hauled the goods, but to keep from freezing in winter, he ran beside the faithful horse the entire distance.

Dangerous thrill rides in the winter included a toboggan trip from the top of The Avenues all the way down to South Temple Street. Little traffic was an advantage in this exciting ride.

Dad's grandfather, David Lennox Murdoch, built a log cabin in Lamb's Canyon east of the City. Dad, with all his eight siblings, his mother, and on occasion Aunts Mary Murdoch, and Jen Murdoch Thompson spent the summers there. Their transportation was one of the first horseless carriages. His father delivered the family to the cabin, and returned back to his grocery business, (and later added a job as Finance Commissioner of Salt Lake City). He visited the cabin weekly during the summer with supplies for the family.

The spartan cabin still stands and is used today. Sold many years ago, it has traded hands several times. There is no plumbing, only an outhouse, and a one block walk to the spring for water. There is no electricity, only a wood stove for heating and cooking.

A personal note: Dad with my mother's father, Tom Clark, and I spent several great deer hunts on this beautiful mountain and canyon. The highest point in the area is named Murdoch Mountain. We always got our buck deer. On one hunt during the war years, 1941-1945, we had only six rounds of ammunition. Ammunition was unavailable due to the war. Venison was vital as a food supply to our family. It was critical our shot be lethal. On one trip, Grandpa Tom, an old cowboy and excellent shot, got two big buck deer with one shot - unbelievable, but true!

Lennox had a great sense of humor and loved to tell stories of his life. He was physically strong, though only 5' 4" tall and slightly built. One of his favorite winter outings was to travel with friends on snowshoes from the mouth of Lamb's Canyon to the family cabin, blazing the trail for others to follow. Dad was a very kind and gentle man and rarely, if ever, lost his temper.

LEFT: *Sigma Chi Party At University Of Utah*
RIGHT: *Graduation From U. Of U.*

Lennox graduation from U. of U. LEFT TO RIGHT: *Bill, Jack, Lennox, Robert in front, William and David Lennox Murdoch*

My father loved to fish and took me and my brother, Mick, on several trips from Silver Lake in Brighton, where he taught us to fly fish; to a trip to Navaho Lake near Cedar City where he set up KSUB Radio as part of the KSL chain; to Idaho's Wood River, and Yellowstone Park. My most memorable trip occurred on my return from Korea and discharge from two years in the Army. Dad took me on a horse-pack trip into the Wind River Mountains of Wyoming, our second adventure into this beautiful and wild place. We were 20+ miles from any other humans, when our guide left us for a week's stay on Blind Lake. We caught and then roped our large cache of Rainbow Trout between two tall pines, pitched our tent and retired early. About 2 A.M. a frightening sound filled the camp. Cans were being thrown about from the garbage pit, accompanied by loud grunts and howling noises; then just a few inches from my head, the soft, but heavy padding of dinner-plate sized feet walked by accompanied by a slobbering, snorting sound. With only a thin canvas between us and a hungry wild bear, we braced for the worst. I only had for protection, prayer, and a semi-automatic Ruger 22 pistol with a nine shot clip. My only thought was to get the gun in the giant carnivore's mouth and keep pulling the trigger. Suddenly lightning flashed and a horrendous thunder burst sent our visitor running into adjoining tents set up by the guide. We quietly discussed our situation and lay awake until daybreak. At about 6 A.M., I heard a zipping sound and horrified saw a large black nose at the base of our tent zipper, slowly raising the zipper until a huge shaggy head appeared. Dad grabbed his boot and screamed as he threw the "missile" striking the startled intruder on the nose. Its head flew up to fully open the tent door, and instead of charging into the tent, fell backward. Our tent had no floor, so I rolled up the side and emptied my pistol into the air screaming my lungs out. Dad remained surprisingly calm and threw rocks at the fleeing beast. We found he had eaten all of our fish; I guess we were next. The rest of our trip, especially at night, was white knuckle, but raising the fish we caught higher on our rope gave us a nice catch to take home. This story was later printed in *Outdoor Life* magazine.

My parents bought eight acres in Cottonwood in 1939, and we left city life on Harvard Avenue. This new adventure was to a true farm. Cottonwood Creek flowed through the property, planted in Jonathan and other apples, Bing Cherries, Bartlett Pears, Italian Plums, grapes, berries of all kinds, and over an acre for vegetable garden.

A full block long lane was lined with 60 giant spreading poplar trees - 60 feet tall.

Dad bought a Guernsey cow, chickens, white turkeys, wild pheasants, sheep, pigs, rabbits and two horses with one Shetland pony boarded yearly in the summer from Auerbachs, the department store owner.

Our nearest neighbor, Pete and Rosa Reva, loaned Dad their giant work horse to plow our garden each spring. I led it down the rows, Dad held the plow and followed. My biggest fear was to be stepped on and squashed like a bug. Mick and I sold our sweet corn and produce every summer out on 6200 South. More horses than cars passed by.

To pay taxes and the home loan, Dad sold our apples and pears to a local distributor, Mike Kesimakis. Grandpa Tom, with Grandma, lived in our basement. Dad, Mom, Mick and I picked the fruit from several acres, wiped, ring-faced, and hauled the hundreds of bushels to Mike Kesimakis in Dad's '39 Dodge car. I got to drive without a license.

Father began work at KSL Radio in 1930. KSL radio was a fledgling station just getting started. Among other tasks, he read the *Deseret News* comic section every Sunday morning, putting himself in the place of the cartoon characters. Listeners of all ages were mesmerized as they followed along in their paper spread out on the floor. His character name was Uncle Tom, and he became the number one personality at KSL. His efforts moved him ahead quickly and he climbed the job ladder.

LEFT: *Lennox reading the comics over KSL radio.*
RIGHT: *New manager for KSL TV*

In the early years of the broadcasting of the Mormon Tabernacle Choir over KSL, the station only had one microphone. One of Dad's jobs was to run across the street from the station to the tabernacle with the microphone, then back again, after their broadcast.

War years were tough on gasoline usage. It was 20 miles round trip to KSL and car pools with neighbors were a necessity. Gas, meat, cream, and butter required food stamps. We grew and hunted meat; pheasants, quail, and morning doves were plentiful on our eight acres. Obtaining venison during hunting season was vital. Most of the rest we grew or received from our domesticated animals. Life was good!

As mentioned, Dad joined KSL Radio in 1930, and at retirement, January 1969, he was Vice President and Assistant to the President of Bonneville International. He was the first General Manager of KSL-TV, named in 1950, and pioneered Salt Lake television. He was the former President of the Utah Broadcasters' Association. He started FM at KSL, pioneered and managed KSUB in Cedar City and KID in Idaho Falls. He was very active in local civic affairs, and one of the founders of the Youth Tobacco Advisory Council. He served as Utah Director of Radio Free Europe, participating in its early development. He was Executive Director of The National Translators' Association.

Always active in the L.D.S. Church, he served two missions for the church - one to Holland from 1926 to 1929, and one with his wife, Ora, as directors of the Oakland Temple Visitor's Center, from 1971 to 1972. He was bishop of the Cottonwood Ward, and on the High Council in the Cottonwood Stake. Our parents always set an example of service. They were always helping others in need. They never spoke about it, but as we grew older we learned by observation of their many good deeds.

A much loved and respected man, he died from a massive stroke at age 77 on November 20, 1978. He is buried with his wife, Ora, in Wasatch Lawn Memorial Park, Salt Lake City, Utah

Ora Maurine Clark Murdoch

In her own words as told to Mick and Connie Murdoch

My name is Ora Maurine Clark Murdoch. I was born July 19, 1909 in Ephraim, Utah. My parents are Anna Marinda Adina Nielsen and Thomas Jefferson Clark. My mother was raised in Ephraim, and my father in the Provo/Springville area. I was born in Grandpa Nielsen's parlor. Niels Peter Nielsen is my grandfather. He helped found Ephraim. He helped quarry the stone for the Manti Temple and chained the road from Ephraim to Manti. This is the same road which is in use today (1995). Grandpa Nielsen's home was a large two-story house made of his homemade bricks. He and his two sons built the home. He married Caroline Christenson. She walked across the plains at age 15.

In our family there were born five children: Ora, Aurilla, David (her twin brother who died at birth), Jay, and Mary Carol. (She was born on Christmas day.) The Clark family owned two or three homes in Provo around the university area. They also owned a fruit orchard up Hobblecreek Canyon in the Springville area. Mother and Father lived at Hobblecreek. I can remember swinging on a swing in the yard, and carrying a forked stick to hold the fish Dad caught in the canal. These were big trout. Our fruit orchard had all kinds of fruit. I had a favorite cherry tree that I climbed in and sat in the branches. We lived in Hobblecreek until I was five years old. In my fifth year I had diphtheria. Everyone was dying with diphtheria, but that year the doctors came out with an anti-toxin vaccine. I was given a shot and it apparently saved my life.

Living at Hobblecreek was an adventure. We had a three-room log cabin farm house. There was no electricity, or indoor plumbing at that time. We had a kitchen, living room, and bedroom. I can still see myself looking down a mouse hole in the bedroom. I thought I saw a lamp in the mouse hole. What I really saw was probably the eyes of the mouse, but I was sure the mice had lamps. We had a dog named Slivers who liked to come into the house and would lay next to the door. Mother would yell at the dog to "get out of here," and he would run outside and knock me down as he went. I was knocked down many times when he would run out.

Mother had a big raspberry field. Mother picked and Grandma Clark would sell the berries in Provo. I would get so tired of Mother picking raspberries. I called myself Yaya. "Yaya's tired," I would say. I was so happy one day when Mother came upon a snake in the bushes. She threw her bucket up in the air and ran out of the patch. I was so happy. Another day I was out visiting a newborn calf we had in a small pen. There was a big blow snake just waiting to wrap itself around the new calf. "Papa, great big long, . . . great big long!" I frantically called. Papa came and killed the snake. They had a big "drag" upon which they piled the picked fruit. It was pulled around the orchard by a horse. I can remember riding on that big drag.

Even though we lived at Hobblecreek in the summer months, and lived in Provo in the winter months, it was a sad day when we had to move. Grandmother Clark was a "visionary" woman. She had a "vision" that they should move to Emery and trade all their property for property in Emery. She said the streets would be one day paved with gold. So they all went. We traded for two homes in Emery and 40 acres in one spot and 60 acres in another spot along with water shares. They made Mother trade her furniture for this old ugly furniture. Grandma Clark took everything she owned with her and didn't trade any of her furniture. She had a piano, but I could never practice on it. She would always be taking a nap. They stayed in Emery for 14 years. Grandmother got the big house with two bedrooms upstairs. My mother got the small house with only two rooms—a kitchen and a bedroom with a big porch and an outhouse. Father was a rancher and a prospector; he was the shoemaker, and veterinarian. There were only 550 people in Emery.

Father did the farming for he and his dad, because his brother Dof wouldn't do anything. Father bred mules. He had a string if ginnys and jacks. You breed a mare and a jack and produce a mule. Mules cannot reproduce. Mules were very strong and capable animals. Dad was a mule skinner. He was a great horseman. I was in Emery about 10 years.

Father got the worst of the land. He got the 40 acres that was not very good soil. Grandpa got the 60 acres which was much better. They raised mostly alfalfa, wheat, and alfalfa seed. They took their wheat to the mill in Ferron to get it ground into flour and germade mush. We lived on a lot of beans with salt pork, and lumpy dick. Lumpy dick is milk boiled on the stove and when it came to a boil, you stirred in the lumps. The lumps were made out of flour, a little salt, and stirred into a dough with cream. We took the dough and rolled it in our hands into dumplings and dropped it into the boiling milk and let it cook until the lumps tested done. Then you ate it with butter and salt and pepper. We had plenty of milk and flour. We had cows, chickens, mules, ginnys and jacks. The ginnys were tame. We could slide off the back of them and they would not kick us. We also had pigs. Mother made bread. I never had a bicycle, but I always had a horse.

As children, we had a good time. On Sunday we got together to play games and make candy and pop corn. We would play run-sheepy-run, kick the can, Anne-I-over, and hide the thimble, among others. We would make burnt sugar candy. We would burn sugar on the stove in a pie tin. It didn't taste too good, but we would eat it anyway. We would have honey candy and molasses candy we would stretch like taffy. I learned to make a one-egg cake.

Ora's One Egg Cake

1c. sugar
1c. flour
1 t. B.P. (baking powder)
1 t. salt
1 egg
1 c. milk

Make consistency of thin cake batter. This was poured onto a cookie sheet so we could make it into a jelly roll after baking. We would dump it out on a dish towel and cover it with jelly and roll up and sprinkle powered sugar on top of it.

I would make it as often as Mother would let me. We had a lot of jerky. Father would go out and kill a deer and then would jerk the whole thing.

I learned how to shoot at age 10. I got my first gun at that age. It was a single-shot .22. I learned that what I shot I had to prepare for dinner. I also had a trapping line. I was supposed to trap gophers. Because all the gophers dug holes in the alfalfa and all the irrigation water would run into their holes, I got the job of trapping the gophers. The first gopher I caught I will never forget. The poor little gopher got caught by the front legs and he was squealing and squealing. I found myself a great big rock and shut my eyes and dropped the rock on its head. Both his eyes bunged right out of its head. That was my first and last gopher. I took the traps back to Dad and threw them on the floor.

Mother would have us look for hen's nests all the time. She would pay us an egg if we could find a nest before the hen sat on it. The nests often had 12 or more eggs in them. We could use the egg to trade for candy at the store. This was our source of eggs as well as "spending money."

I could rope a calf as good as any of the men. When I was eight years old, Father bought *Last Chance*. It was a cattle ranch of 2500 acres. He bought it to have some place to run all his mules, horses, ginnys, and jacks. *Last Chance* was 30 miles southwest of Emery. *Last Chance* became the place we lived in the summer. We had a one-room log cabin with a dirt roof. Mother had biscuits on the top of the stove rising one day. There was a cloud burst and mud came in through the roof and ruined her biscuits. She cried and cried. It was a hard life on the ranch. We returned to Emery in the winter. The ranch was where I learned to rope. I also learned to milk cows. We had a cistern for our drinking water. It was a metal-lined big hole in the ground about five feet deep, and about ten feet across. Once a year I was lowered into it to clean it. I had to scrub out the mud at the bottom because it was filled by a little ditch. This was our drinking water. For the cattle we had a big round pond. There were frogs and polliwogs. The cows' pond was filled by the same little ditch that filled our cistern. The water only came about once a year because it was a run-off type thing. We used our water from the cistern all summer long. The water tasted so bad that mother would make root beer. We had corks for the bottles. I had to take these bottles into the cellar (mud hole) down a ladder so that we could keep it somewhat cool.

In Emery, we had a ½ acre garden. We raised potatoes, beans, tomatoes, carrots, peas, cucumbers, squash, wonderful crisp long icicle radishes. The white icicle radishes were the best I have ever eaten. We had no fruit. Mother had to trade her beautiful bottled fruit at Hobblecreek straight across for the fruit in Emery. It was the worst bottled fruit she had every seen. Mother cried and cried. She refused to use one quart of it. One night Mother made me go out and help her put all the fruit into a hole in the garden.

We had straw-filled ticks on our bed for a mattress. Once a year we would dump out the old straw and put in fresh straw. We also had straw under the carpet. Once each year all the straw was changed for fresh. Grandma Nielsen was a weaver and had woven our carpet for us.

I hated wash day. Mother always boiled her clothes in this copper boiler. There was steam on all the windows as well as a pot of beans for dinner. I hated wash day. We took our bath once a week. We all had to bathe in the same water. We had to haul it from the little muddy ditch. We had a wooden sled with two wooden barrels on it. We pulled it to the ditch and filled the buckets. We would bring the sled home with the old grey mare. Mother would pour a cup of milk into the barrel and stir like crazy. We could watch the mud begin to collect and settle. This was our drinking water, our cooking water, as well as our cleaning and bathing water. Whatever we needed water for, it came out of these little barrels which were filled from Muddy Creek. Aurilla, Mary, and I still have one share of Muddy Creek water. Mr. Christensen rents our water in Emery and sends us a check for $3.50 for each share he uses.

I started in the first grade when I was five when we first got to Emery. We had a school that went first through eighth. The school teachers were usually young girls from out of town. There was a room for each grade. I think it was a two-story brick building. I was a fiend for school. I loved it. I did very well, so I loved it. One year they had had an epidemic of scarlet fever or something. One boy and I were the only two that got promoted that year because the other children had been sick and could not go to school. We had paper and pencils (not slate boards). I loved art and was always involved with crayons and colored chalk. I took the lead in all the school plays. These were three-act plays, and Christmas plays.

The church was just across the street from where we lived. We had a big pot-bellied stove in the middle of the building to heat it. They would get it so hot that it would turn red in color. It is a wonder it did not burn us all to death. If we sat too close to the stove during church, our poor little faces would really get cooked. There was a bell on the top of the church steeple and when something happened they would ring the bell on the steeple. The church was our social center. There was a dance once a week, and my Uncle Earl, from Ferron, brought his movie equipment over and showed a movie once a week. We never had enough money to go to the movie, so we would lay in the ditch and try to see the movie from under the door. Across the street from the church, in the other direction, lived Will Petty who made all the caskets for those that died. He made them out of pine and his wife lined them with this white brocade stuff. (I hated that.) When Will was out on the lawn with his saw, we knew that someone had died the night before. I worried about the fact that we had no white sheets to wrap anyone in. We were too poor to have new white sheets.

I went to church every week. Mother served in the Primary. Dad never went to church. He was dead set against all the sanctimonious Mormons. One man in the bishopric, Will Peacock, had a son that he had caught smoking so he made his son walk home in front of the horse and he whipped him with the buggy whip all the way home. Will Petty, who built the coffins, beat his children unmercifully. Dad said, "If he does that one more time I will go over and beat the hell out of him." He never had to do it. Dad never laid a hand on any of us. Dad would gather up the rejects around town and give them work to do in the barn and a meal to eat. We always had a strange pair of feet under our table almost for every meal. Dad was a true Christian. Jack Anderson's boy from Provo was an illegitimate child who was always made fun of in school. He really didn't have a home life. So Dad took him in and brought him to Emery. For ever after, he lived with us. Dad always gave Jack the best horse and the best saddle, and Mother would get so mad because Jack didn't know how to ride that well, and Dad always looked so straight and tall in the saddle.

At Christmas time, I always worried so much about how Santa Claus was going to get into our house because we had no fireplace. We always went out into the foothills to cut our Christmas tree. We had runners on the wagon instead of wheels. There was no electricity so we had snap-on candle holders. We could only light the tree when we got it all decorated with pop corn and cranberries and paper chains. We did have tinsel. We would light the candles and then stand back and look at the light for one glorious moment. Then Papa would blow out all the candles so we did not set fire to anything. Christmas Eve was the time we lit the candles on the tree. We would hang our stockings behind the front door on string. We tried to find the biggest sock we could. We would send off for things from the Sears Roebuck catalog - a doll, a game or a paint book, and box of crayons. We would hide the boxes when they came until Christmas. We would get one orange in our stocking. That was the only time we would get an orange. We also received a little sack of hard candy and a little sack of nuts in our stocking.

When I was eleven years old, Mother would buy food coloring from the Watkins man. She would hide it so that we could not find it and use it in our lemonade which was made with citric acid. We never saw a lemon. The school had had an outing and we had gone into the mountains for this all-day outing. One of the boys had gotten me a horse and we went with the other children on this outing. When we got back home, Mother just screamed when she saw me. My face was bright red from being out in the sun all day. She sent me into her bedroom to get the face cream that she made out of glycerin, rose water, and flax seed. I went into the room in the dark, as I usually did, reached up on the shelf and got what I thought was the face cream. Instead, I had the red food coloring. I dabbed and smeared it all over my face. Now I was bright red from the sun as well as bright red from the food coloring. The worst part of it all was, I had to let it wear off. It could not be washed off. It took two or three weeks to wear off.

The year I was 13 years old I worked in a restaurant for a lady named Ora Beal. Her husband was Parley Beal. He had the only service station in town. Along with the restaurant and service station, they had all the ice cream, candy, gum, and pop corn. The candy came down from Price (60 miles) twice a week. We were right at the end of the Salina Canyon and everybody coming down would stop at her restaurant. Mrs. Beal had a little daughter, Esther, eight years old. Esther was my helper, and I was Ora Beal's helper. We would serve half a spring-fried chicken with potatoes, a hot biscuit, and slice of tomato for 50 cents. Everybody that came ordered that particular plate. In order to get the chickens we first had to raise them. It took six weeks to get a spring fryer from a baby chick. We would then have to catch the chickens, cut their head off, pull their feathers off, clean them, and cut them up for frying. They were so tender. I had dysentery that summer, and I didn't feel very good.

Mrs. Beal taught me what I was supposed to do, then she got word that her mother was very sick in Price and she was needed to go and stay with her for a week. At the same time Parley decided to go to Salina, so that left me with the restaurant, the ice cream, candy, etc., and pumping of gas. We never knew how many people were coming through the canyon. My mother just lived one block away, but she never came over to the restaurant to see how I was doing. We had no refrigerators and could do very little ahead of time. I was kept very busy keeping the fire going, making the biscuits, catching the chickens, killing them, picking them, cleaning them, frying them, and serving them. We also had the Post Office. We dealt in cash money because all these people were going on to Emery and Price. We were open early until late. I would get so tired.

After 8th grade, in order to go to school, I went to Ephraim to live with my grandmother and my aunt to work for my board and room. Grandma was a weaver of rugs and carpeting. I would help her in the loom room by winding the shuttle, and tying the ends of the rugs. I would take the finished rugs to the post office for mailing. Aunt Lill (mother's oldest sister) had been divorced and came home to live with her mother. She had the only hem-stitching machine in several counties. This was a time when they began using lots of ruffles. Her machine had two presser feet, two needles, two piercers, and two bobbins. The ruffle was finished with a good pique edge. All of this had to be measured. I measured all the finished hem stitching, wrote all of the C.O.Ds, did all the mailing, kept the books, and went to school. I was a straight A student, and took the lead in all the high school plays. I was also the nurse when we had to inoculate all the school children against diphtheria. The children were charged ten cents per shot. The principal gave the shots and I was the nurse that got them ready by rolling up their sleeves, and rubbing their arms with alcohol. I went to grades 9 through 12 in Ephraim.

The depression came and I could not go to the university because I had to get some money real quick so I went to Henniger's Business College. Father raked up enough money to pay the tuition. Dad sold *Last Chance* for $2,000. The fellow gave him $200 and that is all he ever gave him. Dad turned all his animals loose onto the desert. I felt I had to get my parents out of Emery somehow. For about six months I worked for the

Bureau of Mines located on the University of Utah campus. After that, I went to the Federal Reserve Bank. The most I ever made at the bank was $110 a month. I was living at Teeny Nana's house on 70 F Street and First Avenue for $35.00 a month. I lived there while going to Hennigers. I don't know where Dad ever found the money to send me. I had to find them a place to live. On McClelland Avenue I found a furnished house for $28.00 a month. It even had a piano. So I rented that for the folks and for me to live in. They had an old car that they came to Salt Lake in from Emery. They could not afford to feed their animals and I wanted them out of Emery. So they came. There was little for Dad to do up here, but I kept working to support the whole family which still included my brother and sisters. There were really not many jobs.

In the meantime, I had met Lennox when I was boarding with Teeny Nana (Mrs. Anderson) on 70 F Street. Lennox's father had the Murdoch Grocery. I met Lennox in the grocery store. Everyone that lived up there shopped at Murdoch Grocery. We all belonged to the 20th Ward. I met all the guys in the 20th Ward. I had a date every day of the week. There were not enough days in the week to keep up with all the fellows that wanted to date me. Lennox finally convinced me that he was the one for me so I didn't go with any of the other fellows. He "pinned" me with his Sigma Chi pin. He was eight years older than I was. It was shortly after I got my family up here that we became engaged. So now I wanted to get married, but if I got married, there is no money for the family because once I got married, I would lose my job inasmuch as married women were not allowed to work because there were so many men needing work to provide for their families. Lennox and I had dated about two years.

Prior to meeting me, Lennox had filled a mission to Holland. He was about 25 years old and finally asked the bishop, Clarence Neslon, to call him on a mission. He had wanted to go to Scotland where his ancestors were from, but the call came to Holland. Prior to leaving, one day Lennox was walking down Main Street, he saw a fellow he knew had been sent home from his mission. The fellow asked Lennox where he was going, and he said, "I am on my way to get my mission changed."

"Don't even try to get your mission changed," the fellow answered. "I got mine changed and when I got there I broke out in boils and now I have had to come home."

So Lennox turned around and didn't ask for a change. He went to Holland. There was no MTC in those days. No help with the language. He had an old Dutchman for a companion who would chatter away at the doors in Dutch and poor Lennox could not understand a word of anything. Lennox would sit on the dikes and pray they would break. He would become very discouraged and could see no excuse for his being in Holland.

Lennox had a companion, Orv Carstason, that was an atheist. He was a good missionary, but never had a testimony. Later in life Orv died and we went down to his funeral in Richfield. There was Orv laying in the casket in the living room in a black suit. Lennox looked at him and said, "All dressed up and nowhere to go."

My dad had a job selling used cars, but for some reason he became very ill. He would not go to a doctor. He was sure he was dying. He would beat his head against the wall he was in so much pain. He sent mother to the basement to get some of the rock he had brought with him, to make tea out of it. Mother was sure he would kill himself. He began making mineral water from the rock. It started to make him feel better. Dad was a salesman. He talked to everyone about the minerals and the effect it had on him. People began to ask for it, and he began making it out of the rock he had brought. He only had brought up a few sacks of ore. He sold it for 50 cents a pint. Eventually, he got up to $8.00 a gallon, but that was in the 1970s. Dad staked the claim in 1927. Dad was beginning to be able to provide for the family. He traded for a lot of things as well. (The china hutch Connie & Mick have was traded for.)

I had met Lennox after he came home from his mission, and he had graduated from the "U" by the time we decided to get married. There did not seem to be any money for a wedding. But Aunt Jen and Aunt Mary were so happy to be getting Lennox married off that they said we could have our wedding at their big house on "G" Street. Because we got married in the Salt Lake Temple, Dad and Mother could not go. We got married on June 3, 1930. I wore a pale pink lace dress that day. There was not a white one to be found in Salt Lake. I had four bridesmaids in organdy pastel colors with hats. The two flower girls were Aunt Mayme's daughters. Lennox's brother Jack was the best man. Lennox was the last one of the Sigma Chi group to be married. He was 28 years old.

I had to quit my job because I got married. (By then I was doing two jobs at the bank . . . mine and my girl friend's work. She was a girl from Scotland. She was very slow. I would hurry real fast to do my work, and then go over and help her do her job.) When I quit, they could not find another girl to do all the work I was doing. They had to hire two girls to take my place, but I had to go. That is the way it was during the depression. Both wife and husband could not work. Lennox, of course, had his job at the grocery store. However, he went to see Earl J. Glade who had just opened the first radio station in Salt Lake and applied for a job as an announcer. He felt that a man must be making at least $150 per month before he could afford to get married.

We bought a new car, a Model A Ford Coup, for $350 brand new. We went to Bryce, Zions, and Grand Canyons for our honeymoon. We lived in the Piccadilly Apts. on 5th East just off South Temple and paid $50.00 a month. Then we moved over to the Stratford Apts. on 4th East off of South Temple and we paid $50.00 for that one. Aunt Jen wanted us to have an oriental rug. She paid the first $200 on our rug. It is a domestic (made in the U.S.), Oriental rug. (It is now in the library.) We bought our bedroom suite for $150, and we bought a couch, chair, and a kitchen table and we were in business.

We bought our house on Harvard Avenue for $4,200 which included a new roof. We had two peach trees in our back yard. Bill, who was two that first year, helped me peel all the peaches we harvested. We put up 70 quarts.

We had a hardwood toilet seat which needed to be varnished. Lennox painted it one day and warned me about not going to sit on it until it was dry. Off he went to work. I forgot about that warning of course, and went in and sat down, and then remembered about what he had said. I was stuck to the seat. Finally I got unstuck and had a ring of varnish on my bottom. I didn't worry about getting it off until later. Lennox was so mad when he got home and he had to revarnish the seat. I didn't try to clean the varnish off and thought no one will ever know. However, just a few days later, I picked Bill up and fell forward on the kitchen floor and threw my back out. I had the car that day and so my mother and I decided to go to see Aurilla, who was taking care of an apartment. When we got there, I turned to get Bill out of the backseat and my back seized up on me and I could not move. I could not get out of the car or turn around. Mother called Lennox to come home and get me some help. Lennox must have borrowed a car to come out to get me. He took me to his chiropractor on Main (three doors down from South Temple across from ZCMI) Dr. Smith. I had to go up the stairs and it was very painful with each step. Finally, we got into the office and the doctor gave me a gown to put on and then I had to lie down on the table on my stomach. When the doctor looked at me, Lennox said "have you ever seen anything like that before?" "Yes," he replied, "but never in a frame." I still had the brown varnish on my bottom and I thought no one would ever see it, but there I was.

We lived on Harvard Avenue about seven years. Mick was born while we were still living on Harvard. He had a "ga ga" which was a silk stocking that was tied in several knots and which he would take to bed rubbing it on his nose to fall asleep. If he lost his "ga ga", he would wake up in the night and cry. I would have to go into his room and help him find his "ga ga".

LEFT: *Ora with Bill and Mick* RIGHT: *Ora with Janet*

We started looking for property because the boys were always playing in the street. I was sure they would be killed. We had Lennox's Uncle Wallace looking for us as well. We had purchased an acre of ground down by the St. Mark's hospital. It had a little water and one tree. But I wanted more water and trees. I was a farmer's daughter and wanted to get out of the city. Lennox was a city boy. I wanted to raise things. Uncle Wallace kept looking and one day said he had found just the place for us. It was a little more property than we had talked about, but he was

sure we could manage it. This place had been for sale so long the For Sale sign was worn out. Nothing was in bloom when we decided to purchase, so I could not see what kind of trees we had. We moved here just before the trees bloomed. When they began blooming, I was out of my mind with joy. Everything was so beautiful, and we had every kind of tree imaginable. Mick was four and Bill was eight when we came to 6200 South.

The first harvest was really something. Lennox and I hauled so many pears and apples into Mike Kisamakis to sell at his market. One year Aurilla and I picked 80 bushels of plums. Another year my dad and I picked 1,000 bushels of apples and sold them to the government in new baskets for $1.00 a bushel. We were happy to get that because we had so many apples. We bought an apple press and made apple cider. Life on 6200 revolved around pruning and harvesting as well as milking cows and raising chickens.

I had a cute little chicken coop out by the headgate. I wanted to raise chickens like we had in Emery so we could have spring fryers. Pete Reva said, "I will give you some eggs and a setting hen." We called setting hens "scrooks". She sat and sat, but nothing happened. I thought, "I cannot have the hen not have any babies. I will go buy that hen some baby chicks." I went to the Murray Feed and Grain store and bought 13 chicks for the old hen. When I came home, the hen had hatched every one of the eggs. We now had 26 chicks. I knew the hen could not cover all those chicks, so Lennox built an incubator so that we could put half of them inside.

One day Bill asked me "How do you get a wife? Do I just go down to the temple and pick one out? If that is the case, I am going to pick out the prettiest one down there."

After we moved our family out to 6200 South, we needed a little barn. My father and Lennox went back to Lennox's father's place on F Street to dismantle the chicken coop. They numbered all the boards and tore it down a board at a time, brought it out to 6200 South and built it again. That is the shed that Allan and Janet have in their backyard, and which served as our barn as the children were growing up.

This incomplete history was shared with Mick and Connie as we ate dinner and visited with Ora in the last year or so before the development of the property began in 2000.

It is now 2006. Ora passed away October 4, 2003. I, Janet Lennox Murdoch, Ora and Lennox Murdoch's last child and only daughter, will try and finish some of the things my mother has left out of her life history. I am so grateful to Mick, by brother and his wife Connie, for getting mother to write her life history to this point.

Mother was the kind of person who could do anything and loved doing everything. She got her real estate license when I was in high school. She loved working with people and enjoyed that part of her life. She took art lessons and became quite an artist. When they first came to the Cottonwoods, she raised canaries and dachshund puppies. I remember selling the puppies. She loved all kinds of animals and had about every animal allowed on the property. My favorite was the talking pig which she nursed back to health from a runt. The pig was taken away from the mother and Ora feed it on a bottle and it would sleep with the old family dog. People would come from all over to hear the "talking pig,"

Ora's 94th birthday with 10 of her grandchildren

When you picked it up, it would squeak and would sound like it was saying "put me down, put me down!"

She always had time to serve. One of the many organizations that Ora was involved with was the American Cancer Society. She loved to volunteer. When Lennox passed away, she worked for many years at the Shalamar Wedding Chapel, which was owned by one of her dear friends, Helen Knudsen. She loved helping the brides, being the host, working in the kitchen, answering the phones, and even getting some of her granddaughters involved as serving girls. This helped fill up many lonely hours now that Lennox was gone.

In the Church, some of her assignments included, serving as a Ward Relief Society President and for several years she traveled throughout the Church as a member of the Young Women General Board. She was a temple worker in the Salt Lake and Jordan River Temples. She and Lennox were called as the directors of the Visitor Center in Oakland, California. But what she enjoyed more than anything was teaching little children. When I was the Primary President, I asked her to be "Grandma Friendly." She loved coming into Primary once a month and telling a story out of the Children's Friend. All of the children in the ward loved her and from then on she referred to herself as "Grandma Friendly" long after she was released from that calling.

In 1982 she bought a piano and at 73, she started taking piano lessons every week. She was realizing her childhood dream. She started putting some of her dreams and experiences and philosophies into writing poems and short stories. One of her stories was published in May of 1988 in the Children's Friend. It was based on a true story about an incident in her father's life, Thomas Jefferson Clark. It was titled, "High Bid 62 Cents."

She loved having *Molley Woppett* parties for her grandchildren and they loved going to them. What treasured memories they have because she took time to show her love to them in that way. Only her grandchildren can explain what a *Molley Woppett* party was like!

Ora loved life, everyone loved her. She lived life to the fullest and touched many hearts along the way.

POEMS OF ORA CLARK MURDOCH

Beauty Unveiled

As I sat in my own private castle
And gazed at the world at my feet,
Everything out there was Golden,
From my porch way out to the street.
A large bevy of Quail scratched onward
Cautiously searching for seeds,
Some in the new mown grass,
And some in the fallen leaves.
The arms of my GREAT TREES stretched upward,
To the sky which was clear azure blue
And all of the awesome landscape
Was draped in a glamorous hue.
Autumn had come in it's grandeur .. ..
Jack Frost, the artist, we know
Had frantically splashed his colors
On Earth's growing landscape below.
So look up downcast mortal and marvel,
Enjoy what you see as you dream,
This is not something man could make
Happen, no matter how hard he might scheme

written in 1990

I Wonder

I wonder where the years have gone?
I wonder why I sleep so long -
I wonder why the days seem cold
I wonder if I'm growing old?
I wonder why my tree's so tall
Tho I've watched it grow both Spring and Fall -
For fifty years, its claimed that space
While I've rushed on from place to place.
I wonder how I'll ever strive
To keep my wits and stay alive -
If like my tree I'm bound in place
And cannot cope with frantic race?
I wonder, yes, I truly wonder
Which part of life has been a blunder?
My memory's good, my heart is sound -
Tho I do seem closer to the ground..
I wonder if I'll always be
Old to you, and young to me?
But when I lay this mortal by
I'll be at peace - so please don't cry.

written in 1996 at age 88

WILLIAM RICHARD MURDOCH

Bill at Harvard Ave. 1935

My great, great grandfather was William Murdoch, who left Scotland after joining the Church of Jesus Christ of Latter-day Saints and settled in Heber City, Utah. I was born October 19, 1931 at the LDS Hospital in Salt Lake City, Utah. I was the first child born to David Lennox and Ora Clark Murdoch. This was the time of the dark days of the great depression and my parents struggled with the rest of America to survive this calamity. Two more children joined our family a few years later, my brother, Michael Clark and my little sister, Janet Lennox. My years of kindergarten, first and second grade were at Uintah Grade School in Salt Lake City while we lived on Harvard Avenue.

In the spring of 1939, against my best wishes, we moved to what seemed the very end of the world. My father's family thought he had lost his mind, leaving the safety and convenience of the city and moving ten miles south to the remote farming community of Cottonwood, a suburb of Holladay, Utah. We found ourselves in another world. From city life to a full-fledged farm that consisted of every domestic animal indigenous to Utah. We had chickens, turkeys, geese, sheep, pigs, horses, a wonderful Jersey cow, a dog, cats, rabbits, and more. Our eight acres was a regular Noah's Ark.

Throughout the summer months, I spent a good deal of time selling the produce on 6200 South in my little vegetable stand. Sweet corn was my specialty, and I sold hundreds of dozen over the years to the occasional cars that traveled by. Just 35 cents a dozen provided me with spending money and school supplies.

Every morning and night, old Ben Shurtleff would, with his little black and white sheep dog, drive his dairy herd of 35 cows from his barnyard up the street to a gate directly across from our drive. I vividly remember that wonderful day in August of 1945 as I learned from a neighbor who stopped by to buy corn, that World Was II had ended. My brother, Mick and I shut down our little stand and declared a holiday.

I loved to swim and spent a good deal of time from early spring to fall in either the Big Cottonwood Creek behind our house; the old Utah Lake Canal just west of our property; and my favorite spot, Windy Bill's Pond about two blocks east of our home. I always had horses to ride, beginning with Shetland ponies and moving on to larger horses. My Grandfather Clark was an expert horse whisperer and trained the animals without riding them.

Oakwood Grade School was my Alma Mater – second through sixth grades. Marbles was my game and my winning filled an entire drawer in my dresser. Following grade school, I attended Olympus Jr. High School. I played the clarinet in the marching band. It was a great thrill to perform in the Days of '47 Centennial Parade downtown, July 24, 1947. I then attended Granite High School and graduated in 1950. During high school I bought a 1931 Model A Ford. With my brother Mick as my helper, we delivered 135 Deseret Newspapers on a rural route every day. This included the heaviest winter snowfall in history in Salt Lake City 1948 and 1949.

I worked three months at the Grand Canyon Lodge after graduation from high school. I worked at the North Rim as a dishwasher and, finally, as pantry chef. This was a great experience. The $90.00 per month salary covered some of my expenses when I returned home and entered the University of Utah. In addition to attending college, I worked part-time at KSL-TV. This was one of the nation's first television stations. My career began in September of 1950 and continued for two years.

I was called to serve an LDS Mission to the New England States and to leave early in 1951. The Korean War was heating up and all male mission calls in Utah were cancelled. We were asked to either enlist in the regular army or join the National Guard. Since I had begun my education at the University of Utah, I elected to join the National Guard.

In the fall of 1952, I met Arthel Wilkins from Rupert, Idaho... love at first sight. She had attended Brigham Young University for three years and had enrolled at the LDS Business College to go to school and work. She had a part-time job in the promotion department at KSL-TV.

I traveled to Rupert in my father's car in December to ask parental permission and give Arthel an engagement ring. Amazingly, everyone said, "Yes", and I broke the news. My National Guard status had been revoked and I would be leaving for Ford Ord, California for basic training on January 25, 1953.

My unit was "H" Company 1st Infantry Regiment, a heavy weapons company. My Corporal rank made me a squad leader - ten men per squad. Basic Training was hell... penetratingly cold Monterey Bay weather in the winter made our outdoor excursions very uncomfortable. We lived outdoors on field trips day and night.

Several of us were asked to go to Officer's Candidate School. It meant adding another year to my two-year hitch, not something I would even consider. I was sent to clerk's school and then the Adjutant General Corps School. Graduation qualified me a Personnel Management Specialist MOS.

The next stop found me home again and on June 11, 1953, Arthel and I were married in the Salt Lake Temple by President J. Reuben Clark.

I had one more military school to Fort Benjamin Harrison, Indiana and then an assignment to Camp Chaffee, Arkansas as Personnel Sergeant. Arthel and I bought a used 1948 Studebaker and with all of our possessions traveled to Fort Smith, Arkansas. This lasted only until January of 1954, and I was the re-assigned to Pusan, Korea, a war zone and no wives were allowed.

After twenty eight days crammed into the E. T. Collins war ship with 5,000 soldiers aboard we arrived in Sasebo, Japan. Then we traveled on an LST Ship to Pusan, Korea.

This was a difficult assignment as I became the officer in charge of admissions at the Swedish Red Cross Hospital. This was a devastated city with thousands of starving and wounded refugees from the north and central Korea. My first impression of Korea was shock. I had never seen such destruction, nor witnessed the odors. They told us you would smell Korea before you saw it. This was not an exaggeration. With a war-torn landscape, a large ship with only the bow out of the water, and everything seemingly on fire, mixed with tens of thousands of destitute refugees, what else could you expect?

I mostly remember the untold numbers of children, starving and hurt physically with no parents or anyone to help them, sleeping under boxes or bombed out vehicles. During the exodus from North Korea, entire families were separated, many killed and wounded, with no way to get together again. Twenty nine million people in Korea in 1950, and following the invasion from the north only nine million remained above the 38th Parallel. The rest fled south, most trying to get to Pusan, the furthest spot away.

I returned home at the military completion of two years just two days before Christmas 1954. Arthel had found an apartment and we began another life together.

I worked at KSL TV again and finished school at the University of Utah with a B.S. Degree, May 1957. This was a very eventful year. We built our first house on one-half acre of my parent's eight-acre farm. Then, our first child was born, May 13, a daughter who we named Deborah.

In the following years Alison arrived February 4, 1960; followed by Rosemary on October 11, 1968, and William Matthew on January 10, 1970. All are happily married in the temple. Their spouses are Drew L. Winegar, Brian S. King, Jeffrey G. Thomas, and Laura Rose Verbecky. They have added sixteen new members to our family having had four children each - nine boys and seven girls. Andrew Winegar, our oldest grandson, was married last year and he and Pam had our first great grandson, Nolan Andrew.

My church activity has consisted of teaching Priesthood classes, President of MIA and Elder's Quorum. I was called as bishop of the Cottonwood Fifth Ward in December of 1968 and was released in December 1973. I had served as Bishop's Counselor and on two High Councils.

I had the opportunity to work in every broadcast phase over my forty one years at KSL, retiring as Executive Vice-President, General Manager of KSL-TV and Radio in October 1994. I experienced close association with CBS as I served on the CBS Affiliates Board as Chairman of several committees over seven years.

Arthel and I traveled throughout the world as I conducted KSL client relation's trips yearly and other business trips. Everything was first class, as trips I set up a year in advance took us to every corner of the world, Hawaii, Monte Carlo, France, England, Scotland, Italy, Switzerland, Germany, Norway, Denmark, Spain, Portugal, Austria, Hungary, Netherlands, Egypt, Israel, Turkey, India, New Zealand, Quebec, Japan, Hong Kong, China, Thailand. With CBS Board Assignments, Arthel and I had the opportunity to attend two winter Olympic games. One to Albertville, France and one to Lillehammer, Norway.

Following retirement, I worked in the Jordan River Temple as a baptismal supervisor for three years. I also worked at the Blind Center as a service worker, reading radio news for four years.

Much time is spent at the Hearthstone, our cabin, just 30 miles east of our home in Summit County.

It was remodeled since its first construction in 1973. It sits high on a pine and aspen hill on ten acres of heaven. Moose, deer, elk and many other animals and birds abound.

I bought at eighteen-foot Bass Boat and fish Strawberry Reservoir. Secret spots have provided great fishing over the past years.

I look forward to many more experiences with our family.

My two siblings and I subdivided our seven-acre lot in Cottonwood in 2000. Seven lots were sold and we named the place Murdoch Woods.

Arthel Wilkins Murdoch

My history with the Murdoch family began in 1952 when I accepted a position at KSL Television. I had left work at the end of the working day and was waiting for a bus to take me to my Sixth Avenue apartment. Mr. Murdoch was waiting for a bus also. He began talking to me about all kinds of things and, then, our buses came and we left.

A few days later, I received a call from Mr. Murdoch's son, Bill. He asked me to go on a date with him and this is how our Murdoch history evolved.

I was raised in Rupert, Idaho, the seventh child of eight born to Arland B. and Sarah Amelia Reading Wilkins. No record was kept on my weight or length. It was reported that I had black hair and none of my siblings liked the name that my mother and father had chosen for me. Had I been able to talk, I would have agreed with them. I was named Arthel and it has truly been a problem all my life.

I attended a country school. It was a wonderful school with two classes in each room. My mother always made five dresses for me at the beginning of the school year. There was always one for Easter and the 4th of July. In grade school, we learned how to tap dance and twirl a baton which was made from a broom handle with a large ball on the end, all sprayed in silver.

We had wonderful Valentine boxes. The teacher decorated it and we brought Valentines for everyone in the class. We bought them at the M. H. King five-and-dime store. They were two for a nickel or three for a dime. The twenty five cent ones were fantastic. It was the time that cards had moving parts and beautiful red tissue paper.

On Fridays, we went to the band room and had a scripture reading, pledged allegiance to the flag, sang *My Country 'tis of Thee* and had a program. I learned to play the piano and the clarinet.

We received an attendance award if we didn't miss school. I remember the award I received that I loved so much. It was a copy of the picture *The Gleaners* by the artist Millet.

I remember the Amelia Earhart story. It was in 1937 and everyone was worried about what happened to her. We had a Philco radio and I liked to come home from school and sit up on our big round table in the corner and listen to radio programs like *Jack Armstrong, the All American Boy*.

It was on this radio that we learned about the attack on Pearl Harbor. It was horrible news. So many boys in the country had to go to war. My sister's boyfriend was killed and my brother was drafted. This meant a lot of work for me as my dad had no help on our farms. The prisoner of war camp was set up in Paul, a few miles from our home. We were so grateful for this because help was needed to maintain and harvest crops.

I graduated from the eighth grade with about the same children that I started with—there were thirteen of us. We then went to Rupert High School. I always liked school. I played the clarinet in the orchestra. One summer, I played with a band that entertained in the town bandstand on Saturday night. The town was set up like an old European Village with the bandstand where people could come and listen to the music.

I had many friends in high school. We graduated and all went to different colleges. Three went on to become nuns.

Dad and I went to three universities in one day, Utah State University, University of Utah, and Brigham Young University. He was great to take me. We decided on BYU because I would not need to pay out of state tuition. I had a composite major in Foods and Nutrition, Clothing and Textiles, and Child Growth and Development. I really liked bacteriology, zoology, textiles, clothing, and foods.

After my junior year, I decided to work for awhile and went to the LDS Business College. It was a big mistake in a way and then, in another, the best decision of my life. I was sent to KSL to interview for a job in the promotion department. I was hired on a part-time basis while I was going to school. This is where I met Mr. Murdoch, Bill's father.

We were married June 11, 1953, and Bill went to Army training schools. I went with him to Camp Chaffee, Arkansas. We had bought a little navy blue Studebaker car, packed it to the brim and set off for this adventure.

We had a hard time trying to find a place to rent. We had to live on the base for two weeks. I can still hear the taps being played in the morning. We finally found a one-room place to rent. It was a little scary to stay there alone when Bill had to stay at the base.

I couldn't find a job. No one wants to hire an Army wife. We went to the park one day and Bill said that I would have to go home if I didn't find a job because we didn't have enough money. We only had $135 a month. I finally found one working for an insurance agency.

In 1954, Bill went to Korea and I lived with his parents until he came home.

We lived in an apartment on 1st Avenue. Bill graduated from the University of Utah, we had our first child, Deborah, and moved into our first home all in the same year and same month, May 1957. Alison was born February 4, 1960, Rosemary on October 11, 1968, and Matthew on January 10, 1970.

I served in most positions in the ward, Primary, MIA and Relief Society Presidencies, teaching positions.

Bill and I traveled together on many KSL assignments. We have been so fortunate to have traveled all over the world...seen so many, many things. We have met so many people through CBS assignments.

It has been wonderful to see our four children all graduate from the University of Utah. So rewarding to see them all married in the temple to wonderful individuals. Deborah is married to Drew L. Winegar, Alison is married to Brian S. King, Rosemary is married to Jeffrey G. Thomas and Matthew is married to Laura Rose Verbecky.

We have had many happy times together here, at the children's homes and at the cabin. We now have sixteen grandchildren: Andrew, Jesse, Bridger, Sarah-Ashley, Alexandra, Jocelyn, Olivia, Sophia, Ian, Isaac, Gavin, Gabriel, Will, Emma, Joshua, and Caroline.

Our first grandson, Andrew, is married to Pamela Parker and they now have a wonderful little boy, Nolan Andrew.

I pray that they will all have happy lives, be kind to each other, be active in the church and be able to attain the goals they desire.

I have enjoyed being included in the William Murdoch family.

Deborah Murdoch Winegar

My story begins on May 13, 1957 in Salt Lake City. I was the first child born to Arthel W. Murdoch and William R. Murdoch. It would have been nice if I had been born on Mother's Day but I came the day after instead. I have had subsequent birthdays on Friday the 13th and Mother's Day since then however!

I grew up in Holladay, Utah when it was known as Cottonwood. When my Dad was about eight years old, his family moved out to "the country," from Harvard Avenue in Salt Lake City. Grandpa bought about seven acres near the Cottonwood Creek and had a farm and fruit orchards. Each of his three children had a place to build a home. So that is where I grew up. We were quite secluded there. I didn't have many other children to play with but my sister and I had a fun time together just doing simple things like playing with our dolls, reading or exploring outside. We had a long lane of poplar trees lining the drive from 6200 South.

Every season was magical. The trees were golden in the autumn, in the winter the lane was an imaginary skating rink, in the springtime the buds on the trees looked like little caterpillars and in the summer the tall trees made a thick, cool green canopy for us. My grandparents had a swimming pool, which we swam in at least twice a day in the summer when we weren't climbing trees. My Grandma Murdoch was a prolific writer. She had parties for us when we were little to decorate sugar cookies and play crazy games.

Debby, Alison Murdoch (Bill and Arthel's daughters) Janthia, Kathryn and David Murdoch (Mick and Connie's children), Rosemary Murdoch (Bill and Arthel's daughter) Michelle Wilson (Alan and Janet's daughter) and Matthew Murdoch (Bill and Arthel's son.)

My other set of grandparents lived in Rupert, Idaho. We were able to see them several times a year. They had a very large farm and I loved gathering eggs and baking with my Grandma Wilkins. Grandpa tried to teach me how to milk cows once but I wasn't very good at it. There was always a litter of kittens and a friendly dog or two to play with.

My mother was and is an excellent homemaker. She always put her husband and children first. She attended Brigham Young University and LDS Business College. I remember thinking as a little girl that I wanted to be just like her. My Dad worked at KSL Television. He worked his way up the ladder while attending the University of Utah and was eventually made the Vice President and General Manager. He worked very hard to support our family. My Dad would make up fabulous stories to tell us and my Mom took us to the bookmobile, (when I was very small), and later to the library for regular visits. She read to us, with us, and listened to us read. I have fond memories of these special times. She also spent countless hours at the kitchen table helping us with homework assignments.

I had one sister, Alison, through most of my growing up years until I was in the sixth grade. At that time, another sister, Rosemary, was born and about a year and a half later my brother, Matthew, was born. We were almost like two little families. It was so much fun to help take care of my little sister and brother!

I attended Oakwood Elementary, Bonneville Jr. High, and Cottonwood High School. When I graduated from high school I attended the University of Utah. It was during this time that I became engaged to Drew L. Winegar. While he served an LDS mission in New England, I did secretarial work (which I despised), to save money for when he came home. We were married on April 14, 1978 in Salt Lake City, Utah. We lived in Holladay for a year and then moved to Midvale, Utah. Drew worked for his dad for awhile before beginning his own business, Intermountain Sweeper Company.

On August 2, 1979 our first child, Andrew, was born. He had red hair that looked like a golden glow around his head. There wasn't very much of it but we knew it was red. I shouldn't have been surprised because his dad is a red head. He was a very alert baby and learned to talk at an early age. It has always been hard to keep up with him. On March 12, 1982, our second son, Jesse, was born. Two babies couldn't have looked more different. Jesse had a full head of black hair and an olive complexion. I remember checking our hospital I. D. bracelets when nobody was looking to see if they had brought me the wrong baby. Jesse was always hungry, and to this day he is still on a three-hour feeding schedule. In 1984 we moved to South Jordan, Utah. A week later on October 9, 1984, our third son, Bridger, was born. I was again amazed to see another red head. Bridger has a great personality and people love to be around him. He helps me with technology qualms and always has a hug for his sometimes very tired mum. Then when I thought I might perish from the exhaustion of taking care of three young sons, I found out I was going to have another baby. On December 14, 1986, our fourth and last child was born, a sweet baby daughter, Sarah-Ashley. She was born a little early and stayed at the hospital for an extra week. We were so joyful to have her home with us and her three big brothers. She has been a wonderful support to me as I have returned to the University. She is also attending the University. I hope I can help her as much as she has helped me!

Alison Murdoch King

My life story begins in the woods of the Cottonwoods where my father before me grew up. It is in the shade of these magnificent trees where my story begins. Beneath their stately watch and protective boughs are where my best recollections of childhood reside. It is the place which I return to understand my roots. I am blessed to be the daughter of William Richard and Arthel Wilkins Murdoch with sisters Deborah and Rosemary, brother Matthew.

In reflecting on my family and genealogy. I realize the importance of all who have gone before me in my life for the strength I have because of their example. My life is a branch on a tree which has been nourished and sustained and shaped by those who have gone before. I have much to be grateful for; it is because of the preparation of the soil our family has well established roots, for this I am grateful our family landed on this blessed spot.

Trees have always played an important role in my life providing shelter, a land mark, shade and a back drop for magical play. My best recollections of childhood involve the lane.

" My roots are in the depth of the woods." - Galle

My earliest memory is walking down the lane of poplar trees holding my father's hand; we were going to see our new home under construction. The apricot tree on the north side of our house was in full bloom. I remember how beautiful it was. I believe it had just rained.

The front staircase of our house was not yet built. My dad helped me climb up a ladder which reached floor to ceiling in order to get to the living room. I remember how far apart the rungs seemed and how my father helped me position each foot as we went up. I remember carefully climbing until I reached the top. I was so excited finding that we were going to live in a tree house! I likewise remember my disappointment upon learning the ladder was only temporary.

I remember... Grandpa and Grandma Murdoch's lilac bush in the half circle lawn and sitting on the green round metal swinging bench. I remember playing golf on the big lawn with Grandpa Lennox that same summer. All of the cousins would gather sticks and leaves and race them down the ditch from the rock bridge behind Grandma's garage down to the lower bridge.

Every year when the cottonwood trees would release their cotton seeds and the cotton would fly, we knew that endless days of swimming were not too far behind. We played alligator and beauty shop and dipped and draped our hair. We wished there was an under ground tunnel connecting our pool to our bath tub. I remember the way the leaves shimmered against the sky as I floated on my back in the pool.

I remember the sound of my mom calling to me that it was almost time for dinner, and realizing I had been swimming all day! We knew school was approaching when moms calls to get us home, were to try on and hem the new school wardrobe she had made each of us.

I remember the sound of the gate as it shut and putting my hand through the cinder block to lock it up. I remember the foot races we had in the pea gravel down the lane and the contest to see who had the toughest feet.

I remember finding tulips that were lavender and green striped and every color in between from years of cross pollinating behind Grandma's house. The very spot my own daughter's would later call "The Secret Garden" and take me to see being able to rediscover it through their eyes. They were so surprised that I already knew it was there!

I remember gathering wild asparagus for dinner from the banks of the irrigation ditch with Debby near the paddle wheel of our Chinese neighbors. I remember digging a hole to China with Lee Ming in the orchard and having to stop to go to bed, not realizing that her older sister, May Ling, had tricked us until years later!

I remember the Sunday night "Tote Goat" rides our Uncle Mick gave us every week and the snow mobile rides with Dad in the field next door in the winter. He would tell me it was the very spot he as a little boy rode his horse, Black Beauty.

I remember a cousin sleep over on our front lawn one summer night. We lined our sleeping bags up from oldest to youngest. I remember thinking that the trees were protecting us - but they made scary shadows. I remember the predictable lack of trick-or-treaters every year, because of these same scary trees and wondering what we could do to remedy the situation. My dad would always make me feel better when he reminded me how lucky we were to have the best undiscovered spook alley in Salt Lake City!

I remember playing in the grape vines to the north of the house. Debby and I would take a pencil size piece of vine and insert a smaller twig, forming a pencil. We would use crushed honey suckle berries for ink and grape leaves for paper. We also made tiny fairy purses out of grape leaves, tearing a hole in the leaf and pulling the stem through.

I remember spending hours in Connie and Mick's pear tree. Janthia and I would climb bare foot to the top. We would lift paper, pencils, our lunch, and other supplies by a pail with a rope up to where we were. If we were lucky we might get some of Aunt Connies's raspberries in the pail.

I remember Aunt Janet's wedding reception at Grandpa and Grandma's. Laying on cushions on Grandma's screened porch out over the creek, listening to people talk and the sound of china and forks and laughter. Years later I would have my own beautiful wedding reception in my yard.

I remember waiting at the end of the lane for the school bus to come with Debby. We would hide behind the big rock pillars whenever a suspicious looking car would drive pass. I still wonder how many kidnappers those pillars fooled.

I remember my dad holding onto the back of my bike at the end of the lane by Grandma's and Grandpa's telling me how his father had taught him to ride a bike at that exact same place. My father told me he thought his dad was running along side his bike, until he looked down and saw he was riding it all by himself; then I tried it and it worked!

I have memories of smells and sounds and touch that are impossible to relate. It is these memories that made me most homesick after I got married and still do. It was at least 10 degrees cooler down the lane at any given place on the planet at any given time.

I remember many firsts down the lane, first bike ride solo (thanks Dad), first time driving a car (thanks Mom), first kiss! (None of your business!). The amazing thing about memories is that you don't think much about them until years after and then you wish you would have paid more attention to all of the details.

To fill in some of the people and places in my life during my childhood, I start with elementary school. My first school was Oakwood Elementary. I was always so proud to attend the same school that my father had. It is so interesting that three of our daughters attended Uintah Elementary, his first elementary school in the Harvard-Yale area.

I went to kindergarten through 6th grade. I loved all of my subjects, especially science. I loved relay races and four square, but my favorite things to do at recess was hop scotch! We wore dresses everyday and suzy long leg tights during the winter. In my 6th grade year, we were finally allowed to wear "culotte short skirts." These were basically shorts with a flap sewn over the front to look like a skirt. It wouldn't be until the following year we would be allowed to wear pants!

I attended Bonneville Junior High grades 7-9 and continued on to Cottonwood High. I enjoyed many classes and activities, biology, art, pep club and dance company being my favorites. I graduated in 1978.

My first job was the summer I was 15. I asked my mom and dad to drive me to various places I thought might be hiring. The previous summer I had been a candy striper volunteer at the L.D.S Hospital but this year I wanted to make some money. I made a resume listing my qualifications and told my parents I would not come home that day until I had a job!

After pounding the pavement through Fort Union and Holladay for most of the day, I decided to try Dan's Foods on Highland Drive and 7200 South, where Debby worked in the bakery. I got my first job scooping ice cream. I met a lot of friends and had a fun summer.

My next job was during high school was working part time my junior and managed my senior year and into college at a Levi brand clothing store named Al's Garage at the Cottonwood Mall. It was owned by two families in our ward, The Bouds and Bensons. It had a model A Ford on a lift overhead - very unique and an old-fashioned gas pump. I had a good experience there and loved doing the displays in the window and excelled in catching shop lifters. They started paying me $100 for every one I caught!

During my college years and in my first year at the University of Utah, I got a part time job at Nordstrom Clothing Store. I loved display and sales. I worked through college in Sales and Management and became a Pace Setter for the company. During college, I rushed for Lambda Delta Sigma, an L.D.S. sorority. I loved it and joined the Alpha Theta Chi Chapter. I made so many friends and had a great time, eventually becoming the president.

Brian King and I were friends before his mission. We had both worked at Al's Garage during high school and lived in the same ward.. However, it wasn't until after he got home that we really got to know each other. We dated that year and got engaged in January of 1982. We both graduated in June 1982 from the University of Utah. We were married in the Salt Lake Temple two days later!

Following a beautiful reception in my yard beneath the trees, we honeymooned in Coronado, California. We returned to Salt Lake City and lived in the Avenues at 226 G Street (up the street from the historical Murdoch home). Brian attended The University of Utah Law School that fall and I began working full time at Nordstrom's downtown. Never a better dressed student attended the U Law School than those years Brian was there, due to my efforts!

We lived in our apartment with its $90 monthly rent for as long as possible! Upon Brian's graduation we bought our first home in the Sugarhouse area. Our address was 1519 Westminster Ave. We had each of our four daughters in this home. Alexandra born in 1987, Jocelyn 1990, Olivia 1993 and Sophia in 1997. We call them our "Little Women." We had many wonderful experiences in our home. Although we never intended to live there as long as we did, we did so because Brian was in the bishopric, later becoming the bishop. We loved the tree-lined streets and the diversity of our neighbors, especially the elderly ones. After Brian was released as bishop, we moved to our present address 1855 Michigan Ave. It felt like home when I saw the stately sycamores and honeysuckle in the back yard.

"Bread and butter, devoid of charm in the drawing room, is ambrosia eaten under a tree." - Elizabeth Von Antrim

My life has changed since I was a little girl and I now have four of my own daughters. Alexandra at the University of Utah, Jocelyn at East High, Olivia at Clayton Middle School and Sophia at Bonneville Elementary School. Brian and I continue enjoying our busy life together. I am volunteering at the University of Utah Fine Arts Museum and in the nursery at the L.D.S. Hospital and enjoy photography and have portrait painting.

I am who I am today because of the foresight my Grandpa Lennox and Grandma Ora Murdoch had in moving where they did many years ago just as I am blessed for the wisdom of all of my ancestors to lead lives that would ultimately bless their posterity. I have much to be grateful for. Even though the tree-lined lane I walked as a child has changed with the passing of time, the old trees no longer stand as sentinels. In my mind I can return to their beckoning shade, tall shadows, lofty limbs and endless adventures. My roots have stretched further north - we now live on our

LEFT: *Alexandra, Jocelyn, Olivia, Sophia in Murdoch Lane*
RIGHT: *At the beach in Hawaii*

own tree-lined street, Michigan Ave. But a part of me will always remain in "The Lane."

"If what I say resonates with you it is merely because we are both branches on the same tree." - W.B. Yeates
"Though a tree grows so high, the falling leaves return to the root." - Malary proverb

Rosemary Murdoch Thomas

My name is Rosemary Murdoch Thomas. I was born October 11, 1968 in Salt Lake City, Utah at LDS Hospital. My parents are William Richard and Arthel Wilkins Murdoch. I am blessed to have two older sisters who anxiously awaited my arrival: Deborah Murdoch Winegar and Alison Murdoch King. My younger brother, William Matthew, joined our family 15 months after my birth.

I grew up on eight acres of paradise on earth: 2141 East 6200 South, Holladay, Utah. A poplar tree-lined lane with lush greenery on either side. Fruit trees, orchards, ditch banks inhabited by beautiful pheasants and quail. Lilac bushes so large they were trees. Deer would hide in early spring in the orchard and call it home. Unfortunately, they would eat my mother's beautiful rose garden and munch on other floral treats. In the spring we would search out fresh asparagus along the lane. In the winter we would build huge snow forts and snow slides in the orchard. We would slide off Grandma's garage into piles of snow so massive you couldn't see us once we fell to the ground. My brother and I would build huge snowmen in our back yard and loved making snow angels in the crystal snow.

We were blessed to have our relatives as neighbors. My grandfather, David Lennox, and grandmother, Ora Maurine Clark Murdoch, lived at the end of the lane. We enjoyed growing up with seven cousins that were also our best friends.

Each season brought a new adventure for us. Winter snow turned the lane into a crystallized fairyland. We would build extravagant ice huts and snowmen. After large snow storms we would dare each other to slide off of Grandma's garage into so much snow we would disappear after take off. I loved having my dad take all of us on rides on the toboggan behind his snowmobile through the orchards we would sing Jingle Bells and ring a brass bell hung with string.

Spring brought the rebirth of nature. You could smell the buds on the poplar trees and the "worms" that would fall from them covered our lane. The leaves burst on all of the orchard trees bringing a wonderful fragrance of apple blossoms, lilacs, and a beautiful frail white blossoming branch arching over the lane.

One of my fondest memories was when my Grandpa Murdoch took me on a walk down the lane. He always showed us how to love nature and I am so grateful for his decision to purchase such a beautiful playground for us to enjoy. On that particular walk, he took me to a pine tree on the south side of his home, near the lilac tree and over the cobble rock ditch and lifted me up to see a nest filled with robins.

We lived among pheasants, quail and the dreaded magpies, who would destroy the quail nests along the ditch banks. There are many fond memories of the summers in Grandma's pool. My favorite evenings were those watching sunsets glowing against the poplar trees and sleeping under the stars in our backyard.

We enjoyed our trips to Grandpa and Grandma Wilkins farm in Rupert, Idaho, where my mother grew up. My grandfather, Arland B., died when I was four, but I remember visiting my grandmother, Sarah Amelia Reading Wilkins, in Rupert. We loved to sneak into her small barn to see the kittens and smell the beautiful flower garden in between her home and the barn. They had a beautiful white picket fence that surrounded their entire yard.

My mother inherited a love of gardening from my grandmother and also a beautiful talent of sewing and quilting. My mom enjoyed making my dresses and continued to amaze my friends with her expertise in designing any dress without a pattern for proms and other special occasions. My mom is very charitable and always thinks of others before herself. She served as Relief Society President while I was growing up and I would see first hand the Christ-like services she performed for our neighbors.

My father, William Richard Murdoch, worked at KSL-TV for over 40 years. My grandfather also worked at KSL for many years. My father is a great leader and I always admired how he knew everyone's name at KSL from the parking attendant to the television personalities. He mentored many great people and my parents were able to make many wonderful friends around the globe. My father is a devoted member of the Church of Jesus Christ of Latter-day Saints. He served as a bishop when I was a baby and always served those in our ward with compassion and a heart of gold. He has a strong testimony of the gospel and I appreciated the way he honored his priesthood. I have received many wonderful priesthood blessings from my father.

I attended Oakwood Elementary and enjoyed the walks down the lane to catch the bus with my cousins and a few of our neighbors. One of my fondest memories of school was getting a ride in a helicopter with my dad and brother My father arranged for KSL Chopper 5 to take Matt and me to school one morning.

After elementary school, I attended Bonneville Jr. High and Cottonwood High School. I enjoyed spending time with my friends and served as the only girl Student Body Officer my senior year.

Living next to our cousins we were always up for an adventure. We enjoyed playing in our huts along the ditch banks, hiding in our tree house, making movies down the lane, Grandma Murdoch's Molly Whoppet parties, Grandma's basement and dressing up in her fancy hats, Thanksgiving dinner at Grandma's house, playing in Allan and Janet's hammocks in the walnut trees, Aunt Connie's pears and pea patch and, of course, the summer days in the pool. I loved to walk to Chesley Drug and The Store with Michele and buy penny candy.

Our cabin was my family's peace and quiet from the busy life in the valley. We enjoy spending time there with friends and family. Now my boys are experiencing all of the beauty of nature while visiting the Hearthstone.

I was blessed to grow up in a wonderful ward. We were all family. How many people can say that they had their grandma as their Sunday School teacher? My grandma always taught us never to set a tired table (not even for a Sunday School lesson). She always had a creative flair to everything she touched. No matter the topic she always had a handout (individually typed). I also had great youth leaders who I admired and still admire for their sacrifice in all the time they spent with us.

After high school I attended the University of Utah. "Ute" blood goes back a long way in my family. I am the third generation of University of Utah alum in my family. My grandfather, David Lennox, was a cheerleader at the U and my dad graduated from the University of Utah, where he played in the marching band. I rushed both LDS and Greek sororities as a freshman and made many friends in the process. I decided to join an LDS sorority Kappa Theta through the Institute program on campus. It gave me the opportunity to serve as a pledge trainer and president over a group of wonderful young women.

I met my husband, Jeffrey Glenn Thomas, while attending at the U. He had just returned from a LDS mission to Pusan, Korea and we met through a friend. Our first meeting was at The Centre Theatre in Salt Lake at a U2 movie.

My goal was to complete my education prior to marriage and so we had a long three year romance. I had the opportunity to travel abroad to study for a semester to Neuchatel, Switzerland. We traveled throughout Europe prior to our studies at the Neuchatel University. It was the first time I had been away from home. I made many friends and experienced many exciting adventures. While away, I knew that I couldn't be far from Jeff.

He proposed on Christmas Eve 1990. He sat me down at his parent's kitchen table and handed me a beautifully wrapped box. Inside were two coats. He wanted me to choose one of them. Then he handed me another box with gloves inside. He had cross stitched, "I glove you" on the gloves. He asked me to try them on and in doing so a ring fell into my hand. Then he asked me to look out the back window. In flashing Christmas lights it read, "Marry me".

I graduated on June 11, 1991 from the U with a degree in Communication. Fourteen days later I married Jeffrey Glenn Thomas on June 25, 1991 in the Salt Lake LDS Temple. We were married by Elder Carmack. The weather was beautiful and we had many family and friends in attendance. We celebrated at a wedding breakfast at the Lion House and enjoyed a beautiful garden reception at my parent's home in our backyard.

Jeff and I lived in Quailbrook East, a condo complex on 4600 South and 900 East in Salt Lake City. I continued to work at Fotheringham and

Associates, an advertising agency in Salt Lake. We attended the Winder Ward and lived there for two years and then purchased our first home on 1048 East Lafayette Street in Sandy, Utah. It was definitely a fixer upper and we remodeled it from top to bottom. We replaced every door and the entire floor. We added crown molding and Jeff learned how to tile the kitchen and bathrooms and replace French doors. We re-landscaped the entire yard and loved to add to our perennial garden.

Jeff graduated from the University of Utah with a B.S. in Mathematics and a B.S. in Computer Engineering. He also has his MBA from the University of Utah. He has worked at Unisys, Access Software, Alcatel, and is currently a Principal Product Manager at Control 4, a home automation company, based in Draper, Utah.

I continued to work at the advertising agency until the birth of our first son, Ian Jeffrey Thomas, born October 1, 1995. His other brothers joined him through the next few years: Isaac William Thomas born August 30, 1998, Gavin Sumner Clark Thomas born March 22, 2002, and Gabriel Murdoch Thomas January 6, 2005.

With all of the boy energy, we decided we needed a place for them to stretch their legs and run! When Gavin was six months old we purchased a ½ acre lot in Draper and when the sale of our home happened quicker than we planned, my parents graciously let us move in with them until our home was completed. The property that we live on was settled by Ebenezer Brown in the late 1800's. He was asked by Brigham Young to settle Draper and built his family farm on the property where our neighborhood sits.

Our boys are a blessing in our lives. They each add so much to our family and how quickly they are becoming fine young men. Their father is a great example to them and I see a lot of the same characteristics that will help them make wise choices in their futures.

I have had the opportunity to serve in many different callings in the church: Gospel Doctrine teacher, Young Women, Cub Scouts and Primary leader, Relief Society teacher. Jeff has served in the bishopric for nine years and was recently released and called to serve as the Scoutmaster. I am so grateful for my knowledge of the gospel and for the sacrifice that my ancestors made so I can enjoy the blessings of the gospel in my life.

Jeff and I have been blessed to travel with his work and also for fun. We spent time in Korea, where he served his mission. We visited the Red Cross Hospital where my father served during the Korean War. We have also traveled to Amsterdam, Belgium, France, Italy and England.

I would like to have the same wish that my Great, Great Grandma Elizabeth Pinkerton Thyne Murdoch had:

> To keep a green point growing within myself
> Whatever winds be blowing
> To put out blossoms one or two
> And when my leaves are thin and few
> To have some fruit worth showing.

William Matthew Murdoch

1. Return to the beginning

We drove through the Scottish countryside. History passing us on both sides of the highway. As we turned off the main road and onto a small country road, I couldn't help but think of the past. Who had walked these rolling hills. What they talked about. What their dreams were about.

Lost, we saw two old men disappearing up a grassy knoll. Plaid hats. Walking staves. Leather boots. I turned onto a gravel road and called to them, "Where is Muirkirk?".

"Murikirk?" questioned the heavy accent.

"Yes. The town of Muirkirk," I replied.

"Muirkirk," replied the oldest of the two, "It's a goose tune new."

The puzzled expression forced the man to repeat this riddle over and over. "It's a goose tune new." I turned to see Laura and our American traveling companions shrug their shoulders. Finally, in one last attempt, the other man forced out an American accent as he pointed in the distance, "Muirkirk. It's a ghost town now."

Not quite a ghost town, but getting closer by the decade, Muirkirk was a small little village in the middle of Ayrshire County in the middle of Scotland. As we approached the center of town, we noticed very few people. Several small buildings and homes lined the road with expanses of fields in between. Our destination was complete.

We rolled up to the old church, the same church that my parents told me about many years before. Grey stone blocks, dark wood door, and a gated fence to the side.

As we entered the side yard my mind was taken back centuries as I saw the mossy grave markers of my ancestors planted in the dark soil. James Murdoch. Elizabeth Murdoch. William Murdoch. Mungo Murdoch (whom I can't wait to meet on the other side because I'm sure he's going to have a great sense of humor). This is where my Murdoch history began. Right here in this small village.

Laura was three months pregnant with our first child, William, when we made this trek. We contemplated naming him Mungo but thought we'd keep with more direct tradition and name him after me and his grandfather. William, now age eight, recently asked me why our ancestors left Scotland.

"To follow their dreams," was my reply. They were escaping to a world where they could be prosperous and be closer to their faith. I'm certain that when my fifth generation descendants visit my old home site in Holladay, Utah, capitalism will have dramatically changed the landscape, unlike in Muirkirk where it is quite possibly the same sleepy village as it was in the 1800's.

Today, when I travel to Europe, I follow quite close to the same route taken by my pioneer forefathers and foremothers. Approaching Nebraska I think of Wee Granny traveling all the way from Muirkirk and being laid to rest in the shadow of Chimney Rock. I can travel to Europe in less than a day. It took them months to reach Utah.

I live in a fortunate time.

2. My Childhood Home

I was born January 10, 1970 in Salt Lake City, Utah at LDS Hospital. Until my mission to Quebec Canada at age 19, I lived my entire live in the same house at 2141 East 6200 South in Holladay. But this wasn't just a house. It was more than a home. It was an experience.

Eight acres of woods, orchards, gardens a swimming pool and an ice-cold creek were my playground. My protection was a long straight gravel driveway flanked by a hundred poplar trees standing taller than anything one could imagine – girthed with trunks so large that several grown men standing fingertip-to-fingertip would strain to form their circumference.

Cousins were everywhere. My Uncle Mick and Aunt Connie and their four children, Janthia, Kathryn, David, and Michael, lived there as did my Uncle Alan and Aunt Janet and their three girls, Michele, Margo, and Meg. My grandparents, David Lennox and Ora, also lived on the property from the time they bought it in 1935, until their deaths. These cousins were always at the ready to play hide-and-seek, kick-the-can, go swimming in the pool, or build forts in the woods. There was always something to do, and always someone to do it with.

3. Mom and Dad

Mom (Arthel Wilkins) grew up on a farm in Rupert Idaho and, like the saying goes, "You can take the girl out of the farm but you can't take the farm out of the girl."

Mom was always in the garden planting flowers and pruning her incredible roses. She has a deep love for flowers. In fact our kitchen was always overflowing with them. In the windows, on the floor, on the tables. She once brought a single violet leaf home from Greece in a zip-lock bag and from there began a whole colony of violets that she was always giving away to friends and family.

When mom wasn't in the yard, she was cooking or doing something that would facilitate cooking in the future. There was the constant hissing of steam coming from our kitchen. The crock-pot was always cooking with something good for dinner. And in the summer when I heard the sounds of steam it meant I was going to be guaranteed that the cherries, peaches and apricots we picked from our trees would be available throughout the winter because of her massive bottling operation.

At night, when it was too dark to garden, or all of the cooking was done, Mom would sit down and knit or sew. There was always a large inventory of cloth, thread, and yarn. And most of the time there was a cat tangled up in it. She made many of my sisters' clothes throughout their youth and now she makes my daughters beautiful dresses and blankets.

I remember whenever I was ill, she would run to my aid, hold me in her arms, and rock me on a yellow rocking chair for as long as it took to help me feel better. She always sang the same song, "Here comes Peter Cotton Tail, running down the bunny trail..." I sing that song to my kids when they are sick and I rock them in dark of the night in their rocking chair.

Dad (William Richard) grew up on this same land and it was fun to think that he and I played in the same dirt. There is an apple tree in the backyard with a long over-hanging branch. The same branch that dad would ride under, on his pony, and swing from as the horse rode off.

Growing up, I remember my dad in a suit and tie every day. His shoes were polished into glass, and his white shirts always pressed. I liked to play in his ties when he was at work and take out all of his shoe-horns and pretend like they were spaceships. Dad worked for KSL-TV for 43 years. He started as the night-watchman and retired as the President. I will always remember the day my dad was made a vice-president. My mom and I were down at the television station (on Social Hall Avenue in Salt Lake City) and I was left in the car as my mom went inside to talk to Dad. When she came back out she said how proud she was of him, and that he had been working so hard for this promotion. I was proud of him too.

Dad left every day for work at the same time and always got home in time for dinner and the six-o'clock news. He would sit and flip from one TV station to the next, always seeing who was advertising where and getting ideas on how he could improve KSL. I would sit with him as he taught me about marketing, advertising, and politics.

When dad wasn't working at the station, he was at the cabin. This was his escape from the craziness of his job. We would go to the cabin almost every weekend and work on projects – fixing pipes, staining the decks, chopping wood. He loves the cabin. And so do I.

On special weekends I was pulled from my sleep to hear a dreadful noise. The sound of pruning shears busily at work in the back yard. I would pretend not to hear them. But my dad would eventually find me and call me to work. Over the years dad had created the most magnificent tree. The apple tree in the backyard was transformed into an enormous bonsai tree with branches that extended 25 feet from the trunk. The problem is that in the spring, hundreds of sucker branches would sprout out and these needed to be removed. Over the years I grew to love trimming that tree and hauling the sticks to the orchard to be burned with other prunings and dead wood dropped from the poplar trees. In fact, I miss those days.

Several times a year my dad would fire up the old tractor and head to the apple orchard to plow under the weeds and create furrows to water the trees. I would sit with him and ride along, ducking under low hanging branches. Every once in a while one would whip across your face and you would feel a sharp sting. But it was fun to ride on this big machine with

Dad regardless of the collateral damage. I'd always get to raise and lower the hydraulic plow – I didn't think anything could be more fun.

4. Sisters

Being the youngest in a family of four children had its benefits. My parents had already experienced many of the challenges associated with raising children. The only problem is that my three older siblings were all sisters. A "nylon-jungle" is what I often compare my childhood with. Girl things were everywhere, but we always seemed to get along.

Deborah (Winegar) is ten years older and Alison (King) is eight years older. Rosemary (Thomas) is only 15 months older. Debbie and Alison were married and out of the house while I was just a young kid. But I still remember how popular they were at school and taking trips with them to Coronado Island in San Diego.

Rosemary and I learned to walk quite young. My mom says I was nine months old when I was running around and with the two of us it was like a couple of midgets living in the house. In fact in elementary school, a teacher once thought that we were twins. When Rosemary and I misbehaved and were being wild and crazy, my mom would threaten us with the "Spaddle Board". Although many threats were made, not once did I ever get spanked. But I can still see the handle of the board peeking over the side of a high shelf in the kitchen as if to act as a constant reminder that it was there, ready to swat.

Rosemary and I had a lot of adventures together and were always good friends (except for maybe a period of time in the teenage years). I learned a lot from her and credit her for teaching me many successful traits I have today. When I think of Rosemary I think of the quote, "She who laughs, lasts." She has always been very popular and friendly with everyone.

5. My Mission

I had always wanted to serve a mission. Ever since I was a young boy I loved to hear the returned missionaries recount the experiences of their own service.

I left for the Canada Montreal Mission in December of 1998, a month before my 19th birthday. I spent two months in the Missionary Training Center in Provo, Utah learning French and a dialogue called Quebequois.

I arrived in Ottawa in a freezing blizzard in March. It was 40 below zero and my Senior Companion wouldn't let me buy a coat because it wasn't P-Day. All I had was a raincoat, thin gloves, and a scarf. To top it off, all we did was tract from nine o'clock in the morning until nine o'clock at night. I froze. After three days of this, I finally convinced my companion that I had to get a coat or I would die. He agreed.

I spent two years in the service of my Lord. I worked all through eastern Ontario, northern New York, and all over the province of Quebec. I was fortunate to find many people who received the gospel message and were baptized in Montreal, Victoriaville, Quebec City, and Ottawa.

Toward the end of my two years, I was asked to travel around the mission and help train other missionaries. I was able to meet so many interesting people and see beautiful and distant places like Chicoutimi and Rimouski.

My mission taught me to love the Lord and it built my testimony into what it is today. The lessons I learned from this time have help prepare me for my life's journey.

6. Life Lessons

There is no doubt about it. Life is hard. There are many things in life that you could never imagine happening to you. But if life was easy, you wouldn't learn anything. You wouldn't advance and grow. And life is all about improving. That is why we are here.

It's a lot like pruning trees. At the time, it's a brutal reality that you need to spend a day cutting small branches from the trees, getting poked in the eye, and all scraped up. But I look back on that lesson today, and realize that it taught me the value of hard work. I appreciate the fact that my dad gave me the privilege and opportunity to help him, although I certainly didn't think it at the time.

When a favorite pet died, it taught me how to grieve and to work through the emotions. When a friend became unwelcome, I learned how to pick up the pieces and move on. When my father had a massive heart attack, I learned how much he and my mom really meant to me. When someone walked out of my life and said they didn't love me anymore, I grieved, worked through the emotions, picked up the pieces, and realized just how much I truly loved my family.

Difficult situations arise from the most obscure and unpredictable places. You will never know when they are coming or what will happen. But if you have deep-rooted values and you stay close to family, you will be able to work through anything that is thrown at you.

7. One of Father's Most Beautiful Daughters

I worked at a travel agency doing marketing and advertising for them while I went to college at the University of Utah. In this position, I was fortunate enough to be able to travel around the world while I was young.

One day I asked a fellow employee, a really cute girl, if she would like to go to Spain with me and a friend. She said she didn't want to. But she said she had always wanted to go to Italy. This was one of those forks in the road that, if I had chosen poorly, could have taken me to a completely different place in life. It took me about 1.3 seconds to respond, "I love Italy in November! It's a date!"

The girl's name was Laura Verbecky. She was born in Cheyenne at the Air Force base but grew up primarily back east (Ohio, North Carolina, Michigan, Maryland) as well as Colorado and California. She found herself going to BYU and later serving a mission on Temple Square. Luckily, she took a job at the travel agency, and that's where we met.

Italy was our first date.

We toured all over central Italy including Rome, Venice, Florence and Sienna, and got to know each other quite well. By the end of the trip I knew this was going to be something special. And she did too. Italy will forever be our favorite country.

It was the most amazing two year courtship. Instead of simply going to dinner and a movie, our dates consisted of going to dinner and Europe, or the Caribbean, or Hawaii. Side note: We always paid for a friend to go with us to act as a chaperone. Traveling with Laura was wonderful. On a cruise to Mexico, I was propelled to seriously think about marrying her. I had contemplated the thought before, but was very timid in acting upon it because I had been married before and was being cautious.

On July 4, 1998 we flew to San Francisco for the day to take in the sights and eat some lobster. While we walked along the Golden Gate Bridge I knelt down, pulled a ring out of my pocket (fearing that it was going to slip out of my shaking hand and land in the bay) and asked Laura to marry me.

On August 17 we were married in the Salt Lake Temple for time and all eternity.

In my Patriarchal Blessing it contains many personal prophecies. One states that I will marry "one of Father's most beautiful daughters."

This prophecy has come true.

8. Beautiful Daughters and Noble Sons

Another item mentioned in my Patriarchal Blessing is the plurality of the genders of my children, "beautiful daughters and noble sons." This meant at least four children would come into our home. And they did.

On August 4, 1999, William Luke was born with the same intensity then as he has now. Determined, confident and full of life. (Currently age 8)

On April 10, 2001, Emma Rose was born and lit up our lives with her big blue eyes and calming personality. (Currently age 7)

On September 16, 2003, Joshua Matthew was born. His infectious smile and large personality keep us all young. (Currently age 4)

On October 10, 2006 Caroline Lily joined her brothers and sister on

earth with a face that shines when she smiles and a love of life. (Currently age 16 months)

We love our children so much and, as the saying goes, "although our hands are full now, our hearts will be full later."

As we see our children grow, we see our future and our past. The lessons we experience now are similar to those of our ancestors. They are important in understanding where we came from, but also to teach us what we need to know to succeed in the future.

MICHAEL CLARK MURDOCH

Dictated to Connie R. Murdoch beginning January 29, 1995 ending April 2006

I was born on February 28, 1936 in Salt Lake City, Utah, at the LDS Hospital. My parents are David Lennox Murdoch and Ora Maurine Clark. This was a leap year. The doctor asked Mom if she wanted to wait a bit and have the baby on the 29th. She replied, "Enough is enough, let's keep on with this." So I was born on the 28th. My family ultimately consisted of Mom and Dad, older brother William (Bill) Richard Murdoch, and Janet Lennox Murdoch. Bill is five years older than I am, and Janet is five years younger.

I have lived in Salt Lake City all of my life. We lived on Harvard Avenue for the first four years of my life.

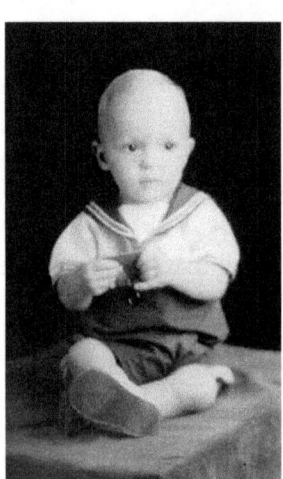

I don't remember anything much about that except the day we were to move to 6200 South. It seemed that our car, an old two-door Dodge, was packed, but I was hungry. Mom went down to the basement and got a bottle of her canned peaches and we had a bite of lunch. I can remember driving down the long driveway at 6200 South. I remember the dining room of the house then was stuffed with furniture. The wood in the room seemed to be of a dark color, with a little dingy light. It seems we all slept on the floor of the dining room that first night.

One of the things I remember from when we first moved to 6200 South, was Mom gave me a bucket to go get some water from the ditch. She must have been planting something and needed water. Buckets in those days were not plastic, they were a galvanized metal and had some weight even empty. I took my bucket and laid down on the foot bridge that crossed the ditch, put the bucket into the water, and was in short order pulled into the ditch. The force of the water filled the bucket quickly and just pulled me and the bucket into the ditch. The water was moving fast for a little boy. When I fell in, something told me to reach up and grab the pipe. (This was an old water pipe which was part of a fountain across the ditch.) I did that and was able to pull myself out of the water. Had I not done this, I surely would have drowned.

I never had my own room, I always shared one with Bill. There was a period of time that we slept down in the basement. We had bunk beds then. One night I came downstairs and turned on the light to our room. I looked down and there was a tarantula next to my foot. I remember only taking one step before I was back upstairs in the living room. However, my remembrance is of sleeping most of the time on the screened sleeping porch. I loved the sound of the stream that went down the back of our house.

At the age of eight, I was baptized at the Tabernacle on Temple Square. Because I was so small, no clothing fit very well. After being baptized, it seemed that the clothes filled up with air and I just sort of floated to the surface, and with a bit of paddling, I was over to the edge of the font.

In Primary every year in the summer there was a parade held in the parking lot of the ward. (This was the building on Fardown Avenue and Highland Drive.) A King and Queen were chosen to lead the parade. One year I was chosen to be the King and Mary Ann Staples was the Queen. I felt quite important.

I attended Oakwood Elementary. In those days it was a small two-story building. The upper grades were on the upper floor. The only ones that could go up there were the kids that were in the upper grades. One day I talked to someone older and said, "You mean when I get out of this school, I will be able to read and write? That will be so neat." Unfortunately, that did not happen very well for me. The methods of teaching in our school then did not match my learning style. I did not read or write very well when I left Oakwood. That would be a continuing problem for me the rest of my life.

In first grade, I remember having to take naps on the floor, and playing in a big sandbox. This was a raised box that you stood around to play in. This box was in the corner of our class room. A most embarrassing moment was a day when I didn't ask to go to the bathroom until it was too late and I wet my pants.

Mr. Worthen was a principal whom I remember. He was a strong disciplinarian and could throw the chalk a 100 miles it seems, with great accuracy. One day I was messing around in the hallway and suddenly I was hit right between the eyes with a piece of chalk. I looked, and he was glaring at me. I knew I had better conform or else.

In the fifth grade, I had a mean teacher that hit you on the top of your head with a ruler if you didn't behave.

The fun time was at recess when we got to play marbles. I loved to play marbles and got quite good at that game. I had some special taws, or shooters. I wanted to buy some really pretty ones. However, when I went shopping I was too Scotch to pay the 75 cent price for one. One day we had a tournament and I made it almost to the end. I was very unhappy when I lost. We also had a very fun playground. There were big rings that we could go swinging hand over hand on; we had teeter totters, swings, and slippery slides, hopscotch, and a lovely baseball diamond. I enjoyed baseball and dodge ball. I was hard to hit because I was so small.

In the 6th grade, I was in the Crossing Guard Patrol and became the Captain. This Crossing Guard Patrol was looked upon with distinction. Later in the year we were taken down town to meet with the police and learn more about the importance of the law.

Every year we had the May Festival. Sixth graders always got to dance the Maypole. However, when my 6th grade year came they did away with that dance. I was so mad.

In 6th grade, we had a very clever teacher. He taught us how to make marionettes. We made them from scratch. Heads were made from paper-mache, bodies from other pieces of wood. Our mothers made clothes for them. We decided to do the play *Beauty and the Beast*. My puppet was chosen to be the prince. We then went around the district putting on our play for the other 6th grades. This was a great experience.

One of the fun things we boys did in the summer was to go up to "Windy Bills" swimming in the old swimming hole. (The swimming hole was located where Crapo's house now stands.) The pond was a round one, but one end was infested with big "water dog pinch bugs", snakes, and moss. But the other end was good for swimming. The boys had devised a homemade diving board out of a plank and rocks. On this particularly hot summer day, we boys had ridden our bikes up to swim. Everyone was diving off the board and having such a fun time, I thought, "I can do that." So, I jumped off the board and sank to the bottom. (I naturally have a negative buoyancy) No one had told me that I also needed to know how to swim. I sat on the bottom of the pond and looked up at all the others swimming around up there. I don't know how I got out, but somehow I must have, because I am here today. I can also remember when World War

II ended, Mom and Dad hosted some U.S. war veterans for a day. It was a hot day, so we took them up to the swimming hole for a cool dip.

Another summer activity I enjoyed, at least in my grade school days, was the summer arts and crafts classes at Oakwood for two or three mornings a week.

I attended Olympus Jr. High, in Holladay. We heard terrible stories about what 9th graders did to the 7th graders, so I was terrified of going to Jr. High. Jr. High was my introduction to shop classes and gym, both of which I loved. Academics were always difficult, however, I enjoyed the sciences. I had a great group of friends: Jim Campbell, Duaine and Charles Applegate, Stan Smith, Dennis and Doug Shipley, Russ Silver, Rowell Sims, Mike VanCott, Jerard Linscholten, Paul Holmes, and Juddy Weiler. These were the closest ones.

I had a bicycle that I used a lot. In the Jr. High years, I would often ride my bike to Holladay two or three times a day. This, of course, was in the summer when we had no school. We loved movies and would often attend a movie at the Holladay Theater. When we were older and had cars or access to a car, we went down town to see movies, or we waited until dark so we could go to a drive-in. Drive-ins were very popular then.

In Jr. High, I also began playing the clarinet. I had a metal clarinet. One day I was practicing and had a really hard piece. I took hold of the end of the clarinet and swung it at the music stand. I put a dent in the bell of the clarinet. "Now, how am I going to explain this to Mom?" I don't remember how I ever did. I marched in lots of parades as a clarinet player. I really enjoyed that. Memorizing the music was hard for me. Bill got me started playing the clarinet because he also played. He even marched in the University of Utah Marching Band.

I attended Granite High School for half of my sophomore year (I broke my leg - story follows) and all of my junior year. I enjoyed shop, aviation, and gym classes a great deal here as well as in Jr. High. On January 2, 1952 I broke my right leg skiing (a 7" spiral break of both bones). I had thumbed up to Brighton and was going to meet the Applegate brothers in the afternoon. I had done really well and so decided to go on the Old Maid run which had not been used much. It must be remembered that in those days the skiing equipment was very inferior, especially by today's standards. My skis were much too long for me, and the bindings wouldn't release for anything. On the Old Maid run there were three big moguls. I hit the first mogul, landed on the third mogul, and found myself with shattered goggles and a leg twisted around in the opposite direction. I lay there in the snow probably for 45 minutes before someone found me. I was nearly frozen before the ski patrol came to get me. It was very difficult because I needed to beg a ride home in order to get medical attention. Someone was found that was going to Salt Lake and would give me a ride.

I was dropped off with my skis at home, but unfortunately left my new gloves in the man's car. We went to the Holladay Clinic to Dr. Daughters' office for the leg to be set. Dr. Daughters picked me up out of the car and threw me over his shoulder like a side of beef, carried me into his office and laid me down on his examining table. I was placed in a cast from my toes to my groin.

Because there were so many stairs at Granite as well as several buildings where classes were held, it was decided that I would do better staying at home and have a tutor come to the house. The next six months were very difficult for me. I was an active boy, and this was my first year of high school. But my friends were so faithful. Someone came every day to visit after school. I also had a tutor, but he was not very good at tutoring.

My leg healed very slowly. In the first weeks after the accident, my leg was quite swollen and would pain and throb. In order to get some sleep at night I would put a wool sock over my toes, take my sleeping bag out to the screened porch, and lay on the bed out there with my leg outside of the bag. The cold would numb the leg sufficiently so that I could sleep. This was repeated many times in those early weeks. Instead of the usual six weeks to three months for healing, mine dragged on for six months. Bone grafts at one time were contemplated. But happily, spring came and by then I was pretty adept at getting around with this heavy cast. One day I was able to get over to Jim Campbell's to play on his rope swing. The weight of my cast made me spin and whip on the rope rather than going back and forth. The tree was quite close to the rope and I came around and smacked the tree with the cast and broke it. Jim helped me splint it so I could go to the doctor where he put a walking cast on my leg. I really feel like my getting up on my leg and getting some activity helped the leg to heal because it finally did.

While my leg was still in a cast, one night I wanted to go out with my friends. None of them could get a car. I had my Model A, but we would have to sneak it out of the garage so Dad would not hear. We decided to push it out the driveway. I got in and steered, and the guys pushed. They pushed it about half way down the drive, then I started it and off we went. The throttle was both a hand and foot mechanism, so I could still drive the car using the hand throttle.

When the cast was finally taken off, the hair on my leg was very long and the leg rather shriveled. I was shocked to see it. Then Dr. Daughters proceeded to bend my knee for the first time by a swift pushing down of the lower leg. This was so painful that I have never forgotten it. Later that evening, I was watching TV and Janet came running through the TV room and knocked the stool out from under the leg. It shot back in a bent position with a big "charlie horse" in it. Much work lay ahead to get the leg up to par. For years I could predict the weather because of the throbbing in the leg.

My Junior year at Granite was fairly uneventful. My Senior year, I started at Olympus. This was the first year for this school, so we would be the first graduating class. We were instrumental in picking school colors of green and gray, writing the school song, selecting the Titan logo, and formulating other traditions. Dr. Farr was our principal. We had a good year. I graduated in May 1954.

Christmas was always an exciting time for us. Dad would always bring the Christmas tree home a week or so before Christmas. It was always a big tree that went to the ceiling. We children didn't decorate much when we were young. Mom and Dad would let us put the tinsel on. There was one favorite gold ball that we loved. When I was very young, I spent my time twisting out and exchanging all of the light bulbs on the tree. It drove Mom crazy. The tree was always in the corner of the living room by the library. We did not have any particular special traditions on Christmas Eve, or for Christmas breakfast. However, Dad just loved to tease us on Christmas morning. He would come in our room and tell us that we may as well just go back to sleep because Santa Claus had not come. He carried that on until we were nearly crazy. (We could not go into the living room until he said we could.) Finally he would let us come out of our bedrooms. Bill would come out one door, and I would go around and come out of the door on the other side of the big fireplace. Our stockings were hung on each end of the fireplace. Our gifts were underneath the stockings. One memorable gift for me was a Craftsman tool box full of tools. I must have been around 16 or 17 because I was working on my Model A. One year I remember receiving a photo cell that was fun to play with. I loved to build things, so as I was growing up I really enjoyed receiving an Erector Set and Lincoln Logs, as well as Tinker Toys. One year I received a fiberglass fishing pole. Fiberglass had just come out, and I thought that this pole was indestructible. When it was put together it could be bent almost in a circle. Later that year in the summer, I was going on a fishing trip with the Scouts. As we were going along, I tried to demonstrate how strong this wonderful new material was that my pole was made from. The pole was designed to be carried in two pieces. I took my two pieces of pole and said, "look how strong my pole is." I then pulled those pieces around my knee like I was breaking a stick. I thought the pole would bend like it did when it was put together. The two pieces broke just like kindling wood. I was mortified. Now I would not have a pole for the fishing trip; and how was I going to tell my father that I had carelessly broken my pole—the gift I had been given. I learned a big lesson that day.

The domestic work I had to do at home was in keeping with a farm like we had. Mom always milked the cows. I would then deliver milk to Wilby

Durham and to DeLoy Evans, our next-door neighbors. We had a chicken coop up by the main head gate, and I had eggs to gather. We had big lawns to mow. Bill would hook me up to the old push mower and I would pull and he would push. Finally Dad went to Sears and bought one of the first power mowers. We were so happy. Of course leaves had to be raked every fall and the fruit picked. I missed many games of football because of picking pears or apples. I got enough football, however, to break my nose. Traditionally we raked the leaves all up and put them into the barrow pits on each side of the driveway, then set them on fire. One year the wind shifted and the whole lane caught on fire. I don't remember whether the Fire Department came, or whether we got it out ourselves. Another time, Dad was burning the ditch next to Wilby's and nearly burned all of Wilby's cherry trees down. We always burned the prunings from the orchard too.

One of the fun things we did was to pasture Shetland ponies for Mr. Auerbach (of Auerbach's Department Store). Every year as part of a promotional, he would give a Shetland pony away. We would board many of these ponies, and we got to ride them whenever we wanted. One of my favorite pass times was to ride a pony up and down the orchard at full speed. I had a smart one that finally learned how to get rid of me when he got tired. He would run under a low branch to rake me off.

We also raised pure bred Columbia sheep for the wool. We had wool shearers that came each year to do the shearing. One fall, a pack of dogs formed and came in our yard and killed or maimed most of our sheep. We also had a pen of bright colored Chinese pheasants, but the dogs attacked them as well. Dad got rid of the sheep and pheasants because he had no control of the dogs.

I did some fun things in my late teens during the summer. My sophomore year, I worked at Zions National Park as kitchen help. This was a new experience for me to be away from home for that length of time. It was not easy. I went with a couple of my friends, Doug & Dennis Shipley, which made it fun. Many nights we were called upon to put on a skit for the tourists. Each night of the week we did a different skit. In July, Mom and Dad came to visit at the Park. For me, that was a big mistake. I still had at least another month left. But seeing them made me very homesick. I did a lot of dumb things after that trying to get fired so I could go home. Fortunately I did not get fired and finished my commitment.

Each of the next two summers I floated the Colorado River (pre-Lake Powell) with Merlin Shaw, who was the Seminary Principal at Granite High. Merlin put the groups together. He and his brother had a company named *Sacatwa*, that ran the river each summer. They only provided the rafts the first year, and we had to provide our own food. The trip took about seven days covering 186 miles. We put in at Hite, Utah, and got out at Lee's Ferry, Arizona. Jim Campbell, Russ Silver (once), Ted Cowley,

Dennis and Doug Shipley, Rowell Sims, and Eddie Barr were some of the ones that went. We were told to pack very lightly because you have to take everything off the river every night. We thought dehydrated food would work well. We forgot about the need for water to re-hydrate the food. We nearly starved to death. We did use the food, but in those days dehydrated food took a long time to prepare, so we didn't get to do all the hiking that everyone else did because we were always preparing food. The next year the food was furnished, but was not of such a great quality. We would dip the dry white bread into the river to moisten it. I still have the hat that I wore on those trips. It has been with me many times to Lake Powell.

Fruit picking in the fall was a big part of our lives. Several things stand out in my mind. One year (maybe 1943 or 1944) during the Second World War, we had a bumper crop of apples. Dad arranged to sell many of them to the government, but they had to be graded and cleaned inasmuch as they had been sprayed with arsenic, lead, and sulphur. We bought cotton gloves to help us wipe the apples faster, and then we had to put all the apples in baskets with lids. What a job to clean, grade, and basket these apples—after picking them all.

Another year we had picked all the apples and sold a lot, but had a lot stored in the barn. It snowed and was quite cold. Dad worried the apples would freeze. So in the middle of the night (or so it seemed) we were carrying bushels of apples from the barn to the basement of the house for safe keeping.

Another year the Elders Quorum had our orchard as a welfare project. They helped pick a bumper crop and get them to Welfare Square. We ran out of boxes and had the apples in great piles underneath each tree. This place had wonderful fruit which took a lot of tending. Dad always paid the taxes with the sale of the pears. He sold the fruit to a vender, Mike Kesamakis. We prepared the baskets for sale by using a special process we called "ring facing." Ring facing can be done to apples or pears. To ring-face apples or pears a special apparatus is needed. This apparatus sits on a small wooden palette, chair height so the operator can sit down. The first step is to fill a terraced lid, called a ring-face lid, with the nicest fruit, arranging it in the most orderly fashion. This would ultimately create a very attractive top to the bushel of fruit. Once the terraces are filled, the next step is to pull up above the terraces a metal cylinder that will hold the rest of the bushel of fruit. The cylinder is filled snugly with fruit to the top. A bushel basket is then placed upside down over the cylinder. The basket is pushed down slowly replacing the cylinder with the basket, (the cylinder obviously can go up and down) transferring the fruit from the cylinder into the basket. When the basket reaches the terraced lid, the operator slips his hands through the lifting handles of the basket, holding on to the ring-face lid. The basket is picked up, turned upright, and the ring-face lid is removed. Voila!! a perfect appearing bushel of fruit with the top layer of fruit neatly arranged in four perfect rings. To more fully enhance, a scalloped purple liner is placed around the outside circumference of the bushel, attach a lid over the fruit, and all was ready for market at $4.00 a bushel. Dad would take the back seat out of the car and load the car and trunk with baskets or boxes of pears each morning to drop off on his way to work. I always felt quite hard done by because every fall when I wanted to be playing football or basketball, I could not do it—it was as though I was chained to the land.

For a few years Grandma and Grandpa Clark lived in our basement. When they were with us, we raised a big garden. Grandpa did the plowing with the help of Pete Reva's horses. (Pete Reva lived in a little house behind what is now the Shalamar) We had two horses, Tony and Cherokee, but these were riding horses. Tony was a big Palomino.

The only way for me to get up on his back was to shinny up his leg. When I wanted to get off, I would slide down his tail. Our garden had rows that ran east and west. We raised a lot of corn. Bill and I would sell it on the street for 35 cents for a baker's dozen (13). (It must be remembered that in those days, there were only about a dozen cars a day up and down 6200 South. It was often a long wait between cars and prospective customers.) We had regular customers that would come, which helped a lot.

One thing we enjoyed doing was listening to the radio. (This is pre-TV days.) There were exciting programs to listen to: Superman, Bat Man, The Thin Man, Fibber Magee & Molly, Inner Sanctum, The Shadow, Amos & Andy, Sky King, Jack Armstrong, Captain Midnight, Buster Brown, and the Lone Ranger, just to name a few.

We had to make our own fun for the most part. One of the things we did was to take our mother's wooden thread spools and turn them into little army tanks by using a rubber band and a match, along with a washer cut from an old playing card. We made guns with rubber bands and clothes pins; cranes out of wood, horse shoe nails and the gears from an old clock. We would play for hours and hours making ramps and having races with these toys. We loved the sand pile. (The spool toys were made and played with the Applegate brothers across the street. The crane made and played with Russell Silver.)

The group of guys I ran around with was a lot of fun, and we did a lot of "things". One evening Stan Smith, Doug & Dennis Shipley, Larry and Charles Applegate and I decided to climb up the Murray smoke stack. We had often wanted to climb up there and paint an "O" for Olympus on it. But this night, we just decided to climb it. At this time, Walt Disney had a lease on the property and there was a care taker there looking after some animals owned by Disney. We sneaked in this particular night having decided to just climb up and look around the city. I was too short to reach the ladder that was our way up the chimney, so I had to be lifted up to reach the first rung. As we climbed up the ladder on the outside, a gust of wind blew Doug Shipley's cowboy hat off, and it landed on an animal pen and startled the animals, who then aroused the care taker. He came out of his shack with a gun. We froze in place on the ladder. The ladder had a cage around it so you could not fall off all the way down. As we got closer to the top, we saw that the brass rungs were getting thinner from acid from the smoke of the smelting process. At the top, the chimney belled out as well as went up. The ladder was really getting rickety with the bolts getting smaller and smaller. We just kept going. The chimney at the top was about 15 feet in diameter with a platform over it and no railing. There we were running around on this platform high above the city. The view was out of this world, and we had no camera. We could see from the State Capital Building to the Point of the Mountain.

Climbing back down was very spooky. Going around the bulging part of the chimney was most difficult. We were also afraid of the animals alerting the care taker before we could all get off the chimney to get out of there. But we made it without getting any buckshot in our behinds. Doug even got his hat back.

My most favorite thing to do in the winter was to hook a ride on the back of cars going along Highland Drive by the church or Fardown Ave. This was often our MIA activity of the evening. The roads were not salted like they are now and were very icy. I loved to do this. One night, Jay Liljenquist brought his dad's big Oldsmobile to Mutual. We would hang on to the back of his car three or four at a time and he would try to throw us off by fishtailing back and forth at a high rate of speed. (Cars went slower in those days, however.) We would knock into each other, but we never seemed to get hurt. One night, we were going down Highland Drive and everyone fell off but me. Jay was going about 60 mph, and my feet were going up and down so fast that they became extremely hot. I could hardly stand it. So, I pulled myself up on the back bumper and held on by the license plate and the handle of the trunk. (Cars had trunk handles in those days.) Everyone thought I had fallen off. After my feet cooled down, and Jay had turned back toward the Church, I dropped down on to the road for another ride. I loved this activity!! (In those days winters were always normal and things stayed frozen pretty much until spring came.)

One day, someone had the bright idea of going sleigh riding on inner tubes. The natural rubber, when it got wet and cold, was very slippery. I found a red tube somewhere and we went up Big Cottonwood Canyon looking for a steep hill. The only steep hills were just below the Spruces and you ended up on the highway. In those days the snow plows threw the snow all onto one side of the road. We decided to tramp a path in the piled up snow so we could come down the hill, go across the road, and up the other embankment. We would try to see how far we could fly when going across the embankment. One night, I had the perfect run. My friends had stopped the traffic on the road and I came whizzing down the hill, came across the road and up the embankment and was air borne. I sailed for about 30 - 40 feet before coming to land in some nice powder—just short of landing in the creek. It was a wonderful ride.

Another fun thing I did with the Applegate brothers was to build a soapbox derby car. I had been thinking a lot about this and had it all worked out in my mind. One day, 6200 South was closed to traffic for some reason, so we decided this would be a perfect time to make our car. We gathered all our "stuff" together. We had steel wheels for the back and some small wagon wheels for the front which we attached to our "chassis". We had it designed so we could steer with our feet as well as a rope. We then took our car up on the hill to 23rd East. We hooked a rope to a bicycle and had one of our friends peddle down as hard as he could to get us started. About half way down, we would let go of the rope and go shooting down the hill and try to turn into Murdoch Lane. We would hit the gravel and dust would fly all over the place. Only one boy could ride at a time, so we spent the afternoon taking turns and enjoying the thrill of the ride. We were glad to have 6200 South closed that day.

Another crazy activity we engaged in was to shoot arrows straight up into the sky and then see how close they would come to hitting us when they came down. (This was with Duaine & Charles Applegate, Jim Campbell, and me.) The arrow would go up as far as the velocity of the shot would take it, then the weight of the arrow head would turn it over and then it would pick up speed as it returned to earth. It would shoot into the ground with a slicing sound. This was really a rather stupid thing to do because we could have really gotten injured. Luckily we always moved before it could cause us any injury.

As Priests in our ward, Bishop Ed Holmes challenged us to obtain 100% attendance at our meetings for a certain period of time. The reward was to be a fishing trip into the Wind River Country. All our Priests achieved the trip. I remember that the only other adult on the trip was Garnett Player. We loaded our stuff in the truck and took off. After several hours drive, we arrived at the ranch in Pinedale, Wyoming for dinner and sleep in the cabins. In the morning we had a big breakfast, went to the corral for our horses, and were on our way to Victor Lake. This was to be an eight-hour horse ride. It seems like there were not enough horses, so we had to take turns riding and walking. That was really a blessing for those who were not used to riding. We were to be at Victor Lake for a week. The fishing was unbelievable. The lake was shaped like a figure eight. Where the top and bottom came together, there was a big rock sticking up and we were jumping and playing. One of the boys threw his line out and tied into a huge fish. It pulled him right off the rock he was standing on. After that we all began catching fish like crazy. One morning we went fishing, jumping, swimming—everything all at once and it did not matter to the fish, they were biting anyway. The last day we were there someone had the bright idea to swim out to an island because surely there would be big fish out there. So we took all our clothes off and carried them on the tops of our heads carefully to this island. When we arrived there, we just did not bother to get dressed because we were having so much fun. We spent most of the day in the nude just playing, fishing. swimming, and having a good time. The thing we were not thinking about was that we were exposing skin to the sun for a long period of time which had never had sun on it. The next morning, we were supposed to ride out. I spent most of the time walking because the tops of my feet and my rear end were so suburned I was in a great deal of pain. The trip had been wonderful, but the going home was mighty miserable. Several years later, I returned to that same area with Dad and Bill.

When Duaine, Charles, Jim, and I were about old enough to obtain a driver's licenses, a neighbor sold us an old Ford V8 for about $15. The car was not street legal, but we had fun in the orchard. We took out the front seat (why, I don't know now), and we had a box for the driver to sit on. We left the back seat in. We probably did some other adjustments as well, but I cannot remember. We would go tearing up and down the orchard having a good time. One day, Duaine was driving and went around a corner sharply, the box tipped over and he fell off. I was in the back seat laughing so hard I could hardly stand it. He was also laughing. However, he was heading straight for a tree. Somehow we missed the tree or he stopped, and we were not hurt.

Another thing we did one day was to take my old Model A up to the Holladay Gun Club area where the old silica mines were located. I was with Dennis & Doug this time. We enjoyed exploring inside these mines. When we came out on this day to go home it was snowing. We piled into the car and decided to cut across the sage brush to get to the part of the road that would take us home. Unfortunately, I high-centered the car on top of a big rock that I had not seen. To get it off, we had to find something to jack up the car. All the time it is snowing. We finally accomplished this feat and got back to the road. We were surprised to see very large cougar tracks in the fresh snow in the road coming from the same area where we had been stuck.

Some time in my early teens, I was looking for fun and Jim, Duaine, Charles, Dennis & Doug and I decided to go over to Oakwood School to see what was going on. They were in the process of remodeling the building. I saw this pipe I thought I could use as a stairway to get up to the second floor. I shinnied up the pipe, which pipe went through a big hole in the floor joist. I let go of the pipe to climb through the hole, but slipped instead. Down I fell to the bottom floor and landed on my back on a pile of bricks. That may have been the beginning of back trouble for me.

Russ Silver and I loved to do gymnastics. We invented what we called the frog leap. We would roll up a mat to use as a spring board, then we would come running along on all fours, spring off the "spring board" fly through the air, then tuck and roll at the end. One day, I missed the roll and just landed on my neck. Another beginning to future neck problems.

I graduated from high school in 1954 and went to work as a hod carrier for LaMar Knudsen. I was too short to push the wheel barrow properly. Because I had to grasp the handles higher up than normal in order to lift the wheel barrow up to move it, I took a lot of ribbing. One day, I figured I pushed about 500 pounds of bricks in each load. That also may have added to my back problems later in life.

In the fall, I attended the University of Utah. Russ Silver and I went together. I had about four quarters there. At about age 18 ½, Russ and I both joined the National Guard. At first, I was assigned to State Headquarters stationed at Fort Douglas. I was known as a Petroleum Specialist. At the two-week summer camp in June held at Camp Williams, our job was to provide the supplies to the other units. My main job was to pump gas.

I worked for LaMar Knudsen through the winter of 1955 and was called to the British Mission in the spring of 1956. I left in May. I was happy I was going to an English speaking mission - or so I thought.

My mission was a memorable experience. Just getting to the mission field was an experience. We did not have an MTC in those days, so I had one week of training at the facility downtown located across the street from the Church Office Building. It was an old school. I think I went home each night so that out-of-town missionaries could be housed in this facility. (This building is now gone.)

We traveled by train from Salt Lake to New York, stopping in Chicago to go to a museum, then stopping at Niagara Falls, then on to New York, all of which took about four days total. We boarded the Queen Mary in New York, and sailed for South Hampton taking one week to get there. That was an experience. We traveled Cabin Class so we had access to all

First Class facilities. The sea got quite rough for May, and one night I was thrown from my bunk. At dinner, we had to put side boards up to keep the dishes from falling from the table. Ropes were strung along the corridors to hang on to for security as well.

When we arrived in South Hampton, we were picked up at the ship, taken to the mission home over night. My Mission President was Clifton Kerr and he was there with his family. His son, Rolfe, is now a general authority (2006). The next day we were taken to Hyde Park where we held street meetings. That was my introduction to the mission. I soon learned to love giving street meetings. A street meeting was a good way to learn the lessons. Our speech was always a rehearsal of one of the lessons. It did take a while to be able to understand what people were saying. There were many dialects.

I served in Liverpool District for one year and then north to New Castle District, where I served in Sunderland for the next year. We had pretty good success in Sunderland. We baptized a family by the name of Self, and another family, the Pearsons. The British saints were wonderful. We had a lot of support in our work.

Our mode of transportation was a bicycle most of the time. If not a bicycle, we walked or took the bus. I learned to love England. The weather was not the best, as it is cold and damp in winter. The scenery is beautiful.

My mission experience was a major factor of my grounding in the gospel. I learned the doctrine, and loved it. I learned to defend that which I believed. Bearing my testimony often strengthened it. I gained confidence in speaking to people just about anywhere. I asked my Mission President how I would know if my mission was a success. He said, "Call me in 30 years and tell me what you are doing." President Kerr phoned me several times in the next 30 years and I was always able to report that I was active in the Church.

After serving my mission, I was able to tour Europe with a missionary companion, Elder James Snarr, which was a very interesting and exciting time.

After my mission, I resumed my previous activities both in education and National Guard. I changed to the 1071st Aviation Company located in Bountiful, Utah. Russ Silver also changed to that unit. I was assigned to the Rotary Wing Unit. (helicopters). Russ was assigned to the Fixed Wing Unit. I wanted to be a pilot. By that time, I was married and Connie talked me out of going to Officer Candidate School. One of the things I remember is helping to take an engine out of moth balls and install it in another helicopter, and then it actually flew. We were very excited. One day at summer camp, I had a startling experience. Our Commanding Officer (C.O.) was sort of a practical joker. I had the opportunity to take a helicopter ride. The C.O. was the pilot. This helicopter had no doors, just a big plastic bubble over us. Everybody knows that helicopters don't fly when the motors shut off. I was leaning out the side looking at the scenery during the flight, and the pilot did what is called an auto rotation, which is sort of like shutting off the engine so that the blades go in reverse. We immediately began to fall just like a rock and I nearly fell out of the helicopter (without a parachute). Thankfully, he turned the helicopter back to regular function and we continued on our way. I'm sure the C.O. got a big laugh out of that, but I was not laughing at first.

After my eight years in the Guard, I was discharged. I achieved the rank of Sergeant. Had I stayed in, the pay would have come in very handy now. However, who knows what kind of war service I might have seen.

University schooling really was not to my liking, so I began attending Trade Tech. (It is now known as Salt Lake Community College.) I started off in a machinist program - completed it in six months. However, I ultimately took a job by the airport with Sperry Univac in the maintenance department inasmuch as the machinist job was out in Clearfield.

In 1960 I met Connie Riley. We enjoyed each other's company very much, and were ultimately married in the Salt Lake Temple by LeGrand Richards on August 12, 1960. Our eternal family was thus begun.

Our children began to come along. Janthia Ann Murdoch was born on May 11, 1961, Kathryn Ilene Murdoch was born on October 4, 1963, David Lennox Murdoch was born on May 11, 1966, and Michael Clark Murdoch, Jr. was born on August 13, 1969.

To support my growing family I was able to transfer from maintenance to the carpenter shop where I was very happy working in wood. I have always loved working with wood. As time went on I learned that our company would pay for classes at Trade Tech, so I enrolled in the Building Technology course. After two years I graduated.

I was a restless worker. I have had many jobs. I worked in home remodeling, I tried small engine repair, I worked at Climate Control as a dispatcher, then went to the University of Utah Maintenance Department, then Sugarhouse Tent and Awning, next was U. S. Welding for 15 years as a torch and regulator repairman, and medical bulk liquid installation, and respiratory medical equipment repair. I later moved on to Interwest Medical doing respiratory medical equipment repair. I retired from there on Friday, September 13, 2002 one month prior to our leaving on a mission to Australia Sydney North Mission.

I will backtrack a bit here to our family:

For a wedding present, my father and mother gave each of their children a half acre of land on the family homestead on 6200 South. That was a great blessing to us. We built a home in 1962, and lived there for 38 years. It was a wonderful place to raise our children. There was space for them to run and play, a swimming pool at Grandma and Grandpa Murdoch's and cousins to play with. It was a good time. We raised a fine garden each year. Our children attended Oakwood School just as I had done. They attended and graduated from Cottonwood High School.

We owned a boat while the children were growing up and usually had a fun vacation to Lake Powell each year.

Our children learned to work through helping us clean the Shalamar Wedding Reception facility after each wedding. We cleaned at least twice each week, and more often in March, June and August. This work was done before they went to school in the morning. We cleaned for 19 years. They also learned to work through helping in neighbors' yards or cleaning houses. We removed trimmings for a professional pruner, John Balmer, and the children helped with this job. All of these things were a blessing to them and to us as they grew to adulthood.

We raised our children in the Church, and they have all been through the temple. Our two sons served missions: David to Scotland Edinburgh, and Michael to Portugal Lisbon North. Our callings in the Church has been varied. We have served in every organization in the Church, and just been willing to do whatever we have been asked to do.

Our mission as a senior missionary couple was a wonderful two-year experience. We managed a microfilm library which supplied microfilm to all the Family History Centers in Australia and New Zealand. We are most grateful to the Lord for that wonderful opportunity.

At this writing, April 2006, we are enjoying our children, grandchildren, and serving in our ward.

CONNIE LOU RILEY MURDOCH

I was born on August 11, 1941 in Salt Lake City, Utah. My parents are Herbert Edgley Riley and Lala Virginia Sturm Riley. I was the fourth daughter born in this family, which ultimately had nine daughters and one son. I was born just before Pearl Harbor was bombed. Dad was drafted into the Army; however, he failed the physical because of varicose veins. That was a very happy day in their lives.

In order of their birth, my siblings are: Geraldine (Gerry) Riley Ewing, Barbara Jeanne Riley Tweed, Beverly Jane Riley Miller, then me, next Judith Ann Riley Black Jeffries, Virginia Lynn Riley Clark Hahn, Janet Deon Riley Mecham, Herbert Michael Riley, Lala Kay Riley Rainey, and Valerie May Riley Adams.

I wish my memory was better than it is, but I will attempt to relate some of the things I remember from my youth. As a very small child I vaguely remember that we lived in a house that had wood/coal-burning appliances for a while. There was a rather tall brown *heatolater*, I think it may have been called, which was in the living room. We had a coal stove in the kitchen for cooking. I remember when my sister, Judy, was born and Mom came home from the hospital with her, we all had the mumps and were sick in our beds. I would have been nearly four at the time. I remember when my dad was enlarging our house with an extension being made to the living room. It was fun to climb out the existing window of the living room with my dolls and play in the new part of this room. One day Mom went to the lumber yard to get something that Dad needed in this building project. She took us kids with her. The man at the lumber yard gave me a pencil and a pad. I can still remember the joy I felt in owning my own pencil and being able to draw.

My older sisters remember a time when we had an outhouse in the back yard. They even tell of playing hide-and-seek and trying to hide inside by holding onto the sides of the holes. Unfortunately one of them fell in. Mother had no recourse but to wash whoever it was off by hosing her down with the garden hose. I don't remember having an outhouse. Apparently when Dad enlarged the house, a bathroom was part of the enlargement.

Our house was located at 1212 East 4500 South in Salt Lake City. It was white shake shingle on the outside. The house consisted of a kitchen, a living room, three bedrooms, one bathroom, and a utility room. After I got married, Dad added a family room onto the back of the house which has been a wonderful addition. We had about two acres of ground. Mother and Dad planted a large garden each spring. Dad also had two milk cows, chickens, pigs, and sometimes rabbits. As we grew up we had responsibility for taking care of these animals, except for milking the cows. Dad always did that job. When I was about 12 or 14 I wanted to try to milk. While Dad milked one cow, I attempted to milk the other cow. He ended up with a bucket full of milk, I had about one inch of milk in the bottom of my pail. From then on, I decided that was a job that was just too much for me.

The garden was a place where we all got a good deal of training in how to work. It was our job to help keep the many, many weeds out of the garden. We also learned to irrigate. Harvesting and bottling the produce was an important part of each summer. Mother was a good manager and we had lots of home-grown, home-bottled fruits and vegetables in our fruit room each fall for winter use. Each year Dad had a beef steer or pigs ready for slaughter for our winter meat. When I was young, I did not appreciate all the wonderful food we had to eat. I thought everyone ate like we did. It was only after I was grown up and beginning my own family that I really began to realize the value of our garden and all the work my parents went to provide nourishing food for all of us to eat. I, at one time, made the rash statement that I would never have a garden when I got married. However, it did not take me very long to realize the value of a garden. I have planted a garden every year since we have had any land on which to plant.

The street we lived on was a friendly street in those days. All the neighbors were about the same age as my parents, and so had children coming along just like we did. I felt secure in my neighborhood. I can still see, hear and smell the sights and sounds of that street of an early spring morning with the sun coming up over the mountains, with birds singing in the various meadows around us. There were large trees on the north side of 4500 South which added to the landscape. Most all of the homes also had large trees in their yards that further softened the landscape. Nights, as I remember, were soft, clear, and with bright stars to be seen. We did not have a lot of street lights or other light pollution so we could see the night sky well and the stars shown brightly. I remember feeling very secure in our home and neighborhood.

We had a wonderful swing in our backyard that Dad built. It was quite tall and very sturdy. Dad had welded large poles together to make the frame from which the swing was hung. A wide board was our seat. Just east of the swing was a "tricky bar" from which we learned to hang by our knees and various other tricks we would think up. We had a plum tree in front of the swing. We would try to swing high enough to see if we could touch the tree with our feet.

Attached to the west side of the swing frame was a cross pole to which Dad connected the clothes lines which ran across the back yard. Many are the batches of clothes that I have hung on those lines. I don't know if Mother ever had a dryer while I was still in the home. With such a large family, it seemed the laundry was never done. In the summer, Mother would wash about twice a week because we could hang the wash outside on the clothesline. But in the winter, she would have to wash something nearly every day. She would hang the clothes up in the utility room on two long lines, and two or three folding wood racks. It seemed like in winter we were never without clothes drying in that room.

One of the special memories I have of the Miller family who lived next door for many years, is Mrs. Miller (Gertrude or Gert for short). She had a daughter, Peggy. Peggy was older than I was, but about the same age as my sister Barbara or Beverly. Mrs. Miller decided to have my older sisters and Peggy have a little sewing circle in which they would get together once a week and embroider something. I felt I was just as big as they were. She was very kind and let me join. I can still remember the little baby bib she helped me embroider during that time. It had a rabbit, which I did in pink, and it held an orange carrot. That was the beginning of my enjoyment of hand work. I was probably 8 or 10. In those days too, Mrs. Miller would often come to our house and sit with Mom and embroider of an evening. It seemed as though there was more time in the day and the evening. Time did not pass so quickly as it does now. (Now being April 9, 2006, the date I am updating my history.)

Some of the neighbors we had on our street were the Harold Sorenson family next door on the east of us. Next to them was the Tom Short family, and next to them was the Veldon Jones family. All of these families are now gone and others live in their homes. On the west side was the Millers, who moved when I was a teenager. I cannot remember the names of the families which have lived in that house since, but there have been three or four different ones. Jo and Glen Burkinshaw lived next to Millers; then the Betty Tenny family, then the Bill Bolander family; Bill and Elith Doxey came next. Most of the people have moved or passed away except for Bolanders. Bill has passed away, but his wife lives on with a son and his family in the home.

Though Betty Tenny lived in our neighborhood only a comparatively short time, she and her family remain strong in my memory for two reasons. First, Betty was a wonderful softball player. She was in our ward at the time I was in MIA and involved in the girls' softball program. She was a great teacher. I can still remember getting up at 6:00 A.M. on Saturday mornings to go to softball practice. She would demonstrate how to smoothly scoop up a rolling ball, and using the proper foot work, move right into position and throw the ball to its appropriate spot - all very fluid and graceful. Our team did very well with her on it. The second reason I remember her was because she had about three children and I often was asked to go and tend them. Now they lived in a very old house onto which they had added a somewhat strange but adequate addition. The old part of the house had an upstairs where the bedrooms were. The only problem was that at the head of those stairs was the scariest Indian mask I had ever seen. I just hated to go up those stairs to check on the children once I had put them to bed. One of the other problems with tending here was that they had no TV and they almost always stayed out until well after midnight. More than once I scrubbed her kitchen floor in order to have something to do to keep me awake and to take my mind off the time and that mask. Because we lived so close, I always had to walk home. You can bet I ran very fast to get there.

Part of our training in our parents' home was learning to do housework and yard work. We each had some cleaning job to do every day, with more in-depth cleaning to take place on Saturday. Mother was a firm believer that the house must be cleaned and scrubbed each Saturday to be ready for Sunday. As I mentioned before, we also had responsibility for animals. For many years it was my job to feed and water the chickens. In the summer it was not too bad of a job, but in winter I did not like it because I always had to thaw the water cans and fill them up with fresh water for the day. I had smelly barn boots and a barn coat that I wore to take care of those chores. We got a lot of eggs from our chickens. Mom must have sold them or something because I can remember gathering upwards of four and five dozen eggs per day for the whole summer. I know we did not eat that many eggs, even with all of us home.

Mom was very frugal. She sold the extra milk to the neighbors, and undoubtedly the eggs. She always saved the money carefully and was able to finance our vacations each year to Yellowstone National Park. Dad loved to fish. He would load up the car every July 3 and we would leave in the evening for Yellowstone. We always had to wait until he was finished with work, and we girls had finished our baseball game. He would drive until he got tired, then stop and lay down on the ground beside the car to sleep. The rest of us just laid our heads on each others shoulder and slept until he awoke and we continued the journey. We were always driving into the Park just as the gate opened. We stayed at West Thumb (which no longer exists as a cabin camp). We had a cabin for a week. Dad brought a rubber raft and little motor, and we fished Yellowstone Lake. He would take turns having several of us girls in the boat and he would help us fish. He would put the worm on the hook and take any fish off the hook. We always enjoyed this annual vacation.

Another fun thing I remember doing as a child was sleigh riding in the winter. Across the street lived Byron Pugh and his wife. Two sons lived close by as well. They owned many acres of land on which they raised hay for their cattle. Part of the land was gentle rolling hills ending at the bottom in a swamp type area. We often went sleigh riding on these hills in the evening after dinner by moonlight. It was a delightful time. We always had to go ask permission, however, no matter how many times we went. That property is now a large baseball complex and park area bordered on the east by 1300 East, and on the west by 1100 East. Some of those sleigh riding hills yet remain.

When it came time for me to go to school, I began kindergarten at the Lincoln Elementary School on 5th East and 39th South. I remember very little of that experience. It was a short five-week course before we were to start first grade. I think first grade was also at that same school. One experience stands out in my mind from that school. We must of had a rule that we could not chew gum in school. I can remember being punished for chewing gum by having to put my gum on my nose as I sat at my table. I can still remember feeling so embarrassed and laying my head down on my arms on the table with my gum on my nose. I don't think I ever chewed gum in school again. I also remember an art project. We painted plaster of Paris figures. I painted a Donald Duck figure. He was bright yellow, as I remember. I believe I did a good job of it.

From second grade on, I attended Woodstock School on the corner of 13th East and Vine Street. I remember nothing of second grade. I remember only a few things about third. My third grade teacher was Mrs. Kemp. She was the sister to Inga Wells, in my ward. She was a very strict teacher. I remember her as a woman with a pointed nose. She taught us to write cursive. I remember papers and more papers full of what I called "springs". This exercise was to help us get used to moving our hand in a fluid way and connect things together. We practiced our penmanship a great deal in her class. The other thing I remember her for was a difficult lesson I learned in honesty. I don't remember all the details of the event now, but as I remember, she had a large piece of green construction paper or something like this covering the top of her desk - probably to protect the top. One day, in somewhat of a mindless fashion, I picked up the one-hole paper punch and began punching holes in that green paper. I punched a lot of them in it. I was more concerned about watching those holes being made than I was worrying about wrecking her desk covering. I don't remember if she came into the room and we ran away from the desk, or just how that all happened. I only remember what happened after that. Somehow she knew it was me but I had said I didn't do it. However, she impressed upon me the importance of telling the truth. I remember how bad I felt lying to her, and I also remember a resolve to tell the truth from then on.

Fourth grade is not bright in my memory. Fifth grade came next. Interestingly, in this school building, it had three floors to it. One floor for 1st and 2nd, one floor for 3rd and 4th, and the top floor for 5th and 6th. I had made it up to the top floor. The only thing that I felt bad about was that during the summer between 4th and 5th grade, the school's beautiful winding staircase was torn out and a straight stairway was installed. I had not been allowed to go up the winding one because you could not go up to the top floor unless you were in the 5th or 6th grade. I never got to enjoy running up and down that beautiful winding staircase. I'm sure they made this change from a safety standpoint, but I was always disappointed that I did not get to go up and down the "fancy stairway". Fifth grade has a few memories. My teacher was Mr. Clayton. He was a kindly grandfather-type of a man. He was an artist at heart. We had many art projects. Art wasn't my great love. About half way through the year, I decided that I was not learning what I thought I should, so I requested to be transferred into Mrs. Smith's class. Mrs. Smith was a strict teacher, but one that really taught you something. Mr. Clayton was quite a bit more laid back. There must have been disorder in the class as well as other things that bothered me, or else I don't think I would have requested the change. As I remember it, my request was granted, but I think the change was made at the expense of Mr. Clayton's feelings. It was unfortunate that I did not worry about that, but in my mind, learning was more important than anything and I wanted to be where I could learn the best. This same action would be repeated in my sophomore year in high school when I made a transfer into a history class that suited my desire to learn better. However, it was done very early in the year, and transfers in and out of a class were not unusual.

Sixth grade was taught by William Lighter. This was a good year. I enjoyed playing baseball and kick soccer. I was becoming a fairly good athlete and so enjoyed these games very much. (Even if we did have to play them in a dress.) I can still feel the warm spring winds blowing through the opened windows of my classroom. The smell of blooming trees and bushes on the wind is still there. We lived in farm country so the smell of freshly plowed earth was a wonderful smell to enjoy each spring. We had a school play while in 6th grade. I was given a part in this play in which I was supposed to sing a solo. I wanted very much to sing this solo, but I was very frightened. So in rehearsal, I would never sing my part. I kept saying that when the performance came, I would then sing it. With no rehearsal, I was even more petrified than ever at performance time. As would be expected, no solo was sung at the performance. I often wonder if I had sung that solo, it may have led to developing a more lovely voice - one of good solo quality. I enjoy singing very much and have always sung in choirs - but have always wished I had a much better quality voice.

When I first began attending Woodstock Elementary School, our playground was all hard-packed dirt. Sometime about my fourth or fifth grade year, they black-topped a section of the play ground. What a wonderful thing that was. We could now bring roller skates to school and skate during recess and lunch time.

Our mother sewed almost all of our school clothes. (One wonders how she did that with so many daughters, as well as keeping up on all the other things a mother has to do.) One of the dresses I remember most was a green and white checked dress with a full circle skirt with very big pockets. As young girls like to do, I pretended I was a lovely dancer and twirled and twirled with the great skirt.

Sometime in my grade-school years, I had an accident. I don't know just how old I was, but I was comparatively young. I was in the car and Mom was driving. I don't know if anyone else was in the car with us or not. I was in the back seat. Mom was going south on 9th East midway between 39th South and 45th South. I must have been playing with the door handle, because the door flew open and I fell out of the car. I don't believe I was hurt very bad, just shook up a bit. I'm sure my mother was a bit shook up as well.

When it came time to begin Jr. High, Mom decided it was time I had a little more grown-up looking hairdo than braids. Up to this point I had worn my hair long and quite often in braids. So off to the hairdresser I went to have a hair cut and a perm. I don't know who this hairdresser was, but she really had a job on her hands with my hair. It seemed the appointment turned into a really long, drawn out thing. But when she was through, I had a very short hair cut, and a very curly perm. I think we called it a "brush-up". My hair would prove to be a struggle for nearly the rest of my school days. I always had a hard time styling it. Finally in my senior year of high school, our neighbors, Jo and Glen Burkinshaw, who were hairdressers, styled my hair in such a way that I could really take care of it. I was so happy. I have worn my hair that way ever since. I now have a talented daughter, Kathryn, who looks after my hair, and she does a great job.

    I enjoyed high school very much. I attended Granite High School. I was there when they celebrated the 50th anniversary of the school. Interestingly enough, some of the teachers that were teaching when I was there, were also at the school when my mother attended nearly 30 years prior. Granite was a good school. I enjoyed attending there. I was in Concert Choir my sophomore and junior years, but did not join my senior year inasmuch as I was in the Pep Club. Granite had good business teachers, so I took typing, shorthand, transcription, and coupled with my English class, helped me be prepared for a career as a secretary after graduation. I had contemplated going to college after high school, but was pretty tired of school, and really had no money to pay for college. My parents did not have money to help. Therefore, I opted to go to work after graduation. Mr. Tripp, the manager of New York Life Insurance in Salt Lake, usually called my shorthand teacher each year if he needed new secretaries for the office. In 1959, the year I graduated, Mr. Tripp called Miss Bosh and asked for referrals. I was one she sent. I was placed as the secretary to the Assistant Manager, Alton White. I made the fabulous sum of $204.00 each month. It seemed like a whole lot to me, and I was grateful. I worked for New York Life for nearly two years. I was married to Michael Clark Murdoch in 1960, and gave birth to our first child in 1961 which necessitated my discontinuing employment at that time.

    Here I will interject the enjoyment I had being in the Granite High Pep Club in 1958-1959. Because of the cost involved for the uniform and other things, I decided I would plant gladiola bulbs and sell the flowers. Our neighbor, Bud Miller, had been doing that, but was now in the Navy, so he gave the bulbs to us. Dad prepared a place in the garden, I planted and cared for the plants. In July when they began to bloom, I put out the sign Bud had used: Gladiolas, $2.00 per dozen or was it $1.00 per dozen? I can't remember. However, I do remember my joy and surprise when someone actually stopped by the house for flowers. This happened regularly, and I was able to earn enough money to pay for the pep club uniform. A lovely blessing. I loved being in the pep club. We marched at all the home games, and it was a thrill to me each time we performed. We had a good marching club and did some fun and interesting patterns. I still remember the first day of practice for us. Marching for 40 minutes was new to our legs. The next day all of our calves were "screaming". As the students trooped up and down the stairs moving from class to class, it was easy to pick out the pep club girls. We were all grimacing with very painful calves. In time, we got conditioned and things were great.

I always loved going to Church. Our social life revolved around the Church as well. I played all the sports while in MIA, I was in the stake play, we did fun Road Shows, I enjoyed attending Girls Camp at Brighton. Every year, my older sisters and I were in the June Dance Festival. What a grand experience!! I can still feel the thrill and excitement of marching with hundreds of other girls onto the track at the University of Utah stadium, standing reverently while the American flag was raised. Tears are close, even to this day, when I stand for the raising of our flag. Mom always sewed our costumes. We never realized the work that took, just expected our fancy dresses would be done in time. Dancing in the June Dance Festival was a much looked-forward-to experience. It continued on even after I was married. My husband and I danced in three or four of these events. Unfortunately, the Church discontinued the Dance Festival because of the growth of the Church and the distances some groups were traveling just to participate.

I began my service in the Church at age 14 as a Jr. Sunday School teacher. Then I was Jr. Sunday School chorister, and my friend, Lola Hansen, was the pianist. During my early years of teaching, the first ward libraries really got going. It was so nice to have this resource rather than hit and miss with whatever we could buy and gather ourselves.

As mentioned earlier, I was married to Michael Clark Murdoch on August 12, 1960. We have had a very good life together. As I write, we will celebrate our 46th anniversary this year (2006). We have a family of two daughters: Janthia Ann Murdoch Reid Hamblin, and Kathryn Ilene Murdoch Reid; as well as two sons: David Lennox Murdoch III, and Michael Clark Murdoch, Jr.

We were able to build a home on the land given to us by Mick's parents, Lennox and Ora Murdoch. This land was one-half acre within the family eight-acre plot. Mick's brother, Bill, and sister, Janet, each received one-half acre to build upon. We lived down "Murdoch Lane" for 38 years. We had a good life with grandmother and grandfather at the top of the lane, Janet and Allan Wilson, and Bill and Arthel Murdoch, and then our home as we come down the lane. Together we raised the 11 grandchildren Ora and Lennox enjoyed. There was a family swimming pool that gave many, many hours of fun in the summer months. We also had a trampoline. Between the swimming pool and the trampoline, as well as trees to climb and property to build club houses on, our children had a wonderful place to grow up.

Another fun thing living down Murdoch Lane was the winter. Uncle Bill would get out his snowmobile and take all the children on rides all over the property. The long lane was frozen most of the winter and it made a great place for the children to be pulled on skis. Mick would pull them with a ski rope and his old truck up and down the lane. Great fun!

When our youngest son was one year old, we bought a boat for water skiing. We owned it with Merlin and Vi Ballard. We enjoyed this boat for many years. The favorite spot was Lake Powell. Every August, we took a week and went to Lake Powell. Many times we planned the trip to coincide with the Ron and Jean Mumford family. A couple of times we rented a house boat, but most of the time we camped on the shore of the lake. In those days, the lake was not so full of visitors as it is now. We had it in the best of times, we feel.

We always raised a large garden. We had a large raspberry patch. Every July I spent many hours picking lovely raspberries. Over time there became so many, that I was able to sell them. I usually sold around 20 cases each summer.

As our children grew, there was always a need for a little extra money. When Mike was around one year old, we began a cleaning job at the Shalamar Wedding Reception Establishment which was located just a half a block west of our home. Our neighbor, Helen Knudsen, owned it. This proved to be a valuable thing in the lives of our children. In the beginning, Janthia was eight years old, Kathryn six, David four, and Mike one. Mick and I would clean the mornings after a wedding, which was usually on Monday and Saturday. We always cleaned before he went to work. The children looked after themselves, with phone calls from Mom to get ready for school. As time went by, we began having them come to help us. This job lasted for 19 years. Our children learned to work, to be dependable, and learned to manage the money they earned. It provided money for our vacations each year, and other things we wanted to do.

In 1976, all of our children were in school all day, so I decided to look for a part-time job. I was very fortunate to find a job as a secretary to Robert B.

Barker, an architect in the stake to which we belonged. It turned into a 25-year position. In the beginning, I worked two days each week, the hours our children were in school. In summer, I only went to the office one day each week. As time went on, I worked three days per week. Then when our sons served missions, Bob conveniently needed a secretary five days per week. It was a wonderful job. The environment was superb. I learned a great deal from Bob, as well as his partner, Nelson W. Clayton. The draftsman, Erling Espedahl, taught me what a true southern gentleman was like.

Our life in the Cottonwood 5th Ward was good. I served in whatever capacity I was called. Over time, I have served in all of the organizations. I want to mention two callings here, just to illustrate the "tender mercies" of the Lord to me. When I was expecting David, I was called to be the Relief Society chorister. We had no piano, and I was most concerned about how I would learn the hymns and practice appropriately to carry out my assignment. I decided we must have a piano. We had little to no extra money. However, I went shopping and found a used piano in the basement of Hart Brothers Music store for $175.00. It was an old upright grand. The dear piano has served our family well for 40 years. I learned some years later when we could afford to have the piano tuned, that the piano was built the same year I was born. Since then, we have had the insides redone, but it still looks the same.

Another calling I received was to be on the stake MIA board as the Mia Maid leader. I was shocked and amazed at the call. I did, however, enjoy serving with Verda Rasband. She was a wonderful Stake MIA President. The challenge for me was that in those days, the stake held leadership meetings once each month, and all the Mia Maid leaders from each ward were expected to come, and I (as the stake Mia Maid leader) was expected to have some enrichment for their lessons for the coming month in some form of take-home items, extra inspirational stories or other things to help lessons to be more interesting or appealing. I am not a very creative person. I wondered how I would ever fulfill this calling; it was so out of my realm. I prayed a lot. Somehow, and I can't even remember how, I was put in contact with a woman who was a stake Mia Maid leader, and was holding monthly meetings in her home for other stake Mia Maid leaders that wanted to come and we would all share our ideas for the coming month. This group saved my life insofar as giving me wonderful ideas to pass on to the Mia Maid leaders of our stake. It was a blessing, pure and simple, provided by the Lord to help me fulfill my calling in a much better way than I otherwise would have.

One other item I would like to be sure to include is that when the Jordan River Temple was going to be built, all the stakes that would be in that temple district were invited to contribute money to the building of the temple. We didn't have a lot, but we were happy to donate to the building of that temple. The Lord always blessed Mick with extra work projects whenever we needed extra. We never had a lot of surplus, but we always had what we needed. We attribute that blessing to our faithful paying of our tithing each month, and the Lord's tender mercies.

Our children had good friends in the ward and at school. They attended Oakwood Elementary, just as their father had done. They attended Cottonwood High School.

Our children were good children. They did well in school. The girls did fun things like choir and pep club. They were comfortable things to go and watch. I can still remember the Veteran's Day choir program at the University of Utah that Kathryn participated in. We didn't even realize such programs took place until she was in one. It's something we try to attend when possible. The boys were a bit different. David played football, as well as participated in drama. Mike was a wrestler. Football and wrestling are a lot more intense from a parents viewing standpoint. I was a nervous wreck. I was glad when David shifted to drama. David played the scarecrow in *The Wizard of Oz*, and did a fabulous job. Mike took fourth in the State of Utah his last year of wrestling.

Our sons each served missions. David served in Scotland, Edinburgh; and Mike served in Portugal, Lisbon North Mission.

In 1988, while Mike was in Portugal, our daughter, Janthia was divorced and came to live with us with her three children - Jennifer, Michael, and Stephanie. She lived with us for two years before buying her own home in West Jordan. She was a very valiant single mother. In 1994 she married Gary Hamblin.

In 1987, Kathryn was married to Kim Reid. They have one daughter, Ashlee.

In 1991, David was married to Barbara Lynn Brooks. They have six children - Amber, Alissa, Spencer, Amanda, Melanie, and John.

In 1992, Mike was married to Rebecca Chamberlain. They have four children - Benjamin, Tracy, Thomas, and Joseph.

In 1976, Mick's father, Lennox passed away. Ora, his mother, was a widow for 27 years. She passed away in October 2003. As his parents were growing older, so were the rest of us. It became harder and harder to keep up with all the property required. There is a lot of work to keeping up nearly eight acres, even when much of it is left to just grow grasses and trees. Irrigating was a summer necessity, which meant that ditches needed to be cleaned annually. The large trees dropped tons of leaves needing to be cleaned up from the ditches as well as lawns. Mother Nature was taking over many areas with heavy growths of trees and vines. In 1999, it was decided to develop the property. This was a difficult decision, but the time seemed to be right, given what was taking place in the Cottonwood area.

Mick and I decided we would move inasmuch as we knew property taxes would escalate. We did not want to have the government eat up whatever value we might reap from the sale of the property. Therefore, on December 17, 1999, we moved from our wonderful home on 6200 South to another lovely home in West Jordan. We lost a great deal of privacy in this move, but had we stayed on Murdoch Lane, we would have lost privacy there inasmuch as huge houses have been built on each of the half acre lots that were marked out in the development. Mick's sister, Janet, and brother, Bill, stayed on the property.

We have enjoyed our new location in West Jordan very much. Our neighbors are very good. Our ward is an excellent ward. Our daughters are both very close, which makes it very nice. They are a lot of help if we need it.

In 2002 we felt we were now in a position to put in missionary papers. We were ultimately called to serve in the Australia Sydney North Mission as microfilm distributors. We were excited to go to Australia, but the microfilm distributor assignment seemed like a very boring idea. We were pleasantly surprised to find our calling very challenging as well as rewarding. We thoroughly enjoyed our two years serving in Sydney. We loved the senior couples we met and served with. We attended Ryde Ward and loved the people there. Australians are very loving people, and it was easy to love them. Our calling utilized all the skills both Mick and I had. All my 25 years of secretarial training was put to good use in the Microfilm Ordering Center. Mick's great attention to detail was put to good use as well. We both felt challenged as well as rewarded in our service.

As I write, it is April 2006. We are enjoying retirement, enjoying interacting with our children and grandchildren. We are enjoying serving in our ward. We are grateful to have the health and strength at the moment to do many things we want to do. The Lord is good to us.

Janthia Ann Murdoch Reid Hamblin

My name is Janthia Ann Murdoch Reid Hamblin. I am the first born child of Michael Clark Murdoch Sr. and Connie Lou Riley Murdoch. I was born on May 11, 1961 and at the time of this writing I am 45 years old. I have one younger sister named Kathryn and two younger brothers named David and Michael.

I grew up in the Cottonwood area at 2133 East 6200 South, Salt Lake City, Utah and had the most ideal childhood. My grandparents are David Lennox Murdoch II and Ora Maurine Clark Murdoch.

They had a plan that has benefited three generations. They bought land. They bought eight acres and it came with a house and apple, pear, peach, and cherry trees. They grew vegetables and raised animals. The lane was lined with two rows of Cottonwood trees. Grandpa also had a swimming pool built. My father grew up with his older brother and younger sister on this property and as each child grew to adulthood they received a gift when they married. The gift was one half acre of land on which to build a home of their own for their family. The house my parents built was the only house I ever lived in until I got married.

I grew up with my cousins and grandparents as close as some neighbors are in a traditional housing development. It seemed like everything we needed was there on the property.

We climbed trees, ran through the woods, played in the ditches during irrigation time, swam in the summer, and watched the leaves change to gold in the fall and when the snow fell, the property became our own winter wonderland.

It is my opinion, that our property defined our family and set us apart in some way. My grandparents were respected and the Murdoch name was associated with that respect. I remember being told, "Remember who you are."

I attended Oakwood Elementary and Bonneville Jr. High. I thought it was really cool that we had our own bus stop at the end of the lane. I graduated from Cottonwood High School in May, 1979 and found employment with the telephone company. At that time, it was called Mountain Bell. I started out as a clerk and felt very fortunate to have such a solid job. I had no idea what I wanted to be when I grew up and college wasn't really encouraged, at least for girls.

I knew I would get married and have children; it was just a matter of time.

That time came on 4 April, 1980. I married Douglas Bret Reid and moved out of my childhood home for the first time. On 28 May, 1981 I gave birth to my first child, a daughter named Jennifer Jae Reid. On 3 October, 1983 I gave birth to my second child, a son named Michael Bret Reid. In October 1985, we began to build a home across the street from my parents. Behind the home of my great grandmother sat one half acre of land. It was as close to the property as one could get and my grandmother agreed to sell the land to me. I felt honored. We moved into our new home in April of 1986. The house was perfect but the economy was not. Both my husband and I were working for the telephone company and for a brief moment, my husband decided he wanted to sell insurance and quit his job. Realizing his mistake, the only way to get back on with the telephone company was to move to Denver, Colorado. We moved in July, 1987. On 22 May, 1988 I gave birth to my third child, a daughter named Stephanie Lynn Reid. I was divorced in March of 1989 and came back home to Utah with my own children and back to my parents' house in Cottonwood.

  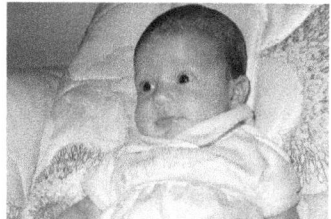

LEFT: *Jennifer Rae Reid* MIDDLE: *Michael Bret Reid* RIGHT: *Stephanie Lynn Reid*

My children, too, had the benefit of living on the property surrounded by their grandparents and my grandmother, their great grandmother, and they climbed trees and ran through the woods and played in the ditches during irrigation time and swam in the summer and watched the leaves turn gold in the fall and when the snow fell, saw the property turn into a winter wonderland.

In May 1990, I was fortunate to be able to build my own home in West Jordan. I was one mile away from my sister, Kathryn, and her family. She was willing to watch my children during the day. I was still working at the phone company but the company was now called US West. I was a service representative in the business office. I talked to residential and small business customers and took orders to start their phone service or answer questions about their bill.

I was very grateful to have my job. It was a good job that paid well and had excellent benefits. Now that I was a single mother of three, it was up to me to provide everything for them. I worked hard to give my children as normal a childhood as possible. But they did have to learn at an early age about responsibility. I had to leave the house early and then when I got to work I would call home to make sure everyone was awake and getting ready for school. Kathryn would come to the house by 8:00 A.M. to pick up Stephanie and make sure Jennifer and Michael left on time for school. When the kids got home from school, they would call me at work and let me know they were home. If they had arguments or questions they would call me at work. I really felt like I raised my children by telephone! The kids did well in school and both Jennifer and Michael played soccer. I was even the coach for Jennifer's team for two years. This made things rather difficult for Michael because if his game was at the same time as Jennifer's, I couldn't be there to watch him play. Stephanie tried playing soccer for one year and decided she didn't like it.

All my children excelled in school. They were driven to do well and get good grades. They were much harder on themselves than I ever was.

In May, 1994, I was asked by a co-worker if I would be interested in a date with her ex-husband. I was rather surprised by this question because if this guy was so nice, why were they divorced? She told me his second wife had recently passed away from breast cancer and his daughters were worried about him. They told her they wished he could meet a nice lady to go out with. One morning as she was getting ready for work, she said that my name just came into her head, so she thought she would ask me if I was interested. Being a single, working mom didn't really leave much time to date and I considered my dating opportunities rather limited. But I decided to take a chance and on 25 November, 1994 I married Gary Elden Hamblin. He is a wonderful man and accepted and loved my children right from the beginning. He grew up in the Ogden area, but moved to my house so the kids wouldn't have to be uprooted. He was working for Jetway, which is the company that builds the walkways that connect from the airplane to the terminal. He also had his own side business as an income tax preparer. He left Jetway after 22 years and began working as an accountant for a trucking company. Each year his tax business would grow and he dreamed of the day when he could just work for himself. In January, 2006, his dream was realized. He quit his full time job and became his own "boss". He passed the test to become credentialed as an Enrolled Agent. Hamblin Tax & Accounting Services, Inc. can prepare your personal or business taxes, do your bookkeeping and accounting and if necessary, represent you in an audit.

Murdoch Lane

Jennifer married Bryan Newel Boyce on 1 November, 2003. She graduated in 2005 from Utah State University with a Bachelors Degree in Computer Electronics Technology. On 24 September, 2006 they welcomed their first child and my first grandchild into the world. His name is Brayden Newel Boyce. Jennifer works for Convergys, which is a call center that handles customers of Direct-TV satellite service.

Michael married Sonya Avery on 2 July, 2005. They do not have any children yet, but they do have three dogs and two cats. Right now, I consider their pets my "grand-puppies" and "grand-kitties". Michael develops and designs web pages.

Stephanie married Andrew David Reese on 29 July, 2006 and moved to Tulsa, Oklahoma. She wants to be a dental hygienist or maybe even a dentist!

After 23 years of working for the telephone company, I was laid off in February, 2002. There I was, 41 years old and I still didn't know what I wanted to be when I grew up. The phone company, which was now known as Qwest, actually called me back as a temporary employee and I worked there until September, 2003. I had learned a lot about the telecommunications business and found it was difficult for potential employers to see me as a good candidate. Mostly it was because of my previous wages, but the other part was that I had no college education. And so it became time for me to go back to school. I enrolled at Stevens-Henager College in December, 2003. I chose the Medical Assistant Program. One of my favorite television shows was *ER* and I enjoyed watching the show even more after I started my courses. I learned medical terminology, radiology, medical billing and coding and phlebotomy (drawing blood). The program also offered several different avenues I could pursue after graduation. I love learning new things and found that although I liked many areas I was drawn to the billing and coding aspect of the medical field. In some ways, this was like work I had previously done for Qwest. I am detail oriented and this is a good trait to have when sending billing claims to insurance companies. I graduated in May, 2005 with an Associates Degree in Medical Specialties and maintained a GPA of 3.95. My school had an employment placement program and they had received a call from a podiatrist's office needing someone to handle the front office. I went to the interview and was offered the job. A Doctor of Podiatry is considered a specialist and the doctor works Monday thru Friday from 9:00am to 5:00pm. I get all the major holidays off and don't work on weekends. I love my job! I am the office manager and handle all aspects of running an office. Again, my phone skills really helped, and I get to do all the billing and coding!

I am now 45 years old and have learned that time marches on and the only thing constant is change.

The property has changed, too. It has now been developed into "Murdoch Woods Place". There are seven new homes that have been built and the original Cottonwood trees which lined the lane have been replaced with new trees. These new trees will grow and the look of the property will change, but in my heart, the memories I have will forever stay the same.

Kathryn Ilene Murdoch Reid

I was born 4 October 1963.
 I was born in Salt Lake City Utah.
 I am the second of four children.
 My parents are Michael and Connie Murdoch.
 My childhood memories are full of happy times! Where I grew up we were surrounded by big, tall poplar trees, and lots of property to run

around on and play childhood games, lots of hide and seek, and playing in the irrigation ditch. That was a fun one where we would have one of us up at the head gate of the ditch and another down stream and we would send notes to each other in plastic Easter eggs. We had a treasure chest where we would keep all our supplies, like paper, matches for burning the edges of the notes, and the plastic eggs. That was a lot of fun! Good times! We lived on eight acres of land shared with my Dad's family. There was Grandma and Grandpa's house at the end of the long lane that was lined with poplar trees, then his brother's house, his sister's house, and then our house. We were spaced far enough apart that it was very private. One of the best things we shared was the swimming pool that was located up at Grandma and Grandpa's house. We all looked forward to opening the pool each summer. There was work involved but we all pitched in to get it cleaned out from the winter and ready for a fresh coat of paint. Then it was ready to put the hose in and begin to fill it. What a happy day it was when the pool was finally full and we were able to get in. I also remember that it was getting close to pool time when the cotton was flying from all the cottonwood trees. To this day, the memory of the pool is brought back each year when the cotton flies. We always had to wait until after the cotton was done flying. The long summer days spent at the swimming pool are some of my happiest! With cousins around to play with added to the fun. I also enjoyed all the leaves that fell from the trees in the fall. There was a lot of raking and hauling off of the leaves. It was a lot of work but it was also fun. I really have a lot of fond memories of where I grew up. It was unlike any other place. I really miss it!!

My grade school days were spent at Oakwood Elementary. I enjoyed almost all of my teachers there and even the principal was a good memory. The principal was Mr. Bond and he was very friendly and made you feel safe at school. He would even join you for a game of *four square* during recess. I can remember all of my teachers. I started off with Mrs. Harris for Kindergarten. She seemed ancient to me. I thought she was at least 90 or so, that being from the point of view of a five year old. She was nice anyway. Kindergarten was spent mostly on the floor on our rugs. I mostly remember nap time and snack time. Our snack was graham crackers and milk which is something I still enjoy. We didn't have a desk or anything like that, just our rug. I think Kindergarten back then was a time to get use to being separated from our mothers during the day. I don't remember learning anything. In first grade, my teacher was Miss Donnelly. She was nice and pretty too. Finally, we had our own desk to sit at and boy did I feel grown up. One thing I remember about 6th grade was our French day activity. We all rode our bikes to school and we ate French bread and cheese out on the big lawn and we rode our bikes around the play ground. It was a fun day. I can still see me standing at the window in 6th grade classroom looking out and thinking it will be forever before I will be in high school.

I attended Bonneville Jr. High School. I really enjoyed jr. high. I loved having seven different classes and having a locker and different teachers throughout the day. The school was so big. I enjoyed 7th and 9th grade the most. One of my favorite classes was band. I played the clarinet.

I attended Cottonwood High School, which was a great school and very big. It was easy to get lost, which I did on the first day of school. I was early because I had early morning seminary but still managed to be late to my first class because I couldn't figure out the map they gave us. I'm still not good with maps. I enjoyed high school but was glad to graduate! I graduated in 1982. Some of my favorite classes were shorthand, typing, choir, and math.

While in high school, I worked at the Arctic Circle, a fast food place. It was a fun job because we were all friends that worked there. It was just a drive-up, take-out place. It was always fun to work there until one night we were the victims of a robbery. It was a night I have never forgotten. The robber came in wearing coveralls and a motocross helmet. He jumped over the counter and I screamed and he pulled out a gun and put it to my head. Later, during the robbery, he put the gun down while trying to open the register and bumped his bag and the gun went off. That night was one of the scariest of my life. I quit working there and moved up the street to Dan's Food Store. I worked in the bakery and snack bar. It was lots of fun and I felt safer working there.

After graduating from high school, I wanted to go work as a nanny. I have always loved kids and did a lot of tending. I had a couple of friends who got jobs as nannies working in New York. I asked them to find a job for me. It didn't take long and I received a letter from a family who was looking for a nanny. I was so excited! The family only had one child. He was two years old and his name was Daniel. The parents were Jill and David Lehv. Jill was a high school teacher of French and Spanish, and

David was a lawyer and worked in Manhattan. I accepted the job and left in August 1982. This was so exciting; I had never been on an airplane before. The flight to New York was very bumpy. It was kind of scary for me. It was raining when I landed at the airport. The family lived in White Plains. It was very beautiful there. I wasn't quite sure what to expect. My thoughts about New York were lots of tall buildings and no trees, but to my surprise there were tons of trees. I was so happy. Trees make me feel safe, having grown up with lots of trees around. The family I worked for was a nice Jewish family. I got to learn about another culture. Some of my duties were to drive the husband to the train station every morning and pick him up in the evening. I got to drive his car which was a yellow VW bug. I had always wanted one of those. It was fun to drive. My nanny experience was great! On the weekend my friends and I would go into the city and have fun exploring all the sights. Sometimes we would go to West Point and enjoy a football game or even go to the dances there. Good times! My nanny responsibilities were for the day time only. I had my evenings and weekends free. Not a bad deal. On Sunday, I would go to church in Westchester. The ward was very nice and there were tons of nannies. Sometimes we would go to church in the city. There was so much to see. My whole experience was positive. In March 1983 my sister, Janthia, came to visit me. That was very nice. However, at the time she came, New York was having a transit strike and the only way to get around was by bus. There were lots of people taking the bus, but we managed to make the most of it. Needless to say, we missed all the major sites, no Statue of Liberty, no Empire State Building. But we did manage to get to Bloomingdales, Neiman Marcus, and Florsheim Shoes. We bought some great shoes! Some of my favorite New York food was the meatball pizza and pumpernickel bagels. So my time in New York was from August 1982 through July of 1983. When it was time for me to return home, my family came to pick me up. They drove out in a motor home from Utah to New York. We toured the Mormon Trail on our way home. It was lots of fun! It was quite the trip. I have kept in touch with the family over the years. Jill even came to Utah for my wedding, which was a special treat.

When I returned home from New York, I attended Cosmetology School. I enjoyed doing hair for many years. I have been doing my Grandma Riley's hair every other Saturday for many years. My cousin and I rotate Saturdays. It is a special time that I have with my Grandma. We have had some great conversations. She inspires me to never give up. She just turned 93 on October 27, 2007; she is legally blind and still lives on her own with her cat. She is amazing to me. One of her favorite sayings is "it's a great life if you don't weaken." Also that "we must endure to the end."

Some of my favorite family memories were spent on vacation each summer. We would go water skiing. We often went to Pine View Reservoir.

That is where I learned to ski! I really loved it. My Dad was very patient in teaching me. We also went to Lake Powell and once we went there that was the only place for us. When we started going to Lake Powell we would either camp in the campground or camp on the beach. One year we rented a houseboat and that was so cool! That is the only way to go. What a beautiful place to enjoy with the rock cliffs and sandy beaches. We always found a private place to call our own. I love going there! My favorite was to lay out and soak up all the sun and get that golden tan. Lake Powell still remains one of my favorite places because that is where I met my husband. My parents always worked hard to save money so that they could take us on a vacation.

My favorite color is purple. I have always been drawn to this color. My bedroom growing up was purple and pink with purple shag carpet. I loved it! I also had this purple coat that was like an Eskimo coat. My couches in my living room are purple leather. What can I say, it is a great color!

Some of my favorite pets I had growing up were gerbils, and I also had a rabbit. One of my best friends, Kathleen Browning, had rabbits and when her rabbits had babies, she gave me one. I took it home and my Dad built a hutch for her. Dad was awesome, he could build anything!

In the summer of 1986 I went on a trip to Lake Powell. My sister and her husband and a group of friends rented a houseboat. One of the couples had to cancel so there was an opening and they invited me to go. I was so happy! It was on this trip that I met my husband, Kevin Kim Reid. He had been invited to be the houseboat driver. The group of people on this trip were all couples and we were the only single ones. We had a great time getting to know each other. There was definitely that spark! When the trip ended our relationship continued. We saw each other everyday for a year. We got engaged on Easter 1987. We were married on July 21, 1987. Kim worked in sales for 20 years. He worked selling Kirby vacuums door to door. He is very talented and can do most anything. He is very handy around the house.

My faith was strengthened after becoming inactive in church for a few years and then deciding to become active again when our daughter, Ashlee, was to be baptized. My husband called the bishop of our ward and asked what we needed to do to have her baptized. The ward missionaries were assigned to us and came weekly to teach her. Soon after her baptism, the bishop called us in to give us each a church calling. They called my husband, Kim, to be the scout master. He was excited about being in scouts because he really enjoyed scouts in his youth and is himself, an Eagle Scout. I was called to teach the Sunbeams in Primary. I was pretty excited! I love children and my class was the three year olds. What a fun age. I have always loved children so this was a good place for me. In teaching the three year olds the basic principles of the church, it was also reteaching me. It brought the light of Christ back into my life. Then the bishop asked my husband if we were paying tithing. He replied no, that we couldn't afford to. The bishop offered a challenge to my husband and told him if we would pay tithing, we would be blessed, and if we weren't able to pay our bills after paying tithing he would pay them for us. Well needless to say, we have not had to ask the bishop to pay any of our bills. It has been a great testimony of faith. We have been very blessed. Once we got our life back on track, then there was the question of going to the temple. It was something I always wanted for us - to be sealed together. But I wanted my husband to want it too. I didn't want to force anything on him so I kept this to myself. I just kept silently hoping for that day to come. Soon the ward missionaries were inquiring if we would like to take the Temple Preparation Class. It had been five years now that we were actively going to church and making the changes we needed. We did start to take the Temple Preparation Class. We were both excited but nervous as well, knowing this was a big and important thing to do. When it came time to decide on a date to go to the temple, we chose September 28, 2002. My parents were preparing to leave on a mission to Australia. We knew we wanted to do it before they left. We wanted them there with us. It was one of the best days of my life! I will never forget that day. Just like the bishop had told us during one of the interviews, that the moment Ashlee entered the sealing room, it would be very special and he was right. She was 13 years old and looked so beautiful in her white dress. She was glowing just like an angel. I love going to the temple and I am grateful we are blessed with so many temples around us. So the happiest day of my life and also the most important thing I have ever done, I would say, is the day we were sealed together as a family in the Jordan River Temple.

The interests my spouse and I share are many. We enjoy camping. We love the mountains. One of our favorite spots is in the Uintah Mountains at the Moose Horn Campground. I love it there. I love being by the water and there is a lake at the base of Mount Baldy. We also enjoy fishing and bird watching. We just enjoy being with each other. Going on long drives (before the price of gas became outrageous at over $3.00 a gallon) and listening to music, talking and laughing. We also enjoy going to Snowbird, which is up Little Cottonwood Canyon and enjoying the spa at the Cliff Lodge. That is our little get-away spot.

My father is Michael Clark Murdoch. The most important thing he taught me was patience. But it seems I am still trying to learn it. He is the most patient person I know. He is also a very service oriented. He will do whatever he can for others, never complaining always serving. I want to be just like him when I grow up. He is my inspiration!

My mother is Connie Riley Murdoch. The most important thing she taught me was the value of hard work. When I was in second grade, our family took on the job of cleaning the Shalamar, a wedding and reception hall. We took this job on as a family. The extra money enabled us to take vacations and help with any other things we needed. We would get up at 5:30 in the morning and clean before school. Dad would help until he had to leave for work. It taught us to work together and also to appreciate what it took to clean up after people. We did this for many years. With hard work, we learned you get out of it what you put into it.

We had a large vegetable garden that took hours of work, weeding, and harvesting the vegetables. We would can them as well. I enjoyed it some of the time but now I appreciate having been taught these things - the value of self reliance. Home grown vegetables were the best. The homemade grape juice was such a treat, and Mom would use it like medicine when we got sick. It tasted great and we did feel better. Mom also had a huge raspberry patch that took her hours to pick but she did it and we enjoyed raspberry jam all winter long. Sometimes she sold cases of raspberries for extra money as well. Mom also taught me to be thrifty and to spend my money wisely.

My first and only child was born August 4, 1989 at 9:30 A.M. at Alta View Women's Center. We were so excited and I was also very scared. This being my first child, I didn't know what to expect. After several long hours of labor, things changed and the delivery ended up as an emergency C-section. I was very relieved when the baby was out and we found out it was a girl! We named her Ashlee Kae Reid. She was such a cute baby with lots of dark hair and dark brown eyes. She was a very good baby. I never thought I was only going to have one child. I had always imagined at least two maybe even four. But that was not how it worked out for me. I felt bad for Ashlee being an only child. I can still hear her as a small child in the back seat of the car saying to me "Ok, I am ready for my brother or sister now." It broke my heart. I had a miscarriage a year before. It was very sad and I feel for anyone who has gone though one themselves. I found joy in tending my sister Janthia's kids. This gave Ashlee her siblings she wanted so badly. It was good for all of us. Stephanie is the youngest of her kids and was one year older than Ashlee and so it was like they were sisters. In fact they are double cousins. Janthia's first husband is my husband Kim's brother.

The birthday I remember most was my 40th. We had spent the day up at Utah State University for a marching band competition that Ashlee was in. It was a beautiful fall day. While there, my brother Mike called me to inform me that Grandma Murdoch was being moved from her assisted living place to another one. She was sick needed more care than they could give her there. Mike was sure the move would be too much for her. We thought she might pass away shortly after the move. On the drive home from Logan that night, the sunset was unlike any other I had seen. I couldn't get my Grandma out of my mind. But the sunset had me captivated. All I could think of was what a beautiful painting it was. The colors were so pretty. I had the feeling that my Grandma had passed away and this was her final painting. She was very artistic and it just seemed like something she would have done. I felt a calmness about me while looking at the sky that night. When we got home I received a call that Grandma did pass away. I was sad. I thought what a horrible remembrance of a birthday that was dreaded anyway. I didn't want to be 40, but now that I think about it, it was a nice way to celebrate her. Each birthday I am reminded of her. She was 94 when she died. She was a great part of my life. I really miss her.

My wedding day was a nice summer day. I was married on July 21, 1987. We were married at the Shalamar. We were married by the bishop of my parents, Dr. Craig Davis. It was a nice day. We had a nice wedding luncheon at Little America. But most of all we were anxious to start our life together. We spent our first night together at the Airport Hilton in the honeymoon suite. That was a very nice gift from my friend, Linda Ronne. The next day we headed to Bryce Canyon where we spent the rest of our honeymoon. We had a great time!

At the time of this writing, Ashlee graduated from high school in June, 2007, and has started college. I am 44 years old, still working and enjoying life as a mother and wife. There is still a lot of life yet to live.

David Lennox Murdoch

I was born on May 11, 1966 in Salt Lake City, Utah. I am the third child of Michael and Connie Murdoch. In my family there are a total of four children. I have the distinct privilege of stating that I was born on the same day as my oldest sister Janthia. The catch is she is five years older than I am. After Janthia came Kathryn, who is is 2½ years older than I am. Kathryn is the only member of my family in which I was able to attend school with (at the junior and senior high level). This made it easier for me when I was just starting junior high and high school because I knew I had an older sister that I could go to for help if I needed it. My younger brother, Michael (Mike), was named after my father. He was born with red hair and untold amounts of energy. Janthia isn't far behind Mike, but Mike generally was the one causing us to be tired by watching him run all over the place.

LEFT: *Easter 1970 on Murdoch Lane* RIGHT: *David and Michael 1972*

For some reason, Mom and Dad decided to name me after Dad's father, David Lennox Murdoch. Grandpa was in turn named after his grandfather, David Lennox Murdoch. Therefore, if you want to get fancy, my full name is David Lennox Murdoch III (on my birth certificate it does not indicate "III"). Bearing my grandfather's name has been of great value to me. With Grandma Murdoch's assistance, the honor and respect associated with this name has been instilled in my heart and mind. Unfortunately, Grandpa died a few months after my 12th birthday, on November 20, 1978. I will always be grateful for the legacy and honorable reputation which my grandfather left me to follow.

Before Grandpa's death he took me to a clothing store. I think it was ZCMI. I remember weaving in and out of the round racks which held all the articles of clothing. I remember Grandpa taking me to a rack which had several leather belts hanging on it. I would soon be receiving the Aaronic Priesthood, afterward being ordained a Deacon in The Church of Jesus Christ of Latter-day Saints. Grandpa understood this was an important event in my life. He wanted me to look nice as I passed the sacrament, so he was taking me to buy a belt. I still have this belt today but unfortunately I don't have the same waist size to wear it. Instead, I have a priceless memory which I will always have in my heart.

Continuing on a religious note, because of my parent's membership in The Church of Jesus Christ of Latter-day Saints, I was born "under the covenant." This means I am sealed to my parents in this life and in the life to come; to one day be able to live and associate with them while living in the presence of a loving Father in Heaven. It also means I have been blessed to have the protection and power of the Priesthood in my home throughout my life. Once more, I will always be indebted to my parents for being the source of this and many other blessings.

Three generations of David Lennox Murdoch

Where I lived

I have many wonderful memories of where I grew up in the Cottonwood area. Sadly, the home and surrounding property has dramatically changed over the past decade. My parent's house is no longer standing; my grandparent's home suffered the same demolition fate. And the trees, well, the dozens of glorious poplar trees that once lined the dirt driveway leading to the homes situated on "Murdoch Acres" have all been replaced with new, younger trees. Hopefully the new trees will grow to the same splendor that their predecessors did. In spite of these dramatic changes that have transpired, I would like to give a brief history of the property and describe what the property was like as I remember it while living as a youth with my parents.

My grandparents moved from Salt Lake City to what was then "the country" when my dad was a wee lad. They purchased a large plot of ground (about 7.5 acres) that had a long dirt driveway just off of 6200 South and just below 2300 East. The dirt lane was lined with over 50 huge poplar trees and led to a beautiful house which was built right next to a stream used for irrigating the property. The years passed and my father and his siblings grew to adulthood. As a wedding gift, my grandparents gave each of their children (Uncle Bill, Dad, and Aunt Janet) a half acre of land, sectioned off from the original 7.5 acres, to build their homes. Consequently I had the unique opportunity of growing up with my aunts, uncles, cousins, and grandparents as neighbors.

Our home was surrounded by trees, bushes, wild flowers and all types of critters (quail, pheasant, squirrels, robins, raccoons, garden snakes, owls, gophers, bats, etc.) We would play for hours outside making forts, digging holes, building "hideouts", and climbing trees. Our property truly was a small piece of heaven and a secure haven to live in while growing up as a young boy. I love the trees and outdoors primarily because of the beautiful "wilderness" that surrounded our home.

Club Houses and Hiding Places

Growing up I remember my father as often wielding a hammer, saw, and tape measure. If you needed a piece of wood for this or for that, he was always able to provide it. Not only could he provide it but he could help you use it in whatever product you were building or project you were engaged in. As a young boy, the project I wanted to complete was that of building a clubhouse.

Dad built a clubhouse for my brother Mike and me which stood tall and strong. I was able to help him with some of the hammering, measuring etc., but he did the majority of the work. Being the independent little boy that I was, I wanted to build my own clubhouse. Mom and Dad gave me permission and I began construction. I must admit, my construction plans were not as refined and detailed as my father's were. As I rethink through my design, I realize my problem was in the foundation. You see, my father, knowing that the foundation of any building (or any principle) must be strong and properly built, took the time to select the proper building materials and construct a solid foundation. I on the other hand, did not think through this process thoroughly. As a result, the floor of my quickly built clubhouse deteriorated over the years. This was caused by the irrigation water which often flooded this area of the woods in order to water the trees and plants. It was a nice clubhouse for a few years, but it didn't last as long as the clubhouse Dad built.

While this small structure was in its prime, it served as the location for my club, otherwise known as "Club 51". It was a wonderful establishment. We collected club funds, had club meetings, and even had our own set of club rules.

Rules of Club 51 (1977)
Obey the chief (Since I was the chief, I think this was a pretty good rule)
Don't fool around with things
Don't yell
Don't act dumb and don't be dumb

Don't interrupt the chief or anyone else
Don't lean on table or wiggle table
Obey the rules
Be quiet
Call me chief
Don't tell club secrets to anyone
Don't feel sorry for yourself
Don't start crying
Don't talk back to anyone
Don't slam door
Pay club fund
Listen to who is talking
Don't steal
Don't call people names
Lock door
Don't grab
Don't lie
Don't ask questions
Come to club meetings
Don't let Mark in clubhouse
No girls aloud

Now I'm not sure which Mark was referenced in #24, but you get the idea that we had quite a club. It was a place where we often played, held meetings, drew up treasure maps then went out and actually hid small boxes of money in the ground. Sometimes when we would sleep overnight in the clubhouse, it would start to rain and you could hear the drops falling on the tin roof. We could always hear the rustling of the leaves as the gentle breeze cooled the night air.

In addition to the clubhouse, one of the many other hiding places I had was in the loft of the garage. Dad had lots of wood and boxes stored up there. It was a bit hot and stuffy, but it was exciting to be hidden from view. I would run home from school, go into the kitchen, gather my food rations (graham crackers and soda crackers), and then climb into the garage loft. It was great up there because no one knew where you were, but if they came into the garage you could peek through the cracks in the loft and watch them look for you.

Birds, Trees and Other Animals

Due to the amount of trees on the property, we always had birds flying around. We also had two large gardens which ended up being prime targets for the pheasants. Every now and then we would hear them "crowing" and moving through the woods. Whenever I would see them, I would always marvel at their size and beauty. One day I decided it was time for me to crow like a pheasant. So I got up early the next morning, just before the sun began to rise, went out into the middle of the driveway, squatted down just like I thought a pheasant would do, tucked my hands in my armpits, and began to crow. What a sight that must have been!

On two other occasions, I was able to see a huge eagle and a beautiful peacock. The eagle was over by the irrigation ditch (no water in it). There were feathers everywhere and it was obvious this eagle had caught some other type of bird. I didn't know eagles caught other birds to eat. The peacock had escaped from a neighbor's cage. I remember is simply strutting around as if it owned the place. A beautiful bird, but I think it had an attitude problem.

Grandma's Molly-Whoppet Parties

Grandma Murdoch had the incredible ability to take her creative ideas and bring them into reality. One such idea was that of holding Molly-Whoppet parties. She dubbed herself Mrs. Molly Whoppet and would spend several hours baking sugar cookies of all shapes and sizes. She would then set up enough card tables and chairs to facilitate the occupancy of all her grandchildren (eleven in all). At each child's work station she would provide three or four bowls of candy, such as candy hearts, M&Ms, chocolate chips, marshmallows, etc. There would also be one or two bowls of icing along with a knife and the cookies she had baked. Prior to the party she would make beautiful invitations and deliver them to all the grandchildren. At the appointed hour we would all go to Grandma's home with great excitement and anticipation. She would have all the grandchildren take their assigned seats, and for the next 45 minutes or so, we would all invent different ways of decorating and icing the cookies she had made. After the cookie decorating we would play various games that always resulted in winning some type of prize. When we were all finished we all went home with our prizes and cookies to eat, enjoy, and remember the fun we had at Grandma's house.

Mom's Cooking

Mom says it took her a few years to develop the cooking skills she has today. But as far as I can remember, Mom has always been the world's greatest cook. A few of my most favorite items on the menu are apple pie, fresh baked bread, and cinnamon rolls ... all made from scratch. Yes she can cook other things in addition to these lovely baked items, but it has always been the pies, cakes, and rolls which I have loved the most.

One of the disadvantages of Mom's cooking was that we didn't always get to eat it. Mom was always making this or that for someone else in the ward or in the neighborhood. More than once I remember asking Mom if

I could have a cookie or sample the rolls she had just baked. She would kindly tell me "I'm afraid not . . . they are for someone else." She would on occasion let us lick the bowls or the spoons which were used to mix the batter. I loved that. I even enjoyed eating the leftover pie crust dough. What a blessing it was to have a mother that knew how to cook wonderful food.

Working, Breakfast, and Toast

While growing up, I was taught the principles of work and frugality. Dad was always working on extra money-making projects in the garage, or out in the neighborhood. Mom had her share of extra work as well. A few blocks west of our home there was a wedding reception business called Shalamar. It was a very nice establishment and housed many weddings and wedding receptions. Next to Shalamar there was another wedding reception home called The Crystal Room. Both of these businesses were owned and managed by one of our neighbors. As with all establishments, someone needs to clean and vacuum the building. This is the extra job Mom began when I was about five or six years old. As a cleaning crew, Mom had Janthia and Kathryn help her. When Mike and I were old enough, we too began to help clean. Every Sunday, Mom would get down her calendar and tell us what days we would be cleaning that week. It wasn't always on the same days because weddings occurred sporadically. The big dread of all dreads was when Mom would inform us that we had to "clean two." This meant there had been a wedding or wedding reception in both the Shalamar and The Crystal Room. That's when it was really hard.

On the appointed morning before school, Mom would wake us up and tell us to get ready to go and clean. She would then go downstairs to the kitchen and make us breakfast (one of the benefits of getting up to clean was Mom made us breakfast). For breakfast, we religiously had toast and Ovaltine. I became very adept at dunking my toast and letting it soak for just the right amount of time. Then before it became too soggy and fell into my glass I would quickly place the soggy toast in my anxiously awaiting mouth. To this day, I still enjoy the act of dunking my food (generally graham crackers) and eating toast.

School

Some of the best advice I was given prior to entering high school was to "get involved". Being involved in extracurricular activities made school a lot of fun. I played two years of American football, competed in drama competitions, worked on the stage crew for a few musicals, and even had a few acting roles myself. My favorite role was that of the Scarecrow in The Wizard of Oz performed for our school's "Children's Theater". I still remember the look of excitement and amazement on the faces of the children that attended the performance in our big school auditorium at Cottonwood High School. They were amazed to see a tornado blow us to and fro, and they couldn't believe their eyes when they saw a witch fly across the stage.

After graduating from Cottonwood High School, I attended Brigham Young University for a year prior to serving a full time, two-year mission for my church. I really enjoyed my experience at BYU. It was the first time I had lived away from home for an extended period of time and it was the first time I had experienced homesickness. The realities of life were slowly coming into my life; I was growing up. I stayed in the dorms (John Hall in Helaman Halls) and made wonderful friends. For the most part, we all got along well and built lasting memories. One of the challenges of being in the dorms was privacy. There really wasn't any place to go if you wanted to quietly be by yourself to ponder and pray. One day I noticed the door to the janitorial closet was open. I peeked in and found there might be enough room to kneel in prayer. For several months this tiny "room" became my prayer room when I needed a quiet place to be alone to pray.

As my 19th birthday approached, I knew it was time to submit my papers to notify the church that I had a desire to be a full-time missionary. I submitted my papers and waited for their reply. Several weeks later my parents called and indicated that a large envelope had come to the home from church headquarters. It was my mission call! I arranged for a friend to take me to the bus stop where I took a commuter bus from Provo to Salt Lake City where my parents picked me up. With great anticipation we gathered the family around up at Grandma Murdoch's home and I opened the letter. With wonder and excitement I read that I had been called to serve in the Scotland Edinburgh Mission for a period of two years. "Unbelievable," I thought ... "but where exactly was Scotland?"

Mission Experience

Shortly after receiving my mission call, I turned nineteen. A month later, I entered the Mission Training Center (MTC) in Provo Utah (1985). I was there for about three weeks learning how to be a missionary and learning a bit about the Scottish culture. At the conclusion of my training, I flew to Scotland with about six other missionaries. Two missionaries met us at the airport, helped us load our luggage into the mission van, and then drove us to the mission home/office where we met our mission president and his wife, President and Sister Dunn. As we traveled on the road, I truly thought we were going to die. My brain had been conditioned for 19 years to drive on the right side of the road. In Scotland (and all of the UK) I was introduced to driving on the left side of the road. Every corner we took and every vehicle that approached us, made me think we were going to crash. Somehow, we made it to the mission home without hitting anything. To me it was a miracle.

As I entered the mission home, I was amazed at how thick the walls where. They were all made from big blocks of sandstone, probably a foot thick and the ceiling in the rooms must have been twenty feet high! Everything was so old and so beautiful. I sat down on a couch and quickly learned what jet lag was. Within seconds, my eyes became so heavy that I felt like I could sleep for a week. I tried to fight off the urge to sleep but I lost that battle; I was out. I don't remember when I met the mission president (before or after my unconsciousness) but I do remember having immediate respect for him and his wife. I could tell they were great people that cared about us as missionaries and were there to help us adjust and get on with why we were there; to teach the Scottish people about the good news of the restored gospel of Jesus Christ.

While serving in Scotland, I was given the opportunity of serving with twelve companions (one stake missionary and 11 full-time missionaries) all of which taught me something about the gospel, myself, and life. Over the next two years I was given the opportunity of living in Elgin and Forres, Saltcoats, Stornoway (Isle of Lewis), Aberdeen, Paisley, and Edinburgh. These areas provided me with a good view of both the highlands and lowlands of Scotland. I quickly fell in love with the beautiful country and its wonderful people. There were times when I became discouraged and there were times when I was filled with joy. On one occasion, I was struggling with keeping my motivation where it needed to be; I was feeling quite discouraged. We had spent hours and hours knocking on doors and no one really wanted to talk to us about the gospel. We came to an older house that had a sandstone ornament or fixture above the front door. It contained two simple words: "Stand Fast". This powerful phrase had a great impact upon me. I realized that I needed to pick myself up and not allow myself to become discouraged; I needed to stand fast in what I knew was right and in what I knew I had been called to do. To this day, those two words resonate powerfully in my heart and mind as something I need to do and want to do; standing fast in that which I know is right and true.

University and Dating

I loved being a missionary because I could stay focused on something that really mattered. But my two years quickly passed and it was time to move on to the next stage of my life. I returned home in the summer of 1987 and returned to BYU that fall. I continued with my plans to graduate with a degree in Computer Science, but more importantly I started to search for an eternal companion.

One day on campus I bumped into a friend from my mission, David Brooks. He and I had touched basis a few times since our return from

Scotland and I had attended his wedding a few months prior. On this day, I think we were in line to give blood. He reminded me that he had a younger sister at BYU and that she and I should get together on a date. He gave me her phone number and also informed me that it was her birthday that week. A day or two later, I gave Barbara a call and sang Happy Birthday to her over the phone. I then asked her if she would like to go out on a date. Kindly, she accepted. On the appointed date, I went to Barbara's apartment and picked her up. She looked beautiful. Not having a lot of money the date was simple but fun. We ate dinner at the Cougar Eat (a dining area on campus) where we enjoyed a nice meal which included a large helping of chocolate pudding. Unfortunately, the pudding was so good that we ended up eating too much which resulted in not feeling too well. We then made our way to the Harris Fine Arts Center were we located a room with a piano. I knew Barbara played the piano and I thought it would be fun to play the piano and sing songs together. I think we both enjoyed ourselves that night. I know I felt great hope that perhaps "this was the one!"

Barbara and I dated off and on for the next several months. Soon I was hooked and couldn't stop thinking of her. I would write little notes to her and leave cards for her at her apartment. On one date, I had the distinct impression that Barbara was the one I should marry. She was everything I was looking for in a wife and a mother. I looked at myself and hoped I was what she needed in a husband and a father. Marriage was a big step but I knew it was the right thing to do.

As time progressed, I learned that Barbara had a desire to serve a full-time mission for the church. I knew this would be a wonderful experience for her and supported her in this decision. I realized that a mission for her would mean that she would be gone for eighteen months and a lot could change in that time period. We discussed the implications of this decision and we both understood that there were no guarantees that our feelings for each other would remain unchanged by the time she returned. Barbara submitted her mission papers and soon received her call to serve in the visitor center at the Oakland California Temple. Barbara moved home with her parents in Coolidge, Arizona to get ready to leave on her mission. When Barbara was set apart as a full-time missionary, I flew down to Arizona to be there for this important event. Once she was a full-time missionary, it became very awkward because I could no longer give her a hug or hold her hand. Instead I gave her a warm and mighty handshake. I loved Barbara and knew I would really miss her while she was gone.

For the next eighteen months I wrote faithfully to Barbara. I'm not a big letter writer but did my best to send supportive letters to her. I dated a few times during that eighteen months but I knew that if Barbara was willing to marry me I needed to wait for her to return. Time passed and soon Barbara would be home. I had moved to Texas to work for IBM for a year.

A week or two after Barbara returned home from her mission I flew from Texas to Arizona to see her again. See looked great and had grown in many ways. She had served faithfully as a missionary and I was very proud of her. My love for Barbara was burning in my heart and I wanted to ask her to marry me. I met with Barbara's father and asked for his permission to marry Barbara and he kindly gave his consent. I concluded that continuing in a distant relationship would not be ideal and wondered how I could propose to Barbara. Before I was scheduled to fly back to Grapevine, Texas, Barbara and I decided to go to a performance by a BYU dance group at a local community college near Coolidge, Arizona. After the performance, I remember putting my arm around Barbara and asking her what her plans were now that she was home from her mission. She paused a moment and indicated she was planning on continuing her education at BYU. My heart jumped a bit and I realized "it was now or never" but I didn't know how to get the words out. Somehow I managed to say "How would you like to spend that time with me?" She thought about the words I had spoken, turned to me and said "David, are you asking me to marry you?" I swallowed real hard, looked into Barbara's big beautiful eyes and replied "Barbara, will you marry me?" Again she thought for a brief moment and then said, "Yes". I was so grateful she said, "Yes". Somehow, in the matter of a few seconds, we had just gotten engaged. This wasn't really how I had planned it ... I wish I would have been a bit more prepared and a lot more romantic about the whole thing, but that's how it worked out. A few months later, Barbara and I drove to Salt Lake City, Utah and had the tremendous blessing of being married and sealed in the holy Salt Lake Temple for time on this earth and for eternity.

Marriage and Family

Growing up I never moved once. After getting married, my life was just the opposite. Following our wedding ceremony in the Salt Lake Temple we enjoyed a simple, beautiful wedding reception near my parent's home, then we drove to Coolidge, Arizona to attend an enjoyable open house near Barbara's parent's home, then we made our way to Grapevine, Texas to begin a new and exciting chapter in our lives. Since that time we have moved eleven additional times.

In December of 1991, after I was finished with my internship with IBM in Texas, we moved back to Provo to finish our education. The apartment we moved to was so small that when we learned Barbara was expecting, we were informed that we would need to move because the apartment was only zoned for a maximum of two people. We moved to BYU married student housing and in October of 1992, we were blessed with the birth of our first daughter, Amber. When Barbara and I graduated from BYU (Barbara with a degree in Elementary Education and I with a degree in Computer Science), we were no longer qualified to live in the BYU apartment because we were no longer students. We then moved to Grandma Murdoch's basement apartment in Salt Lake City. This was a unique opportunity for us to spend some time with our Molly-Whoppet Grandma Murdoch and live once again on "Murdoch Acres". While living in Grandma's basement apartment, our second daughter, Alissa, was born; it was January 1994 and there was lots of snow on the ground. We treasured our time and experience with Grandma Murdoch. Having a desire to pursue a Masters degree in Computer Science, we then moved back to an apartment in Grapevine, Texas where I began a Masters program part-time at the University of North Texas and worked full-time at IBM. Unfortunately, I was unable to continue with my educational interest and I put this goal on hold. Shortly thereafter we were blessed with the opportunity of purchasing our first home, which resulted in another move across town. We loved our home on Cimarron Trail but after accepting a six month project with IBM in Phoenix, Arizona, we moved again to an apartment in Mesa, Arizona. This gave us the opportunity of living much closer to Barbara's brother, David, and his family as well as Barbara's parents, who were about an hour south in Coolidge. We moved in early spring, which is a wonderful time of year to live in Arizona, but quickly learned what the word "hot" meant as we progressed into the summer months and temperatures climbed consistently above 100 degrees Fahrenheit. After our six month project was completed, we moved back to our home in Grapevine, Texas. A few months after we moved back to Grapevine, we were blessed with the arrival of a beautiful little boy whom we named Spencer. He was our tax baby because he was born on December 31, 1996. As time progressed, I really wanted to earn my masters degree and I knew it would only get more difficult the longer we waited, so we sold our home and moved back to Utah (West Jordan) where I started full-time work in Salt Lake and part-time school at BYU. Life was quite busy with a growing family, work, church, and school and I was struggling to keep up. We had had another beautiful baby by this time, Amanda in 1999, and we were feeling very stretched. We didn't want to quit work and take out student loans because Barbara and I do not like debt. Having Barbara go to work wasn't the right solution for us either. We concluded that if I was closer to BYU it might help, so we sold our home in West Jordan to my parents who were going through a major change of moving from their home in the Cottonwood area, and we rented the top level of a home near BYU in Provo. Sadly, I pushed a bit too hard and my health started to decline; I was consistently getting sick. We concluded that my Masters Degree would have to wait for a different stage of life. No longer needing to rent, and having changed jobs to a new company in Provo, we decided to purchase another home. We found a beautiful ranch-style home one mile north of the Mount Timpanogos Temple in American Fork where we moved in July 2000. While living in American Fork, we set a new record by living in our home for seven years, during which time we added two more precious children to our family - Melanie in 2002 and John in 2004. But then, you guessed it, it was time for a new adventure. For years I had looked into ways in which I could take my family to Scotland to live, work, and experience a new culture and a different country. After much research and work, we finally got all our ducks in a row and we moved to Scotland in July of 2007.

Scotland

Upon moving, to Scotland I opened a subsidiary company, Murdoch Consulting (Scotland) Ltd. of my US based parent company, Murdoch Consulting Inc., which I started in 2004. We provide software solutions and currently specialize in Microsoft® .NET applications. The project I'm currently working on is located on the east coast of Scotland in a city called Dundee.

My family and I are currently living in a wee village called Blairlogie. My wife and I leave our home at 6:00 A.M. and drive to the train station in Stirling, where I take a train to Dundee. I then catch a bus from the city center (UK spelling: centre) to the Ninewells Hospital where I have a three-month contract. Once this project is over, I will locate a new project which I hope will be a bit closer to home; commuting two hours a day to work and two hours a day from work is not ideal for spending time with your family.

Living in the land of my ancestors is a dream come true. I love this beautiful land and I love the people. Sadly, a lot has changed since I lived here 20+ years ago as a missionary. It seems as though the moral framework of this country has greatly been diminished. So many people are now smoking, profanity and pornography are the norm, and the youth have all but lost their respect for those around them.

In spite of these problems I look around me and see so much good, and so much courage and strength. As a family we have traveled to several of the beautiful beaches of Scotland, we have marveled at the fantastic castles and monuments that dot the land, and we have so much enjoyed the green, beautiful country side, the magnificent flowers, the heather, sheep, and all the beauties of nature that surrounds us. And yes, we have even enjoyed the rain.

Next summer (2008), we will evaluate how we are doing and decide if we should move back to America or if we should continue for another year with our Scottish adventure. I would prefer the later, but time will tell.

Conclusion

In writing this historical sketch of my life my understanding of a few things has been deepened. First, the Lord knows me and is working to help guide my life each and every day. I have the agency to accept his guidance or do things "my way"; the choice is mine to make. Secondly, I have an amazingly supportive, caring wife. My marriage and family are vitally important to me and I must strive more diligently to appreciate, strengthen, and uplift my relationships with Barbara and my children. Barbara is my best friend and my eternal companion; I love her. Lastly, life is what you make it. Challenges and struggles will always be part of our existence, and we are given the gift of choice to decide how to handle and work through these challenging opportunities. There is a God in heaven who watches over us all. He provided a Savior for you and for me enabling us to repent and become clean. Life has great meaning and purpose. For this knowledge I am eternally grateful.

Michael Clark Murdoch Jr.

My name is Michael Clark Murdoch Jr. I was born on August 13, 1969 at the LDS Hospital, in Salt Lake City, Utah. I was born to Michael and Connie Murdoch. When I was born the doctor came in and told my mother that I was a fat little red head. I resented that, but I have grown up to really appreciate my red hair. It is what has made me different and unique. I am grateful that I am not fat but I am little. My height stands tall at 5' 2 and ¾" and I am about 145 lbs. I am proud to say that I got my height from my father. He is about 5' 1". I am the fourth child in my family so that makes me the youngest. I am so thankful for my family.

My Grandfather and Grandmother, David Lennox and Ora Murdoch, made a very wise choice many years ago and bought some wonderful property in the Cottonwood area, a suburb of Salt Lake City. It was a beautiful plot of ground seven and half acres of beautiful orchards down a long lane of tall poplar trees.

My grandmother and grandfather had three children who were able to have homes down this lane where they raised their children. Between Uncle Bill's family, Aunt Janet's family, and our family, there were eleven grandchildren to enjoy Grandma and Grandpa Murdoch. Grandpa Murdoch built a swimming pool when raising his children, which was a great blessing to all of us as we were growing up. Each family took turns cleaning and maintaining the pool. We loved all the beautiful foliage surrounding the pool as well as each of our homes.

There are so many wonderful memories on that property. We truly had a paradise. I remember some of the very best times as a little boy was when our Grandmother Murdoch would invite all of us grandchildren to a Molly Whoppet party. She created the very best time for us kids. She would dress up in funny hats and aprons. She would send us some of the greatest little party invitations. After getting an invitation to a Molly Whoppet party, you could hardly wait. At the door, she would give a hug and a kiss to each one of us as we came into the house. Then she would give each of us a number. That was our number that she would call out during the party. She was so organized and so fun. We would each get our own tray with freshly baked sugar cookies. We would also have everything needed to decorate those cookies - little cups of candies and a little bowl of frosting. It was a wonderful time to be a kid. She had the best games too. We would have to find balloons, bean bags, and presents. We would win prizes and play dress up. Grandma Murdoch was the best story teller in the world! Oh how we loved her Molly Whoppet parties. We would go home with some of the funniest things. Grandma would have a prize table with all sorts of interesting things. She would go to the Deseret Industries and would buy all sorts of funny things and then put it on a table for us to choose from. You never know what will strike the imagination of a child.

One thing I really loved about our property was the trees. I loved to climb the trees. I would climb a favorite tree and it felt like I was a hundred feet in the air. At the top I felt I could see the whole world. How I wished I could fly.

Our home was built in the middle of a pear orchard. We always had fresh pears to eat and bottle, as well as give away. We had a big vegetable garden and a big raspberry patch. We had to help with all of this produce. We had a patio swing and would sit there together and husk corn, snap beans, shell peas, or stem grapes. We grew a great deal of the food we ate. We also enjoyed growing pumpkins. One year I took third place in the county fair for the biggest pumpkin.

Work was something that we knew a lot about. My parents taught us a lot about how to work. From the time I could walk, I think, my Mother had a job for me to do. Money was tight so Mom and Dad took extra jobs so that they could provide vacations for us every year and other things we might need. We all helped Mom and Dad clean a place call The Shalamar. It was a wedding reception hall. It was a beautiful place. It was our job to clean it after every wedding. Our parents got us kids up early before school on those days and we would clean before going to school. I hated getting up early to go and clean that place. Now that I look back at it, I am grateful to my mother and father who taught us how to work and clean.

I remember too, working with my Dad. He would get what we called *limb jobs*. He had a good friend who pruned trees for people. He would call us to go and pick up the branches and take them to the dump. He taught us how to properly load a truck with limbs so we could unload at the dump with only a few tugs on key branches. Dad taught us how tie knots and lash loads. Going to the dump was a fun adventure. My Dad never complained. He was always grateful for the extra work.

Oakland, California 1970

With the extra money we would go on a family vacation. It seemed that every year I was gone on my birthday. It seemed like August was the month to go on vacations. My parents were great planners and organizers. For many years, we had a boat and the destination would be beautiful Lake Powell. We all loved Lake Powell. We loved to water ski and collect things from the beach. The sand was red and quite fine. We often enjoyed these vacations with the Mumford family, who had children the same age as our family. We camped on the lake and had such a wonderful time. Sometimes we would take Grandma Murdoch with us. She was sure to always bring some mineral water with her in case we got sunburned. Of course, with my red hair, I usually always did and she would doctor us up with mineral packs.

As time went on and we got bigger and there were a few more available dollars, Mom and Dad rented a houseboat. We really loved that. We could lay up on the top of the houseboat at night and see millions of stars. We had great spots on the lake to camp. We would sometimes bring fireworks and set them off at night. I really loved doing that. One of my favorite activities was cliff jumping. There were some great places to cliff jump.

I always wanted to go to Hawaii but our family never had the money to go. However, when I was sixteen years old, I found a way. I still don't know where I heard that you could go work in Hawaii to pick pineapples, but somewhere I heard it and my mother and I ended up at the Whitmore Library listening to a man talk about jobs in Hawaii. As he talked about the job and the activities I remember thinking to myself, "this is for me." I could see myself climbing up trees and picking pineapples with a machete in my hand. Little did I know that pineapples grew on razor sharp plants that you pick by hand on the ground. So I signed up for it. The cost was $750 dollars and my parents made me pay at least half of it. At first Mom didn't want me to go but it was Dad who convinced her. I would only make $3.41 per hour there, and I even had to pay room and board. They told us this isn't a money making experience. We did have to work 40 hours a week and sometimes more. Overtime was great because you got paid time and a half. They actually saved your money for you and gave you a little to spend out of each paycheck, but even after six months, I didn't have a lot of money saved. I didn't mind because I knew it was a work experience.

It was a bit scary leaving home to go so far away with people I really did not know yet. I loved the rush of the plane as it took off. I was finally flying. Landing in Hawaii was so awesome! The humid air hit you like a rain storm. You began sweating instantly. I couldn't believe I was on a tiny island way out in the middle of the Pacific Ocean. It was all so exciting.

When we arrived in the field the first day and after first putting on the appropriate clothing, which really amounted to armor, Kevin, our supervisor, or Luna, as he is called in Hawaiian, gave us a quick lesson on picking pineapples. We were to all line up on either side of the boom, which was a slow-moving conveyor belt on the back of the truck. We were to pick the pineapple off the plant, twist the crown off (the sharp spiny thing on the top), and put both crown and pineapple onto the boom to be carried up into the truck. We were excited to get started. After about an hour of doing this, I was getting really tired. My body was sore, and then I looked up and saw miles and miles of pineapples. Then it hit me. I was here for six months. This would be the hardest work I had ever done.

After we got back to camp, our Luna, Kevin, told us to put on our swimsuits because we were going to the beach. The beach! Well now that changed everything. I stopped feeling sorry for myself. I had never been to the beach before. In fact I had never touched the ocean before. Oh boy!! The beach! This is what saved my life. I forgot how my body hurt and I ran right in. I was amazed at the power of the ocean. I didn't know the first thing about waves or how to ride them. After a while I started to catch on. It was the best of times. I fell in love with the ocean that day. I was hooked. I couldn't wait to go back to the ocean.

The Islands are a very spiritual place. I decided to read the Book of Mormon for myself. No one asked me to. I just did it, and it changed my life. I gained a testimony of that sacred book.

Maui was a magical island. Maui Pineapple Company is the last pineapple company in the United States. I enjoyed working for this company. The days were hot and the work was hard and tiresome but the reward for working hard was worth it. I worked hard at having a good attitude. One of the greatest parts was at the end of my time on Maui.

We held a huge camp meeting and it was our final one before we left. We talked about the good times and the bad, the happy and the sad. Then the coordinator, Brian Pickett, read a letter like someone in the camp had sent home. It was a letter telling about the experience that this young man was having there in Hawaii. It was a positive letter and when he ended it, he told everyone some more good things about this young man. He said things that would make any young man feel proud and then he said we would like to award this young man with a plaque for the *Man of the Season Award*. The highest honor given to a young man for that season. He said, "we would like to give this to Michael Murdoch!" I felt something I had never felt before. I felt part of an organization of friends that had become as a family. I felt honored to have served with these great people. I never sought for it. I believe it happened because of the change of heart that I went through and from reading the Book of Mormon.

I graduated from high school and the next great event of my life occurred: I received my mission call. I was called to serve in the Portugal Lisbon Mission. While I was there, my mission split into the Lisbon South

Mission. However, I couldn't go initially to Portugal because of visa problems. Instead, I was sent to the San Bernardino Mission in California. I loved this mission. I spent three of the best months there. I loved doing missionary work. I loved serving the Lord and helping people learn the truth. Finally after three months of waiting, I received my visa. I was actually sad. I was enjoying my mission in California.

LEFT: *Mick Murdoch in Liverpool 1956* RIGHT: *Michael Murdoch in Portugal 1989 Michael compares himself to his father on his mission. Both are standing on chairs.*

Portugal was hard for me because of the language. I had to rely on the Lord to give me the gift of tongues. I had many wonderful experiences on my mission. The Lord even arranged for me to meet my future wife there. She was assigned to our zone just shortly before she was released. While some of us were having dinner at a members home, the member commented that Sister Chamberlain and I should get married when we returned home. She was from California and I was from Utah, a bit difficult for much dating. However Becky sent me a letter a couple of months after we returned home and so began the "getting to know you" period. My mission was a great experience. I really enjoyed being a missionary. When I returned back to America, I remember feeling so grateful for this country. I had a HUGE appreciation for America. I loved our freedoms and beauty that was America. We have so much for which to be grateful.

After my mission I had a desire to go back to Hawaii. I wanted to be a supervisor for Maui Pineapple Company, and give back to the program that gave so much to me. I returned home in October and signed up to go back to Hawaii in January. Becky had begun writing to me and we were corresponding. She had mentioned that she wanted to come and visit me in Hawaii. When I got to Hawaii the work was intense with very little free time. I had to be Mom and Dad to fifteen 15-year olds. So I didn't see how I was going to spend time with Becky. I learned she was going to come the next week. What a challenge to find

a place for her to stay and find some time to spend with her. It all worked out with the help of a good bishop. It was so great to have her there to walk those beautiful beaches in the moonlight. Cupid was doing his work. After my tour of duty in the pineapple field was over, I flew right to California. I spent three weeks living in her home. I finally had to go home. She went to Oregon to run a marathon, but right after that she came to spend some time with me. This time she stayed in my home.

Becky was a marathon runner and was in position to probably qualify for the Olympics. However, she developed a painful problem in her feet that basically put an end to her running career. We were scheduled to get married on August 14, 1991. We both had to overcome some health issues before our wedding day, which happily we did. We were married in the Salt Lake Temple. A temple marriage was so important to us. Both of us had grown up all our lives with this goal to get married in the temple. Both of our parents got married in the Salt Lake Temple. I wanted to get married in the Hawaii Temple but we wanted to have friends and family there. Everything connected with our wedding and the receptions were so memorable and beautiful.

Becky's Dad gave us a honeymoon trip to Maui. So once again we were able to go back to the place where we fell in love. It was so much fun to be together, just the two of us. I couldn't have asked for anything more. I love Maui and how it makes me feel. The spirit of Hawaii is very strong. There is so much love there. It was my goal to someday live there with my family.

Over the next couple of years, Becky and I worked at various jobs and lived in various areas. Our first son, Benjamin Michael Murdoch, was born on December 27, 1994. We were living in California and I had a job with TCI cable. I enjoyed living in California. I loved the ocean and the beach. I learned how to surf at Santa Cruz. I was in the Young Men's Presidency and loved the youth. It was a real happy time for Becky and me. Ben was growing up and enjoying himself. It was fun to be together.

My company decided to go on strike and I didn't want to strike. I called

LEFT: *Maui at Twin Falls* RIGHT: *Maui with the whales*

a friend's brother I knew in Hawaii and asked him for a job. I wanted to return to Hawaii. It had always been a goal of mine to live in Hawaii. He gave me a job so I quit the cable company. Becky was expecting our next child and I went over to Hawaii to prepare the way. I began working with Advanced Landscaping. I really didn't like the work. It was hard. I was taking care of the yards of some resort places and commercial businesses. It was so tiring. I wanted out. Someone in my ward worked for a hotel and luckily I landed the greatest job ever. I worked for the Four Seasons Hotel. At the time it was rated as the number one destination island resort in the world.

We rented a small bungalow and just enjoyed our proximity to the beach and to work. Becky loved taking Ben to the beach and walks along the ocean. I'd often get up early and run to the beach to do a bit of snorkeling before going to work. We didn't have a lot of money, but we were so happy. Christmas was coming and we didn't have much to spend for gifts. A friend from work had given us a tree, someone else had given us lights and ornaments. We bought something small for Ben and decided that was good enough. However, while at a ward party, Santa came to our house and left gifts under the tree. What fun on Christmas morning to see the gifts for Ben were the ones we would have selected had we had the money.

Our sweet little daughter chose to be born on December 29, 1997. Again, Becky delivered at home with the help of a great midwife. We had soft Christmas music playing and the hymn *Joy to the World* was playing when our daughter was born. We named her Tracy Joy Murdoch.

Working for the Four Seasons Hotel was interesting as well as enjoyable. I worked at their Spa, which was a wonderful place to be. I enjoyed booking the massages for the rich and famous.

The best part about living on Maui was the adventure. We loved to get out and experience nature. We were always looking for new hikes and different waterfalls. We would give tours to some of the most exotic places. Some falls were so private that we were the only ones there.

By the time our third child was born, we had moved two more times.

Each move gave us a bit more room and made life more comfortable. On September 23, 2000, Tomas Lyman Murdoch was born. He was a big 9 pounds 10 ounces.

We enjoyed all the things that Hawaii has to offer like geckos, Jackson chameleons, skinks, and anoles. There is something about lizards that the kids just loved. They had big frogs as well.

While we were on Maui, the Big Island received a new Temple in Kona. It was to become our temple. So our ward was able to participate in the dedication of it. I was chosen to be one of those that worked in the temple during the dedications. I helped people put on slippers as they went into the temple. We had President Gordon B. Hinckley come and dedicate it. It was a wonderful experience.

Things began to get pretty crazy in our lives. I had two part-time jobs and one full-time job. Becky was expecting again, and our landlord didn't want to rent to that large of a family. We began looking everywhere but we could find nothing suitable that we could afford. We even tried the island of Hilo. We applied for a loan, but complications arose and the loan fell through. Becky had an ultrasound and they said there was only a placenta, but no baby. Becky had been throwing up for three months for nothing. She then had to undergo an induced miscarriage to get things back to normal. We had no place to go. I had plenty of work, I just couldn't find a place to live. About this time Mom called me to let me know they were going on a mission to Australia. She said "why don't you come to our home and housesit for us while we are gone." I agreed and so our time on Maui came to an end. We left on September 11, 2002.

It was nice to be back among family, but we did miss Hawaii. After about a year of working different jobs, I interviewed with R. C. Willey and was hired. Our lives stabilized a bit more then. We were able to buy a little old house in American Fork with a nice piece of property. We moved in July 2004, the year my parents were returning from their mission.

Our life has had its ups and downs and some challenging adversity. We have added two more sons to our family - Joseph and Peter - and they are doing well. The drop in the economy in 2008 has caused some real trauma for us as a family. Presently I am working two jobs to provide for our family. With faith and work we hope things turn around for us in the near future. Living through a depression is very difficult. We rely on the Lord and work hard to keep the commandments. We are grateful for all the blessings that are coming our way.

JANET LENNOX MURDOCH WILSON

I was born June 18, 1945 in Salt Lake City, Utah at the Latter-day Saint Hospital. I am the youngest child and only daughter born to David Lennox Murdoch and Ora Maurine Clark Murdoch. I have two older brothers William Richard Murdoch and Michael Clark Murdoch (Bill & Mick).

I was named Linda Maurine for about two weeks. Mother kept looking at me and didn't feel that was the right name for me so they paid to have my name changed to Janet Lennox Murdoch, after my father's aunt.

I called her Aunt Jen. I was the first in the family to be named this name for over 56 years. She was so thrilled at the time of my christening that she started a bank account for me and gave me some of her treasures. When she passed away, she left me her diamond engagement ring (which I had made into a ring for my husband when we got married) and her beautiful wedding dress, which I wore at my wedding. My mother spent many hours remodeling it to fit me. She also left me her luggage, her lovely linens, and her gold thimble. She was a fine Christian woman and one I admired greatly. My name means a great deal more to me than if I had been called Linda.

The greatest thing my father taught me was how important it is to have a good reputation. The 2nd thing was the importance of being a loyal person. How did he teach me that? Through example! He had the greatest reputation and was one of the most loyal people I knew. He taught me that if I said I was going to do something, I better be prepared to do it and do it on time and go the extra mile, if that's what it took. I was always so proud of my father. He may have been small in stature (5 ft. 2 in. tall), but he was a giant to many. He had many great, influential, important people he had to deal with every day, through his work at KSL Radio and then KSL

LEFT: *Janet Lennox Murdoch Thompson and Janet* RIGHT: *Janet, age 4*

T.V. He became the Manger and Vice President of KSL T.V. I remember I loved going downtown to visit him at his office. Even though he associated with Prophets of the Church and important people in the community here in Salt Lake and other states in the United States, he was a very humble man who would rather be home than traveling. He treated everyone he knew with dignity and respect and was a very wise, down-to-earth man. I loved December to come so I could go out to the mail box and gather the Christmas Cards. The box was always crammed full from Dec. 1st until Christmas Day with loving cards and notes, almost too many to count. My father and mother were respected, loved, and cherished because of the wonderful giving, loyal people that they were.

The most important thing Mother taught me was by her example also. As I watched her serving others, I realized that is what truly brings you happiness. Our kitchen, from the time I was a small child and growing up, was always in a mess. When Mother wasn't cooking and canning, or bottling fruit & jam, she was baking, making and taking goodies to people in the ward or neighborhood. The kitchen floor was always sticky and the counter tops were always cluttered with her open cookbook and pots and pans and recipes everywhere, but the joy on her face as she boxed up her bundles of goodies to take to the new person who just moved in, or the lady who had just had a baby, or the sick family down the street, helped me realize what serving others meant.

I loved Christmas Eve because that was the night mother played Santa and I got to be her helper. When it got dark we were off depositing presents and goodies (anonymously) on the front steps of homes in the neighborhood and always finding ourselves down town where she had a very dear friend and my father's Aunt Mary. Then it was time to go back home. I would crawl into my bed and she would spend the rest of the night getting my Christmas ready, usually sewing me something she hadn't quite got around to finishing. Serving others truly does bring great happiness to the soul and I thank my mother for teaching me that.

I was so blessed to be raised on about 7 1/2 acres of beautiful property in the Cottonwood area. Because of the foresight of my father and mother and because they were not afraid of hard work, and because they didn't listen to everyone who told them they were crazy to go that far out of Salt Lake and they might as well go on to Provo, Bill, Mick, and I had an ideal childhood. We were not only able to grow up on this beautiful property which was like our own private park, with apple trees, peach trees, pear trees, plum trees, cherry trees, and a huge open green space to run and play on, but we also had many animals ranging from chickens, pigs, horses, sheep and cows to entertain us. One of the fondest memories I have of animals was Duchess, the Dachshund. Mother decided she could have puppies and we would sell them. I loved watching them play with each other. They would trip over their long ears chasing each other on their short, little legs. What a funny sight. I loved them all, but I knew when they grew old enough they would be sold. I remember the big basket we would put them in when someone would come to buy one. We would tie a red bow around their necks. One by one, as the days passed, they were all sold. I felt so sad to see them go, but I knew I would still have my Duchess.

When Bill, Mick, and I got married, we were each given one-half acre of land as a wedding present. Thus, we grew up here and raised our children on this incredible piece of land with a mountain stream running though it and a seven hundred foot long lane lined with about 57 HUGE poplar trees. The Wasatch Mountains framed the picture making it one of the most beautiful lanes in the valley. The trees could be seen from all over. As the seasons changed, there is no way to describe this fantastic lane, but, I will try. In the fall there were a billion crisp "potato chip" leaves making the lane a fantastic color of yellow. Jumping in all the raked leaves and then dragging them off to the orchard to be burned was fun but quite a challenge each year.

Tons of white fluffy snow during the winter would make the lane a glittering fairyland and a fun place for sleigh riding and watching cars getting stuck in the ditch on the side of the drive way. Spring was my favorite when the long brown seed pods (which we would respectfully call "worms") would start to fall so the wonderful dark green leaves could form on the branches of those HUGE, incredible trees. It was like driving down a living green tunnel all summer long. One of my favorite days of the year was the last day of school. The school bus would drive up to the lane and let me out. As I walked down the lane smelling the delicate smells of late spring and the beginning of early summer, knowing I had three whole months without any school, I could hardly contain myself!!

I guess I take after *Wee Granny*. Not in her strength and courage, but like her, I only grew to be 4 ft. 8 in. tall. Wee Granny has become a very famous pioneer. Her picture at Chimney Rock has been in the Ensign a number of times. They have erected a monument in her name at Chimney Rock where she died with her famous saying, "Tell John I died with my face towards Zion." I am very proud to know she is my great, great, great Grandmother.

Along the way I found a friend, Jannette Wozab, who was almost the same height as me. We were in 1st grade together and people thought we were sisters. We became best friends all through grade school, junior high, and high school. She lived on Fardown Avenue, not far from me, and we would ride our bikes back and forth from school to her house to mine. We loved riding our bikes down to the corner to Chesley Drug store and buy candy, then back to my house and swim, laugh, and talk the summer away.

Strange how things go! After graduating from high school, I went to Brigham Young University and made many new friends. Jannette didn't go onto college and we lost track of each other after all those years.

I must mention my grandfather and grandmother, on my mother's side. They both played a real part in shaping my life. My father's parents died before I was born, but my mother's parents came to live with us the year after I was born. They lived in our basement for many years. Then they built a home just across the street from us. I loved to go to Grandma's and have her cook me a steak (of all things), but she had a very special way of cooking it which mother never could get right. I can still taste how good it was!

Bill, my oldest brother by 13 years and Mick being 8 years older, made it seem like I was an only child growing up in the home. By the time I remembered Bill, he was getting ready to go on a mission, but the Korean War prevented that from happening and even though he had his mission call and his farewell, he had to go to the Korean War. I remember how terribly sad we all were that he wasn't able to go on his mission and how much we missed him and worried about the horrible war and the fact that he was there and not allowed to do the Lord's work like he wanted to be doing. The Lord did protect him and He did answer our prayers and Bill returned home with honor. After he got home from the war, it seemed like it wasn't long before he got married to Arthel Wilkins in the Salt Lake Temple.

Mick was always gone with his friends and about the only time I saw him was at the dinner table, then it was time for him to go on a mission for our church, to England. I do remember feeling heartbroken to see him climb on the train that morning, knowing I would not see him again for two LONG years. Although I didn't want to admit it, I knew that I was going to miss him. I was going to miss the teasing and joking and the fun we had together. In fact, before he returned, I even missed the arguments we used to have. In spite of it all, though, the time seemed to fly by quickly and one night at the dinner table, about a month before it was time for Mick to come home, Dad calmly said, "Janet, how would you like to take a trip with your mother and me to New York to pick up your brother?" These words stand out in my mind vividly. Before I could hardly turn around, I found myself and my parents in a wonderful big, new, exciting world. I could hardly believe my eyes at the towering buildings and the unbelievable sights we saw there, the many interesting museums, the Empire State Building, the world-famous U.N. Building, the Yankee Stadium, and then, our boat trip around Manhattan Island. I will never forget how I felt seeing Mick as he came walking down the gang plank of that huge ship, The Queen Mary, and the fun we had running to greet him. They let us go aboard that beautiful boat and I remember getting sea sick walking up the plank. What a wonderful experience it all was. I had never seen a ship that big in my life! While we were all back East together, Dad suggested that we go on to Washington, D.C. and visit the many points of interest there. It was all very educational and exciting.

After Mick had been home for two years, he decided to get married to Connie Riley in the Salt Lake Temple.

It seemed like mother and dad always had projects going on. I remember when they decided to build a big outdoor fireplace and a patio across the ditch. The project was finished bringing with it great summer parties roasting hot dogs, hamburgers, and marshmallows, sitting around the fire and singing and talking. Those were the good old days. As the years went on, it became a great place to use as a hide out or a fun place to explore. It even got the name "The Secret Garden".

When I was about 12 years old, it was my misfortune to have to spend six months in a cast which covered two thirds of my body. During my sojourn in this tight enclosure I learned many things. I learned all about doctors and nurses and hospitals and suffering. The doctors never could decide what was wrong with my femur bones, but they were bowing out from the hip to the knee, so they decided if they sawed them in half and straighten them with rods and put me in a cast which covered both my legs and came up to my waist with only my toes sticking out and a bar between my legs that it would take care of the problem. The doctors thought I would heal in six weeks and that would be that. Well, that wasn't that. It took my bones six months and by the time they finally took the cast off, I was in Physical Therapy for another six months learning how to bend my knees again and walk. I missed a year of school, but I did have a teacher who came to the home. It was an education I will never forget and I am not talking about what the teacher who came to the home taught me, it was an education in pain, both physical and mental. I learned to appreciate my legs, what was left of them, and that I could finally scratch an itch when I had to! When it was all over with, my parents built me a very beautiful swimming pool and it was here I learned to walk again. I remember I would rather swim than eat or sleep. I became a real water baby and needless to say, I spent every possible minute of every summer deep in the heart of the pool. The pool became my best friend.

I consider our family a happy, religious family. While I was growing up, I remember my father being the bishop of our ward (Cottonwood 5th Ward) and my mother was the Relief Society President for many years. Her main love was her calling to the General Board of the Young Women and the traveling she did throughout the church. My father and mother were called to be directors of the Visitor Center in Oakland California. After that, they were temple workers at the Jordan River Temple for many years.

I have lived in the Cottonwood 5th Ward all my life. There are not many people who can say that! The only time I left this ward was when I went to BYU in 1963 after graduating from Olympus High School. It was there that I met my dear husband (Charles) Allan Wilson. My roommate, Kay Heaton, grew up with Allan in Burley, Idaho and she asked him if he would like to come over to our apartment and clean our walls and we would cook him dinner... thus, we met and as luck would have it, the girls' Preference Dance was coming up in December so I asked Allan. He accepted, we started dating and the rest is history. Allan proposed to me the day after Valentines (1968) and we were married five months later, July 12, 1968, in the Salt Lake Temple.

After we were married, our first little home was in Provo, Utah. It was a cute little "OLD" white home with a living room, a huge kitchen, a bedroom, and bathroom. We were actually able to afford the rent ($65) but not much else. We were both in school at the "Y". Allan worked at night in a favorite Mexican restaurant called the El Azteca. He was the cook and he learned how to cook great Mexican food. He truly enjoyed his job since his major was Spanish and he served a mission in Central America (Guatemala, El Salvador, Nicaragua, Costa Rica, Honduras and Panama.)

I was majoring in Elementary Education and I only had my student teaching to do and a few classes after that before I got my degree. Our first daughter, Michele, was in a hurry to get here I guess, and at that time they would not let you do your student teaching if you were pregnant. All I ever wanted was to be a wife and mother so needless to say I was so excited. I did not complete my degree in college but started a new degree in motherhood. I certainly used my education however when our last child, Meg, was only 2 years old and I began teaching at a pre-school and taking Meg with me. I was only going to do it for extra Christmas money that year, but I remained doing it for 15 wonderful years. It was like teaching Kindergarten and that was what I was going to do when I graduated from BYU Preparing so many children for Kindergarten was a fulfilling and rewarding thing to do. Often, I will be in a store or somewhere and a mother of the child, or the child I taught, will come up to me and ask me if I am "Miss Janet." Of course it is hard for me to remember them since the last time I saw them they were five years old and now they are twenty, but it makes me feel good, as I talk with them, to know that they have gone on to be well educated, contributing citizens and that they remember the fun they had in pre-school.

After Allan graduated from BYU, with a major in Spanish and minor in English, we moved into the basement of my parents' home. This was the first home for our daughter, Michele. This is where she took her first steps. We lived in their basement for about two years and then when my parents were called on their mission to Oakland California, we moved upstairs and rented the basement out while they were gone. We also started building our home at that time. I was pregnant with our second child, Margo. We finished our home just before Mom and Dad returned from their mission. It was fun to finally have our own home and a nursery we could fix up for Margo. This home is where Margo took her first steps. About four and a half years later, Meg was born. We have lived in our home going on 33 years now. It has been wonderful raising our children on the same property I grew up on. It was a very innocent, peaceful time to raise children. They played with their cousins (who were their neighbors) swam in the pool during the summer and spent many hours at Grandma and Grandpa Murdoch's home. Mother loved having "Molly Whoppet" parties for the grandchildren and it gave us busy mothers (Arthel, Connie and myself) a break which we needed and were grateful for. The children will always remember those precious memories they spent with their Grandmother, Ora Murdoch.

Allan's parents remained living in Burley, Idaho. They would visit us often and we would visit them. In fact, Grandpa and Grandma's home in Idaho was where Meg took her first steps during one of our visits there The children loved going to the farm. There were cows and horses and plenty of room, as far as the eye could see, to ride the motorcycle and shoot the BB gun, and learning how to make homemade noodles with Grandma Wilson. What fun. Grandpa and Grandma Wilson always planted a very large garden and the home grown tomatoes were to die for. Every year we would go up to get a few sacks of those wonderful Idaho potatoes and walk the ditch banks looking for fresh asparagus.

Allan's father died at the early age of 65 of pneumonia. His mother is still alive at the age of 94 and living in Burley in an assisted living center.

Our children didn't lack for things to do with the fun trips to Idaho and being raised on the large expanse of beautiful property, complete with a pool and a stream of running water going through it gave all of them an opportunity to let their imaginations soar, and what one didn't think of the others did.

It was wonderful. I didn't need to worry about them. When they were little, I just put a life jacket on them in the summer and I always knew if they were not in the house, they were either in the pool or at the cousins or at Mom's. When they got older they were always home with friends in the pool all summer long or thinking of things to do on the property.

At that time of our lives, Allan was busy teaching Spanish at Central Junior High School. Since school teachers were not paid much he had to get a second job. He worked at night for J.C. Penney's. After about four and one-half years of this he decided to make a career change and started working for the United States Postal Service. He started at night and worked his way up to a level 19. Along the way he held many titles. The job he enjoyed most at the post office was during the years he was the Manager of Training. He was asked to go to Washington D.C. to Postal Headquarters to develop a training program. And then went around the country teaching this course to new training managers. He was then in the Personnel Office where he was responsible to hire the employees for the State of Utah. His last job with the Postal Service was Injury Compensation Specialist and in April 2004, he retired after working there for 31 yrs. We celebrated and went on a Caribbean cruise, which was wonderful. Allan took one month off and then decided retirement wasn't what he wanted to do right now so he started working for Thatcher Company and has now been there for two years.

I have enjoyed being a wife and mother now for 36 years. The challenges that come with being a parent are all worth it, especially when the grandchildren started coming! We have been very blessed to have such fantastic children, and grandchildren.

I have also enjoyed my many church callings. I love working with children and had the opportunity of being the Primary President twice. I have taught about every class in the Primary and been a counselor a number of times. I have taught in the Sunday School and also the Young Women's organization. Many years have been spent in the Relief Society as secretary, and Counselor to four different Relief Society Presidents. I love the Gospel and am so happy to have a testimony of the truthfulness of it. I gained my testimony as a young girl when I decided to start reading the Book of Mormon on my own. I had just started reading the first verse of the first chapter in Nephi, when a very calm peaceful feeling came over me and I heard a voice say "This Book is true." This is something I will always remember and cannot deny!

We have been very blessed to have three beautiful daughters, three wonderful sons-in-law and six beautiful grandchildren.

Michele graduated from BYU with her Bachelors Degree in Art and married Barry Cunningham in the Salt Lake Temple. Barry also is a graduate from BYU and has his Masters Degree in Market Research and they have two beautiful children: Janessa and Spencer.

Margo graduated from the University of Utah, the "U", with her Bachelors Degree in Psychology and then went to BYU and graduated with her Masters Degree in Social Work. She married Rick Lybbert in the Salt Lake Temple. Rick is a Physical Therapist and graduated from the "U". They have three beautiful children: Lindsie, Troy, and Mallory.

Meg graduated from the "U" with her Bachelors Degree in Psychology and her Masters Degree in Social Work . She married Jeremy Cunningham, Nov. 25th 2006 with their marriage sealed in the Salt Lake Temple Nov. 2007. Jeremy is a Senior Computer Specialist and they have a precious little boy who is eight months old. His name is Cameron Adam Cunningham.

Changes happen and I am sad to say that the beautiful property which we all lived on for so long is now in the process of being sub-divided. It became too much to take care of after our parents passed away and the taxes went through the roof leaving us with this hard decision. Dad passed away November 20, 1978 of a stroke. He was 77 yrs. old.

Mother passed away 23 years later. October 4, 2003. She was 94 years old. In the year 2000, the decision was made, by the three of us, that we would have to sell the property. Bill, my oldest brother and his wife, Arthel, decided to stay and so did my husband, Allan, and myself. My other brother, Mick and his wife, Connie, moved and went on a mission to Australia. They are now back and living in South Jordan, Utah.

I feel as though I have moved. We have a new address, Mom and Dad's home has been bulldozed down, the pool is gone, and the huge popular trees in the lane no longer exist. New homes are being built all around us. We did put a time capsule in the river rock wall which now surrounds Murdoch Woods. All of us as families have placed our memories of the beautiful property that once was. I wonder what year someone will open it up and try to understand what this precious, incredible spot was really like. How could they ever know? They were not here to hear the laughter and feel the love. They can only imagine. They cannot bulldoze away the wonderful memories I have of Murdoch Lane which I carry in my heart and memory.

The rich experiences I have had of living here all my life and raising our children here, where I grew up, are special blessings which I will always cherish. How thankful I am that Dad and Mom bought the property when they did and they didn't listen to everyone who told them they were crazy! Hopefully we will be able to stay right here and someday try to tell all the stories, this property holds, to our beautiful grandchildren.

CHARLES ALLAN WILSON

Born: November 2, 1944, Jones Maternity Home, Rupert, Idaho
  PLACE: Rupert, Minidoka, Idaho
  PARENTS: Charles Murwin Wilson and Dorcas Janette Smith
  SIBLINGS: Edna Diane Wilson Ellis, Kenneth Smith Wilson, and Robert "L" Wilson, who died when 4 days old
  SPOUSE: Janet Lennox Murdoch, daughter of David Lennox and Ora Maurine Clark Murdoch.

My early memories begin with living in a community northwest of Burley, Idaho, called Emerson. My father farmed and we had cows, chickens, and I remember a mean bull, that we had to be careful of when we crossed through the corral, and a horse named Ginger, that loved sugar cubes. The winter of 1948 and 1949 was an extremely intense winter. I remember we were snowed in and no one could get out of their places and the snow plows did not come. The milk trucks could not come and pick up the milk and so we had milk all over the house in wash tubs and various containers and eggs everywhere in the kitchen. Finally Dad, with another neighbor, was able to take the horse and sleigh to town to get some groceries. Being four years old, it seemed like the snow was as high as the telephone wires. We did not have a phone in those days, however, the Heckendorns, our neighbors to the northwest, had an old wooden crank phone. The Mays were our other neighbors across the street to the west. The Emerson Ward was a wonderful ward. I remember Dad playing on the ward men's baseball team and we spent many summer nights at the ball field.

We also went with the ward to many 24th of July celebrations. One I remember the most was at the Bosteder area above Oakley, Idaho. We actually slept over night. We had races and I won a race and got a chirping bird that you put water in, and it chirped, but a friend also, won a play watch and I wanted it and so we traded. I remember wishing I hadn't traded.

We moved from Emerson to another community called Unity, south east of Burley, Idaho. Once again, Dad farmed for the Congleton family. We lived in a little house down the lane off of the main road, close to the Congleton House. Bill and Edith Congleton had two daughters, Rachel and Eunice. Rachel had married and moved to California as Rachel Forth, and Eunice never married and taught school in Pocatello, Idaho. When her parents died, we helped with the upkeep of the yard. I mowed the lawn. She was a good friend of the family besides being the owner of the farm.

I attended Southwest Elementary School up to the 5th grade. When I was in the first grade, I was hit by a car on Easter Sunday, and spent 33 days in the hospital. I had a broken leg and had to have a cast like a pair of pants on me with a bar in between. They had to put a plate with 3 screws in my leg to hold the bones in place. I missed the last few weeks of the first grade. I attended Burley Junior High starting the sixth grade.

During the 8th grade I was elected Student Body Secretary and enjoyed the time in school. In fact, I loved school since it was my out from having to do farm work all the time and I got to see all my friends. I moved on

LEFT: *Age 8* MIDDLE: *Age 10* RIGHT: *Age 16*

to Burley High School starting in 9th grade. I was active in many clubs. As an officer in Key Club, I went to the International Key Club convention in Long Beach, California. The Key Clubs of Utah and Idaho chartered a bus and went to the 1962 World's Fair in Seattle, Washington and then on to the convention in Long Beach. I was a member or officer of the following clubs: Spanish (president), French, (president), Thespians, Bel Cantos (singing group), School Photographer, Year Book staff, and was an exchange student to the Intermountain Indian School. I was in the freshman class play and a three-act play comedy. My favorite teacher in high school was Maurine Andrus Parker. She taught Spanish. Because of her, I developed a love for Spanish and a desire to become a Spanish teacher.

Upon leaving Burley High School and graduating in May of 1963, I went to Brigham Young University, in Provo, Utah. I took the normal required courses, but focused on Spanish as my major, with English as a minor. I attended one year before I was called on a mission to the Central American Mission, with headquarters in Guatemala City, Guatemala. The mission consisted of Guatemala, El Salvador, Nicaragua, Honduras, Costa Rica, and Panama. I served in El Salvador, Nicaragua and Guatemala. I traveled to Honduras to renew my passport. The mission was split and I remained in the Guatemalteco-Salvadorena Mission consisting of the two countries of Guatemala and El Salvador. I enjoyed my

mission and Hispanic people of Central America. Some of my baptisms from there live in Phoenix, Arizona and I call or email on occasion. I left the mission October 21, 1966 and flew to Washington D.C. where I met my parents at the airport. We all planned it so we could visit with my sister, Diane, who lived in Virginia. We did the touristy things all around Washington D.C. I had applied to BYU and started there soon after arriving home from Washington D.C.

I ran into an old friend from the farm, Kaye Baker Heaton. She said that she would feed me dinner if I would come over and help wash her walls. She had just moved into the house and wanted to clean it up. While I was there her roommate was bringing some of her things up from Salt Lake to move in. We were introduced. Her name was Janet Lennox Murdoch. The interesting thing about this is that my freshman year I remember seeing Janet walking across campus at a distance. She had on a black and white dress with big, yellow flowers. It came to me shortly after meeting her of that day three years later. We were engaged and married in the Salt Lake Temple.

LEFT: *Margo, Meg, Janet, Michele, Allan*
RIGHT: *Laura Wilson, Kenneth Wilson (Allan's brother), Dianne Ellis Wilson (sister), Merlin Ellis, Janet and Allan Wilson. Dorcas Jeanette Wilson, mother.*

I graduated from BYU and starting teaching school at Central Junior High School. I worked with County Recreation during the summer months and at JC Penney's at night to make ends meet. Then I took the Postal Exam. I scored high enough to get called right in and hired on. I taught school during the day and worked as a clerk at night at the Post Office. By Christmas time, I quit teaching school and only worked at the post office.

Michele Diane was our first daughter. She is married to Barry Cunningham and has two children, Janessa and Spencer. Margo Ann, our second daughter, is married to Rick Lybbert with three children, Lindsie, Troy and Mallory. Meg Elizabeth, our third, daughter, is married to Jeremy Adam Cunningham and they have a son, Cameron Adam Cunningham.

I worked my way up in the Postal Service. I held positions in management as Manager of the Training Facility. After that, I became the hiring officer and hired for all of Salt Lake City. I worked there for 31 years and retired April 2, 2004. I then began working at the Thatcher Company as a customer service representative and now as a staff accountant.

During my many years, I have served in many positions in the LDS Church: Sunday School teacher, Sunday School counselor and president, Elders Quorum counselor and President, High Priest Group assistant, Executive Secretary in seven bishoprics, and Executive Secretary to two stake presidencies.

Michele Diane Wilson Cunningham

I was born in Salt Lake City, Utah on October 6, 1969. My parents are Janet Lennox Murdoch and Charles Allan Wilson. I am the oldest of three sisters. Margo Ann Wilson Lybbert is next and then Meg Elizabeth Wilson Cunningham is the youngest in our family. It wasn't always easy being the oldest. But now when my sisters and I get together we laugh about all the things we did to each other. I was known as "the princess" because I was always trying to do what was right and keep the peace in the family and I guess my sisters thought my parents treated me like a princess.

I was fortunate to live in the beautiful Holladay area of Salt Lake surrounded by big beautiful trees and my neighbors were my grandparents and aunts, uncles and cousins. I had such a wonderful childhood. My cousins were my best friends and we played and had fun adventures down what we called, Murdoch Lane. The lane and the trees were such a great backdrop for these adventures. We also had a swimming pool. So if we weren't busy making forts out of twigs and leafs we would be in the pool playing fun games like Marco Polo. With each new season came fun and exciting things to do.

We practically lived outside in the spring and summer and we even slept out on my cousin Mike's trampoline. Who needed a house when you had clubhouses, forts and a huge umbrella of trees to live under? In the spring the smell of blossoms filled the air and we had fun watching the mother quail and her little baby quails following after her, scurrying down the lane. The sound of the birds singing and things coming to life was an exciting thing to watch. Summer, of course, was the best because we got to swim and play all day long. Another favorite for my cousins and me was to go roller skating! We just couldn't get enough of it. There was nothing better than skating to the music! It was a regular disco! It didn't matter if it was on the patio in our back yard or in my cousin Rosemary's garage, as long as we had music and skates we were in heaven!!!! I also loved to climb the tall trees. I never could get as far up as Mike could, but I would try. I was definitely a tomboy, and I could keep up with the boys!!

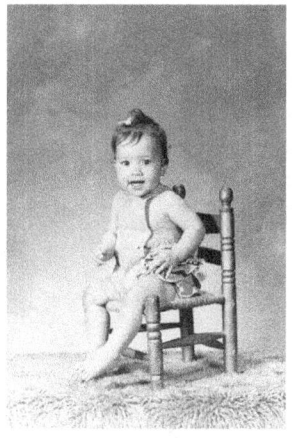 

Fall and winter were just as fun. It was a magical time of year. The leaves fell by the dozens and we would make piles as big as we could and jump in them. In the winter, a beautiful glistening blanket of snow would cover the trees and the lane became a sledding paradise. We would tie a rope from the sled to the car and my dad would drive, pulling us up and down the lane and it felt like we would slip and slide for miles and miles down that marvelous snow packed road.

Of course the most memorable times were when the whole family got together to celebrate the holidays or when my Grandma Murdoch would have one of her famous Molly Whoppet parties. They were just for the grand kids, and it really made me feel like I was someone special being invited to a fun party and frosting cookies with all sort of yummy goodies and coming home with all sorts of treasures. Thanksgiving was always a big day down Murdoch Lane and we could hardly wait to go to Grandma and Grandpa's house for the biggest feast ever! All the cousins, aunts, and uncles would be there and we would have so much fun. The best part was when we would go down in the basement and dress up in old clothes and costumes and pretend we were whoever we wanted to be.

Christmas day was also a favorite of mine because we would have a progressive dinner and it would start at My Aunt Connie and Uncle Mick's house with a yummy cheese soup. Then we would come to our house for a salad bar. Next we would go to Uncle Bill and Aunt Arthel's for the main course and then we would end up at Grandma and Grandpa's for dessert. I was sad when over the years after we started getting married and having to go to other places on Christmas and Thanksgiving that our wonderful traditions had to finally come to and end. The one thing these traditions and experiences taught me was that family is the most important thing and that although we can't always be together all the time on this earth, if we live the gospel of Jesus Christ and follow His commandments, we will all be together forever in the next life.

LEFT: *Michele's high school graduation 1988*
RIGHT: *Barry and Michele's graduation from BYU*

Such wonderful experiences with my family always made me anxious for a family of my own. In my Patriarchal Blessing, it basically said that in due time I would get married and the sweetest fruits would come in motherhood. While I was patiently waiting, I filled my time, with furthering my education at Brigham Young University. That was a very challenging time in my life. I was learning to be independent and studying harder than ever. I felt like I was barely able to tread water. I met my husband, Barry, my junior year. He lived in the same apartment complex and his roommates and my roommates had Family Home Evening together. I thought that he would be fun to take to the girls preference dance. Little did I know that he was hoping I would invite him. We were married on July 19, 1991 and not only was it my wedding day but it was also my Grandma Murdoch's birthday. It was an honor to be married on such a special day. She was a wonderful person and I wanted to be just like her. Once again, the beauty of Murdoch Lane played an important part on my wedding day. I'd always dreamed of being married in the Salt Lake Temple and having my reception in our backyard.

And I wanted a picture of me with my husband in the middle of the lane with all the trees around us. I was so lucky to have those dreams come true. I will always remember how beautiful the lane looked and how hard everyone worked to get it to look so perfect.

Our first apartment was just south of the BYU campus and we both continued with school. One of the best feelings in the world was when I graduated. It was such a relief. I was so happy that I was able to persevere and that it was finally over! I am proud to say that on December 18, 1992, I finished my degree of Bachelor of Arts!

One of my favorite things to do is arranging flowers. I was able to work while going to school in a flower shop called Forever Flowers. It was a small place and people would walk up and order flowers through the window, like a drive through. It was a good experience but I was glad to have an opportunity to work for another floral shop called The Planted Earth. That was where I learned the most about the floral business. I thought I would be working there for a while, but I had my daughter, Janessa Kristin, on April 5, 1995 and shortly after that our new little family moved to Colorado. That was a challenging experience. Here I was, a new mom in a new state. There was so much to learn, and at times it was overwhelming. But, I proved to myself that I was stronger than I thought and that I could survive living outside of Utah.

The reason for the move was an answer to our prayers. Barry wanted to have a better job and be able to provide for our family so I didn't have to go back to work while raising our children. But although I didn't need to have a job for extra income, I started to feel like maybe I should work a few days a week and interviewed for a job at a floral shop. The woman wanted to hire me and I had things worked out with a neighbor, who was in our ward, to watch Janessa. Things seemed to go smoothly, but I wasn't sure if it was worth it because by the time I paid my neighbor to watch Janessa and the taxes that would be taken out, there wouldn't be much left and so I didn't know if I should take the job. We did a lot of praying and we got our answer very clearly the next day when I was talking to the lady about the job and she said that I could start right away and when I told her that I had plans to go to Utah and that the airplane tickets were already bought, she said that she didn't know if that would work because they really needed someone right away and they didn't provide vacation time especially right off the bat. She said she would talk to the owner to see what they could do. The next day, she called me back and said that she was sorry but if I went to Utah they couldn't hire me. It was at that moment that I felt such an overwhelming feeling of the Spirit whispering to me, "why question the Lord? You prayed for your family to be taken care of so you didn't have to work and here you are trying to go against that." I felt a great relief and was glad that they couldn't hire me. I knew that I was supposed to be at home taking care of my beautiful little daughter. That was all I had to worry about everything else would be taken care of. What a powerful experience. I will always be grateful for the power of the Spirit. If I hadn't listened, I would have missed out on many things. I know that staying home is what I was supposed to do and I loved watching Janessa grow and develop. What a fun time that was. I wouldn't have missed it for the world.

We stayed in Colorado for five years. That last year, in 1999, we were blessed with another child. Spencer Allan was born February 25. I was so happy to have a boy. Now I had one of each. It was perfect. Since I never had a brother it was a new experience to have a little boy around. What a great time in my life I was now enjoying the sweetest fruits of motherhood as told in my Patriarchal Blessing. During all of this, Barry was finishing up his Masters Degree in Business from Regis University. We knew we wanted to move back to Utah and within a couple of months, Barry was hired for a job and we moved back.

I don't think we would ever have been prepared for all that would happen to us in the years to come. The year 2000 arrived. We were happy in Utah for that year and then in June of 2001 with out any warning, Barry lost his job. We were devastated because we knew that getting another job in Utah was going to be hard because they didn't pay as well as other states. So, when Barry interviewed and was offered a job in White Plains, New York, he accepted and we moved there the end of August. The cost of living was so high to live in New York, so we decided to find a place to live in Connecticut that was just a 30 minute or so drive to NY where he was working. The company put us up in a townhouse while we looked for a home. We found a new subdivision in Danbury, Connecticut and were able to get a house that was almost finished and would be ready to move into at the end of October.

September came and Janessa started 1st grade I couldn't believe she was already old enough to go to school all day. Each morning I would take her out to the bus stop and once she got on the bus I would take Spencer for a walk in the stroller. I will never forget the morning of September 11, 2001. We were on our morning walk when a lady passed by me. She was listening to her walkman and had a terrible look on her face. She asked me if I had heard about a plane that had just crashed into one of the World Trade Center buildings. I thought how horrible! I rushed home to turn on the news. They were showing the building with the plane smashed into it. And it was on fire. I quickly called Barry and asked if he had heard what happened. He had and was looking out his window towards Manhattan and said he could see the smoke. He was about 45 minutes away from there. I sat there and watched and couldn't believe what was happening. It was especially scary for us because only six days earlier for Labor Day, we went into Manhattan and had been up on the top of one of the towers looking out over New York City. Who could have imagined that this would happen? As I sat there and watched, a second plane came and crashed into the other tower. I couldn't believe what was happening! Then they were reporting a plane had crashed into the Pentagon! And another one had crashed in a field in Pennsylvania. This was so horrible! There was no way to describe how I felt. I thought the world was coming to an end! Then the towers started falling down. Everything was happening so fast. I didn't know what to do. Barry called back and said that they were sending everyone home and then the school called and said they were sending the kids home too. The world as we knew it was no longer the same. In an instant everything changed. We were lucky we didn't loose anybody that day. But there were kids at Janessa's school who did. What a tragedy.

As a result of this terrorist invasion, Barry lost his job. On November 1st, instead of moving into our new home, we were moving back to Utah to live with my parents until we could get out of the mess we were in.

I will always be so grateful for the wonderful parents that I have. They were so willing to let us stay with them and to help us out with whatever we needed. I know that I can always count on my parents for anything. We stayed with them for almost four months. Janessa had to get used to another 1st grade class. She went to the same elementary school that I had gone to and my mom had also gone there as well. Oakwood Elementary hadn't changed much. It was neat to see the old school and reminisce about the good old days.

In February of 2002, Barry received a job offer that would take us to the beautiful state of Maryland. We lived in Frederick and Barry would commute to work in a small town in West Virginia called Charlestown. Living in a place that was so rich in Civil War history was great and we would get out and explore every chance we got. Gettysburg was only 30 minutes from where we lived. We had several chances to go there. And of course Washington D.C. was very close as well. We spent a lot of time there. With all the museums and monuments, it never got boring. Frederick was best known for several Civil War history sites such as the Barbara Fritchie Home and Museum in downtown Frederick. This was only 10 minutes from where we lived. Fritchie was a 96 year old woman who confronted General Stonewall Jackson to spare the country's flag and the town of Frederick. I had never heard of her, but when my Dad found out we were going to be living in Frederick, he was so excited because that was where Barbara Fritchie lived! Of course he had to tell me who she was. He had learned about her in grade school and had to memorize a poem about her. When my Mom and Dad came to visit us for the first time, guess where my dad wanted to go first?

We really enjoyed living in such a wonderful historical place. But Barry wasn't too happy with his job and before long he got another job that he thought would be a place where he could stay for along time. Well, everything happens for a reason and for some reason Barry and his boss didn't always see eye to eye and he quickly found out that this was not the right job for him. We really wanted to get back to Utah so we could be around family. So, we decided to throw caution to the wind and leave Maryland behind. I couldn't believe we were actually going to go back without a job or even a plan, after all, we had lived here for three years and that was the longest time we had ever lived in one spot. Even in Colorado we moved three times in the five years we were there. With a lot of praying yet again, we knew that somehow things would work out. My sister, Margo, knew someone who had a condo we could rent right by where they lived, in Saratoga Springs, so right after Christmas we left for Utah.

I had always thought it would be so exciting to own a floral shop, so we set our sights on buying a business. But this was clearly not the path we were supposed to follow as we received a lot of advice from family friends that told us this was not a wise thing to do. We were so confused. We were determined to find a business that we could control ourselves and that Barry could be his own boss and forget about the corporate world with all the headaches of the unstableness he felt. A tow truck business looked like it would be a very good and lucrative business to get into and again we went full steam ahead and when things weren't fitting into place, it was clear again that this was not the right thing to do. We were so worried that we had made a horrible mistake. But out of the blue, a job that Barry had interviewed for wanted him to come back for another interview and eventually he was offered the job. We were back!!! What felt like years had only been a few months, but I will never forget that feeling of being unsettled and we are so grateful again for the promptings of the Spirit leading us down the right path.

We have been living in South Jordan for a little over two years. And all is well. (knock on wood) Barry is really happy with his job. He finally feels valued and has been promoted to a Director over his group. Janessa is now 12 years old and loves sports. Her favorites are soccer and basketball. She is so smart and mature for her age. I feel like I'm talking to an adult most of the time when I am around her. Spencer is now eight years old and was recently baptized. He is such a character. He is always inventing something with his creativity. He loves to spend time with me cooking and doing projects. I can't believe the things he makes and builds. And I sill get to stay at home and enjoy being with my children, even though they can make me crazy at times, I know that this time will not last for long and I am grateful for the time I have with them. We are so grateful for taking a leap of faith and putting all our trust in the Lord. I have a strong testimony of prayer it has obviously been shown to me time and time again that whenever you are in doubt, all you need to do is pray and if you are in tune to the Spirit, you will be guided down the right path. No matter what happens in the years to come, I know I can always find comfort in prayer and I am so grateful for the gospel in my life. I'm grateful for my ancestors who crossed the plains and who died for this belief, and for my parents and grandparents who taught me the gospel and were such wonderful role models in my life. I hope to carry on this wonderful legacy and be a great example for my children to follow. I don't know what the future has to hold, but I am looking forword to it and all the challenges it has to offer.

Written: May 8th, 2007

Margo Ann Wilson Lybbert

I was born on October 17, 1972 to Janet Lennox Murdoch Wilson and Charles Allan Wilson. I am the second of three daughters. We grew up on 7 ½ acres of property my Grandmother and Grandfather (Ora and Lennox) bought in Holladay, Utah. As each of their children got married, they each inherited an acre of property to build a house on. So, I grew up with my grandparents and cousins right next door. It was the most beautiful area I have ever seen with a creek running through it and forests of trees everywhere you looked. I was very fortunate to have grown up there.

I have many wonderful memories of playing with my sisters and cousins for hours every day. Most of my favorite memories were at our family swimming pool, which turned our summers into nothing but swimming from sun up to sun down. Our swimming pool had the most springy diving board I had ever been on. I can still hear the sound it made as you jumped off into the water. One favorite memory was when my mom was all dressed up to go to a wedding. She decided she had better give us "life saving" lessons just in case something happened while she was gone. She grabbed a long pole to show us how to give the pole to the person who needed help getting to safety. As she was demonstrating to us how this was done, she tripped and fell into the pool, high heels and all. We laughed and laughed at my mom's safety lesson.

One of the best parts of my childhood was living right next door to the most wonderful Grandma one could ever ask for, Grandma Ora Murdoch. Everyone loved Ora. She had a way about her that everyone grew attached to. Her grandchildren were very important to her and I could feel her love for me every time I was around her. Every so often, each grandchild would receive a special invitation to what she would call a "Molly Whoppet Party." Ora would transform into a character named "Molly Whoppet" and the grandchildren got to come enjoy all kinds of fun games and prizes. We would always look forward to these fun parties. Something I will never forget is the special bond I had with Grandma Murdoch. When I was young, I would make a visit to her house for my daily dose of "mush" (it was really called Cream of Wheat). No one could make a bowl of mush like Grandma could.

Christmas was a time for family traditions, all of which I have great memories of. Because we all lived so close, we would put on a progressive dinner every Christmas afternoon. We would start at my Uncle Mick and Aunt Connie's house for cheese soup. Then, off to our house for salad, followed by Uncle Bill's and Aunt Arthel's for the main course. If we weren't too full, we would finish at Grandma Murdoch's house for dessert. It was so much fun to be together as an extended family and share all the wonderful gifts we had received for Christmas.

Family vacations were always a hit in our family. The usual scene would consist of Mom and Dad stressfully packing the station wagon with our belongings. Mom was sure to pack the Velveeta cheese and Ritz crackers to eat along the way. Once we were all in the car, the fun would begin. I usually sat in the middle of my two sisters. Somehow, I would always find a way to bother them by taking up my share of the back seat. Michele would quickly lose patience with me and the fights would begin all the way to Disneyland.

I loved going to visit my Grandma Wilson in Burley Idaho. My Grandma would always come running out of her door to greet us, screaming and yelling with joy. My favorite part of the farm was riding the motorcycle and the minute we arrived, we began riding all over the farm. My dad was so grateful when I was old enough to drive it myself and he didn't have to spend all day driving us around. We had fun exploring the old barns, feeding the cows, seeing how potatoes were harvested, and running up and down the irrigation ditches.

My childhood years quickly passed, and adolescence was knocking at the door As a teenager, I loved to be with my friends. My goal each day was to have fun, and that is what I did. I quickly made friends with anyone who loved to laugh. I laughed my way through junior high and high school. My teachers would always tell my parents that I was getting good grades, but I talked too much. My main focus at school was to socialize. My 9th grade year, I was Student Body Historian – I didn't even know what a "historian" was, but it sounded fun, so I ran for it and I ended up winning.

I got my first job when I was 14 years old. I was bored one summer day and I decided it was time to start earning some money. I told my mom "Goodbye, I'm going to find a job." I walked down to Taco Time on the corner and asked if they were hiring. I returned home that day with my employee uniform and work schedule. Now as I look back on that opportunity, I realize how much I learned from my first job. My parents helped me learn how to be responsible and keep my commitment to my job – I was not to call in sick or not show up at work for any reason. There were times I had to go into work when I would have rather been with my friends (but usually they would just come buy tacos from me). I was able to earn enough money to buy my first car when I was 16 years old.

During high school, I continued to have fun with my friends. Throughout the summer months, my house was the "swimming" party house. Every day, my friends would show up for a day in the sun at our pool. I remember one day some of my guy friends bought 100 gold fish and released them into the pool. We played games trying to catch all the fish and had a blast throwing them around. I was able to save one of the fish to keep as a pet. I loved the summer days of swimming all day, going to down to the corner for a hamburger for lunch, and watching movies with my friends at night.

As I was getting older, I knew I needed to have some direction in my life. As a sophomore in high school, I decided I wanted to go into Child Psychology. I started volunteering at Primary Children's Center for Counseling. This is where I made many wonderful connections which helped me achieve my future goals.

After about a year of volunteering, it turned into a full time job as a Medical Secretary. The counselors were so great and quickly took me under their wing as they gave me experiences in helping with groups for children of divorce and allowing me to observe therapy sessions.

After high school, I went to the University of Utah and majored in Psychology. This is where I met the man of my dreams, Rick Lybbert. It was a fairy-tale romance that continues on to this day as the best thing that ever happened to me. Rick and I met in Abnormal Psychology class. Rick was studying to get into physical therapy school and needed to take this class as a pre-requisite for P.T. School. It was a night class, held weekly for three hours. Rick and I sat together every class and got to know each other slightly. It wasn't until the end of the semester, when Rick asked me to study with him for our take home final, that the rest of my life started to begin. After finals week was over, Rick called me and asked me if I wanted to come over and watch a movie with him and his roommates. I accepted the invite and was expecting him to ask where I lived so he could come pick me up. The next words out of his mouth were, "great – I'll see ya in about 20 minutes, and would you mind picking up the movie on your way." I've been in love with him ever since. We dated for about eight months when he proposed to me on the Golden Gate Bridge in San Francisco. He surprised me and flew me out to his parents' house in California. I was so shocked over the surprise of being on a trip for the weekend, I didn't even consider he may be proposing to me. We took a walk across the Golden Gate Bridge and all I was thinking about was how good I was going to spit off the bridge at the first lookout point. When we got to the lookout point, he put the ring on my finger, got down on one knee, and asked me to marry him. My response was "Shut up—I can't believe this!" After my shock, I responded with a "yes." We got married on June 25, 1994 in the Salt Lake Temple. It was a perfect day. We had a beautiful reception in my parents' backyard. This year we are getting ready to celebrate our 13th wedding anniversary.

Over the next few years, I finished up my undergraduate degree, worked full time at Primary Children's and put Rick through Physical Therapy School. After Rick graduated from P.T. school, he worked hard and put me through social work school at Brigham Young University. During the college years, Rick and I enjoyed ourselves probably more than the average person. We have a lot of common interests, so we filled our spare time camping, mountain biking, snow skiing, hiking, playing golf, and tennis. We were constantly playing. After social work school, I worked full time as a therapist for one year and then the real fun began – we started our family.

Life has never been the same since the birth of our first boat. It was a 1990 Ski Centurion. We were so excited about this purchase, as Rick and I both love to water ski. This purchase changed our lives dramatically, as we relocated our home to our dream neighborhood on a lake in Saratoga Springs, Utah. This is the only neighborhood on a lake that exists in Utah. Shortly after the boat, came our first daughter, Lindsie Lybbert, born May 24, 1999. I had always dreamed of being a mother and after 5 ½ years of marriage I got that chance. I spent my days playing with Lindsie, taking her jogging in the jog stroller, and laughing at all the funny things she would say. She was a very determined baby and learned to talk at an early age, walked at eight months, and was potty trained by age two. We took her out on the boat almost daily and she spent the early years of her life thinking all kids have a daily boating/skiing routine.

A couple of years later, we decided Lindsie needed a sibling, so along came Troy Daniel Lybbert, born September 2001. Troy has been a pure joy in life. He has a very happy nature about him and a contagious laugh. He is very athletic and loves to ride his bike. Right after he was born, we bought some land in Saratoga Springs (just down the road from where we were living) and Rick built us our dream home with a beautiful view of Utah Lake and Mount Timpanogos. It was a lot of work, but when Rick sets his mind to something, he never gives up. Troy also has grown up (all five years so far) with water skiing as the center of our family fun. He was on the boat by the time he was 10 days old.

On April 15, 2005, our third child, Mallory Lybbert, was born. Lindsie and Troy were so excited to help care for a new baby. Mallory has a very easy-going nature and hardly ever even cried. She is currently two years old and we find ourselves laughing at her every day. She is our blue-eyed girl and we nick named her the "destroyer" as she loves to destroy anything in sight.

We have been very blessed with three healthy, smart, darling children and the ability for me to be a stay at home mom. Rick is a very hard working husband and currently owns four physical therapy clinics and is working on a project to build a private water ski lake that will also include a disabled water ski program. He is in the middle of this huge project and someday we will find out if it comes to be. It will be called *The Last Chance Ski Ranch*.

I feel so grateful to have the family I have. My parents did such an excellent job raising us with the gospel as the foundation for our lives. As I look back on my life, I owe everything to my very loving and understanding parents who knew when to be firm, and when to let go at times. I can only hope that I can do as wonderful of a job as they did. I am just beginning my journey as a parent and pray every day that I can provide as wonderful of a childhood for my children as my parents did for me.

Meg Elizabeth Wilson Cunningham

My name is Meg Cunningham. My parents are Charles Allan Wilson and Janet Lennox Murdoch Wilson. I have two older sisters, Michele Cunningham and Margo Lybbert. I always wanted a brother, but never got one. I was born May 20, 1977 in Salt Lake City Utah. Everyone was expecting me to be a boy and my parents even had the name Mark picked out for me (they liked the letter M, I guess). Anyway, I surprised them and they got another girl. My sisters gave me a warm welcome when I came home from the hospital and Margo told my mom to "take her back to the hospital." I am happy to say they let me stay and eventually Margo and I became friends.

My childhood memories are very rich and deep. I can close my eyes and vividly remember all the days I spent in the family swimming pool or exploring on the eight acres of property. I was fortunate to have grown up down a long lane of gigantic trees surrounded by my aunts, uncles, cousins, and grandparents. I felt like the luckiest kid alive. I lived my summer days in the swimming pool. There was nothing better than playing Marco Polo and other games in the pool on a hot summer day. I always loved to explore on the property, play hide and seek with my cousins, jump on my aunt and uncle's trampoline and swing on cousin Mike's rope swing. My best friend, Lindsay, growing up lived behind me and I could get to her house by walking through my back yard and through a gate into her back yard. We were inseparable and I was always at her house or she was always at my house playing. When we were growing up, 6200 South wasn't a busy street and our parents would always let us walk down to the corner drug store. We looked forward to saving our money and walking down there on a Saturday to buy the penny candy. I thought it was so cool how much candy we could get. I was always thinking of ways to make money and things I could do to earn it besides my weekly allowance. I laugh at all the crazy things we came up with. We would buy a lot of different candy at the store and then set up a table on the street by her house and sell the candy for double the money (I'm not sure we sold much.) I also remember brushing her cat and collecting all the fur, over a long period of time, and then making the fur into things. We went door to door selling cat fur saying it could be used for doll clothing or whatever else we could think of. I'm sure the people thought we were crazy and just laughed at us. Then there was the time I wanted to sell frozen Otter Pops with another friend of mine that lived down Walker Lane. Well, I was in charge of getting the Otter Pops and freezing them. The next morning I was in a hurry to get to our meeting spot down Walker Lane and set up our stand. My mom was helping me get ready when we

discovered the Otter Pops weren't even frozen. I was so upset, "How can we sell Otter Pops that aren't even frozen... it's a hot day and these were supposed to cool people off, now nobody will buy them." My mom attempted to calm me down and I remember her telling me that I would laugh at this some day (not exactly what I wanted to hear then), but it was true. I also think we made $25 selling them that day.

I have always been a very independent and determined individual in every aspect of my life. If there was something in life I wanted, I set my mind to doing whatever it took to get it and wouldn't let anything stand in my way of achieving it - good grades, making a sports team, getting a job, graduating from college with my undergraduate degree, going back and getting my master's degree, becoming certified in skydiving, getting a motorcycle (dirt bike) and riding around, starting a vinyl lettering/craft business, etc. I recall wanting to start making my own money and got a job when I was 14 at my friend's parents' Italian restaurant. From there I always had a job and was very dependable. My parents have been exceptionally supportive of my decisions and have been there to help me. I had bought and paid off four different cars all before I was twenty three. I was so determined at one point to have a specific car and couldn't find any for sale in Utah. While my family was on a trip, visiting my sister and her family in Colorado, I decided to look in the newspaper ads for cars. I found the dream car I was looking for, but there was one minor detail... we were on vacation in Colorado! My dad, being the supportive and loving dad that he was, helped me find a solution to this problem. After driving to look at the car, test driving it, and falling in love with it, my dad had some money wired into my brother-in-law's account from his bank in Utah. We got the cash from the account and bought the car. I drove my new car home from Colorado to Utah and don't think I stopped smiling the whole way home. I was able to pay my parents back every penny for the car, but I won't ever be able to pay them back for their encouragement and support.

Unfortunately, I never had the opportunity to really know my Grandpa Murdoch (Lennox). He passed away when I was just one year old. My mom told me that I was his favorite grandchild though (oops guess the secret's out now). She told me he would walk down every morning and watch my mom give me a bath and then he would play with me. He loved to put his hat on my head and would take his belt off for me to play with. He wanted me to have his belt and hat when he passed away, so my grandma gave them to me and I have them in my cedar chest. They are the only items I have and my only memories of him. Now my grandma and I were very close! I LOVED going to her house and playing her piano. She would listen to me make up songs and she would record them as I sang. She loved to write stories and poems, I guess I got my creative gene from her. She encouraged me and helped me write stories, songs, and poems.

I even had one of my stories I wrote in the 5th grade published in the Friend Magazine. My grandma was so proud of me. My mom always tells me how much I remind her of Grandma Murdoch (Ora). She says that I get my determination, creativity, and no fear attitude from my grandma. As I got older (in high school), I would mow her lawn every Saturday. She had a few good sized lawns and it would take me about an hour to mow them. As she got a little older and it was hard for her to do house work, I would also help with her house work on Saturday. I loved cleaning her house, doing her laundry, and washing her hair because it gave me the opportunity to spend more time with her. We were very close and our bond and friendship grew more each year. It was difficult for me when she passed away several years ago and there are days when I feel like she is still alive. My memories of Thanksgivings at her house with all my aunts, uncles, and cousins will never fade. I will always remember the big long table she had set up for all of us. She would decorate everything so nice and used her fine china. And who can forget the football games we played on her big lawn after we stuffed ourselves? I have to laugh as I think of Grandma Murdoch and her "un-birthday gifts"! She always made us feel special even when it wasn't our special day. If we were having a birthday party for someone she would give them a present, but also give all of us an "un-birthday gift". I would always look forward to what it would be... as she got older however, you would sometimes open up a present that you could have sworn you had seen on her shelf before!

My other grandparents lived in Burley, Idaho. That is where my dad was born. My Grandpa Wilson (Dick) also passed away at a young age and I never got to know him either. My Grandma Wilson (Dorcas) has always been a key part of my life too. I would love to go to Idaho to her farm and see where my dad grew up. She lived in a little house on a big farm with cows and horses that we loved to feed. I remember climbing all the big hay bails and shooting her BB gun at tin cans. She had an old Honda motorcycle that was so much fun to ride around in the potato fields. We had a blast every time we would go visit her. She was always singing in the kitchen when she was cooking and she loved to knit. My parents say the spunky, feisty, athletic part of my personality from Grandma Wilson. My family will never let me forget the day my grandma was saying something that I didn't agree with and I boldly said, "Oh bull, grandma!"

I am very lucky to have a rich heritage of pioneer ancestry that goes far back. I am related to Wee Granny, who traveled over from Scotland with the Martin Handcart Company. Their company left too late in the summer and ran into bad weather. Wee Granny became a victim to the bad weather conditions and passed away before she made it into the valley. I am sure a lot of my strength and determination is a product of my pioneer ancestry.

I started pre-school when I was two! My mom and her friend opened a pre-school in her friend's basement. My mom had a degree in teaching and always wanted to teach school, but was hesitant at first because I was so young and she didn't want to leave me with a babysitter every day. She knew I was only two and the pre-school kids had to be at least three. She told her friend she would try it out and see how it went, but that she would only do it if she could bring me. Well, my mom tells me I was a handful at first and she thought she was going to have to tell the lady it wasn't going to work out. Evidently I was very territorial and didn't want to share my mom with twenty other kids. I finally figured out that it was a fun place and I could make friends and share my mom. I loved going to pre-school. I have so many fun memories of being there and having my mom teach me along with other kids. She was so good at what she did and made learning fun.

We would go on lots of field trips and made a lot of creative things. I loved painting time and especially loved singing time. They had people come and bring things for us to learn about. I remember one time they had someone come and bring a big huge snake that we all got to touch. I could talk about all my fun pre-school memories, but that would take about ten more pages! I went with my mom to pre-school for three years before I started kindergarten. My mom continued teaching pre-school for fifteen years.

Some of my best childhood memories are of my birthday parties. My parents always let me have elaborate parties. I was really creative and never wanted to just have a boring old party. I remember having a *backwards, inside-out party* and my friends had to wear all their clothes backwards and inside out. It was always some sort of dress up theme. My mom went to a lot of work making me feel special on my birthday and my parties were always so much fun. We would play lots of fun games, eat pizza, ice cream, watch movies and they were always sleep-over parties. The next morning my dad would make us waffles and then take everyone home. I remember my mom throwing me a few surprise parties too. I was always excited for my birthday to come. Every year we would work hard to get the swimming pool open and ready before my birthday.

I have wonderful memories of all the holidays, especially Christmas. My mom would decorate the house so nice and we always had a gigantic tree that was at least 12 feet because we had a vaulted ceiling. The best memory of Christmas, and growing up down the lane with all my relatives on my mom's side, was the traditional progressive dinner. It was so much fun to get up in the morning and open the presents from Santa. I remember every year my mom would make the most delicious breakfast wreath (what's funny is as a kid I pretended I liked it, but really didn't eat a lot of it...then as I got older I guess my taste buds grew up because it was the best pastry ever). Lunch time was when the progressive dinner began. We always started at Uncle Mick and Aunt Connie's house with cheese soup. Then everyone "progressed" over to our house for a make your own salad bar. Next we all walked over to Uncle Bill and Aunt Arthel's house for sandwiches and then ended up at Grandma Murdoch's house for dessert. The best part about going to the different houses was the fact that you got to see what Santa brought everyone for Christmas. I would always wear the new outfit I got and loved playing with everyone's toys!

My other favorite holiday was Halloween. I remember getting to go to school in my costume and enjoyed the parade where we would walk around for all the parents and other kids to see us. We would usually have chili or something warm for dinner and then my dad would always take us trick-or-treating. He would drive us around the neighborhoods to each house.

Family vacations are definitely on my long list of memories. I don't remember how many times we drove to California to go to Disneyland, but I do remember how much fun we had. I specifically remember stopping in Barstow, California each and every time we would go just so we could eat in the McDonalds train. I remember both grandmas came with us on one vacation to Disneyland and I thought that was so cool. I also remember a few trips to Hawaii. One particular trip I will never forget and my family won't let me either. Margo had been bothering me all day and singing a song saying that I liked a boy I didn't like. She really knew how to get to me, but also knew how to look so innocent to my parents and get away with picking on me. After numerous times of asking her to quit singing that, it escalated into fighting and finally resulted in me deciding to remove myself from the situation. We were in the middle of Hawaii looking at waterfalls and doing some tour when I had endured enough of her. I quickly hopped on the closest tour bus that was leaving and waved goodbye to my family. I wasn't quite sure where it was going and was even more sure that I didn't care because I was glad to be away from her. Well, needless to say my parents panicked and got on their own tour bus to find me. I think I was only twelve at the time and wasn't thinking rationally.

I looked forward to having Family Home Evening every Monday night. My mom would always plan a fun activity and some sort of dessert that we all could help with. We spent many Monday nights reading the scriptures and drawing pictures on the pages that related to the stories. My mom was a good artist and she helped me do a lot of my pictures. I enjoyed the

Family Home Evenings when we would write a letter to the missionaries. I recall writing once a month to my cousin David. I thought it was neat writing him because he was in Scotland and at the end of each letter I would say "Cheerio"... I think that is how they say goodbye. One particular Family Home Evening that I will never forget was in October. We usually made caramel apples for Halloween (well, this was another thing I never liked as a kid... I think they were too hard to eat or something. I always pretended I liked them so I wouldn't hurt my mom's feelings). So on this particular night that we made caramel apples, I figured out a solution to my problem of not liking them. I quietly took my caramel apple (stick and all) with me to the bathroom; it was a fail-proof plan! All I had to do was place the apple in the toilet and flush all my problems away. Back to the kitchen I went and hoped nobody would comment on the record timing of how fast a seven-year old polished off an entire caramel apple. I was safe until someone went to the bathroom only to find the clogged toilet overflowing.....oops!

I attended Oakwood Elementary School. My friend would come over in the morning and we would walk down my long lane to the end and wait for the bus to pick us up. Sometimes her mom would drive us, if we missed the bus. As we got older we were able to walk to and from school. I liked when we rode our bikes to school the best. However, I remember one day I rode my bike to school and was so excited to get home after school, because I was having a big Friday the 13th party at my house, that I forgot I rode my bike and took the bus home. I still remember to this day the horrible feeling I got when I realized I left my bike at school. When we went over to the school, my bike was gone! Someone had stolen it. That was a horrible feeling as a kid to have someone take something from you! My parents were always there for me and were so loving and understanding. They helped me earn some money and helped me to get another bike. I went to Sears with them and was able to pick out another bike.

Junior high came fast and I spent my days going to school at Bonneville Junior High. I have lots of great memories of junior high! I ran for Student Body Officer (SBO) for my 9th grade year. I had fun campaigning, making posters, doing skits, and all of the stuff that went along with running for the office of historian. I remember how nervous I was in the assembly that day they announced who won, but when they called my name I was so happy and excited. My 9th grade year was my favorite year. I had so much fun planning assemblies, doing fund raisers and activities, taking pictures of everyone and all the events, putting together a slide show at the end of the year to music, and being a leader for the school. I was involved in so many activities, sports and with friends that I was having the time of my life.

Cottonwood High School was where I would spend the next three years of my life. I thought high school was fun. When I was a sophomore I had a boyfriend who was a senior, so I thought I was pretty cool because we would always leave campus and go to lunch with his friends. I played center field and left field for Cottonwood High's softball team. My coach called me his "weapon" because he said I was the fastest one on the team. That meant that I had to bunt a lot. Usually when you bunt, you sacrifice yourself getting on 1st base so the person who was on 1st can advance to 2nd base, but I usually made it to 1st base in spite of bunting. I loved game days and traveling around for competitions. In between 9th and 10th grade, I tore my ACL in my left knee and had to have a ligament replacement, so I was happy to get back to sports and being active. I hated being out for an injury and missing out on doing the things I loved to do. I got my first car when I turned sixteen my junior year. It was a white Honda CRX. I was so happy to finally be able to drive and not have to have my dad drive me to school. Looking back on it now, I really don't understand why I was so embarrassed to be seen by my dad dropping me off. I should have been grateful... something that most teenagers are not.

Well, high school came and went. I found myself spending the next four years of my life at the University of Utah, where I earned my undergraduate degree. I majored in psychology and minored in sociology. I worked in various jobs related to my field including residential treatment centers, boarding schools, and other treatment facilities. I enjoyed all the jobs I did, however I really wanted to do more treatment and counseling. In order to get hired anywhere as a therapist you have to have your Masters in Social Work. So after taking a few years off of school (remember I started going to school at age two...I needed a little break) I went back to school to get my master's degree. I spent about six months in California before starting graduate school at the University of Utah in 2002. I graduated with my Master's degree in Social Work the summer of 2004.

It was challenging, but very rewarding and was a wonderful experience. I had several ups and downs during these few years which presented challenges for me, both emotionally and spiritually. I had met someone while I was in California, we dated for six months and then I returned to Utah to start school. After six more months of long distance dating, he moved to Utah and we got married six months later in the Salt Lake City Temple. I began my second year of graduate school and was feeling the pressures of trying to balance school with marriage and house work etc. A few months into our marriage things began to change and become uncertain. After several more months of living chaos, fear, and stress, I decided it was an unhealthy situation and we needed to seek some marriage counseling. After a few more months and no changes or commitment on his part, I decided to counsel with our bishop. After many hours of prayer, sleepless nights, tears, and trips to the temple, I knew it was in my best interest to get out of the toxic marriage. I felt strongly that I needed to leave before we had children. It was not an easy decision and one that I spent many hours on my knees pleading with the Lord for direction and comfort. I know he answered my prayers and provided me with love and comfort through my family and friends. They say everything you go through in life is designed to make you stronger and provide you with a learning experience. I am still trying to figure out what I was supposed to learn from that experience, but I am sure one day I will know. What I do know is I am thankful I didn't turn away from the church and that I relied on my faith and testimony to get me through my trials. I know that Heavenly Father answers our prayers and if we remain faithful and worthy he provides us with blessings. I know this is true because after about a year of struggling through things and not knowing which direction my life was going to go in, things started to fall into place. I am sure that because I had put all my faith and trust in the Lord, up to this point, he opened doors for me and people were place into my life. I felt my life had been completely destroyed and up-rooted and had no idea how I would be "normal" again. When I least expected it, things started to fall into place for me and I began to get my life back together. I was introduced to someone whose job was looking for a social worker and ended up getting hired for the University of Utah Psychiatric Department. It quickly became one of the biggest blessings in my life and a wonderful job. I was sad to have to leave this job after one year of working there. However, there was excellent rationale behind the decision... my motivation is all explained... keep reading!

Another blessing re-entered my life during this same time. A long time friend contacted me, after a few years of no contact, once he heard of my divorce. Jeremy and I met when I was fourteen and he was fifteen. My sister (Michele) married his uncle (Barry) and my family flew to one of their wedding receptions in West Virginia (where Barry was from). Jeremy and I hit it off right from the beginning. We had so much fun together the few days that we were there. He thought he was so cool because he had his learners permit and could drive. I have to laugh when I think of us sneaking out of the reception line to "steal" his dad's mini van and take it for a spin in the church parking lot... that was his way of showing off for me. Anyway, the trip ended and I went back to Utah to begin 9th grade and Jeremy stayed in West Virginia to begin 10th grade. After we left he told his grandma, "She is so beautiful. I am going to marry her someday." We wrote some letters back and forth between 1991-1995 (a few of the letters I still have). His dad and sometimes he and his brothers would visit Utah for ski trips and for Thanksgiving. They seemed like part of the family and would stay at our house. His brothers went to BYU and we would have them over for Sunday dinners since they didn't have any family around. I went to the MTC (Missionary Training Center) to see both his brothers off on their missions, as well as seeing Jeremy off on his mission. We wrote letters and kept in touch while he was on his mission. We continued to keep in touch, over the phone and some visits to Utah through out the years after his mission. We lost touch around 2001 and didn't have contact again until around 2004. We began talking on the phone more (he was living in Texas at this point) and planned a few fun trips. Finally, one day he got the courage to tell me he has always liked me and he felt like he missed his opportunity to be with me once I got married. He said he was upset with himself for never expressing his feeling and didn't want to miss his opportunity again. I was in shock and didn't really take him seriously at first (you have to understand... we were rarely serious, we are always laughing and joking). I think it took several months of us talking on the phone and visiting each other before I realized he was serious. We had been friends for so long and knew each other so well that getting married seemed like the natural next step. With Jeremy living in Texas and myself living in Utah, we wanted to get married soon so we could be together. We were faced with the decision to wait 6-12 months for my temple cancellation to go through so we could get married in the temple, or get married civilly and get sealed in the temple a year later. We chose to be married on November 25, 2006 in the Joseph Smith Building and got sealed in the Salt Lake Temple a year later November 24, 2007.

Jeremy had been promoted in his company and was relocated to North

Carolina a month before we were married. Therefore, after our wedding, we loaded up a U-Haul with all my belongings and towed my jeep and drove across the country. It took us four days and we drove through some bad weather. At one point, the roads were closed due to snow storms and ice so we had to get a hotel. It made me think of the pioneers and how they traveled across the country in bad weather, but didn't have the shelter that we had. It was hard to leave my family in Utah and move to a new place, but I believe we had a purpose for being there. I worked for LDS Family Services as a Social Worker part time and also opened up a vinyl lettering business called *Let Your Walls Do The Talking*. Jeremy developed my website and it really started taking off. After about one year of living in NC, Jeremy approached his boss and discussed the idea of being an independent contractor for them. They agreed...which meant he could work from home...so why would it matter if the home he worked from was in North Carolina or Utah?? We worked out a plan to move back to Utah and he would fly back to North Carolina every so often when they needed him too. We moved in with my parents and thought it would be for a short time. We ended up living with them for one year while we were waiting for our house to sell in North Carolina (it is STILL for sale and it's almost been 2 years!) I got my job back at the University of Utah Department of Psychiatry as a social worker and also worked as a school social worker at Rosepark Elementary School. Then I found out I was pregnant and four months into it, I stopped working. We started looking for a house in Utah (stressful) and flew back to North Carolina to load up all our stuff, since we left the house furnished and everything in it (stressful). We moved into our house two weeks before I gave birth (stressful) and are still trying to get settled.

So this is where my story ends.....or should I say begins?? The next chapter of my life is starting, I am a MOM. We have a precious little baby boy named Cameron. He was born on May 27, 2009 and is five months old! He brings so much joy and happiness to our lives. I LOVE being a mom, it is such a rewarding and fun job! Cameron makes me laugh and smile every day. I feel so blessed to have such a sweet little spirit in my home and am excited for all the adventures he will bring. I love adventures and enjoy exploring new things in life. I believe we choose our destinations and create our happiness. I use my Grandma Murdoch as my example of someone who had a true appreciation for life and living it to its fullest. She was the most optimistic and positive lady, even in the midst of pain and adversity she never lost her sense of humor. I loved to listen to her stories of her life and the adventures she would tell. I hope that one day I will be able to tell my stories to my grandchildren and I can inspire them as I have been inspired by the people in my life. I have been very blessed to be born into such a loving and supportive family. I have so many memories of growing up and my life so far that I could write my own book. I wouldn't be who I am today if it wasn't for my parents and for the gospel in my life.

Chapter 7

Mary Smith Murdoch and Gordon L. Weggeland

Mary was born August 10, 1904 to William Murdoch and Jeannette Smith Murdoch. She was the second child of nine children. She was born in a small house next to the grocery store operated by her father at 72 F Street, Salt Lake City. Being the eldest daughter in a large family of children, she was expected to help her mother in caring for the succession of younger siblings. She would say that she became a second mother to the younger children.

At a early age, she was assigned the duty of obtaining the family's daily milk and dairy products by taking a very early walk of over a mile to the dairy operated behind the home of Brigham Young. She would do this in all types of weather and well before breakfast. Household refrigerators were not then available, and only until much later did the family acquire one.

Her father was the bishop of the ward in which the family lived and was a strict disciplinarian. He operated the grocery store, was generous and well liked in the community. In the late 1930's and early 1940's, he was elected to serve as a member of the Salt Lake City Commission.

During the summer months the children lived in a rustic cabin with their mother in Lamb's Canyon in the nearby Wasatch Mountains. They would stay for three months each summer, visited on weekends by their father, who would bring provisions for the following week.

Their father's sisters, Jen and Mary, often visited them at the cabin for several weeks each year.

Mary attended Salt Lake City schools, graduating from East High School. She graduated from the University of Utah School of Education and taught for several years in the Salt Lake City public schools prior to her marriage. She contributed almost all of her earnings as a teacher to support her older brother, Lennox, on his mission to Scotland.

Mary married Gordon L. Weggeland in the Salt Lake Temple. Always very active in Church activities, she served as President of the Relief Society in several wards in which she and her husband lived in Salt Lake City, Honolulu, Hawaii, and in Hong Kong.

Mary was the mother of five children: Mary Barbara, Gordon Gail and Warren Murdoch. Twins Jeanette and John died as infants shortly after their birth.

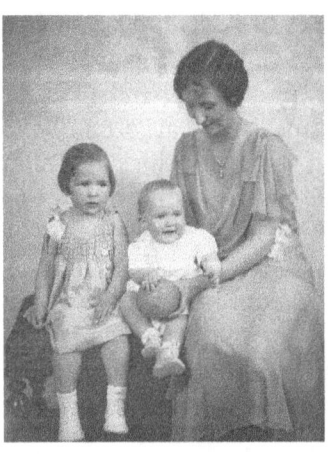

Devoted to her family, the Church and all who needed her love and help, Mary was always there in time of need. She was a beautiful woman, a wonderful mother, excellent cook, and an expert seamstress. She was gracious, generous, and supportive of good causes. She had many friends. She had a great intellectual curiosity, and she loved reading poetry and wrote some very lovely poetry from time to time.

She died in Salt Lake City on December 29, 1985.

MARY BARBARA WEGGELAND SMITH

March 10, 1929 – October 22, 1990

Mary Barbara Weggeland was born March 10, 1929 in Salt Lake City, Utah. She was the first born of Gordon Leroy Weggeland and Mary Smith Murdoch Weggeland. Although named for her mother, Mary Smith Murdoch Weggeland, Mary Barbara was known by the name Barbara throughout her life.

Barbara enjoyed a lovely childhood. She grew up in a loving home with her two younger brothers Gordon Gail Weggeland and Warren Murdoch Weggeland. Barbara and her brothers were taught the gospel by the example of their loving parents. Gordon and Mary Weggeland were both active members in the LDS church and attended regularly.

Beginning at the early age of seven, Barbara began studying piano. She became a talented pianist. Much of her time was spent practicing diligently four hours every day. Barbara also loved helping her mother care for her younger brothers Gail and Warren.

At the age of seventeen, Barbara entered the University of Utah. She was affiliated with the Chi Omega Sorority, Mu Phi Epsilon, received recognition from many scholastic organizations and in 1950 earned a degree. Following her university years, Barbara acquired an elementary teaching position, continued her love of music playing, accompanying and teaching piano lessons.

On July 31, 1950, Barbara married Wallace Burbidge Smith. Together they raised three daughters; Martha Gay Smith, born March 18, 1953, Sandra Kay Smith, born March 16, 1956, and Mary Jane Smith born April 23, 1962. Later divorced, Barbara relocated to Provo, Utah and Boulder, Colorado to further her education, receiving a Master of Arts from Brigham Young University in 1972 and a Doctorate of Philosophy from the University of Colorado in 1979.

A teacher, lecturer and pianist, Barbara Weggeland Smith continued her career as a music educator and pioneer of the group piano method of teaching. Dr. Barbara Smith was a Professor of Music at James Madison University in Harrisonburg, Virginia and later an Assistant Professor of Music at Ithaca College in Ithaca, New York.

In 1981, Barbara returned to Salt Lake City where she established and directed the Intermountain School of Keyboard Arts. She was a devoted teacher and successful businesswoman. Barbara was the author of many articles on group piano techniques and a popular lecturer. She served in many official capacities in the National Music Teachers Association, the Virginia Teachers Association, and Mu Phi Epsilon.

On a cold day in December 1985, Barbara was diagnosed with breast cancer. The stage of the disease was severe. Barbara underwent several treatments with an optimistic attitude. Then, on March 31, 1989, her youngest daughter, Mary Jane Smith, age 28, died. This tragedy was devastating for Barbara and her family.

One year later, a beloved mother, sister, grandmother, and friend, Mary Barbara Weggeland Smith lost her long and courageous battle against breast cancer. She died at the age of 61, on October, 31, 1990. Throughout her short life, Barbara touched others by her kind loving presence and exceptional talent. Those who knew and loved Barbara appreciated the beautiful spirit she possessed.

GORDON GAIL WEGGELAND

Gail was born July 6, 1930 in Salt Lake City to Gordon Leroy and Mary Murdoch Weggeland. They were loving and gifted parents. With brother, Warren, and sister, Barbara, they had a happy childhood in the Garden Park area of Salt Lake City. He attended public schools and graduated from East High School. He was a good student, active in sports, skiing and hiking the Wasatch Mountains.

At the University of Utah, he was a member of the Sigma Nu Fraternity. He received a degree in Political Science and in 1955 a law degree. At the age of eighteen, he left for South Africa as a missionary for the Church of Jesus Christ of Latter-day Saints. He was among the first group of Elders to open the country of Southern Rhodesia (Zimbabwe) to missionary work. He has been active in the church, serving in many positions and callings.

In 1953, Flora Ann Cannon and Gail were married in the Salt Lake Temple by President David O. McKay. They have made their home in Salt Lake City, except for the period of the Korean War when Gail was in the Army. Children, Mark Cannon Weggeland (1955) and Mary Lynne Weggeland (1957) were born in military hospitals. Leslie Ann was born in 1962 in Salt Lake City. All of the children graduated from the University of Utah and are active in the Church. Gail remained active in the Army Reserve and commanded Infantry and Judge Advocate Units. As a Colonel, he served as the Staff Judge Advocate for the 96th ARCOM, a corps size unit.

Gail started his career in law by clerking for Justice Worthen at the Utah State Supreme Court. In 1958, he was employed as an attorney for the U.S. Security and Exchange Commission. For 27 years, he was the "Attorney in Charge" of the Salt Lake City office (one of 11 field offices), directing investigations and prosecuting civil and criminal cases throughout the western states. He practiced law for ten years after leaving the government.

Gail has many hobbies. With his wife, Flora, he has traveled from the Arctic Circle to the Antarctic Circle, and has visited the major cities and countries of the world. He is a good artist and an ardent white water river runner, spending most summers with the family running wilderness sections of the western rivers. He flew an experimental biplane, rode motorcycles, and has an elaborate model railroad layout in his basement. He is active in political and community service organizations.

WARREN MURDOCH WEGGELAND

I was born at Salt Lake City, Utah January 17, 1935, the youngest child of Mary Murdoch and Gordon L. Weggeland. My sister, Mary Barbara, was seven years older than I, and my brother Gordon Gail was five and one half years older.

I grew up in a beautiful home in the eastern section of Salt Lake City, a home filled with love, culture, and purpose. The neighborhood in which we lived was a wonderful neighborhood, with nine other boys my age. We explored the gully created by Red Butte Creek which ran between Yale and Harvard Avenues. We built tree houses, fished for trout, threw rocks at porcupines and squirrels, and played baseball, football, tag, and kick-the-can in the street on Yale Avenue or on Douglas Street. On occasion we even stole the neighbors' cherries or apples as they ripened on the trees.

I attended Salt Lake City public schools, graduating from East High School. I then attended the University of Utah. I interrupted my education to join the U.S. Army during the Korean War. During my military service I was stationed at the Supreme Headquarters of the Allied Powers Europe (SHAPE) in Paris, France. Following my service I was discharged from the Army in Paris and travelled extensively in Europe, the Middle East, and parts of North Africa.

Upon my return to Salt Lake City, I resumed my studies at the University of Utah. I graduated with a B.S. Degree in Political Science in 1959 and J.D. Degree from the University of Utah Law School in 1960. I started practicing law upon my admission to the Utah State Bar in 1960 and worked for the Salt Lake County Attorney's Office (now known as the District Attorney's Office) as a prosecutor in the Criminal Prosecution Division. During my service in that office, I tried many felony and misdemeanor cases. I then served as an Assistant Attorney General in the office of the Utah Attorney General. My duties were trying civil and criminal cases and handling and arguing appellate cases before the Utah Supreme Court. I resigned from that office in early 1968 to devote all my attention to my clients in my private practice.I practiced law in Salt Lake City from 1960 until my retirement in 2005, maintaining throughout those years a very active practice involving both transactional work and litigation. During that time I was admitted to practice in all courts of the State of Utah, the United States District Court for the District of Utah, the Tenth Federal Circuit Court, the Ninth Federal Circuit Court, and the United States Supreme Court. I was also admitted to practice on a temporary basis in many other state and federal courts for the purpose of litigation in that particular court.

In 1956 I married Barbara Ray. We had two children: Steven, born in 1956, and Karen, born in 1958. We were later divorced. I later married Susan Ostler and we had two daughters: Heidi, born in 1966, and Amy, born in 1971. We later divorced. I have twelve wonderful grandchildren.

Since 1993, I have been blessed with the companionship of a fascinating and wonderful woman. She is brilliant, beautiful, highly educated, compassionate, generous and witty with a great sense of humor.

My avocation was music. I played saxophone and clarinet. For many years during college and thereafter, I had a small jazz band. We played many private parties, weddings and on occasion, in nightclubs in the Salt Lake City area.

Aside from my music, I have enjoyed traveling, river running in the Intermountain area, and fly fishing, particularly saltwater fly fishing for bonefish, tarpon and permit.

EDITOR'S NOTE: *Warren died on August 18, 2010 in Salt Lake City, Utah.*

WARREN WEGGELAND

Warren Weggeland 1935 ~ 2010 Warren Murdoch Weggeland died of natural causes on August 18, 2010. Born to Gordon Leroy and Mary Murdoch Weggeland on Jan. 17, 1935, Warren was raised in a home he described as a place "filled with love, culture and purpose." Growing up in the Gilmer Park neighborhood of Salt Lake City, Warren attended Douglas Elementary, Roosevelt Junior High and East High School. At an early age, Warren developed a love of learning that continued throughout his life. He loved history, art and music, which came naturally to him. Warren played the saxophone and clarinet and in his college years enjoyed performing with a small jazz band. Warren was an undergraduate student at the University of Utah when he enlisted in the Army. He was stationed at the Supreme Headquarters of the Allied Powers Europe in Paris. After his discharge, Warren returned to the University where he received his B.S. and J.D. degrees. Warren practiced law for 45 years, including positions as Chief Deputy Salt Lake County Attorney and Assistant Attorney General. Warren loved to travel and would prepare for trips by studying the language and history of each country he would visit. His trip to Paris, Capri, Sorrento and Rome last year was among his favorites. Andros Island in the Bahamas was a familiar, much loved spot for salt water fly fishing and relaxation. When he was not fishing or traveling abroad, Warren was most happy playing golf at the Alpine Country Club with friends. Warren is survived by his close friend, Barbara Liebroder; children Steven (Jenny), Karen Hale (Jon), Heidi, and Amy Rogin (Bill); stepsons David Perkins (Kris) and Terry Perkins (Jill); brother Gail (Flora); 16 grandchildren and five great-grandchildren. He was preceded in death by his parents; infant siblings, Jeanette and John; sister Barbara W. Smith; and granddaughter Chelsea Hale. Friends may visit with Warren's family on Wednesday, August 25 at Larkin Mortuary, 260 East South Temple, from noon to 2 p.m. A graveside service at Salt Lake City Cemetery will be held at 2:30 p.m. In lieu of flowers, contributions in Warren's memory may be sent to the S.J. Quinney College of Law at the University of Utah.

Chapter 8

John Thyne Murdoch and Ruth Streeper

By Bruce Murdoch

Jack Murdoch (John Thyne Murdoch) was born September 7, 1905 in Salt Lake City, Utah. He married Ruth Streeper in Salt Lake City and they moved to Boise, Idaho in the late 1930's. Jack died at the age of 69 after 30 years in the small business he owned called, Jack Murdoch Finance Co. Jack had a very likeable personality and was known as *Smilin' Jack Murdoch, Your Loan Arranger*. Ruth lived to the age of 91, having never spent a day in the hospital, other then giving birth, until she had a stroke at 90. She dedicated her entire life to her five boys hardly ever leaving the house. She was very active around the house cooking, cleaning, working in her flower garden, etc. Her lifetime goal was to be Jack's wife and our mother and she truly was successful at both. She could cook like no other and bake beyond belief. She had a large home with lots of property, a big family and that suited her just fine. I know they did not see the Mormon way as their way, but both always spoke highly of the Mormon people; there was no animosity, it just wasn't for them.

The oldest of the five boys was John Streeper Murdoch. He looked so much like Jack when he was younger; pictures were hard to tell apart. John was much older then me, maybe 15 years, so I have but few memories. He joined the Air Force at around 20 years of age and became a jet pilot. While home from flight school, he was flying with another pilot and had to eject. The chute failed and John died at 21 yrs. old. He left behind his wife, Martha, who at the time was pregnant with my niece, Jahn. It was a very sad time.

Second oldest is Thyne Streeper Murdoch who is now approximately 67. He is a widower (Teresa) and had three lovely daughters, Shannon, Melinda, and Brandy. Shannon died in a car accident soon after graduating from Denver University. She had just started working for a stock brokerage firm here in Boise when it happened. I was very close to Shannon, a favorite niece. Melinda is married to Tim Randol and they have two children, Jeb and Breanna. They live in Idaho Falls. Jeb just got out of the Army after a tour in Iraq and is going to Boise State University. Breanna is still in the Army and stationed in Korea. Thyne is a realtor here in booming Boise and does quite well. He stays very active and we see or talk regularly.

Next in line is Charles Stephen Murdoch. He is somewhere in his 60's. He and his wife, Ann, have no children, travel the world, enjoy their cabin in McCall, and play lots of golf. Steve was a Stock Broker, owned a fitness center for many years, and does some property development. For the most part he is retired. He reminds me a lot of Ruth; very even tempered and cool headed. They reside in Boise.

James Phillip Murdoch was the 4th son. Jim had a tragic bike accident when he was in the 7th grade which left him in a coma for nearly a month. When he came to, he had to learn how to do everything all over again. Some things he never learned again. Brain injuries are at times very hard to understand and Jim was no exception. He lived with Ruth and Jack until their deaths and then lived in the same house until June of 2005 when he was diagnosed with acute leukemia. He passed away three days after the diagnosis, refusing any treatment. I think that he just wanted to go; his life was unfair but he did the best he could and we did the best we could for him. He had a lot of Jack's wit and displayed it right up to the last day. He never married.

Last of all is myself, Richard Bruce Murdoch. I am 57 years old and

LEFT: *Jim and Steve* RIGHT: *Jim, Bruce, and Ruth*

Jim, Ruth, and Jack

not afraid to admit, a mama's boy. I loved her dearly; I'm not so sure the feeling was mutual at times. I'm sure I put her through the ringer more then once. I forgot to mention that we all graduated from Boise High School and Steve and I both got our college degrees in Business. Steve from Woodbury Business College in Los Angeles and me from Boise State University. I have two children from a previous marriage; Jonathan Van and Sydney Brooke Murdoch. Jon was in the Marine Corp Tank Division and was with the first division to reach Baghdad at the onset. He made it out safely and is now working for me at Murdoch Finance. He has not married and is 30 years old. Sydney (29) is living in San Pedro, California and graduated from Southwestern School of Law in Los Angeles. She is married to Michael Mehall who is also a lawyer. I also have two children with my wife of 22 years, Mary Ann. Katherine Ruth Murdoch is our oldest (18) and just graduated from Boise High School and will be attending the University of Arizona in the fall. She has been a cheerleader since the 8th grade and on the varsity golf team since her freshman year. Good kid. Our youngest, Meredith Lynn Murdoch (17), was born premature and only weighed 1 lb. 5 oz. at birth. She spent 89 days in the neonatal intensive care unit. It was a roller coaster ride with her health for several years but she grew out of it and is now a very normal healthy child. She struggles with school and needs tutoring but all considering we'll take that. She is a lovely child and runs cross country for Boise High School. Besides the Finance Business that I have owned for the past 20 years, we also own an Assisted Living Facility called Plantation Place in Boise, Idaho. We built it 10 years ago. I was hoping to complete it before Ruth died, but no cigar; she would have loved it. It has 40 units and sits on the 11th green of Plantation Golf Course, Boise's oldest golf course. I was fortunate enough to partner with an old friend that had been in the health care industry for many years. We also are involved in residential and commercial development in our valley which is really booming right now. Who knows for how long. We have done several subdivisions and business parks and because Thyne and Steve are involved, it has kept us very close. So, as you can see, our family has had its ups and its downs. I'm sorry that I never got to really know our relatives in Salt Lake City. I never knew my grandparents. I only saw my mother's dad once before he died. I remember Lennox a little, Bill, Jean, Mary, Bonnie, Bob, I know there were more. I met them all I think. I saw Jean and Dave in Arizona one year and had dinner with them.

Pictures of Jack as an infant and young child

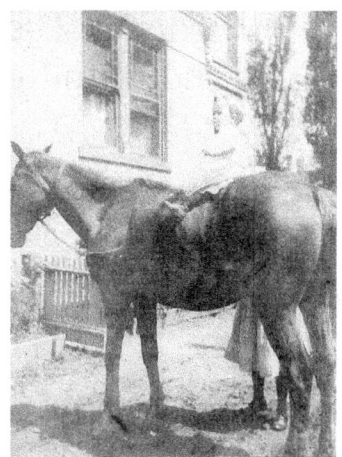

LEFT: *Jack as a child*
RIGHT: *Jack on the horse with his Aunt Afton holding him from behind*

Martha Murdoch's History of Jack (John Thyne) and Ruth Streeper Murdoch

contributed by Martha Murdoch, wife of son, John
November 26, 2007

John Thyne "Jack" Murdoch was one of the hardest working men I have ever known. Jack was a completely "self-made" man and he was 100% totally dedicated to his incredible wife, Ruth Streeper Murdoch, and his five sons.

When Jack was about fifteen years old and attending East High School in Salt Lake City, he pulled a boyish prank by putting a "stink" bomb in the furnace at the school in the dead of winter. The entire building had to be shut down for a week or two. After that incident, Jack's father sent Jack to work on a sheep ranch in Nebraska.

Jack later returned to Salt Lake City where he met Ruth Streeper while both of them were working at First Security Bank. Ruth was from the Centerville-Farmington area where Brigham Young had sent her pioneer ancestors. Ruth's father was Charles Streeper and her mother was Susan Van Fleet. Susan Van Fleet's father, William Van Fleet, was one of the last Pony Express riders, lovingly referred to by his fellow riders as "Ragged-Assed Bill". Jack and Ruth were married in Salt Lake City. Years later, they would regale us at the dinner table with stories of their courtship and of the fun they had at Salt Air and parties they attended in the Utah canyons.

Their first son, John Streeper Murdoch, was born in Salt Lake City April 22, 1935. When John was about four years, old First Security Bank sent Jack to Boise to work at their Boise Branch. After they were in Boise a few years, Jack opened his own business, The Jack Murdoch Finance Company.

When the Second World War broke out, I was living in San Francisco with my mother who was a partner in a book store and my father, a civil engineer, who was commissioned a Commander in the Navy and was scheduled to design airfields all across the Pacific. My mother was very gifted in math so she went to work for the government in California for the first four years of the war. My parents decided I should go to Boise to live with my aunt and uncle because the coastal areas of the country were getting pretty dangerous and they didn't know what was going to happen next. As it turned out, my uncle and aunt lived two doors down from Jack, Ruth, and John Murdoch.

We were a little gang of kids, two little neighborhood boys, myself, and John Streeper Murdoch. The boys included me in their games and I remember clearly how John would pull me in his little wagon. After a hard morning or afternoon of play, we'd "somehow" find our way to Ruth's house because she always had fresh peanut butter cookies or some great treat. As it happened, during the summers my Campbell relatives would include John in our trips to the family ranch near New Meadows. In earlier times the Campbell's, who had all the cattle in the area, and the Carrs (the other cousins), who had all of the sheep, would tell of the range wars between the cattlemen and sheep men in the same lands between New Meadows and McCall, Idaho.

The Murdochs would also include me when they went on trips. We would go to Zion's, Bryce, and once we went to Kanab to see Hollywood stars filming westerns.

We once visited the old Murdoch family home in the Avenues, (which had been sold by then to a new owner, however the owner let us visit and come in and see Jack's childhood family home). Jack's father brought a hand-carved Scottish thistle banister from Scotland and the banister was still in place. His father had also imported some beautiful wallpaper from Scotland and some of that original wallpaper was still there in well-taken-care-of condition.

We would spend time with Bonnie and her family and I met Jack's darling little red-haired Aunt Mary Murray Murdoch, who also lived in the Avenues area of Salt Lake City. Great Aunt Mary was a real live wire, she was very elderly then and she had never married. We so enjoyed visiting with her and hearing the stories of her early life. I just wish that I could remember some of those stories.

On our Salt Lake City forays, we would include a visit with Lennox and Ora Murdoch. Lennox's family lived almost a mile from my Uncle Boyd and Aunt Zola Martin on Walker Lane. The Martins had purchased about four acres from the Anderson Farm just after the Second World War. (The Greek Orthodox Church on Highland Drive now stands at the center of the old Anderson family farm.) Ora remembered the Anderson farm in the early days and told us of her own growing up in Holladay and how hard they had all worked in those early days on her Clark family farm.

When I was ten, I was sent away to a private school but still remained very close to the Murdochs. By then Ruth and Jack had added Thyne, Steven "Charlie" Charles, and James "Jim" to their family and Bruce was on the way. I spent holidays and summers in Boise and finished my last year of high school with John at Boise Senior High.

Except for brief vacations, Jack was constantly working yet he always came home for lunch and no matter whatever any of us did throughout the day, we all came together for supper. Ruth had her hands full with those five boys; however, they were the very center of her universe and I was privileged to be included in her circle of love. Ruth's home was always immaculate, she was a terrific cook, and always so spunky and fun. I loved her just as much as my own mother.

Holidays, especially Christmas and New Years, were major events in the Murdoch home. Absolutely none of the holidays were as much fun as New Year's Eve. It was so suspenseful for all of us to wait until Jack did his "First Footing". According to Scottish tradition, the eldest darkest male always at the stroke of midnight on the last day of the year, "first foots"—meaning he brings one of the finest things he can across the threshold to his wife to insure health and prosperity to the family for the coming year. Some of his first footings were especially memorable. I remember her enormous four carat diamond ring, the huge elaborate complete solid silver tea service, a beautiful full length mink coat, a new Cadillac at least every other year, etc. Yet no matter how extravagant each year's gift, nothing compared to his constant complete and total love and devotion for Ruth.The most memorable times of all though were after we had finished supper. The stories, laughter and the fun could go on for hours.

John excelled in sports and scouting and when he was 13, he represented Idaho at the National Boy Scout Jamboree back in Pennsylvania. Although very fun loving, John was always a leader. He was president of his class and of his fraternity. John was very caring and had a very compassionate heart. Even in high school, he led a drive among the business leaders in Boise to help disadvantaged families.

John and I studied pre-med together in college and we were married in Boise on May 26, 1956. John had been in the ROTC in high school and in college. So even though he had been back east to John's Hopkins, where he planned to finish his medical studies, he decided to go into the Air Force early and prepare to become a flight surgeon to help pay for his advanced medical studies. He loved his flight training and all the lovely people we met while he was completing his flight training. While on the way to our new base, John and I made a visit home to our families in Boise. During that time he went on a flight with a Utah National Guard pilot as principle pilot. The canopy of that jet had a flaw and shattered while they were in flight. John was riding in the back second seat and was killed as the shattered canopy struck him on April 3, 1957. Ora Murdoch had made the effort to come to our wedding the previous May and her beautiful poetry for our wedding and at this tragic time in April meant so much to me.

Our daughter Jahn Streeper Murdoch was born in Boise October 2, 1957. Shortly after Jahn's birth, John's brother Jim was involved in a terrible bicycle accident. Jim was such a "full-of-the-dickens" fun little ten year old, a loveable spark plug for the whole family. His accident on top of the loss of John deeply traumatized all of us. Many specialists were brought in to Boise, but very little could be done. Jim lived with the effects of that accident until he died in 2006.

Bruce, Jahn, Steve and Thyne 2005

The sadness we all felt was so overwhelming that Jahn and I moved to California where I had accepted a teaching position in the Los Angeles City Schools and later at the University of Southern California where I trained returning Peace Corp volunteers to become high school teachers.

In California, Jahn and I joined the Church of Jesus Christ of Latter-day Saints. We didn't move to Utah until Jahn went to BYU.

Ora Murdoch had always made the effort to keep in touch. She sent one of her heart-felt poems at every major occasion of our lives.

Even with tremendous challenges throughout her life, Jahn was a very ambitious young lady. Jahn Streeper Murdoch held many responsible callings in the Church and during her schooling. She graduated from BYU in Provo, started her own business, married in the Los Angeles Temple, and had six children. Jahn's living children are Caminiah, Zachary, Tajah, Tory, and Hollan. Her youngest, Stevie Ann, died before Jahn could bring her home from the hospital.

I taught high school biology for many years and then after several graduate degrees, taught at the University of Utah until I retired.

Chapter 9

Elizabeth Murdoch, George John Ross, and LeMoyne L. Hatch

Written by Carolyn Ross Hultquist and George Ross

Elizabeth was the fourth child of William and Jeannette Murdoch. Her fond memories and wonderful stories made her childhood seem ideal. Mother was born at 73 "G" Street the day after Christmas, 1908. She died November 22, 1994. The stories we begged to have her tell over and over where about good times at Lambs Canyon, ballet classes with Jeanette, high school events and MIA dances with her best friend, Lorene Romney, working at Makoffs to help her father put her siblings through college (she said someday it was supposed to be her turn, but it never happened), meeting our father when he returned from his mission to Germany, and how they survived during the depression while our father attended law school in Washington D.C.

Mother truly enjoyed living in various parts of the country while our father worked for the FBI, but was thrilled to return to Salt Lake and her family. Although our father faced death and danger as an agent for the FBI, it was after they returned to Salt Lake, working as an assistant attorney general for the State of Utah, that he died as a result of injuries he received in an automobile accident in March 1944. At that time, Mother faced life with three small children ages 2, 6, and 11.

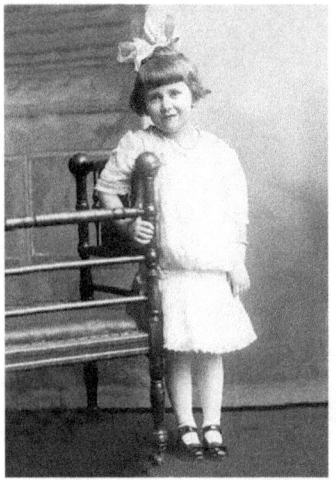

LEFT: *Young Beth* RIGHT: *Jeannette, Jean, and Beth*

She would have preferred to stay at home with the children, but faced with feeding and caring for three children, she was thrust into the work place. She realized she needed more than a job to properly care of us, so she pursued and achieved the designation of Registered Record Librarian. This was the highest level of achievement in her field and she was one of only 75 in the country at that time. Having achieved this designation and being recognized for her outstanding work at the LDS Hospital, she was recruited and accepted employment at the Veterans Administration Hospital in Salt Lake City. She worked there until she retired.

George and Beth about 1937

Mother always made time for each of the children. She always had to work a half day on Saturday and this was also her only day to wash, clean, grocery shop, etc., but she still managed to make Saturdays a special day for us as well. Saturday evening we would read together, listen to the Hit Parade, and share her yummy divinity, fudge, or famous chocolate cake.

She did what she had to do without ever

Beth and George Ross

complaining and never expressed any self pity. The strong Murdoch clan rallied to help her. Since Mother didn't drive and her bus ride took forever, transferring at State Street and South Temple, Bill and other brothers would often give her a ride. At one point Bill, Lucy, and their girls lived on the street behind us. Bill would hop the fence and come by to visit and help Mother with home maintenance tasks and getting the Christmas tree in the stand. Aunt Jen and Aunt Mary would take us for rides to the Homestead or to Snelgroves in Sugarhouse in Jen's 1936 Buick. What a treat this was, since we didn't have a car. Lennox and Ora offered George several wonderful summers out in the country. Jeannette would take care of Carolyn when our Mother had to travel with her work, and Mary would invite us down for warm chocolate chip cookies, and then load us up with tons of goodies to take home. All of us remember the day Lennox brought us our first television.

Mother was a wonderful cook. After being married, we always looked forward to the invitation for dinner. She would set the table with her best china. Her pot roast was second to none and she loved vegetables, particularly brussel sprouts. Mother also loved going to the the coffee shop at the Hotel Utah for lunch, the Empire Room at ZCMI, talk and laugh on the phone while sitting on he chaise lounge or at the kitchen counter, and to visit often with Aunt Afton Warner whom she dearly loved.

In 1954, 73 "G" was the scene of another blessed event. Mother married LeMoyne Hatch. The reception was at the Murdoch family home and the Murdoch sisters worked in the kitchen preparing all food. Lemoyne was an answer to our prayers. He cherished Mother and was devoted to her while setting a wonderful example to us children. They enjoyed going to the theatre with Aunt Mary Murdoch and visiting with Aunt Afton. Life was simple and for 40 years they were like a couple of love birds.

The greatest lessons Mother taught us by example: A strong work ethic, the principle of tithe, the importance of education, to be kind and soft-spoken, and to be thrifty. Mother's lesson about tithing is worth sharing. Mother was working in a doctor's office in the Medical Arts Building across from the church office building. Things were not going well for her at the time. One day, she had this urge to walk across the street and pay her tithing, but put it off several times. Suddenly the urge was overwhelming. She had only enough money to pay tithing, no more. She paid it. When she got home from work, she began to wonder what she was going to do and prayed for help. The next morning, when she was getting ready for work, she changed purses and when she opened the purse there was $20.00 she didn't know she had. She always admonished us to be honest with the Lord and he would always bless us.

LeMoyne Hatch

Children
William Murdoch Ross - Born: May 3, 1932, Died: July 4, 1997
George John Ross III - Born: October 17, 1937
Carolyn Ross Hultquist – Born: April 6, 1942

Ballet Class. Far left is Jeannette and third from left is Beth

WILLIAM MURDOCH ROSS

Bill was born in Washington D.C. but lived his entire life in Salt Lake City, except for time spent in the Army. One of Bill's first jobs was to be an usher at the Uptown Theatre. They liked his work so much they offered him a job at the Villa Theatre on Highland Drive. So it was the Uptown during the day; the Villa in the evenings. He did that for a number of years. Bill didn't drive so most of the travel between jobs was by bus. Most of his career, he worked at the University of Utah. Bill enjoyed the times he shared with Aunt Mary Young and Grandmother Ross. He had a great sense of humor and loved music, especially classical and was fond of attending the symphony at the Tabernacle when he could. Bill passed away, having never married, July 4, 1997.

GEORGE JOHN ROSS III

Wife: *Diane Rosella Miller*, Married December 26, 1958
  Children:
  Kimberly Ross Parker, born October 17, 1960
  Married Danial Vinton Parker on September 11, 1981
  Four Children: Broc, Brittnee, Brooke, Brady
  Stephanie Ross Thomas, born November 21, 1961
  Married Kurt Thomas on July 6, 1985
  Three Children: Zachary, Taylor, Sidney
  Stacie Ross Stoedter, born June 29, 1965
  Divorced
  Children: Mallori, Alex, Makenzie, Maverick
  Bradley John Ross, born May 11, 1968
  Married Julia Eckhardt on June 30, 1988
  Children: Madison, McCall, Brody, Boston.

Although our father died when we were very young, Mother wanted us to know what a great person he was and his achievements. He attended George Washington University Law School during the depression. He was the secretary for J. Edgar Hoover, the director of the FBI, while he was attending the university. Mother would tell us, and we heard the story many times, of how they lived off of potato soup. Although we didn't have anything, we didn't know it. We all thought life was wonderful and grateful to have such a loving wonderful mom. I think Mother just told us about the soup to put things in perspective in case we ever felt picked on. While our father was working as an FBI agent in Chicago, he was involved in the arrest of some bad guys know as the Mafia. We didn't ever get any details, however.

One thing that has always been important to me was the fact that Mother thought she had had a miscarriage while in Chicago. Dad had to leave immediately for an assignment in Los Angeles so she couldn't take time to see a doctor before leaving. Father dropped mother off at their new apartment and had to leave again. Mother didn't drive so didn't go to a doctor being in a strange city and not knowing a single person. So as time went on she kept growing as though still pregnant. On October 17, 1937 she took a taxi to the Saint Vincent Hospital and I was born that day. The doctor told mother that she had been pregnant with twins having lost one which was the event in Chicago. I believe I will have the opportunity to see my twin someday.

I will forever be grateful for Mother's testimony and teaching us the principle of tithing. I am sure that the shock of losing her husband was terrifying for her, but we never heard her complain about her circumstances. I am sure she wet her pillow with tears many nights wondering how she was going to provide and raise three children, but she never once let on that this was a challenge or a burden. Her great example and positive attitude has shaped the lives of all three of us for which we are forever grateful.

CAROLYN ROSS HULTQUIST

Married Richard Arthur Hultquist, August 24, 1964

We were raised in a loving, caring environment and I have nothing but fond memories of growing up. Mother was such an outstanding example for us. Whenever I have had to face overwhelming problems in my life, I have the example of my mother's faith, strength and courage to draw on. I was so young when our Father died, I can't really remember him but Mother kept his memory alive for all of us with wonderful memories. After graduating from the University of Utah, I married Richard and moved to Washington. I missed my family so much but feel blessed that they weren't so far away and I could visit often. Mother and LeMoyne came up at least once a year for several years and we went home to Salt Lake during the holidays as often as possible. As George said, dinner at Mothers was always a treat and during the holidays it was amazing. A favorite memory during the holiday season was when Mother and I walked from their apartment on South Temple and "Q" Street to the Hotel Utah one snowy evening. It was a winter wonderland. We had French onion soup to warm us, walked through Temple Square, and then caught a cab back home. As much as I miss my family, we have had a wonderful life. What we enjoy most is digging for clams, putting out crab pots and sharing our seafood feast with our family and friends. Our family has been blessed and we all live a short distance from each other.

Children:
Richard Hultquist, born January 28, 1967
Married to Jill Hetherington on October 23, 2000
Children: Jackson Ross, Margaret (Maggie) Riley.
Rich works in insurance benefits and Jill is the Tennis Coach at the University of Washington.
Sarah Hultquist, born November 23, 1968
Married to Hunter Graham Goodman on August 7, 1999
Sarah works in the software industry and Hunter is an Assistant Attorney General.
Ashley Hultquist, born October 16, 1973.
Ashley is a graduate student at the University of Washington.

(The following poem was written by Ora Murdoch in January 1985 and presented at a dinner Mother hosted at the Hotel Utah Roof Garden.)

Elizabeth

"Twas the night after Christmas and all was serene.
Everything in the big house was pronounced 'squeaky clean!'
As Mama in her 'kerchief and Pa in his cap
Had just settled themselves for another long nap –
When a wee baby girl so lively and quick,
Gave to Mother a most frightful kick -
The lights all came on the stove was restoked.
Grandma got so excited she practically choked.
Doctor Richards was summoned, the bed was made right;
But why need it happen in the Black of the night?
Aunt Mary was running in one room and out...
Mama's poor head was splitting, "Oh, please don't shout!
When the battle was over, the baby was here-
Oh, isn't she precious? that sweet little dear.
But, where is her hair? no fuzz can I feel.
Her wee head was as bare as a smooth lemon peal
Then one look from Lennox and Mary and Jack
"Aw, gee, can't you try putting, just putting her back?"
They named her Elizabeth for you and for me,
Because was born at 73 "G."
In Elizabeth's bed on the second floor
That night after Christmas behind a closed door.
And now she's survived for many a year -
Seventy six, the number I secretly hear.

She's a noble example of who can survive -?
Being happy and useful and staying alive.
Since your Father she buried many years ago-
When you precious kids were too young to know
The struggle and strife-the grief and the pain
That beset her life.
She could not sit by and watch you all grow-
There were bills to pay mouths to feed – and so,
She buckled her belt on right good and tight
And went out in the world to put up a fight.
She's made of good fixins' this brave Mom of yours
And her faith and her courage opened numerous doors.
A Medical Librarian isn't born every day but she studied and struggled
And made this job pay.
She put you through school like the "down of a thistle"
Til LeMoyne spied her one day and gave her a "whistle."
And I hear them exclaim "ere they drove out of sight
We've lived a good life and for us, we're just right.

Ora Clark Murdoch, 1985

Chapter 10

Jeannette Murdoch and Wendell Bitner Romney

by Janet Romney Hull, July 2007

Jeannette Murdoch was born on January 14, 1911 in Salt Lake City, Utah. She was the 5th child of William Murdoch and Jeannette Cousins Smith Murdoch. The next day, her twin brother, William, was born.

Jeannette's father, William, owned and operated the Murdoch Grocery next door to their home on 78 "F" Street. There were nine children in the family and both parents worked very hard to care for them. When Jeannette got older, she worked at the store helping with orders. The store had a delivery service.

Among the happiest memories of Jeannette's childhood were those of the summers spent at the Murdoch Cabin in Lambs Canyon. The day after school was out, her father would load the kids in the car and away they would go to the cabin for the whole summer. On Fridays, father William would come up with a load of groceries for the week. The children's Aunt Jen would go up to supervise the kids, and also a helper or two. Jeannette and her siblings would roam the hills and make their own fun. No other entertainment was available.

Jeannette, Lexxie (a friend), and Beth

At night they would all sleep out on a huge screened in porch. A couple of the older boys had small guns. They would lie in wait for the pack rats to climb the screen and then they would let them have it. Jeannette and her sisters shivered with fright. Sometimes, one would get away and the next morning they would find an old, dirty bar of soap in the place of someone's shoe or slipper which the rat would take. This was how they would spend their summers for many years, going home the day before school started in the fall.

Jeannette and her sister, Beth, loved dancing. Together they took ballet from William Christensen, Sr. There are pictures of them with beautiful ballet dresses performing in dance recitals.

As a child, Jeannette attended Lowell School. Little did she know that right across the street in a red brick house lived the boy she would someday marry! After Lowell School, she went on to Bryant Junior High and then to East High. After East High graduation, Jeannette went to the University of Utah. She joined Kappa Kappa Gamma Sorority and was later the chapter president. She majored in elementary education and graduated with a teaching certificate.

On July 15, 1935, she married Wendell Bitner Romney.

For the next few years they worked very hard saving money so they could build a home. Jeannette worked at the Murdoch Grocery and Wendell worked at ZCMI department store as Credit Manager. Finally, their home on 11th Avenue was finished. They moved in and a year later on June 19, 1941, I, Janet Romney, was born. Four years later, Nan Murdoch Romney was born on July 12, 1945. Jeannette was a wonderful mother. She worked very hard keeping a perfect house, ironing all our fussy dresses, cleaning, and cooking delicious meals.

As Nan and I got older, Mother had things outside the home that she enjoyed doing. She was active in the Garden Club and also volunteered at LDS Hospital as a Pink Lady. She taught Primary and worked in the M.I.A. She loved getting together with her sisters. They always celebrated their birthdays. Mother was always a peacemaker and spread love and kindness wherever she went.

When I got married, she and Dad would come to Hawaii for visits. They loved getting away in the winter to the beautiful tropics. It was wonderful for Clyde and me and our children. Our daughter, Allyson, still remembers her Nana making cookies while in Hawaii and letting her help. It is a memory she cherishes.

In the late 1970's, Mom began suffering from mini-strokes. These occurred more and more often until her mental faculties became greatly impaired. In November 1982, Clyde brought her to Hawaii to give Dad a break before he was to join us December 16 for Christmas. On December 4, Dad had a heart attack and on December 16th, the day he was to join us, he died in the LDS Hospital. By this time Mom's mind was mostly gone and caring for her was very difficult. She fell and fractured her back and the doctors told me that she belonged in a nursing home. If not, she would probably fall again and break her hip. After caring for her in Hawaii for 10 months, Nan came over and together we took her back to Salt Lake to the Wasatch Villa. This was terribly difficult. After a couple of weeks, I told her I loved her, kissed her, and said goodbye. I knew this would be the last time I would see her. This was in August of 1983. On October 27th, her beautiful spirit left her body. At last she was free from her sick, inadequate body.

My mother, Jeannette, has now been gone almost 24 years. For some reason, it seems longer. I feel so blessed to have been raised by such a wonderful and righteous woman. I look forward to the day I shall see her again.

LEFT: *Sisters, Jeannette and Mary in Hawaii.*
MIDDLE: *Janet and Jeannette.*
RIGHT: *Jeannette and Wendell in Hawaii.*

Wendell Bitner Romney

By Nan Murdoch Romney Williams

Our father, Wendell Bitner Romney, was born on March 5, 1906 to Sarah Lydia (Lillian) Bitner and William Stevenson Romney. Our mother, Jeannette Murdoch Romney, called him Wen but his brothers and sisters and their families always called him Wendell. He was a handsome man - with a twinkle in his eye, wavy brown hair and a great sense of humor. He was the second of eight children: Elmer, Wendell, Lorene, Jean, Lillian, Dorothy (stillborn), William, Jr., & Adele. He was raised at 367 Third Avenue in Salt Lake City – a home that became the center for many of our happiest memories as children. It was there that we gathered for Thanksgiving dinners (with everyone dressing up in Sunday best and the cousins at the "childrens' table") and many family get-togethers with aunts, uncles, and cousins visiting from Mexico and Florida. The great picnics in the backyard with yummy orange chiffon cake baked by our Aunt Lillian were always a lot of fun. This beautiful home remained in the family until May, 2009. The sale of the "Romney Family Home" definitely closed an era for our family. It is rare to have a family home create so many decades of memories – over 100 years worth!

As a child, I remember going with my father to "367" and watching him stoke the family furnace with coal that had been delivered down a coal chute into the basement. Because Dad was the only living son in Salt Lake City, he helped with this chore until a gas furnace was installed. Dad was always ready and willing to help his mother and two sisters who lived in the home in whatever way he could.

Dad's parents were well-respected in the community – his father being active in many church and community activities. William was the treasurer of ZCMI (Zions Commercial Mercantile Institution) – a popular local department store and the first department store in the United States. Dad would later become the Credit Manager of ZCMI.

Lydia (Nana Romney) had a great personality. She never liked anyone to be very serious and was a real practical joker. She had long hair, which she wore in a bun on the back of her head. I remember watching her brush her long hair with a silver handled brush and thought she was so beautiful. She had a wonderful singing voice and was a member of the Mormon Tabernacle Choir and traveled with the Choir when they performed at a World's Fair. When she was younger, she performed in plays at the Salt Lake Theatre in downtown Salt Lake.

Lydia Bitner Romney's mother was the sister of President Gordon Bitner Hinckley's mother. President Hinckley was the Prophet for many years of The Church of Jesus Christ of Latter-day Saints. Because of this relationship as cousins, Dad and Pres. Hinckley's family created many memories together. Bitner Ranch was located up Emigration Canyon and was the site for the Bitner cousins to gather. Pres. Hinckley fondly recalled delivering peaches to "Aunt Lill's house" (on 3rd Avenue) and talking and laughing in their kitchen.

Pres. Hinckley spoke at our father's graveside services in December of 1982. In his busy schedule as Prophet, he always found time for Dad's family — whether going to the hospital to give blessings or to attend Lorene's 80th birthday celebration at "367".

Dad's family was blessed to have many strong church members as relatives – each of whom cherished their family ties.

Elder Joseph Bitner Wirthlin, an Apostle of the Church of Jesus Christ of Latter-day Saints, was Dad's cousin. He also attended our father's funeral and was always a great support and example.

Henry Romney Eyring, a renowned scientist, was the president of the Romney Family Association for many years. Henry Eyring's sister was Camilla Eyring Kimball — the wife of President Spencer W. Kimball. Elder Henry B. Eyring, a current Apostle, is Henry R. Eyring's son.

President Marion G. Romney was Dad's cousin. Our father's family was instrumental in helping Pres. Romney's family leave the Mexican Colonies. As a result, a bond existed between the two families. My sister, Janet Romney Hull (Clyde), and I, Nan Murdoch Romney Williams (Dwight), were blessed to have Pres. Romney seal both of our marriages in the Salt Lake Temple. My favorite wedding picture shows Pres. Romney coming through our reception line and shaking our hands. A very special memory!

Dad's grandfather, George Romney, was the first bishop of the 20th Ward located on Second Avenue and G Street and his picture remains to this day in the Bishop's office. Grandfather George learned the art of woodworking from his father, Miles, who was called by the Prophet Joseph Smith to be the foreman in charge of the woodwork for the Nauvoo Temple. George moved with his father, mother (Elizabeth), and his eight siblings from England (where he was born) to Nauvoo. After Nauvoo the family moved to Utah when Miles was asked by the new Prophet, Brigham Young, to be in charge of the woodwork in the new St. George Temple.

Following that assignment, George was asked to direct the work on the woodwork in the Lion House and Beehive House in Salt Lake City. George envisioned the site and building of the Hotel Utah. He and six other men met with President Joseph F. Smith. The plan was approved and George was put in charge of its construction. It was reported by many people that he visited the site everyday of its construction. When the Hotel Utah was completed, he was asked to travel to the east coast and help to select the furniture. He travelled extensively throughout the United States and Europe and was referred to as "the greatest traveler in the state of Utah". He was also called the "grand old man of Salt Lake". It was this George who started George Romney & Sons Company and was President at the time of his death – just as Dad was President at the time of his death.

Dad attended Lowell Elementary School, located across the street from their home. Around the same playground and on the same property, my generation of cousins played — ducking in and out of the window wells as we played hide-and-seek.

Dad then attended Bryant Jr. High School located on First South. He played football on their school team and loved to joke with us saying he was so thin he could have been knocked over with a feather and doesn't know how he survived the football experience. Dad graduated from Salt Lake High School which would later become East High School in Salt Lake City.

After high school, Dad graduated from the University of Utah in Business. While at the University, he joined Phi Delta Phi Fraternity. Dad was a huge fan of the U of U sports teams — especially the football team. He had season tickets to every home game for as many years as we can remember and always with the best seats located on the 50-yard line. We were convinced that he sincerely felt they couldn't play a game without his presence!

Upon his graduation from college, he was accepted at New York University for the Masters of Business Administration Program. He wanted desperately to accept this opportunity but it was a difficult decision. It was in the middle of the depression and a challenging time for everyone. His father had been successful but lost a lot in the stock market during that time. His family felt that perhaps he should remain in Salt Lake City, find a job, and be accessible to his family. After much consideration, he felt he should accept the graduate program in order to prepare for his own future and that of his future family.

Dad had many great experiences while living in New York City. He accepted a part-time position as "floor walker" at Macy's Department Store. In those days, as part of great customer service, high-end department stores had someone employed to mingle among the customers as a friendly representative of the store and make certain everyone was being well served. A secondary duty was to keep an eye out for shoplifters.

He often spoke of the Macy's Thanksgiving Day Parade which he attended each year while living in New York City. He recalls how cold it was but what a fun thing to do. New Year's Eve on Times Square was also an amazing experience for Dad, although he also mentioned that it was a lonely evening as well — being "alone" among the thousands of people in attendance.

One year while living in New York City, he sailed with friends to Bermuda — three single guys, what an adventure! We have a photo taken on the ship and he looks so dapper with his dress hat and long dress coat.

When he returned to Salt Lake City, he took the position as Credit Manager of ZCMI, a position he held until his retirement in 1968. Everyone loved and respected Dad at ZCMI. He made friends with everyone. We often were told how he always spoke and made conversation with all employees. Being the "boss" of that department, he was the only man among perhaps 20 women. The Credit Department was located on the 3rd floor. The department was set back and enclosed with a glass partition but Dad's office was a separate office in front. I remember with great fondness going to visit him in his office. His staff always made a fuss over my sister and me. While attending the U of U, I worked downtown and loved to go visit him. Unless he was in a meeting, he kept his office door open. I will always remember the twinkle in his eye as he would see me approaching. What daughter wouldn't love to visit their father with such a welcome! As part of Dad's sense of humor, he loved to say how impossible it was to get away from women. With an office full of women, a wife, two daughters, and a female French poodle at home, he was surrounded!

His wonderful wife, our mother, Jeannette Murdoch Romney, lived fairly close to the Romney family during their growing up years. The Murdochs lived at 78 F Street. Both families belonged to the 20th Ward. Mother's father was the City Commissioner and owner of Murdoch Grocery located through their property on F Street. Although they knew each other when young, they didn't begin dating until after Dad's return from New York. They were married on July 15, 1935.

In 1941, they built our family home at 709 – 11th Avenue. Dad designed the home and it was a great home and area in which to live. Their house was among the first few built on that block and many years later, Dad felt

he had made a mistake not purchasing the entire block. Hindsight always seems wiser! Janet and I sold the home in 1983 following Dad's death. As with all family homes with special memories, it was a difficult thing to do. Because Dad lived so close to his work, he came home everyday for lunch. Mother would have his lunch prepared and after eating he would lie down on the sofa in the living room and have a 15 – 20 minute nap. He would get up feeling refreshed and return to work. Dad was excited when the first branch of ZCMI was built and opened at the brand new Cottonwood Mall – the first store on that property. Now Dad would be in charge of both Credit Departments. At that time, the Cottonwood area seemed quite a distance from downtown Salt Lake City, and it was a unique thing to have two branches of the same store in the same valley. One Monday night a month (the only night of the week the store was open in the evening) Dad would work from the Cottonwood location.

Dad loved to travel. Probably his favorite place to visit was Hawaii to spend time with Janet and her family. He loved the beauties and the climate and, of course, spending time with his first grandchildren. He and Mom did a lot of traveling with his brother and his wife – Bill and Helen Romney. Bill and Helen lived in Mexico City where Bill was Vice President of American Chicle Company. They would travel to Mexico, the West Coast or to Las Vegas and have a great time. Dad & Mom also travelled a lot with close friends. They traveled to Canada and to the Canyons together. We know that our Mom always regretted not being able to travel to Scotland, the land of her Scottish heritage. Dad never wanted to travel to Europe so they never went. According to him, everything was "too old there". We always thought that was a crazy statement because that's exactly what makes Europe so interesting — its history, etc. Every summer and almost every spring, Dad saw to it that we took a trip as a family. We would go to Las Vegas and stay a few days on the way to California – both southern & northern. All of us, however, especially loved our trips to Jackson Hole, Wyoming or to the Canyons. When we travelled to those spots we often went with their friends who had children our age. We all stayed in log cabins and had a great time in that beautiful setting. The Homestead in Midway, Utah was a favorite destination for weekend escape and fun.

Dad was very creative and loved to film and animate all of our Christmas mornings. He would film us going to bed on Christmas Eve, waking up Christmas morning and going downstairs to see all that Santa had left for us. He didn't stop there, however. He put all of our dolls and playthings into motion — the dolls climbing into the little high chairs and everything that could move under the tree was seen moving without any hands involved. It must have taken great patience on his part but what wonderful memories for us! I think even at today's standards, he and Mother spoiled us at Christmas!

Dad was very involved in community and professional organizations. For years he was treasurer and then president of George Romney & Sons Company – a property development company in the City. He was president of the Salt Lake Lions Club, the Credit Bureau of Salt Lake, and of the Ninth District National Retail Credit Association. Everyone valued and respected his ideas and leadership.

Our little French poodle, Gygi, loved Dad and he returned that love. She would sit on a chair in front of the dining room window watching for him each night when he came home. As soon as she saw his car, she would jump down, bark and run to the door waiting for him to walk in. She snuggled next to him each morning and night when he read the newspaper on a big overstuffed chair in the living room. At breakfast, Gygi would sit at our Mother's feet in the kitchen until she was told to go get Dad to come to breakfast. She would run into the living room barking and not leave until he was following her into the kitchen. Another girl in his life—but he loved it.

As Dad and Mother got older, Mother suffered memory loss as a result of several mini strokes. Dad took great care of her at home, which wasn't easy physically or mentally. In November, 1982 they planned to spend Christmas with Janet and her family in Hawaii. The plan was for Mother to go first then Dad would join her a few weeks later. When Mother had been gone about one week, Dad had a heart attack, his 2nd, on December 4. It was necessary for him to have a ventilating tube down his throat which made it impossible for him to speak. Because Dad was always the person in charge, this was a very difficult situation for him. While in the hospital, he wrote notes fast and furiously to me. He was very concerned about Mom's well being and gave me implicit instructions on everything that needed his attention. He passed away on December 16, 1982 at the age of 76.

A few months after his passing, my family was attending our church's Stake Conference. I was in the foyer with our youngest son, John, who was then two years old. I was holding him on my lap and he suddenly said, "There's Granddad". I didn't respond and a few minutes later he said, "Granddad's here". I'm certain Dad was present that day and it is very sweet to think that he would want to be with us and that John was pure enough to see him.

I hope that Dad knows how much we love him. He left a great legacy. Because Dad never had any sons, I wanted to be certain his name was carried on, so we named our second son, Wendell Romney Williams. He goes by Romney and I am grateful he bears his granddad's name.

In writing Dad's personal history, it has been choice to take the time to think about him and his life. My sister and I are grateful to be his daughters and for the life he gave us, our heritage, and many wonderful memories.

JANET ROMNEY HULL

I was born Janet Romney on June 19, 1941, in Salt Lake City, Utah, the daughter of Wendell Bitner Romney and Jeannette Murdoch. She and her twin brother, William, were the fifth and sixth children of William Murdoch and Jeannette Cousins Smith. My father was the second child of William Stevenson Romney and Sara Lydia (Lillian) Bitner. Four years after my birth, another girl, my sister, Nan was born on July 12th, 1945. She and I were the only children, and we lived in the same house at 709 11th Avenue all of our growing up years. It was a nice comfortable house with a large living and dining room. On the second floor were two bedrooms and a bath. My sister and I shared one of the bedrooms. These were large rooms also, so the sharing worked out fine.

Dad worked as credit manager at ZCMI, known as America's first department store. Sadly, this store is no longer there; however, I still have fond memories of going to town with mother and having lunch in the Tiffany Room. Back then I could have a chicken salad sandwich and a drink for 50 cents. A very nice dress cost $17.98. Beautiful shoes were $5.00 a pair. These were the prices when I was in my early teens. Earlier things were even cheaper.

In the old store (in the early 60's, it was remodeled) my father's office was on the 4th floor. If we had time on a shopping day, Mom would take Nan and me up to see him. All the ladies in the credit office would stop their typing etc. and smile and say hello to us. One special lady named Miss Spall was Dad's assistant. She added much joy to every Christmas. On Christmas Eve day, ZCMI florist would deliver a beautiful centerpiece for our dining room table. About a week before that, Dad would bring home a box of homemade English cookies she and her friend had made. Oh, they were so delicious. Miss Spall had been born and raised in a town in England and her cookies were like none we had ever tasted.

I began my schooling at age five at Ensign School—the old one on 10th Avenue. It has since been torn down. Since no one went to pre-school in those days, kindergarten was quite a shock and a little scary. I was a somewhat fearful child and a little shy. I usually sat on the steps when Dad would drop me off in the morning. I sat there until the bell rang. This went on for about a month. Then all was well.

It's funny the things you remember from your childhood even though many many years have gone by. One of my memories goes back to when I was two. I had long blonde hair and one day, Mom and my Aunt Jean Buckwalter, Mom's sister, were sitting in the kitchen and I was in the living room. I had a toy broom and there was a fire in the fireplace. I remember looking at my broom and wondering if it would burn. To find out, I stuck it in the fire and, of course, it caught on fire! I got scared and dropped it on the carpet. It left a nice, large and very noticeable burn on the carpet.

Shortly after the incident, Mom and Dad got a small throw rug to put in front of the fireplace to hide the burn.

Another incident took place when I was about seven. I was down at my Nana Romney's house. She had been making a rag rug. These were popular in those days, made from scraps of plain and colorful rags one had. Well, Nana had stitched it wrong and had to take out the stitches. I was helping her using the index finger of my right hand. On and on I went, one stitch after another, each catching in the first crease of my finger. Finally, I had quite a cut. It didn't really hurt, so I paid no attention to it. The next day, my finger was red and swollen. The day after that, it was more swollen and obviously infected. After looking at it, Mom told me she was taking me to the doctor after school. Well, I worried all day what the doctor might do to my finger. The girl sitting next to me said: "Oh, what if he has to cut it off". That did it!! I wasn't going home after school!!!! When the bell rang, I left and instead of going home to 11th Avenue, I went down and wandered around the lower Avenues. I don't remember how long I stayed away, but finally went home after what seemed like a long time. Mom was waiting for me and we went to the doctor. He deadened it and drained the infection. My whole finger was bandaged for a week or so, but I was glad I still HAD a finger.

Time passed and before I knew it, I was in Bryant Junior High. I remember how much I hated gym. I was not an athlete and had no desire to become one. I would have scrubbed the halls on my hands and knees if it had meant I could have gotten out of gym. Nevertheless, I lived through it.

I loved the times when Mom would let me buy lunch. I cringe now when I think about what I had. Bryant had the best soft rolls, chili, and mashed potatoes and gravy. This was always what I bought, at least while in the 7th grade. It was usually followed by a big candy bar—not a great diet, especially for one who ended up with heart disease. Oh, I almost forgot the apple pie—WONDERFUL!

My years at Bryant ended, then on to East High. I loved it. I got to pursue what I loved— speech and drama. My junior year, I was in the school play, *January Thaw*. I loved every minute of all the after school rehearsals every day. All of us in the play loved it and I had the opportunity to be with some really talented kids. We all worked hard. My senior year at East High didn't start off to well. During the summer I came down with Mononucleosis and missed a lot of school in the first half of the year. I was so weak and tired, I couldn't do anything but sleep.

Finally I overcame it and returned to school. I wasn't too far behind because a friend had brought me my homework while I was out. The teachers were great and I was able to graduate with my class. The summer of 1959 passed quickly and I started the University of Utah in the Fall. I majored in English with a minor in speech and drama. I also joined Delta Gamma and made some good friends.

I had an aunt and uncle who lived in Hawaii. During the summer of 1964, I went to visit my mother's sister, Mary Murdoch Weggeland, and her husband, Gordon Weggeland. They were wonderful people, so kind and generous. One day my Uncle Gordon mentioned that he had to go to the Orient on business. This meant he had to get someone to teach his Gospel Doctrine class. He told Aunt Mary, "I think I'll ask Brother Hull." Well, Brother Hull came to their place to get the books and little did I know at the time, I was sitting across the room from the man who would be my husband. I loved his good looks and handsome smile. He was so sweet and friendly. We dated the rest of the time I was there (I stayed a month altogether.) I went home and we wrote all that year. Then one day, I got a letter from him saying he was coming home that summer. He did and we dated the whole time he was there. Toward the end of his visit, he asked me to marry him. Obviously, I said "yes", then back to Hawaii he went until December. We set the date for December 30. On that day, we were married in the Salt Lake Temple and our reception was that evening in the Empire Room, which, by the way still exists, even though the building is no longer the Hotel Utah, but instead the Joseph Smith Building. The next morning we were off to San Francisco for a short honeymoon before leaving to make our home in Honolulu.

Hawaii was another world for a little gal who had grown up in Salt Lake City. I immediately met many wonderful people of many races and nationalities. I loved the beautiful mountains and beaches. I loved the soft air - so good for your skin. The main attraction though was the people. They had a way of making me feel so welcome and loved. It was impossible not to love them back. They took me under their wing and I became a part of Hawaii and Aloha.

Our first home was a studio apartment. It was very convenient to Ala Moana Shopping Center and a grocery store. I could walk to both.

We also became a part of Makiki Ward and I became the 2nd counselor in the Relief Society. I was in charge of the "work meetings". Talk about a baptism by fire! Wow!! What did I know about homemaking? I had just gotten married!! As it turned out, the Relief Society was full of lovely sisters who willingly helped and I learned fast. I also worked with a wonderful president.

Months passed and I was busy. I missed my family and friends back home, but didn't have much time to think about it. I had also gotten a job in the credit department at Liberty House, a large department store. Most of the employees there in the credit office were military. They, too, were away from home and missed their families and friends.

The summer of 1965, Nan, my sister, came over with some of her friends to live and work for the summer. It was great to have her around and we had many fun times. One thing we always liked to do was go to Queen's Surf Beach in Waikiki for sunset potluck dinners. We would sometimes take our hibachi and grill teriyaki beef. Everyone, (including Nan and friends and ours) brought something. It always turned into a real feast. This fast became a tradition that we did all the years we lived in Hawaii.

During that same summer, another exciting thing happened! We found out we were expecting our first baby!! In September of 1965 we bought a condo, a short distance from our studio apartment. It was nice to have a brand new and more spacious place. Time passed and on February 28, 1966, our son Scott Romney Hull was born. Clyde called Mom and Dad and told them they now had their first grandchild. Mom began making plans to come to Hawaii to help. She arrived a few days after Scott's birth, much to the joy of all of us as well as Mom. She was thrilled with her new little grandson.

Mom stayed with us for six weeks and was there for his blessing at Makiki Ward in the Honolulu Tabernacle. My aunt and uncle were still there and came to the blessing also. After we were treated to a delicious dinner at the Weggeland's apartment. My Aunt Mary, like my mom, was a wonderful cook. Having her there was a blessing for me. We went many places and did a lot of fun things together. When Scott was six months old, she and my uncle moved back to Salt Lake to be with their children and grandchildren. We missed them very much.

During the summer of 1966, we took Scott and traveled back to Salt Lake to show him to his new relatives. We stayed first with Clyde's folks in Ogden and then with Mom and Dad in Salt Lake. Scott was a most popular little visitor. He had big brown eyes and beautiful blond hair. We had a photographer come to the house to take his picture. Yes, we were very proud parents.

When Scott was born, we lived in a condo in Honolulu. Soon after 1967 was ushered in, we were expecting our 2nd baby. On October 16, 1967, our son, Mark Stephen Hull was born. What a doll! He had dark curly hair, and long eyelashes. He was a happy baby, always smiling.

In March of 1967, we moved into a nice house with a yard—just what we needed with two little boys. We had nice neighbors and one of them had two boys just the ages of Scott and Mark. It was so nice to have a yard for Scott to play in while Mark was growing up and learning to walk.

Clyde was still with Island Homes, selling real estate and sometimes his hours were very long. Often the boys and I had to eat dinner before he got home. Usually though, he got home in time to read the boys stories and put them to bed. The stories the kids loved the best, though, were the ones Clyde made up.

When a mother is home all day raising small children, it really helps to develop good friendships. We were then in Kahala Ward and there were mothers there with children the ages of mine. We would get together often either at someone's house or at the beach or park. We would watch the kids play while we sat and chatted. Some of those friendships are still here today, nearly 40 years later!

On May 13, 1970, our daughter Allyson was born. She was six weeks early—labor induced. I had toxemia and it was necessary to get the baby delivered. She was a beauty. I finally had my girl and Scott and Mark finally had a little sister. It worked out well because I was unable to have any more children.

In November of 1972, we said "goodbye" to Niu Valley and moved to Hawaii Kai. This was the house we would stay in all the rest of our lives in Hawaii. Everyone loved it. We had a pool and a nice backyard, with a strawberry patch, grapefruit tree, lemon tree, papaya trees, and banana trees. The fruit was wonderful!

One thing that made Hawaii such a special place was the fact that Mike and VaNetta Hull, Clyde's brother and his wife and family lived there too. They had five children, their last three the same ages as ours. We did so many things together. On holidays, such as the 4th of July, Labor Day, or sometimes just ordinary weekends, we would pack food and go either to

Bellows Beach or to the North Shore. The kids would play on the beach and in the water. VaNetta and I would fix the lunch. Then we'd find a scenic spot (not hard to find) and eat lunch. Sometimes our dear friends, Jack and Cathie Richards and Puao and John Sothern and their two children, Sheylani and Vincent, would join us. Late in the afternoon, with everyone tired, burned or tan, we would home—another choice experience for the memories bank.

Other holidays we all spent together were Thanksgiving and Christmas. We would take turns. Someone would do Thanksgiving, then someone else would do Christmas Eve, and the other one, Christmas day. Christmas is such an exciting time for children and ours were no exception. They spent much time looking and playing with their toys and each others. Scott and Kerry (Mike's son) usually got some of the same toys, as did Mark and David and Julie and Allyson. David, Mike, and VaNetta's son was a little younger than Mark, and Julie M and V's daughter, was a little older than Allyson, but they all had great times together. To this day, these children are all still close due to so many bonding experiences they had.

While our children were growing up, many animals lit up our lives. I always have felt it important to teach my children to love, care for, and be kind to animals. We had guinea pigs, who had many babies. We had rabbits, who also had many babies and three dogs. Our first dog was named Muffy and she was a terrier mix. Our other two were poodles. First we got Heidi, then we bred her to our groomer's dog and she had two black males. We kept one and named him Ruggles. The other we sold to the Ed Browning family. He was the head of the Episcopal diocese in Hawaii. A few months later, they moved and he became the head of the diocese of the United States.

Time passed quickly. The kids grew up and went on missions. In December of 1988, I was diagnosed with heart disease. I was 47 years old. Heart disease runs in my father's family. On the December 22, I had double bypass surgery. It was rough, but by the end of March, I was back at Iolani Palace where I was a docent. I loved this! The palace was beautiful—fully restored to the days of the kings and queens. It was especially wonderful because Hawaii is the only state that was once ruled by kings and queens. I met many wonderful people who were also docents, as well as many interesting tourists.

At this time, Scott was home from his mission and away at Ricks College. One day, we got a phone call telling us that he was engaged to Paula Sommerfeldt. We were delighted. We had met Paula and she is a lovely girl and we loved her immediately. Where had the time gone? Our "little" Scott was about to be a married man! They were married in the Salt Lake Temple and made their home in Logan where both were going to Utah State University.

After that Allyson went on her mission to Holland. A few months later, Mark went on his mission to California, San Bernardino.

Eventually, both Allyson and Mark were home and busy with school and work. Allyson became engaged to Carlo Bos, whom she had met at the Missionary Training Center. They were married in the Salt Lake Temple on a snowy November day.

As the months went by, we became grandparents! How exciting this was. We were blessed with two grandsons, six months apart. Hunter Romney Hull was born on May 5, 1995. On November 15, 1995, Christian Carlo Bos was born.

One fine day in October 1997, Mark was married to Lachelle Wilson in the Arizona Temple. We all went down for the big day, including our two year old grandsons. At that time two more grandchildren were on the way. Clyde and I had now moved back to Salt Lake to be with our families

We now live in Murray where in 2001, I became Relief Society President. I enjoyed this calling so much. It gave me a chance to really know the sisters, and strengthened my capacity to give and to love.

Today, I direct the ward extraction program, which I love. This program aids the church in redeeming the dead.

In one week from today, June 19th I will be 65. I feel as though I've had a wonderful life - full of challenges and blessing. I have learned a great deal about myself. I've tried to make changes where necessary and nurture that which is good. Today I have nine grandchildren and every one is a gold mine. If I may say so, these children have been born of goodly parents who are doing their best to raise them right—so far, so good.

I'm extremely blessed and so grateful to my Heavenly Father for everything. I know firmly that if we keep the Lord's commandments and follow His path, we will find our way home to Him someday. I feel safe and comforted by this knowledge.

CLYDE L. HULL

Everywhere around the world people gather to celebrate my birthday. Being born on New Year's Day is both good and bad. Good, because everyone is in a festive mood. Bad, because everyone is tired of gift giving.

I was born to Clyde John Hull and Dora Arave Hull on January 1, 1933 in Ogden, Utah. I was the first baby born in a hospital in my family. In spite of a fun but rough and tumble childhood, I've never had a broken bone. I think my dad tried a few times, but though deserving, I was resilient.

I graduated from Ogden High School with very good grades—largely because I avoided all subjects which were likely to require too much homework or had words in the course title I couldn't pronounce. Weber College was fun and I applied the same techniques that had served me so well previously with pretty much the same results.

From the time I was twelve, I worked at my dad's service station. Inmates at Japanese prison camps enjoyed pretty much the same benefits I got. When I started at Weber, my mandatory sentence was over and I was free to take a job at First Security Bank as a warehouseman, which by contrast was a piece of cake. Before starting at the Y (Brigham Young University), I worked for a summer at the Bank of America in downtown L.A. as a teller. That fall I completed my first quarter in Provo before leaving for a 2 ½-year mission for The Church of Jesus Christ of Latter-day Saints in Uruguay, upon completion of which I finished at the Y and worked briefly for United Airlines before accepting a job with Husky Oil Co. in Cody,

Wyoming. After a year in Cody, I tendered my resignation and returned to Ogden where I taught business subjects at Ben Lomond High School for three years.

In 1961, I flew to Hawaii to visit my brother and sister-in-law. I decided I'd rather be on the beach at Waikiki than shoveling snow in Ogden, so after completing my teaching contract in 1962 I moved to Honolulu. Having sold real estate part time in Ogden and doing well, I decided to give up teaching for a career more financially rewarding. At that time Hawaii had a two year residency requirement, so I taught two more years—one at a business college, and one at a public high school near my Waikiki apartment. Janet's uncle introduced me to her as I was about to begin in real estate, and we were married in Salt Lake in 1964. Three children followed in two-year intervals, Scott, Mark, and Allyson.

I had been with Island Homes for 20 years when the owner died in 1984 and his grandson inherited the company. Since I had been the broker in charge, I was invited to buy 49% of the company, and for three years Brent Christensen and I thoroughly enjoyed running the company. In early 1987 Brent and his wife decided they wanted to move to the mainland, so I purchased his 51% that March. One year later, a Japanese company wanted to buy me out, and made me an offer I couldn't refuse. As part of the sales agreement, I agreed to stay on as principal broker for three years, making three trips to Tokyo and receiving increasingly bizarre instructions. It was a great relief when my responsibilities with the company were over, but sad to see how the new owner mismanaged and ultimately ran the company into bankruptcy.

During my 34 years in Hawaii, we visited Utah almost every year and additionally made many trips abroad and to other parts of the U.S. We took a half a dozen cruises, built a cabin in Idaho, and thought our stay in Hawaii would be permanent. However, with our kids moving to Utah and the arrival of our first grandson there, Utah's pull became irresistible, and in 1996 we returned to live in an investment property we had in South Salt Lake, and within a year had begun the construction of the home we now occupy and love, keeping busy with a variety of Church callings and maintaining a busy social life with a multitude of friends and family.

Scott Romney Hull

My name is Scott Romney Hull. I am the son of Janet Romney Hull, who was the daughter of Wendell and Jeannette Romney. I was born in Honolulu, Hawaii on February 28, 1966. That is where I lived until my LDS mission took me to Utah, at the Utah Salt Lake City Mission in the fall of 1985.

Growing up in Hawaii was great fun and interesting. I loved my years growing up there and became very adaptive to the local culture and got along just fine. I grew up loving the water and one of my favorite pastimes was body surfing at Sandy Beach, not too far from our home in Hawai'i Kai. I grew up loving all sports and participated in little league football and basketball.

After my mission in Utah, which I served between 1985–1987, I went to Ricks College in Rexburg, Idaho. I had a great time there and ultimately met Paula Rae Sommerfeldt, who later became my wife. We got engaged while I was at Utah State University and she was finishing up at Ricks. We got married May 18, 1991 in the Salt Lake Temple. After we were married, we both attended Utah State University. In June of 1994, we both graduated from the College of Education. Paula got her degree in teaching school and I got mine in Parks and Recreation.

Shortly after graduation, we moved to Bozeman, Montana. We quickly found the cost of living was too much for the simple jobs that we worked to make ends meet. After a few months, we moved back to Utah.

On May 5, 1995, Hunter Romney Hull was born to us. It was a very happy day! We lived with Paula's parents in Draper while we built a house in Riverton. We moved into our new home in July of 1995. On May 31, 1998, we were blessed with the birth of our daughter, Kailee Ryann Hull.

We lived in Riverton for four years and then, through my job, we moved back to Logan in August 1999. We were lucky to have our home sell within a few short days after putting it on the market. We both felt really good about moving back to Cache Valley and have always felt this is where we are supposed to be. In March of 2000, we bought a spec home in Providence, just south of Logan.

On August 28, 2000, we were blessed yet again with a 3rd child – Nathan Dax Hull. He completed our family. Although we would have liked more kids, the Lord had other plans.

As of October 2009, we are still in the same Providence home and still very much enjoy Cache Valley and all the outdoor recreation opportunities that it offers. In the summer we love to hike, camp, and spend Saturdays at the beaches of Bear Lake. In the winter, I love to go to Hyrum Dam and ice fish. I can easily spend several hours sitting on a bucket on the ice, staring at my floater. I find it really thrilling when it starts to jig. I catch a lot of perch and rainbow trout. I have also taken my kids many times and they really seem to have a good time as well. At their current ages of 14, 11, and 9, they are all very seasoned in the sport.

My family is my pride and joy. I love spending time with them...hiking, camping, going to USU Aggie games, local high school games, etc. I have gained a firm testimony on the importance of family and our awesome responsibility as parents to raise our children properly. We are a very active, church-going family. As of this date in October 2009, I am the Stake Young Men's secretary and my wife is the ward Young Women.s President. We love our callings!

Hunter just completed his Eagle Scout Award. As of this entry, we are planing his Eagle court of honor date for the formal presentation. Both he and Kailee play piano and have taken lessons. Nathan may soon be starting as well. Right now, he is still ALL about playing with his trucks in the garden dirt pit, riding his bike and skateboard, and playing catch with the football.

We have been very blessed as family. I feel we were clearly lead to Cache Valley. All though job fluctuation caused me to have to commute to Salt Lake for over two years to work, between 2001 and 2003, the dust has long since settled. I am currently working as an independent broker for Carpet Direct, selling floor coverings direct from the mill. It is a mobile show room with all the samples in my van. It is by appointment only. Every day I am meeting with people at their homes, businesses, and often times, even in parking lots to show them samples and go over costs. I love what I have to offer, as nobody can compete with my prices! I just always hope that word continues to spread around the valley. I have been at this now since June of 2006. It has been up and down. Currently, with the economy in bad shape, business has dropped off. Fortunately, the Lord has blessed us and helped sustain ourselves with the help of family. Luckily, things are picking back up again, but this last year had been quite a challenge.

The Hull Siblings - Allyson, Mark, and Scott

Mark Stephen Hull

Written July 2009

I was born on October 16, 1967 to Clyde LaMont and Janet Romney Hull in Honolulu, Hawaii at Kapiolani Hospital. I have an older brother, Scott, and a younger sister, Allyson.

The majority of my childhood was spent in Honolulu, Hawaii in Hawaii Kai at 731 Kokomo Place in Mariner's Cove. We lived in that house until my parents sold it and moved to Murray, Utah in 1994.

Each summer we would go to the mainland to visit my grandparents in Utah. My Granddad, Wendell Bitner Romney, and my Nana, Jeannette Murdoch Romney, lived in Salt Lake City. My Grandpa, Clyde John Hull, and my Grandma, Dora Arave Hull, lived in North Ogden. We would take trips to our cabin on the Snake River in Island Park (Last Chance), Idaho.

We had several dogs throughout the years: Muffy, Heidi, and Ruggles.

I attended preschool at Mohalapua in Nui Valley and Aina Haina Elementary School for Kindergarten through 6th grade. During my 6th grade year, there was a teachers' strike and all public schools were closed for a time. My mom enrolled me in a private Catholic school, Holy Trinity, on Kalanianaole Highway.

For junior high, I attended Niu Valley Junior High and also one year at Clayton Junior High in Salt Lake City, Utah. In 1987 I graduated from Kaiser High School. After my mission I attended Ricks College (now BYU-Idaho) in Rexburg, Idaho for a year.

My love for surfing started at a young age. I surfed various spots all over Oahu wherever the waves were good. However, my favorite spot was Half Point at Sandy Beach.

LEFT: *Mark and Miles* CENTER: *LBI Parasail Business* RIGHT: *Allyson Bos & Janet Hull 2007*

I worked at jet ski, dive boat, and parasailing companies out of Monalua Bay. I went to school to get my USCG (United States Coast Guard) certified captain license and did so in 1988. I worked as a parasail captain for Sea Breeze Parasail and traveled the globe, helping train other captains how to safely operate parasail operations. I went to St. George's Bermuda, Key West, and Saipan Micronesia. I started my own parasail company in May 1997 in North Myrtle Beach, South Carolina. I then worked for another parasail company in Sea Isle City, New Jersey for the summer of 1998. In May 1999, I opened L.B.I. Parasail & Watersports, Inc. on Long Beach Island, New Jersey. I operated 10 successful seasons there before selling the business in early 2009.

I served a mission in the San Bernardino California mission from March

6, 1991 to April 6, 1993. I had two mission presidents, President D. Earl Hurst and President Calvin R. Stephens (from Morgan, Utah). I served in Lake Isabella, Redlands, Apple Valley, and Rancho Cucamonga. For the last nine months of my mission, I served as an assistant to President Stephens and was on splits all over the mission.

President Stephens taught me everything I know about how to truly make the gospel come to life. I am forever blessed to have made his acquaintance as my priesthood leader, teacher, and am still friends with him and his wonderful wife, Lynette.

In 1996 I went on a Church History and American History tour with Calvin Stephens as the guide. I met Ann Alexander on this tour. She gave me the phone number of her son-in-law's sister, Lachelle Wilson. Lachelle was from Mesa, Arizona but was living with relatives in Lindon, Utah. I was living in Salt Lake City, Utah at the time. We dated from November 1996 until I left to start my parasailing business in South Carolina in May 1997.

Once in South Carolina, I missed her and we talked about her coming out to help with the business. We were "unofficially" engaged over the phone and Lachelle came to visit me in July 1997. While she was there, I took her parasailing and when she came down I asked her to marry me on my parasail boat about three miles off shore in the Atlantic Ocean. I had a grocery bag of fireworks that we enjoyed after we were officially engaged.

We were married in the Mesa Arizona Temple on Saturday, October 11, 1997. That was five days before my 30th birthday and 15 days before Lachelle's 27th birthday.

For the first three years of marriage, we tried to have children. Finally on Sunday, June 25, 2000 at 8:16 P.M. our first child and son, Miles Romney, was born in Manahawkin, New Jersey. He has been a source of tremendous joy in our lives. He is an excellent son and brother. We were blessed to have our first daughter, Malialani, on Thursday, October 31, 2002 at 6:03 A.M. in Mesa, Arizona. We call her our "treat" because she was born on Halloween. She had the darkest, curly hair with brown eyes. Her mission in life is to keep me happy and make me laugh.

TOP LEFT: *Mark with Malialani, Alissa, and Miles.* TOP RIGHT: *Baptism day for Miles*
BOTTOM LEFT: *Mark* BOTTOM RIGHT: *Janet Hull with Lachelle, Alissa, and Malialani*

Five and a half years later, on Friday, May 30, 2008 at 12:44 P.M. in Gilbert, Arizona, we welcomed a second daughter, Alissa. She was a beautiful baby with surprising bright blue eyes. While Lachelle and Alissa were still in the hospital, I left to get on a plane and go back to New Jersey to start up our 10th parasailing season. Three weeks later my family and my mom came to New Jersey for six weeks.

In September 2001, we started Aloha Glass Pro, a residential window cleaning business. We also did new construction cleaning. In 2003, we began selling window treatments (shutters and blinds) under Aloha Window Coverings. We changed the name of our business to Aloha Window & Construction Cleaning in February 2005. In October 2007, we sold that business. I started working as an independent contractor for Carpet Direct in November 2007.

I am gratefully for the privilege to be a member of the Church of Jesus Christ of Latter-day Saints. It has been the source of tremendous blessings in my life. I've had the opportunity to serve as the Elder's Quorum President and in various presidencies (branch, quorums, Sunday School), ward mission leader, ward missionary, and many years as a youth and adult Sunday School teacher.

Allyson Hull Bos

I was born Allyson Hull on May 13, 1970 in Honolulu, Hawaii at Kapiolani Womens and Childrens Hospital. I was the third of three children. My oldest brother is Scott Romney, then Mark Stephen.

My first two years were spent on Haleola Street in Niu Valley, Then, we moved to 731 Kokomo Place in Mariner's Cove in Hawaii Kai. I was raised in that house and loved it because my room had a great breeze from the mountains and we had a pool.

I first went to the Nutcracker Ballet at age five. I knew then that I had to take ballet. Mom started me in classes but soon took me out because of my lack of coordination. She started me again with the same teacher when I was seven and things went much better. Ballet became my passion. Things took off for me when, at age 10, I began taking classes from Nolan Dingman. I started Pointe classes and danced in Hawaii's Nutcracker in 1980 and 1982. In 1981, my family went to Salt Lake City for seven months so my mom could help out with my Nana who was suffering from mini strokes and it was becoming a real strain for my granddad. I went to 6th grade at Emerson Elementary. While in Salt Lake, I also attended Christensen Academy where I studied ballet. I auditioned for Ballet West Nutcracker and got a role in the party scene. Three hundred auditioned for the party scene but only 16 were chosen. It was the part I'd played the two years before. I loved being identified on stage by my own unique dress.

I had an amazing school year that was fun. My teacher, Mrs. Monson, had the class put on a Shakespeare play called, *A Midsummer Night's Dream*. I was Puck, a funny character who wrote a play within a play.

In March of 1982, it was time to go back to Hawaii. Mom felt she had done all she could for Nana. I resumed 6th grade at Kamiloiki School. Then I went on to junior high at Niu Valley, then Kaiser High School.

At 15, I was taking up to eight ballet classes advancing to the highest level, including pas de deux classes and private lessons. One day, I learned that Nolan Dingman was moving and the Honolulu City Dance Center would be no more. There was no other ballet teacher as qualified as he, so I didn't continue.

In 1987, I was 17 and a senior in high school doing half day with two jobs. I worked at Honolulu City Book Store and part time at Orange Julius. I deeply missed ballet and wanted to do something with it, so I decided to teach. I was able to rent the cafeteria at Koko Head Elementary School on Saturdays. It had a stage with ballet bars. I started teaching a 10:00 AM class and within a couple of months I had to create an 11:00 class. The 10:00 was five to seven year olds and the 11:00 was eight to ten. I loved this and taught until I left for Ricks College (now BYU-Idaho) in August of 1988 for a year. That was enough for me. Rexburg was boring. The following year was spent at BYU Provo. This was a turning point for me. I had gone home for the summer and was back with all of my high school friends. After a few weeks, I began to realize that my testimony was a bit lacking. I was outside one evening looking at the stars and pondering my life's events. Suddenly an overwhelming thought struck me: sink or swim. I knew that if I didn't move forward in strengthening my testimony, I'd lose it. After that I gained a strong testimony and knew I wanted to serve a mission. I had read and studied the Book of Mormon and decided to prepare for my mission. That year, I hungered and thirsted for the scriptures.

I served my mission in the Netherlands. I first went to the MTC in Provo where I learned Dutch and the discussions. I was the only sister in my class. A few weeks into our learning there, a new missionary arrived and joined our class. He was Elder Bos from the Netherlands. I thought he was handsome, but tried not to think about it. I was going on a mission for one reason—to spread the gospel. Elder Bos was going to Suriname. Some in the class were going to Belgium. When it was time for our group to leave, we all put our names and addresses on the board so we could keep in touch. We felt like a family. I was impressed by Elder Bos. He was focused and hard working but could have fun when it was appropriate. He seemed more mature than the others. I secretly hoped our paths would cross again.

I loved my mission! My first two companions were a bit trying.. I came down with the flu and it was the first Sunday with my first companion. She strongly suggested I fast, go to church, and then go tracting afterwards.

Wanting to do the right thing, I did as she asked. By the end of Sacrament Meeting, I was forced to lie down on the bench. I had chills and was feverish. I told her I was miserable and that I needed to go home. She told me to have faith and that we needed to go out tracting. I went out not knowing how I'd make it. After an hour of feeling like I was ready to pass out, I finally told her I was going home with or without her and I did. She went with me. She would tell me after a prayer to let the spirit guide me to the spot on the street map where we should go that day. That always felt uncomfortable to me. I felt that if we were living right, the Lord would direct us in a more natural way. I never said anything. I went along with her wishes because she was not only the senior companion but she was my trainer and I wanted to respect her. We were companions for two months and it was the end of her mission

My second companion presented a new kind of trial. She preferred naps over work. She liked long lunch breaks, talking to elders on the phone at night, and any other form of rule breaking that she could get away with it. She too was my senior companion, but not my trainer so I didn't feel the need to tolerate the disobedience that affected my efforts at missionary work. She didn't like me at all and called me (to the other fellow missionary slackers) Sister White Handbook. One evening some neighbors, whom I knew somewhat from the previous few months, invited us over for hot chocolate. They asked what we were doing in Holland. I bore a little testimony of the gospel and in a casual manner asked a few questions which led into the first discussion. My companion clammed up. When we left, she yelled at me saying "They invited us over for hot chocolate, not for religion." That was when I began my letters to the mission president asking for one of us to be transferred. It was a long month but afterward I was transferred up north. Here, I had an amazing companion. We both wanted to work hard. We got along great and had many successes. We worked together for three months. I trained my remaining five companions and loved it. We taught many wonderful people and had quite a few baptisms.

Throughout my mission, Elder Bos and I were writing to each other. It started when at our 1st mission conference, one of the elders from our class gave me a letter Elder Bos had written to all of us. I was the last to get it and was happy to keep it so I could write back. We were both happy to be in touch and were great supports to each other. He was a great missionary and I admired him.

After my mission in the fall of 1993, I decided to attend Utah State University where my brother, Scott, and his wife Paula were going to school. I loved it. Carlo and I kept in touch. The following July of 1994, Carlo came to Utah to visit his grandparents. He later confessed it was to see me and find out if we were right for each other. Three weeks later, we got engaged. He called his parents and asked them to send his things because he wouldn't be returning home. We were married on November 26, 1994 in the Salt Lake Temple. Three months later I was expecting our first baby. Christian Carlo Bos was born on November 15, 1995. On May 18, 1998 James Romney Bos was born. Thomas Frans came along on October 29, 1999. Two summers later, our daughter, Malia Allyson, was born.

I love being married to Carlo, who honors his priesthood, works hard, and clearly loves his family very much. He got a degree in Computer Science from the University of Utah a few years after we were married and started his career as a software engineer. He's always loved computers and began creating his own computer games at age 12. He is currently working for 1-800-Contacts creating software for various departments within the company. He also does consulting on the side. He happily accepts church callings and always does his best. He serves now in our bishopric as the First Counselor and works very hard with no complaints.

LEFT: *Milia* RIGHT: *1990 family trip to Holland to visit Oma and Opa*

I'm a stay-at-home mom—which means driving kids around, running errands, attending soccer games, helping in the kids' classrooms, and going to the gym. I'm able to be with my children and deeply appreciate that privilege.

My children are all doing well. Christian is nearly 12. He works hard in school and is a good student. He has many friends and is kind to everyone. He is studying piano and is a green belt in Tae Kwon Do. James is 9. He likes school but not the work. He is a real people person and they love him. He looks like his dad but his body and many mannerisms and behavior are like his Uncle Mark. He smiles a lot. He likes skateboarding and Tae Kwon do. Thomas is 7 and very much his own person. He has definite likes and dislikes and clear ideas of how things should go. He's a great soccer player and consistently scores the most goals on his team. He's good at any sport he tries and kids like him slot. Malia, age 6, is a spunky, social butterfly who wants to be with friends every moment. She's strong willed which makes her a good leader. She is also very nice. She loves anything pink and can't wait to start ballet lessons.

Christian and Thomas, November 2009

Milia's baptism

Jackson Hole, August 2002

Lake Tahoe, July 2009

Thomas, July 2009

Christian and Hunter at the cabin

Now, a few childhood memories that I hold dear:

Baking cookies, especially molasses ones, with my Nana, Jeannette Murdoch Romney, when she would visit us in Hawaii. She was always so sweet to me.

Getting a soda at Jolly Rogers with Mom before ballet at Mrs. McKenzie's.

Eating mangos cut in little blocks on the peel prepared by Dad out by the pool, or anywhere.

Scott's silly made up songs on the way to the cabin.

The cabin on the Snake River at Island Park, Idaho.

Camping out in Mark's room when we were adding onto the house (about 1982)

Sleeping on cots in the basement of Grandma and Grandpa Hulls's house with Mark and Scott.

Sleepovers and outings with my cousin Julie.

Shopping at Ala Moana Mall with Mom and my aunt and cousin—especially at the Hello Kitty Store, Liberty House, and Shirokiya's.

Saturdays with Dad and my brothers at Bellows Beach in Waimanalo, followed by malasadas.

Staying with Nana and Granddad and looking through boxes of Mom's books, dolls, etc. in their basements; also rolling down the hiss in the backyard.

Visiting Aunt Nan and Uncle Dwight and my cousins and going to Brother Volheye's house. He was known as the candy man of their ward.

NAN MURDOCH ROMNEY

I was born during my favorite season, Summer, on July 12, 1945 in Salt Lake City, Utah at the LDS Hospital. I am the second of two children born to Jeannette Murdoch and Wendell Bitner Romney. My older sister, Janet, is four years older than I am – born on June 19, 1941. My name, Nan, was the name of a favorite actress of my parents, Nan Grey. I have never seen a picture of her nor do I know anything about her, but perhaps she had something to do with my wanting to be one of two things when I grew up: an actress or a waitress. I have never experienced either professionally, although I frequently served both roles while raising my children. Of course, I have been asked all my life if my "real" name is either Nancy or Nannette. I always say no but have never explained its origin and have always been amused that people just naturally think it must be a nickname. My middle name, Murdoch, is my mother's maiden name. I am grateful to have a name from each of my parents.

Both sets of grandparents gave me a rich heritage. Both the Murdoch and Romney families have been a positive influence in my life. My mother was one of nine children and my father was one of seven children. Their examples and the stories that I have read about their involvement in church and community have made me a stronger person – giving me a desire to be strong for my own children and posterity.

With just two kids in the family and, being the youngest, rumor has it that I drove Janet crazy – the pesty younger sister. Dad was meticulous in filming us as we grew up and many of those home movies reveal how much I imitated everything she did. Dad was really creative and the movies have kept memories alive.

The only home I ever lived in before I was married is the home my parents built in 1941 at 709 11th Avenue. The lot and cost of building equaled $4000. That home was the site of wonderful memories with friends, lemonade sales in the summer, our own Mickey Mouse Club in the basement performed by my friends and me, ice cream cones with my family on the front porch on hot summer nights, and many more memories that make me grateful for a happy and full childhood.

Mother's cooking was always the best and the smells that came from her kitchen have stayed with me – wanting to recreate those memories with my own children. I know I have my mother to thank for my love of cooking. I loved watching her – her yummy nightly dinners for our family, her gracious family gatherings at our home (always with a beautiful centerpiece) and, as simple as it sounds, her tuna fish sandwiches.

A great memory was helping my dad cut the front lawn. Our front yard was a steep slope and it wasn't easy maneuvering the lawn mower back and forth. Of course, Dad did most of it but I felt I was a big help. He often referred to me as "half pint" because I was so small. If anyone else called me that it would have been an insult, but from him it was endearing.

We had great family vacations – either during spring break around Easter or in the summer. When we got our French Poodle, Gygi, she always accompanied us on these trips. We traveled to southern California often, stopping in Las Vegas on the way. With no air conditioning in the car, it was a long, hot drive but we all enjoyed being together. We also traveled to San Francisco a few times but our favorite spot was Jackson Hole, Wyoming or to the Canyons. Often on these trips, friends of our parents would go with us. The Homestead in Heber City was a favorite place to spend a summer day, swimming and eating breakfast or lunch.

Thanksgiving was always fun at Nana Romney's house – with the cousins sitting at the "kids' table". Each year this holiday got us in the mood for Christmas – a holiday that our parents always made memorable and so much fun. Dad filmed our Christmases and animated all of our dolls and anything else that he could put into motion. Our house looked beautiful decorated with all the colors of the season – both inside and out. Even today, the smell of a fresh Christmas tree brings back all the warm memories. No wonder it is my favorite holiday!

I think my sister was a budding playwright. When I was about eight years old, she wrote a "play/musical" which several of the neighborhood kids practiced and then performed. We invited everyone else in the neighborhood – children and their moms. They sat on the stone steps in our backyard and I can't imagine how the adults kept a straight face. I don't remember the script or anyone else's part in the program, but I vividly remember my cousin and me singing and dancing to "Utah We Love Thee". We were perfectly serious but it must have been hilarious to watch. I don't remember how much we charged but every cent we earned we gave to the Primary Children's Hospital. I think it was a sweet gesture for a group of kids to do with their summer vacation.

At Nana Romney's house was a beautiful piano which I loved to pretend I could play. Finally our parents bought a piano and my first piano teacher was my cousin, Barbara Weggeland, the daughter of Aunt Mary Murdoch Weggeland (my mother's sister). At one of our recitals, my sister and I played a duet, "In the Woods". It was fairly complicated to keep in sync with each other. About half way through I forgot my part. I looked at the audience and laughed. Janet didn't see any humor in it. At least I didn't run from the stage crying. That probably would have embarrassed her more. As an interesting side note, our son, Romney, and our daughter, Ann Marie, took piano lessons from Barbara many years later. By then, she had her own studio with several pianos.

Growing up, my friends and I spent a lot of time in the downtown area of Salt Lake City. We took the bus to swimming lessons at the Deseret Gym and after we walked to ZCMI and bought a yummy hot dog in the basement. My father was Credit Manager of ZCMI and occasionally we would visit him. I loved to read and going to the public library was fun and I always brought home a few books to read. I read through all the Nancy Drew books and always thought her life sounded so exciting!

My mother was a great mom and role model. She was a great cook and I know I got my love of cooking by watching her in the kitchen. I love looking through cook books and trying new recipes. To this day, I love baking chocolate chip cookies on rainy or snowy days. When our kids were growing up, I didn't even realize this was something I did until they told me how much they looked forward to them after a cold day at school. It was something I did instinctively and didn't even realize it! From my mother I learned to be a gracious hostess, the importance of love, family loyalty, looking nice for my husband (very important to my mother), the love of flowers and gardening and French Poodles (especially Gygi, our dog growing up), and always supporting my kids through everything – no matter what!

Nan, Jeannette, and Janet

Aunt Mary Murdoch, Nan, and Janet

From my Dad I learned the value of hard work, family loyalty, importance of laughter, my love for the Yankees, admiring hotel lobbies (family inside joke), never leaving something unfinished, and an inquisitive mind.

I attended Ensign Elementary School – located on 10th Avenue between D & E Streets. It was a fun time walking to and from school with good friends – through deep snow in the winter and through crisp, dry autumn leaves in the Fall, buying penny candy at the store across from the school, sleigh riding on our steep front lawn, fun bike rides and summer fun with friends or eating tuna fish sandwiches with Mother and Janet under the Pussy Willow tree next to our house.

My junior high memories were not the best. The school was wild with some really scary kids. We called them greasers then. I didn't care for the subjects I had to take (particularly painful was geometry) and didn't much care for the teachers. But, like everyone else, I survived!

My high school years were great! I loved East High and everything that went with it: Pep Club (as Marching Chairman, I made up the marches and it was fun), Dance Club, great friends (girls and boys), crazy experiences, great teachers, interesting school subjects and overall, just the best of times.

After high school I attended the University of Utah. I pledged Delta Gamma Sorority. My junior year I was the sorority Secretary and really enjoyed that. I loved my friends and all activities associated with my sorority membership. Best of all, my senior year I met my future love and husband, Dwight Bradley Williams. Dwight studied his first year of college at Stanford, returned to the U his second year, and then served a Church mission in the Germany Hamburg Mission. He was transferred in the middle of his mission to serve in the newly-formed Italian Mission. At the U, we were in a Political Science class together but formally met through a mutual friend. We started dating in January. We were "pinned" (he was affiliated with Beta Theta Pi Fraternity) in May and married September 1, 1967 in the Salt Lake Temple by Elder Marion G. Romney.

Dwight graduated in June in Political Science and I graduated in August in Sociology. Two weeks after we were married, we moved to New York City for Dwight to attend Columbia Law School. With Dwight's love for travel, foreign languages, foreign people and foreign food, his specialty has been international law.

LEFT: *Fraternity Pinning* RIGHT: *September 1, 1967*

We lived in New York for four years – four great years. I wasn't able to use my college major but, because I had kept up with my shorthand (which hasn't been taught for years) and type; I was able to have some interesting jobs – secretary to the President of Rolls Royce of America (scarier than prestigious), secretary to the Director of Public Relations for The Martin Marietta Corporation (a real father figure), secretary to the Executive Vice President of Diners Club (a man I will always admire) and secretary to the Director of Fashion for Donohue Sales (my only, my last, and I would never consider it again, female boss). That sounds like a lot of jobs in four years but, because I was the bread winner for our little family while Dwight was in law school, each job paid better and helped us survive that big, expensive city.

After graduation, Dwight got a job with a law firm on Wall Street. After one year of that life style (always at work, never seeing our baby and realizing all attorneys, young and old, worked that hard), we knew we should return to Salt Lake. We moved into a duplex just on the corner from my parents. It was fun having them so close and they enjoyed their two new grandsons—details about our children later.

After living in the duplex for about one year, we built a home on Virginia Street behind Shriners Hospital. It was a good family home. The boys had good friends and we enjoyed the area.

Two years later we bought an older home on Arlington Drive, which we enjoyed remodeling. After adding two daughters and another son, the home became too small so we moved on.

In October 1980, we moved to Berkeley Street where we lived for 20 years. It was a wonderful family home and most of our children's "growing up" memories evolve around that neighborhood. As the children went on missions and/or got married, the home was too large. Dwight was traveling a great deal for his work and we knew it was time to get something on a smaller piece of property. In April 2000, we moved to our current home in Holladay. It's just right for us, our children, and 16 wonderful grandchildren.

Dwight and I are blessed with five wonderful children. They are the greatest blessings we have. Each is such a good person – faithful members of the Church, love for each other and Dwight and me and demonstrating it in all they do, hard workers, and wonderful loving parents to their adorable children.

Our first child, Dwight Bradley Williams III, was born in New York on December 3, 1970. He was a real joy, so alert and inquisitive from the beginning. When it came to learning, he was like a sponge. At 18 months old he was counting from 1 to 10 in five languages and he will never stop learning. With many talents in many areas, his mind works overtime in creating. He graduated from the University of Utah in Political Science. He served a mission for the Church of Jesus Christ of Latter-day Saints in the Zurich Switzerland Mission. Brad married Raina Bradford on September 2, 2000 in the Louisiana Baton Rouge Temple. Raina served a church mission in the Arizona Tempe Mission and is a graduate of Brigham Young University in Recreational Therapy. Shortly after they were married, they moved to London where Brad received a graduate degree from The London School of Economics. His career has been focused on ventures primarily in media and entertainment. They are blessed with five precious children: Annabelle Marie (Jan. 20. 2004), Luke Bradley (Nov. 22, 2005), Andrew Bradford (Oct. 27, 2006), Lillian Claire (Lilli) (Nov. 19, 2007) and Alice Mae (March 7, 2010). They live in Salt Lake City.

Wendell Romney Williams (Romney) was born on July 3, 1972. We named Romney after my father who never had a son to carry on his name. From the beginning, Romney had a calming spirit and has always been a peacemaker. He has a great personality, is very loyal to family and friends, and brings out the best in everyone. He graduated in Political Science from the University of Utah. His career has centered in entrepreneurial endeavors and he has been instrumental in formatting the foundation for several companies. Romney served a church mission in the Switzerland Geneva Mission. He married Alecia Thompson in the Salt Lake Temple on October 19, 1996. Alecia served a mission in the Germany Dusseldorf Mission and graduated from the University of Utah in Political Science. They are blessed with four precious children: Thomas Romney (April 19, 1999), Lauren Kathryn (May 18, 2001), Christian Thompson (May 28, 2004) and Sophie Nan (May 22, 2006). They live in Salt Lake City.

Ann Marie was born on December 29, 1976. We were so thrilled to get a daughter. She never had a chance to wear anything but pink! From the beginning, Ann Marie was soft-spoken and very feminine. She loves her surroundings to be attractive, and it is reflected in her home and garden and she loves a good laugh. She served a mission in the Italy Padova Mission. A few years after her return, she married Brent Kenney on June 27, 2001 in the Salt Lake Temple. Brent graduated from the University of Utah in Accounting and served a church mission in the Spain Malaga Mission. After they had been married a few years, Brent received his Masters of Business Administration from Westminster College and works at Hewlett-Packard. They are blessed with two precious children: Jonas Brent (Nov. 6, 2002) and Alexander Smith (Alex) (April 25, 2005). They live in South Jordan.

Elisabeth was born on April 12, 1978. She was spunky from birth and has always enjoyed meeting new people. When she was a toddler, she asked complete strangers if she could try on their shoes. This ease with people has transferred to her adult life and she makes friends easily. She is very creative and loves teaching herself new skills. She graduated from the University of Utah in Art History and did a study abroad in Siena, Italy. Elisabeth married Jesse Theurer on October 28, 2000. Jesse graduated from the University of Utah in Communication and served a church mission in the Germany Dresden Mission. He owns a business in the mortgage industry. They are blessed with two precious children: Ellie Ruth (Sept. 10, 2004) and William Romney (June 30, 2006). They live in Salt Lake City.

John Bryson was born on July 23, 1980. He was doted on and greatly enjoyed by his two older brothers and two older sisters, who gave him over a dozen endearing nicknames during his childhood. John's great personality wins him instant trust and friends. He is very loyal, a hard worker, and extremely kind and loving. He attended the University of Utah. John served a church mission in the Italy Catania Mission. Upon his return, he moved to southern California. He works in the direct marketing industry – mostly international. Not long after moving to California he met Jodie Shiotani. They were married in the Salt Lake Temple on August 1, 2003. Jodie graduated from Brigham Young University in Communication and after their marriage received her Masters of Business Administration from Brigham Young University. They are blessed with three precious children:

Stila Haruko (Dec. 22, 2005), Alexa Shiotani (August 24, 2007) and Brody Shiro (July 30, 2009). They live in Ladera Ranch, California.

As the kids were growing up, we had many fun family vacations. We all enjoyed going to California, Las Vegas, Hawaii, and Jackson Hole. Although it was often crazy traveling with everyone in the car, those are wonderful memories.

We love our children's spouses dearly. We are so fortunate to have them in our family. Our children and their spouses approach life with faith and hard work. It brings Dwight and me such joy to see them enjoy each other – good laughs, fun times, and helping to lift and bless each other. They live and exemplify their testimonies of The Church of Jesus Christ of Latter-day Saints. They are what make Dwight and me want to become better people. They bless our lives every day. Few relationships can equal those of parents and their children—unless it's the love and complete adoration we have for our grandchildren. To us, they are the dearest people in our lives. Each one brings such joy. I look forward with great anticipation to see what their futures bring. I hope they know we will always be here for them – loving and encouraging them in everything they do. We will always be their greatest cheerleaders.

In November 1984, Dwight received a call from Elder Bruce R. McConkie's office. He was a member of the Twelve Apostles of our Church. His secretary said that Elder McConkie would like to meet with Dwight and me in his office. We had no idea what this meeting could be about. We met with him. He was loving and kind, and told us that a list was being compiled of future mission presidents. He interviewed us asking many questions about our family, Dwight's work, and our testimonies of the Church.

We left his office feeling that possibly we would be put on a list for some future time when our children were grown. It was a humbling experience, but we didn't think we would be hearing any more about it for years.

Two months later, on the first Sunday in January 1985, as we were getting ready to rush out the door for church, the phone rang. The caller said, "This is Gordon B. Hinckley. Is Dwight there?" I handed the phone to Dwight and rushed (pushed) the children out the back door so neither party would be distracted by five not-so-happy-to-be-going-to-church children.

President Hinckley apologized for the informality of the call but said he was so consumed with his responsibilities that this was the only way it could be handled. At the time, President Hinckley was the 2ndCounselor in the Church to the Prophet Spencer W. Kimball and the 1stCounselor, Howard W. Hunter, both of whom were very ill. He asked if Dwight would accept a call to be a mission president starting July 1. He did not state where it would be—only that it would be a foreign mission. We were asked not to discuss this with anyone (other than our children) until it would be announced in March.

I was shocked and overwhelmed. At that point of time, the focus of my thoughts was the anticipation of moving five young children (ages 5 years–13 years) to a foreign country, what to do with the house, what happens with Dwight's law practice, how do we tell the children, and how exactly does one function as a mission president and his wife? With these thoughts weighing heavy on my mind, it was difficult to focus on the spiritual aspects and the great blessing it would be for our family.

We told the children a few weeks later and we received every reaction possible. Needless to say, Brad and Romney were the most concerned. They were 13 and 12 years old, respectively. Brad would be entering high school and Romney would be the next year. As time went on, we all realized what a great blessing it would be for us to serve our Heavenly Father and the experience of doing so in a foreign country would be an added blessing.

Our formal structured preparation was really minimal. We spent a few hours over the course of two or three days at the Missionary Training Center in Provo, Utah. There were general talks of inspiration and instruction given to all the new presidents and their wives. It was wonderful, but filled us with more questions that we knew couldn't be answered, except through first-hand experience in the mission itself. There was no language instruction. Dwight, of course, knew Italian from his mission but the kids and I wouldn't begin our study until arriving in Italy.

We were called to serve in the Italy Catania Mission in Southern Italy. Arriving there was unforgettable – two excited but bewildered adults, five excited but frightened children and many, many pieces of luggage. We were met at the airport by the out-going mission president and his two missionary assistants.

We began our Italian instruction with Signor Paci. The children caught on immediately, but it was more difficult for me and was a learning process for the entire mission. Signor Paci was the head master of the children's school—The English College.

Immediately we felt a bond with the missionaries. They were all wonderful to us and loved the kids. To the missionaries, our children were a piece of home for them. I can't even begin to describe the love I felt for the missionaries. They were so dedicated to their missions and so kind to our family. Many were serving while trying to handle very difficult situations at home. Their service strengthened my testimony.

The Church members had many struggles remaining strong in the faith and they were wonderful people. In some instances, they had to travel long distances to get to Church, but they did so faithfully. They were really the pioneers in Italy. They were so generous with their time and resources

– feeding the missionaries and helping each other—and us. Three weeks after arriving in Italy, John turned five years old. All the mothers and children from the Church branch came to our home with balloons, lovely gifts, and a beautiful delicious birthday cake. It is the only birthday party John has ever had where he didn't know anyone there! What wonderful loving people!

The mission home in Catania was at the top of the city. It was on a quiet street across from a monastery surrounded by an orange grove. The fragrance of the orange blossoms in the springtime is indescribable. Dwight drove the kids to school on his way to the mission office everyday and a couple of missionaries from the office would pick them up and drive them home.

The curriculum of the school was very different than what they would be learning in the States. John, who would be starting kindergarten at home, was required to write the Italian script when he didn't even know how to write in English. Ann Marie and Elisabeth got along fine in their classes and their teachers really liked them. Brad and Romney's curriculum was very strange and it became apparent almost immediately that, upon returning to the States after three years, they would be way behind their fellow classmates.

The real disturbing thing, however, was that every student, except Brad and Romney, was allowed to smoke in the classroom for seven hours, six days a week. The boys became physically ill, and we were very alarmed about their being in such an unhealthy setting. The Missionary Department in Salt Lake agreed that we could not allow them to remain in that environment. Elders Russell M. Nelson and Joseph B. Wirthlin assured us we would be transferred to another Italian mission when one became available in July. Until then we had no choice but to send the boys home to live with friends of the family. They were in different homes but saw each other at church and school.

We missed the boys terribly but we were so proud of their strength and determination to make the most of the situation. We knew we would be reunited the end of June. Although in some ways they were content to return home, they endured many challenges of their own—some of which we didn't learn about until after the mission. I am so proud of their maturity at such a young age.

In April, Elisabeth turned eight years old and was baptized in the Ionian Sea with two other children. Dwight's parents were able to visit and share that with us.

We made preparations to be transferred to the Italy Rome Mission the end of June. Brad and Romney returned and we all traveled throughout the mission to say goodbye to the missionaries and members we had grown to love very much. It was definitely a bitter/sweet experience.

Rome brought many changes for our family. The children's school, The American Overseas School of Rome, was an incredible experience for each of the children. Students from about 30 countries made up the student body and the curriculum was amazing. All five children perfected their Italian, made great friends, and lived a life that has influenced them to this day.

The mission home was located on a secure gated property next to the building that contained the mission office. From the balcony that extended out from the office, the missionaries could watch our children play outside. John would often stand on our property and call to the missionaries to come over "to play". Occasionally their mission president would give them permission to do so.

There is always a pull for a mission president's wife when they have a young family and it was no different for me. We traveled throughout the mission every six weeks to hold zone conferences. Our mission was very spread out and this was done over a four to five day period. Sardinia, a beautiful island, was part of the mission and the missionaries often felt isolated there. I felt a real need to go with Dwight to as many as I could – several times a year. When I was at home with the kids, I felt I should be with Dwight and the missionaries and when I was away at zone conferences, I felt I should be with the kids. At times we were able to take Ann Marie, Elisabeth, and John with us but Brad and Romney's school courses required a steady attendance.

It has been 25 years since we left for our mission and the memories are vivid and will always be a strong common bond in our family. As a family we talk often of the mission, Italian Church members, and missionaries (our missionaries, our family). We see and keep in touch with many of them. The mission shaped our lives and our testimonies. Each of us follows with close attention, everything that goes on in the Church in Italy. We are grateful to have been given this blessing at a time when our children could be part of it.

Upon returning from Italy, I took a job at Highland High School in the Attendance Department. With about two months left in the school year, the principal of the school, Dr. Cendese, asked me if I would be interested in helping him form a scholarship department in the school. His vision was to have me study and learn all I could about the various universities that the students would be attending, and advise them on the availability of scholarships at those schools and work with them to qualify and be accepted. It was truly overwhelming but I loved it. I worked at that position for two years. These students were very dedicated to their futures and I felt honored to be a part of that.

The local office for the International Visitors Council was looking for a new Director. At that time, Dwight was serving as the National Chairman.

Although it seemed like nepotism to me, the local board asked me to consider filling this position. I decided this would be something I would thoroughly enjoy. Under the administration of the State Department in Washington, D.C., professional business people and educators are selected to come to the United States and meet with their professional "counterparts" in various parts of the country. Over the course of many previous years we had hosted several of these guests in our home and it was something from which the entire family benefited. The local office maintained a small staff and we worked very hard to provide these hand-selected foreign visitors professional experiences that would be of importance to them and their careers. While our son, Romney, was a student at the University of Utah, he worked as one of our programmers.

I worked for three years at International Visitors. It was quickly becoming apparent, however, that with Dwight's busy travel schedule and my stressful job there was a void at home that needed to be filled. The kids were very busy in important phases of their lives and we felt that home was where I should be. Dwight is still serving on the local board and we continue to enjoy our association with the program, but the decision we made about my staying home has never been regretted.

For the past ten years I have served in the Salt Lake LDS Temple as an ordinance worker. Words can't describe my love for the Temple and the work performed there. I serve two days a week and they are the best two days of the week. I pray for continued good health so that I may serve for many years to come. In the Temple, I have had many experiences that confirm my belief in the truths that are taught there and in my Savior, Jesus Christ. It has given me a deeper eternal perspective.

My life is rich and full. My testimony of The Church of Jesus Christ of Latter-day Saints increases almost daily. Of course, I have challenges in my life and in the lives of Dwight and our children. I have peace, however, knowing that we are a strong family woven with the same values and hope for our future and that of our posterity – like those of my wonderful ancestors.

DWIGHT BRADLEY WILLIAMS

I was born October 27, 1943 at St. Mark's Hospital in Salt Lake City, Utah, during World War II. My mother, Janet Jardine Williams, had been notified that my father, Dwight James Williams, had been seriously wounded in action in Sicily in August. At the time of my birth, she didn't know whether my father was dead or alive. Fortunately, my father survived, although he had suffered a major head wound while the squadron he commanded was providing cover for Allied troops invading the mainland of Italy. I remember my father's testimony that he could not have flown the 90 miles back to his base or landed the Spitfire in his condition. He nearly died during surgery to remove shrapnel from his brain and then caught Malaria while recuperating in Northern Africa. Dad was firmly convinced that the Lord took over the controls of his Spitfire and brought him safely home.

My father was assigned to a series of Army Air Corps (that was before the US Air Force had been organized as a separate military branch) bases in Texas until World War II. I don't have any memories predating my family's move back to Bountiful where my parents rented a small yellow-brick home next to the Bountiful Mill Creek at 602 South Main Street, only a block south from my Grandma Jardine's home. My grandmother, Ada Bryson Jardine, was a very important influence on me as a boy. Above all, she was a saint. Grandma Jardine had been widowed since the early 1930s. My grandfather, Frank Jardine, died from "blood poisoning". Somehow Grandma managed to raise her three youngest children on a Spanish American War Veteran's pension that, with the federal government's generous cost of living increases, was only about $38.00 per month at the time of her death in 1973. Grandma always paid her tithing and recounted many instances when she had no money left. A former client or colleague of her late husband would drive out from Salt Lake City to visit her, saying: "I just couldn't get Frank out of my mind." Invariably they would give her money which tied her and her children over.

Grandma Jardine was the daughter of two pioneers from Glasgow, Scotland, Samuel Bryson and Isabella Nixon Boag Bryson (Samuel's second wife). The Brysons had experienced significant miracles in their lives. Samuel's mother was, as far as we can determine, the first female convert from Northern Ireland (County Down) to the Church of Jesus Christ of Latter-day Saints. One night in the early 1840s, Margaret Cowan Bryson, a widow whose husband John, a Sergeant in the British Army, had never

Dwight at two years old with his father

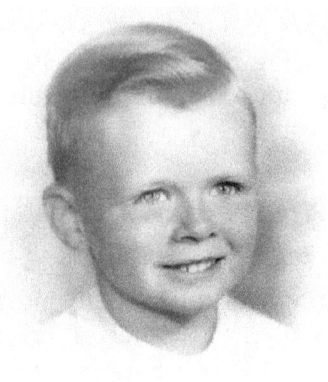

Dwight at age four

returned from the Battle of Waterloo, dreamed she heard heavenly music and saw two men giving her a book.

A few days later while at the market square in her village, Sister Bryson heard two Mormon elders singing the very same hymns from her dream. The missionaries, who had barely arrived in town, presented her with a copy of the Book of Mormon. When Margaret began to read it, she immediately knew it to be the word of God. Margaret joined the Church and prepared to gather with the Saints in Nauvoo, Illinois. But first she traveled to Glasgow to teach the gospel to her only child, Samuel. Samuel, his first wife, and their children all accepted the Restored Gospel and were baptized. After a short time, Samuel received the Priesthood and was set apart as the branch president.

After Samuel's conversion, Margaret left Glasgow for Liverpool where she embarked on the journey to join with the Latter-day Saints in Nauvoo, Illinois. On her arrival, Margaret secured a job as a nanny to the children of Mary Fielding and Hyrum Smith (the Church Patriarch and brother of the Prophet Joseph Smith). In June 1845, Margaret was living in the Smith home when news arrived that Joseph and Hyrum had been murdered by a mob at Carthage, Illinois. Sister Bryson remained a close friend of the Smiths and recounted how whenever she would attend General Conference in the Salt Lake Tabernacle, Joseph F. Smith, who had become an apostle and eventually became the Prophet and President of the Church, would come down from the stand to embrace her.

Isabella Boag and her sister lived in the same building as the Samuel Bryson family and joined the Church while Samuel was presiding over the

Mormon congregation in Glasgow. About twenty years later, Isabella immigrated to Utah, where she married Samuel Bryson. They later became my great grandparents. So we see that my little Grandma Ada Bryson Jardine, a daughter of Samuel and Isabella, came from powerful stock. Although she only had completed the 4th grade, Grandma ended up marrying Frank Jardine, an Englishman who had earned a degree in mining engineering at the Colorado College of Mines. Grandma read every book in Grandpa's vast library of literary classics as well as her own collection of many books written by LDS Church authorities. Grandma Jardine was not only well versed, but had a natural wisdom and exuded love and kindness for her grandchildren.

Grandpa Jardine was born in Northampton and came as a young man to stay with his uncle's family in Idaho. Frank was close to his cousin, William M. Jardine, who later became the U.S. Secretary of the Interior. During the Spanish-American War, Grandpa Jardine was one of Teddy Roosevelt's "Rough Riders". While training in Florida for the assault on San Juan Hill in Cuba, his horse fell on top of him. That incident resulted in a case of "blood poisoning" that was believed to be the cause of Grandpa Jardine's death decades later. Because Grandpa remained an Anglican but was married to the daughter of a prominent pioneer (Samuel Bryson was one of the Presidents of the 7th Quorum of Seventy in the Bountiful Stake), he was a perfect bridge between the Mormons and the non-members, many of whom had come to Utah because of the mining industry. This universal respect for Frank Jardine was reflected when he was named Chaplain to the second session of the Utah State Legislature.

I was terminally bored in grade school and as a result distinguished myself as a practical joker or, for those who lacked patience or a sense of humor, a problem student. That all began my immense loss of faith in the public school system and its "one size fits all" programs in general. A long time before I was old enough to enter kindergarten, I began to plead with my mother to teach me how to read. Mom responded: "Oh, no, Dwight B., I couldn't do that. I haven't been trained as a teacher and I might teach you the wrong way." I was disappointed but eager to see how an official public school teacher, who had been trained for the calling, would show me the right way to read. Unfortunately, my educational experiences at the Stoker School Kindergarten and first grade and second grade at Bountiful Elementary School were huge disappointments. I had the same teacher, Mrs. Twining, for all three of those years. She wasted large portions of each of the three years teaching the same colors, shapes, and numbers.

In the middle of my second grade year, my father was transferred from the Salt Lake City Airport to the Oakland Air Traffic Control Center. My family rented a small house on Harmony Court in Hayward in the East Bay. My brother, Mark, was born in April of 1951. For some reason my mother was not happy when I came down with a case of measles shortly thereafter. Jean also contracted them, but Mark did not. We all survived and during the summer, my family moved into a new tract home in nearby San Lorenzo Village. In November, I was baptized and later confirmed by Bishop Orval Ostler. We attended church in the Hayward Ward, about a half hour's drive away. I attended the third grade at the David E. Martin School in San Lorenzo, California. My main memory from that year is that it seemed to rain every day from late October until early May. I had a yellow rubberized, long raincoat with a matching yellow rubberized hat and galoshes. That gear kept the rain out, but I sweat so much inside them that it really didn't keep me dry walking to and from school.

The summer of 1952 my father was able to be promoted and transferred back to the Salt Lake Air Traffic Control Center. My parents moved back to Bountiful, which happened none too soon for my mother. My sister Barbara was born a couple of years later. From 1952 through 1958 we lived on over an acre and had various kinds of animals including, from time to time, rabbits, chickens, pigs, a Jersey calf named Sugar, and even a Shetland pony named Flash. They were all delicious. During my fifth grade year my neighborhood was bussed a long distance to West Bountiful Elementary. Our teacher, Drew Christensen, fortunately preferred reading classics to the class rather than following the usual, boring lesson plan.

Along the way I took piano lessons for nearly four years, beginning with a neighbor, Carolyn Smith, then with Joyce Greenhalgh, a nice lady in Bountiful who had studied at Julliard, and finally with Ed Stoker, a professional pianist in Salt Lake City who taught me chords. I also played the mellophone, sort of a wannabe French horn, but with the same kind of valves as a trumpet. Eventually, my dad bought a real trumpet for me, which I played from about the sixth through the eighth grades. The last three years I marched with the Bountiful High School band in the Ogden Days of '47 parade each summer. I began to enjoy school to a certain extent at Bountiful Junior High and made some good friends, most of whom were "band turkeys" like me.

Because my piano playing had given me more general exposure on assemblies, I enjoyed the ninth through twelfth grades at Bountiful High School even more. The Key Club officers invited me to join their club so that they could have an entry in the talent contest at the Utah-Idaho Regional Convention in Burley the spring of 1959. I won first place which also earned an invitation to compete at the Key Club International Convention that summer in Toronto, Canada.

During the summer between my ninth and tenth grade years, my family moved to 375 East Millcreek Way, which was just a block from Bountiful High School. About a year later the George Fisher Orchestra invited me to join them as their pianist when Garn Ford went on a mission. Although I preferred jazz to "moldy fig" dance band gigs, it was the latter that kept the band busy, often over ten jobs per month.

My classes at Bountiful High School were not very challenging, but I enjoyed several extra-curricular activities, including Key Club president, Jazz Club co-founder, newspaper staff, Utah Boys' State and Rotary Youth Leadership Conference. At the end of my senior year, I was accepted to Yale, Stanford and the Air Force Academy. Although I had dreamed for years of attending Yale, I ended up accepting the offer from Stanford.

During the summer following graduation from high school, I had a dramatic brush with death. My friend had been given a Triumph Herald convertible sports car for graduation and he suggested we drive it to Wendover, Nevada one afternoon. On our return, a violent rainstorm brewed up from out of nowhere. Although we were not driving faster than fifty miles per hour, the car hydroplaned. I suddenly found myself flying through the air. I only had time to exclaim: "God help us!" before ending up lying upside down in the dark with the car over me. My first sensation was the taste of salty sand in my mouth. Then I heard my friend yelling for me. John opened the door and I crawled out. My back was sore and I had a thin one inch long cut on top of my right wrist. Other than that, I had miraculously not been injured. I learned from the accident that God answers prayers. My friend, who attended the Community Church, scoffed at my claim and accused me of being superstitious. I thought it curious how two people could walk away from a brush with nearly certain death with such disparate observations.

My freshman year at Stanford was an awakening in many dimensions. Throughout that year I observed that although my contemporaries had come from diverse religious backgrounds, all of us were merely parroting the traditions in which we had been raised. I realized that I didn't have a testimony of the truthfulness of my own faith, but that didn't bother me too much until in February 1962 when a friend's parents told me what great respect they had for their Mormon friends in Palo Alto, including their mayor, David Haight.

That was a turning point for me. I decided I really needed to know whether the Church of Jesus Christ of Latter-day Saints was true or not. If it was true, I would do my best to live its teachings, but if not, why should I be bothered with the sacrifices, strict rules, and inconveniences? In any event, I didn't want to be a hypocrite. For me, it would be all or nothing. During Spring break while I was at home in Utah, a friend was also in home in Utah from Yale. Bob had been blessed with a strong testimony while in high school, in connection with which he had also built a base of gospel scholarship. Bob told me I was in an ideal position with the Lord because I was sincere about knowing the truth. Bob pointed out Moroni's promise at the end of the Book of Mormon (Moroni 10:4-5).

I decided to dedicate a thirty day period during which I would study and pray sincerely to learn whether the Book of Mormon was true. I hadn't noticed or felt anything happen until I woke up the next to last day in May 1962 and clearly knew it was true, that Joseph Smith had seen God the Father and His son, Jesus Christ, just as he had said, and that the Church of Jesus Christ of Latter-day Saints had been restored through messengers from heaven. I didn't know all that many details, but the pillars were all there. I didn't have any more doubts and I had the motivation to live the Gospel and have faith in the Lord. I am thankful to have had that faith continuously since that morning in May, 1962.

With substantial urging from my parents, I returned to Utah and transferred to the University of Utah for my sophomore year. Although I had not mentioned it to a soul, I had determined to serve a mission for the LDS Church the next summer. It seemed that I could prepare more effectively in Utah than in the über-liberal environment at Stanford. Most of my classes at the U. of U. were easy and required minimal homework. That left ample time for extra-curricular activities. I was asked to fill a vacancy as a National Student Association representative to the student senate. Through that connection I met great people and was encouraged to participate in fraternity rush winter quarter, which culminated in my pledging Beta Theta Pi. Being a Beta was a positive experience, especially because of the chance to meet a number of recently returned missionaries who reinforced my desire to serve a mission.

On Mother's Day 1963, Bishop Beckman interviewed me for a mission call, which I announced at lunch that day. I was excited to receive my call signed by President David O. McKay to serve in the North German Mission with headquarters in Hamburg. I began my mission at the end of June 1963. My first city was Emden, in East Friesland on the Dutch border. It was a shocking disappointment not to find the cultural mecca I had assumed to be present in all of Germany. The missionary work was difficult and few people were willing to speak with us. We had no "golden contacts". Fortunately, my companion was branch president and the members were great saints, so I enjoyed serving them. In late October 1964, I was transferred to the small, backwater village of Heide in Schleswig/Holstein. Once again, the members were great people and very supportive. On the other hand, although my companion and I worked very hard, the people there were mostly closed minded and we had no missionary success except for one good family that gained testimonies but didn't accept baptism because the husband, Herbert, couldn't stand the ridicule he received from his colleagues at work.

I was transferred to the mission office staff in Hamburg at the end of May 1964. The mission home was a marvelous experience. President Myers assigned me to be the *Propagandaminister* of the mission, with duties to publish the mission newsletter and then to assist the mission secretary. Not long after, Elder Ezra Taft Benson, who was presiding over all of the European missions at that time, had just announced that it was time to reinitiate missionary work to the Italian people for the first time since Lorenzo Snow had served there around 1850. President Myers had been informed that approximately 10,000 *Gastarbeiter* ("guest workers", a euphemism for cheap foreign laborers who were willing to handle the jobs Germans refused to do) were employed by the Volkswagen plant at Wolfsburg in our mission. Elder Benson asked that a new Italian-speaking district of four elders be opened there as soon as possible. President invited me into his office and inquired whether I had any Italian ancestors, to which I responded: "Well, my mother's maiden name is Jardine, which could have originally been spelled 'Giardini', although we haven't been able to trace it back to Italy yet."

The President asked me searchingly if I would be interested in working with Italians. I immediately responded sincerely: "If it's all right with the Lord, I would love to". Then, following a long pause, I told President Meyers that with all of my heart, I just wanted to teach honest people who would be willing to listen and that I was willing to pay any price for that blessing. In a few days I found myself back in President Myer's office. He had obviously received a confirmation that my personal desire was right with the Lord. My call to work with Italians was another defining moment. It was as though for the first time during my mission the lights suddenly came on, and I knew with perfect clarity that I had indeed been called to the right mission, but that the Lord had to keep me on the shelf and work on my humility, patience, and perseverance while He was pulling the other factors into place. The Lord knows the beginning from the end. This means that He also knows that we all have enough time to be patient in preparing for the special callings He assigns to us.

We had great success in teaching many good people in Wolfsburg and eventually baptized some Italian pioneers there. In August 1965, I was transferred to Brescia, Lombardy, Italy. President Rendell N. Mabey assigned me to be the District Leader of the Milano District, the Italian Zone of the Swiss Mission. The final four months of my mission could not have been more enjoyable. One to two hours of door-to-door tracting would fill up an entire week of teaching appointments. Even rejections were generally friendly and considerate.

During my mission I had decided to prepare myself for law school and looked forward to returning to complete my undergraduate studies at Stanford. The day after I arrived home, I felt an overwhelming impression that I should stay home and finish my undergraduate studies at the University of Utah and that I would meet my future wife there. I had very mixed feelings about abandoning my goal to receive a Stanford degree, but then learned that because of the Vietnam War, I would have to remain in ROTC and that I could not complete the sequence at Stanford without delaying law school for an entire year, so I reconciled myself to graduating from Utah.

My experience at the Beta house and reconnecting with my fraternity brothers helped me reenter the world after two and an half years of monastic life in Europe. I immersed myself in extra-curricular activities and took heavy academic loads as a political science major in the honors program along with several foreign language courses. I applied to law school at Stanford and Columbia (with the University of Utah as a backup) and felt I had a reasonable chance of being admitted somewhere.

During all of 1966 the dating scene was unsatisfying. I had come to the conclusion that I was finished with sorority girls and that perhaps I had misinterpreted the message not to return to Palo Alto. That all changed in January 1967 when I met Nan Romney in a political science class taught by Professor J.D. Williams. Nan was lovely, unpretentious and, as one of her friend's mothers told a friend of my mother, "Nan is the cutest of all the Delta Gammas and just as nice as she is cute". Not long after I met Nan, Columbia Law School accepted me in the Class of 1970. I was also accepted by Stanford Law School, but because of my focus on international commercial law, I opted to study at Columbia.

It didn't take long for me to fall in love with Nan. After an initial "I'll have to think about it" response to my offer of my Beta pin in April, which I interpreted as a complete rejection, to my great joy after a serious conversation, Nan accepted it. We became formally engaged just before my graduation the end of May and set a date to be married in the Salt Lake Temple on September 1 following Nan's graduation in August. We were sealed by President Marion G. Romney, Nan's father's first cousin. We enjoyed a beautiful reception in the Empire Room of the Hotel Utah (now the Joseph Smith Memorial Building). Incidentally, Nan's research over forty years later revealed that her great-grandfather, George Romney, had been the leading developer of the Hotel Utah. Nan and I only had a few days to find an apartment before my classes were to begin. Housing near the Columbia campus was very expensive, but we located a modest but cozy converted coal room with pink and blue tile walls in the basement of a nice town house on 106th Street near Riverside Drive. Our landlord, Tony Sava, a retired master tile layer from Puglia in Southern Italy had installed the tile walls himself. We enjoyed attending the Manhattan Ward. Our bishop, Earl C. Tingey, understood the time pressures on the many graduate students in the ward and his leadership provided a healthy activity level sufficient to stretch the members without an overdose of mere busyness. The quality of the speakers, the music, and the teachers was unsurpassed in my church experience. During our first year, Nan and I were in charge of Ward Activities. The next year I was Ward Executive Secretary, which was in reality leadership training. I didn't realize until years later that Bishop Tingey did most of the job while leading me to believe that I was doing the work.

Winifred "Winnie" Bowers, a friend from the Manhattan Ward, introduced me to Professor (Emeritus) Julius Goebel, Jr., a distinguished legal historian. He hired me as his research assistant during the summer following my first year and part time during my last two years of law school. During that time I cite-checked every single reference in Volume I of the History of the Supreme Court, the definitive study of the high court funded by the Oliver Wendell Holmes Permanent Devise. Professor Goebel even mentioned me in the credits. The good professor also let me work on the Legal Practice of Alexander Hamilton, of which he was editor-in-chief.

During my second year, I was finally able to take a number of international courses at Columbia Law School, which I found much more engaging than the first year foundational subjects. At the end of that year I was fortunate to be hired by Chadbourne & Parke as a summer associate. I preferred the work immensely more than the classroom. At the conclusion of the summer, Chadbourne offered me a full-time position following graduation.

At the beginning of my third and final year of law school, Bishop Tingey called me to be Elders' Quorum President. That was a challenging but very enjoyable calling. The next year, President George Watkins of the New York Stake called me to serve as an assistant stake clerk, which involved attending monthly stake leadership meetings in Westchester County. Our first son, Dwight Bradley Williams III (Brad), was born at Woman's Hospital on December 3, 1970, which was also Professor Goebel's birthday. Nan shared a hospital room with a new mother from Harlem who named her son Jambooli.

A few months later, I received an unexpected offer from a friend at Van Cott Bagley to join their firm in Salt Lake City. Nan and I flew home and decided that would be best for us and Brad. The level of professional opportunities in Salt Lake City was a letdown compared to Chadbourne, but in retrospect the decision to raise our family in Utah was nonetheless the right one. Nan and I enjoyed the blessing of being near our respective parents, all of whom except my mother passed away in just over a decade. When we completed our move to Utah, Nan and I rented an apartment on 11th Avenue, just two houses away from Nan's parents. Our second son, Wendell Romney Williams, was born there on July 3, 2002. About the time Romney was born I began serving in the 142nd Military Intelligence (Linguist) Company of the Utah National Guard, which I finished three years later. Not long after Romney's birth, we found an opportunity to purchase a building lot on upper Virginia Street behind the Shriners' Hospital, on which a friend built a nice, modern home for us.

Around the same time my friend Gordon Gee moved east and offered me to take over his job teaching Business Law in the College of Business at the University of Utah. In 1974 we purchased a Georgian home on Arlington Drive in Federal Heights. We were blessed with three more children while we were living there. Ann Marie was born December 29, 1976, Elisabeth April 12, 1978 and John on July 23, 1980. It became apparent that the home, which was an ideal size for a family with two children, was far too small to accommodate five. Because of the lot dimensions, adding on to the residence would not have been feasible.

While we lived on Virginia Street, our home was in the Federal Heights Ward, Salt Lake Emigration Stake. Our new home on Arlington Drive was also in the Federal Heights Ward. Around 1976, nearly all of the active elders in our ward, including me, were ordained to be seventies in the Emigration Stake. I had great church experiences as a seventy and was called to be a president in the stake seventies quorum, including the opportunity to teach and confirm a Japanese friend in direct response to Stake President Ralph O. Bradley's promise of success in missionary work.

I also was blessed with a marvelous friendship with Bruno Livio Gerzeli, a former professional soccer star who had joined the Church in Toronto, Canada. Bruno told me humbly that President Kimball himself had repeatedly admonished him to prepare for a mission call to teach the gospel to his people. Around 1980, Bruno asked me to travel with him to South America to check out a potential real estate acquisition. It became apparent very early in our trip to Chile that the business opportunity which had brought Bruno and me there was not going to be viable. Notwithstanding, the week turned out to be a divine gift in the form of a one-on-one tutoring session. A most unique experience presented itself when Bruno raised a young boy from the dead who had been hit in the head by the bumper of a large truck.

Not long after that experience, Bruno became ill and eventually passed away. Nan and I attended his funeral service, where the keynote speaker was Elder Thomas S. Monson. Beginning the eulogy, President Monson shared with the audience that the First Presidency not only had known and loved Bruno well, but they had actually spoken about him among themselves year after year when the Missionary Committee would forward recommendations for new mission presidents. Elder Monson admitted that President Kimball and his counselors had remarked whenever an opening for new mission president would come up in Italy, how strange it seemed to them that once again Bruno's name did not appear at the top of the list. The First Presidency had been vividly aware that the Lord had been planning for some time to call Bruno on a mission to his people. President

Monson explained that sometimes, as in Bruno's case, even the First Presidency might misinterpret certain details of truths which the spirit makes known to them. What they didn't get right was the venue, he admitted. "We knew that Bruno would soon be called to take the gospel to his people. We just hadn't understood that Bruno's call would not be to the country of Italy, but instead to the Italians in the spirit world."

Nan's father had a second heart attack and passed away in December of 1981. His cousin, Elder Gordon B. Hinckley, spoke at Wendell's graveside service. Nan's mother was living in Hawaii with Nan's sister, Janet. Eventually Janet brought Jeannette back to the mainland to live in an assisted living center. That summer we located a home on Berkeley Street and 21st South in Parley's First Ward. We lived in that home for almost twenty years. Nan's mother died in October, 1982 – just nine months after Wendell's death.

Around Thanksgiving in 1984 I received a phone call from Elder Bruce R. McConkie of the Quorum of the Twelve Apostles. He wanted to see me in his office. I began to worry whether I had done something wrong, but the fear left me when he asked if I would bring Sister Williams with me. When the interview arrived, Elder McConkie put us at ease by explaining to Nan and me that we were being considered in a pool of potential mission presidents. We had the impression that if a call were ever to come to us, it would be in several years, until in January 1985 the phone rang early on a Sunday morning. Nan answered, looked over at me and mouthed the announcement "It's Gordon B. Hinckley". She scurried to round up the children to leave for Stake Conference while I accepted our mission call over the phone. Driving to stake conference, my first impression was that the mission would be in Italy and that, ironically, I would be privileged to carry on for Bruno there. I also finally understood why the Lord had given Bruno and me that marvelous, ethereal week together in Chile a few years earlier. Both Nan and I were humbled by this calling and we looked forward to serving the Lord with our five children.

My favorite professor from the University of Utah, Elder Neal A. Maxwell, then an Apostle, set Nan and me apart to preside over the mission in Italy, he told Nan that she too had been foreordained to that calling. Clearly we would have been unlikely candidates had I not served that preparatory mission in the 1960s.

We arrived in Catania, Sicily on a beautiful sunny day, July 1, 1985. Because of the size of our family, a larger residence was provided in the village of Sant'Agata Li Battiati ("St. Agatha baptized them") about a third of the way up the slope of Mount Etna. The beautiful, spacious home had just been built in a planned unit development known as "Parco Inglese". The English reference was to note that the development was located on the last piece of property originally given to Lord Admiral Horatio Nelson by the Princess of the House of Catania.

Not long after we arrived in Sicily, Nan and our children checked out the available schools. They settled on English College. The Headmaster, Signor Paci, a former Roman Catholic priest, agreed to be their Italian teacher during the rest of the summer. Although classes were set to begin in early October, because the weather was still hot, the school didn't bother to open until near the end of that month. Brad and Romney's school situation was less than ideal. At ages 15 and 13 respectively, they were the only students who did not smoke during class, six days a week. Elders Joseph Wirthlin and Russell Nelson told us the Church could not allow its youth to be exposed to such serious health risks. They promised us that if we would endure the rest of the year, they would arrange for us to be transferred to one of the other Italian missions at the beginning of July. As a result, the boys returned to Utah, lived with friends of the family and finished the school year.

The Catania Mission covered the entire Island of Sicily and all of Calabria (the front of the boot), Basilicata and Apulia (the instep and heel of the boot) on the Italian peninsula. There were three districts and no stakes in the mission. That meant I had to conduct regular leadership meetings with the district presidencies. We tried to visit each district for missionary conferences every six to eight weeks and would coordinate our interactions with the local leaders and members with those visits. Our first visit to Bari occurred not long before the Italian vacation period, during which most of the members attended the temple in Zollikofen, Switzerland. I remember conducting interviews until nearly 2:00 A.M. Saturday night to accommodate all of the members needing to obtain or update their temple recommends.

Italy Catania Zone Conference with Elder and Sister Joseph Wirthlin

Zone Conference, Catania Mission 1985

Because there were no stakes in either the Catania or Rome Missions, the Mission President had to interview each person who went to the temple for the first time even though they had already been interviewed by their Branch President and District President. To avoid the long, stressful road trips, I flew a couple of times to Bari, but because it was necessary to transfer in Rome, the entire air trip ended up taking about six hours, the same as by car. Just at the end of my year in Catania, Alitalia finally initiated a daily direct flight between Catania and Bari.

We were transferred to Rome July 1, 1986. Brad and Romney returned to Italy the end of June. The Rome Mission was vastly easier in every way. In the beautiful villa in the Monte Sacro neighborhood, Nan had ample running water, the electricity and telephone always functioned, and the heating system worked well.

She was able to walk to a great open market just down Via Cimone. The children were blessed to attend the American Overseas School of Rome ("AOSR"), which was an excellent educational and social experience for each of them. They all thrived. Thanks to their experience in Catania and Rome, all five of them speak Italian well. Our missionaries became big brothers and sisters, best friends and role models to our children, which was a great blessing. The younger children enjoyed accompanying us to missionary conferences and district conferences in Florence, Naples and Cagliari. The childrens' interaction with the missionaries served as good preparation for their own future missions.

We had many great experiences and met many good people during our mission in Italy. One Sicilian brother, whom I was privileged to baptize, had been violently opposed to his wife's activity in the Church for decades. At his baptism, he wife bore a testimony that her husband "could not have been baptized one day earlier or one day later than today, because this was the day that he had agreed in the spirit world with the Savior to join His church". She then paused before concluding with the startling declaration: "My husband and President Williams were good friends in the pre-existence, and President Williams promised him that he would come and find him wherever he might be in order to baptize him on this day." I felt so humble and honored to be there and to have performed that sacred ordinance for my old friend.

That experience helped me to understand why my mission had begun in Sicily, notwithstanding the fact that two Apostles had informed me less than ninety days following our arrival in Sicily, that the missionary department appeared to have made a mistake in our assignment and that we would be transferred north at the first opening the next summer. In retrospect my baptism by fire in Sicily proved to have been immensely effective preparation for my next two years as president of the Italy Rome Mission. In fact, I am convinced that I was blessed through that preparatory calling to accomplish much more in every aspect in Rome during only two years there than I would have done in three years, had my service been spent entirely in the Rome Mission. On many occasions during my mission, both in Sicily and Rome, I felt Bruno Gerzeli's presence.

The missionary work progressed well in Rome, primarily because of the number of refugees and foreign laborers that just seemed to be led to our missionaries. Over the two years we were in Rome, the total number of convert baptisms doubled, while the number of Italian converts remained constant. A protestant pastor from Africa stopped two of our missionaries in a park one day and introduced them to a highly educated Iranian banker, Mohammed Amin Sani. The reverend told the Elders that Brother Sani's ideas about religion sounded like he was a Mormon. By the time Brother Sani had completed the missionary lessons and was baptized along with his wife and teenage son, Reza, he had brought several other Iranian refugees, a Czech and some Polish people, including a pediatrician, to the missionaries. Sani referred so many Iranian refugees to the missionaries, that I called four of our elders to learn Farsi. They called their district the "Persian Immersion". During the period I was in Rome, their district baptized over thirty Persians.

I had the privilege of interviewing the only child of the President of the Karl University in Prague, prior to her baptism. She did not speak English or Italian and I didn't speak Czech or Russian. Fortunately, we both spoke German, as did one of our sister missionaries who taught her the missionary lessons. Sister Reinholdova's father was a German communist who had ended up in Czechoslovakia after World War II and ingratiated himself with the party bosses. He was disgraced when his daughter fled communism for freedom in the West and embarrassed even more when she accepted Christianity and was baptized a Latter-day Saint.

One day, two of our elders came to the Mission office to report enthusiastically that the evening before they had been looking up a referral on the ground floor of an apartment building in Rome, when the lights went out and suddenly a crowd of people showed up in the lobby. The missionaries heard voices in an unintelligible language until suddenly someone asked in broken English: "You teach us your church?" It turned out to be a group of 18 young Hungarians who had fled communism to Italy. One of them spoke enough Italian to explain their desire to learn about the Restored Gospel, but none of the Hungarians spoke any language other than Hungarian at the level necessary to understand the missionary lessons. Although we didn't have any missionaries who could speak Hungarian, just the day before I had received the non-member mother of a sister missionary would soon be stopping in Rome. To her daughter's surprise, she agreed to interpret for me and the elders. By the end of the meeting, two of the Hungarians asked to be baptized. Eventually all 18 joined the Church.

Following our mission, I resumed my law practice. As a result of many wonderful spiritual experiences during the mission, I had lost the "killer instinct" that unfortunately is an important aspect of a lawyer's skills. I was grateful not to be a litigator. Because many new laws, such as the Tax Reform Act of 1986, had eliminated vast areas of my client base and a major client had just died in a tragic plane crash while I was in Italy, it took considerable time to reestablish my law practice.

I enjoyed callings in the Parley's First Ward as Gospel Doctrine Teacher teamed with Leonard Arrington, High Priest Quorum Instructor teamed with W. Cleon Skousen, High Councilor to President James Parkin of the Parley's Stake and later to President Bill Lloyd of the University Fourth Stake. I currently serve as Gospel Doctrine Instructor in the Cottonwood First Ward and as a veil worker in the Salt Lake Temple.

I am proud of each of my children. They have all married in the temple. Most of our children and their spouses have served a mission and each of them has achieved as much education as they desired. We have been blessed with 16 grandchildren who are the source of greater joy than I could have imagined. I have been greatly blessed with good health, a great family, good friends and marvelous experiences throughout my life. I gratefully acknowledge the hand of the Lord in all things. My greatest desire is to endure to the end and to be able to serve my family, the Lord's Church, and my fellow men in the future.

Dwight Bradley Williams III

Brad was born on December 3, 1970 – the oldest of five children. He was born in New York City following his Dad's graduation from Columbia Law School and one year practicing law with a New York law firm. We named him Dwight Bradley after his father and grandfather but always knew we would call him Bradley. When he was just six months old, we moved back to Salt Lake City to his first home in Utah on the corner of 11th Avenue and "K" Street – just half a block from his grandparents, Wendell and Jeannette Romney.

LEFT: *Brad as a baby* RIGHT: *Brad 6, Romney 5*

Brad was the first grandchild for Dwight's parents, Janet and Dwight J. Williams, the fourth for mine and the delight of everyone. From birth he was very alert, staying awake from 3 – 4 hours at a time. He seldom cried but completely enjoyed observing everything around him and, of course, loving to be entertained. At an early age he was like a sponge, soaking up every learning opportunity around him.

He began talking (very well) at 12 months. At eighteen months he could count from 1 – 10 in five languages. It was at this point that Dwight's parents made the comment, "You're not raising a child. You're raising a trained seal!"

At eighteen months Brad was sought after by the older kids in the neighborhood. He was one of them. They made him a partner in their lemonade stand, placing him front and center on the corner yelling, "Lemonade for sale." That was a successful summer business for all of them! Brad had a real love for cars. He could spend a long time just standing (he couldn't reach the steering wheel sitting down) on the front seat of the car pretending he was driving. With one car in the family, his favorite thing to do in the morning was "Take Daddy to work".

When Brad was 19 months old his younger brother, Wendell Romney (Romney) was born on July 3, 1972. He now had competition, which was not welcome.

We built a home on Virginia Street behind Shriners' Hospital and moved there when Brad was two years old and lived there for about three years. Brad had a neighborhood of friends and these little two and three-year olds began calling him Brad. At that point, we knew our desire to use his formal name of Bradley would not happen. To this day his wife addresses him as Bradley more often than anyone else.

At age three, Brad clearly needed more structure than we could provide him. He was bored and quite the challenge. We knew Rowland Hall had a very good Nursery School but the enrollment age began at 4 years. We applied and he was accepted. He immediately became the source of attention and curiosity for all the teachers. They observed that he was the smallest in the classroom (being the youngest) but, at the same time, caught onto everything the quickest— craving to go on to the next learning experience. They asked if they could meet with us and find out more about Brad. In theory, he became a "case study" for them.

When Brad was five, we moved to a home just a few minutes away on Arlington Drive. In this home three more siblings were added to the family, Ann Marie (Dec. 29,1976), Elisabeth (April 12, 1978), and John Bryson (July 23, 1980). In October, 1981 we moved to Berkeley Street where we lived until April, 2000.

Brad attended Wasatch Elementary, Roslyn Heights Elementary, Hillside Jr. High, Highland High School, and graduated from Rowland Hall, which he attended following our family mission in Italy.

Brad's first exposure to learning a foreign language was in Jr. High where he took a German class. The teacher had never taught German before and, because Brad had learned quite a bit of German from his Dad, he corrected the teacher on several occasions. It wasn't a pleasant experience for either one of them but it became evident that Brad had a talent for foreign languages – which would aid him later in life.

As an advantage or disadvantage, academics always came easily for

Brad – receiving high grades without having to work hard for them. His athletic talents are equally strong. Brad's interests have included skiing, snowboarding, tennis and running and biking.

In January 1985, Brad's Dad was called to serve as Mission President in the Italy Catania Mission. Brad was devastated, which we could understand, because he would be entering 9th Grade (high school) – an exciting time for anyone. His best friend had served a mission with his family in Washington, D.C. and their entire family assured Brad that it would be a wonderful experience for him. This was an encouragement we all appreciated. Before we left for the mission, both Brad and Romney received their Eagle Scout awards.

Our family packed up and moved to Italy in July, 1985. Unfortunately, because of the poor curriculum and unhealthy school conditions in Catania (everyone but Brad and Romney smoked all day long in the classroom), Brad and Romney had to return to Utah in January, where they lived with friends' families. Brad lived with the family who had been so encouraging to him. This was a great blessing because they assured him things would be much better for him when we were transferred to Rome in July, which definitely was the case

In Rome all the kids attended the American Overseas School of Rome. Brad had a great experience and opportunities while living there. The school had students who represented several countries and he made lasting friendships. He was elected Vice President of the Student Body, participated in the Model UN at the Hague in the Netherlands, and enjoyed a week-long Renaissance trip to Florence. His Italian was flawless. Friends from Utah visited and stayed with us in Rome which made the summers very enjoyable.

Returning to Utah after the mission, Brad graduated from Rowland Hall  and began his studies at the University of Utah, joined Sigma Chi Fraternity and majored in Political Science. After attending the University of Utah for one year, Brad served a mission for The Church of Jesus Christ of Latter-day Saints in the Switzerland Zurich Mission. Both he and Romney were on their missions at the same time and they had the opportunity to serve one day together in Romney's mission, Geneva, when Brad was renewing his visa. That day they had the opportunity to use the Italian they knew well on the family's mission in Italy.

During the 1996 Summer Olympics in Atlanta, he was asked by World Travel Partners to help manage a 7-month project. He enjoyed it and enjoyed living in Atlanta. His last year at the U of U, he served on the cabinet as Director of Student Programs. This experience is what began his passion and interest in working in the entertainment and sports industries. He was contacted by Capitol Records to be a Marketing Promotions Representative which led him to become an individual concert promoter.

Brad was the co-founder of the Spitfire Tour, a national spoken-word tour featuring celebrities, artists, and musicians which included Woody Harrelson, Bill Maher, Chuck Dee, and Kenneth Cole. The focus of this tour was not entertainment but rather the celebrities speaking about global issues of which they were passionate. They presented this on several college campuses around the country for two years and it proved to be a sought after and successful tour.

Upon graduation, Brad began work for Campus Pipeline, a ventured-backed technology company. He managed all of their entertainment, strategy, and partnerships. During this time he met Raina Bradford on a blind date. She was originally from Louisiana. Raina graduated from Brigham Young University in Recreational Therapy and served a mission for the Church in Arizona Mesa Mission. She was and still is a beautiful addition to Brad's life. They were married in the Baton Rouge Temple on September 2, 2000.

In September 2001 they moved to London, England where Brad had been accepted in a Masters Program at the London School of Economics. They took advantage of living in Europe and traveled to various countries during that time.

Returning from England, Brad and Raina moved to Boston where Brad accepted a position to work for Clear Channel Entertainment where he was in charge of marketing. Accepting an offer to work in Virginia for Ruckus, another venture-backed media and entertainment company, he joined them as their Vice President of Product Strategy.

Returning to Utah in 2006 Brad, was recruited by Skullcandy, a headphone and audio products company, to lead their brand marketing and business development. Brad is currently Vice President of Marketing and Brand Management for Siege Audio. His private consulting includes contracts for Monster Cable, Beats by Dr. Dre, Nitro Cirus, and other lifestyle brands.

Brad and Raina are blessed with five beautiful children: Annabelle Marie (January 2004), Luke Bradley (November 2005), Andrew Bradford (October 2006), Lillian Claire (Lilli) (November 2007), and Alice Mae

(March 2010). They are wonderful parents. Each one of their children has a zest for life, a vitality and enthusiasm that are so evident in both Brad and Raina. At the same time, they are teaching their children a love for their Savior and the importance of good values, love and service to their family and others and integrity.

Brad is a talented and unique person. His life has been blessed with a wonderful wife, precious children, and a testimony of the gospel. He will have many opportunities to bless the lives of those around him and pass on a rich heritage to his own family.

Wendall Romney Williams (Romney)

I was born on July 3, 1972 at LDS Hospital in Salt Lake City, Utah. My dad, Dwight Bradley Williams (born in Bountiful, Utah), was 26 years old. My mom, Nan Murdoch Romney Williams (born in Salt Lake City), was 24 years old. They named me after my maternal granddad, Wendell Romney. My older brother, Bradley, was born 19 months earlier. My sister Ann Marie was born in 1976, Elisabeth in 1978, and John in 1980.

My earliest memories of life are very happy ones. I always felt loved by my parents and safe at home. I can still remember what my soft white blanket (which quickly went dirty gray) smelled like and felt like against my cheeks – until it disappeared "mysteriously" when I started first grade. I was too young to remember, but my parents tell me that I never crawled. Instead, I "scooted" forward on my behind by pulling myself forward with my heels, regardless of the terrain. Fortunately, and contrary to the theory by some child developmental experts, I still learned how to read. My parents made bed time special by tucking us in "the daddy way" or the "mommy way" and telling Brad and me stories when we shared a room. While lying on one of our beds, my dad often taught us German vocabulary and expressions, in addition to playing a game called "Light and

Dark" with us in order to instill a sense of right and wrong. We went on some very memorable vacations to places such as Jackson Hole, San Diego, Disneyland, and Hawaii (where I learned – painfully – about the need to protect my fair skin from major sunburns).

Until the age of nine, I grew up in a neighborhood by the University of Utah in Salt Lake City called Federal Heights. Brad and I had a lot of fun playing together when we were young kids (once we graduated from sharp pencil attacks by the older of us two). In the basement, we played a lot of football and watched our fair share of NFL football games, The Price is Right game show, Saturday morning cartoons, and a kid's show called The Electric Company. My parents had a stereo that was such a huge piece of furniture that it literally spanned the wall of our living room like a credenza. I have fond memories of Brad and me pretending to play the guitar or drums in that room while listening to the "Sergeant Pepper's Lonely Hearts Club Band" Beatles album or Brad's "Saturday Night Fever" Bee Gees album. I realized how competitive our relationship was around age five, when I declared myself a Pittsburgh Steelers fan (because he was one at the time), only for his unexpected response to be "Okay, because I love the Dallas Cowboys" (the Steelers' biggest rival, whom he had detested up until that moment). Brad was a lot better at soccer than I was, but I didn't care, because I thought it was boring and considered it the sport you had to play until you were old enough to play the cool sports, such as baseball, basketball, football, and tennis.

I loved playing with my friends. Until about the age of seven, I played a lot with Wood Moyle, whose mom and my mom were best friends since high school. The two of us had quite an imagination for playing Star Wars, which we played with our friend Mike Hinckley. I had three close friends on the street where we lived when I was in pre-school: Jonas Armstrong, Trent Rockwood, and Allison Holman. Star Wars was a common theme when we played, as were "CHIPS" (a TV show about police officers), Army, and "Cowboys and Indians." Modes of transportation were primarily big wheels and dirt bikes with mag wheels. A nice old man in the ward, named Brother Volhei, treated Brad and me like the grandkids he never had. We made frequent visits to his house, where we played games and ate a lot of candy. He took each of us individually on the bus to Deseret Book downtown in the ZCMI Center before we were baptized, so that we could pick out our very own set of scriptures (with our name engraved).

My quality of life increased unexpectedly but dramatically at the age of seven, when my friend, Jonas, introduced me to the game of baseball. After a few minutes of playing catch with a tennis ball and Jonas' baseball gloves, I felt an unexpected connection with baseball that was far greater than anything I had experienced to that point in my life – with the exception of Star Wars. A couple of months later, Russell Farnsworth moved into our neighborhood. He had actually played on a baseball team the previous year and invited Brad and me to play on his little league team that spring. Russell and I became close friends and played a lot of baseball and Star Wars together. As third graders, Russell, Jason Johnson, and I were convinced that we could control the minds of the girls we had crushes on by whispering into the tops of our Chapsticks (lip balm) like the magic instruments they were. That theory was never disproven.

One week or so before my 8th birthday, I fell out of a tree while playing with my friend Trent Rockwood and broke both bones in the middle of my right forearm. I ran down the street toward home – with sheer terror and panic shooting through my mind – yelling, "My arm is broken! My arm is broken!" A visitor coming down the front steps with my parents commented calmly, "Why yes, it certainly is." Though I was worried I wouldn't be able to get baptized with a cast on (since they didn't have waterproof casts back then), my parents creatively wrapped my cast with an enormous black plastic garbage bag. During my baptism at the Salt Lake Tabernacle on Temple Square, a small pocket of air in the bag caused my arm to float to the top of the water. So my dad baptized me twice in order to ensure full immersion. That sequence of events, combined with how clean I felt upon exiting the baptismal font and our trip afterwards to have ice cream sundaes at Snelgrove's ice cream parlor, made my baptism day particularly memorable.

Certain things stand out in my memory about my grandparents. My Mom's parents, Wendell Bitner Romney ("Granddad") and Jeanette Murdoch Romney ("Nana"), were kind and very mild-mannered people. They were very proper and dignified. It seemed to me that my Nana always wore a turquoise dress with a diamond pattern. My Granddad's slicked-back silver hair and noble demeanor made him look like a true statesman. Their house on Eleventh Avenue in Salt Lake was always incredibly quiet and clean and smelled like Sanka. My favorite memories with them were drinking Nestle chocolate or strawberry milk and eating tuna fish sandwiches with chopped-up pickles in them. I also remember going with them on different occasions to The Tiffany Room in the ZCMI Center in downtown Salt Lake for an extra fancy egg and hashbrown breakfast or cup of hot chocolate. My Granddad was a big sports fan, so I liked to sit next to him on the living room couch and watch him while he watched games. Until the passing of my Granddad when I was nine, we had a tradition that I loved of opening their gift to us on Christmas Eve, which was often a pair of pajamas. My Nana died approximately nine months later while living in Hawaii with my Aunt Janet (my Mom's only sibling) and her family.

My dad's parents, Dwight James Williams ("Grandpa") and Janet Jardine Williams ("Grandma") lived in Bountiful, Utah. We visited them many Sundays for dinner, which seemed to be roast beef and mashed potatoes most of the time. Brad and I always seemed to find and consume several rolls of my Grandma's homemade apricot fruit leather. They were always very nice to us, though they recognized there was always a 70% chance that Brad and I would either break something valuable of theirs or permanently stain their couch or car seats (which explains the hard plastic cover on virtually everything upholstered that they owned). My Grandpa and I had a special bond through sports, because he was the only family member of mine living in Utah who liked to talk sports with me after the age of 10 (which was when I started to follow scores and stats). I loved that my Grandpa would pull out a bag of black liquorice and share it with me as "our secret" (he had a strict diet due to his heart problems). He had a small collection of amazing model airplanes (British Spitfires, B-52 Bombers, etc.) in the basement that I used to stare at for long periods of time with great pride that my Grandpa was a war hero. In fact, my Grandpa's life was saved miraculously after being hit from behind by a German fighter pilot and spiraling out of control toward the ground. My Grandpa passed away in 1990 after an unsuccessful heart surgery. While praying for comfort after his passing, I had a strong impression of the reality of the resurrection and that I would see him again one day. At the time of this writing, my Grandma is living in a retirement center. She is experiencing constant physical aches and needs a walker for support, but her mental faculties seem strong.

I'm embarrassed to say that not only was I an abnormally picky eater who didn't dare to try anything that didn't look like a plain hamburger, cereal, or white rice with soy sauce, but also that I gave my mom a hard time for making anything that wasn't on my short list of "approved" meals. To this day, I'm still amazed at my mom's capacity to love unconditionally and forgive.

School played an important role in my life from a young age. For Kindergarten through 3rd grade, I attended Wasatch Elementary. My 1st grade teacher, Mrs. Frech, informed our class that a little elf named Jeremy slept in our classroom at night. So at the end of many days at school that year, I built a bed and four walls out of small blocks and folded a tissue for a pillow, so that Jeremy would have somewhere to sleep. I laugh at myself now, but I appreciated my teacher's imagination and making me feel needed by a little elf.

When I was about seven, I learned that my dad had achieved some great academic accomplishments. From that point on, I wanted to follow in his footsteps and get straight A's for the rest of my life in order to attend Columbia University (like my dad, though I had no clue at a young age what that really meant). Starting in elementary school, I tried my hardest every day and loved spelling, reading, math, and recess. My dad reassured me that getting a B in handwriting was okay and didn't count toward my goal of straight A's, because (in his words) "the smartest people never have good handwriting." That still makes me laugh (and my handwriting is still hard to read – often times even for me).

When I was nine, my parents sold our house in Federal Heights. Unable to find a house to buy that felt right to them, we rented a house a couple blocks south of East High School on 13th East in Salt Lake. Brad and I attended Lowell Elementary that year. A couple weeks before my 5th grade year (in 1982), we moved into a house on the corner of Berkeley Street and 21st South in the Parley's area of Sugar House in Salt Lake. My Mom's cousin, Margaret Christensen, lived close by and I signed up for little league football before we moved in, so I knew some of the kids in our neighborhood before school started at Rosslyn Heights Elementary. It was an intimidating area to move into, due to some extremely strong personalities of certain parents and their kids who dictated what was cool. Luckily, I was accepted by some of the cool kids and felt at home sooner than I guessed I would. My closest friends my age were Dave Brinton and John Roberts.

By the age of 10, I was sure I wanted to play professional baseball for the New York Yankees (because my Mom and Granddad loved the Yanks). My friend, Matt Willey, and I rotated at shortstop and pitcher on our little league team, which was the first and only championship team I've ever played on in competitive sports. My favorite sports memories from that year were my first over-the-fence homerun, pitching a few no-hitters, and a 58-1 victory in baseball, though in hindsight I wish our coach had ended the game early or asked us to show some mercy toward the other team. My baseball hero was Ricky Henderson, who set the all-time record for most stolen bases. While watching Major Leagues Baseball's "game of the week" and other sports programs alone on Saturdays in our basement,

I dreamed of breaking his new record and practiced stealing bases for countless hours.

My 7th grade year was a new adventure with a larger group of friends and experiences. I took German and some new subjects that I really liked. I continued to love sports – especially baseball – and had my first "serious" girlfriend. I started to have a difficult time concentrating on topics that either disinterested me or did not come naturally to me, which meant I had to spend a lot longer than normal on assignments in those subjects. I realize now that symptoms of ADD (attention deficit disorder) were kicking in, but had no clue at that time what was happening.

Just when I thought things were going as well as they could for me in 7th grade, my parents informed us in March or so of that year they had been called by Elder Gordon B. Hinckley of the Quorum of the Twelve Apostles in the LDS Church to preside over a mission in Catania, Sicily for three years – starting that July. The move to a foreign place and subsequent transition were very difficult for Brad and me – and our negative attitudes didn't help the situation. I was slow to adjust to the reality of life in Sicily. I missed my friends immensely (I wrote several letters per day) and felt ripped off about the fact that we rarely had running water (we bathed in the non-working shower with bottled tap water) and our electricity and heat went out a lot. The missionaries were our only friends. My parents must have asked the office staff to look out for us, because they treated us like their own brothers and invited us to work with them some evenings and even let us have sleep-overs at the office. Though Catania was roughly the size of Salt Lake City, I only remember seeing one traffic light in the entire city. It was a crazy place. For fun away from the mission office, we rode our skateboards on our street. Brad and I joined a baseball club, but quit a couple weeks later when we learned that games were played on Sundays.

The school situation in Catania was the most challenging aspect of our life there. My parents found a school for all of us that had a very friendly headmaster, named Signor Paci, who spoke English and tutored us in Italian until the school year started. Little did we know that in school, Brad and I would be in the same class with former school drop-outs ranging in age from 15 to 21 (and Brad and I were in the 8th and 7th grade, respectively). To make matters more challenging, all of the other students and teachers smoked in our small enclosed classroom all day long. We came home from school sick every day. It seemed like we had a headache and sore throat for three months straight. In January, my parents felt our only option for receiving academic credit for that year was to send Brad and me back to Salt Lake, where I stayed with my friend Dave Brinton and his family for the remainder of that school year. Those were very long and lonely months for me, as most of my friends were really hard on me for reasons I wasn't aware of, I rarely saw Brad (he stayed most of the time at a friend's house in a different neighborhood), and it was too expensive to call my mom for support. That trial taught me some good lessons, however. It was during that time that I really thought about what it means to be a true friend and discovered the power of pleading for comfort and strength through prayer.

During that time away apart from my parents, my dad was informed that we were going to be transferred to Rome for the last two years of our mission, since the school situation there was much more conducive for an American family. At the end of that school year in Salt Lake, Brad and I went back to Sicily for our family to pack up and tour the mission to say farewell to the missionaries and members. It was clear immediately that our experience in Rome would be much better; we had many of the amenities of American life, the mission home was right next door to the mission office (which meant we could hang out with missionaries at the drop of a hat), and we enrolled at the American Overseas School of Rome. Brad and I frequently rode the bus downtown and explored a lot of Rome's amazing history and monuments. Our school was truly unique; the student body was made up of kids from over fifty countries and each grade had only roughly thirty students. My basketball team alone had players from China, Philippines, Taiwan, Iran, Philadelphia, Somalia, Italy, Sweden, Texas, Israel, and New Jersey. There was a wild social scene, which made for many uncomfortable weekend outings, but fortunately I made some good friends and ended up enjoying the experience. Brad was the big man on campus. He was a lot more confident than I was in that setting, so I watched him and slowly overcame my shyness in uncomfortable social situations by pretending to be outgoing. (The concept of "fake it until you feel it" became a valuable tool for me in challenges over the course of my life.) The combined workload of school and basketball was very demanding, but rewarding.

The highlight of my time in Rome was taking a Renaissance Humanism class my sophomore year with Mrs. Giammanco, which included a weeklong field trip to Florence at the end of the school year to see everything we had studied. Her passion for and insight into the Renaissance and its artists and Humanist thinkers who literally changed the world opened my eyes to a new way of thinking (which ultimately sparked my passion for entrepreneurship). Through my interactions with so many people from around the world and the chance to study Italian and French grammar and literature, I also gained a love for international affairs and foreign languages. One of the most unique experiences during my time in Rome was the unexpected chance at the end of my freshman year to co-star in an Italian movie (called "Maramao") on the island of Sardinia, where my mom and I lived for six weeks in a nice bungalow on a beach resort and ate every meal in the hotel restaurant with the other actors.

The countless miracles we observed in missionary work (such as the formation and growth of the International Branch and the conversion of Dr. Muhammed Sani and his family, who had fled Iran in search of freedom and truth) opened my eyes to the converting power of the restored gospel and how Heavenly Father provides hope and answers to all of His children who truly seek the truth.

At the end of our three years in Italy, I had very mixed emotions about moving back to Utah, but was excited to re-connect with friends and baseball. Soon after our return home, I wasted my movie earnings on a small Italian sports car, but loved the flexibility to get around on my own. As a junior at Highland, I played baseball (pitcher and center field, but never got my timing back completely after two years off), got involved in student Senate, worked as a dishwasher once or twice a week at a restaurant, and spent a lot of time with my friends. My experience at Highland had some negative aspects that motivated me to look into a local private school named Rowland Hall-St. Mark's, where Brad attended upon our return from Italy (his senior year). It had a lot more in common with our school in Rome, in particular its smaller classes and emphasis on helping students get into top colleges. My final decision to attend Rowland Hall was inspired by the movie Dead Poet's Society, based on a prep school with a teacher who challenged all of his students to "seize the day." But because I applied for admission and a scholarship a couple of weeks before the start of the school year, all the scholarship money had been allocated. However, as a complete answer to prayers, a large portion of the tuition came out of nowhere as a donation to the school. I loved my senior year at Rowland Hall and felt very lucky to be there. Due to the extremely heavy workload, college applications, and extra-curricular activities (I played baseball and was involved with student government), it was common to study until 1:00 or 2:00 A.M. and pull all-nighters a couple times a month for papers or tests. Since there were few LDS students there, I felt others observing me constantly to see if I was LDS by name or by action. On weekends, I hung out quite a bit with old and new friends who attended East High and worked each Saturday night during the school year in the kitchen of an Italian restaurant in order to earn spending money.

Though I had always wanted to go to Columbia University to be like my dad, when it came time to decide on college, I wasn't sure where to go. This was due in part to how much more expensive it would have been to attend Columbia over the other schools where I had been admitted. I decided to attend Tufts University in a suburb of Boston, due to its International Relations program. Though I had some good experiences and met some amazing people at Tufts, my freshman year there was far from what I had anticipated it would be. A few weeks into the first semester I was diagnosed with a severe case of mononucleosis and strep throat. Immediately upon being diagnosed, I slept all day for a week straight in the on-campus health center, waking up in the evening to eat. Due to the risk of rupturing my spleen from physical contact, I dropped out of fall baseball. Though I knew baseball was no more than a hobby for me at that point, it was hard to accept that I would no longer play the sport that was the first true love of my life. The most trying aspect of my bout with mono was the incessant panic I felt that I would no longer achieve my goals for graduate school and business, due to the inevitability of receiving bad grades that semester (I was only able to drop two of my five courses). But that experience made me rely on the Lord and realize that I had to trust in Him to navigate my course in school.

When I submitted my mission papers while in Boston, I had the clear impression that I would be called to the Switzerland Geneva Mission (which was the French-speaking mission with the most Italian speakers). I was so sure about it that I told people at Tufts that was where I was going long before I had received my call. I returned home after my freshman year pretty sure I would not return to Tufts, but excited to get ready to go to the Missionary Training Center (MTC) in Provo, Utah in July and afterwards to Geneva (where I was called to serve). That summer, I realized if I gave my whole heart to my mission, my college plans would work themselves out afterwards.

From the first day in the MTC, it was painfully clear I had a lot to learn about the gospel and my testimony needed a lot of help. While there, I was blessed with undeniable experiences that strengthened my spiritual foundation and assured me that I was in for many life-altering opportunities. Early on, I adopted the "fake it until you feel it" motto when I needed to gain a testimony about a certain doctrine or lacked enthusiasm about difficult things, such as companions or tracting when I was tired or facing discouraging circumstances. It is difficult to summarize such a life-changing two year stretch of life, but we saw countless miracles. We were unquestionably doing the work of the Lord. As with any form of service, I grew more than anyone I served. I had the blessing of working with some great companions and amazing people. Some elect people did join the Church – some of whom are still strong members of the church today. I served in a total of five cities (Renens, Sion, Geneva, and Lausanne in Switzerland, and Lyon in France) and had over ten companions. Local food favorites (and delicious comfort foods on long, cold days) included Swiss chocolate, cheese fondue, tomato fondue, warm baguettes, and melted Raclette cheese.

Approximately eight months into my mission, I had the opportunity to work one day with my brother, Brad, who was in the neighboring mission in Zurich. This was orchestrated by our mission presidents who understood how much such an experience would mean to both of us. We had the privilege of ending our day together by committing to baptism one of my investigators who spoke both French and German. Brad was a great mentor and role model to me throughout my mission. My mission was all more than worth the sacrifices and hard work. Anyone with the opportunity to serve an LDS mission should go and give 100%; the blessings and growth that come will take your life to an entirely new level.

After my mission, I decided to live at home with my parents and go to the University of Utah in order to enjoy a balance of academics, church, and social life. My short-term plan was to pledge the Sigma Chi Fraternity (Brad and many of my friends had joined before their missions) and then apply for a transfer to Stanford. But as a welcome twist of fate, I ran into Alecia Thompson two months after my return home, which was one week before the start of fall semester. We didn't know each other well, but Alecia's family lived one street down from the house we moved into when I was 10 (she was 9 at that time). On our first date, it felt like I had known her well my whole life and we were just re-connecting. On our second date, I found myself in total amazement about her charismatic personality, curious intellect, mature perspective on life, and numerous talents. I sat at lunch with her, thinking to myself, "I'm either a weird returned missionary who thinks everything is revelation... or I'm talking to my wife." On our third date, I knew I wanted to be with her the rest of my life.

That January, after my initiation into Sigma Chi with 44 pledge brothers (some of whom will be life-long friends), I joined Alecia for an internship in Washington, DC. After several memorable months, we noticed that something was missing in our relationship. We didn't feel ready to discuss marriage, so we decided to break up and see if things would change in time. After three heart-wrenching months apart, Alecia told me she was literally (and unexpectedly) called on a mission while sitting in church. So she submitted her mission papers, was called to Dusseldorf, Germany, and left on December 6, 1994. We made no post-mission plans regarding our relationship, but we agreed to write each other. My heart ached daily for her to come home and I didn't think the time would ever go by. But because I knew how impactful my mission was on my life and my testimony, I was excited for her and supported her 100%.

While Alecia was on her mission, I got heavily involved with my coursework (my major was Political Science), student government, and Sigma Chi. I worked part-time at International Visitors - Utah Council (IVUC) with my mom in order to have enough money to get by. Later, my cousin, Mark Hull, and I decided to start a parasailing business together, which fueled my interest in doing entrepreneurial ventures over the course of my career.

Upon graduation in March of 1996, I got a full-time job at Utah Technology Finance Corporation in downtown Salt Lake. The President, who was also Chairman of IVUC, placed me as interim Executive Director at IVUC after my mom retired from that position. After what seemed like a decade, Alecia returned home in May.

I was amazed to see how she had remained her wonderful self, but had gained such a strong foundation in the gospel. It was so natural for us to be together that we got engaged in August and were married two short months later in the Salt Lake Temple on October 19th. After a long courtship, we were finally able to start our lives together officially.

We have always loved spending time with each other. Some of our favorite activities in our first year of marriage included going to movies at the dollar theater, making smoothies, and getting bagels and watching college football games in bed on Saturdays. We saved up money that entire first year in order to take a trip to Alecia's mission, my mission, and Rome (with a day trip to Florence). It was a once in a lifetime trip for us. We loved every minute of it. I can't wait to go back to Europe with Alecia.

Shortly after our wedding, Alecia and I began managing a condominium complex near the University of Utah (called Arlington Place). Once we were in a position to pay our bills with that income and free rent, Alecia encouraged me to pursue the parasailing start-up full-time. But shortly after Mark and I had secured a location to operate in North Myrtle Beach, South Carolina, he and I decided to pursue separate entrepreneurial paths.

For my next job, I joined an internet start-up in the early phase of the internet boom (1997). But when both Alecia and I lost our jobs one month after purchasing a starter home in Sugar House, I was introduced out of the blue by a friend to Ted Hoff, who was a partner in a management development firm in Boston that had spun out of Harvard Business School. The job and move proved to be an invaluable opportunity to learn from a brilliant mentor, have our marriage solidified by having to rely solely on each other without family around, and gain life-long friendships with sharp couples in our ward.

Soon after I started my job in Boston in August of 1998, we were elated to find out we were expecting our first child. A couple months into the pregnancy, two different tests indicated our baby had Downs Syndrome. But after Alecia received a Priesthood blessing from her dad that the baby would be perfectly healthy, another test confirmed that a miracle had indeed occurred. Thomas Romney Williams was born on April 19, 1999 (Patriots' Day in Massachusetts, the day of the Boston Marathon). From very early on, he was very intense and strong-willed.

While in the middle of the application process for business school in the year 2000, I had the opportunity to interview at an early stage high tech start-up that had spun out of MIT, called SMaL Camera Technologies. The founders offered me a position that I would have hoped for coming out of an MBA program, which was to lead marketing and business development as the sixth employee. After we accepted the offer, we bought a small townhome in a neighboring suburb called Arlington. We loved our new ward from the beginning, had some positive learning experiences through various ward callings, and eventually cultivated several life-long friendships. We were also able to observe the examples of numerous church members in the Boston area who were literally changing the world in their professions while faithfully raising families with a strong foundation in the gospel.

2001 was very exciting for us. Our little company debuted its first product at the International Consumer Electronics Show in Las Vegas, where we won "Best of Show" for digital imaging. That exposure immediately catapulted the company on the global stage, generated high-profile press coverage throughout the US and abroad, and positioned us to raise funding and line up solid customers. It was a highly intense experience that I felt lucky to be a part of (and Alecia was very patient with the demanding workload). More importantly, our first daughter, Lauren Kathryn Williams, was born on May 18, 2001. Lauren was extremely pleasant and highly charismatic from day one. When she was a couple years old, we started calling her "La dee dah" and "La" – nicknames that stuck.

The following two years, which were very enjoyable for our little family, included a move to a 1930 colonial in Arlington that Alecia transformed into a place we loved (a process she referred to as "getting rid of Grandma's wig").

2004 was also a very eventful year. Our third child, Christian Thompson Williams, was born on May 28 of that year. He had (and continues to have) the happiest eyes and a very sweet disposition. He never ceases to melt my heart with endearing sayings such as, "Hey dad... you're my buddy." A week before Thanksgiving, we sold our house, said goodbye to good friends, the Red Sox, and a beautiful part of the country that we called home for more than six years, and moved to a suburb of Dallas called Flower Mound. We were close to selling SMaL and I wanted to pursue my own start-up, so I secured the rights to be area developer for a franchise concept in the auto glass industry.

The warm winter weather and people were some of the many things we loved about Texas. Many struggles with employees taught me that very few employees who do not have ownership in a company care about the owner's dreams and risks in the business. After only six months, a sudden shift in the auto insurance industry cut my margins by 40%. The corporate founders and I realized that the shift reduced our chances for achieving our goals in the business so dramatically that we decided to shut down the franchise program and for me to join them as a partner in Utah in hopes of re-inventing the business.

Left to Right: John, Brad, Elisabeth holding William, Ann Marie, and Romney in August 2006

Though Alecia and I had planned initially to stay in the Dallas area for five to eight years, in July we sold our house and relocated back to a suburb of Salt Lake called Sandy. Though the circumstances of the move were not ideal, it was nice to be reunited with family and old friends in Salt Lake. On the business side, we analyzed various ways to evolve in the auto glass industry, but concluded ultimately to shut down the business entirely at the end of the year. It was a difficult realization, but in hindsight it was the right decision.

Since 2005, the entrepreneurial path has taken some eventful twists and turns. Through my company, Entrepreneur Launch Group, I've been able to advise or consult for various entrepreneurs and business owners, including an enjoyable opportunity to work with my brother-in-law, Jesse Theurer. In two situations, I was hired on full-time in exhilarating but short-lived positions. The first was to lead marketing for a local company called AK Designs that designed and sold chairs in retail stores nationwide. Most recently, I ran an international prepaid debit company with an amazing mentor named Joe Kwiatkowski, an industry veteran from American Express.

2006 brought some big milestones for our family. On May 22, 2006 our fourth child, Sophie Nan Williams, was born. She looked quite a bit like Lauren, minus the chubby cheeks and had a sweet demeanor. In October, Alecia and I celebrated our tenth wedding anniversary. I have been deeply blessed to share my life with someone who has such an ability to love unconditionally and willingly take care of so many of our kids' and my needs. She has always been an unwavering support of me and my unconventional wiring as an entrepreneur, despite the roller coaster nature of that professional path. The highlight of 2007 was Thomas' baptism and confirmation. It felt strange to be old enough to baptize my own child, but it was an amazing blessing to be a part of. The gift of the Holy Ghost has had an indelible softening effect on Thomas. In May 2009, I had the privilege to baptize and confirm Lauren. In the summer of 2009, we sold our house in Sandy, Utah and moved to the Sugar House area of Salt Lake by my brother Brad and my sister Elisabeth and their families.

It has been exciting to watch all of our kids grow and develop their talents and interests. Thomas loves Star Wars, Legos, architecture, playing on the computer, reading, and sports. Lauren gained a love for reading at a fairly early age, always seems to be dancing or performing in some way, and enjoys playing with Polly Pockets and dolls (especially her American Girl doll that looks like her). Christian really looks up to Thomas, loves playing with any type of ball, and doesn't quite understand why he can't play on Thomas' baseball and basketball teams. Sophie has been a source of real joy for our entire family and makes us laugh with her funny faces and cute sayings. Alecia and I have absolutely loved seeing the impact our parents and siblings have had and continue to have on each of our children. We are grateful for our blessings and look forward to the next chapters in our lives.

Ann Marie Williams Kenney

I was born on December 29, 1976 at LDS Hospital in Salt Lake City, Utah. I was born to amazing parents for whom I have a great deal of admiration and respect. My father is Dwight Bradley Williams and my mother is Nan Murdoch Romney Williams. I was the third child and first daughter born to them. My older brothers are D. Bradley Williams III, who was six years old, and W. Romney Williams, who was four and a half years old when I was born. When I was 15 months old my sister Elisabeth Williams Theurer was born and when I was three and a half, my brother, John Bryson Williams, was born.

My earliest memory is from when my brother John was born. I remember my dad telling us we needed to be good at the hospital when we went to visit my mom and the new baby. He told us if we were he would take us to 7-Eleven after to get a treat. I remember being so excited to see my mom again. I missed her a lot the few days she was gone. I can still remember my dad holding me up to the window of the newborn nursery to get my first look at my new baby brother.

I had a very happy childhood. My parents were so kind and showed us a lot of love. I always felt safe and protected at home and around my parents. My dad had a love of languages and food and taught me to as well. He loved teaching us words in German, French, and Japanese.

I was a very shy little girl. I never left my mom's side. I remember my sister, Elisabeth, being all over the place and not being afraid to talk to strangers. I will never forget the day I didn't want to go to Preschool at Small Wonders in Salt Lake. I was probably four years old. Elisabeth and I were only a year apart in school so we went there together but in separate classes. My mom was dropping us off at school and I did not want to get out of the car because I wanted to stay home with her. She took Elisabeth in and I remember crying and hiding in the back seat hoping I wouldn't be found once she came back. She came back with my teacher and they both pulled me out of the car kicking and screaming. I was crying so hard, and of course, all of the kids were staring at me. My mom eventually left me at school heartbroken and very nervous. Now that I am a mom, I look back and know I would have done the same thing. She was probably just as heartbroken to leave me like that, but she knew it was the only way I would learn that I could be okay when I wasn't with her.

When I was five, my family moved from the house I was born in on Arlington Drive to a rental house on 1300 East. They wanted to shop neighborhoods and wards before buying a new house. I remember while we were living in the rental house my parents bought a bright yellow VW Vanagen. It had a sunroof almost as big as the roof of the van. I got my finger shut in the sliding door the day they bought it.

I loved having a sister so close in age. It was like having a constant friend around. That is, when we got along! We shared rooms up until my brother, Brad, went on his mission and I got his room. We loved playing with our dolls and Barbies. We often played house and I always pretended my name was Stephanie. My mom had given us a glass tea set that she played with when she was a young girl. We loved to pretend we were at a tea party. Unfortunately, we weren't too careful with the tea set. I think only a few pieces weren't broken.

We spent a lot of time at my mom's parents' house in my early years. My Granddad was Wendell Bitner Romney and my Nana was Jeannette Murdoch Romney. They lived very close to us on 11th Avenue in the house my mom had grown up. They were very kind people. I loved going to their house. It always smelled like coffee. My Nana was a very classy lady. She was always very well dressed. She usually made us tuna fish sandwiches mixed with cut up bread and butter pickles. I never did like tuna fish, but for some reason my Nana's always tasted good to me. My Granddad's favorite drink was Countrytime Lemonade and he always shared it with us. My Nana got Alzheimer's and my mom and her sister, Janet, decided she should go live in a Nursing Home. I still remember the smell there from when we'd visit. It made me sad to see my mom go through seeing her mom forget who her own daughter was. She passed away when I about five years old. My Granddad died from a heart attack the next year.

My dad's parents were a big part of our life also. We often had Sunday dinner at their house in Bountiful. My Grandpa was Dwight James Williams and my Grandma Janet Jardine Williams. They loved to travel the world and I liked looking at the souvenirs from their trips. My Grandpa was a very sweet man. He had a warm smile. My Grandma made sure we always had fun when we came to visit. She taught us how to make wheat bread from scratch. She even showed us how to grind the wheat. We loved making "Shrinky Dinks". We'd color a picture on a special paper and she'd put it in the oven where it would shrink and turn hard. We loved teasing Grandma by going out in her garden and eating a few pieces of fresh chives. When we went back inside we'd pretend to give her a kiss, but instead we'd breathe our chive breath on her! She had concocted an interesting dish she called "Potato Hoggabush". It had ground beef, potatoes, and different spices. It looked disgusting and probably was, but Elisabeth, John, and I loved it. My Grandpa passed away when I was 14 years old after one of his many heart surgeries. My Grandma will turn 90 in a few months. A few years ago she became unable to go up and down the stairs of her house due to severe back pain. She decided it was time to move to a Care Center where there would be help for her if she needed it. She has a hard time getting around, but her mind is still very sharp. I always enjoy seeing her when we have family gatherings.

I remember Elisabeth and I always had matching outfits. I would usually have the pink version and she'd have the yellow or purple version. We of course had matching shoes as well. Clogs were popular when we were preschoolers. I had a red pair of the sandals and she had a white pair. One day, we must have gotten into a fight because Elisabeth threw her clog at me. It hit me on the forehead and cut it open! My mom quickly piled me, Elisabeth, and John into the car. She dropped Elisabeth and John off at my grandparents' house and took me to the hospital to get stitches. I still remember holding a wet washcloth over the cut while on the way to get it fixed.

Just a few months before I started Kindergarten, my parents bought a home just off of 21st South and 2300 East on Berkeley Street in Salt Lake City. We would live in this beautiful home for 20 years. I attended Rosslyn Heights Elementary School and we were in the Parley's 1st Ward. My Kindergarten teacher was amazing! Her name was Mrs. Bitner. She was a distant relative of my mom's. My 1st grade teacher was Mrs. Clark. She was really strict and had a time out box she would make her students sit in if they did something wrong. I made sure I never had to sit in that box! My 2nd grade teacher was great and her name was Mrs. Cundick. I remember her reading us the book *Charlotte's Web*. I was really lucky to have a great group of friends in my ward. These friends were Rachel Scalley, Ann Christenson, Amanda Harris, and Katie Holman. Hailey Bateman was a good friend as well and she was in the Parley's 6th Ward. I loved spending time playing with my friends. I remember we liked playing with our Barbies, Strawberry Shortcake dolls, and our Cabbage Patch Kids dolls.

A big love of mine was dance. I started taking ballet when I was 4 years old. When I moved into our new neighborhood I took ballet classes with my friends at Miki Cassalino's and later on at the Children's Ballet Theatre. I became pretty good at it and was so excited when I made it to Pointe. In the 8th grade I quit because I was too lazy to get out of bed on Saturday mornings for an 8:00 A.M. class. This is a huge regret of mine.

A huge turning point in my life came while I was in the 2nd grade. One night towards the end of that school year, my parents sat us down in our family room. I can still remember where everyone was sitting. My dad told us he had been called to serve as the Mission President in Catania, Italy for our church, The Church of Jesus Christ of Latter-day Saints. He was only 41 years old. I was so young that I didn't fully understand what he was saying. I just knew we were moving to a place I'd never heard of and we'd be learning a new language. My brothers, Brad and Romney, were very upset. They were in the 6th and 7th grades. I remember them yelling and slamming doors in anger. They did not want to go! Looking back now, I realize how much faith my mom and dad had to answer a call like that from our Heavenly Father. My dad was willing to leave his job as an attorney for three years and move his family to a foreign country, and my mom was incredible to support my dad and take all five of us kids along.

We left for our three year adventure the last week of June 1985. On our way to Catania, my parents took us to Paris, France, and Rome, Italy to do some sightseeing. I remember thinking they were beautiful cities.

We arrived in Sicily July 1, 1985. The mission home was beautiful. It had marble floors throughout. Even though it was in a beautiful neighborhood, we were without electricity a lot and often had to take baths in bottled water my mom would heat on the stove. We took Italian lessons from one of the professors at our new school, English College. His name was Signor Pacci. He was a very nice man who spoke English well. He smelled of coffee and cigarettes. He taught my mom, my siblings, and me Italian six days a week until school started that October. We learned quickly that Sicily was a very relaxed place. The summer weather was so nice that year, that the school officials decided to move the first day of school from September to October so the Italians could spend more time at the beach!

I was very nervous to start the 3rd grade. I didn't know any of the kids in my class and I didn't speak the language well at all. Before arriving in Italy, I only knew how to say "ti amo", which means "I love you". I had often heard my mom say that to my dad at the end of phone conversations. My teacher was a very sweet girl. Her name was Maestra Laura, which means "teacher Laura". She was very kind to me and made me feel comfortable in such a strange place. I found out quickly that I was pretty far behind the Italian students when it came to math. In America, I'd only learned the 2, 5, and 10 times tables. Well, in Italy, my classmates already knew their times tables up to 12! I was forced to learn them on my own at home. I remember my mom spending a lot of time with me trying to help me memorize them. It didn't do any good. I knew I was already behind and my brain just shut off when it came to math. To this day, I dislike math greatly!

My parents realized a few months after we were in Catania that the school situation for Brad and Romney wasn't going to work. The junior high and high school kids at the English College were all put in the same classroom, and most of them were dropouts in their twenties who had decided to go back to school. On top of that, they smoked all day in the classroom the size of a bedroom. My parents had to make a very hard decision to send Brad and Romney back to Salt Lake City to finish up that school year so they wouldn't get any farther behind. I remember how sad my mom was to send them back to Utah. They each stayed with families of their friends.

My mom tried to make the best of our situation. Sicily was a lot like a third world country. It was dirty and old and smelly. She wanted life for us to be a lot like it was in America. She signed Elisabeth and me up for ballet lessons. I remember the studio was far from the mission home. She'd drive us there once a week and wait until our class was over. The studio was old and very small. It felt like a dark cave. And of course, it smelled like cigarettes because our teacher smoked constantly during class. I remember we had a recital and we wore beautiful white leotards with a white tutu.

My dad drove us to school every morning on his way to the mission office. One morning in particular sticks out in my mind. We were very close to arriving at our school. We turned a corner and came upon a store that had been bombed the night before. There were policemen all around it and it was taped off. My dad explained to us that the store owner had obviously not paid his "protection money" to the Mafia. This is when I learned that the Mafia has a lot of control over the Sicilians. I remember a trip we took to Palermo, which is the city of the Mafia headquarters. We were there for a Zone Conference with the missionaries in that area. While driving on the freeway outside of the city, we came upon a car that had been blown up. This also was the Mafia's doing. It was pretty scary to see things like that every now and then.

The English College was a very small school. The playground was incredibly small. It only had one slide for the students to play on. We were the first Americans the students had ever met. Elisabeth and I would get asked all of the time to teach the kids English. All Italians take English lessons starting in elementary school. Since our teachers didn't know what to do with us during English lessons, we had to take English as well.

After one year in Sicily my dad was transferred to Rome, Italy to be the Mission President there. The First Presidency of the church realized that our family could not spend three years apart. Brad and Romney came back to Sicily just in time for us to make the move to Rome. We were so excited to go to Rome. We'd visited the mission home on our way to Catania and knew what it was like. We attended a very good private school there call the American Overseas School of Rome (AOSR). It was an international school with the American Curriculum. Some of the countries represented in my class were America, Italy, Finland, Japan, Israel, India, Sweden, and Saudi Arabia.

My 4th grade teacher was named Mrs. Opal. She was a Jewish woman from New York City. She was quite the character. She reminded me of

Miss Piggy. She had bleached-blond hair, wore a lot of makeup, and wore very nice clothes. She'd always wear a fancy silk blouse, long pencil skirt, and stiletto heels that seemed to be too big for her. She thought she knew everything about Joseph Smith. I met two very sweet girls who became my best friends while in Rome, Sara Levi and Aili Pyhala. Sara had been born in Rome. Her mom was American and her dad was an Italian American. I spent a lot of time at her house for sleepovers. Aili was from Finland. They were great fun.

During my 4th grade year in school, we studied Greek history. We learned all about Alexander the Great. We actually took a week long field trip to Greece so we could see everything we'd studied! It was an incredible experience for me. Elisabeth went as well with her class. We went to Athens and Crete. The only thing I didn't like about that trip was the Greek food.

I had a wonderful 5th grade teacher at AOSR. She was from England and her name was Mrs. Calvary. She was very nice and proper like you'd expect someone from England to be. I still struggled with math and had to go to a math tutor once a week. Towards the end of the school year, we took a weeklong field trip to a beautiful city called Ravenna to visit some of the sights we studied. Ravenna has some of the most beautiful mosaics in the world. My mom was able to chaperone that trip. We had fun together.

The mission home was over a hundred years old. There were two large wrought iron gates at the entrance of the driveway. One night after getting home from somewhere, I went to shut the gate. After having shut the gate I turned to walk back to the house. I couldn't figure out why I wasn't able to move forward even though I was moving my legs. Something was holding me back. I soon realized I had shut my finger in the gate! It scared me and I started screaming for help. Of course my parents and everyone with us ran to help. They tried pushing the button that opens the gate, but the gate wouldn't budge. The only way to get it to open was to push it in on my finger. At the time we had a young Italian girl in her twenties living with us. Her name was Olivia Fantauzzo. She started yelling, "We need some wine, we need some wine!" She was convinced the wine would help take away the pain. My finger was fine, but my middle fingernail eventually fell off. I kept it in a little box with my baby teeth!

My eyes were opened a lot during those three years in Italy. I got to see that the church I belong to operates the same way in Italy as it does in America. The several hundred missionaries we met became like brothers and sisters to me. They treated me so nicely and I loved them like they were family. I got to see how blessed I was to have been born in America. While living in Rome, I remember one Christmas very well. There was an international branch that met at the church. The meetings were in English.

The members and investigators who attended were refugees from all over the world. Iran, Poland, Russia, and Africa are a few of the countries I remember. These people left their countries with basically the clothes on their backs and nothing else. I remember one family with three young children. The kids didn't have any toys. They lived in a hotel close to the mission home. My parents decided we would bring Christmas to them. My mom and dad took me, Elisabeth, and John to their hotel to give them their presents. I will never forget the looks on their faces. They were so happy. It was then that I realized how blessed my life had been.

My parents were great about taking us all over the mission to spend time with the missionaries. We went to several Zone Conferences. We'd often sit at the back of the chapel and make faces at my parents while they were speaking. I grew to love everything about Italy; the people, the food, the language, and of course the beautiful country. We were lucky enough to be able to see many cities in both Sicily and in the boundaries of the Rome mission. I learned to speak the language quite fluently. I loved to eat at the McDonald's by the Spanish Steps any chance I got. Even though I loved the Italian food, I really missed not being able to get any American food there. It was a huge treat when someone with access to the American Army base brought food to us.

I think my parents are amazing to have shown such faith to move their family to a different country. Those three years are still and will always be the most special and memorable time of my life. My family grew so close while there. Me and my siblings' friends lived so far from us that we were forced to spend a lot of time together. We became so close and have such a strong bond because of it. Whenever I talk about my childhood, I phrase it as being "before Italy" or "after Italy". I even got my social security number while living there. We had to get it through the American Embassy in Rome. You'd never know I was from Utah by looking at my number. It shows I should be from New York.

I was sad to leave my friends in Italy but my family and I were so excited to go back to the States. We left Rome on July 1, 1988. My parents wanted us to have the chance to see London, England before returning home, so we went there for six days. I will never forget how funny we must have looked to everyone. Sure we were on vacation, but people had no idea that we were also moving home after living three years abroad. We had to pack everyone's summer clothes into suitcases. We'd shipped everything else home, and the things would take a few months to get to the States. There we were at the London airport, all seven of us, with about 14 suitcases! We got some pretty strange looks. I remember riding the neat red double-decker English buses, and looking out the windows and pointing to all of the American stores and restaurants. We were so excited to see a Pizza Hut, McDonald's, and even a Safeway grocery store. During one bus ride, we were sitting by a lady who was clearly homeless. She smelled like she had bathed in urine. Since we were in a country where English was spoken, my siblings and I started saying in Italian how smelly she was. The next thing we know, she turned to us and in Italian said, "Basta!" which means "stop it". We were shocked she understood us! I remember it rained five out of the six days while we were in London.

We returned back to the States on July 6, 1988. I remember being pretty nervous to see my friends again. I didn't know if we'd still get along like before. We had a lot of family and friends greet us at the airport. All of my friends were there. They invited me to have a sleepover with them at my friend Rachel's house. Everyone was very nice to me and made me feel like I hadn't missed anything during those three years. I started 6th grade and remember having a hard time feeling like I fit in. All of my friends had taken skiing lessons, tennis lessons, sewing lessons, and ballet lessons while I was gone. They'd all gotten really good at them too. I hadn't taken ballet while we were in Rome and I really wanted to take again. My mom signed me up at a different ballet school so I wouldn't be so self conscious. She also tried to get me to take tennis lessons, but I refused.

I attended Hillside Junior High for 7th and 8th grades. I didn't hang out with most of my friends from my neighborhood. Those two years were not my favorite ones. I started taking French in 7th grade and found it was very similar to Italian. It came somewhat easily for me. I took a French state test and placed 4th in the state. I remember feeling excited about that. I attended Highland High School and graduated in 1995. I didn't like my schoolwork but still managed to do okay. I had a great group of friends that made my high school years very memorable. I began doing things again with the girls in my ward. We had a great bond. We loved to have fun and laugh together. My closest friends were Amanda Harris, Catherine Bowers, Hailey Bateman, Katie Bradley, Rachel Scalley, and Holly Burbidge. We were all in the Pep Club together our junior year. I am still close to most of them.

I took Jazz dance classes the whole time I was in high school. I loved dancing. It was my dream to be in the Dance Club. I finally got the courage to try out for it my junior year. I made it all the way to the final cut but was not accepted. I was heartbroken. I remember walking home all alone feeling very sad. I look back now and know I never could have fit it into my class schedule my senior year.

My favorite class was French. I took French all four years of high school, having AP French my senior year. Madame Davis was the teacher and she happened to be my favorite as well. My interest and love for foreign languages grew.

I was a big music junkie. If there was a good concert coming to town, I'd have to go. My friend, Scott Romney, and I went to a lot of concerts together because we had the same taste in music. My friend Holly was a big runner and she got me to join the Cross Country team my freshman year. I soon realized running to compete was not a love of mine. I dropped out after finding it impossible to run three miles in under a certain time. Soon after, I got a job at the hair salon where I got my hair cut. I worked as the receptionist three days a week after school. My junior year I got a second job at the neighborhood gas station around the corner from my house. It was called Uptown Service. The owner, Dale Aramaki, was fun to work for. I'd work both jobs six days a week after school and on Saturday. I quit the salon my senior year and just worked at the gas station. I was able to save a lot of money and began to realize I needed to be careful how I spent it.

Ann Marie, Brad, Elisabeth, John, and Romney 1994

During my senior year I took a Humanities class from Julie Hewlett. She was a great teacher. It was fun for me to study a lot of the art because I'd seen most of it in Italy. That summer I was lucky enough to travel to Europe with My Humanities teacher and a counselor from school, Dean Collett. Most of my closest friends went as well. I earned enough money to pay for half of the trip. My parents were nice and helped me with the rest. We visited Italy, France, Switzerland, Denmark, Norway, Scotland and England.

That fall I started my university studies at the University of Utah. I pledged with the Delta Gamma Sorority and made some great friends. My mom was a Delta Gamma while she was at the U of U and she was excited I chose that sorority. I realized that I did not like school too much and I had a really hard time doing well on my tests. I took an Italian class which was the only class I did well in that first semester. I was more into socializing than my studies. I lived at home and took the bus every day to school. After my classes were over I took the bus downtown to my dad's office where I worked as the receptionist in his law firm. I then drove home at night with my dad.

I look back on the chance I had to work for my dad with fond memories. It was great to see him interact with the staff. He treated them as equals, whereas some of the attorneys did not. It was often that people would tell me how much they respected him and admired him. I feel that we grew closer during that time because we saw so much of each other.

The winter of 1997, I received my mission call to serve for my church in Padova, Italy. I was so excited when I opened my call. In my mind that was the exact mission I wanted to go to, but never thought I'd get to actually serve there. I cried I was so excited. I entered the Missionary Training Center on March 4, 1998. The district I was in couldn't get our Visas, so we were sent Stateside until our Visas came. I was sent to Columbia, South Carolina and served for a month and a half in Clemson. I was happy to be there but I really wanted to get to Italy.

Ann Marie serving in the Italy Padova Mission

I got to Italy the end June. My first city was Bolzano. It is a small city on the border of Italy and Austria. It didn't look like the typical Italian city at all. It had a lot of Austrian influence. A lot of the people spoke German and Italian. While I was serving there my sister, Elisabeth, was studying in Siena, Italy for a few months. I got permission for her to come spend a day with me and my companion. She was able to watch us talk to people about our church. It was a lot of fun. I was there for three months and was transferred to Florence where I served for eight months. The members there were so great. I had déjà vu the first time I walked into the church there. I had been to that church a few times while my family lived in Italy when I was younger. I had those types of experiences often on my mission. There were a handful of members in the cities I served who had been missionaries when my dad was Mission President. It was great to see them again after so many years. My last city was Mestre, which is about 15 minutes away from Venice. We'd spend our P-days in Venice.

My love for the Italian people grew so much while on my mission. They are wonderful people. I was blessed to have many spiritual experiences that shaped my testimony of Christ's Gospel. I will never doubt my faith because of the experiences I had as a missionary. It wasn't easy. Our days consisted of knocking doors and talking to people on the streets. It brought me a lot of joy seeing people change their lives and join the church. I think about my mission often and am thankful I was able to go on one.

I returned home from my mission the end of August 1999. I had a hard time adjusting to normal life again. All of my friends were either married or on missions. I was lonely and missed serving others.

My parents moved from the house I grew up in to a home in Holladay, Utah about one year after I returned home. I didn't want to attend a family ward for church so I decided I'd go to a church for singles. Shortly after I started going to that new church, I met a very attractive and nice guy. His name was Brent Kenney. I wanted to get to know him better and had told one of my friends about him. He was my home teacher and I had learned he liked to ski. My friend suggested I ask him to go see the Warren Miller movie that was coming out shortly.

I got up the nerve to call and ask him to go see the movie with me. He said yes, and we had a great time. That was early November of 2000. From the very beginning, we were comfortable with each other and had a great time together. It was easy to fall in love with him. I loved being with him and he treated me so well. I knew I wanted to spend the rest of my life with him. We were married June 27, 2001 in the Salt Lake Temple. It was the happiest day of my life! We bought a home on Claybourne Circle in Salt Lake City.

On November 6, 2002 our first child was born. We named him Jonas Brent Kenney. He was a large baby, weighing in at 8 lbs. 15 oz. He had strawberry blond hair and was so handsome. The night we brought him home from the hospital, Brent let me go to sleep while he stayed up with Jonas. Brent came in at 5:00 in the morning and I asked him why it was so late that he was coming to bed. He told me he and Jonas had stared at each other all night. I realized then that Jonas would not be a sleeping baby. He slept only a few hours a day as a newborn. When he was about four months old, he started taking two - thirty minute naps a day. Since he never slept, he was ready to go to sleep at night by 6:00. Brent would come home from work around 5:30 and most of the time I'd have Jonas bathed and in his pajamas.

Jonas loved to laugh as a baby. He was a tow-head blond with the most beautiful blue eyes. He was a handful and I was very tired at the end of the day. He woke up every morning between 5:00 and 5:30 until he was two and a half.

We found out we were having our second boy in 2005. We sold our house and bought a home we would build in a new development in South Jordan, Utah. Brent worked in South Jordan so it was a no brainer for us to move out south. His commute was cut down to four miles. We lived with my parents for a few months while we waited for our house to be finished. During that time our son, Alex, was born.

Alexander Smith Kenney was born on April 25, 2005. He had dark brown hair and was a lot smaller than Jonas, weighing 7 lbs. 6 oz. He was just as handsome as his big brother. He slept a lot from the very beginning and it was then that I realized how much different Alex was from Jonas. He was very easy going. When he was ten days old, we moved into our new home where we still live.

When Alex was around four months old, we realized his head was tilted to the right and that he rarely moved it to the left. His pediatrician told us he had Torticollis, which was when the head leans to one side and not the other. We took Alex to a physical therapist who showed us some exercises that would help his head stop tilting. Fortunately it worked and his head rested normally between his shoulders.

When Alex was around fifteen months old, his hair started going very curly. He has the tightest curls and gets asked what ethnic background he comes from all of the time. People don't think he belongs to me. He has Brent's olive skin, and combined with his hair he looks almost black in the summer. He resembles my sister, Elisabeth, when she was younger minus her skin tone.

Being a mom full time brings me a lot of joy. I love my boys so much. I am grateful that I am blessed to stay home with them everyday. Jonas is currently in the first grade and he is extremely smart. He has a great memory. He excels at math and reading. He loves all sports but has a real love for soccer and baseball. Alex is in his last year of preschool. He is such a happy boy and still loves to snuggle with me. He is very social and could play with friends all day and watch TV all day if I let him. He likes sports as well and they come very naturally to him. He has played baseball and soccer.

I enjoy exercising. I like to run and go to exercise classes. It's very therapeutic for me. I volunteer up to three times a week in Jonas' class at school. I help his teacher with math and find it rewarding to be able to help the kids. I also love to be able to spend time with Jonas during the day and to see him interact with his classmates. I enjoy cooking but find it a bit frustrating right now. My boys are very picky eaters and hardly eat anything I make. I have had several callings in my church that have helped me grow a lot. I currently teach Relief Society and really enjoy it.

I feel so blessed to be married to Brent. He is the best husband and such a great father to our boys. He recently coached Jonas' soccer team. We like to do fun things together as a family. There is a lake in our neighborhood that we like to fish in during the summer or go for bike rides around. We spend a lot of time together which I think is very important.

Elisabeth Williams Theurer

I was born on April 12, 1978 at LDS Hospital in Salt Lake City, Utah. I was born to Nan Murdoch Romney Williams and Dwight Bradley Williams. I was the fourth child out of five children. D. Bradley Williams III, W. Romney Williams and Ann Marie Williams were my older siblings. Two years after I was born, my youngest brother John Bryson Williams was born. I always felt very blessed to have such amazing parents and siblings and to be born into such a great family

Most memories of my childhood were those spent with my siblings. I remember getting into a lot of trouble with my little brother, John. We had some great times together. It was fun having siblings so close to my age. When I was young I wasn't shy. I have always been told that many times I would walk up to complete strangers and strike up a conversation. I used to ask complete strangers if I could try on their shoes. My mom has often told me that she knew when it was coming. She said I would get his look in my eye and then I would either go take their shoe, or ask them if I could try it on. I remember my older sister, Ann Marie, being constantly by my mom's side as I caused mischief. I think she was the reason I got caught most of the time. She made sure my mom knew when I was getting dirty, or causing problems. I have always loved having a sister so close in age. For most of my childhood, we shared a room. Many great memories came from these times. My side of the room was always a mess and hers was always spotless. She used to tell me that my house was always going to be messy while hers would always be clean. She taught me a lot.

I remember living on 1300 East in a rental house and I broke a bowl and stepped on a piece of the glass, having to go the hospital to have it removed. I remember being so worried that my mom was going to get mad at me because I broke a bowl, and then the relief I felt when she wasn't mad at all. She was always so patient and loving. When I was about three years old, I was being naughty at a shopping mall and I was playing on the escalators and running up the down. I tripped and cut my lip open. Fortunately, I don't remember any of it, but my family tells me that there was blood everywhere. I can only imagine how upset my mom must have been. It sounds as though I was quite mischievous and silly. I know that one of my parent's dear friends, Art Swindle, told my parents that he hoped school wouldn't stifle me.

Growing up we spent a lot of time with our grandparents. My mom's parents, Wendell Bitner Romney and Jeannette Murdoch Romney, we referred to them as Nana and Granddad. They were such classy people. I remember the smell of their house and how my Nana always looked so beautiful. My granddad loved Countrytime Lemonade and my Nana made the best tuna fish sandwiches. I still remember playing with my mom's old dolls at their house. I wish I remembered more about them. They were such amazing people and I love looking at pictures of them.

My dad's parents, Dwight James Williams and Janet Jardine Williams, are also amazing people. They used to babysit us when my parents would go out of town. I loved sleepovers at Grandma and Grandpa's house. We used to help Grandma make her famous pickles; the spicy ones were our favorite. Grandma was known for her dried fruit leather, shrinky dinks, peach jam, and her yummy homemade wheat bread. I enjoyed making all of these with her. I used to love being at Grandmas and looking at all of her own art work. She used to paint and I always loved the paintings she did of her roses. I loved that she had painted them herself. I still remember when my grandpa passed away. I was in Junior High School. I'll never forget my sister coming into the TV room to tell me and John that Grandpa was probably going to die. I remember doing everything possible to try and keep from crying. He was such an amazing and loving man. I have been blessed with great examples in my life.

When I was seven years old, my dad was called to be a Mission President for the Church of Jesus Christ of Latter-day Saints in the Italy Catania Mission. I remember being very confused. My brothers were older and quite furious when they heard the news. I was so young that it wasn't as hard for me to pick up and move to a foreign country. What an amazing experience this was. I often wish I had been older so I could have soaked it all in even more. I was baptized not long after moving to Catania. I had the opportunity of being baptized in the Ionian Sea, on my birthday, April 12, 1986. My dad baptized me, my grandpa confirmed me. The two assistants of my dad's, were the witnesses. I still remember what a special experience this was. I can still picture standing on the beach with my family before I entered the water. The mission home was beautiful. It was cold due to all of the marble floors and we often didn't have running water. I remember my mom having to boil bottled water to bathe us, while our neighbors had elevators in their homes and were always watering their lawns.

The first year in Catania was a tough year. My brothers had a horrible school experience and were sent home to finish the school year. Once the First Presidency of the church heard we had been separated as a family, they transferred us to the Rome Mission. What an amazing experience we had there. We were one of the few families that where LDS. This was the first time I really gained a testimony of our Savior and his gospel. Even at a young age, I remember having to stand strong and not let my love for and belief of my Savior waiver. My siblings became my best friends. This was a very bonding experience for us as a family.

Elisabeth's baptism in the Ionian Sea

While we were in Rome attending AOSR (American Overseas School of Rome) we had some amazing experiences. I had the opportunity of going on a field trip to Greece, with my Greek History class. I remember it was beautiful, but it rained a lot and the food was horrible. I'm sure I would feel differently now. When we lived in Rome we did some modeling. This was a fun experience. My brother Romney was cast in a movie where he played one of the leading roles. I had the opportunity of filming a few commercials. I still remember one was for a meat company and another was for a dessert company, similar to Hostess. I remember thinking the desserts were awful. One day my brother, John, was watching TV and one of my commercials came on and he quickly turned the TV off, thinking he paused it, as he ran to find me. These were fun experiences.

We returned home in July of 1988. I was so excited to come home to see my friends. I was also very nervous. What if no one remembered me and what if my friends didn't like me anymore? When we walked off the plane, the gate was filled with friends and family to welcome us home. Although none of them were friends my age, I remember feeling such love and relief at the same time. I spent the night at the Scalley's home with Catherine.

I was so glad to be home and had a wonderful time. The Scalley's were always so good to us as a family.

I enjoyed being home and also made some new friends. My best friend, Katy Hanseen, moved from Minnesota at the same time we moved back. We were inseparable. We spent every minute we could together. People even used to ask us if we were twins. I loved it. We spent many weekends and summer nights toilet papering, crank calling, playing truth or dare, and staying up all night talking and laughing. I remember dressing up as Large Marge and walking the streets. We had some great laughs together.

Junior High was another experience. I attended Hillside Intermediate School. My friends changed in my desire to fit it. I didn't like Junior High at all. I quickly learned that being popular wasn't important at all. Being a good friend was what was important. I couldn't wait for Junior High to end.

I attended Highland High School and really enjoyed it. I was on the Senate Committee and was on the Pep Club Team my Junior Year. I enjoyed spending time with friends. We spent many spring breaks in St. George, Utah. When I was in high school, I spent my summers as a Nanny for the Angstman family. When I was a junior, I started working at Uptown Service Station, the local Phillips 66 Gas Station. I loved my job. Dale Aramaki was my boss and I had a great time working there.

My junior year in high school, I'll never forget my family doing a sub-for-Santa and delivering the gifts to the mobile home of these dear people. It was the most humbling and one of the most memorable Christmases I had as a child. I quickly realized how blessed I had always been and how grateful I was for the life I had been given. Another Christmas memory from growing up was every Christmas morning, my dad had to be the first one down the stairs to see if Santa had come. He would turn on all the Christmas lights and check to make sure he had come. We then got to line up youngest to oldest. My mom always made holidays such a special time. No matter what the holiday was.

It was my junior year in high school where my testimony was tried and strengthened. I had a good group of friends, but many of them made different choices than I did. I was very grateful that I had been taught to choose the right; this saved me in many situations. My parents had taught me to choose the right and to stand strong and make good choices. I was so grateful that I had a testimony and knew how important it was to follow my Savior's example.

When I graduated from high school in 1996, I took my Senior Trip to Hawaii. We had waited a month after graduating to go, so that we would meet the Rugby team after they finished touring. We had a great time. I was hesitant to go because over that month my friends had changed and I was no longer spending time with the friends I had in high school. Nonetheless, I had a great and memorable time.

I attended the University of Utah and pledged Delta Gamma in the fall of 1996. I loved it. I began to form stronger friendships with girls I had grown up with, but whom I had drifted from. I was so grateful for this experience. Some of my closest friendships came from this experience. Once again I had to remain strong and stand up for what I believed in. This is where important decisions I had made in my life paid off. To this day, two of my closest friendships came from the time spent at the DG house. I met my dear friends, Amy Hyde and Katy Hanseen, and I began to hang out again. I wouldn't change this experience for the world, although during my junior year, I chose to drop out of the sorority.

During my junior year of college, I did a study abroad through the Italian program at the U of U. I spent four weeks in Siena, Italy studying the language. I loved every minute of this. I went early and traveled through many of the cities that I lived in, or places I had spent time in while living in Italy as a child. I ate more Gelato in those those four weeks than I could possibly in a lifetime. Italy is such a beautiful place. It was because of the experiences I had as a child that my love for art and food began. I graduated from the University of Utah with a degree in Art History. I knew this was a major that I most likely wouldn't use for a profession, but I loved the culture and art so much that I had to explore it more.

It was during my senior year in college that I met my now husband, Jesse Smith Theurer, son of Craig Brook Theurer and Carol Galloway Theurer. We dated for a brief month and then broke up and lost contact for a year. When our paths crossed again, I remember telling my mom that he was perfect. This was before we had begun dating again. I told her he was so easy to talk to, attractive, funny, caring, and so much fun to be with. It was three short months later that we were engaged to be married. He proposed to me at the top of the Joseph Smith Building, in a room where the first presidency holds many important meetings. The view of the temple from this room is amazing. As we looked down over the temple, Jesse explained how important the temple was to him and he bore his testimony of the temple and told me he wanted to take me there. I'll never forget how much peace I felt when I said yes. We were sealed in the temple on October 28, 2000. What a memorable and perfect day. We were married in the Salt Lake Temple and had our reception at Heritage Gardens in Sandy, Utah. After the ceremony and pictures, we met my family at Hires for lunch. Jesse will never let me forget how uptight I was because I did all the flowers for my wedding and I had to hurry to finish them and go set up. Not the wisest decision, but I enjoyed making all the arrangements. We had our honeymoon in Maui, Hawaii. What a wonderful week we spent there. One of our favorite things to do was to discover that we both have a great love for good food and good restaurants. Some of our favorite meals were had on our honeymoon.

It was after my wedding that I chose to explore the world of Floral Arrangement. I began to do weddings on my own under the company name of Tulips. Later I teamed up with Summer and Ashley Jensen and worked under their company name of Petals. This was a fun experience.

Our first apartment was in the Avenues on the corner of A Street and 3rd Avenue in Salt Lake City. It was such a happy place. I remember how much fun I had putting it all together. Things were so simple and small, and we were so happy. I'll never forget our first Christmas together, the heat in our apartment went out and we would crank the oven up and cuddle to keep warm. It was so cold you could see our breath, but what a memorable time. Six months later, we bought our first home in Sugarhouse on 1500 East and 2491 South. This home and the experiences we had in this ward brought so many blessings to our lives.

Jesse was put in as the Ward Mission Leader and we were so blessed because of all of his hard work and the many sacrifices he made to serve the people in our neighborhood. Our next-door neighbor, TJ, quickly became Jesse's buddy and he spent so much time at our house. He lived with his grandmother and Jesse quickly became his father, friend, role model, and mentor. We both still miss that little house and that wonderful ward. It is here that I learned the importance of serving and what it means to truly be selfless. I learned all of this through Jesse's example. My parents had always taught me this, especially my mom, but it was here that I experienced it first hand. In this ward we had an amazing bishop, whom I'll never forget. His name was Bishop Ed McConkie. He was such an amazing example to both of us. He taught me so much. It was in this ward that I had my first miscarriage. I remember feeling so alone, mad, and I even doubted my faith for a while. I don't quite remember what it was that Bishop McConkie said to me, but I'll never forget how his words made me feel. This was a very difficult, but rewarding time in my life. It did cause me to doubt my testimony, but at the same time it strengthened me. It taught me to never forget the Lord, that I can't do it alone.

After two great years in this ward, we moved to Bountiful, Utah. We built a home in Scenic Circle. This home was beautiful, but it was also a place that I felt so comfortable and so at home. Our ward was amazing. Shortly after we had moved there, we found out I was pregnant with our first child. I was ecstatic. Ellie Ruth Theurer was born on September 10, 2004, five days before my actual due date. At about 4 o'clock in the morning my water broke, waking me up from a deep sleep. We quickly got ready and headed to the hospital. I remember being so uptight, because here I am sitting on about five towels and Jesse is driving on the freeway under the speed limit. We made it there and I had a long labor. They said that she wasn't ready to come out, that she had just kicked my bag of water and broken it. After 16 hours of waiting, she finally came. Her heart rate was dropping quickly, so Dr. Stephen Lamb had to use the vacuum to get her out quickly. She was quickly rushed to the NICU (Newborn Intensive Care Unit) station that was set up in my room, to be checked. She had a mild fever, but was perfect. I couldn't believe how much love I felt for this sweet child. We used Ruth as her middle name, naming her after Jesse's sweet grandmother Ruth Elizabeth Theurer. She is an amazing women and someone Jesse has always adored, and now I do too. Ellie is so honored to be named after her. Ellie was a beautiful baby and such a sweet heart. She and Jesse had such an adorable bond. He loved holding her on his chest and taking a nap.

After two years of living in Bountiful (Ellie was 8 months old) we moved in with Jesse's parents as we started the adventure of building another home. We lived there until we found out I was pregnant with our second child. We moved into a condo above Hogle Zoo and then sold that and moved in with my parents just in time to welcome William Romney Theurer into our family. He was just precious. He was born on June 30, 2006. I was induced, originally due on July 7th. His labor was a breeze. He has been such a wonderful addition to our family. He immediately melted our hearts. Ellie was so sweet to him and just adored him. He was such a sweet baby. He instantly became our lil' buddy. William was named after my maiden name and my mom's maiden name. Two great names he carries.

After living with my parents for a while, we moved back in with Jesse's parents because our home on Claybourne was taking much longer than expected. When William was about eight months old, we were finally ready to move into our beautiful home. Our home was beautiful, but it never quite felt like home. We sold it about one year later and moved to Princeton Drive. This move was one that was done completely by faith. I have never fasted and prayed so much in my life that everything would work out. I prayed that we would find a home that would be a wonderful place to raise our family. A place where our children would be surrounded with amazing examples, a great peer group, and a place with great leaders to help teach them. We found it. This experience definitely strengthened my testimony of prayer.

Ellie is now five years old. During these five years, we have loved every minute with her. She is such a joy to be around. She loves to dance and sing. She takes ballet and is very good at it. She can be quite dramatic, but this is what makes her so silly. She is such a caring and concerned little girl. She is always thinking of others and making sure no one is left out. I love this quality about her. She loves to be together as a family. She loves Jesus and loves to pray. I am so grateful for her.

William is now three years old and keeps me on my toes. He is crazy and silly. He loves to go, go, go. Anything to do with climbing and jumping, he loves. We always say he is a crazy as his curly hair. William loves to say the prayer and if it isn't his turn he will just interrupt whoever is saying it and say his own. He and Ellie have such a bond, it makes me so happy and I hope it continues. They love being together and when the other one is gone they miss each other. Their relationship reminds me of the one I have with my little brother, John.

We love spending time together as a family. We have gone on many wonderful trips together, mainly to Newport Beach, California, but others include Hawaii and Island Park, Idaho.

This year, 2009, I have had three miscarriages. These experiences have definitely made me realize how much I have been blessed. I adore my children and thank my Heavenly Father every day for them and for their health. I am constantly praying that I will be a good mother to them. That I will teach them to do what is right and to find happiness through the gospel of Jesus Christ. I have been blessed with such an amazing husband and best friend. My life was forever changed the minute I met Jesse. I love him with all my heart. I, too, thank my Heavenly Father for him daily. I have been blessed.

John Bryson Williams

Written in November 2009

My parents are Nan Murdoch Romney Williams from Salt Lake City, Utah and Dwight Bradley Williams from Bountiful, Utah. I was born on July 23, 1980 in Salt Lake City, Utah. I wish I could tell you that I was immediately given my name that day, however, my birth certificate reads: "Unnamed baby boy Williams". My family called me "Junior" for a short time but I am grateful they eventually chose to name me John. I am the youngest child in the family and have two brothers and two sisters. Being the youngest, I received the most attention from everyone growing up. I was the beneficiary (or victim, depending on how you look at it) of probably hundreds of nicknames. Perhaps these names were welcomed considering the unnamed baby boy incident with which I started my life.

As I write this, I am flooded with memories of growing up in such an amazing family. Of course we picked on each other, as families do, but I have always felt so loved by my siblings and have always had a deep respect and love for my parents. My brother Brad was born in 1971 and Romney in 1972. Ann Marie, my oldest sister, was born in 1976 and Elisabeth in 1978.

I grew up in Salt Lake City, Utah on 2109 Berkeley Street. I can still remember the smell of that home and remember what it felt like to run around the large yard as a small child. I remember having so much fun with friends and family there. Some memories that I have from around the age of three or four are barbecues with relatives and playing with neighborhood friends. At the age of four, a friend of mine named Morgan Scalley and I chose to give ourselves haircuts. Apparently it didn't turn out too well but at least it was perfect timing - just before a family picture. I am sure my parents were thrilled.

When I was four years old, my parents gathered the family to tell us that we would be moving to Catania, Italy on the island of Sicily. My father had been called to preside as Mission President over the Catania, Italy Mission for a three-year period. As a four year old, I had no idea what that meant, but if that is where mom was going... that is where I was going. I am sure that my older siblings didn't feel that way, but there is also a nine year difference between myself and my oldest brother, Brad.

In July of 1985, we moved as a family to Catania, Sicily. One of my first memories was my 5th birthday celebration that the local LDS branch gave me. I remember opening gifts from children and families that I had never met. I remember how I felt and even the smell of that basement room in the Catania Mission Home. That day, my parents took a picture of me that still stands out in my head of how I looked and felt as a child, with big blue eyes and blond hair (the hair changed over the years to brown).

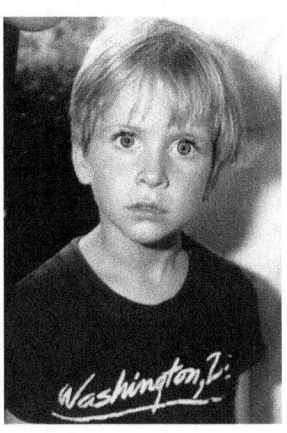

The schooling situation was not the best, especially for my older brothers. They unfortunately were stuck in a classroom with a wide range of ages and all the kids smoked cigarettes throughout the day. Needless to say it was not ideal and no condition that should be permanent. This caused my parents to send them back to the States to live with family friends. One year after moving to Catania, my parents were transferred to the Rome, Italy Mission. This was a complete change and the schooling was incredible. We all went to a school called American Overseas School of Rome. We had such a great experience there and I remember so many fun experiences that we all gained there. I was at that time in the first and second grades.

Being so young, I learned Italian very easily although I was very shy to speak around strangers. This experience in Italy was just a start for my love of Italy and Italians. As a child in Italy, I was lucky to have so many missionaries around that wanted to play with me. I remember playing soccer in our yard in front of the mission Villa with cheap plastic balls that are easily found in Italy, painted to look like a soccer ball. We were lucky to have the mission office just next door to our home. I sometimes feel that the mission home in Rome is still "home", even after all these years. I feel extremely blessed to have had the opportunity to live in Italy as a child because it taught me to appreciate other cultures and it also left me thirsting for more. Although I was very young, it had a great impact on my life that is priceless. We returned home to Utah in the summer of 1988. I remember the ride home very well... mostly because I was so exhausted that I couldn't wait to use the bathroom and decided sleep was more important. Upon arriving home, Dave Brinton (Romney's friend) picked me up and probably wondered why my shorts were so wet. I remember the feel of that summer night and how light it was outside and the smell that came off of the Great Salt Lake. I couldn't wait until the next day to see my old best friend, Morgan. That day we had a pool party at his family's home and it felt good to be with my old friends again.

When I was 12 years old, I had a unique experience of being able to travel to England all alone. A friend's family was called to preside over the Bristol, England Mission and my friend, Edward, moved to England for three years. My parents allowed me to travel all alone to England to spend a couple weeks with the Pugsley family. I now look back on that and realize that even today, times have changed and I wouldn't feel comfortable allowing my child to travel alone....but it sure was fun. This experience sticks out in my mind because once again at a young age, I was exposed to another culture and people. This helped continue my desire to see the world and be exposed to other cultures. I turned 13 years old on that trip.

I attended Hillside Junior High and Highland High Schools. During those years I had many groups of friends. I realize how great it is to have many friends and many types of friends. During those years, I found it easy to make friends with people from other local schools. This helped create some good relationships that continued into college years. I believe creating good relationships with people, is a key to living a happy and successful life. I learned this well from observing my older brothers, Brad and Romney. They always seemed to be genuinely interested in what others had to say and they made friends very easily. My advice to my children during these junior high and high school years would be to be yourselves and accept people for who they are. Stay strong in the gospel of Jesus Christ and decide early to be unique by choosing to stand for what you believe in.

Brad and Romney had always been good to me growing up and from a young age they would take me up to their fraternity house at the University of Utah. While coming to an end of high school, I couldn't wait to move on and involve myself with the Sigma Chi Fraternity. I had a cousin, Brian Watkins, who was active in the fraternity during the time I graduated from high school. Immediately the same summer of high school graduation, I was already spending time at the Sigma Chi house with my cousin Brian. I became active in the Sigma Chi Fraternity at the University of Utah and spent a lot of time there during my time at the University. I was blessed to build many very strong friendships that will last an eternity. Being a part of something bigger than myself, I learned to appreciate people with different backgrounds, beliefs, and personalities. I believe that this experience served me in order to prepare for a mission.

During this time, my sister Ann Marie was serving as a missionary for the Church of Jesus Christ of Latter-day Saints in the Padova, Italy mission. After a year of University, it was time for me to send in my papers to serve a mission as well. Growing up I always knew I would serve a mission and am so grateful that I was blessed with the circumstance in our family that allowed me to gain a testimony of the gospel of Jesus Christ. I was convinced I was going to Asia on my mission for some reason, but was very surprised to find out that I was called to serve in the Catania, Italy Mission - the exact mission home in which I had turned five years old!

My mission changed my life. I am overcome with emotion even now as I write this because of the gratitude I feel for the blessing of that experience in my life. I not only grew more on my mission than I would have imagined possible but I also gained a personal testimony of the restored Gospel of Jesus Christ and know that His church has been restored on the earth as the Church of Jesus Christ of Latter-day Saints.

All missionaries have great experiences but I was blessed with some incredible experiences having lived in the same mission as child. Many of the church members remembered me and mostly my father, who had an impact on many people during his short year there as a Mission President. Many times I would be in a city or walk into a church building and be flooded with memories and the knowledge that I had been there when I was five years old. I had the unique opportunity to have three Italian companions while on my mission. There were only about six Italians or so in the mission so I felt blessed to have this opportunity. This allowed me to learn the Italian language much better than I would have otherwise.

When I left my mission in Catania, I knew my work there was not complete. I am drawn to Italy and the Italian people and I believe this was something that was set in motion long before I was born. I often think about my connection with Italy and I believe it started when my grandfather, Dwight James Williams, who fought in World War II. While he was flying a plane, he was shot down over the Straits of Messina, which separates Sicily and Italy. This was a miraculous story because he had been badly injured in the head and was guided back safely and actually landed the plane with no problems. I asked my father just a couple of months ago if he had been born at the time and his answer was, no. Apparently my grandmother who was then pregnant with my father had been notified that his airplane had been shot down. She had no idea if he were alive or dead. It wasn't until after my father's birth that she was notified that he was alive but was critically injured. This story for me is the beginning of our family connection with Italy.

The connection still continued after that experience when my father was called to serve a mission in Germany. Missionary work in Germany was difficult for him, but after a series of events occurred in his mission, my father was given the unique opportunity to teach Italians living in Germany as workers. He was chosen as one of four missionaries from his mission to join small groups of other missionaries from the surrounding missions to start missionary work for the Italians. They were the first missionaries to start teaching Italians since Lorenzo Snow and his companion had taught in Italy. Because of that experience he was able to be called back as a Mission President as described earlier. Only because he was called back was I able to go to Italy as a young child which allowed me then to be called back as a missionary. When I had that feeling of my work not being complete, I didn't know what it meant and may not fully understand it now, but I have made the effort ever since returning to keep my ties and love for Italy alive. I have had the unique opportunity to travel often to Italy and each time I go, I am reminded that we are put here on earth for such a great purpose. I am blessed with many opportunities to learn and to teach but I hope that by being an example to a people I love so much, that someday I can see one of them join the Lord's restored church here on the earth.

I returned home from mission in December 2001. After returning home from my mission, I wasn't quite sure what I wanted to do but I continued where I left off at the University of Utah. After a year being home, I was given the chance to move to Los Angeles, California. Growing up I always liked to do various voices and would joke around by making personalities around these voices. My family still to this day will embarrass me by having me do a voice. On many occasions my dad would embarrass me the most by asking me in front of his clients whom, to me, were strangers. So when I was given that chance to move to L.A. to be an assistant to an animator, I jumped on it. I saw it as an opportunity for me to do something that could potentially interest me, so I did. I have heard my mother say that she knew when I left that day, with the car packed full of my things, that I was never coming home. Now that I am a father, I dread that day but am so grateful that I had parents that loved me and supported me in my life and a new opportunity.

I moved to Los Angeles in December of 2002 with optimism for the future and an excitement I hadn't felt before. When I arrived in Los Angeles, I decided right away that I would be involved in the singles ward north of the Los Angeles valley where I was. After three weeks of attending the singles ward near my home, I decided that I would check out the Los Angeles first singles ward near the temple. I had heard good things about it and I knew that there would be a bigger crowd and therefore, more people to meet. Not knowing what time the ward meetings actually started on Sunday, I showed up early and had some time to kill before the other singles arrived. I sat down near the back of the chapel and waited patiently for the others to fill the chapel seats. I will never forget one of the first people to walk into the chapel, because I immediately realized how beautiful she was. She was an incredibly pretty Asian girl with short hair. I didn't take my eyes off of her as she found a seat just a few rows in front of me in that empty chapel. Throughout the Sacrament Meeting I would glance over at that girl wondering who she was. After the Sacrament Meeting ended I found myself alone in the hallway not knowing where Sunday School was held. I had wandered halfway down one hallway and looked back to see what direction that girl had gone and of course my plan was to follow her. After turning around, I realized she was headed in the same direction as I was, and I realized the correct classroom must have been the one directly in front of where I was standing. I entered the classroom and came up with the bright idea of sitting down and leaving one seat open next to me on the aisle. My plan worked! The same girl I had noticed from the first second she walked into the chapel had fallen right into my plan and into her seat next to me. I found it funny that her roommate followed her into the classroom and asked her why she sat down there when there was no room for her. I understood that maybe this mystery girl had a plan too. That is when I introduced myself to her and found out that her name was Jodie Shiotani. We immediately hit it off and I got her phone number before leaving church. Her calling in the singles ward was Family Home Evening and she invited me to come to the activity at the ward the next night. That same Sunday night we exchanged some messages and made the connection that Jodie knew my sister Elisabeth and so did her brother Kelly. The next night I couldn't wait to arrive at the church to see her. After the activity, we went with a group of people to get ice cream sandwiches at Diddy Riese in Westwood. Before leaving that night, she told me that a group of friends got together at her home to watch a TV show and invited me to come the next night. Once again I couldn't wait to get there and spend time with her. That Tuesday evening, I asked Jodie if she would like to go out with me on Thursday evening. I was confident she wouldn't say no and I was right. That Thursday night, we went out on our first date. We went to the Cheesecake Factory Restaurant and after we made our way to the Santa Monica Pier. I remember how being with her seemed so easy and natural. That night my life changed and we have been together ever since. One day a few months later, we were sitting on the sand at Zuma Beach in Malibu and I turned to her and said, "Do you think we will get married?" I asked that as if that was a normal question to ask... but everything felt so comfortable with her that it felt like a natural question since I did think we would be married. She said, "Yeah, I do." After that, I moved home to Salt Lake City to start working and a couple months later Jodie moved back to Utah before our wedding.

In that time we were apart, I flew to California and surprised her with an engagement ring. I took her out to dinner once again at the Cheesecake Factory and after we wanted to go to the Santa Monica Pier because that is where we had gone on our first date but it was raining. We decided to go anyway and while we were out there in the rain, I got down on my knee and proposed to her. We were married in the Salt Lake Temple on August 1, 2003 when I was 23 years old. That day she made me the happiest man in the world.

We lived in Lehi, Utah for two years while Jodie attended the MBA program at Brigham Young University. After graduation, we moved back to California but this time to Orange County. We knew we wanted to get back to California and decided Orange County was the place we wanted to be to start our family. We moved to Ladera Ranch, California and were so excited for our new life together. I have loved living in southern California and am so grateful to be here. Going to the beach is one of my favorite things to do and I appreciate having nice weather year round. Not long after moving to California, we found out that Jodie was pregnant with our first child. Our oldest daughter, Stila Haruko Williams, was born on December 22, 2005. We felt it was important to keep some of Jodie's Japanese ancestry alive through our children's names. Stila's middle name, Haruko means *Spring* in Japanese and is the name of Jodie's grandmother. I never would have imagined that having a child could bring so much joy and love into our life. Stila was so sweet and I loved being able to spend so much time with her. Stila continues to blow us away with how smart she is and how much she loves to participate in her church and school activities. Our second daughter, Alexa Shiotani Williams, was born on August 24, 2007. Alexa gets her middle name from Jodie's maiden name which means *Salt Valley* in Japanese. Once again, that same feeling of love and joy came into our lives. Alexa was so similar to Stila in so many ways she almost seemed like a clone at first. Alexa developed her own unique and very spunky attitude and still keeps us laughing and shaking our heads. She is just as smart as her sister and they keep us on our toes. After having two girls we were ready for a third, since we already knew how to raise girls, but we then found out Jodie was pregnant with a boy. We were nervous at first to have a boy, I think just out of fear of the unknown. Brody Shiro Williams was born on July 30, 2009 and has been such an incredible baby. Brody's middle name, Shiro, is a short version of Jodie's father's Japanese name. It is amazing how that joy and love comes with any child welcomed into a family. He is so sweet and brings the needed balance to our home. As I finish writing this, we are in Utah for the Thanksgiving holiday and I will bless little Brody tomorrow night.

I am so grateful for what Heavenly Father has blessed me with in my lifetime. I often think how important it is to live up to our responsibility and potential, having been given so much. In life we go through good times and difficult times, but it is imperative that we confront all situations with gratitude and a positive attitude. I love all my family and thank them for all they have given me and look forward to the many years of memories that we will create together. This is just the beginning...

Chapter 11

William Murdoch, Jr. and Lucy Deanne Parkinson Nibley

By Susan Murdoch Briggs

This is the story of my parents William Murdoch Jr., born in 1911 and Lucy Deanne Parkinson Nibley Murdoch, born in 1914. My twin sister, Anne, and I (Susan) were born January 31, 1939. We were born seven weeks premature and through the excellent care of our parents, we survived. Another sister, Jane Nibley Murdoch Gardner, was born June 23, 1948.

Mother went to Wasatch Elementary, Roosevelt Junior High, East High School and the University of Utah. Dad also went to East High and the University of Utah.

My parents were wonderful, successful people. My father was manager of the West Chemical Products Company and my mother was a real estate agent for Gump and Ayers and the Ramsey Group.

My parents always strived for the best. They were hard workers and successful in all that they did. My father went to England on a mission as

Bill and Jeannette

a young man and my parents served in the New York Mission in the late 1970's and the Liberty Stake Mission in the early 1980's. The LDS church was very important to them and they loved and lived the gospel.

Dad grew up on "F" Street where he and his eight brothers and sisters were raised. His father, William Murdoch Sr., ran the "Murdoch Grocery Store." The Murdoch Grocery Store and the family home were next store to one another. Dad learned to work there as he labored side by side with his father. They helped the poor and each week they would put free baskets of food out for the needy. William Murdoch Sr. was Commissioner of Salt Lake City and served in many positions in the city government. Grandma Jeannette Murdoch was a "stay-at-home-mom" and cooked for all of the store employees.

My parents were married in 1936 in the Salt Lake Temple. My mother was the daughter of Preston Nibley, whom was the LDS Church Historian, and also the author of many LDS Church books. Her mother was Ann Parkinson Nibley from Logan, Utah.

The memories of growing up were filled with fun family dinners, picnics, trips to Brighton, Utah, and cookouts by the fire. This is where I learned to love nature and the wonderful, beautiful mountains. My father's interests and hobbies were hunting, fishing, gathering and canning choke cherries, and collecting coins, pocket knives, and trinkets. My mother loved reading, traveling, and giving fun parties. When I was in Junior High and High School, our mother made all of our school clothes, dresses, and formals. She was a beautiful seamstress. She also loved trying new recipes.

My parent's helped the poor and the needy. My dad traveled a lot with his work and he never passed anyone in need on the road. He would pick up hitch-hikers. One time, the man he picked up put a gun between them on the front seat. Dad stopped the car, said he had a family to support, and asked the man to please get out of the car. The man then left the car and my father never again picked up another hitch-hiker. My mother would gather clothing and food from her family, neighbors, and friends to take to the needy church members on the west side of town. She and Dad were then serving in the Liberty Stake Mission. They were deeply loved for their thoughtfulness, unselfishness, and caring.

My parents were wonderful, supportive grandparents. Dad would tell the grandchildren funny stories that he made up and always gave them coins and candy. Mother made delicious meals and constructed dolls out of towels for her granddaughters. She also used to have a button box and would thread buttons to make necklaces and bracelets with the grandchildren. She had a wonderful personality and would laugh with us for hours.

Dad passed away March 31, 1999 at age 89. Mother longed to join Dad and she passed away December 2, 2005 at the age of 91. Their reunion must have been so very special.

Their legacy: the twins, (1) Anne Murdoch McQueen, 4 daughters, 13 grandchildren, (2) Susan Murdoch Briggs, 4 children (2 sons and 2 daughters), 2 grandchildren, (3) Jane Murdoch Gardner, 5 children (2 sons and 3 daughters), 3 grandchildren.

In closing, I'd like to express my gratitude and thanks for the fine wonderful parents I had and also for the wonderful teachings and examples that they gave us.

ANNE MURDOCH MCQUEEN

I was born in Salt Lake City, Utah on January 31, 1939. I have an identical twin sister, Susan, and I am one minute older. My father was William Murdoch Jr. and my mother was Lucy Deanne Parkinson Nibley Murdoch. In 1948, June 23, our sister, Jane, was born.

I attended Uintah Elementary School, Hillside Jr. High, and East High School. I had many happy years as a teenager. I attended the University of Utah and graduated in Secondary Education. I was a member of Chi Omega Sorority. After graduation, I taught Physical Education and Health at East High School.

Anne and Susan

On June 7, 1963, I married Craig Hugh McQueen in the Salt Lake Temple. It was a joyous day. I taught school and put Craig through medical school. He is an orthopedic surgeon.

We have four beautiful daughters. They have been a joy to us. They were all honor roll students, class officers, cheerleaders, and obedient girls. All four attended the University of Utah and were members of Chi Omega Sorority.

All four girls married good men in the Salt Lake Temple. They are all wonderful mothers and I love my twelve grandchildren.

We are all active members of the LDS Church and Craig and I are now serving a mission with the Hispanic Inner City. We love our calling and we love the wonderful Hispanic people.

We enjoy many great family traditions. We love Sun Valley, Laguna Beach, and our log home in the Pine Mountain above Oakley, Utah.

Craig loves horses, tennis, art, guitar, reading, and all sports. I rescue homeless cats and dogs and I take care of three "ferel" cat colonies, trap them, have them neutered and spayed, get shots, and release them back in their own locations. I love cats. They are wonderful animals. I go to these colonies every day – rain or shine. I have done this for 18 years.

I love life, I love serving the Lord, and I love keeping the commandments. Because of these things, I experience peace and joy in my life.

Melissa Anne McQueen Anderson

I was born to Anne Murdoch McQueen and Craig Hugh McQueen on August 24, 1966. I had a very happy childhood with many experiences and opportunities. We are a very happy family. There is a lot of love!!

I attended Indian Hills Elementary School, Hillside Jr. High School, and Highlands High School. I had the privilege of being a Senior Class Secretary. I help plan our high school reunions every five years.

I attended the University of Utah and was a member of Chi Omega Sorority. I had the wonderful privilege of going to Europe with a Study Abroad Program. My two sisters, Heather and Becky, went with me also. We had a wonderful time traveling through Europe.

I married Craig Ross Anderson on September 21, 1990 in the Salt Lake Temple. We have been blessed with four beautiful children. Our oldest is Joshua (15), Ashley (13), Jordan (8), and Lucy (5). These children are very special and have many talents. All of them have been in Ballet West's

Nutcracker Ballet. They are following my footsteps. I danced for years in many ballet productions, including The Nutcracker Ballet. The children have had extensive modeling jobs and have appeared in many national magazines. This year, Josh, being six feet tall, will play on the Highland High football team. We are proud of him.

We, as a family, love our ancestors! We are grateful for their sacrifice. We teach our children as often as we can about all their trials and tribulations. We appreciate their testimonies and through their example, we are strong Latter-day Saints. Our testimonies grow every day and we love the Gospel. We love serving the Lord and hope to always keep the commandments.

Heather Jane McQueen Kinnersley

I was born on April 13, 1968 to Anne Nibley Murdoch McQueen and Craig Hugh McQueen, in Salt Lake City, Utah.

I attended Indian Hills Elementary, Hillside Junior High, and Highland High School. I danced for many years and was in Ballet West "The Nutcracker" for five years. In high school, I was a freshman class officer, dance club, and pep club.

I then went to the University of Utah and joined the Chi Omega Sorority. My two sisters and I went to Neuchatel, Switzerland on Study Abroad.

I met Kevin Kinnersley in a class at the University. He also went to Highland High and then served a mission to London, England South Mission. He was a Beta Theta Pi. We were married March 22, 1991 in the Salt Lake Temple. After being married for six years, we adopted a little boy we named Justin and four years later, we adopted another boy we named Jaden. They are now eight and four years old. We are hoping to adopt a baby girl in the future.

We are all healthy and enjoying our lives. Our boys are active in many sports, which keeps us busy. We have a wonderful family on both sides and love being with the cousins, enjoying many wonderful traditions!

Rebecca Susan McQueen Brown

My name is Rebecca Susan McQueen Brown. I was born February 11, 1970 in Salt Lake City, Utah to Craig and Anne McQueen. I am the third of four daughters. I grew up in Salt Lake City. I attended Indian Hills Elementary, Hillside Intermediate, and graduated from Highland High School. I attended the University of Utah and was a member of Chi Omega.

I started dancing when I was three years old and had the opportunity to dance in Ballet West "The Nutcracker". I am not a runner but have run in a few half marathons, the Salt Lake Marathon, and most recently participated in the Wasatch Back Relay.

I married Jamie Brown on May 1, 1991 in the Salt Lake Temple. Together we have raised four amazing children.
Brandon James Brown born October 15, 1992
Madeline Rebecca Brown born December 26, 1994
Jessica Heather Brown born February 20, 1997
Tyler Matthew Brown born Mother's Day, May 9, 1999

I am very grateful for a husband who works hard so I can stay home and take care of my kids. We love to do everything together as a family. We are each others' biggest supporters. There isn't a game or a dance recital or cheerleading competition that we haven't all attended cheering the other on. I love being a mother. It is the most rewarding thing I have done or will ever do. My family is definitely the highlight of my life. My faith is strengthened each time I look at my children and husband. I am so blessed to be the one chosen to be the mother of my family.

I have also been blessed with many church callings. All of which I have grown and learned a lot from - Primary President, Relief Society Counselor, Young Women Counselor, Primary Chorister, Primary teacher, the Young Adult Leader, and Enrichment Leader.

We love to travel and our favorite places are Laguna Beach, California, Sun Valley, Idaho, Jackson Hole, Wyoming, and our cabins up Weber Canyon and Provo Canyon.

My life so far has been full of a lot of ups and downs. Each day is a new challenge bringing us many new lessons to be learned and taught. I am grateful for the Gospel and what it teaches us. I pray my life will continue to go as it already has. I have no complaints.

Jennifer Jill McQueen Green

My name is Jennifer Jill McQueen Green and I was born August 25, 1977 in Salt Lake City, Utah. We are, of course, well known for our LDS culture. I went to Indian Hills Elementary, Hillside Jr. High, and Highland High School. I was a ballet dancer and danced in the Ballet West "Nutcracker" for three years. I participated in Highland High's Dance Company, Pep Club, and was Junior Varsity and Varsity Cheerleader. I graduated from the University of Utah in 2001 with a Bachelors Degree in Family and Consumer Studies and Human Development.

I met Zachary Tyler Green and we were married on June 10, 2000, on the anniversary of our first date. I met him at a wedding in which I caught the bouquet and jokingly told him, "Zach, I know we haven't gone out yet, but we're getting married 'cause I caught the bouquet." Little did I know it really wasn't a joke!!

We had a girl, Rivers Rebekah Green, born on July 11, 2002. Six weeks later, we change her name to Marisa Rivers Green. On February 23, 2005, Jillian Jennifer Green was born.

Zach went on a mission to the Philippines Baguio Mission in 1997 and 1998. He now is Director of Sales for Paramount Acceptance, a computer finance company. He also is a Real Estate Agent for Kincham and Friends Real Estate. I have a little girls' hair accessories company called "McQueen Bows". I make bows, headbands, flower clips, etc. for girls and even clips and headbands for adults. We live in Sandy, Utah

SUSAN NIBLEY MURDOCH BRIGGS

I was born January 31, 1939 to William Murdoch Jr. and Lucy Nibley Murdoch in Salt Lake City, Utah. I was born an identical twin. We were born two months early, sickly, and small. We survived due to the wonderful care and sacrifice of our parents.

I attended Lowell Elementary, Uintah Elementary, Hillside Junior High, and East High School. I had the opportunity of being voted Junior Class Girl's President, and I also was a member of the wonderful Madrigals and the East High Choir. I attended Brigham Young University and was a member of the social unit, OS Travota. I also was a member of the Women's Recreational Association. I then attended the University of Utah where I joined the Chi Omega Sorority and again was a member of the Women's Recreational Association. Here I played on the University of Utah Women's

LEFT: *Anne and Susan* RIGHT: *Lucy holding Anne and Susan (Sorry, but they don't know who is who, so we are guessing.)*

Softball Team and the Women's Field Hockey Team. I graduated from the University of Utah with a bachelor's degree in Physical Education and a minor degree in Health Education. After graduation I taught school for seven years: three years in California, and three years in Salt Lake.

I married John Frank Briggs on March 20, 1969 in the Salt Lake Temple. With his work as a stockbroker, we lived in many places including: Connecticut, New York, California, Georgia, and Hamburg, Germany.

While in Georgia, I had the opportunity of organizing the very first Relief Society in Garden City, Georgia. We held our meetings in a little shack next to a railroad track. Every time a train went by, our whole building shook. I have also had the opportunity of serving in the Relief Society Presidency, Primary Presidency, and taught Sunday School for many years. We

LEFT: *Anne Murdoch McQueen, Jillian Green, Marielle MacDonald, and Susan Murdoch Briggs* RIGHT: *Anne and Susan*

were blessed with four children: Jason Scott Briggs, Jennifer Susan Briggs MacDonald (Kenneth), Jaron Sean Briggs, and Julie Shannon Briggs. I also have two wonderful grandchildren: Amelia Juliette MacDonald and Marielle Elise MacDonald. We returned to Salt Lake City, Utah in 1977.

I returned to teaching and taught school for another 15 years. I was a health teacher at Hillside Intermediate in the Salt Lake City School District. I loved teaching health and I loved the challenge of the twelve and thirteen-year olds. I retired from the Salt Lake City School District in 2002.

I was divorced in 1994 and moved to West Jordan, Utah where I now reside. After moving there, I went back to teaching and taught three years at the "Turnabout Stillwater Academy." This is a lock-up facility for troubled teens. I retired from teaching from this facility in 2006.

Jason Briggs, Vanessa Vettica, Kenneth MacDonald, Amelia MacDonald, Jennifer (Briggs) MacDonald, Marielle MacDonald, Jaron Briggs, and Julie Briggs

Since retirement, I have filled up my spare time with many hobbies. I participate in cat and dog rescues, I volunteer for "No More Homeless Pets," I am an avid gem and rock collector, I do a lot of hiking in the mountains and the deserts, plus I have been a runner for many years winning several ribbons and trophies. I am looking forward to doing future work in the genealogy department. I love my retirement and spending time with my beloved children and grandchildren.

written December 2006

Jason Scott Briggs

I was born in Hollywood, California February 21, 1970. I was the beloved, adopted child of John Frank Briggs and Susan Nibley Murdoch Briggs. On February 25, 1971, I was sealed to my parents in the Salt Lake City Temple. I am the 5th grandchild of William Murdoch Jr. and Lucy Deanne Parkinson Nibley Murdoch.

In my childhood I lived in California, Connecticut, Germany, Georgia, New York, and Salt Lake City, Utah. In Savannah, Georgia I attended a Baptist Church Kindergarten and then attended Pooler Elementary School. We moved back to Salt Lake City in 1977 where I attended Edgemont Elementary, Indian Hills Elementary, Rosslyn Heights Elementary, Hillside Intermediate, and Highland High School.

As a young boy I enjoyed playing football, baseball, and karate. I also danced in the Ballet West Nutcracker for three years performing the role of Fritz. In high school, I was a member of the soccer team and became an Eagle Scout. After graduation, I moved to Hawaii and worked in the pineapple fields making many great friends and also learning to wind surf. After returning, I moved to Alaska and worked in the salmon fisheries.

I have enjoyed many years playing the guitar and singing in a band named, Groove-berry Jam. We were very well known throughout the Salt Lake area and played in many establishments.

I worked for years as an assistant manager at the Judge Café. I also worked many years at the Salt Lake Roasting Company. Presently, I own a coffee shop, "Alchemy Coffee" with my partner Vanessa Vettica in downtown Salt Lake City. It is an atmosphere of great coffee, pastries and live music.

My hobbies and interests are hiking, camping, traveling, music, and reading. I love animals and, with Vanessa, own several beloved pets including: a German Shepherd, German Shepherd/wolf mix, and a cat. I also enjoy collecting rocks and antiques. My current interests are in family history and architecture.

Jennifer Susan Briggs MacDonald

I was born September 8, 1971 in Hamburg, Germany. I am the 7th grandchild of William Murdoch Jr. and Lucy Deanne Parkinson Nibley Murdoch. I am the second child of Susan Murdoch Briggs and Frank Briggs.

As a young child, I lived in Connecticut, New York, California, and Georgia. When I was seven years old, my family moved back to Utah where I attended Edgemont Elementary, Indian Hills Elementary, Rosslyn Heights Elementary, Hillside Intermediate, and Highland High School. My fondest childhood memories were dancing in the Ballet West Nutcracker for five years. I enjoyed high school, participating in many extra-curricular activities including: Dance Club, Pep Club, and Choir. I also served as a Student Body Officer, Secretary of the National Honor Society, and graduated in the top ten of my class.

After high school I attended the University of Utah where I served in the student government and was affiliated with the Chi Omega Sorority. I was privileged to live with my grandparents during this time of my life so that the money I earned from my job as a nanny could go towards tuition. I feel so blessed that I was able to earn a B.S. degree in Biology, and a minor in Chemistry in 1996. I later earned another B.S. in Psychology in 1998. Without the support of my grandparents, I would not have been able to attain such accomplishments and am eternally grateful to them for providing me with this opportunity.

On July 19, 1997, I married my soul-mate, Kenneth Ian MacDonald, (born August 25, 1969) in the Red Butte Gardens in Salt Lake City, Utah. Kenneth is the second son of Colin and Wendy MacDonald. Kenneth, a British citizen, spent his childhood in England and South Africa. When he was 10 years old, his father was transferred to Utah, and Kenneth later graduated from Brighton High School. He also graduated with a B.S. in Biology from the University of Utah. Kenneth converted to the LDS church six months after we were married and we were sealed in the Salt Lake Temple on February 5, 1999. We share the common interests of outdoor recreation and travel. Together we have visited Malaysia, Japan, Singapore, Australia, Mexico, Canada, as well as San Francisco, Moab, Las Vegas, Mesa Verde, Jackson Hole, Boston, Washington D.C., Palmyra, The Hamptons, Montauk, Chicago, Fort Lauderdale, Pennsylvania (Amish Country), and Manhattan.

In 2001, I earned a masters degree in Clinical Psychology with an emphasis in Health Psychology from Argosy University in Phoenix, Arizona. I worked as a counselor in the Maricopa County Burn Unit and also as a crisis counselor with ChildHelp USA, a national child abuse hotline. When my husband and I moved to Dallas, Texas, I worked with adolescent sex-offenders in the Collin County Juvenile Detention Center. When we moved again to Long Island, I started a program that counseled adolescent sex-offenders living within the community. Hopefully, my education has helped me to better society and help those in need; qualities both my grandparents and parents tried to instill in me and demonstrated themselves.

We now live in Ramsey, New Jersey, which is only 20 minutes away from the George Washington Bridge into Manhattan. We feel so very blessed to have two healthy daughters. Amelia Juliette MacDonald was born May 27,

2003 in Stony Brook, New York. She is energetic, fun, smart, and always the life of the party. Marielle Elise MacDonald was born November 11, 2004 in Ridgewood, New Jersey. Marielle began to dance a week after she learned to walk. She loves to sing and especially loves being silly with her big sister. I love being a mother, and feel so privileged to be able to raise these sweet little angels. My husband is a perfect father and enjoys spending every extra moment he has with his girls by reading to them, taking them on hikes and bike rides, teaching them golf, and "cuddling."

My ancestors sacrificed a great deal to better their lives and the lives of their children. Many of them crossed the plains for religious freedom. I have also been told of their struggles during the Great Depression and the World Wars. I am grateful for their sacrifice and hope to honor them by living my life with integrity.

Jaron Sean Briggs

I was born December 24, 1974 in Savannah. Georgia. My parents are Susan Nibley Murdoch Briggs and John Frank Briggs. I was a Christmas baby. The hospital nurses brought me to my parents in a big red stocking. It was a wonderful and exciting time for my parents. We lived in Pooler, Georgia.

I was 3 years old when we moved back to Utah. I went to Rosslyn Heights Elementary, Hillside Junior High, and Highland High School. In my elementary years, I played soccer and football. I also was in the Nutcracker Ballet for three years. My friends and I tried out for the Nutcracker together and we all made the party scene. It was one of my favorite things, especially since I had been born on Christmas Eve.

In junior high, I won many art contests. One of my art designs was picked to be on the school's student directory.

In high school, I was voted Freshman Class Secretary, and participated in many school activities. When I was a senior, I was the Senior Class Vice President. I also won many art awards (Reflections). My painting of the Berlin Wall took first place in my high school. This painting also took first place in regionals and state. It was a great honor to win these awards. It was also in high school where I learned about film and movies. This became my passion.

After graduation from high school, I served a mission to Berlin, Germany. I had an experience there that I will never forget. My companion and I were walking on a bridge by some railroad tracks when I spotted a man laying on the tracks. In the near distance, I could hear and see the train coming. I immediately jumped off the bridge and pulled the man off the tracks just as the train sped by. He was drunk, depressed, and wanted to end his life. We got him home and kept in contact with him. He soon wanted to hear the missionary lessons. I was transferred and wonder to this day what happened to him. Soon after, I was hit by a car while riding my bicycle at night, and returned to the States.

In Utah, I attended the Salt Lake Community College and the University of Utah where I studied film and advertising. To pay for school, I worked years at the Monaco Hotel. I am presently attending the "Art Center" in Pasadena, California. I am studying film, directing, and advertising. This school only takes 12 students a year, and I was lucky enough to be accepted. It's been a wonderful honor.

In my spare time, I make films with my friends and I enjoy camping and hiking in the Utah mountains. I also love music, reading, and traveling.

Written December 2006

Julie Shannon Briggs

I was born June 21, 1982 in Salt Lake City, Utah. My parents are Susan Nibley Murdoch Briggs and John Frank Briggs. I was the fourth child. I had one sister and two brothers. I went to Rosslyn Heights Elementary, Indian Hills Elementary, Hillside Junior High, and Highland High School.

When I was eight years old, my father taught me to play the violin. We had the opportunity to do many duets together for church meetings and social gatherings. I have many fond memories of playing the violin with my father. At this time, I also took ballet and loved it. I danced for six years.

In junior high, I won two awards. One was the "Terrific Kid Award." This was given to me because I helped the mentally handicapped girls get ready for their P.E. classes. I also won second place in the Salt Lake City School District's Chess Tournament. I enjoyed singing in the choir and was given the opportunity to perform two solos.

In high school, I played on the girl's basketball and softball team. I was in Pep Club my junior year and also sang with the Junior Choir. As a senior, I sang in the Senior Choir and the Girl's Barbershop Quartet. At this time, I also participated in some modeling and worked in the ZCMI Fashion Show.

After I graduated from high school, I worked as a nanny for two separate families. I truly loved these children. I currently work for a family with a special-needs child, who was born without the ability to feel pain resulting in many tragic accidents. I have formed a strong bond with this little special spirit.

In 2002, I had the opportunity to live in New York where I worked at a health food store called, "Wild by Nature." I was also able to spend many hours with my new little niece. I returned to Salt Lake City in 2003 to attend the Mountain West College. I graduated with an associates degree and am a certified medical assistant. I am 24 years old and looking forward to getting married and having a family. I enjoy camping, hiking, animal rescue, movies, fashion, and travel.

JANE MURDOCH GARDNER

I am William Murdoch's youngest daughter Jane. I grew up in Salt Lake and had an ideal childhood. I loved having so many extended family members on both sides who my parents dearly loved.

I have memories of going to Uncle Lennox's beautiful home and picking apples from the wall of apple trees that lined his driveway. We would swim in his pool where Dad taught me to dive. I remember trips to Aunt Mary Murdoch's for a tour of her cozy apartment and offers of interesting goodies. Although I didn't see a lot of Dad's family, I loved them because he loved them so much. I will always remember how, as Dad's family passed on, he sweetly talked of them and how he devoted hours to the upkeep of their graves. He would bring flowers in the warm months and place wreaths on their graves in the winter. He would weed and water and lovingly make things look nice. I even remember a scrapbook he kept of the headstones he cared for. Dad's favorite family quote was, "remember your ancestors" and he always did. My parents' example of service to family was powerful.

I attended BrighamYoung University and the University of Utah, and married Marty Gardner in 1968. We had the chance to live all over the country as he pursued his career as a Law Professor. We lived in Indiana, Alabama, Massachusetts, and then settled in Lincoln, Nebraska. Along the way, we had five wonderful children which will always be my greatest blessing. Through the busy years of raising children, I kept even busier with church work, civic duties, and volunteer work. It was a fun and fulfilling life. I am now working in a retirement community environment with dozens of seniors and their families. I find myself really caring and giving helpful and needed service to other peoples' relatives. My parents' devotion to older family members comes to mind everyday. I learned from them to revere, respect, and serve those that have lived long lives and now need to be cared for.

Joshua is our oldest son and was born in January 1970. He was always amazing and I am in awe of his abilities. He graduated from Trinity University in San Antonio, Texas with degrees in Philosophy and Religion. At Trinity, he played on the basketball team and had a wonderful time. After college, he went to St. Petersburg, Russia on a mission. He was one of the first missionaries to serve in that area and what an experience! He has kept up with his Russian language by teaching English as a second language and also tutoring Russian students. He then earned his law degree from the University of Nebraska Law School. He is currently working as a cognitive skills trainer helping students with learning problems. He has a wonderful wife, Paula, and two daughters, Thea, 3 years and Willa, 18 months. They are more than busy with work, church, and family.

Erin is our oldest daughter and was born in August of 1971. She sang

Susan, Bill, Jane, Anne, and Lucy Murdoch

and danced her way through life, attending BYU as a musical dance theater major. She then moved on to the University of Utah, where she received degrees in both Psychology and Social Work. She earned her master degree in Social work and is currently a mental health therapist in Lincoln. She is married to Mike Kramer and has four children: Sunny, 14, Gardner, 13, Sailor, 2, and Bridger, nine months.

Bryn was born in 1976 and is our middle daughter. She was a gymnastic champ in high school and also sang and danced in many productions. She graduated from the University of Nebraska with a Masters Degree in Social Work. She works with at risk and abused teenagers.

Lynsey was born on the 4th of July in 1979. She is attending the University of Nebraska and majoring in Early Childhood Development. She also sings and dances. All three girls are health nuts running miles on the Nebraska running trails.

Jacob was born in September of 1987 and is a junior at the University of Nebraska majoring in English. He is the lead singer and guitarist in his rock band, The Black Hundreds. They plan to go on tour on the west coast when the school year is over.

All the kids are interesting and capable adults and I am more than thankful for them. "My cup runneth over!"

As I look at the careers that my kids have chosen, I can see that my dad's example of service to others is strong. I love being a Murdoch and living in Nebraska, where Wee Granny traveled and is buried. This makes me feel close to her. I am grateful for my ancestors, and as Dad hoped, I will remember them.

William Murdoch, Jr. and Lucy Deanne Parkinson Nibley

Clockwise from top: Willaim and Jane; Josh and family; Jacob with band; Sunny, Gardner, Sailor Bridger, Jane's daughters Erin, Bryn, and Lynsey

Chapter 12

Ellen Jean Murdoch and David Jesse Buckwalter

Ellen Jean Murdoch Buckwalter was born October 2, 1918 in Salt Lake City, Utah to William and Jeannette Cousins Smith Murdoch. She is the 7th of nine children.

David Jesse Buckwalter was born November 10, 1913 in Pittsfield, Massachusetts to Jesse Otto and Louise Marie Buckwalter. His brothers and sisters are Robert C., George E., Donald, and Grace Buckwalter Edmonson. He was a middle child.

Their Story - In 1940, David Jesse Buckwalter rode into Salt Lake City on his Indian motorcycle. He had the good fortune to meet Ellen Jean Murdoch. The rest, as they say, is "history". David Buckwalter arrived from Pittisfield, Massachusetts having graduated from MIT with a chemical engineering degree and worked in Texas (oil field), California, and Nevada. He eventually married Jean on September 21, 1940 and in 1947, young David Murdoch Buckwalter arrived on the scene.

The Buckwalters lived in Salt Lake City for several years while David Senior worked in the copper and oil business. In 1960, his friends in the cop-

LEFT: *Jean with Mary Murdoch* RIGHT: *Jean*

per business convinced him to move to Peru. The family returned in 1963 and lived all over the United States as David Sr. had a very successful career in the copper business and related industries. Jean was extremely supportive and was greatly involved both as a mom and as housewife/social director for all the different places they lived. She was a supreme hostess where people naturally gravitated to her endearing personality. Much of Dave's success was due to Jean and her ability to make everyone welcome and feel appreciated. Jean and Dave carried on their later years in Tucson, Arizona and are now at peace in Salt Lake City, where it all began. Jean died on March 10, 1993. David died 22 July 2002.

LEFT: *Lennox Murdoch, Jean and Dave Buckwalter, and John Leonard*
RIGHT: *Sisters: Mary, Bonnie, Jean, Beth, and Jeannette*

DAVID MURDOCH BUCKWALTER

Born: 18 September 1947 in Salt Lake City, Utah

He is the only child of David Buckwalter & Ellen Jean Murdoch Buckwalter

David graduated from Michigan State University with a Master's Degree in Marketing and Advertising with a Bachelor in Business Administration. The degree gave him a position at Southern Arizona Bank working as a investment banker in December of 1971… increasing the banks financial corporate equities and through bank mergers, he maintained the investment accounting division through First Interstate Banking (Wells Fargo). Once leaving the banking industry, his career path led to mortgage brokering for 10 years and after the market fell, he worked at Cudahy Meat Company as a corporate financial manager. When the company closed the main office, his job direction switched to the retail truck area with responsibility of inventory, selling, and accounting. Deciding to branch out from retail., he currently works at Bank of America where he happily seems back in his niche.

ELVA AGUILAR DESJARDIN BUCKWALTER

Born: 24 October 1952 in Tucson, Pima County, Arizona
   She is the middle child of Rudolph & Guadalupe Aguilar Desjardin.
   Elva Buckwalter grew up in Tucson, Arizona and attended Palo Verde High School.
   On February 2, 1972, Elva met Dave at Southern Arizona Bank where she was a Benefits Insurance Liaison. They dated for two years and were married January 19, 1974. They were married at Oro Valley Country Club where her fiancé/spouse was a member. Employment has always been insurance related (auto as well as the medical industry) and is still employed and working for United Health Group through multiple mergers for twenty years as an auditor. Happily married and blessed to have a satisfying career with being a Mom and a Grandma to Jadon Cade.

Ashlee Pilar Buckwalter

Born: 22 June 1977
   Birth Place: Phoenix, Maricopa County, Arizona
   1st Child
   Parents: David & Elva Buckwalter
   I was born June 22, 1977 and was an only child until I was nine. My two siblings arrived back to back and gave me a rude awakening and a large dose of reality. My grandmother, Ellen Jean Murdoch Buckwalter, was the best grandma a child could ask for and was always there for me. No longer did the world revolve around me (according to my parents Elva and Dave Buckwalter,) but my grandmother made sure that when I was with her, the world still did. I couldn't have asked for a better grandma. She was attentive and so loving, and not a day goes by without me thinking about her. I miss her very much. My grandmother always made me feel special.
   Don't get me wrong... my parents were great too. One of my most memorable memories was when I was six (pre-sibling era), and my mother asked me what I wanted for my birthday. I had a huge imagination as a child, and when she stated that I could have anything I asked for, she kept her promise. I requested a huge party that would be held in my honor in Tucson, Arizona. I wanted dance music, including live music from mariachis. I wanted the whole family and all of my friends to attend. I asked for balloons, cake, ice cream, etc. My ideas were somewhat grandiose, but my mother surprised me and had every detail down to the requested floating flowers and candles in the pool. You could imagine the arrival of my sister, and then soon after my brother was an abrupt and challenging change for a spoiled brat like me.
   I attended a private traditional Christian school during grade school, and then transferred to a public school during junior high. In high school, I

attended Xavier College Preparatory and after sophomore year transferred to Washington High School where I graduated in '95. Throughout grade school and high school, I was involved in swimming and much of my time was devoted to working out and swim meets. When college came around, I grew tired of swimming and decided I needed to do some traveling. I ended up attending Phoenix College and through them I received two scholarships. One scholarship was a chance to study in Guanajuato, GTO for a summer and the other was an academic full scholarship for Arizona State University. I graduated ASU with a degree in Communications in 2000. Since then, I fell into government sector and have had the opportunity to work for the State in Human Resources and I now currently work for the City Of Phoenix in their Personnel Department. I make recommendations to the City Council concerning job classification and pay. I enjoy it thoroughly and I plan on retiring from the City Of Phoenix. Additionally, I am in the process of getting my Master in Public Administration through Arizona State University.

I am very fortunate to have purchased a home very close to my parents. In fact, they are only two blocks away, and despite the age difference between my sister, brother, and I, we are all very close to this day.

Children:

Jadon Cade Murdoch Aguilar Desjardin Buckwalter
July 10, 2006, Phoenix, Maricopa County, Arizona
Jadon Cade enjoys Veggie Tales, Spiderman, and the Bee Movie.

He has been counting to ten since he has been 18 months old. He will be two and a half this December and is bilingual (English and Spanish) at this juncture. He is such a delight.

Courtney Bianca Buckwalter

Birthdate: 20 April 1986
  Place of Birth: Phoenix, Maricopa County, Arizona
  Middle Child
  Parents: David & Elva Buckwalters. My earliest childhood memory is that of my grandmother, Ellen Jean, or Grandma Jean, as I would call her. She was making the best tuna fish sandwich I have ever had with a side of Wheat Thins®. Still to this day, I have never tasted such a delectable sandwich! The grandparents lived in Tucson, Arizona at this time, but would visit every other weekend - or what I thought to be eternity. She would always bring holiday themed sugar cookies from our local grocery store; which never failed. Grandma Jean was the most wonderful, thoughtful grandmother a child could ask for. I also remember fishing with my grandfather, David "Buck" Buckwalter near Payson, Arizona. That day, I didn't catch any fish, but all of my bait was gone! He was a very patient grandpa!

I am currently attending college in my sophomore year at Phoenix College. I am a full-time honors student attending with a full-ride scholarship. I also am an active member in various clubs through the community college. I am transferring to Arizona State University to the renowned WP Carry School of Business in January 2007. My program of study is global business with a minor degree in Spanish. The summer of 2006 I will be living in Mexico for the second time to be immersed in the Latin culture.

I dedicate most of my time to my studies as well as volunteer work with The Phoenix Children's Hospital. I also work part-time with a promotion agency marketing various products in Phoenix, Arizona and surrounding areas. In my spare time I am focused with my dancing. I have been involved with the Primavera Folklorico Dance Co. since 1994; studying my Mexican culture through ballet folklorico. I also belong to the Arthur Murray School of Dance where I am currently taking ballroom classes, focusing mainly on the Latin style dances.

David Jesse Buckwalter, Jr.

Born: 11 May 1987
  Phoenix, Maricopa County, Arizona
  Youngest Child
  Parents: David & Elva Buckwalter
  I am currently apprenticing in cabinetry in Tucson, working for my grandfather, Rudy Desjardin. I have always been a 'hands on' type person. My grandfather has a cabinet business and I have always enjoyed wood shop. I am installing, staining, and drafting....plus enjoying the opportunity to spend time with relatives that I rarely visited when living in Phoenix. This career hopefully, should provide a lifelong enjoyment in

remodeling or homebuilding. My employer (Grandpa Rudy) is Rudy's Tops & Cabinets is diverse and we build libraries, kitchen cabinets, tables, doors and moldings... and at this juncture of my life... life is very good. As I improve on my skills, I have the hope to take over my grandfather's business when he retires.

Chapter 13

Robert Gail Murdoch and Betty Lue Clark

Robert Gail Murdoch was born in Salt Lake City, Utah on June 10, 1921, the eighth of nine children to William and Jeannette Cousins Smith Murdoch. Bob was very proud of his Scottish surname. He loved to hear bagpipes and always wanted to go to Scotland. He grew up in the family home at 78 F Street on the Avenues. His father owned a neighborhood grocery store called Murdoch Grocery, where the men of the family all worked. One of the main selling points of the store was the delivered and boxed up groceries to the customers. Bob began driving the truck when he was only 12 years old and because he was so short, had to sit on a cushion and had blocks on the gas and brake pedals. He was always very serious about putting in a hard day's work.

His grandfather, David Lennox Murdoch, built a cabin in Lamb's Canyon, which is where the Murdoch children spent their entire summers for many years. Bob always told stories of summers at Lamb's Canyon.

 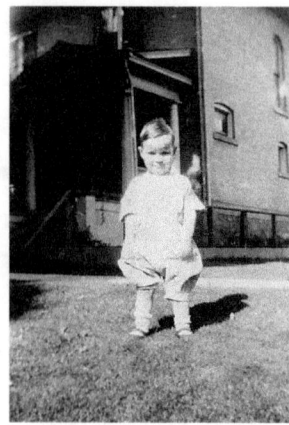 

LEFT: Bob about 2 years old. MIDDLE: Bob about 18 months. RIGHT: 11 1/2 years old, taken December 1932.

When they returned home at the end of August, his mother had made each of them a hat and coat for the coming winter. Bob's Aunt Jen and Aunt Mary tended the children during this time. One of the chores they made them do was sweep the dirt road leading to the cabin. They also had to chop and stack wood. When Bob got older, he would sit patiently on the front porch waiting for gophers to pop up and then shoot them with his .22 rifle. This proved to be a good thing later on in his life. After he joined the Army, he received many sharp-shooter medals. Bob was a very strong young man. He wrestled in high school and boxed at the University of Utah while in college.

He met his future wife, Betty Lue Clark, in the grocery store one day. Eventually he asked her out and they always had a great time together. She says that he was very funny and loved to make her laugh. His father, William, died before Bob served his mission.

In 1940, he was called on a mission for the Church of Jesus Christ of Latter-day Saints to the East Central States Mission, which included Kentucky, Tennessee, and North Carolina.

It was a difficult mission because of the distances they were required to walk – some days they would walk 20 miles. They were also required to always have $10 in their pockets so they wouldn't be arrested for vagrancy. They were asked many times to go "without purse or scrip", which means without money or food and rely on the Lord for guidance. This was  always a difficult thing to do because the people in the backhills were often very poor and could barely feed their own families. On one occasion, Bob and his missionary companion didn't have any luck finding a place to sleep and came across a little church in the mountains. They found that a door was unlocked so they went inside, took down the drapes and used them for covers for the night. The next morning, they re-hung the drapes, went outside and found some apples trees. They helped themselves to the apples for breakfast. In looking for places to sleep, many times they had to sleep on the hay with the animals in the barn. The experiences of his mission must have had a profound effect on his ability to endure the difficult trials of serving in the Philippines during World War II. His faith in the Lord to guide and comfort him during the war most likely had its beginnings from the challenges he faced on his mission. Many times growing up, if we saw missionaries, Bob would hand them some money from his pocket.

After returning from his mission, he and Betty were married in the Salt Lake Temple on March 30, 1942 by David O. McKay. Within a short three months, he enlisted in the Army and was sent to Camp Walters, Texas for Basic Training. He then went onto Luzon in the Philippines and directly into front-line combat in the Zombali Mountains.

During his service in the Army he had an experience in which he was forced to stay for 30 straight days in a foxhole. This was because there were no replacements for him and his platoon. He became very discouraged and had to rely on the Lord for comfort. Prayer was a very important part of his life while serving in World War II. After the Japanese surrendered, Bob was sent to Tokyo, Japan as a Chaplain's Assistant. He always said that it was something no one ever thought would happen - that they would walk down the streets of Tokyo. One day his Chaplain sent him and two other Japanese civilians to find and bring back some Christmas trees. This was supposed to be a difficult assignment because many of the trees had been cut down for firewood. But they found several trees, cut some down and returned back to the Chaplain's office. The Chaplain was absolutely amazed that they had found several trees and asked where they had gotten them. Bob explained the route he had taken and was told that those trees belonged on the estate of the Emperor Hirohito! He always said, "I'm probably the only person of the face of the earth who cut down Christmas trees on Hirohito's estate!" Bob received the Bronze Star after the war. His mother, Jeannette, died in Salt Lake City during his time at war and was not able to attend her funeral. He loved his mother very much so this must have been very hard on him.

After an honorable release and after returning to the States, Bob and Betty moved to Boise where Bob went to work for his brother, Jack Murdoch, at Jack Murdoch Finance. Soon after, their oldest daughter, Janice, was born while they lived in the north end of Boise at 1404A Lemp Street. Later they moved to 2308 N. 19th Street towards Hill Road and that is where Bette Ann and Sherri were born.

A new church house was being built on Hill Road, not far from their house. Dad literally helped to build that chapel and would come home with sore hands from laying the bricks.

One of his favorite past times was to go fishing. The girls always got a thrill when he brought home catfish because they thought they were so interesting and because they lived a long time out of water, he would put them in the bathtub to swim around. One time, Bob got really sick after a fishing trip, and Betty had to kill 28 of them all by herself. There were many weekend fishing trips with the family because Bob had heard of that "special" fishing hole during the week.

Because he had yellow jaundice during the war, mosquitoes wouldn't come near him, but they came near everybody else! Bette Ann remembers going fishing with Bob while the family was staying in Yellowstone Park. She was immediately eaten alive with mosquitoes. Bob would simply say, "Don't let little things like that bother you." Bette Ann went back to the cabin and Bob continued fishing.

The time came for the family to have a new car. The girls were sick of the green Studebaker, so Bob went shopping. He and Betty came home with a red and pink Rambler station wagon. The girls were embarrassed of the color, but the car was big. One reason for buying this car, besides the fact that it had overdrive, which was new at the time, was to pick up church members who lived a long distances from the church on Sundays. Some Sundays he made two trips before church to pick people up. He had many church callings, including serving in the bishopric of the Boise 2nd

Ward located in the old Tabernacle on the corner of Washington and 10th Street. He also served for years in the Stake Sunday School. He was a natural-born teacher and was a wonderful Sunday School and Seminary teacher.

Bob was a banker. While working for the Bank of Idaho, he attended and graduated from the American Institute of Banking at the University of Washington in Seattle. He enjoyed his visits up there with Carolyn and Richard Hultquist. Carolyn is his sister Elizabeth's daughter. Bob retired from First Interstate Bank, formally Bank of Idaho, in 1982. He was already living in Eagle on a golf course and loved it. He played golf everyday with a group of his friends. This was a wonderful time for him and loved to share golf stories. Once while golfing at the Eagle Hills Golf Course, he got a hole-in-one, a dream come true and something he always loved to share with anyone who would listen.

As time progressed, Bob began showing signs of Alzheimer's Disease and it was evident that he could no longer live by himself. The difficult decision was made to take him to a retirement home and then into the Boise Idaho Veteran's Home located in the northern part of Boise, where they cared for veterans with Alzheimer's Disease. He lived there for seven years, where he received compassionate care from his family and the wonderful staff. From the time of his diagnosis until his death, he lived with that disease for 12 years.

Throughout his professional career, Bob was involved in many worthwhile community services. He was appointed by Governor Andrus to the State of Idaho Task Force to review efficiency of the various state agencies. The bank appointed him to fund raising committees for the United Way and American Heart Association. Upon his retirement, he was instrumental in raising funds and planning the construction of the Eagle Senior Citizen Center. He was very active in church and held many leadership positions.

Some fun memories of Bob—

While they were still dating, Bob wanted to take Betty bird hunting. He took her down to the Murray area, south of Salt Lake City. When they got in the field, Bob explained to Betty to walk about 20 feet in front of him. "If I yell 'Drop Louie', drop quick because I am going to shoot", he said. Well, a bird flew, Betty dropped, and Bob shot. Unfortunately, Betty had dropped right into a pile of mud and manure. A stinky mess! Bob made her walk while he drove the big black Buick, the family car, to the nearest farm yard so she could wash off. A lady let her use her pump in the yard and Betty was able to clean up enough to get back in the car. "It ruined my new mittens. It was all down my pant legs and it was awful." Betty never went hunting with him again.

Bob wanted to take her golfing. When they got on the course, Bob told Betty that her assignment was to carry his bag, in other words, be his caddy. ("Bob could talk a bird out of a cage", Betty always said.) Needless to say, Betty never went golfing with Bob again. Except for one time . . . Betty went golfing with a friend while he was off at another course with some friends, or so she thought. She and her friend, Mary Bell, were out on the course and Betty didn't see that Bob had been following them from tree to tree watching her every move. She was having a difficult time hitting the ball and he had finally had it! He stepped out from behind the tree and said, "I'll show you how it's done." He took the club and in his perfect form, hit the ball. It only went about 10 feet, bouncing all the way. Betty and her friend couldn't stop laughing but Bob didn't like that. So he took another swing at the ball and it flew.

Janny used to spend lots of summers in McCall. One summer before her senior year in high school, not long before school started, she decided to put red highlights in her hair. Now you have to realize that she had dark skin and black hair. Bob even called her, "Dark Cloud." He did not approve of her dying her hair. After putting the dye in her hair, she wrapped it in a towel and laid on the couch for a bit while her hair processed for the 25 minute maximum time limit. Unfortunately she fell fast asleep. When she woke up 45 minutes later, she had a new red and black hair color. When she got home and had no more than taken two steps inside the front door and Bob saw her with her tan skin and black/reddish hair, he said, "NO daughter of mine is going to look like that!" He almost wouldn't let her into the house.

Janny also remembers her dad having a sweet and caring spirit. He was always concerned for others, and was always a good example for his daughters. When Janny was young, Bob put her on a stool and taught her how to box. She still has a powerful punch today. After Janny hurt her back from falling from a horse, Bob would go around saying, "Head up, shoulders back, and stomach in." Bob always said to be proud of your Scottish Heritage. Janny took this to heart and served as Historian for the Boise Chapter of the Scottish Society of Caledonians.

Bette Ann's favorite memories were of their fishing trips. Bob would come in and wake her up on Saturday mornings and off they would go fishing. They usually went up to the middle fork of the Boise River. Bette Ann got to be pretty good at fishing and picking out fishing holes. They would whistle to signal to each other when they had caught a fish. Bob could only do a little whistle. It was not too loud. But Bette Ann could give a really loud wolf whistle. She soon learned that the whistle only brought her dad over to take over her fishing hole, while she spent forever taking the fish off of the hook. When they went fishing on the middle fork of the Boise River, they always stopped at a little spring by the side of the road. They would drink from it and gather a little watercress to take home to Betty to put in a salad. One time when they went by, there was a sign there that read, "Do Not Drink this Water". They just looked at each other and laughed. Bob decided the first summer of their fishing trips, that they needed a lucky song. He decided that it would be *We'll Sing in the Sunshine*. If they ever heard it on their way up to fish, they were in for a lucky day of fishing. He taught Bette Ann to love and appreciate the beauties and wonders of nature.

When Sherri was just a little girl, she remembers getting up one morning and when she went into the bathroom, she got scared because the bathtub was full of live catfish swimming around. Sherri remembers her dad always being keenly aware of people's needs. She remembers that he had noticed that a young boy in the ward needed shoes. So, he gave money to the bishop to give to the boy's family. This happened several times when he noticed a need and gave someone money to help them. When Sherri was a teenager, Bob was offered a manager's job at the Jerome office for the Bank of Idaho. The family took a Saturday and drove to Jerome. Sherri cried the whole way over and the whole way back, not to mention the entire time they were in Jerome. Needless to say, Bob turned the job offer down. When the Nampa managerial position came up, he took the job before he told Sherri. When Sherri was graduating from Ricks College, Betty and Bob went to Rexburg for the graduation. Bob was afraid they weren't going to get a good seat because he always liked to get up front where he could see and hear. Of course, they got to the gym late, but they had wonderful seats up front. Why? Well earlier in the day, Bob had gone over and put signs on the chairs that said, "Reserved for President Eyring's Relatives." (President Henry B. Eyring was the president of Ricks College at the time).

When Bob got older and had a hard time with his Alzheimer's, Sherri and Betty Lue spent many hours at the Veteran's Home taking him for walks and helping him get used to being there. When she would visit, he would call her over to his side and whisper in her ear, "See those guys over there? They're crazy." Even after Betty and Bob divorced, she always was concerned and reached out to help him there. Bob was very blessed with the angelic service of Betty. She spent several days each week visiting Bob at the Veterans Home and taking care of him.

LEFT: *Bette Ann, Sherri, Jan, and Jane Murdoch at the Murdoch graves 1956.*
RIGHT: *Bob's headstone at the Salt Lake City Cemetery, buried next to his parents.*

Bob loved his grandchildren. He would take them out to eat, buy them things and take them for drives. He always had them over for pop (ginger ale) and to feed the ducks at the pond. He lived at Eagle Hills Golf Course, so feeding the ducks was a huge hit with the children. Bob would give his many found golf balls to his grandsons.

Bob died at the Boise Idaho Veteran's Home in Boise, Idaho on March 5, 1998. He is buried in the Salt Lake City Cemetery next to his parents.

Bob's favorite quote was from Heber J. Grant:

> *"That which we persist in doing becomes easier to do, not that the nature of the thing has changed, but our power to do so is increased."*

At Jack's house Christmas about 1960. Back: Jack, Bob, Betty, and Jan. Front: Bette Ann, Sherri, and Sabina Clark Alder, Betty's mother

WORLD WAR II MILITARY SERVICE

As told to Sherri Murdoch Porter by Betty Lue Clark Murdoch

Bob was serving a mission for the Church of Jesus Christ of Latter-day Saints, in the East Central States Mission (Kentucky, Tennessee and North Carolina), when the war was really heating up. Pres. Roosevelt allowed missionaries who were out, to finish their missions. Missionaries were not called on missions again, until after the war. He served his mission from 1942-1944.

Bob returned home to Salt Lake City from his mission and three weeks later, on March 30, 1944, he married Betty Lue Clark in the Salt Lake Temple. Three months later, he was drafted into the Army and three months after that, headed off to boot camp and then to California to board a ship to head to the *Pacific Theater*, as they called it. When he was inducted into the War, he was in the Infantry First Cavalry Division, trained in Mineral Wells, Texas. He was in the Rifle Division and was an excellent marksman.

It was very hot in Mineral Wells, and it was very common for the soldiers to pass out from the heat. They couldn't understand why Bob would never pass out from hikes or standing at attention. He always told them it was because he didn't smoke.

Bob said while on the ship to the Philippines, they had Spam for breakfast, lunch, and dinner. He never liked it later on and would refuse to eat it. His boots hurt his feet something terrible and hurt the entire time he was in the war. They never fit him right because he had flat feet and the boots had arches.

He was involved in the fighting on the front lines. He hated foxholes and hated digging them. When he was on the Island Leyte, in the Philippines, their assignment in the First Cavalry Division was to protect Ipo Dam. This dam was very important because it was the main water source for Manila. They were in foxholes for over 30 days because they had to wait such a long time for the relief troops to come and the Japanese were trying to take the dam. They were in such danger, and surrounded by the enemy; no one could go in to help them. The General finally came to them and with tears in his eyes explained to them that they had no relief coming because of the danger. They needed to stay there because of the importance of the dam and he would send relief as soon as he could. It was a long time spent in that foxhole and he always said how much he hated it.

His platoon was in enemy territory when a fellow comrade was wounded. The group needed to move on so Bob volunteered to stay behind until medical help came for him. They had very little food. By the time the medical helicopter came to the rescue, Bob had become very sick. They could only take the wounded comrade to safety. Bob had to stay behind in enemy territory by himself. Being behind enemy lines was very dangerous and now Bob was alone. He needed to get back to his platoon, so he followed colored wires back to his unit. Along the way, he went into an abandoned hut to rest and he fell asleep. He suddenly heard a voice tell him to get out of the hut. He immediately ran out and the hut blew up. He was unhurt. When he found his way to his platoon, it was dark and he was scared to death his buddies would shoot him thinking he was the enemy, so he kept saying, "Murdoch, Murdoch" and they recognized his name and voice. He later in life received the Bronze Star Medal for his bravery. This story was always a testimony to Bob of listening and following the Holy Ghost.

Bob continued to get really sick so they sent him off shore to an Army hospital ship. He had yellow jaundice, hepatitis, and eight different tape worms. One night, after the doctor left, Bob copied his diseases from the clipboard at the end of his bed into his Bible. He was down to 90 pounds.

One night, he said that he was so sick that he decided to just give up. He actually died that night in the hospital. He opened his eyes and there standing around his bed, all dressed in white, were his mother, Jeannette; his father, William, his grandfather, David Lennox and grandmother, Elizabeth. They were holding out their hands to him to come and join them. He then realized his deep love and devotion for Betty and decided to fight and get better so he could go back to her. When he started to feel better, they fed him a lot of Zagnut candy bars (the center of a Butterfinger - without the chocolate) to help him put on weight. He always loved eating them. He eventually got back to his platoon.

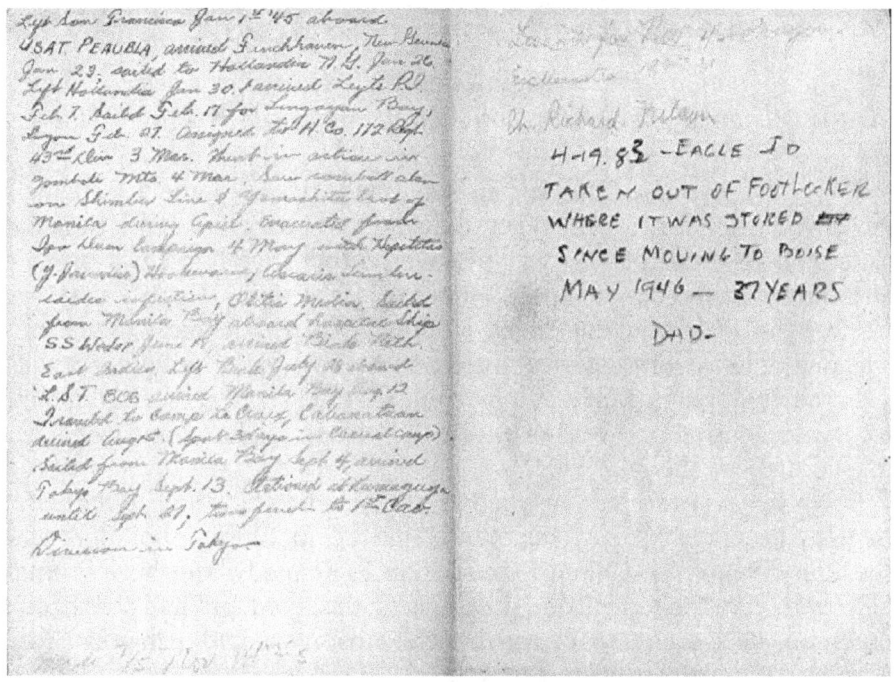

Bob wrote down his diseases in his Bible

He served most of his time in the Philippines fighting. The war was very difficult on Bob because he was such a peaceful-type person. He said he was never sure he killed anyone, but we can't imagine that being the case considering they were living in a foxhole on the front lines, running a machine gun and shooting.

Lucy Murdoch (Bill) once told Bette Ann, that Bob was different when he came home. One can only imagine what he must have gone through and can sympathize with veterans and what they have gone through to defend our freedoms.

After the war, Bob served as an Assistant Chaplin with a Baptist Chaplin in the Army of Occupation, in Tokyo, Japan. Finishing the war and walking down the streets of Tokyo, was something no one ever thought would happen. He always said it was a surreal experience.

Both pictures taken in Tokyo in 1945, after the war.
LEFT: *Bob on far left.* RIGHT: *Bob is on the very right next to the building.*

When in Tokyo, the Chaplin told Bob to take two men and a Jeep and go cut down a Christmas tree. When they did and brought it back, they were asked where they got it. It was discovered that they had cut it down on Hirohito's Estate (the Japanese Emperor at the time). Luckily they were not caught. Everyone sure loved kidding them about that experience. It was one of his favorite stories to tell and he always told it with a laugh.

In the Philippines, Bob was a machine gunner. He also received a medal for *marksmanship* and was an excellent shooter. He lost some of his hearing because of this.

Bob had never received his medals of which he knew he had earned, so in 1962 he wrote his congressman, James A. McClure, who approached the President of the United States, John F. Kennedy, and he was finally able to receive the long awaited medals he deserved and had sacrificed so much for. He received many medals, the most respected being the Bronze Star Medal. The certificate reads:

> THE UNITED STATES OF AMERICA
> TO ALL WHO SHALL SEE THESE PRESENTS, GREETING: THIS IS TO CERTIFY THAT THE PRESIDENT OF THE UNITED STATES OF AMERICA AUTHORIZED BY EXECUTIVE ORDER, 24 AUGUST 1962 HAS AWARDED
> THE BRONZE STAR MEDAL
> TO: Technician five Robert G. Murdoch, United States Army
> FOR: Meritorious achievement in ground combat against the armed enemy during World War II in the Philippines.
> Other Medals and Ribbons: Asiatic Pacific Theater Service Ribbon, Philippines Liberation Service Ribbon, Good Conduct Medal AR 600-68, Victory Medal, Japanese Occupational Medal, Marksmanship Medal

He was released from the Army in June 1946.

Betty Lue Clark Murdoch

On September 28, 1922, my twin sister, Sherri, and I were born in Los Angeles, California. My mother, Sabina Clark, had separated from my father, John Burt, who was from Salt Lake City. She moved to Los Angeles to have what she thought was one baby but later found out she was having twins. She had a broken pelvis from an auto accident in 1918 and the doctors were amazed that she was carrying twins having had such an injury. We came into the world at the teaching hospital so my grandmother could save money on the delivery. We lived in Los Angeles for another year or so and eventually moved back to Salt Lake City and lived with my mother's sister, Ella, and her husband, Harry Eccles. We lived with them for about four years and attended kindergarten at Hawthorne Elementary School. We then moved to the Blackstone Apartments, which later became the Royal Arms Apartments, on the corner of North Temple and West Temple.

When I was two years old, Mother had hired a lady to take care of us so she could work. The lady had been sewing on the couch and apparently lost a needle. She sat me down on the couch next to her, not thinking the needle could be there and I sat on it. The needle went in the upper part on the back of my right leg. She called Mother and they rushed me to Dr. Middleton's office, the Clark's family doctor. He took an X-ray and when he decided to operate on my leg, my Aunt Hazel (Mother's sister who drove us to the doctor's office) told him that he should take another X-ray because she was afraid it had moved. He said that he wouldn't because he knew right where it was. He cut into my leg and checked and it wasn't there. He took the knife and cut it farther and finally put his hand inside my leg and felt around and couldn't find it. As a result, he tore it about three more inches up my leg. Aunt Hazel finally told him to stop it and he sewed it up. He left me with a huge scar that today is about 6 inches long. It is very deep and goes into my leg about one half inch to one inch. Recovery must have been horrible and Mother always felt so bad for me. Later as I grew, it always hurt because it stretched and pulled. They never found the needle and I always wondered if the needle just went down into the couch cushion or if it was even there. I will never know.

LEFT: *Twins Sherri and Betty Lue at Saltair by the Great Salt Lake*
RIGHT: *Betty Lue and Sherri*

I grew up mostly around Temple Square in Salt Lake City. I have fond memories of the Temple grounds and my Aunt Evelyn taking us to see the flowers. We met and became friends with the gardener, Brother Nowman, who would tell us all about the flowers and his designs. Sometimes he would give us a flower to take home to our mother. He had been the gardener for the German Kaiser at the Palace in Berlin, Germany during World War I. I would have loved to have known his conversion story. He would take us to the greenhouse and show us his drafting table and his plans for his designs, such as the *fleur de lis*, and other beautiful arrangements, that made Temple Square so beautiful.

When we were living in the Royal Arms Apartments, we were watching a man put in some steps in the back of the building. When he saw us, he told us that he would make the steps shorter so we could climb them better. We always called them "our steps". We lived in the 17th Ward, Salt Lake Stake, a historical ward located at 1st North and between West Temple and 1st West. It had a beautiful stained glass window of Joseph Smith in the Sacred Grove that I always loved to look at and have always wondered what happened to it when they tore the building down.

We lived with our mother and her sister, Evelyn, who helped raise us. My mother taught business at Henagar Business College and later sold insurance at Hogle Insurance Company in downtown Salt Lake City. When the Great Depression hit, she lost her job. She was without work for a long time and finally got a job at The New England Bakery on Main Street and 1st South. It was very hard on her because of her pelvic injury as she had to stand on her feet all day. She would bring home wonderful chocolate éclairs and we loved them (she used to love to make them for us when she lived with us later in her life). We would meet her at the street car stop at Main Street and North Temple and she would sometimes have two bags of groceries from the Piggley Wiggley. She always told us she couldn't have made it without our help. I could never figure out how she even got on the bus with those big bags of groceries. She always amazed me. Somehow, she always managed to support us and we never knew how she did it. We always felt like we were fortunate to have the mother we did and how smart she was.

We were quite poor, but as little girls, we never thought about it. We just went along and I am sure that Mother and Evelyn didn't want to worry us. They were so great and never missed an opportunity to teach us in so many different ways. There was a little boy, Pee Wee Jones, in our neighborhood who was a really bad bully and always picked on us. One day after another episode where he hit us and we were crying, we went to Mother and told her our sad story. She looked at us and said, "Well girls, there is only one of him and two of you." We looked at each other, ran out the door, and beat him up. He never bothered us again. When we were about four years old, Mother must have saved up some money and took us to the Hotel Utah to eat because Sherri and I wanted to go and see the inside. She bought us little dresses, white gloves, and hats. A nice looking black man greeted us at the door and took us to the dining room. Another black man took us to our table. We were on cloud nine. We thought it was so amazing. He shook the napkin and put it in our laps. Mother said she wanted to take us out to eat to teach us how to eat at a restaurant and how to act in public. We really did learn a lot about how to act when we went out by that experience. I look back and think that Mother must have had some kind of training in manners and how to be polite. We were never allowed to interrupt a conversation and were always told to use out best manners.

During the Depression and when we were about ten years old or so, I remember that times were very bad and so many people lost their jobs. Many of these men would ride the trains and we would call them bums, because they would bum a ride on the train from city to city trying to find a work. Evelyn felt sorry for them because these were bankers and other types that were once respected men in their communities. She would never let us go down by the train depot. We always had a chain on the door of our apartment and the men would ring the doorbell and Evelyn would open the door partially. The men would ask for something to eat so she would tell them to go sit on the steps and she would get them something. She would make them a sandwich and then hand it to them through the chain in the door but always told us not to tell our mother because it was such a hardship to provide for us, let alone anyone coming to the door begging. Once someone came to the door, Evelyn opened it partially with the chain on and he was yelling to let him in. Evelyn couldn't get him to leave and he was reaching into the door trying to get to the chain to open the door. I finally went over and told him to take his hand out because I was shutting the door. I gradually started shutting it and finally was able to shut it all the way. Evelyn said, "Oh my goodness, you were so brave. How did you know what to do?" All I could think of was that we needed to get his hand out of the door. Evelyn always said I could figure things out. We used to sing, "Hallelujah, I'm a Bum."

> *Hallelujah, I'm a bum,*
> *Hallelujah, bum again,*
> *Hallelujah, give us a handout to revive us again.*
> *Oh, I went to a house and knocked at the door,*
> *And the lady said, "Bum, bum, you've been here before,*
> *Hallelujah, I'm a bum,*
> *Hallelujah, bum again,*
> *Hallelujah, give us a handout to revive us again.*

My Aunt Evelyn always did a lot of genealogy and loved to write and receive letters from people who would help her connect genealogy lines. She wrote down so many stories and even made up songs about her ancestors. She had volumes of records when she died in 1977. She made it possible for hundreds and hundreds of people who had died to have their temple work done. Aunt Evelyn taught us many things and one of my favorite memories is that she would let us write out the temple sheets for her to take to the temple. We loved doing that. We used to love to do baptisms at the temple and would do at least 100 at a time. She was so good to us and when Pig Latin was becoming the rage, we were trying to learn it but were having problems and couldn't quite speak it right. A lady from upstairs heard us trying and yelled out the window and asked if she could teach us Pig Latin. So, with our newly acquired skills, we loved to talk in front of Mother and Aunt Evelyn, who told us they didn't understand it, so we felt free to talk about anything we wanted. Swearing was really on the outs and Sherri and I were not allowed to say bad words, but one day we were playing in the sandbox right under the living room window and having a big conversation in Pig Latin. One of us said, "amday" and Evelyn poked her head out the window and said, "What are you girls doing talking like that? Get in here right now." I remember saying to her, "I thought you didn't understand Pig Latin." Then I knew we couldn't use Pig Latin in front of Mother and Evelyn because they knew what we were saying all along.

Growing up on the north end of Salt Lake City meant there were steep hills on the west side of the Capital Building, which was north of our apartment. One day, Sherri and I put on our roller skates and decided to go up to 3rd North and skate down the steep hill to West Temple. When we would get to the bottom of the hill, we would grab the old mail box, which had a box on top and a pole down to the ground. This would prevent us from going into the busy street. We would swing around the pole bringing ourselves to a stop. All the way down the hill, our feet were wobbling back and forth so fast that I don't know how we even stood up. I look at that hill today and wonder, "What were we thinking?" We did it a lot but never told our mother what we were doing.

I was always an adventuresome person and Sherri was more cautious and timid. I had recently seen something about parachuting and decided I wanted to try it. Airplanes were something new. I got one of mother's umbrellas and decided to parachute off the garage roof in the back of the Royal Arms. The garage had a flat roof and was just big enough for cars to get in, so it wasn't too far off the ground. Sherri was crying and pleading with me not to jump because she didn't want to be left an only child. She just knew I was going to get hurt or die. Finally, she got down on her knees and started praying. I remember looking down on her and decided while she had her eyes closed, I would jump. So I did. I wasn't hurt, I didn't die, and when Sherri opened her eyes, I think she was pretty relieved. She was surprised I had done it while she had her eyes closed.

When we were in the Royal Arms, David O. McKay lived next door in the Miller Apartments. We would be out on the sidewalk playing when he went out the door for work. He always wore striped pants and a swallow-tail coat and I loved to watch him walk because he was tall and stately. He worked at the Church Office Building and was President of the Sunday School. I always remembered his beautiful, soft wavy hair. He was always so kind and friendly to us. His youngest son, Bobby, was a playmate and we would play kick-the-can and other fun things at night until about 10:00 during the summer.

We had a lot of friends and the people in the ward were always nice to us. Aunt Evelyn would tell us to go visit old people in the ward to give us something to do. We loved doing it and they always seemed to welcome us and loved to visit with us. One was Brother Cowley. One day, after church when Sherri and I were about seven years old, we decided to stop and visit with the Cowleys. When Sister Cowley answered the door, she said, "Come on in and tell Brother Cowley goodbye." She let us over to his coffin by the fireplace and there he lay. We didn't know why he was laying there in the coffin not moving. We were just staring at him when she picked us up, one at a time, to have us give him a kiss goodbye on the forehead. She lifted me up first and I remember he was ice cold! She then lifted Sherri up. We were both so stunned that we wanted to get out of there quick. We told her we had to get home, so we ran home and told Mother what had happened. She told us yes, that he had died and she explained to us that Sister Cowley was just being nice. We always loved him but I don't remember ever going back to that house again.

We went to the LaFayette Elementary School east of State Street, between Main and State on North Temple. In the center of the hallway  was a huge dinosaur that was always amazed me. I used to love to stand there and study it. I went to Horace Mann Junior High School and then graduated from East High School. I went to the University of Utah for only a couple of semesters but decided it was too expensive for Mother to keep both Sherri and me in college. I went to work for the Presiding Bishop's Office (PBO) at the Church Office Building on South Temple for a couple of years, working under Marvin J. Ashton. I then went to work for the Federal Housing Administration under Gordon Weggeland (Bob's brother-in-law) who was the State Director of the Federal Housing Administration for Utah while Bob was on his mission and also during the war. I started as a file clerk, then a priority clerk, and worked up to an administrative secretary. While I was priority clerk, I had to process requests for housing supplies and because it was war time, those types of things were rationed. I became overwhelmed with the requests and got behind, so I worked until 10:30 at night to get things done. I can't believe that I walked home after work because the street cars didn't work that late. I had to walk home to 1st Avenue and F Street from two blocks off Main Street, ten long Salt Lake City blocks, usually in high heels. What was I thinking?

Mother married George Alder and we moved to 455 1st Avenue. It was one block north of South Temple. Sherri and I were just out of high school. We lived there for about a year or two and within that time, I met Bob. One day George was out watering the lawn and had a heart attack and died. It was very sad because George was such a kind man. I used to go to the Murdoch Grocery Store, which was the neighborhood store, to buy meat or whatever. Bob saw me at the store and wanted to get to know me better, so he came to the house to meet me. We had a milkshake maker and he loved to come to the house to have a homemade milkshake. If he didn't come, I would invite him down and use the milkshake as an excuse. We went out many times. One of the funniest memories I have is when he took me to the Murdoch Cabin in Lamb's Canyon. He wanted to introduce me to his aunts, Mary Murdoch and Janet Thompson. When we were barely out of the car, he introduced me to his Aunt Jen and before you could shake a stick, she handed us each a broom and told us to go sweep the road. Well, the road in front of the cabin was dirt and I couldn't figure out why anyone would want a dirt road swept, but that is what she had us do. Bob just laughed and said that everyone had to do it.

Jeannette Murdoch and Sabina Clark Alder, Betty's mother-in-law and Betty's mother

Bob decided to go on a mission and was called to the East Central States Mission and served mostly in Tennessee, North Carolina, and West Virginia. World War II was already going on in the Pacific and in Europe but Bob got a deferment to serve a mission. When he returned home from his mission, we were married three weeks later on March 30, 1944. Three months later, he was off for basic training for the Army in Mineral Wells, Texas. He then went to California and when he was ready to be shipped off, I took a bus from Salt Lake City (I had barely been out of Salt Lake, let alone travel by myself to a strange place) and eventually made it to Pittsburgh, California, where Bob would leave for the Philippines to fight in the Pacific Theater. I went down to spend Christmas Eve and Christmas day with him. We weren't sure when he would be shipped out and it was all hush-hush about his departure day and time. I was scared to take a bus and I was scared to death to go that far away from home. I made it and ended up staying at the YWCA in Oakland. A very nice taxi driver helped me get to where I needed to go. The next morning, I took another bus to Pittsburgh, California, which is where Bob was and we finally met up.

On Christmas night, we walked all over the place trying to find a place to eat that was open. We finally found a diner. The owner said all he had left was a piece of salmon and a piece of halibut. I ordered the salmon and Bob ordered the halibut. I got food poisoning from that salmon and was sick all night. The bathroom was down the hall and it was a very long night. The next day, I wanted to let Mother know I got there. I went to the post office and stood in line to mail a postcard. All of a sudden I felt awful and I passed out right there on the floor. I woke up and found myself on the couch in the post master's office. He asked me if I was feeling better and if I was having my period. I stayed for a little while and felt a little better and left. I went back to the hotel, laid down for a while but thought if I ate something, I would feel better. I went out, found a diner and sat at the counter. I ordered some soup and looked up at the waitress when it came and asked if she had a restroom. She said it was only for employees and I immediately threw up in the soup. There were two men on either side of me and I was so embarrassed. I saw Bob later that day and then he was confined to his quarters and I never saw him again before he left.

I was able to take care of Bob's mother, Jeannette Murdoch, during some very difficult health problems, one of them being Alzheimer's Disease. She was a darling, small woman, so kind and sweet. I remember her beautiful deep-set blue eyes and her very sweet face. You could tell she had been a very beautiful lady. I had to give her a shot every day and because it was during the war, I had dull needles. I told Mary Weggeland and she called the doctor and told him and finally got some sharp needles. To this day, I think the needles were dull because they gave us used needles. I took her on walks every day after work because she loved to go outside and we both enjoyed those walks. When she died, it was difficult, not only because I was attached to her, but because Bob was not home to say goodbye.

Finally in August of 1945, Japan surrendered but Bob continued to stay on in Tokyo as a Chaplain's Assistant for eight months in occupied Japan. He finally came home and called me from the train station in Salt Lake City. He said he needed to go to Fort Douglas to finish up paper work and get his discharge. I decided I need to cut the lawn and that I had time to do it. So, there I was out in the front, racing around mowing the lawn with no makeup, my hair in curlers, and my pretty new dress all laid out on the bed. My plan was to quickly mow the lawn, take out my hair and comb it, put on my makeup, and be all ready in the pretty dress when he came in the door. Well, so much for my plans – I could hear a car and some loud voices coming around the corner, but I thought to myself, "No, that's not him." When I looked up, there he was in a car with some other GIs and I ran toward the house. I could hear Bob yell, "You'd better run, Louie!" He ran in the house, gave me a big hug and kiss and ran out to the car to go to the Fort Douglas to finish up his paper work. I was so mad that I thought I had time to mow the lawn and not get caught. I still think about that and laugh but I was so disappointed.

We rented an apartment right away in Salt Lake City, but Jack offered Bob a job with his finance business and we moved to Boise, Idaho. We lived in a hotel for a while and then lived on Lemp Street in the north end of Boise. Janice (Janny) was born on April 22, 1947. We eventually moved to 2308 N. 19th Street, a little two bedroom house with a basement. Bette Ann was born on October 17, 1949 and Sherri was born February 19, 1952. We had irrigation ditches all over the neighborhood and children we always falling into them and drowning. I became an advocate of covering the ditches and we were finally successful.

We lived very close to Hill Road and the church decided to build a chapel there. Bob would come home from work, get on some work clothes, and off he would go to help build that chapel. Members of the church built a lot of the buildings in those days, and Bob would come home with cuts on his hands from laying the bricks and bruised thumbs from missing the nails. When the building was finally finished, it was truly a beautiful building and we were so proud of what had been accomplished.

At the time, Bob went to work for the Continental State Bank, which later became the Bank of Idaho. He originally worked as a collector, then a loan officer, and later became a senior vice president. He retired from there when it was the First Interstate Bank.

We moved to 1102 N. 17th Street, buying the house from Jack and Ruth Murdoch. Our daughters loved living in that neighborhood and had a lot of friends there. The house was bigger and closer to town. It was one block off of Harrison Blvd., which was a beautiful row of very large elaborate homes. Our girls went to Washington Elementary School and North Junior High School. We attended the Boise 2nd Ward on Washington and Tenth Street, which was called the Tabernacle. Mother was having some arthritis problems and it was decided that she should come and live with us. She lived in the basement in a small bedroom with a half bath.

I worked as a secretary for the Western Equipment Company, which sold heavy equipment. I later worked for the State Department of Employment. After many years there, I became a monitor for federal programs and my job was titled as a *Grants Operations Analyst*. I traveled throughout the state visiting different companies who had contracts with the state to make sure they were honoring their contracts in running federal programs. I really loved this job. In Twin Falls I was investigating a Boy Scout program that was not recording things correctly. I snuck papers out of the office under my coat and went to the newspaper and copied all that was fraudulent. I got two awards for my efforts, but the raises I got were even nicer.

I always felt it was important to give blood during the blood drives. The Red Cross would call me because I had A negative blood, which they needed quite a lot for heart surgeries. It was always close to my office, so I usually just walked over. I got pins for the many gallons of blood I gave.

We moved to Inverness Way in the Hillcrest area of Boise to give Mother more room. She had a very difficult time going up and down the stairs. She later died while we lived there in 1964. The house was such a well-built and nice home and we loved living there.

LEFT: *Bob and Betty visiting Lennox* RIGHT: *Bob and Betty in Hawaii 1967*

We moved to Nampa, Idaho for Bob to manage a branch of the Bank of Idaho. Janny and Bette Ann were out of the home and Sherri went to Nampa High School. We lived there for a couple of years. We moved back to Boise and bought a home on Oakmont Street. After 32 years of marriage, Bob and I divorced in 1974. I moved to a small apartment and later bought a small townhouse on Phillippi Street, where I still live. I continued to work and retired in 1984 after 28 years with the State of Idaho.

Bob began to deteriorate from the ill effects of Alzheimer's Disease and was eventually put in the Boise Idaho Veteran's Home in the Alzheimer's Ward. Sherri and I made frequent visits and took him clothes and things he needed. I visited him every day or every other day. I fed him and did whatever he needed. I used to take him on drives until one day he told me he didn't want to go back and wanted to get out of the car. He tried to open the car door while I was driving. It scared me and I never took him in the car again. It was hard to see him deteriorate and Bette Ann, Sherri, and I saw him just before he died on March 5, 1998.

LEFT: *Twins Sherri and Betty* RIGHT: *Ora, Bill, Lucy, and Betty about 1994*

I have always loved to travel and have visited some very interesting places. I have gone to Europe and visited Switzerland, Austria (saw the beautiful and amazing *Passion Play,* which is only put on every ten years), Germany, France, and Italy. I loved Venice and we were serenaded in the gondola but people would slam their windows shut when we went by. I have also gone to England and Scotland, which was wonderful. I have been on three cruises to the Caribbean. I took Janny, Bette Ann, and Sherri on a cruise to the eastern Caribbean for a week and we had so much fun together. I went to Alaska on two cruises. I went to Nova Scotia to see the leaves change and fell and broke my arm. I had to come home early. Bob and I went to Hawaii in 1965 and I went again later. I have also gone to Lake Louise in Banff Canada. I also went to Vancouver Island and visited Victoria and Buchardt Gardens. I have fond memories of all my travels.

I have been blessed with three beautiful daughters, 14 grandchildren, and 39 great grandchildren. They are all so wonderful and I love talking to them and visiting with them. I feel so blessed to have such a wonderful family.

JANICE MURDOCH

I was born on April 22, 1947 in Boise, Ada, Idaho. I am the oldest of three girls born to Robert Gail Murdoch and Betty Lue Clark. The first place we lived was on Lemp Street in a little stucco duplex on the corner. It was about a block from the Washington Grade School where I later went to the 3rd – 6th grades. The second home was on 19th St. near the north end and ending at Hill Road, a narrow two lane road with foothills on the north side and residences on the south side. Along on the south side about 1.5 miles from our house was a small farm and the owner was Mr. Brown or Farmer Brown. One night a week in the summer he would come into the neighborhood and surrounding streets to take little kids for a hay ride – those were great rides. I remember he wore a big straw hat and bibbed overalls.

Our ward was a great red brick one on Hill Road. During this time, my Dad was on the Stake Sunday School Board and every so often he would let me go with him to visit the different wards. This included wards even out in Eagle. This was way out in the country and it was a small wooden white building. I remember the entry was at an angle and was a vestibule that went straight into the chapel with wooden floors. In Sunday School we sat on little wooden chairs. The weather was overcast that day and sprinkling a little. By the time we got to our classroom the rain was coming down harder. Our teacher wanted us to sing Itsy Bitsy Spider and just then the roof started to leak with rain was running down the wall and as the song says "... it washed the spider out".

While in this house on 19th St., I started to ride horses. I was going down an alley and two gals on horses were coming towards me. They were sisters, Chris and Cathy Hedstrom. Cathy and I ended up being best of friends – she lived one street over and south a bit. Their pasture was about two blocks west and I think this was to get me out of my Mom's hair, Cathy and I rode almost daily for four and a half years up in the foothills. Since I started riding when I was four years old and Smoky was a full size horse, it was a bit of challenge to get back on after getting off but he had a lot of patience. Mom would pack me a lunch and send me on my way to ride horses.

Besides my love of horses, I also managed to pick up any stray dogs and bring them home. More times than I could count at the time, I was told to quit bringing dogs home. But one was a favorite. He was a golden St. Bernard and we named him Banana. He would let us ride on his back for a few steps and then sit down and we would slide off.

I started kindergarten while in this house. It was a ways from our home and actually in the basement of an old church across from the ward we went to for many years by Boise High School. (The church was torn down to be a gymnasium for the high school.) My hair was braided and down to my waist and every single time I would get to the bottom of the steps, a girl named Kathy Weaver would grab my braids and yell "giddy up horsey". I wanted my hair cut so bad but Mom wouldn't do it. My grade school was Lowell School off State Street.

By the time I was to enter the 3rd grade, my parents bought the house, with furniture, from my Uncle Jack and Aunt Ruth at 1102 N. 17th & Alturas, off Harrison Blvd. My new grade school was to be Washington Elementary School. This home had some wonderful, wonderful memories for all of us. This is where my Mom taught me, with her tennis racket, how to play tennis on the side of the building. I kept that racket until I got married and somehow misplaced it several years later.

So where do I start with the memories? Well, my bedroom was actually the sunroom and had five windows on the east side and three windows on the north side. These were old windows that went down inside the wall of the house with ropes. In the summer, Mom would open the east windows and when I was waking up I could smell the mint that was planted outside my windows. It was great.

One that I will never forget was the time Mom thought that it would be neat to have chickens in the back yard. She was tired of all the slugs in the garden and heard that chickens eat them. She decided to get a rooster from one of Bette Ann's friends. This didn't go over very well with the neighbors because the rooster would crow every morn at 5:00 A.M. even when she covered the cage up. So the rooster and the cage all went back to where they came from. And speaking of something from the country, Mom was notorious for looking for asparagus when we would go for family rides. Asparagus, of course, grows by the ditch bank so when she saw some she would tell Dad to stop the car and she would jump out and grab some – us girls were on the floor of the car not wanting to be seen while our mother "stole" asparagus. Her excuse was that it was on a ditch bank so just sitting there, not in a field.

I was still a cowgirl though – my new best friend was Jane Tennyson. For my birthday one year she gave me a western shirt – burgundy with silver threads – just like hers. So we had our matching shirts, jeans that were so dirty they could stand up in the corner, and our boots. We were inseparable.

Kids our age went swimming a lot in the summers and, of course, we had to walk to the swimming pool at Lowell Grade School. It cost 10 cents. We'd swim and swim and swim and then have to walk home. Also, we would go to the movies – of course, we had to walk there. There were two theatres downtown, the Penny Theatre and the Ada Theatre, now called the Egyptian Theatre. I was given 35 cents – 25 cents to get in and 10 cents for a candy bar which was usually a Butterfinger. To me it was approximately 2.5 – 3 miles one way from where we lived but we were talking and gabbing all the way so it didn't make it feel like a long way. Also, my Dad took me to every *Francis the Talking Mule* movie that came out.

Dad was a great, great fisherman. Because he was a commercial banker, he met lots of businessmen and they would always talk about fishing. One of them became his best friend, Trev Baugh, who owned a siding company. One thing Dad liked to tease us all with was to get home late at night and fill up the kitchen sink or even the bathtub and put catfish in one or the other. When Mom would get up during the night to get a drink of water and get splashed by the catfish, and she would yell "Robert!!" He loved to tease us.

Because they got good gas mileage, my Dad's favorite car was Studebaker. We didn't just have one, we had two! Ugly as they were to us, Dad thought they were wonderful. We used to ask when we could have a "real car".

Our grandmother, Sabina Clark Alder (Gram), was living in Salt Lake City and every so often we would drive down to visit her – this was long before there was such a thing as a freeway. Eventually, Gram came to live with us and many times in the summer Dad and Mom would take all six of us to California in the Studebaker to spend time with Mom's twin sister, Sherri, and her four kids. We also went to Disneyland and loved the great times there. I actually caught a little fish at the dock of Tom Sawyer's Island when I was about 12 years old. One time Dad wanted to leave early so he left work, came and got us, and he drove us to Tonipah, Nevada. We were on the second floor of this old hotel – so old that the only key was a skeleton key. We heard Bingo being played all night. Dad was craving a steak so he and Mom went someplace for a steak at like 2:00 A.M.

Jan at Disneyland

While we lived on 17th Street, my grandmother taught me how to knit, crochet, do crewel work and she tried to teach me how to do tatting. I still have the hat and gloves that she taught me to knit one summer. In the 3rd grade, Mom started teaching me how to play tennis with her racket. I practiced all the time on the south wall of Washington Grade School – I had to count up the rows of brick to match the height of the tennis net. I played tennis until my freshman year in college. I also played a lot of tetherball – in the sixth grade I was the girls' and boys' champion.

I went to North Junior High School and then, still with my friends from grade school, I went to Boise High School. Then when I would have started my junior year of high school, Mom and Dad moved us to the other side of town and I was to go to Borah High School – the cross town rival of Boise High School. That was a weird feeling. Our parents bought a nice house on Inverness Way. This was a great house. It had a big backyard and an orange kitchen which was on the west side of the house so when the sun was setting it looked like it was on fire. At Borah, I played tennis and was in the Pep Club for two years. My Mom learned then that asking me to pull weeds was something she would never do again. In the backyard, she had seven "islands" for lots of flowers. Since I used to suntan a lot she asked me to pull some weeds while I was out back. "Sure," I told her, "no problem". So I pulled weeds and cleaned up those islands nice and pretty and was really proud of myself. But when she got home from work, she went to check my work and it turned out I hadn't pulled weeds but some expensive special flowers that she had bought. Oops! Another time she told me to get rid of some fish that she hadn't cooked and to use them for fertilizer out front. So, I just put them on the ground under

the bushes that were under the kitchen window. It was in the summer and hot. We could not figure out where this awful smell was coming from. It turned out she meant for me to dig a hole and put the fish in the hole for fertilizer, not just throw them under the bushes. But the one smell that kept me out of the house all day was when my sister, Bette Ann, wanted cow's tongue for her birthday dinner. I tried every excuse in the book not to come to that smell but it didn't work.

My first year of college was at Boise College (it was going from Boise Junior College to Boise State University so this was the only year it was Boise College.) My second year was at Ricks College in Rexburg, Idaho – br-rrrrr. My history class was actually in the lamb sheds – the only heat was a parlor stove in the corner and we had to keep our coats, hats, and gloves on during class. I had a lot of good memories there. I didn't graduate because I lacked two credits. Living in Rexburg, the wind is always blowing – always! I told myself I would never, ever live there again. WRONG!

That summer, I got a job with the State of Idaho in an office close to where Mom worked. And nine months later, I got a job in the same building so we could carpool. I had a jazzy '64 Chevy Nova Rally Sport, bright red with white convertible top and loaded with chrome. I used to say it was *All Show, No Go* but I loved that car. I got a little apartment on Warm Springs Avenue with a friend of mine. Since I couldn't even boil water for a hot dog, this was quite the experience for me. We had natural hot water with that awful smell so if we made Jell-O, it had to sit in the refrigerator for three days in order for the smell to go away.

One night I got a call from a Chuck Boyd who I vaguely knew in high school. He had just gotten home from his mission to Australia. He was Assistant to the Mission President and the gal that worked in the mission office on her mission was a dear friend of mine, Annette (Nettie) Raymond. When he got ready to come home, she told him to call me. We began to see a lot of each other and on the way to my cousin Janet's wedding reception in Holladay, Utah, he proposed. We were sealed September 13, 1968 in the Salt Lake Temple and our reception was in the Lion House.

Chuck was in college and working for the Idaho Highway Department. He worked for them while he was in high school. We lived in a mobile home out in Meridian and rode to Boise for school and work on a 125 CC Honda motorcycle. Gas was about 25 cents a gallon. I tried going to college at night but it didn't work quite as I had expected. Chuck went to school the last two years straight through in order to finish. He got his degree in Accounting with a minor in Finance and a minor in Engineering. One day at work he had mentioned that if there was an opening in the Rigby, Idaho office, he would like to be considered for it. (He didn't ask me if I wanted to go back to eastern Idaho.) Well, he got a job there and traveled for three months back and forth from Meridian to Rigby. We finally moved to Ammon, which is close to Idaho Falls and he drove about 12 miles to work. His good friend from his mission lived in Idaho Falls so they hung out a lot together. This was when Chuck got his first motorcycle which he parked in the kitchen area because he didn't want it to get cold in the garage - it was wintertime.

At the little house in Ammon is where we had our first son, Eric Charles, who was born September 20, 1973. The next year we bought a great brick house in Idaho Falls and moved into a great ward. We loved it and made some great friends. This is where Lance Robert was born – August 17, 1976.

We did a lot of work on that house to fix it up. But our ward had gotten quite large and was going to be divided. All our friends were in the newer part so we bought a brand new home at 2234 Mesa. I loved that house – we had lots of room inside and out. This home is where Charles Murdoch Boyd (known as CJ for Chuck Jr.) was born – November 4, 1977. While we lived there we had ten motorcycles. Camping and motorcycling riding were big family activities for us and there are lots of great, great memories living in eastern Idaho. Jackson Hole was just two hours away, so we took many rides through Yellowstone Park, into Jackson Hole and then back home. We had two camp trailers while at that house but when we went camping we almost always slept outside under the stars and did most of our cooking around a campfire.

At this time, I was working for the Idaho National Engineering Laboratory. My marriage to Chuck ended in June 1989. Eric stayed with his Dad and Lance and CJ

Eric, Lance, and CJ

came to live with me. Two years later, I was transferred to Rocky Flats Engineering Laboratory in Golden, Colorado. This was in January and the company put us up in Marriott short-term living condominium set-up in Boulder, Colorado. We brought our Basset Hound, Bass, and our spaniel, Elsie. The housekeepers loved those dogs. We lived in two houses in Westminster, Colorado just a few blocks from Standley Lake which we loved. These houses were not far from open spaces so there were lots of little animals and two beautiful eagles to watch. Rocky Flats was beginning to shut down and the new company took my seniority away. Lance, CJ, and I moved to Meridian, Idaho where I worked for DirecTV in several capacities. While in Meridian, Dad passed away after being at the Boise Idaho Veteran's Home for about seven years. I was so glad to be able to spend some time with him. He was a very, very special person. My son, Lance, has Dad's laugh and chuckle.

A year later to the day, CJ entered the Missionary Training Center in Provo, Utah to go on his mission to the Pennsylvania Harrisburg Mission.

Lance got married to Mandy Starr and today they have two little boys, Jaden and Zadyk. Lance is a contractor lineman, so he works for long periods of time in different states in the west. They live in Kuna, Idaho.

Lance, Mandy, Jaden and Zadyk Boyd

CJ and I moved back to Denver and were there for several years. He became the father of a little girl named Kaytie Elise Stankiewicz-Boyd, who was born on November 24, 2002. I was working for a law firm at the time and the partners decided to disband. I had always wanted to live in western Oregon, so I moved to a little town called Lebanon, 11 miles east of Albany. This is an area where there is a lot of timber brought down from the hills (elevation 350 ft. above sea level) and lots and lots and lots of sheep. Less than one month after I moved there, CJ and little Kaytie came to live with me. We had a great time. The coast was only about one hour away so we went as often as we could. It is beautiful there. Not far from where we lived were two of the many, many waterfalls in Oregon – Royal Terrace Falls and McDowell Creek. We hiked those many times. Even Kaytie hiked up Royal Terrace Falls and that is one mile one way! We went on lots picnics. Our favorite park was on the Willamette River and in the little town of Waterloo. Kaytie learned how to skip rocks and did fantastic. Because of legal issues with Kaytie's mother, Nichole, in September 2007 her other grandmother and

Nichole came to take her back to southern Colorado to the small town of Sanford. I was working for a title company and they were cutting back on employees because of the economy. I asked to be laid off and I went with Kaytie to Sanford. In December 2007, I moved to Littleton, Colorado. In August 2009, Kaytie's mother asked me to move to Pueblo and I went to be near her.

Cousins Eric Boyd, Chad Porter, Jennifer Johnson, Richard Christensen, Heather Pruitt, Mike Porter, Kim Allen, and CJ Boyd

CJ is still in Oregon. He married Amy Lynn Brimacomb on July 27, 2007 and today they have a little boy, Zacharias, born on June 16, 2008 and Hailey, born on August 18, 2009. Another child is due in December 2010. My oldest son, Eric Charles, lives in Littleton, Colorado and works as a Master Waste Water Technician. He is married to Tracy Lynn Davidson. They do not have any children. Eric's first wife, Jennie, lives in Modesto, California with their 14 year old daughter, Sierra LaNae.

I have had a great life. And I am so thankful for my great parents that put up with me and raised me by setting such good examples for us girls and those around them. I am thankful for all the wonderful, wonderful memories of growing up. Today I have lots of challenges and know I can't stop but must move forward. The following is one of my favorite scriptures that keeps me going ...

"Learn of me, listen to me, walk in the meekness of my spirit and you will have peace in me." D&C 19:23

BETTE ANN MURDOCH CHRISTENSEN

I, Bette Ann Murdoch, was born of goodly parents, Robert Gail and Betty Lue Clark Murdoch, in Boise, Ada, Idaho on October 17, 1949. At the time I was born, we lived at 2308 N. 19th Steet with my older sister, Janice (Janny), who was 2 ½ years old when I was born. Two and a half years after I was born, my sister Sherri was born. Mom always told me that she thought I was an angel because of my blond curly hair, blue eyes, and sweet disposition. When I was an infant, my mom was doing the laundry in the basement. She looked over to see Janny carrying me down the cement stairs by my head and saying, "Here Mommy." Mom calmly thanked Janny as she walked over to get me from her. Whew! I luckily made it through that scary moment.

Next door to us, the neighbors had a black Cocker Spaniel dog named Elsie. She was with us all day long and Mom called her our *protector*, which proved to be true, especially on one occasion. All the backyards in that neighborhood had irrigation ditches, which when.dammed up, flooded with yards to water them. One day when I was about two and a half years old, Janny wanted to go play at little Billy's house, a couple of houses down and took me with her. Mom made her promise she would watch me carefully. A little while later, Billy's mom came over carrying a wet Bette Ann and told her that Elsie, my protector, barked and when she looked out the window, there I was floating face down in the irrigation ditch. She ran out and pulled me out by my hair. Elsie is in many of our pictures and I can still remember her.

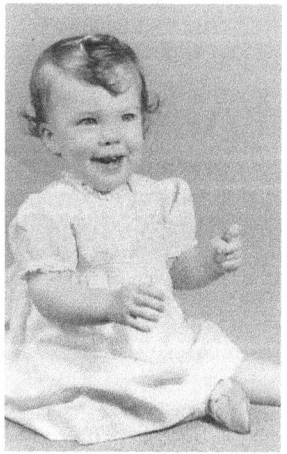 

LEFT: *Bette Ann, 9 months* RIGHT: *Bette Ann and Elsie, her protector*

I was very young when I learned to ride a bike and the only one we had was a regular, women's size that was blue. I was about four years old and rode all over the place. I must have looked so funny on that thing.

Once I rode with no shoes and rather than hit a car because I couldn't use the brakes in time, I used my toe to stop, which turned into hamburger. Needless to say, my next memory is of me soaking it in the bathtub at the house.

We moved to 1102 N. 17th St. when I was five years old. This was Jack and Ruth Murdoch's old house. I always loved the neighborhood and the friends we made there. We went to Washington Elementary School, which was several blocks away across busy Harrison Blvd. We always had to wear dresses to school, but on really cold days we could wear pants under our dresses, which we had to take off in the cloakroom. My teachers were from first grade: Mrs. Gray, Miss Cantrell, Mrs. Koski, Mrs. Mason, Mrs. Wandell, and Mr. Lythgoe. We had a principal, a secretary all the time, and a nurse each Thursday. At the end of 5th grade, some of us were selected to be crosswalk patrolmen and we had a hat, a red wooden stop sign, and a bandoleer with a badge. We were official! I also had this job in 6th grade and loved it.

We did walk in some pretty deep snow to school and it seemed uphill in both directions. The winters in Boise were quite brutal and we had a lot of snow. We also made some pretty cool snow forts and had snowball fights with the neighborhood kids. We had some great kids in our neighborhood and spent many a late night out playing in the summer. One of our favorite things to do in the summer was float the Boise River. We would have someone's mom take us up to Diversion Dam where we would hike through the bushes to get to the river, put in our innertubes, and float down to Ann Morrison Park. It was really fun.

The city bus came right by our house, so it was easy to catch a ride downtown and all of the neighborhood kids would go to the movies. We lived just a few blocks from Hyde Park, an area with a few little stores. My grandmother would send us over to the cobbler to get our leather shoes fixed, and I always loved to walk into the store to the smell of the leather and seeing the owner in his leather apron with all the tools for repairing shoes.The first Albertson's Grocery Store was just a few blocks away and Gram (our grandmother) would send us to the store for yeast so she could make bread. We loved to walk down the alley for four or five blocks and then a couple of blocks to the store. Sometimes Gram would give us a little extra to get some ice cream. She made delicious bread and made scones, which was just bread dough that she fried and put maple syrup on top.

The house on 17th Street was not very big, but was much bigger than the one on 19th Street. The front of the house had several stairs leading up to a porch on one side. Inside the front door was the living room with a fireplace at one end and on the left side was a set of double doors that you could open into the master bedroom that had a small walk-in closet. Going to the back of the house from the living room was the dining room, which had a door that connected to the hall by our bedroom. It had red flocked wallpaper (that Mom hated) and a beautiful crystal chandelier in the middle of the room. My grandmother was an expert at growing African Violets and she had a two-tiered glass table by the window for them. They were amazing and beautiful. My mom had her dining room table and hutch in there. In 1958, there was a huge earthquake by Yellowstone Park in the middle of the night. We could feel it in Boise and it woke us all up. We all ran into the dining room and Mom yelled, "Just hold something!" She tried to keep the crystals on the chandelier from hitting each other. Beyond the dining room was the kitchen with a small area for the table. The floor was black linoleum with a white line around the edges, which my mom tried her hardest to keep clean. She didn't like it because it showed everything. Turning left in the kitchen and going down the hall, was the one full bathroom in the house. In the back corner of the house was Janny's bedroom which had small windows all across the two outside walls. Turning left down the hall, Sherri and I shared the middle bedroom. It had a small closet and we had two twin beds. We had a long white bookcase where we kept our toys, which was always hard to keep clean. We had pretty white chenille bedspreads on our beds. Our bedroom window looked out the north side of the house. I think that because Sherri and I shared that bedroom, we were not only sisters but were best friends. Mom and Dad's bedroom was the next room down the hall and I always loved to go in there. The furniture was so pretty and they had a nice walk-in closet, where one year just before Christmas, Janny took us there to show us our presents. Off the kitchen, were the stairs to the partial basement. The washer and dryer were down there along with a fruit room, a small bedroom, tiny half bath, a very small family room to watch TV, and a crawl space where Mom kept the Christmas decorations. I think the huge furnace took up most of the space. In the backyard, the one-car garage was clear across the yard. Along the backyard fence, we had the most beautiful double petal lilac bushes that were a deep purple and in the spring, they smelled heavenly. We also had a funny, huge fireplace (probably meant for a barbecue) in the corner that we never used that I can remember. We had a swing set which we loved.

When I was about eight years old, I decided I was adopted. Janny and Sherri were both very dark with brown eyes. Janny's hair was black and Sherri's was dark brown. I was blond with blue eyes. I thought a lot about this for several weeks and wondered where I came from. One day, I went to Janny and Sherri and in a very serious tone asked them to come to my bedroom so I could tell them something important. I sat on one bed looking across at Sherri and Janny on the other bed and told them the truth – I was adopted. Janny immediately jumped up and said that was the stupidest thing she had ever heard and told me I wasn't adopted, which shocked me. She left the room and I just sat there dumbfounded that she didn't believe me. I am sure Sherri didn't know what to think. The seriousness of the occasion was dashed to bits and my confession was ridiculed. I eventually realized I wasn't adopted.

Every Christmas day in the afternoon, we would go to Jack and Ruth's lovely home in the foothills of Boise. Ruth always made her Scottish Shortbread cookies. They were so delicious and we always loved our visit. They had a beautiful view of Boise out their big back windows and Ruth would always have a cute present for each of us. Mom would buy something for the boys in return. Jack loved buying new things and had one of the first color TVs in Boise. It was amazing to watch, but he was constantly trying to perfect the colors and spent most of the time "adjusting" it. We loved to go swimming in the summer in their lovely pool and Ruth was always so gracious to let us come. After I was married, I wrote a letter to Ruth asking her if I could get her recipe for the Scottish Shortbread. She quickly replied with a hand-written copy of it (which I still have) and told me that she had gotten the recipe from Mary Weggeland.

Scotch Shortbread

½ lb. butter
½ C. sugar
2 C. flour
Cream butter and sugar until well blended. Add flour and knead with hands. Roll between waxed paper to ¼ in. thickness. I cut mine in squares and prick with fork.
Bake at 275 degrees until lightly browned.

I love to make it at Christmas time, but it seems like it never tastes as good as when Ruth made it.

Our vacations during the summer were usually spent visiting relatives. Dad was a very early riser and would wake up at 4:00 A.M. and we were on the road by 5:00. Sometimes we went to California to visit my mom's only sister and we loved to go to Disneyland. Traveling those long, desert roads was awful without air conditioning and poor Mom was always affected by the heat. We would roll down the windows and she would use water on washcloths to cool down. Lucky Sherri always got to sit in the front seat because she got car sick so easily and after throwing up a few times, we all decided it was a good idea. Other trips took us to Salt Lake to visit Dad's relatives. The road to Salt Lake was long and boring. By the time we got to Brigham City, we were ready for it to be over, but from Brigham City to Salt Lake City was along the side of a mountain and took forever, even though we thought we were almost there. On those trips to Salt Lake City, my dad's Aunt Mary (we called her "Red-headed Aunt Mary") would take us to lunch in the Tea Room at the ZCMI. We had to dress up and enjoyed the girls' time together. One of the things all of us remember is that she always made us eat our parsley which was just a garnish on the plate. She said it would keep our breath fresh. It tasted awful. We loved to visit Lennox and Ora and loved to drive down their beautiful lane. Ora always had something fun to do and we loved sleeping on the screen porch in a big, soft bed. I could hear the water from the stream and the birds. It was heaven. Bill and Lucy were always so gracious when we stayed there and we all loved them dearly because they loved us back. Once we had a reunion at Jeannette and Wendell's and we ate dinner in the backyard. We met David Buckwalter Jr. for the first time and we were impressed that he had lived in Peru. It was a beautiful backyard and fun to see everyone.

Our grandmother, Sabina Clark Alder, came to live with us when we were just little girls. She suffered from bad arthritis and had a hard time living in her apartment in Salt Lake. She made the most delicious chocolate éclairs, something I have never been able to duplicate. She was a really great cook and loved doing it. She taught me how to crochet and knit, but I picked up the crocheting and continue to do it today, having made many afghans and 20 baby afghans for my grandchildrens' baby blessings. She lived in the little bedroom downstairs. She loved to sew and made us pajamas. She would tell us stories of growing up in New Mexico (she was born Luna Valley, New Mexico in 1884) and told us a story of the Indians coming so her brother grabbed her and her sister and ran to hide in the corn fields. She used to sing funny songs, which we loved. For a few months, she sometimes went to live with mom's sister, Sherri, in California, but mostly with us.

During the summer of 1963, we moved to Inverness Way in the Hillcrest area of Boise. We loved that house and all the great features, such as an intercom, built in mixer/blender, cedar closet, nice family room, and the neighborhood was very nice. It was a three bedroom house and there was a room for Gram, so she didn't have to go up and down stairs. She died while we were living there in 1964 and is buried in Boise at the Cloverdale Cemetery.

I had a friend, Jeanene Dahlquist, that lived just a couple of doors down and we were great friends. I took a Home Economics class in junior high and loved the sewing part of it. I have been making clothes and sewing ever since. Jeanene and I used to love to sew our own clothes and would run down to each other's house with our projects to show each other what we were doing. We had some pretty nice school clothes and were very well dressed. Jeanene's grandfather gave her a tandem bike and we rode all over Boise on it. I think our longest ride was out to the Dry Creek Cemetery, which was almost to Eagle, a ride of about 25 miles round trip, to find (unsuccessfully) the grave a girl we knew who died and was buried there.We lived in the Boise Seventh Ward and had some good friends there.

I loved to go to Seminary, which was held at the Cassia Stake Center. During my junior year, I was asked to be the chorister. I didn't know anything about music but I did learn to lead and 4/4 time was my favorite. The kids got pretty tired of singing, "There is Sunshine in My Soul Today". I loved to read the Book of Mormon and read it every night before I went to bed. I knew it was true and loved its doctrine, stories, and messages.

I attended South Junior High and then Borah High School. I had some friends, but never very many. My mom told me many years after I was married that Dad was very concerned about this and was going to take me fishing to make up for it. He did and boy, did we ever have fun on those Saturday mornings! He was a fisherman from way back and knew all the places to go. Our favorite place was above Arrowrock Dam outside of Boise. It took a while to get up there, but because we were both early risers, we were on the road by about 6:00 - 6:30 A.M. every Saturday during the summer and into the fall after school started. I loved the ride up there and the beautiful scenery. He loved to take me because I turned out to be a pretty good fisherwoman. Our favorite song was, "We'll Sing in the Sunshine" and he just knew we would have good luck if we heard it on the radio. We went many places to fish, including a trip to Yellowstone Park. The family was staying in a cabin  and Dad wanted to go fishing, so out we went. I didn't get too far because the mosquitoes were thicker than I have ever seen, kind of like something you would see in your worst nightmare. They were attacking me like I was their only food source. I noticed that none of them were landing on Dad. He had yellow jaundice during the war and mosquitoes apparently didn't like his smell or blood. I told him I was going back and he told me, "Don't let little things like that bother you." Ugh, are you kidding? I made a quick beeline back to the cabin. We had so many fun memories that we talked about for many years after and I treasure those times we had, just the two of us.

In December of 1967, a friend of mine introduced me to Wynn Christensen. He needed a date to a party at a friend's house and asked me to go. I remember sitting there playing a game and looking over at him wondering if I would marry him. After dating for while, we pretty much knew it was meant to be. He was funny, a hard worker, and I loved being with him. It just felt comfortable. He came from a wonderful family, whom I fell in love with also. He left for the Franco-Belgium Mission in June of 1968 and I waited for him. He returned in September of 1970 and we were engaged on Christmas Eve of 1970. .We were married on June 4, 1971 in the Idaho Falls Temple. Four weeks before our wedding, I had surgery on my right knee, so I limped through everything. I was the third bride in a line of thirteen as we went up the long stairs to the first room. I had to climb the steps one at a time and held up ten other brides behind me. The temple was more than full and I remember how hot it was and my dad sitting on the arm rest of someone's seat during the session because it was standing room only.

After graduating from Borah High School, I attended Boise College for one year. I then transferred to Brigham Young University in Provo, Utah. I lived with two good friends about three blocks from the south end of campus. The walk in the winter was brutal because we couldn't wear pants on campus. I majored in Speech Therapy but fell in love with the Learning Disabilities aspect of it. If I would have continued on, I probably would have specialized in it. I made a lot of friends there and loved college life. The next year, I moved to a different apartment building and lived there only a semester because I wanted to move back to Boise because Wynn was home from his mission. After we were married, he transferred to BYU and majored in electrical engineering, his call in life. We found a little basement apartment in an elderly lady's otherwise, huge house. Alene Simmons was our landlady and was always so kind to us. We both went to school and worked during that first semester after we were married. I worked in the Chemistry Department as a secretary, usually typing up tests for the professors. I got the job because I was so good at typing numbers on the old typewriters. Wynn worked at Boise Cascade Lumber Company and drove a delivery truck. I became pregnant with our first baby and I had a spiritual feeling that I wasn't to stay in school and that I was to stay home to raise my children. Wynn gave me a blessing before the birth of our daughter and there was a phrase in it caught my attention, but I didn't say anything to Wynn at the time. It was - that I wouldn't feel the birth. I just remember thinking it was kind of a strange thing to say.

About midnight on April 6, 1972, I started labor and 40 hours later, on April 8, Jennifer was born by Cesarean Section. She had lots of black hair and the nurses would bring her in with her hair combed and styled. She was adorable. Recovery was tough because I lost so much blood and didn't feel good for about a year. We had combined our savings when we got married and had $1500 in the bank, of which Jennifer took all but $30 of it. It was a testimony to us of the law of tithing.

We lived in that cramped little apartment for about two years and I became pregnant with our second baby. Wynn was one third of the way through his Master's Degree but we decided we couldn't afford to pay for another baby. We left BYU for China Lake, California and Wynn worked for the Naval Weapon Center. He worked there for twelve years on the guidance systems for missiles, including the Harpoon and the Sidewinder. Ryan Wade was born also by C-section on April 16, 1974 in Ridgecrest, California, which is the town adjoining the base. We lived on the base for another couple of years and started looking for a house in town. We moved to 723 W. Haloid the same week that Richard Warren was born on October 28, 1976, also a C-section. Reed William was born on June 30, 1978 and Russell Wayne on June 16, 1981, all C-sections. The house had three bedrooms and a nice backyard. We planted grass in the front yard and worked all summer to keep it green because the heat of summer killed just about everything we planted. We had one of two yards in the neighborhood with grass. The kids had a blast on the front yard and it sloped to the street. They played soccer, baseball, and the slip-and-slide was perfect on the slope. We attended the Ridgecrest 2nd Ward and made so many good friends there. We had many church callings and loved living there. I grew in confidence and learned to do things that I never knew I could. Wynn was called into the bishopric when he was 27 and then as bishop when he was 34 and served for two and a half years before we moved to New Mexico.

One day, Wynn got a call from a friend who lived in Los Alamos, New Mexico asking him to apply for a job at the Los Alamos National Lab. We didn't think too much of it because he was a bishop and we didn't think it would be a good idea to move in the middle of that calling. I didn't want to live with white sand all around me. We flew to New Mexico just to look it over and fell in love with the place. It was in the mountains and had four seasons, instead of our two – cool and hot. We went home and prayed for a long time and finally decided to move. I packed up the house and painted every room, except the bathroom. I told Wynn I couldn't paint one more room, so he made time to help me. His bishop calling was overwhelming and was gone until 10:00 every night. He rarely had time for anything else. We finally sold the house and left in our big white van. We made it to White Rock, a suburb of Los Alamos, in February of 1986 arriving with lots of snow everywhere but on the roads. We rented a house from a lady who was serving a mission while we looked for a house. We had a difficult time finding anything big enough for our family and finally the realtor called and said there was a five-bedroom house that just listed. I told her I wanted to be the first one to see it and, while Wynn was working on the stranded van on the highway, Jennifer and I went to see the house. I bought it on the spot having a spiritual feeling as I walked in the door that this is THE house. We have lived here for 24 years. The kids had instant friends as there were LDS kids all over our neighborhood their ages. They loved growing up here and it has been a great place to raise children. The kids loved the bike and hiking trails and there was always something for them to do.

On December 30, 1986 Michelle came into the world, another C-section, born in Los Alamos. She is the first to be born in New Mexico since my grandmother, Sabina, who was born in Luna Valley by the Arizona border in 1884. I always knew there would be another girl in the family because my patriarchal blessing said, "many sons and daughters". What a delight she has been.

I began to have surgeries on my right knee and after another injury in December 2002, I went into the surgeon and told him I wanted my knee replaced. I couldn't walk, go shopping, or be on it for any length of time. He told me I was too young but I told him that I don't have a life if I can't walk. On January 13, 2003, I had a total knee replacement and it has been wonderful. I made an amazing recovery and worked for weeks on my therapy. I actually walked into the physical therapy office without crutches, which no one there could believe. It was a huge decision, but it has been so wonderful not to live with the constant knee pain.

I have always loved to sew and made a lot of things for my kids, including button shirts and shorts for the boys and dresses for the girls. Who knows how many things I have sewn over all the years. It is wonderful to sit down at the sewing machine and just sew something. I also love to quilt and have made many for my children as well as charity. Genealogy has always been fascinating to me and I have had many spiritual experiences as I search for ancestors. The veil is very thin as we do this great work and I have felt help from the other side on many occasions. I was the Family History Center Director for two years and was able to help many ward members find their ancestors, which means many names have been taken to the temple. It is a wonderful feeling to know I helped in some way.

Gradually our children have grown, gone to college and gotten married. Jennifer married Kendahl Johnson and they have four children – Kaylee, Konnor, Kenna, and Kamryn. Ryan married Kim Johnston and they have five children – Cami, Michael, Kylee (triplets), Ashley, and Luke. Richard married Heather Stoddart and they have four children – Elise, David, Ella, and Maxwell. Reed married Sara James and they have four children – Owen, Matthew, Meghan (twins), and Rachel. Russell married Emily Lundwall from Ridgecrest, California. Her mother was the Relief Society President when Wynn was bishop. They have three children – Parker, Hannah, and Olivia. Michelle is living in St. George, Utah attending Dixie College.

I have been greatly blessed having been raised by wonderful parents, who loved and taught me. I have a wonderful husband and children. My testimony of the Gospel of Jesus Christ has always been a priority to me and is constantly being nourished with the spiritual experiences of life. Priesthood blessings play a great part of my testimony as I have seen their promises come to pass. In studying my heritage, it has taught me that what we do in this life is what our descendents will appreciate as time goes on. I hope my life is an example of a Christ-like life to them.

RANDALL WYNN CHRISTENSEN

I was born in Salt Lake City, Salt Lake County, Utah on April 4, 1949. I was the second of five children of RW (Chris) and Naomi Knowles Everton Christensen. My older sister, Rebecca (February 3, 1947), had already claimed the best side of the bedroom as she had a two-year head start on me. Perhaps that is why I cried when there was seemingly no reason. When I was born, my father worked as a clerk for the FBI and was in the process of building our house in Salt Lake. We lived in the house for a short time, long enough that I have a memory or two of the circle where it was located. We didn't live in the house long (about a year) as Dad was promoted to the rank of Special Agent and was transferred to Milwaukee, Wisconsin. I decided that I would leave my beautiful Salt Lake birthplace and the mountains with streams full of trout and go with them. I have a few memories of Milwaukee, mostly bad. Let's just say that the wading pool across the street had cracks in the bottom that were terrifying to me.

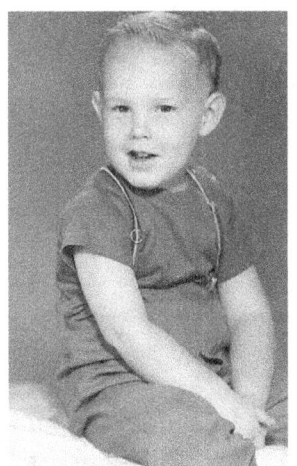 

LEFT: *Wynn at two years old* RIGHT: *Wynn and his reaction to poison ivy.*

The next transfer was to the Philadelphia office. We lived in Collingswood, New Jersey for a year or so before moving on to a more permanent assignment in Norristown, Pennsylvania. We spent the next 10 or 12 years in various homes in the Norristown area. The first was a rented house at 1932 W. Marshall St. in Norristown itself. It was here that I started to develop my love for sports and had my first best friends,

Ralph(y) Davis, Roger Hebner, and David Dowhan. I learned early that you should learn the terminology of a sport before you play it. When I was about 5 years old, I was playing in my first baseball game with the kids in the neighborhood in a field across the street from our house. I managed to get to 3rd base and on an overthrow my teammates started yelling, "Go home! Go Home!" I thought it was a strange request but I didn't want to disappoint, so I crossed the street as fast as I could and sat down in my front yard. I waited for them to call me back but they just kind of stared at me, shrugged their shoulders, and played on.

My father grew tired of driving an hour to church every Sunday and convinced the District Presidency to let him start a dependent Sunday School in Norristown. The Sunday School grew to become a large branch, built a meeting house, and became a ward. It is now a stake.

I entered school as a 1st grader, having missed kindergarten somehow, and completed the 2nd grade at West Norriton Elementary School. Also during this time, our family added my sister Laureli (May 14, 1953), my brother Roy (March 9, 1956), and my brother Bruce (September 16, 1958). Bruce only lived a day or so as he had complications from Rubella. We don't know exactly where Bruce is buried.

It was during this period that I began my engineering career. My parents bought me an Erector Set for my 6th birthday. I had poison ivy so bad that year that I could barely see through my swollen eyes but I was excited. I had a scheme to build a motor using some magnets. My mother told me that what I was attempting to do would not work because it was a perpetual motion machine and that was impossible. I, of course, took it as a challenge and made a goal to get it working by the time I was 10. I had one other goal for my 10th birthday - to put back together my mother's alarm clock that I had taken apart. The gears and assorted parts were sitting in a box. I accomplished neither goal but I had fun trying and never lost my fascination with science and engineering.

While living in Norristown, we made our first trip back to Utah. Dad made a bed in the back of our '53 Chevy station wagon for my sister and me. We left in the evening and mom and dad took turns driving all night while we slept. When we woke up and the sun peaked up on the horizon the scenery had changed to the cornrows of Iowa. Back then it was a two lane road from Chicago all the way to Utah. As we continued west, I had my first glimpse of the Rocky Mountains rising out of the plains of Colorado. It was an amazing sight for an easterner, both beautiful and frightening. In Utah, I was introduced to a new world of western ruggedness, clear blue skies, fireworks, and fishing. I would always love the west.

Our next stop on the house rental circuit was Woodland Ave. in Trooper, Pennsylvania. I was enrolled in Audubon Elementary School where I attended 3rd and 4th grade. I have good memories of this time in my life. On April 6, 1957, a day I remember very clearly, I was baptized by my father in the Philadelphia Branch meetinghouse. This building served as our meeting place for district conferences. During this period our district would hold our Father and Sons outings in Harmony Pennsylvania, at the location of the actual priesthood restoration. This event each year had a great impact on my fledgling testimony. I caught my first fish on the Susquehanna River, I would guess within a stone's throw of where the restoration took place. My memories of this time of my life were generally very good. I took up the clarinet, played my first organized baseball team, started cub scouts, learned to swim, and had some great memories of friends in the area.

Our next move was to a rental on Old Eagle School Road in Wayne, Pennsylvania. We only spent about one year in this house. I was enrolled in the 5th grade at Old Eagle School Elementary School. I had probably the best teacher of my school career here, Mr. Roselli. I had good friends in the neighborhood in Lou and Don Priem. We spent hours playing football in their backyard. Baseball was also a passion and because our backyard was quite deep, I spent hours throwing the baseball up and hitting it, trying to break the world's record, which I did several times. Dad was called to the Philadelphia District Presidency during this time. He was with the District President when, in a hard rainstorm, they slid through the railing of a wooden bridge near Valley Forge Park and fell to the railroad tracks below. President Clark was killed in the crash and Dad broke his arm. The crash was hard enough to knock off the back cover of dad's watch. At the hospital, he noticed it when the hairs of his arm got caught up in the workings of his watch. Nobody wore seat belts back then.

As a family, we finally decided that we wanted to stay in Pennsylvania rather than hope for a move back to the west, so we bought a house. The house was located at 493 Hansen Road in King of Prussia, Pennsylvania. I was in the 6th grade now, and I picked up a paper route and became one of the richest kids in the neighborhood. I knew everyone for blocks around. It was a great time in my life. I was ordained a deacon during this time, joined two scout troops, one outside the church and then our ward scout troop when it was finally organized. We stayed in this house until midway through my 9th grade year.

My father was given the opportunity to transfer to the west to Butte, Montana. We decided to go and sold our house to a Philadelpia Eagles football player. We left around the first of January 1962. As we drove west, Dad received word that the destination was changed to Boise, Idaho and so were our lives. Boise became our family center to this day. We moved into a rental for a short time on Sunny Brook Lane, within a block of the current location of the Boise Temple. Dad began construction on our final house on 5706 Lynwood Place. During this time I finished the 9th grade at West Jr. High, 10th grade at Borah High School, and my junior and senior years at Capital High School during its inaugural two years. Like most people, my years in high school were a mixed bag of good and bad experiences. My friends were mostly composed of members of my Teachers and Priest Quorum. They were great friends and we had some great experiences together that will be found in the larger plates.

Through the help of my good friend, Paul Crookston, I was able to land my first real job at a lumberyard called Cash and Carry. This job financed my first year in college at Boise College (later to become Boise State College and then Boise State University). I had known since the 9th grade that

I would be an electrical engineer so I began in earnest toward that goal. During my year at Boise College, I was introduced to a young lady named Bette Ann Murdoch after a basketball game through mutual friends. I had two jobs at the time, the lumberyard and I also cleaned out milk tankers in Meridian, Idaho at night. One night, while busy cleaning the milk tankers, I decided that I should call Bette and ask her out to a party. She agreed, much to my surprise, and the rest is history.

Six months after meeting Bette, I was called on a mission to the Franco-Belgium mission. I left on June 10, 1968. I spent two months at the Language Training Mission (LTM) in Provo, Utah, three months in Brussells, three months in Thionville, France, three months in Metz, France, three months in Liege, Belgium, four months in Charleroi, Belgium, four months in La Louviere, Belgium, and three months in Lille, France. The work was difficult and I had but one baptism while I was there but it was worth every second.

Upon returning from my mission, Bette was at BYU and I began my sophomore year at what was then Boise State College. On Christmas Eve, 1970, I proposed to Bette. We were married on June 4, 1971 in the Idaho Falls Temple. We were very poor. Our whole honeymoon to Jackson Hole, Wyoming cost less than $40 and then we moved to Provo and started life together. Ten months later, we welcomed in our first child, Jennifer. I was taking electrical engineering classes and Bette was supposed to be putting me through school. Now, I would have to go to school and support a family too. We used all of our savings to pay for Jennifer's birth (April 8, 1972). But it all worked out and I left school with a bachelor's degree in Electrical Engineering in January 1974. While I was going to school I worked at another lumberyard, this time for Boise Cascade. I was a delivery truck driver and had a lot of interesting experiences delivering lumber to home sites throughout the Provo and Orem area. I was part way through my Masters when our second child's eminent birth required us to leave, as we had no savings left to pay for Ryan (April 16, 1974). I was offered a job at the Naval Weapons Center in China Lake, California, which I took in January 1974. I absolutely loved working at the lab at China Lake. I was able to work on the Sidewinder missile, the Harpoon missile, and several other projects. During our 12 year stay in China Lake/Ridgecrest, I had callings with the Young Men Presidency, Sunday School Presidency, Sunday School Teacher, Stake Sunday School Presidency, Elders Quorum Presidency, two Bishoprics, a member of the High Council, and finally as Bishop. We welcomed in three more children during this period, Richard Warren (October 28, 1976), Reed William (June 30, 1978), and Russell Wayne (June 16, 1981). Our home was getting quite crowded so we began an addition to our home. In the middle of the construction, I was called as Bishop and the rate of construction slowed considerably. In November 1985, we received word from our friend Rollin Jones of an opportunity at Los Alamos National Laboratory at a significant increase in pay. We visited in December and were taken by the beauty of the area. We decided that it would be best for our family if we took the job, so with much sorrow at having to leave a place that had grown on us, we sold our house and left for New Mexico in February 1986.

Upon arrival to Los Alamos, we found ourselves in a huge sellers' market. We were finally able to buy a house but we had to do it before it came on the market and only Bette had a chance to look at the house. Of course in this environment, there was no dickering; it was a take it or leave it. We were blessed to get a house that was big enough for our family. It wasn't fancy (still isn't) but it did the job. At the end of the first

Four generations - Reed, Owen, RW, and Wynn

year in Los Alamos, we welcomed in our 6th and final child, Michelle (December 30, 1986). During our time in Los Alamos, I was called to various callings in the Ward Young Men, Cub Scouts, High Council, Bishopric, Ward Missionary, High Priests Group Leadership, Stake Young Men, and at this time my dream job of Ward Clerk. At Los Alamos National Lab, I worked on a huge laser system, the Super Collider, an imaging satellite, a bomb detecting bee box, and several weapons projects. During my career I shunned management positions as I thoroughly enjoyed the technical work. Our life in Los Alamos has been ideal and a great place to raise our family. During the 25 years that we have been here, our children have one by one left home, gone on missions, graduated from college, married in the temple, and returned home from time to time bringing our wonderful grandchildren with them. We have been thoroughly blessed by the good decisions that they have made and continue to make.

Jennifer Christensen Johnson

I was born on April 8, 1972 in Provo Utah. My parents, Randall Wynn and Bette Ann Murdoch Christensen, were attending Brigham Young University at the time. I was their first child and first grandchild on both sides of the family. When I was 20 months old, we moved to China Lake, California so that my Dad could take a job at the China Lake Naval Weapons Center. We lived on the base for over two and a half years and then moved into the adjoining town of Ridgecrest. My years in Ridgecrest are full of great memories. We lived at 723 West Haloid St. I made many friends in Ridgecrest. My best friend, Amy Bullock, and I met in 1st grade. We were inseparable and did everything together. I began taking piano lessons from her Mom, Doris, when I was eight years old. I attribute all the piano skills I know to her and what she taught me. I still use that talent today to play both the piano and the organ in church.

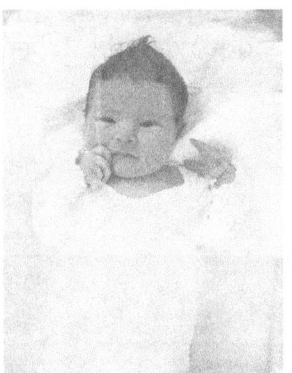

I was baptized by my dad in May of 1980. I still remember that day and how I felt. I have four brothers and one sister. I am the oldest and each time a sibling was born, I would hope (and pray) that it was a sister. But as each came along, it was always a boy. By the last one, I told one of the ladies in my ward that I was going to send the baby back if it was a boy. However, after I saw Russell and how cute he was, I avoided that lady because I was embarrassed that I had told her that.

When I was in 8th grade, my dad took a job in Los Alamos, New Mexico. I was sad to leave my friends but excited for a new adventure. It was just a few months after moving there that my Mom came in one morning while I was brushing my teeth and getting ready for school to tell me that she was expecting a baby! I remember my heart skipped a beat – because I KNEW it was the sister I had always longed to have. And sure enough, on December 30, 1986, my baby sister, Michelle, was born. I couldn't have been more thrilled!

In New Mexico, I made new friends – but continued to stay in touch with ones from Ridgecrest. I went to Los Alamos High School. I started teaching piano lessons after school as a freshman and continued all four years of high school. It was a great start to something I would do even up until now. I attended all four years of early morning seminary which was held before school at the high school.

After graduating from high school, I went to Brigham Young University for the summer term. Little did I know the day my parents dropped me off and drove away of the future that was in store for me there in Provo, Utah. I took three classes that summer, and while I was homesick, I enjoyed some of the funnest times of my life. I lived in Helaman Halls, Budge Dorm. During the fall, I moved to the dorm next door and it was there that I met life-long friends. My roommate was my best friend from Ridgecrest, Amy Bullock. We made an agreement the day I moved from Ridgecrest that we would keep our grades up through the years so that we could get into BYU and room together. And we did! My freshman year was great. I did a lot of learning and growing and made some wonderful friends. One memorable experience was taking an organ class and playing the Tabernacle Organ on Temple Square.

LEFT: *High School graduation* RIGHT: *Playing the Tabernacle organ*

I went home during the summer and worked at the Los Alamos National Laboratory. It was a good paying job and I enjoyed the people I worked with. I returned to BYU and moved off campus to 515 North 400 East, Apt 5. I had always wanted to be an elementary teacher, and so I began to pursue that degree. The following year (my Junior year), after coming back from working at the lab, a group of friends from Los Alamos decided to get together one early morning to go stand in line to get football tickets together. My roommate, who was also from Los Alamos, happened to see a guy who had lived in Los Alamos years before but his family had moved to Arizona when he was young. She invited him to join us. At the first football game, I just happened to sit next to this young man. We cheered the BYU football team on – and chatted throughout the game.

After the game was over, we started walking home. He happened to live south of campus like I did and so we started walking back together. We got to a point where he lived one way and I lived another way, so we just stood on the corner and kept talking. After two hours of chatting (among other things, we had decided he would be our flag football coach), my friend who was with me and I, decided we should get home. He gave me his phone number and we went our separate ways. As we got across the street, my friend turned to me and said, "You are going to marry him." I blew it off. I had JUST met him. What were the chances? Highly unlikely. We called him up and set up our flag football team. He began coaching us and he and I also started dating. At the end of the semester, I realized that we were getting pretty serious and I had a decision to make. The time was coming when I could go on my mission, something I had always wanted to do since I was a child, or I could continue dating him and probably get married. The decision was a tough one. I fasted and prayed to know what to do. Both decisions were righteous ones, which made it even harder. One night at a fireside (which wasn't even on missionary work) the Spirit bore witness to me that I should serve a mission. And so as soon as the fireside was over, I walked up to my bishop and told him that I needed to fill out some mission papers. Kendahl and I broke up so that I could concentrate on going on my mission, although we stayed close as friends.

In March 1993, I received my mission call to the Salt Lake Temple Square Visitors Center Mission. I was thrilled. I had just gone there to visit a few weeks before and had seen sister missionaries there. I had thought to myself what an awesome place it would be to serve a mission. Interestingly enough, on my mission call, it said I would serve for a period of "19 months." This wasn't normal. Normally it says "18 months" for sister missionaries. I later asked other sisters that I served with on Temple Square if anyone else had 19 months on their mission call and no one else did. I still to this day wonder about it and why I was the only one. I did end up extending my mission, partly because of what my mission papers said. I have to think that perhaps there was someone I met on Temple Square in that last month that needed to hear the Gospel.

My brother, Ryan, also turned in his mission papers the same time I did. He was born almost exactly two years after I was. He was called to serve in the California Anaheim Mission. We were even called to go into the Missionary Training Center on the same day (that got changed later – they ended up asking me to go in a week after my brother). So on May 12, 1993, I entered the MTC. My companions were Sister Cintra (from Brazil) and Sister Cano (from Florida). It was a humbling, exciting time and I couldn't wait for everything ahead of me.

I had many amazing experiences on Temple Square. I remember once giving a tour to a Jewish man from Jerusalem. He looked exactly like the men from the movie Fiddler on the Roof. I also had many experiences where I felt like I was in the right place at the right time to meet certain individuals to share my testimony of the Gospel with them. It was a unique, wonderful mission, something I still treasure and look back on everyday. While serving on Temple Square, missionaries have the opportunity to serve in a different mission somewhere in the United States when there aren't as many visitors to Temple Square. Each month, a list would be posted of the sisters who were going and to which mission they would be serving for four months. We never knew when or where, so it was always a surprise.

LEFT: *Ryan and Jennifer serving in California Anaheim Mission*
RIGHT: *Jennifer on Temple Square*

One day, I walked into the room and there posted on the door was "California Anaheim Mission" and my name was underneath. This was amazing to me since first of all, they had never called any missionaries from Temple Square to serve there, but also because my brother, Ryan, was currently serving in that same mission! What were the chances?! I was so excited but didn't want to tell anyone just in case they might change it. I did tell the Assistant to the President and she told me, "Sister Christensen, it is where the Lord wants you to serve." After that I was so excited to get on a plane and get to California. I didn't have time to write Ryan and tell him I was coming to his mission (I was leaving in just a couple of days) so I knew I would just have to go surprise him. When I got there, I was having my interview with the mission president and I told him that my brother was serving in the mission. He kindly put us in the same zone so that we were able to see each other. That day, my mission companion surprised me and drove me to his house. I'll never forget the look on Ryan's face when he looked and saw me standing at his doorstep. We enjoyed four months together in the mission field and were the "hit" of the mission! We would be at zone conferences or other places and if we were together, all of the other missionaries wanted to get their pictures taken with us at conferences (because it was rare to have a brother and sister serving in the same mission.) I loved my mission and am appreciative of all of the wonderful experiences I had while serving the Lord.

I returned from my mission on December 7, 1994. And in January, I went back to BYU. I continued my education in Elementary Education and enjoyed meeting up with friends from before my mission. Kendahl had continued to write me faithfully throughout my mission, but when I got home, I just didn't have a huge desire to date him at the time. I knew he wanted to get married and I knew if I married him, that I would probably drop out of school to support him. While that is not a bad thing, I just had this feeling and desire that I should finish my education before getting married. And so we lost touch with one another. I continued my education but had to change majors. I graduated in August 1997 with a degree in Family Science. I moved to Orem and lived with some missionary friends. I worked at 1-800 Contacts in Draper, Utah while looking for another job. The job finally came in January 1998. I was hired at the Kirton & McConkie Law Firm in downtown Salt Lake City as a legal secretary. I was the legal secretary to three patent attorneys. I was also the secretary to Tom Monson, son of President Thomas S. Monson. (It was while I was his secretary that he took me and introduced me to his father, President Thomas S. Monson, now president of the Church) – a day I will never forget!)

I moved to Murray, Utah in order to be closer to my job in downtown Salt Lake. I worked on the 18th floor on the corner of South Temple and State Street and so every day I got to look down onto Temple Square and the memories of my mission always came flooding back.

One day I received a call from someone familiar, Kendahl Johnson. We reconnected and began dating long distance. He was working for a minor league baseball team in Oregon, but that didn't stop us. Our relationship progressed to a beautiful engagement on the beach and on August 27, 1999, we were married in Salt Lake City. We were sealed for time and all eternity in the Bountiful Utah Temple by my grandfather, RW Christensen, on September 2, 2000.

Now for a little about Kendahl. Kendahl was born on October 24, 1970 in Mesa, Arizona to Norma Joan Hewett and Kendahl James Johnson. The family moved to White Rock, New Mexico when he was very young and they lived there for four or five years. The family moved to Tucson, Arizona where he grew up. He served in the Idaho Boise Mission, where he met his future grandmother-in-law and grandfather-in-law, Naomi and RW Christensen, who served in the mission office. He then attended BYU. He has an older brother, Hugh, who died when he was only 19 months old in a car accident and four sisters, Kendra, Kellye, Kristi, and Karleen.

We moved to Colorado Springs, Colorado where Kendahl took a job working for the Air Force Academy in the Athletic Department. I also got a job in the same department, working for the Air Force Men's Basketball coaches as an administrative assistant. But I quit that job when our first child, Kaylee Anne Johnson, was born on April 2, 2001. She was beautiful and sweet and our lives have never been the same. We bought our first home and settled into life as parents. Just two years later, on May 15, 2003 we welcomed Konnor Hugh Johnson into our eternal family.

During this time I served in the ward Primary Presidency and then the Stake Primary Presidency. I made wonderful friends and so I was very sad when Kendahl got a job offer in San Antonio, Texas. We only had five weeks to sell the house and move to a place we'd never seen before. But the Lord was watching over us and everything went smoothly. We drove into the large city of San Antonio in June 2004. We lived in an apartment for four months while our house was being built. I was put in as Relief Society President one day after finding out that I was pregnant with our third child. Kenna Lynn Johnson was born on June 6, 2006 and had lots of black hair that stood straight up. When she was just a couple of months old, we found out that Kendahl had been offered a job at another Air Force Base in Warner Robins, Georgia. After just two years, we were moving again! But we felt it was the right thing for our family. Our house sold in a matter of days and we were off on a new adventure to the deep south.

We bought our third home in Bonaire, Georgia and have settled into life here. Our fourth child was born in Warner Robins, Georgia on June 2, 2009. We named her Kamryn Jenae Johnson. Kendahl is currently working at Robins Air Force Base in the Public Affairs Office. I have the opportunity to stay at home with my children. I am also teaching piano lessons and love photography. I am currently serving as the Primary President and Kendahl served as Elders Quorum President for almost four years. He is now the Assistant Ward Mission Leader. We are enjoying living in the southern part of the United States and being able to see this part of the country. We feel that we might be here for awhile, which is fine with us. We enjoy the people here and have made wonderful friends. We do miss living close to family, but we know that eventually we'll be able to move back out west and have that opportunity again. The children are all growing and are healthy and happy. We feel very blessed.

Ryan Wade Christensen

I was born April 16, 1974 in Ridgecrest California. I was the second child of my parents, R. Wynn Christensen and Bette Ann Murdoch, having an older sister, Jennifer, born two years earlier. Ridgecrest was the town adjacent to China Lake Naval Weapon Center. My father, Wynn, worked for the laboratory there. I remember a little bit from when my family lived on the base. When I was two, we moved from the base to 723 W. Haloid in Ridgecrest. This would be our family's home for the next 10 years.

All of my brothers were born in Ridgecrest as well. We spent a lot of time outside as kids. We had computers and Intelivision, but still liked being outside playing sports or riding bikes. My best friend, Danny, lived right across the street from us and most of my time outside was spent with him. We rode bikes, skateboards, played soccer, football, baseball, and sometimes basketball. This translated to school as well. Sports dominated the playground during recess for me. In 5th grade, my elementary school had a track meet and I had the fastest time in 5th grade in the 100 yard dash and was the lead-off runner on our school's team at the city track meet.

I remember our house had a big window in the front living room. The front yard also was pretty big and had no trees making it a perfect place for playing sports. Needless to say the front window was broken a few times from soccer balls being kicked through it even if the ball was a Nerf. We spent most of our playing time in the front yard as we lived in a cul-de-sac. Ridgecrest was always hot in the summer time. There was a local number you could dial on the phone that would give you the current time and temperature. The hottest I remember it getting was 117 degrees.

I also experienced a few earthquakes while we lived there. Being next to the San Andreas Fault meant earthquakes were something people got used too. We used to practice earthquake drills in school by ducking and covering under our desks. Since I went to school on the Naval base, we also practiced bomb drills. For this we left the classroom and walked to the football/soccer fields. It never made sense to me why you would walk to an open field if your city was being bombed but apparently that is what you do. I always loved seeing the jets fly overhead and especially loved it when the Blue Angels came to town.

When I was nine years old, my dad was called as Bishop of the Ridgecrest 2nd Ward. We didn't see much of him during this time but when we did, we had lots of memories. We would build model rockets and shoot them off by the community college. He would take us on long drives on his motorcycle. I remember he would let me get in front and let me be in charge of the throttle. He would steer and make sure we didn't tip over while I controlled the speed. Pretty fun.

In February of 1986 when I was 11, we moved to Los Alamos, New Mexico. I remember snow on the ground when we first got there which was something new for us. We moved into our home at 112 Aztec in the summer of 1986. I attended Los Alamos Middle School and Los Alamos High School. Since the town was small, we had to be creative when it came to doing things. We were so close to the mountains and to the Rio Grande that the outdoors was the place to be. I spent a lot of time camping and hiking with friends. The most popular place was the Blue Dot Trail by Overlook Park, where we could hike down to the Rio Grande and camp. Mainly it was overnight camping but sometimes we spent a couple of days down there. Our parents could check on us by going to the overlook and we could yell back and forth to each other but we were so far down there that it was ineffective. I went on several campouts with the Explorer Troop from the ward, which were week-long camping trips. The biggest one was the trip to Durango, Colorado. We took the Silverton/Durango steam train and hopped off half way to Silverton when the train stopped to fill up with more water. We hiked about six miles into the mountains right at the foot of three 14,000 foot mountain peaks. We climbed to the top of one of them and it seemed like you could see forever.

During middle school and high school, I had a couple of paper routes. In Middle school, Richard and I had an Albuquerque Journal route in the morning. It was an everyday paper so we had to get up early every day including holidays. We also were responsible for collecting the money from the customers. This led to some good tips but it was a pain to go collecting. When high school started, so did early morning seminary so I took over a Los Alamos Monitor afternoon route. It was a good way for me to learn responsibility and work ethic.

When I turned 16, I was able to get a job at Pizza Hut earning $4.25 an hour. The summer of my junior year, I worked at both Pizza Hut and for Los Alamos County in the Finance Department. I worked at the county during the day and about three nights during the week would work at Pizza Hut. I was able to save a lot during this time as college and mission got closer. Growing up, our parents had us save 50% of everything we earned and put it in our mission fund. This was hard at the time to put away so much of my money but I was glad when it came time to paying for school. I graduated from Los Alamos High School in May of 1992 and after spending the summer working and playing golf almost every day, left for Brigham Young University in the fall. During one of those rounds of golf, I got a hole-in-one on Hole 15, a 191 yard par three at the Los Alamos Golf Course.

My freshman year at BYU was great and I made many new friends that are still good friends to this day. It was nice to have religion classes mixed in with the core classes. I struggled with the huge class size but still managed to get a 3.0 GPA at the end of my first year. It was while I was at BYU when I received my mission call to the California Anaheim Mission. I was very excited to be going to California. By this time I was really getting sick of cold weather and snow and was looking forward to the warmth of California.

I reported to the Missionary Training Center (MTC) on May 5, 1993. There were three of us in my district going to Anaheim including my companion, Todd Phillips, who was from Boise Idaho. My sister, Jennifer, entered the MTC a week after I did on May 12, 1993 to serve in the Salt Lake Temple Square Mission. It was kind of nice to have a familiar face to see sometimes. After three weeks in the MTC, we flew into Orange County and were taken to the mission home. We were assigned our companions and then taken back to our new areas. My first companion was Brian Malcarne from Connecticut. He was a convert to the church and was the only member in his family. He was a hard worker and was a good trainer for me to start off my mission. I had many spiritual experiences on my mission and learned about the power of prayer and the Holy Ghost. My testimony of the Savior grew as I depended on him for strength during the many trials that came during my mission. I saw many people change their lives as they chose to accept the gospel despite the adversaries many tries to stop them. I also saw many reject the gospel even though they had felt the spirit and knew what they were being taught was true. During my mission, I served in Huntington Beach, Placentia, Yorba Linda, Anaheim, Fullerton, Orange, Santa Ana, and finished my mission back in Yorba Linda. While I was serving in Huntington Beach, I got a phone call from one of the sister missionaries saying she was going to drop off some things for the zone leader since he lived closer to us than to her and it would save on his monthly miles allotment. When she came to the door, she asked if we could come out and help her bring the box in. As I walked through the door, I saw her new companion on the right kind of hiding on the porch. I thought how she looked like Jennifer and had to do a double take to see that it actually was Jennifer! She had been called to go to Anaheim for a four month proselyting mission away from Temple Square. We were in the same zone with each other for two months as she served in Newport Beach. It was a great treat for us both and for others in the mission to see a brother and sister serve together in the same mission.

After my mission, I worked for Foxfire Construction in White Rock on a remodeling job before going back to BYU.

This was my first taste of construction and I really enjoyed it. I was able to do some framing, sheetrock work, trim work, hung cabinets, paint, and some tile work on the house. It was because of this experience that I decided to major in Construction Management at BYU. So when I went back to school, I started the Construction Management Program and would be in school full time including summers for the next three years.

My roommates were friends I had made my freshman year, Brent Hartzell, Jay Meldrum, and David Rice. David was a friend from White Rock and we all still keep in touch with each other to this day.

In May of 1996, our student ward boundaries switched around. My roommate, Jay, became the Elders Quorum President and thus was able to setup the home teaching routes. This is how I met my future wife. I was assigned to home teach Kim Johnston (Kimberly Sue Johnston) from Preston Idaho. We both had common friends with each other which helped kick start our relationship. I had a good friend from my mission who was from Preston and it turned out that he was marrying Kim's best friend in high school. We started out just talking with each other, sometimes late into the night. We had our first date with Jay Meldrum and Jen Thompson Meldrum to Johnny B's Comedy Club. We had ice cream after the comedy club and then a movie to follow that up. Our second date a week later was to the Buzz game in Salt Lake, then up to Preston to meet Kim's parents, go to the rodeo and to see friends. A couple of months later, I asked Kim to marry me and was so glad she said yes. We were married December 27, 1996 in the Salt Lake Temple. My grandfather, RW Christensen, performed the sealing which was a tremendous blessing to have him be able to do it for us.

Kim was born May 22, 1975 in Malad Idaho. She is the only child of Harry Johnston and Debra Jean Hobson Johnston. She and her family moved to Preston when she was five and she attended Kindergarten through 12th grade in Preston. Upon graduation she spent time in Connecticut as a nanny before returning to Utah to attend BYU where we would eventually meet.

Upon graduating from BYU, we had places to choose between for employment, Phoenix and Dallas. After deciding we would go to Phoenix, we both prayed about our decision and felt like I needed to go to work for Grand Homes in Dallas. So that is what we did. We arrived in Dallas on Saturday May 2, 1998. My parents drove our Dodge Neon behind the moving truck. Our first apartment we rented sight unseen and it was disgusting. My dad and I unloaded the truck and then we took my parents to the airport to fly back to New Mexico. On Monday, I was reloading the truck as we moved to another apartment building that was much nicer. We had two fellow BYU grads that came to work for Grand Homes and we were all in the same apartment complex which made our Texas transition easier.

In the summer of 1999, we bought our first home at 4133 Driscoll in The Colony, Texas. It smelled horrible and needed a lot of work which was just what we wanted. Our plan was to fix it up and sell it. This did not quite happen like we would have liked and three years later we were still living there. During our time on Driscoll, Kim became pregnant with triplets. We were a bit surprised and tried to get the house ready for the new family members. With help from friends, family, and ward members we were able to get things in order.

Kim's mom and grandma stayed with us for the last couple of months of Kim's pregnancy and kept the house clean and Kim and I fed. The last seven weeks before their birth, Kim went on hospital bed rest. I stayed with her and mainly went home to change clothes and mow the lawn. Kim had a lot of visitors and we made a lot of friends with the hospital staff. Kim made it 33 weeks and on March 30, 2001, Cami Sue, Michael Wade, and Kylee Brook were born and would change our lives forever. They all were taken to the NICU and would stay there for about a month. When they all came home, and gained a bit of weight, we put them on a strict schedule to save our sanity. It worked and life was easier. This schedule would save our sanity as it would help us get out and do things we needed even though three kids could sometimes be a little overwhelming. My mom came and she and I washed 24 bottles, filled them, and put them in the fridge for the next day.

We adjusted pretty well and were blessed to have some really good kids. We were able to go on trips in the car with them to see relatives and even made a trip to Sea World in San Antonio, Texas before they were two. In 2002, we started building our own home at 3832 Windward in The Colony. I designed the home and was also the general contractor, which saved us a lot of money and let us build it the way we wanted. It was a two story home so we had to teach the kids to go up and down the stairs. Cami had the toughest time and fell down the stairs three times. Each time she did, Kylee and Michael cried harder than Cami did.

LEFT: *Ryan crossing the finish line at Hyrum, Utah Triathlon in 2008*
RIGHT: *Russell, Ryan, and Reed*

In 2003, our daughter Ashley Jean was born on September 11. It was a planned C-section so we did not have much say on the date. I called my mom and told her we named her Kaitlyn Liberty because she was born on 9/11. My mom told some of her friends at her ward's Relief Society Enrichment meeting the wrong name and had to tell everyone again what Ashley's name really was. (I love playing tricks on my mom.) We had a pretty rough time the week after Ashley was born as she had spinal meningitis and had to be hospitalized for a week. When Ashley came home for good, Kim came down with pneumonia and had a collapsed lung. She spent about four days in the hospital which was pretty crazy period in our lives. Our testimony about the power of the Priesthood was definitely strengthened by this experience.

About one year later at the end of 2004, on December 2, Luke Joshua was born. With only about 15 months separating Luke and Ashley, the two have become really close. We now had five kids, with the oldest three being nine years olds. It sounds crazy on paper but we have enjoyed the opportunity. Luke keeps us all laughing and we could not have been happier to have him in our family. Our three bedroom home that we built had quickly become too small for all of us. Thus we started making plans to build our next home. We completed our new home at 6417 Hampton Court, which was one block away from our home on Windward. It was a home custom built for us with two very large bedrooms upstairs, one to fit three girls and one to fit two boys. We even had a media room which we loved using for family movie night and the occasional ward activity up there as well.

In 2008, I left Grand Homes and started my own homebuilding company, Summerstone Homes. At the time the market everywhere else in the country was starting to decline but the Dallas market seemed to be doing just fine. About five months after leaving Grand Homes, the Dallas market started to decline as well in new home sales. Summerstone Homes was building two homes, one spec and one sold job. We were very nervous that the spec home would not sale but we were blessed to sell it about three weeks after completion. Due to the slow market, it became necessary to find another source of income. With much prayer and fasting, we were led by the Lord for me to go back to school. In about a two week period of time, many miracles crossed our path and led us to Texas A&M in College Station, Texas for me to pursue an MBA Degree. I applied four weeks before the start of classes and got accepted two weeks before classes started. In the two weeks leading up to school and with Kim and the kids in Preston, I found a house to rent in College Station that fit our family, picked up my family in Preston, picked up my mom in White Rock and drove them all back to Texas, leased our home in The Colony and with the help of parents and friends, had our home packed up in two trucks and were on our way to College Station.

I have finished my first year here at A&M and will graduate in December of 2010. It is a very intense program, where I spent about 80 hours a week studying and preparing for classes each day. Where we go from here is a good question. We are putting our faith in the Lord as he has guided us this far and we truly feel blessed with the guidance we have received in our lives up to this point.

Richard Warren Christensen

My name is Richard Warren Christensen. I was born in Ridgecrest, California on October 28, 1976 at approximately 8:30 A.M to R. Wynn and Bette Ann Murdoch Christensen. As you may have heard, the nurses all gathered 'round and gazed in wide wonder at the joy they had found. I have an older sister, Jennifer, an older brother, Ryan, two younger brothers, Reed and Russell, and a younger sister, Michelle. Being born the third child makes me a middle child but I brought a lot of personality to the family. My mom told me that when I was little, I was the first of any of her children to write on the walls. One day, I found a permanent marker, pulled the bottom off, and scribbled all over the kitchen floor. My mom didn't know you could take off the bottom of a permanent marker and she scrubbed that floor forever trying to get it off. It finally just faded away over time.

I loved living in Ridgecrest, mostly because I didn't know anything better. Ryan, Reed, and I would spend countless hours out in the desert riding our bikes or hiking around looking for bugs and lizards. I didn't really have any friends that lived close to me in our Ridgecrest neighborhood. When I was 9 ½, it was heartbreaking for me to move to White Rock, New Mexico when my dad took a job at the Los Alamos National Lab. I think the worst part for me was leaving our stupid dog, Ruff Ruff, behind.

White Rock was a great place to grow up. White Rock and Los Alamos were on the way to nowhere, so there were no transients in the town. Most people were fairly well off because of the government lab there, where my dad worked as an electrical engineer. I had several friends that lived close to me as I grew up there. The outdoor activities were endless in that area.

LEFT: *Richard and Ryan at Temple Square*
RIGHT: *Ryan, Jennifer, Reed, and Richard*

I had some very good friends at Los Alamos High School and we had a lot of fun. I had a few paper routes for 6 ½ years until I turned 16. I then got a job at the Pizza Hut in town and after working there for a while, decided that a college education would be a good idea after high school. I also participated in track my junior and senior years in high school and we won the New Mexico State Track tournament my senior year.

I had a tough time with school. When I was in high school and younger, I had a difficult time concentrating. I remember so many times in 5th grade sitting through the teacher going, "blah, blah, blah," as I sat there day-dreaming about who knows what. Then the bell would ring and we would be going out to recesses, and I'm wondering what just happened. Then a week or two later the teacher asks all the kids to turn in their assignments, and I had no earthly idea what she was talking about. By the time I got to college, I didn't have that problem so I think just getting older and paying attention to paying attention when I'm supposed to, has turned me around. I was very proud to have graduated with a 3.5 GPA from college, despite the mediocre grades in my first couple of years.

I graduated from Los Alamos High School in June of 1995. After high school, I went to Eastern Arizona College in Thatcher, Arizona for two semesters. While there, I gave my parents a heart attack by buying a 1967

Plymouth Barracuda and then getting a girlfriend. Despite their heart attacks, buying that Barracuda ended up leading me down the road of my future educational emphasis and occupations. EAC was a good time for me. I made some very good friends that were roommates of mine in the eight-student rental home I lived in.

After EAC, I worked for a while at home in New Mexico doing mostly yard work. I put an ad in the local newspaper as "college student with pickup will do yard work". The phone rang off the hook and I eventually had to pull the ad because some of the jobs became permanent over the span of the summer.

I left on my mission in November 2006 to the Oregon Eugene Mission for The Church of Jesus Christ of Latter-day Saints. I remember after my first week in Salem, Oregon looking out the window and realizing that I had not seen the sun since I had arrived. For some reason most of my memories about Oregon seemed gloomy, but I'm sure it is because it's mostly cloudy there all the time, except for in the summer. The summer in Oregon is amazing. The plants have all the water they need and just go crazy. I had the worst seasonal allergies in my life in Oregon and wrote my parents to remind me to never move here. The one place that was different was Kalamath Falls. It was on the east side of the mountains that divided the gloomy weather from the sunny weather. That was probably my favorite area. My mission was invaluable to me because I learned the gospel so well and learned to listen to the Spirit. There is nothing like being a missionary.

A few weeks after my mission, I headed off to UVSC, Utah Valley State College" (now Utah Valley University) in Orem, Utah. I eventually got two

Associate Degrees and one Bachelors Degree. While going to school there, I met my wonderful wife to be, Heather Ann Stoddart, from Sandy, Utah. We were married on November 16th, 2000, a year and a few months after we met. While still going to college, we had our first child on May 16, 2002. Her name is Elise Abigail Christensen. Elise has always had a unique, cute laugh that I've always adored. Elise is our computer nut. Not too long after learning how to walk, she was learning how to operate a computer to play games.

I graduated from Utah Valley State College in December 2003. While going to college, I worked at a local car dealership in Provo called Harmon's Downtown Auto Center in the body shop in various positions, but mostly in the paint shop. I worked there for

3 ½ years. When I graduated, I was lucky enough to be hired by Sherwin-Williams Automotive Finishes. They threw me right into a branch as a Branch Manager on January 4, 2004 in Houston, Texas. While in Texas, we had two children, David Richard Christensen was born October 26, 2004 and Ella Margaret Christensen was born October 3, 2006. David is a very energetic boy. He loves boy things, like toy guns and wrestling. Ella is Heather's clone. She is just like her mother in a million ways.

After being in Texas for some time, we found an opportunity to move to Phoenix, Arizona. I stayed with Sherwin-Williams, but took on a larger branch in Glendale, Arizona. We moved to the nice community of Surprise in February 2008. The weather here is so wonderful, except for a few months in the summer. We had our fourth child here, Maxwell Warren Christensen. He was born on June 23, 2009. Max had issues at birth, and was in the NICU for two weeks. We almost lost him a few times. Now he is 90th percentile in his weight, height, and his head is "off the charts". At my last calculation, Max cost about $90,000 to be born into this world - $12,000 of which was a helicopter ride...Lucky!

We continue to live in Surprise, Arizona and my shop business is doing great, despite others being closed. Elise was baptized on June 5, 2010, and both sets of grandparents attended, which made for a special day for her.

Reed William Christensen

I was born on June 30, 1978 to R. Wynn and Bette Ann Murdoch Christensen in Ridgecrest, California and the fourth of six children. I remember well growing up in Ridgecrest. As far as I can tell, my earliest memory was when I was two weeks shy of being three years old, a kid in the neighborhood ran over me on his bicycle breaking my leg.

Ridgecrest was pretty dry and desolate, but as a kid you don't know any different. I remember riding on bike trails and the adventure of just going around the neighborhood and outrunning stray dogs that would nip at your feet. It seems we were always outside growing up – building forts, exploring the desert, and biking. I attended Las Flores Elementary until second grade. I remember being very good at soccer and often scoring goals in games. I also seemed to be very quick of foot as a kid. I usually never lost a race until later in life in 5th and 6th grade and actually won the 50-yard dash in a multi-school track meet after we moved to Los Alamos.

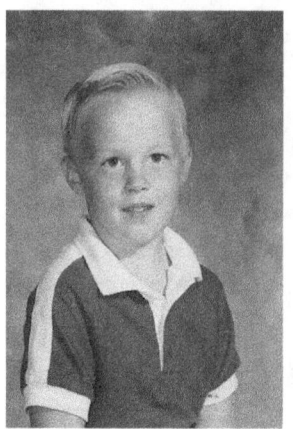 

In second grade we moved to White Rock New Mexico. I remember when we arrived in New Mexico in February 1986 and it being covered in snow. I thought we had moved to somewhere near the North Pole. We were quick to make friends with the Rohrer family in the neighborhood as they seemed to have a child that matched up age-wise with each of us. As I now reflect back on growing up in White Rock, I would have to say there was no better place to grow up. Most of my days were spent on my bike at some point. Whether it was doing an early morning paper route (from fourth grade until ninth), or taking jumps on the "back-trails", I was usually found on my bike. White Rock was a unique place in that it was surrounded by either Indian land or Department of Energy land, so the town would never grow in size. This made for many trails to explore as well as Indian caves to visit. Frequently we would take hikes down to the Rio Grande and swim in the river and streams. A favorite activity was visiting "Heck's Hole" (actually called Hell's Hole but being good Mormons we didn't say that word) as we would call it and squeeze down through narrow shafts and caves to a large cavern at the bottom. Looking back now, I wonder how I ever survived these early years, but boy were they fun.

I graduated from Los Alamos High School in 1996 and attended Utah

Valley State College. I took my first courses in business management there and found that I was very adept at my studies there achieving straight A's my first semester. I was also able to live with my brother Ryan in Provo before he was married and enjoyed this time together after his mission.

    Shortly after arriving home from college, I received my mission call to Barcelona Spain. I spent nearly three months at the MTC, one month longer than normal waiting for my visa to come through. My first area in Spain was Murcia and it was probably the most formidable six months of my life. My first companion was about as perfect a trainer as you could have your first two months. When he was transferred after two months, I was crushed and remember going in to the bathroom and weeping like a baby. He taught me the basic principles about being a missionary and teacher of the gospel that I carried through to the end of my mission. Although I've had a lot of people inspire and change my life, I must say he is up there at the top. In Murcia, we had a lot of success as missionaries. We baptized several people and on one occasion baptized eight or nine African men one memorable evening. Our little area that had previously been avoided before (I learned this later in my mission), turned into the hot spot of the mission and a place where people thought they could go in order to get baptisms. I was transferred from Murcia to Castellon de la Plana and spent two hard months there with little success and the only companion with whom I didn't see eye to eye on how to do the work. I was then transferred for a few weeks to Gandia, then to Valencia for three months, another very enjoyable time in my mission where we enjoyed success again in baptisms. After Valencia, I was transferred as a senior companion in Albecete, the only place in the mission that wasn't near the coast it seemed. There we worked hard to find a family, and eventually did (which was baptized after I was transferred). I was transferred to Villajoyosa, a small village on the coast. There I had a companion that helped me keep my sanity. It was just the two of us, and the area we covered was sparsely populated with a branch consisting of two families. I was the first counselor in the branch presidency. I recall the branch president being pretty strange with a sizeable ego. One time during the service, he leaned over to me and offered me a cigar in his pocket. Another time he recounted a story about how he had found a long lost brother and had a glass of champagne with him which I later told my mission president about, and which he cornered me about prior to my being transferred. Villajosa was the hardest part of my mission, and one of the best. I was put to the test, and felt like I came out a stronger person. My next stop was Elche – the palm tree capital of Spain. Here I was able to enjoy more success with several baptisms. My companion and I were with each other for so long that we would often finish each other's sentences. My last two months of my mission were spent on an island in the Mediterranean – Palma de Mallorca. Here, four of us missionaries tried to help find and baptize people on the whole island of 700,000 people. We were really outnumbered! Our apartment was right on the dock where we would watch cruise ships and even US aircraft carriers dock and stay for periods of time. It was a great way to spend the last two months of my mission.

After returning home from my mission, I took up residence again in Orem, Utah attending UVSC again and living with my brother Richard. There I set a goal to marry within a year of returning from my mission. One of my roommates caught me in a good mood one day and asked if I would go visit some friends of his, and I agreed to go. There at the apartment I met the James sisters and their roommates. Growing up, I had taught myself to play the guitar and developed the ability to create songs on the fly. This talent served me well as Sara James was impressed. A little while later, Sara and I attended a fireside together and had fun goofing off during the meeting. I think the things that caught my eye about Sara were her beauty, sense of humor, and overall sweetness. She has always had a strong testimony of the gospel. I called her up a couple days after the fireside and asked if she would go on a date to a free school play, *Antigone*, and some ice cream afterwards at Leatherby's – she accepted. During our first date, my stomach growled like crazy because of some bad indigestion. But it didn't seem to bother her and we talked the entire evening, often forgetting we were on a double date with one of my roommates. We never spent a day apart since. I proposed about three months from the day we met. I took Sara to our favorite park in Provo where we ate Taco Bell and took two 50 cent rolls of pennies to made wishes in the stream, asking her to marry me on the last wish.

A little about Sara - Sara Ann James was born on November 4, 1976 in Owensboro, Davis, Kentucky to Roger Lyle and Trudy Fay Alexander James. She has two sisters, Shaloah and Myra, and a brother, Sam. Sara attended BYU and graduated after we were married, with a Bachelors of Science in Geography.

The date: July 29th, 2000, more or less one year after arriving home from my mission, Sara and I were married in the Albuquerque New Mexico Temple and held a reception in my hometown of White Rock. That night we left for our honeymoon to my Aunt Sherri Murdoch Porter's cabin in Cascade Idaho. After returning, I concentrated on getting accepted to Brigham Young University, and was accepted in late 2000. I worked hard my first semester at BYU to get accepted into BYU's prestigious accounting program – and eventually was. The accounting program was difficult and time consuming, but prepared me well for my career in accounting. In July 2002, Owen James Christensen was born into the family and we made room for him in our tiny apartment in central Provo. In December

2003, I graduated from BYU with my Bachelor's in Accounting and Masters in Taxation. I also accepted a position with Novagradac and Company in San Francisco, California. We moved to Concord, California which is one hour away from San Francisco in January 2004, and spent six months there before moving to Austin, Texas with the same CPA firm. Prior to leaving for Austin, we found out Sara was pregnant with twins. In Austin, we enjoyed having a larger townhouse with a garage, but had a rough time with the hot and humid climate and frequent bouts with flying cockroaches in our apartment. There in Austin, Matthew Wynn Christensen and Meghan Naomi Christensen were born on November 25, 2004 and spent two weeks in the hospital being four weeks premature. The next months are literally a blur, dealing with numerous dirty diapers, midnight feedings, and three little mouths to feed. We didn't enjoy Austin much, in fact, I often look back on Austin as some of the most miserable months of my life. We struggled to make friends in the ward, the neighborhood was not inviting, and we were down on our decision to be there. One day, Sara spotted a job in Albuquerque, New Mexico with KPMG, a big four accounting firm. We made a quick trip out there, got the job, and bought a house all within a day or two.

Our first house was the perfect starter home with something unique in Albuquerque, as it had grass in the front and backyard (most houses just have rocks). Our house also had a very large tiered backyard where the kids spent many an hour exploring and playing. After dealing with some harsh traveling requirements to the Navajo Nation in western New Mexico, I took a job with PNM, the local utility company and loved every minute of it. When PNM announced layoffs, I started looking at other options and found a similar position in Coeur d'Alene Idaho. So in September 2007, I submitted my resume on a whim and got a call from the Controller and fellow BYU graduate, John Hunter. He talked us into visiting Coeur d'Alene, which we did and fell in love with the area. It was gorgeous and the kind of place we could see raising a family. Although we loved Albuquerque and being close to my parents, Coeur d'Alene seemed like the small town similar to White Rock where the kids could grow up and have a breadth of experiences. I accepted the position and with a heavy heart prepared the house for sale. We moved to Coeur d'Alene in January 2008 and we immediately met with some of the worst snow storms in Coeur d'Alene history. Shortly after arriving, we welcomed our fourth child into the family, Rachel Mae Christensen, born April 20, 2008. She is a sweet and well-natured baby – our first that wasn't colicky!

While in Coeur d'Alene, my new boss introduced me to the sport of triathlon. After injuring my ankle, I began swimming in the pool in the building at my work. In 2008, I signed up for a triathlon when I got to the point I felt well enough to compete. Ryan and Russell also signed up for the same triathlon. The thought of doing triathlons kept me up at night for about a week, and I had no idea why. It could have been a mid-life crisis or something, but it became somewhat of an obsession. My first triathlon was in Hyrum Utah with my brothers where I did an Olympic distance event. But looking back on this event, the most important memory for me is that my grandfather, RW Christensen, was there to witness it prior to his death in November 2008 as well as attend the blessing of our daughter Rachel. Sometimes I look back at my desires to enter the sport as Heavenly

Ironman in Coeur d'Alene, Idaho

Father's plan to get us to see him one last time before his death. Later that summer, I did a Half-Iron Distance Race (1.2 mile swim, 56 mile bike, and 13.1 mile run) successfully. I continued to have ankle problems through the winter, but set a goal to do the Half-Ironman in Boise on June 13, 2009 (partially as an excuse to go down and see family). During the training, my ankle was hurting too much only allowing me to run once a week. I was concerned and one day took my concern to the Lord and asked whether I should stop training, but felt inspired to run on it, which I did. My ankle was strengthened and I successfully completed the Half-Ironman in 5 hours and 38 minutes while running the entire half marathon. The next week I signed up for the Ironman in Coeur d'Alene and hoped my body is able to take the training regimen I was to submit it to. Throughout my training however, I am always wary to spend as much time with my wife and children and make them my priority. On June 27, 2010, I successfully did the Coeur d'Alene Ironman in 12 hours, 32 minutes and 52 seconds. I was quite sick the week before and had never run a full marathon before this race as I have a torn carlige in my hip. My mom came to witness the event and I was glad she was able to come.

Russell Wayne Christensen

I was born on June 16, 1981 in Ridgecrest, California to R. Wynn and Bette Ann Murdoch Christensen. I was told that I was a beautiful baby with black locks that made any other mom jealous. (My mom had to cut my bangs when I was four weeks old because they were down in my eyes.) I lived there until the age of four when we moved to Los Alamos, New Mexico.

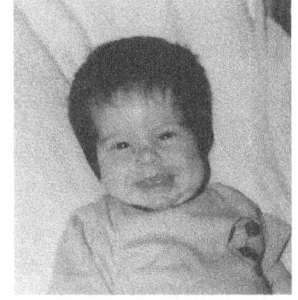

I remember a lot about Ridgecrest including a lot of my friends. I always tried to remember as much as I could about living there and later in life it would be to my benefit. Moving to Los Alamos, New Mexico was exciting to me, and it became more exciting when we saw all the snow. Living in White Rock, a suburb of Los Alamos, provided the perfect childhood environment. I quickly befriended half the kids on our street and spent most of my summers riding bikes and building forts in the arroyo behind our house. My best friend lived next door which was very convenient for me. We were on the same sport teams most years, which made for a lot of fun.

One of our favorite things to do was to explore Rattlesnake Hill, which was only a block from our house. It was a small hill which we constantly explored and made some amazing forts but never saw any rattlesnakes. I was always grateful that I never had to move after I started school. A lot

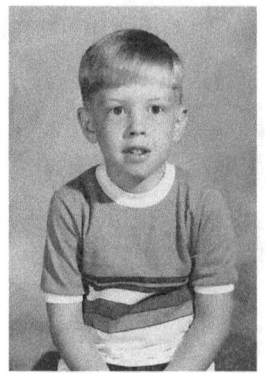 

of my closest friends were with me from kindergarten all the way through to high school graduation. In school I always enjoyed math. It was like solving a puzzle for me, so my mind was always entertained. This and my love for cars and anything to do with car and home stereos fueled my interest to become an engineer. My Dad was always an inspiration in that regard as well. I was always impressed at his engineering mind and ability to fix almost anything. My Mom was also an inspiration in my life. We were able to bond a lot doing paper routes together and I always cherished those early mornings together. During my teenage years, I finally quit the paper route that I had for eight years and became a bagger at Smith's Grocery Store. It finally felt like I had a real job and I took it very seriously. I later worked for Los Alamos National Bank as a handyman, of sorts. That was also the time I started to snowboard and fell in love with it. When I finally got the nerve up to buy a season pass my senior year, the ski hill didn't open once all winter because of lack of snow.

After graduating from Los Alamos High School in 1999, I went to what was then Rick's College in Rexburg Idaho. I took college extremely seriously my first year to the point where I would leave at 7:00 in the morning and would stay on campus until the library would close most days. Becoming an engineer intimidated me at first and I felt like if I wasn't studying, I was falling behind. I did manage to have fun every once in a while and went snowboarding when I could. Towards the end of the year I ran into one of my Ridgecrest friends while playing Frisbee and he informed me of all the Ridgecrest, California kids attending Ricks that year. One of them was Emily Lundwall, who I had always remembered playing with as a small kid. I emailed her and asked if she remembered me and she did give me a simple reply, but nothing else came of it.

It was at Ricks College that first year that I received my LDS mission call to Minnesota Minneapolis Mission. My mission really helped me to grow as a person. I had an amazing mission president, Lonny Gleed, who inspired us to work hard and to love the people in Minnesota. I fell in love with the people there as well as the scenery. My first area was Duluth, where our apartment had an amazing view of Lake Superior. A few times we got to drive up the north shore to Thunder Bay and enjoy the amazing views. My first winter there was truly awful. I remember waking up Christmas morning to -40 degrees F standing temperature. Our car was dead and we attempted to make visits on foot but quickly gave up. Seeing the first blades of grass in the spring was truly exciting to me.

After my mission I returned to Rick's College, which had become BYU-Idaho while I was away. My first Sunday in my new ward I was surprised to see two good friends from Los Alamos there. Then a gorgeous young lady got up and introduced herself as Emily Lundwall and I about fell over. I quickly ran up and introduced myself and told her I remembered playing with her as young kids in Ridgecrest. She didn't quite share the same clear memories I had, but we started to hang out more and more. After a few snowboarding trips together, I knew it was to be. Emily is also an amazing piano player, which really impressed me while we were dating. We were engaged six months later and got married the next summer in the San Diego California LDS Temple on June 27, 2003. For my parents, it became somewhat of a reunion to be back in Ridgecrest, as our parents were already friends with so many of the people and my dad had previously been the bishop of the ward.

Emily and I attended BYU-Idaho one more year together and Emily graduated with a Bachelor's Degree in English. After that, we decided to transfer to Utah State University to allow me to finish my Mechanical Engineering Degree there. Just after moving there, Parker Wayne was born on November 28, 2004. My parents were kind enough to buy a townhouse 4-plex and let us manage them while I went to school. I learned a lot about fixing toilets and repairing drywall, which would come in very handy later. I made it through college working at Sign Pro as a sign maker and finally graduated in May 2007 with my Bachelor's Degree in Mechanical Engineering.

A couple weeks after graduating, Hannah Emily was born on May 24, 2007 in Logan, Utah. She was a beautiful baby, but Emily's pregnancy with her was anything but fun. We were relieved that the delivery was over, and then two weeks later we moved to Minden, Nevada to start my mechanical engineering career at GE Energy. We fell in love with the area and especially being so close to Lake Tahoe. A year after moving here we bought our first house in Carson City and have enjoyed being able to fix it up to our liking thanks to the skills learned at the townhouses in Logan. Since being here we have made a lot of close friends, and have had a lot of opportunities to serve in the community and our church. I have had the opportunity to serve as a scout leader and Emily teaches and plays piano for the choir.

Olivia Mary was born on June 22, 2010 and has added much to our family. We are excited to see where life leads us next.

Michelle Christensen

I was born on December 30, 1986 to Randall Wynn and Bette Ann Murdoch Christensen in Los Alamos, New Mexico. I was the sixth child and the second girl, with four brothers born between me and my older sister. Here is the birth order – Jennifer, Ryan Wade, Richard Warren, Reed William, Russell Wayne, and me, Michelle. Jennifer, my only sister, was 14 when I was born. Just when I knew what was going on in life, she went off to college.

I had a lot of fun memories growing up, most of them when I was in preschool with my friend Kelsi Painter. Our moms got us together a couple time a week and had a little pre-school where we learned the alphabet, made cool stuff, and went to Bandelier National Monument and played in the stream. I remember going to the dinosaur museum in Albuquerque and being terrified of the T-Rex there. My brother, Russell, kept teasing me about the dinosaurs coming alive and eating me. I was very mad at him that day. I also remember playing a lot with Dalan Rohrer down the street. We would ride our bikes, play outside a lot, and watch movies, with *Bambi* being our favorite.

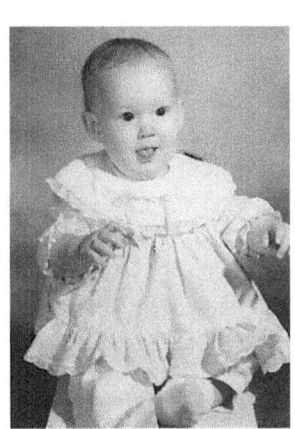
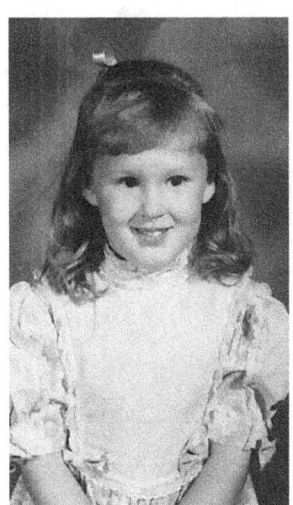

My most memorable birthday had to be when I got a new mixer toy that actually worked. I remember trying to mix cookie batter in it. It didn't work too well, so I gave up. I did like to help Mom make cookies with her big mixer and she let me sit on the counter. I also remember getting my new stuffed dog at Toys 'R' Us, and my mom asking me what I was going to name it on the way out of the store. I told her, "Fretchy, because when you throw a ball for a dog, they go and fretch it." I realized later that there was no 'r' in fetch. I still have that dog today though and it always reminds me of that day.

My baptism was either on my birthday, or the next day. My dad baptized me and I also remember making the bathroom floor really wet. Grandma Murdoch gave me new scriptures and a scripture bag with a pink cover. I also remember the white cake I got from Sister Peterson.

I always loved helping my brothers do their paper routes and I got really good at folding papers when I was about four or five years old. When I got old enough, I had my own paper route when Russell quit his. I also remember going to the orthodontist with my brothers for their appointments. The doctor was always checking my mouth to see when it would be time to start widening my mouth for braces later. That began in kindergarten and I eventually wore braces until I was a sophomore in high school.

When I was in first grade, my teacher was Mrs. Davis, who I thought was really mean. I was humming one time in class doing an art project and she yelled, "Who is making that noise?" and all the other kids pointed at me, then she said "Go write your name on the board." I didn't like her very much after that. My mother used to come in and help in her class and she asked Mrs. Davis why my name wasn't on any list. She told my mom that I was there and pointed to the name, Crystal, on the list. I was always mad that my parents didn't give me a middle name, so I made that one up and told my teacher to all me Crystal. My second grade teacher, Mrs. Fisher, was a really nice teacher and what I remember the most from that grade was doing all the plays and such.

Going to third grade was my favorite with Ms. Morrison. She wanted us to have a great year and we had music to memorized multiplication facts. My fourth, fifth and sixth grade years I don't remember too well, but I had Mrs. Parsons for my sixth grade year. That was the year I remember that all the teachers were trying to get us prepared for middle school. One of the things they told us was that cursive was going to be used a lot and scaring us that if we didn't know how, they would fail us. We got to middle school and I don't remember ever using cursive like they said I would.

When I was in fourth grade, I wanted to take violin lessons really bad and they offered it on Thursday mornings before school. I also took lessons from a lady in the ward. I played from fourth grade through ninth grade and finally decided I had had enough. School was getting harder and I didn't have the time or desire to practice anymore. I did learn a lot and was in the orchestra for each of the schools. During middle school, we went to several competitions and always took first place. Violin is not an easy instrument to play but I think it helped with my thinking abilities and learning music was a great experience.

When I was in 6th grade, I decided that the friends I had were not the best and needed to find new ones. My mother told me a story of someone she knew who didn't have any friends when she was a little girl, so she prayed. I decided that I would do that too. I started to pray for a friend and it took a while but one day I was walking on the playground and Whitney Burkett asked me if I wanted to play with her and her friends. It was the start of a great friendship and I went to Lake Powell with her family for three summers. We had a blast on the house boats they rented. Whitney was a great friend and a good example of how to be a friend.

High school seemed to go by fast. Freshman year was the year that 9/11 happened and I remember that day and where and with whom I was with.

I was in the library with my friends and someone came up to us and told us that a plane crashed in to one of the towers. We were watching the big screen TV in the library that morning and then the school was let out after first period, which was a computer typing class. The teacher was letting us listen to the radio the whole time. I remember not being able to concentrate very well. When I was a sophomore, a boy in our ward, Jacob Frogget, asked me out to Prom. He gave me a video and on it asked me in several different ways to go with him. It was really clever and I am sure unique. After that Prom, I was asked out on almost every dance. It was fun, but by my senior year, Prom didn't seem as fun anymore. I was getting tired of the pictures and standing around at the dance saying nothing to each other. Mom always made me some pretty amazing Prom dresses and I loved how unique and pretty they were.

I graduated in June of 2005 from Los Alamos High School and graduation was very memorable. It was a great feeling to be done with high school and Los Alamos. I went to Eastern Arizona College in Thatcher, Arizona for two years and got my Associates Degree in General Education. Life in Thatcher was great and it was a fun and great two years! I loved the small town (it was very small) and the small campus which is only three blocks long. I went to Hawaii during my last year for Spring Break with three other friends. We found a deal online for a round trip plus a hotel for four days for only $360.00! We saved a lot of money and we had a blast! We went on the Pearl Harbor tour, the Polynesian Cultural Center (where a friend got us in for a good price), toured the BYU-Hawaii campus, went snorkeling at a really cool place where the fish were so close to us it was amazing, and went swimming every day at the beach which was a block from the hotel.

After Arizona, I went up to Provo, Utah to work and to figure out what I wanted to go into as a profession. I decided to work for a year to get Utah residency and in-state tuition. I worked for Reem's Grocery Store for most of that year, until it closed. Being out of school for a year, I decided that I didn't like it. After a year of trying to decide where to go, I went down to St. George, Utah to look at Dixie State College. I saw that they had a really nice elementary teaching program and decided to take the chance. I called my mom and told her I was moving to St. George, and I already had an apartment. She asked if I knew anyone down there. I didn't but decided I needed to go there anyway. I have made some great friends and I love being in a warmer climate.

I am now down at St. George, Utah working my way through Dixie College for a teaching certificate. I love it here.

SHERRI HEATHER MURDOCH PORTER

My name is Sherri Heather Murdoch Porter. I was born February, 19, 1952 in Boise, Idaho at St. Luke's Hospital. Dr. Reynolds thought 10 month pregnancies were fine so my sisters and we all weighed over 9 lbs. I was named after my mother's twin sister, Sherri.

I was born to Robert Gail Murdoch, born in Salt Lake City, Utah, June 10, 1921, and Betty Lue Clark Murdoch, born in Los Angeles, California. September 28, 1922. I am the youngest of three girls. My sisters are Janice Murdoch, born April 22, 1947 and Bette Ann Murdoch Christensen, born October 17, 1949. They were also born in Boise.

I lived at 2308 N. 19th St. until I was about three years old, so I don't remember too much about the house. I did have my picture in the paper with another girl, Julie Taylor. We were licking the beaters after our Mom's made cakes to sell to raise money to cover the ditches that ran through our neighborhood.

When I was three, we moved to my Uncle Jack Murdoch and Aunt Ruth's old house at 1102 N. 17th St. It was right by Harrison Blvd., the most beautiful street in Boise. I remember the house being really big but going by now it wasn't so big after all, but very charming. The formal dining room had wallpaper and a crystal chandelier that when we had to clean it, we washed each crystal one at a time. There were three bedrooms upstairs and a basement.

My parents room had French doors with gathered sheer drapes, opening into the living room. This was the place my sister Janny, who was always very curious, snuck in to peek at my parents in the living room on Christmas Eve. She ran and woke up Bette Ann & me, and revealed the truth about Santa. Every Christmas after we opened our presents, we would get dressed up and go to Uncle Jack and Aunt Ruths house. She always made wonderful Scottish shortbread.

We had a great front porch where dolls and many a game of jacks were played. We had lots of dandelions in our lawn in the spring, and Dad would pay us one penny each to dig them up. If we didn't get the root, however, we didn't get paid for it. We also were assigned to rake leaves. We would rake them into "rooms" and play house.

We had lots of flowers and bushes that I can still remember. We would make dolls out of the Hollyhocks, and had Lily of the Valley, Syringa, and Lilac bushes. Janny and Bette Ann cornered me in the backyard flowerbed once and wouldn't let me leave until I ate a worm. I finally bit it in half, threw it at them, and ran away.

We had lots of friends in the neighborhood, and loved playing outside until after dark playing kick the can, no bears out tonight, hopscotch, jump rope, roller skate, jacks, marbles etc. One of my best friends was Carol Hansburger whose dad was the president of Boise Cascade. They lived in a very big house on Harrison Blvd. It was four stories with secret passages, a sunroom swimming pool, and a sit-down elevator. Her Mom was our Girl Scout Leader. They remodeled their attic for our meetings. We had a puppet show once and I put off making my paper-mache "Dragon" for so long that I ran out of time. I remember staying up really late one night to do it, crying with every strip of gooey newspaper I applied. It turned out great though. We also made up plays with commercials and had our families come.

Dad worked as a banker. Mom worked for the Department of Employment. My Grandmother, Sabina Alder, lived with us a lot and taught us how to knit, crochet, and sew. She would have our friends over for taffy pulls, and she made wonderful cinnamon rolls and chocolate éclairs.

One funny memory is when Bette Ann and I took swimming caps and sewed yarn on them to look like wigs. Mine was bright yellow yarn, (I always wanted to be a blond), and it was sewn down the center and then I took the yarn and braided it in two long braids. Bette Ann and I got on our bikes and rode around the block. I thought I looked like a gorgeous blond. I remember some guy whistling at me and I really thought I was hot and that I had fooled him. Now I laugh because he was probably making fun of me.

I had a horrible fear of shots. Back then shots were a lot more common to give when you were sick. We used to get shots for vaccines and they gave them in the gym at BJC (Boise Jr. College) now Boise State University, on Capital Blvd. Because I was so bad about going, Mom would trick me into going somewhere in the car, but when we got on that street I would start screaming because I knew where we were going and what was up. We used to get the polio vaccine on a sugar cube we would have to eat.

We walked to the stores in our neighborhood such as Hyde Park to get our shoes repaired and Joe Albertsons first store was on 17th and State. There was another store by it called, Bosco. I would save my money and go buy plastic dress-up shoes. We would also take a wagon through the neighborhood and collect pop bottles for the deposit money and by ice cream and candy. We went to the Capital Building once and signed our names on the registry as foreigners and started talking with an accent. I am sure we fooled everyone.

We went to church at the 2nd Ward in the Tabernacle, downtown, which has since been torn down. We had lots of "Gold and Green Balls", plays, and events there. I was baptized there. Dad was in the bishopric and was always concerned about members getting a ride to church. He bought a brand new pink Rambler station wagon, with a 3rd seat (turned backwards), so he could go pick everyone up and take them to church.

When I was five, I went to kindergarten at the neighbor's house, Mrs. McClannahan, in her basement. I went to Washington Grade School from 1st to 5th grade. We moved to 2708 Inverness Way on the Boise bench, during that summer after 5th grade, and I then went to Hillcrest Grade School for 6th grade, then South Jr. High, and Borah High my sophomore year. Then Dad needed to manage a branch of the Bank of Idaho, so we moved to Nampa my junior and senior years. I went to Rick's College, (now named BYU-Idaho), in Rexburg, Idaho, for two years, 1970 -1972. I then went to Brigham Young University in Provo, Utah for two more years, graduating in 1974, with my BA in Interior Design.

When I was at Rick's, I tore my cartilage in my knee and had to come home in the summer and have surgery. I ended up having three knee surgeries during my four years in college. It was very difficult getting around BYU in a full cast in the snow and on crutches. Everyone wanted me to stay out that semester but I was determined to continue, concerned I may not finish school and graduate. I am so glad I was able to graduate.

When I was home from BYU the summer of 1973, I was asked to organize a group of people from BYU to help "orient" the new students coming in the fall. I asked my friend Kay Ridgeway Hadley to help me invite people that were home for the summer to come. This is where I met David Porter. It was love at first sight. We dated and went back to school and were engaged in October. During Christmas break, I had my 3rd knee surgery. We were married April 18, 1974 in the Salt Lake Temple even though I was on crutches. Two months later, I graduated from BYU with at BA degree in Interior Design. We continued at BYU and Dave graduated with his Masters in Accounting.

We started our family:

Ami: February. 12, 1975, born in Houston, Texas while Dave was doing an internship with Exxon.

Chad: June 15, 1976, born in Provo, Utah while Dave was finishing school.

Mike: Oct. 9, 1977, born in Salt Lake City. We lived in Murray, Utah while Dave was working for the Internal Auditors office in the Capital Building.

In 1978 we moved to Boise, Idaho. Dave worked for the Internal Auditors office.

Heather: Nov. 29, 1979, born in Boise, Idaho. Dave started working for Joe Albertson as his personal accountant.

Kimberly: May 24, 1985, born in Boise, Idaho.

I worked as a free lance Interior Designer through our years of raising the children. My business' name is *S.P. Interiors*. It was the perfect profession for me so I could always schedule appointments around the school, sports, and church activities.

Dave worked for Mr. Albertson for 15 yrs., then for a developer at Columbia Village. This is when he started to love the building industry and we decided to start building houses. Our first house was for his Dad, Preston Porter. It was in Nampa, Idaho and was the nicest house on the block. We started building and loving it because I was doing what I love and he was enjoying the business aspect of it. We eventually built up the business and started building full time. Our son-in-law, Vaughn Pruett, eventually worked for us. Our business' name is *D&S Homes*. I have decorated a lot of model homes and Parade of Homes, but when we did our Parade Home in 2007, we took 1st in almost every category.

Ami enjoyed gymnastics, Girl Scouts, and played the flute in marching band at Meridian High School. She played in the Boise River Festival every year. She graduated from ITT Technical College, and also graduated from the church's Institute Program, where she also sang in the choir. Ami married Glen Butterfield and had two children - Alan, born 15 June 1998, and Elizabeth, born 24 August 2000. Ami and Glen later divorced.

Chad loved to play football, basketball, and baseball. When he was a junior in High School, he broke his femur in a football game. He had to have surgery with a rod hammered down into the bone. He has had many accidents in sports, on his dirt bike, (once was air flighted to the hospital) in cars, driving his semi truck , kayaking, and other adventures. He got his Eagle Scout award. He married Andrea (Andee) Garn who was born January 10, 1979 from Rexburg, Idaho in the Boise Idaho Temple on August 16, 2002. They both graduated from Boise State University in Accounting and Chad got a second degree in Computer Information Systems. They have four children: Maija, born 22 January 2004, Rocco, born 5 May 2005, GiGi, born 5 December 2006, and Bianca, born 4 June 2009.

Mike also played football, basketball, and baseball. Dave coached their teams throughout. Mike had a group of nine that ran around together. They were all great guys. He didn't just love school and would much rather be playing a sport than studying. He got his Eagle Scout award too. He went on a mission for the church to the Vancouver British Columbia Mission. He went to Ricks College and later went one semester of college at BYU-Hawaii, where he met his future wife, Amber Chase, who was born June 1, 1981. She is from Pocatello, Idaho. They married in the Boise Idaho Temple on December 20, 2002. Amber graduated from Idaho State University in Communications. They have two boys, Caiden, born 6 June 2006 and McKai, born 10 January 2008. Mike graduated with his Masters from the College of Idaho in Public Relations and is currently getting a second Masters in Theology from Lubbock Christian University in Texas. He is going to be an LDS Chaplin in the Army.

Heather was in 4-H and dance. She played softball with Dave as her coach. They won the 1st place trophy and those girls never stopped screaming. She also played, softball, basketball, and soccer in high school. She went to Ricks College and her first year majored in Interior Design, then later changed to Interpersonal Communication. She served a mission in the California Riverside Mission. When she returned, she married a high school friend, Vaughn Pruett, born August 3, 1980, in the Boise Idaho Temple on September 12, 2003. He also had just returned from his mission to Hawaii. They have three children; Brooklyn, born January 26, 2005, Jackson, born October 11, 2006 and Londyn, born June 25, 2009. Vaughn graduated from BSU, December 2008 in Business. He works for our business, *D&S Homes,* and on his own.

Kim was five years behind Heather and so she was dragged to all the games etc. She finally got a little tired of that. She played basketball in grade school and was really short but always made the baskets. She went out for track in middle school. In high school, she took up golf and got *Most Improved Player.* Kim loves to travel. Her junior year she went to Europe. She and I traveled to Washington D.C. and after high school, she worked at a resort in Cape Cod, Massachusetts. I picked her up and we went to New York City, Palmyra, and Niagara Falls. Dave and I took her to Hawaii to see Mike in November 2001. She attended some schooling at Boise State University. Kim is a very hard worker and is currently working at a jewelry store. She married Todd Allen on June 30, 2007 in the Boise Idaho Temple. Todd went on a mission to Brazil. He is a personal trainer and attends BSU majoring in Business.

I think our childrens' fondest memories were going to our cabin in Cascade, Idaho. We celebrated many a birthday there with family and friends and a few Christmases. Everyone enjoyed playing in the snow and at the lake. Chad and Mike and their friends would rig up the little bike with "noodles" and create a jump into the lake where the bike would float. They also played paintball in the woods. We would often go up for the 4th of July for family reunions, and watch the fireworks over the lake. The 4-wheelers were always used especially to go up to the Skeen Lake waterfall, and fly off "Michael Jordon" jump. Heather had many a wreck as she was a crazy driver. A lot of hunting trips, card games, and our favorite, *Pictionary*, were always played. A tradition for many years was to go up to the cabin for Thanksgiving. One year I asked Mom to bring the dressing, (she is famous for her dressing). When I had the turkey ready to stuff, I asked her for it, she got a funny look on her face, and pulled out a bottle of *Ranch Dressing*. So that year we didn't have any stuffing for the turkey. After we ate we would go out on snowmobiles or in the car, and cut down our Christmas tree in the woods. Often my nephew, Russell Christensen, would come and spend it with us. We loved the year he was into crocheting beanie hats. Everyone was obsessed with making them. Mike had a little bit of a tight grip on the hook because, his turned out the size of a "preemie" baby... and maybe not even that big.

One family trip took us to Disneyland in Anaheim, California. We flew the whole family down. Ami decided to conveniently get lost and ended up walking back to the hotel while the Disneyland staff and her family were looking for her. We went to the Oregon Coast one year and when Mike came home from his mission, we went up to Canada.

Dave and I have taken trips to Florida, Hawaii, Lake Powell, Sedona, Arizona, and cruises to the Caribbean. We went to Martin's Cove in October of 2008 and the surrounding areas, and felt the spirit of our pioneer ancestors. I must say, I do have a rich heritage and I am so thankful for these wonderful families, who left *my* family a proud legacy of strength and commitment - an example for which we are eternally grateful.

DAVID PRESTON PORTER

I am David Preston Porter born in Idaho Falls, Idaho on January 28, 1951. My father is Preston Peterson Porter, born May 10, 1918 in Preston, Idaho to Albert and Mary Porter. My mother is Dorothy Mae Parson Porter, born August 15, 1920 in Logan, Utah to Edgar A. and Anna D. Thompson Parson. My siblings are Larry Porter, born December 10, 1942, Deborah Porter, born December 11, 1950, and Ann Christine Porter, born March 10, 1954. We lived in Idaho Falls for three years and moved to Twin Falls for two years then moved to Boise. My father worked for the IRS for 30 years and in 1976 he retired.

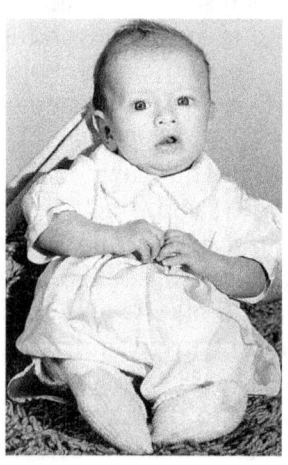

I went to Cole Elementary School, West Jr. High, and Capital High School, graduating in 1969. I was always involved in sports, namely basketball, football, and baseball. I played intramural soccer in college. In grade school, I loved to play marbles and could beat almost anyone. In 5th grade, I won the marbles championship and got my picture in the paper. I was very strong and could do many pull ups. In 6th grade, I was the Pull-ups Boise City Champion, and hold the record to this day, which was 29.

My dad's family is from Preston Idaho, and I loved going to the annual family reunions in Preston every year. My Uncle Ralph and Aunt Fawn Porter, lived on a farm and raised dairy cattle. It was fun to go there and ride horses and play. Later when I had my family, we would still go to the reunions and our family loved the farm experience. One year the boys brought salamanders home they had caught in some water. One escaped in the garage much to Sherri's panic... it was never found. Uncle Ralph's farm house was later in a movie that was very popular called *Napoleon Dynamite*.

Growing up in Boise, we lived at 7644 Cambridge Dr. I worked a paper route, and as a bag boy at Albertsons when I was young. I saved my money and in high school bought a silver, 1965 Mustang.

We went fishing a lot with Dad. We would go salmon fishing on the Middle Fork of the Salmon River and catch a bunch of fish. At night, we would hang them up in the trees so the bears couldn't get them. One night the bears came into camp and ate the tail end of several fish, going up as far as they could reach.

When I was a Boy Scout, we floated down the Middle Fork of the Salmon River on a high adventure with RW Christensen (Wynn's father) who was an FBI agent. We ran into a hermit in the mountains and talked to him and then came into camp and told everyone. Pretty soon, RW left and found the guy. The next thing we knew, he had radioed in a plane that arrived at a landing strip not far away. RW flew out and left us for the rest of the trip. In the next few days, the FBI flew back and captured this guy. He was wanted for some crime.

We grew up in the Church of Jesus Christ of Latter-day Saints, so I was always involved in the activities there. We went camping a lot, played church basketball, and did dance festival. After high school, I went to Boise State University for one year then from June 6, 1970 until June 6, 1972, I went on a mission for the church to the England Southwest Mission. My mission president was John M. Madsen, who is a General Authority now. It was very hard to eat the food in England and I was a very picky eater. I soon discovered I needed to eat or starve, so I ate the very greasy fish and chips dripping in oil and wrapped in newspaper, and other strange foods like blood pudding. I baptized a very interesting man, Brother Matthews. He was an artist and worked with oils. I had him paint my portrait and my companion's portrait. He had many oil paintings, and I brought several scenery paintings home to give to my family, along with my portrait. It was always very damp and cold there and our clothes and shoes were never dry. I had some choice experiences in England. I baptized several people in the ocean. I taught and baptized a Baptist preacher and his wife. We toured many old castles, etc.

After my mission I went to school at Brigham Young University in Provo, Utah. When I was home for the summer, I got a call from Sherri Murdoch to help with an orientation for new BYU students. We talked for over an hour and I was thinking she is fun but probably not cute. I agreed to help and first met Sherri at the orientation event. It was to be held at her friend Kay Ridgeway's house. Boy, was I wrong! I was in love with her at the first meeting, but didn't know it. I already had a date for that weekend, so I had my friend Barry Jenkins call her up and ask her out so we could double date. Sherri already had a date and couldn't go. I finally couldn't take it any longer, so I gave Barry two days to ask her out and then I would move in. We had many fun dates that summer like Julia Davis Park, Ann Morrison Park, running through the corn field, go-cart racing, etc.. I fell fast in love with this sweet, lovely, pure angel. We went back to school together and were engaged in November 1973. At Christmas break, she went home for another knee surgery, and much to the pleading by her parents not to go back that semester, went back in a full cast, (hip to ankle), on crutches in the snow at BYU. We were married in the Salt Lake Temple, Sherri still sporting crutches, on April 18, 1974.

Sherri graduated with her B.A. in Interior Design, June 1974. I was now in the Masters program in Accounting. I did my internship at Exxon in Houston, Texas. Our first child, Ami, was born there February 12, 1975. Sherri's mother came down to help out. We were only there four months and moved back to Provo. I graduated April 1976.

Our second child, Chad David, was born in Provo, June 15, 1976. The Provo Hospital maternity ward was very overcrowded and Sherri was in a "ward" of 11 women who had just had babies. The hospital was very strict would not let anyone but the husbands in to visit. My sister, Ann, was also attending BYU and decided to get in to visit.

She put on a very short white skirt, and a blouse and nurses hat that her roommate had and tried to find her way into the "ward". She looked so out of place because the other nurses' skirts were to their ankles and no one wore a hat. She acted like she knew the place and opened a door that turned out to be a closet, and pillows fell out. She then went out the emergency exit and went to another floor and tried to get in. She was locked out. She eventually found the room, but never did see Chad.

I graduated with my Masters Degree in Accounting in 1976. I went to work for the Utah Legislative Audit Department at the Capital Building in Salt Lake City. We first lived in North Salt Lake in an apartment. Within six months, we moved to our first home on 76th Street, in Murray, Utah. It was there that we had our third child, Michael, who was born in the Holy Cross Hospital on October 9, 1977.

We decided that we wanted to move back to Boise, so I started searching for a job in Boise. We sold our home and moved to Boise on 5103 Silver Spur in 1978. I started working for the Idaho Legislative Auditor's office. That is when we had our fourth child, Heather. She was born in Boise at St. Luke's Hospital on November 29, 1979.

I decided to find another job, because I did not enjoy the one I had.

I landed a job working directly for Mr. Joe Albertson, working with his personal estate. I stayed with him for 14 years when he finally passed away at the age of 88.

During that time, we had our fifth child, Kimberly. She was born on May 24, 1985. Having five years between her and Heather, she was always the "little sister" to the friends.

After working some accounting jobs, Sherri and I decided to see if we could build my Dad a home. We did and it turned out so great we decided to continue to build part time, later evolving into full time. We are a great team with my accounting background and Sherri's interior design. We have built a number of homes in the Boise area and entered houses in the Parade of Homes. We love the building industry and continue to build and do remodels.

My mother, Dorothy, passed away March 6, 1992. She had terrible arthritis and a number of medical ailments. In 1999 Dad married Mildred Whitaker.

Ami Porter McKay

My name is Ami Porter Butterfield McKay. I was born in Houston, Texas on February 12, 1975 in the Sharpstown Hospital. My parents are David Preston Porter and Sherri Heather Murdoch Porter. I am the oldest of two brothers, Chad and Mike, and two sisters, Heather and Kimberly. I weighed 5 lbs 13 oz. and was very tiny. My Mom described my legs as "chicken legs" because they were so little the plastic pants that covered the cloth diaper wasn't even close to doing the job it was intended to do. My Dad was in Houston on an internship for Exxon Mobile. He was to give a big presentation that day and wasn't very excited to call them to let them know the baby was coming. They lived there only four months. My grandmother, Betty Murdoch, came down to help out. We had a ton of roaches in our apartment and one night I was crying and my Mom turned on the light to get me up and a roach was crawling across my face. My Mom was obsessed with killing them and could not sleep after that.

We moved to Provo, Utah so my dad could finish school. We then moved to North Salt Lake, (Bountiful, Utah) for a year, then into our first house in Midvale, Utah. We lived there one year then moved to Boise. I liked growing up in the house at 5103 Silver Spur, Boise, Idaho. It was the best house ever! My favorite game I used to play as a kid was, There Are No Bears Out Tonight.

When I was eight, I crashed and burned on my bike. The only thing I remembered was breaking two teeth and my mouth looked like hamburger. I had seizures for two years after that. When I was 13, I went swimming at the old Warm Springs Swimming Pool in Idaho City. I did a cart wheel into the pool, slipped and smashed my face. I had to be taken to Boise in an ambulance to the hospital. The next day, I had to go to Driver's Ed. I was embarrassed because, I had a black eye. I had it for, three weeks.

Once I was pumping Kim on my bike, and Kim's leg accidentally got caught in the spokes. A neighbor, Ann Takasaki, cut the spoke to get Kim's leg out. I was so freaked out.

I started gymnastics, when I was eight years old and continued until I was 13 years old. Dad made me a balance beam and covered it with carpet and I used it in the backyard. I also loved the trampoline and could do flips on it. My favorite birthday was my 16th. We went (Mom and my friends) to the Holiday Inn and had pizza and spent the night and played and swam.

While attending Lake Hazel Middle School and Meridian High School, I played the flute in the band. I played in the River Festival and sang in the Institute Choir. I graduated from Institute and graduated from ITT Technical School.

I moved out of my parents' house at 22. I started to go to the student ward at the Church of Jesus Christ of Latter-day Saints. That is where I hung out with Glen Butterfield. I met Glen at a church dance.

Glen & I were married November 27, 1997. Our son, Alan Joseph, was born April 15, 1998, in Boise Idaho.

Our daughter, Elizabeth Ann, was born August, 24, 2000. Both were born in Boise, Idaho at St. Alphonsis Hospital. We divorced in 2004.

Alan is now 11years old and goes to Meridian Middle School. He went to Chief Joseph Elementary School and received Citizenship Award of the Year for two consecutive years. He is very good at science. He likes to play computer games and wrestling. He loves being in scouts.

Elizabeth is in 4th grade and goes to Chief Joseph Elementary School. She is a good reader and loves to help. She too has received Citizenship Award of the Year.

We love family trips to the cabin, Lagoon, Bear Lake, the Oregon Coast, and Disneyland. We have taken a couple of trips down to New Mexico to visit Uncle Wynn and Aunt Bette and their family.

I married Rob McKay. It lasted 9 months.

I got into an apartment at 180 E. James Court, Meridian, Idaho, on June 15, 2004. This is where we currently live.

I have medical issues where I am unable to stop tremors and shaking. It is similar to Parkinson's but has some different symptoms. It is getting worse. I am currently in a wheelchair and have trouble walking. The doctors do not know what it is and tell me it is very rare.

Chad David Porter

My name is Chad David Porter. I was born on June 15, 1976 at 3:43 A.M. at Provo Hospital in Provo, Utah. I weighed in at 7 lb. 2 oz. and was 20½ inches long. My parents are David Preston Porter and Sherri Heather Murdoch and I was their second child. I have one older sister, one younger brother and two younger sisters: Ami Porter McKay (2/12/75), Michael John Porter (10/9/77), Heather Porter Pruett (11/29/79), Kimberly Porter Allen (5/24/85).

My dad was born January 26, 1951 in Idaho Falls, Idaho. His father is Preston Peterson Porter (5/10/1918) and his mother is Dorothy Mae Parson (8/15/1920-3/6/1992). My mom was born February 19, 1952 in Boise, Idaho. Her father is Robert Gail Murdoch (6/10/1921-3/5/1998) and her mother is Betty Lue Clark Murdoch (9/28/1922).

I grew up in Boise, Idaho and went to Silver Sage Elementary School, Lake Hazel Junior High School, and Meridian High School. I graduated from high school in 1994. I then attended Ricks College, in Rexburg, Idaho, and graduated with my Associates Degree in Accounting in 1997. I attended Boise State University in Boise, Idaho. I graduated in December 2000 with a Bachelor of Business Administration in Accountancy. I continued on at Boise State University and in December 2001, I graduated with another Bachelor of Business Administration in Computer Information Systems.

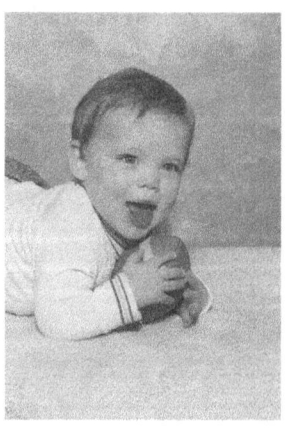

On June 30, 1984, I was baptized a member of the Church of Jesus Christ of Latter-day Saints and then confirmed July 1, 1984. I was endowed in the Salt Lake Temple on August 10, 2002.

I met my wife, Andrea Dee Garn (Andee), at the Boise State University LDS Institute. She was born on Wednesday, January 10, 1979 at 6:10 A.M. at Madison Memorial Hospital in Rexburg, Idaho. She weighed in at 8 lb. 12 oz. Her parents are Phillip W. Garn and Christina Helena Myntti Garn and she is their seventh and last child. Her dad was born December 6, 1940 in Rexburg, Idaho and died there on May 14, 2009 from Pulmonary Fibrosis. Her mother was born April 12, 1943 in Vasa, Finland. She has three older sisters and three older brothers: Kae Charisse (Kaesi) Garn Johansen, Derek Daniel Garn, Tricia Lynne Garn (1969-1974), Phillip Tyler Garn, Sharlie Jenae Garn Leslie, Cameron M Garn.

On Friday, August 16, 2002 we were married and sealed in the Boise Idaho Temple. We had our first child, Maija Christina Porter, on January 22, 2004. Rocco Chad Porter was our second child and he was born on May 5, 2005. Our third child, Gigi Sheree Porter, was born on December 5, 2006. Our fourth child, Bianca Gwen Porter, was born June 3, 2009.

After I graduated from college, in 2001, I worked as an accountant for Washington Group International in their tax department. The company was struggling at the time so they were not able keep me on full time. I went back to work for Apex Excavation, a company I had work for out of high school and off and on through college. I wanted to help Apex more as an accountant but since I knew how to run all the equipment, I would get stuck picking up the slack and running equipment and the crews. I enjoyed this because the work was outside and kept me active, but it also wears you out and beats up your body.

After four to five years of working for Apex, I was offered an opportunity to start a trucking company and haul landscape block for a company in Boise, Idaho. I was a little nervous about starting a business but my ultimate goal in life was to get an accounting degree, gain a strong business background, and then start my own business. I realized this was my chance. We finally found a bank to fund us and we bought a semi truck, flatbed trailer, and a forklift (18 wheeler). A few months after starting *Porter Hauling*, we were facing the problem of not being able to keep up with the work load. So we bought a second setup and hit the ground running. We had up to four trucks running at one time during our busy times. Once I was fully loaded (80,000 lbs.) and my brakes went out on a 6% grade going into Horseshoe Bend, Idaho which is a 25 mph town. I was very lucky to be alive and thankful to avoid any casualties as I blew through town going 95 mph. My brakes were smoking pretty bad but did not catch on fire. If traffic would have been busier it could have gotten ugly. I just prayed the whole way down and my legs were shaking like a wet dog. Someone was watching over me!

In 2009 we wanted to diversify a bit and play in the real estate market. We started a company called Whitewater Investments, LLC. During the down economy there are some unreal deals on real estate so I have been currently doing a real estate investment education to help my learning curve on how to take advantage of these deals. My Dad and I were able to work a deal together in 2009 and turned a pretty nice profit. This has me very excited for the future. We have had some challenges along the way but we have been very blessed and I think these business opportunities have changed our lives and made us better people. Andee and I recognize the Lord's hand in all things and the many blessings we receive by following his commandments.

Although I have a wonderful family and love being with them, I have been known to disappear some days and spend time in outdoors. Andee feels that over the years I have obtained too many recreational hobbies, but I can't resist. I love being in the outdoors. Below I will list a few of my passions and a quick story that relates.

Rafting: As far back as I can remember, my dad would take me rafting and fishing down the South Fork Boise River. When I was 12, my Dad wrapped the boat around a rock in the middle of *Devils Hole* rapid. I was so scared. The boat filled up with water and we were stuck bad. We all had to stand on the rock in the river while they tried to free the boat. When the boat came off the rock we were so full of water he could not guide the boat so we went over every rock and almost ripped/popped the boat. The river has nothing but canyon walls surrounding it and we would have been in trouble, but we came through in one piece and escaped the punishment of the river. I have my own raft now and love taking the family on little slow water adventures. I can't wait till they get a little older and I can introduce them to the craziness of whitewater.

Kayaking: I took a kayaking class at Boise State and was completely addicted. I was not married yet and spent three days a week on the river. I loved the adrenaline of being in a small vessel and having waves pound you in the face while trying to stay upright. I started out my first summer running smaller class two and three rapids on the middle fork of the Payette River. I wanted to progress to the big stuff, so I gained confidence and started running the south fork of the Payette River, which has class three and four rapids which are more technical and bigger runs. Midway through the summer, I felt I was ready to tackle the class five rapids on the north fork of the Payette River. I remember being super nervous because instantly I was pouring over into a class five rapid called *Hounds Tooth*. It instantly flipped me upside down so quick I didn't know what to think. I felt my helmet brush a rock (which I was lucky it wasn't my nose). I quickly rolled upright and was pretty shaky. I tried to stay composed because I had three more class five rapids to go plus all the constant rapids and holes in between. The rest went well and I continued to run the north fork of the Payette River for a few years till I had kids. Luckily, I have realized the importance of family and cut back on the high risk activities.

Dirtbiking: I started dirtbiking when I was about 10 years old with my dad and brother. It was all I could think about. We would go deer hunting up to the Danskin Mountains and ride dirt bikes. We crashed a lot trying to go where Dad wanted us to, but that taught us how to handle crazy situations. I flipped the four-wheeler (without a helmet on) once while speeding through deer camp and almost crunched my head, but I got lucky. Dad was a little mad at me for bending up the four-wheeler, oops. Another time up at the cabin, I rolled the four-wheeler onto my non-helmeted head and had to get stitches at the ER in Cascade, Idaho. I don't think I learned my lesson because in 2007, I had to get life flighted out of the St. Anthony sand dunes in Eastern Idaho. A bunch of buddies and I were on a ride at the dunes when I jumped off the tip of a dune wrong and lost my bike and flew 35 feet through the air and landed on my shoulder. It felt like I broke my back but luckily it was only a broken my collar bone, three ribs, and a minor punctured lung.

Deer Hunting: Ever since Rick's college in 1995 the tradition started. When the warm nights turn to cold nights and the leaves start changing colors, I can't sleep at night. This is when I go into rut and know that soon it will be time to go to deer camp and hang out with the boys, eat good food, tell stories around the camp fire, dirt bike, and chase big bucks. I love it.

Elk Hunting: In 1995, I came home from college for a weekend and snuck up to the cabin with my buddy, Barry Hill. It was the last day of the elk hunting season. We got up late and didn't get a good start, but our luck was good that Saturday. We walked right into a herd bull with six cows. I knelt down shot twice and the elk ran away. I asked Barry, "Why didn't you shoot?" He said, "I forgot to put a bullet in my gun". To make a long story short, I thought I missed until an hour later we found a single blood drop in the snow. We were pumped. We tracked this elk for three to four hours and then lost his trail on a logging road. I went off a hunch and followed a trail downhill. I remember looking down into a tree stand and seeing a massive 6 x 6 elk laying there. I gave a loud yelp to Barry and the fun began... packing it out. We left it overnight and our Dads came up to help us. We found a good way into the elk with four-wheelers and made for an easy pack out. It has been 15 years since I got lucky on that bull and still haven't shot a big bull like that one - and believe me I've tried.

Bird Hunting: Growing up, Dad would take me bird hunting with his friends. I remember getting a BB gun and thought I was big stuff. I also remember them saying that if a bird flies behind us, you'd better duck because we are shooting away. We had lots of fun memories with Dad and Boomer, our Brittany pointing dog. Now I have English Pointers and love taking them chukar hunting. Nothing like seeing a few dogs on point and rewarding him with a good shot on a bird.

Snowboarding/Wakeboarding: Before I got married, I thought it was fun to show off on the snowboard and wake-board. My buddies and I were always trying do the fancy tricks, spins, and flips. I was glad when I got married so I didn't feel pressure on having to show off for the females anymore. I quickly realized that if I pulled off a cool flip or trick, I would look to the boat and noticed Andee wasn't even looking. I remember some of the worst wrecks would come from boarding and my body would hurt for weeks. Now – no pressure.

Fly Fishing: This is where my passion is right now. Fly fishing is a lot easier on my body. My favorite thing is to be on the river with my raft and trying to convince fish to eat our flies. It may sound boring but something about it is very addicting and fun. Maija and Rocco have caught some fish and love it. I can't wait till the kids are older so we can be on the river together. Hopefully we can do some week long Salmon River adventures with the whole family. I can't wait!

Michael John Porter

I was born two days before October 11th, specifically, October 9, 1977 in Salt Lake City, Utah, to David Preston Porter and Sherri Murdoch Porter in the Holy Cross Hospital at 10:23 P.M. I thankfully cannot recall anything that happened that glorious day; however, I do look back on life now with thankfulness for the chance to come to earth and take on the challenging test of life. I am the third child with an older sister, Ami, older brother, Chad, and younger sisters, Heather and Kimberly. Yes, that makes me the middle child.

My childhood was that of fun and games all the time. However I was taught the value of being a good worker. I do not recall many times growing up that I was ever bored. I was privileged to have a wonderful big brother to run around with, as well as friends who made great decisions. One particular time, three of my friends and I were running around the neighborhood in search of something adventurous to do. We came across an outdoor party down by Silver Sage Elementary School. I had this brilliant idea to go get our rubberband sling shot that three people have to manage in order for it to launch 100 ft. or so. We decided to shoot rotten apples from off our neighbor's trees. We were thinking it was so much fun until one lady got hit by the apple and started saying words we had never heard before, and threatening to come chase us down. We left and played the safe side in that situation since they all were drinking at the party and we didn't know what they would do to us if they did catch us.

Other childhood memories include many cabin trips, fishing, rafting, camping, soccer, football, baseball, and basketball with Chad and Dad. Dad was often my coach with many creative strategies for having fun. We didn't always win, but Dad did a great job working with the guys. When I was about 10 years old, he ordered a fishing net from a fishing establishment in Oregon and when it came it smelled like rotten fish. Dad used that net to build a huge batting cage in our backyard. All the neighbors were wondering if we were getting exotic birds or something. Lots of hours were spent in the cage practicing with a pitching machine he bought. The teams loved it. He would always schedule one-on-one time for the boys that didn't have a Dad or didn't have support at home.

One Christmas, Mom and Dad bought a trampoline for the backyard. We used to spend hours jumping on it and quickly learned to do flips and other tricks. Once my Grandma Betty Murdoch and her sister, Sherri Jensen, came and were willing to get on the trampoline with us. We bounced around them, making them fall and they couldn't get up. We were all laughing so hard. They were good sports about it.

One year in the fall all my friends and a few Moms went to our cabin in Cascade, Idaho to play paintball in the woods. We protected ourselves with goggles, snowmobile outfits, hats, etc. and Mom took us up on West Mountain and let us off. We had teams and played paintball for hours.

That night we played *Truth or Dare* and we had to do some crazy things. It was a blast.

I remember being a frustrated child when it came to school. I did okay in school but thought it was boring and wanted to be outside playing sports. I got passing grades, mostly "C"s, in order to stay in sports. In middle school, I came home one day, and proudly announced to my Mom that I was ready to go on my mission now! I even thought I would much rather watch paint dry than stay in school. High school didn't excite me either. I wanted to drop out of school really bad in the 11th and 12th grades. I remember my good friends would not allow it and my good buddy, Jeff Hymas, would tutor me in math during our lunch hours my senior year so that I could pass and graduate. I graduated from Meridian High School in 1996. I look back now and wonder how I did it.

I wanted to serve a mission for the church and turned in all my papers. I received my call to serve in the British Columbia Vancouver Mission. It started out rough with a less-than-enthusiastic trainer who would do anything but missionary work while I read and studied the scriptures to pass the time. Eventually things turned around and my mission was a wonderful experience. I served my first area in Victoria, on beautiful Vancouver Island, and later was there again as a District Leader. Places I served were Victoria, Vancouver, Prince Rupert, Burnaby, and Vernon. In Victoria, I had a wonderful experience, and baptized Delvanir Cahavalu in the ocean. After returning home from my mission, our family drove up to visit my missionary areas and we went everywhere but Prince Rupert (which is half way to Alaska) and even visited the Bakers on Salt Island.

When I returned from my mission, I thought things would automatically fall into place for me, as far as what I wanted to do in my life. I thought college was out of the question because school was difficult and going to college was not for me. I got a job doing manual labor working alongside my brother, Chad. I really didn't like the job and realized that I needed to go to college if I wanted to have any type of future. I finally decided that anything would be better than working that job. I had the impression that I should apply to Rick's College in Rexburg, Idaho. I really questioned that because my ACT scores and high school grades were not great. Fortunately, the Lord followed through in my behalf and I was accepted. It was one of the greatest days of my life. I had direction and was happier than I had ever been before.

School was still a struggle but I was managing to pass my classes. Every birthday when I blew out my candles, I would wish that someday I could get all "A"s in all my classes for a semester. It was a very unlikely goal for me at the time. I thought about it all the time but didn't let it get me down because I was meeting and helping many people there that were just as needy as I was.

One particular experience was a kid who lived down the hall from me by the name of Mike, also known as Toothless Mike. He had been hit by a car and had a few brain problems, bad leg, and missed a few front teeth. He was a great kid, but because of his condition he could also flip at any moment and become the most violent kid as well. I remember becoming his friend and he would tell me how much in love he was with girls that who would say, "Hi" to him. One time a girl actually talked with Toothless Mike and he became madly and obsessively in love with her. He told me that he was making a knitted hat for her, a bracelet out of hemp, and a necklace. In my mind I was thinking, "Don't you think that is a little too much?" He tried and tried to find her to give her the things he made for her but she was afraid of him now and in hiding. I would talk with Toothless Mike trying hard to tell him to let her go, move on, but he could not. He would describe how beautiful she was, how her smile was that of pure joy and happiness, and her personality was truly the nicest he had ever known. I remember thinking I wanted to meet this girl myself. I had this image of her painted in my mind just by his description of her. I really wanted to meet her to say sorry for what Mike was putting her though, but I never did get to meet her at Rick's.

I had a feeling that I should go to BYU-Hawaii and did as I was prompted to do. At first I wondered why in the world I needed to be there. After a couple of weeks, I met a nice girl with a great personality and wonderful smile in a church prayer meeting. I had noticed her at a few events and we hit it off as friends quickly. Soon we got a little more serious, and one night we were talking on the beach about people we knew at Rick's College. The topic of Toothless Mike came up. It dawned on me that she was the girl Toothless Mike was talking about! I also realized that Toothless Mike was not far off with his description of her. She did have the nicest personality I had ever known, beauty beyond anything I had known, and her smile was as penetrating as any joy or happiness I had felt. This was THE girl and I was starting to fall in love with her. Now I knew why Toothless Mike was so obsessed with her - the girl that we had talked about for so many hours. This was her! The girl I always wanted to meet. The rest is history, as they say. I married Amber Chase, the love of my life, in the Boise Idaho Temple of the Church of Jesus Christ Of Latter-day Saints on December 20, 2002. We are so blessed.

Amber grew up in Pocatello, Idaho. She is the youngest of 7 children. Her parents are Carol Lynn Browning and Richard Whitaker Chase. They owned the Pocatello Greenhouse where Amber worked all through her growing up years, driving a skid-steer at work and coming home to feed their llamas on the farm. She graduated from Highland High School in

1999 and graduated from Idaho State University in May 2004 with a Bachelor's Degree in Speech Communications. She was then an academic recruiter for ISU, traveling around recruiting from community colleges and high schools. She was also an academic counselor advising ISU students. Amber did this until the best part of our lives changed things - KIDS!

Our oldest son, Caiden Michael Porter, was born on Thursday, June 7, 2006. We adopted Caiden four days after he was born on the June 11, and were sealed six months later in the Idaho Falls Temple on December 16, 2006. This date is so special because this is the day we all became an eternal family. This temple is special because it is where we had our answer to adopt and fell in love with Caiden's spirit before we even met him.

Amber then gave birth to our beautiful, chubby baby boy, McKai Chase Porter, on January 10, 2008. We feel so blessed to have Kai and feel it is a miracle that we have two of the cutest kids ever. Caiden and Kai are the best of buddies. We hope to have more children to bless our lives and to bring us happiness and entertainment!

US Army Chaplain Graduation December 2010 at Ft. Jackson, South Carolina

Back to my schooling, I never liked it. I did finish with a Master's in Human Resources Training and Development from Idaho State University, mainly to say that I could do it. My last semester in college, about seven years after I set my goal, I received straight "A"s in all my classes!

However, Human Resources and Training Development was just okay to me. My real interest is in the program I am in now to which I can say that I do love. I am working on a Master's of Divinity from Lubbock Christian University. Currently I am a LDS Chaplain Candidate for the Military. Once I finish school, the hope is to become a full-time Chaplain for the Army National Guard.

I pretty much hated school growing up and thought I would be a high school dropout. But, I have been in college now from 1999-2010. The Lord truly makes our weaknesses become strengths if we will put forth the faith, time and effort.

Heather Porter Pruett

I was born on November 29, 1979 in Boise, Idaho at the St. Lukes Hospital. It was a glorious day! I remember it well! My parents are David Preston Porter, born January 28, 1951 and Sherri Heather Murdoch Porter, born February 19, 1952. We had a wonderful childhood filled with playing, wrestling, singing, fighting, laughing, and crying. Life wouldn't be normal without all of those things in a family of seven.

I often think of how grateful I am that I was able to be born into a home where the gospel was known, practiced, and embraced. I am so grateful for parents who taught me the gospel. Where would I be without it? They truly are my heroes, and I look up to both of them immensely. I love them so much.

I am the fourth of five children born to my parents. Ami, born February 12, 1975 is the oldest and was four years old when I came to this earth. Chad David, born June 15, 1976 was the second child and was three years old when I was born. Then comes Michael John, born October 9, 1977 and he was two years old. I was the next child born and then six years later,

Kimberly was born on March 24, 1985. So every year for four years my *wonder-woman* mother had a child. How she did it, I don't know. My dad was 28 years old and my mom was 27 when I was born. This is amazing to me because right now I am almost 28 and only have two kids. I can only imagine four and having them one per year! Yet another reason I look up to my parents, especially my mom.

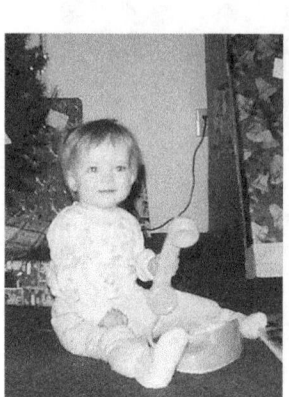 

In September of 1978, Mom & Dad bought the home in which I would spend my growing up years. (5103 Silver Spur off of S.Cole road and Snohomish in Boise Idaho). That very November they brought me home from the hospital to live there. I then lived in that house all the way until I went off to Ricks College after high school, when I was home for the summers, and after my mission. Mom & Dad ended up living there for 28 years, after which they built themselves a home in Eagle, Idaho. Lots of memories were had in that house I called home.

Right down the street from our home, was Silver Sage Elementary School. All five of my brothers and sisters attended that elementary school; not to mention that all of us went to the same Lake Hazel Middle School and Meridian High School as well. I have to say that it was a trick following in my big sister's and big brother's footsteps. Their reputations were hard to match, especially Chad's! I was often asked if I was Chad Porter's little sister by the teachers. I was reluctant to answer that question and often pleaded the fifth!

I was baptized on December 5, 1987 by my father David Preston Porter and confirmed the next day in church. Some things that I remember about my baptism were:

I was baptized the same day as my friend, Brianne Lowry.

I thought it was so silly I was in a dress in the water.

I got my first set of nice scriptures from my grandparents and we went to eat pie afterwards.

The next day at the confirmation, I remember my mom telling me that I should imagine during my confirmation that the Holy Ghost was descending upon me like a dove.

I remember a distinct image in my mind as the confirmation was taking place that a dove came out of the heavens and rested upon me.

I was really overcome with the Spirit from the confirmation.

I wanted to bear my testimony so badly but was afraid I would cry from my strong emotions.

I went up on the stand and came back down after sitting on the bench for a while. I decided I couldn't do it.

It was always an exciting privilege to get to spend the night at Grandma Murdoch's and Grandpa Bob's houses. I remember that we had to take turns going and we were more than thrilled when it was our turn. With Grandma Betty Murdoch, we would always go on walks and I remember watching the news at night with her. At Grandpa Bob's house, I remember getting ginger ale, English muffins, and him showing us his quarter collection, which he later gave to me for some reason! My brothers and sisters were so jealous, so I shared with them. He always had tons of golf balls around and it was definitely a guy's house with duck and golf décor (thanks to my mom!).

A few of the jobs I have had over the years are: paper route, Mervyn's, Snoshack (Carrie's, Sherri's, Tawna's), Meridian Water, Ricks College Academic Office (Max Checketts, Jim Gee, Bergstrum, Wylene Jensen, Barbara Sharp.), substituting school, and at the Bank of America Center as an event planning.

After graduating from Meridian High School, I attended Rick's College for two and a half years, graduating with an associate's degree in Interpersonal Communications. In October 21, 2000, I received my endowments in the Boise Idaho Temple. Shortly after that on January 3, 2001, I was set apart as a full-time missionary for the Church of Jesus Christ of Latter-day Saints and served a mission in the California Riverside Mission. I served in Corona, Palm Springs, Palm Desert, and Riverside under the direction of President Edward Heyes.

I came home from my mission and began working at Joey's Only and substituting in school to pay my way through college at Boise State University. I was very active in my student ward and loved being social. Vaughn Pruett, a friend from high school who had gotten home from his mission around the time I did, asked me to go to a returned missionary class with him. We soon started dating after that and fell fast in love. He swept me off of my feet with his amazing charm and smile. He was so incredible and everything that I had hoped and prayed for in a spouse. We were married and sealed together in the Boise Idaho Temple on September 12, 2003. Vaughn and I were both 23 years old.

A year and a half later Vaughn and I completed building our first home, a lot of which he built. I graduated from BSU earning my Bachelors of Communications, and was nine months pregnant. Soon after, we gladly welcomed our first child into our lives.

Brooklyn Heather Pruett was born January 26, 2005 in Boise, Idaho at St. Lukes Hospital. Twenty and one half months later, our second child, Jackson Vaughn Pruett, was born in the same hospital on October 11, 2006. And our third child, Londyn Mae Pruett, graced our home this past summer on June 25, 2009. She was also born at St. Lukes and all three children were delivered by our amazing Doctor, Timothy West.

Kimberly Porter Allen

My Name is Kimberly Porter Allen. When I was young everybody wanted to call me Kimber and I hated that name. I think that is why my mom picked that name hoping I would go by Kimber, but it didn't stick with me. I just go by Kim. If I were going to be a boy my name would have been Matt.

I was born May 24, 1985 in Boise, Idaho. I went to Silver Sage Elementary, Lake Hazel Middle School, and Meridian High School. I graduated from high school in 2003 and then attended Boise State University.

Growing up I played the piano, until my teacher made me sing my notes as I played. I'm a terrible singer! I played the flute through middle school and I loved it. I even learned the *Titanic* theme song.

In high school I played soccer and golf. For my graduation present I went skydiving. We're talking lots of butterflies, people!

I met Todd Allen at the LDS Institute at Boise State University. We were at a dance and I was dressed as an 80's diva and Todd was dressed as a 70's hippie. After exchanging phone numbers, we became inseparable. Todd was born in Boise, Idaho on February 6, 1984 at St. Luke's Hospital. He is the youngest of eight children, most of which were born in Boise, Idaho Falls, Rexburg and Provo. Todd and I were sealed in the Boise Temple on June 30, 2007. Our reception was held at my parents' house in Eagle Idaho. Todd is currently attending Boise State University and majoring in finance and works at The Fitness Company as a personal trainer.

I am a workaholic. My first job was when I was 15 years old at my cousin's Sno Shack. I was a hostess at Red Robin and Chili's through high school. I was a waitress at a few different restaurants after that. In 2006, I moved to Massachusetts to work at a resort for the summer. I was a bookkeeper for two years for a construction company. I currently have three jobs. I work full time at Jared the Galleria of Jewelry, bookkeeping for my brother Chad Porter, and I am a Scentsy consultant.

We recently bought a house and are loving being new homeowners. Life is busy but we are loving it.

Chapter 14

LaVonne Bonnie Murdoch and John Granville Leonard, Jr.

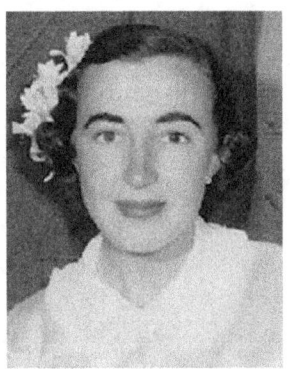

Bonnie was born in Salt Lake City, Utah, to William and Jeannette Murdoch, on August 13, 1923. She was the youngest of nine children in a prominent Mormon family. Her father was very involved in Utah state politics. He served in the House of Representatives, was Acting Mayor of Salt Lake City, City Commissioner of Finance, and was to be the Democratic Party's nominee for the U.S. Senate when he died suddenly of pneumonia. All the children worked in the well-known Murdoch Grocery Store that provided home delivered gourmet food items to the wealthy as well as to the destitute members of the community.

Bonnie attended public schools in Salt Lake City and in 1946 received her Bachelor's Degree in Sociology from the University of Utah. She was an active life member of the Chi Omega Sorority. During her high school and university years, she had the burden of caring for her mother, who suffered from dementia.

During World War II, she enlisted in the WACs (Women's Army Corps) on September 6, 1944 and was trained at Fort Des Moines, Iowa. She was a recruiter, wrote and narrated radio shows, handled publicity, and managed recruitment offices in the Western States. Her scrapbook is filled with scores of newspaper clippings documenting her WAC activities. She attained the rank of Sergeant and was honorably discharged on June 23, 1946.

Bonnie's professional life brought her to San Francisco where she was a runway model and Assistant Blouse Factory Manager for I. Magnin & Co., Publicity Director for the San Francisco Chamber of Commerce, and Publicity Associate and Personal Assistant to the Vice President of Marketing for PC&E. She also took language and philosophy post-graduate classes at the University of California and completed a two-year course in advertising at Golden Gate University. During this time, she was active with the California Children's Home Society, American Association of University Women, and was the Publicity Chairman for the San Francisco Mental Health Society.

While living at the San Francisco Resident's Club, Bonnie was reintroduced to her future husband, John Granville Leonard, Jr. (born in Ogden, Utah, August 20, 1921). Bonnie and John had known each other at the University of Utah in 1940-1943, but never dated. John was starting his lifelong career as a salesman for American Can Company and lived in a "bachelor's pad" with his best friend. Bonnie and John's first date was March 31, 1950. Their whirlwind romance culminated in marriage on September 19, 1950 in Salt Lake City. They lived in a Pacific Heights apartment where their children John III ("Hap") (John Granville Leonard III, b. April 6, 1952, San Francisco, California), and Penny (Patricia Ann Leonard, b. September 13, 1953, San Francisco, California) were born. Bonnie continued to do maternity modeling work for I. Magnin & Co. during her pregnancies. The family eventually moved across the Golden Gate Bridge to homes in San Rafael and Fairfax in Marin County.

1948

On April 6, 1958, the family moved to Chappaqua, New York where John was promoted to Assistant Manager of Sales Analysis and Research for American Can on Park Avenue in New York City. In August 1958, daughter Jane was born (Bonnie Jane Leonard, b. August 10, 1958, Mt. Kisco, New York). The pressures of a grueling daily commute and overwhelming work schedule took a toll on John, who requested a transfer back to California. The family lived for 18 months in Ogden, Utah, where

John's mother, Grace Davis Leonard (b. 1883, Indiana) lived, before a new sales position was available in the San Francisco office. John became responsible for two of the company's largest sales accounts, Standard Oil Company and Clorox. John was instrumental in designing and manufacturing the first plastic Clorox bottle, which revolutionized the containment industry.

The family purchased a new home in Walnut Creek, California where Bonnie, a homemaker, was an avid tennis player and lap swimmer, dedicated to her "mile a day" workout at Heather Farms, rain or shine. She was also involved with the J.S. Bach Festival Association, East Bay Chi Omega Alumni, and the Relief Society of the Church of Jesus Christ of Latter Day Saints.

Her beloved John died of a sudden heart attack on Thanksgiving Day, November 22, 1973 in San Francisco. Thereafter, Bonnie embarked on an intense educational program to prepare for a new career. She completed a rigorous Medical Secretarial Course in June 1975, where she learned medical stenography and office management. Subsequently, in 1976, she worked in a radiologist's office and soon after managed the offices for three orthopedic surgeons. She was also a volunteer Candy Striper for three years at John Muir Hospital in Walnut Creek.

In June 1978, Bonnie completed a two-year course via the Life Underwriter's Training Council. She sold life insurance, became a member of the National Women's Leaders Round Table, and was an active member of the Walnut Creek Chamber of Commerce Publications and Insurance Committees.

In 1979, Bonnie decided to "retire" and moved to Tucson, Arizona to be near her sister, Jean. She purchased a new condo and for the next few years she relaxed under the Arizona sun. Throughout her entire life, Bonnie was a dedicated "sun worshipper" – so Tucson seemed to be "the promised land." However, in 1983, she missed her friends in Walnut Creek, moved back to a townhouse in Pleasanton, California, and started to commute to Walnut Creek to visit her friends.

In 1984, Bonnie began to show the early signs of dementia, so her children relocated her to an apartment in Walnut Creek, within walking distance of her old neighborhood. She continued to enjoy reading, music, needlework, swimming, and bridge. As her condition slowly worsened, Bonnie lived in a series of board and care homes in Alamo and Walnut Creek, where her children could visit her on a regular basis. Bonnie's last residence was at Manor Care in Walnut Creek. She was a very popular resident because she was always smiling and laughing – forever friendly and pleasant, until she passed away at the age of 77 on the evening of May 30, 2001. Her children, John, Penny, and Jane were at her side.

Bonnie, Jennifer and Penny

Back: Bonnie and Beth. Front: Jean, Mary and Jeannette.

A private graveside service for the immediate family was held at Oakmont Memorial Park in Lafayette, California on June 2, 2001 where her husband John also rests.

Bonnie's radiant smile and sunny disposition will be missed by all who have known and loved her.

John Granville Leonard Jr.

John was born on August 21, 1921 in Ogden, Utah. His father John Granville Leonard was born March 26th, 1881 in Shelly County, Indiana and died on November 8th, 1940 in Ft. Knox, Kentucky. His mother, Grace M. Davis, was born on December 14, 1883 in Crawfordsville, Indiana and died in December 1974 in Ogden, Utah. John and Grace were married on September 27, 1905 in Indiana.

Starting at age 13, John Sr. started to work at the Boston Dry Goods Company in Indianapolis (April, 1893 - Oct. 1894). Eventually, he became a salesperson for American Can Company from 1915-1940 and spent the majority of his career in Ogden, Utah. He received a gold Hamilton Watch from his co-workers the day he retired. He passed away later that year in Kentucky.

John Jr. was the youngest of five children: 1) *Geraldine Marion Leonard* was born on October 20, 1909 in Indianapolis, Indiana and died 1987(?) in San Mateo, California. She was married to General George Coolidge – a graduate of West Point and a liaison between the Joint Chiefs and the White House during WWII and later was the US Army commander of Heidelberg, Germany. 2) *Erma May Leonard* was born in Newcastle, Pennsylvania on April 20, 1914 and died in Ogden on September 7, 1927 of disease. 3) *Ruth Ellen Leonard* was born in Ogden on May 9, 1916 and died in Ogden in the late 1960s. 4) *Mary Elizabeth Leonard* was born in Ogden on October 22, 1919 and died on March 4, 1932 of disease.

John attended Ogden High School before graduating from the University of Utah with a B.S. Degree in Business in 1942. He was active in the Beta Theta Pi Fraternity. Upon graduation, he enlisted in the US Army and attended Officer's Candidate School and received additional training in the Artillery at Fort Benning in Georgia. On the eve of being sent to fight the Japanese in the South Pacific, he was involved in a training accident that changed the course of his life. While acting as an official observer of an infantry training exercise, a rifle grenade exploded within a few feet of him. Although most of the men around him died, John survived but was seriously injured by shrapnel that perforated his intestines. He spent the next year in the hospital undergoing intense penicillin treatments to stem the infections. It was a terrible injury that left huge scars on his abdomen, yet he was lucky that he missed his deployment to the war zone since his entire battalion was slaughtered by the Japanese. He was eventually reassigned to *The Presidio* in San Francisco where he was a First Lieutenant involved in defense of Fort Point near the base of the Golden Gate Bridge.

After the war, he followed his father's footsteps and went to work for American Can Company. He started in the sales office in San Francisco and was reintroduced to Bonnie Murdoch, whom he had known but never dated at the University of Utah. They were married on September 20, 1950 in Salt Lake City at the home of Wendell and Jeannette Romney (Bonnie's sister). Her older brother, Lennox, gave her away. John and Bonnie continued their careers in San Francisco while living on Webster Street, between Nob Hill and the Marina. Subsequently, John III and Penny were born and the family relocated to San Rafael and eventually Fairfax.

On April 6, 1958 the family moved to New York where John became Assistant Manager of Sales Analysis and Research for American Can at their corporate offices on Park Avenue in New York City. The family moved into a new home in Chappaqua, New York. They lived there for almost five years. Their third child, Bonnie Jane, was born on August 20, 1958. Sometime in 1962, the family relocated to Ogden, Utah for a period of 18 months where John managed the local sales department. In the spring of 1963, the family moved back to the San Francisco Bay Area. John worked in the sales department office south of Market Street where he was responsible for managing some of the company's largest accounts, Standard Oil and Clorox.

John suffered a massive heart attack in front of the St. Francis Hotel in downtown San Francisco on Union Square in the early afternoon of November 20, 1973. He passed away two days later on Thanksgiving Day at San Francisco General Hospital.

John will always be remembered for his incredible work ethic, sense of humor, and ability to play the piano by ear.

JOHN GRANVILLE LEONARD III

John was born on April 6, 1952 in San Francisco, California. He was the first child of John Granville Leonard II and Bonnie Murdoch.

John's father was a salesperson for American Can Company and Bonnie was a homemaker.

On John's sixth birthday, the Leonard family (including his sister Penny who was born on September 13, 1953) moved from Fairfax in Marin County, California to Chappaqua, New York.

John attended Roaring Brook Elementary School until half way through the fifth grade when the family relocated to Ogden, Utah for a period of 18 months, where he attended Wasatch Elementary School. Just prior to the end of sixth grade, the family moved to Walnut Creek, California. Although John had graduated sixth grade in Utah, he attended Walnut Acres Elementary School for the final six weeks in order to make new friends. He attended Oak Grove Middle School in Concord for the seventh grade and was in the first graduating class of Foothill Intermediate School. Subsequently, he attended Ygnacio Valley High School in Concord, California. He was a varsity swimmer specializing in butterfly and long distance freestyle, elected Student Body Vice President and President of the Student Senate, and was involved in numerous extra curricular activities. Subsequently, he attended Willamette University in Salem Oregon, the oldest university west of the Mississippi, from 1970-1973, where he studied English, was elected Student Body President, was on the Varsity Swimming and Tennis Teams, was active in the Big Brothers program, and was an Honor Roll student. He transferred to University of California at Berkeley in 1974 and eventually graduated from University of California at Santa Barbara with a BA in Film Studies in 1977 and was on the Dean's List. During his time at UCSB, he fell in love with Jennifer Beth Sutin (born December 2, 1957 in Albuquerque, New Mexico). After seven years of dating, they were married on September 1, 1985 in Oakland, California in a garden ceremony at their home.

From 1978-1987, John worked in the advertising business in San Francisco where he became a partner and creative director for Taylor Spencer Granville whose clients included Lucasfilm, CBS Radio (San Francisco 49ers, Golden State Warriors), San Francisco Ballet and Opera, Meyer Corp., Marriott Hotels, and numerous retailers and radio stations. In 1987, he started his own marketing consulting firm called *The Granville Group*, which represents many San Francisco radio stations, Raiders, San Francisco Giants, Web Communications Group, a casino, and does pro bono work for various organizations including LEGS (Innovative, Low Cost Prosthetic Limb Technology for the Developing World via LeTourneau University in Longview, Texas).

From 1979, after she graduated Phi Beta Kappa from UCSB in Art History and Anthropology, Jennifer worked in art galleries in San Francisco, managed an art poster store in the Embarcadero Center, and then pursued a sales career in the watch industry, working in various sales and management roles at Gucci Timepieces, Montblanc and Ebel. In 2007, she went to work for Time Concepts and is currently the brand manager for Body Glove Time.

In 1987, John and Jennifer moved from the Oakland Hills to Alamo, California where they lived in three different residences until 2005 when they relocated to Grass Valley, California in the Sierra foothills.

Their first son, Benjamin Granville Leonard, was born on August 17, 1987 in Oakland, California. He grew up in Alamo, California graduating from Monte Vista High School in 2005. He graduated from Chico State University in December 2009, with a degree in Economics and now works in the mortgage banking industry. His interests include music, playing guitar, art projects, nutrition, and working out. Their second son, Zachary John Leonard, was born on October 11, 1990 in Oakland, CA. In 2009, he graduated as a Valedictorian from Nevada Union High School in Grass Valley. Zak was co-captain of the high school golf team and played in many Northern California Golf Association and First Tee tournaments. He is currently enrolled in the Orfalea School of Business at Cal Poly in San Luis Obispo, California.

PATRICIA ANN LEONARD (PENNY)

Penny (née Patricia Ann) was born in San Francisco, California to Bonnie Murdoch Leonard and John Granville Leonard, Jr., on September 13, 1953. When the family lived in New York, Penny attended elementary school at Roaring Brook School in Chappaqua, New York.

When the family moved to Ogden, Utah for a brief time in 1962, Penny attended Wasatch Elementary School. When the family moved to Walnut Creek in 1964, Penny attended Walnut Acres Elementary School, Foothill Intermediate School, and graduated from Ygnacio Valley High School in 1971. Penny was active in drama and school activities, and was voted as Homecoming Princess and Best Personality at YVHS. She was also elected President of the Senate at YVHS. She took piano lessons for six years from Doris Marliave in Walnut Creek.

Penny attended Utah State University in Logan, and graduated in 1975 with a Bachelor's Degree in English Literature. Upon returning home to the Bay Area, she began her career at Bank of America and then began selling memberships at Crow Canyon Country Club in San Ramon, California. At that time, she was married to Gregory James Goggin of Walnut Creek. They were divorced in 1989 without children.

Penny extended her sparkling personality, interpersonal skills, and management expertise to successively more significant roles within the Club Corp organization, and traveled extensively, both internationally and domestically. She developed and taught management-training programs and has made numerous presentations at industry conferences, workshops, and retreats. She was responsible for membership sales and marketing for hundreds of city, athletic, and country clubs for Club Corp. Penny retired from Club Corp in 2008 as Senior Vice President of Sales.

Penny's love of people, her eagerness to help those in need, and her compassionate spirit have endeared her to all those with whom she has worked, and all those whose lives she has touched, both personally and professionally. Her nephew and nieces especially appreciate Penny's perspectives on matters of education, career development, and life in general. Penny applies her father's wonderful sense of humor, her mother's gracious spirit, and the Murdoch fortitude to all that she sets out to accomplish.

BONNIE JANE LEONARD

Jane was born in Mt. Kisco, New York, to Bonnie Murdoch Leonard and John Granville Leonard, Jr., on August 10, 1958. She was the youngest of three children, with older siblings, Penny and John.

Jane attended kindergarten in 1963 at Wasatch Elementary School in Ogden, Utah, where the family lived for a short time.

When the family moved to Walnut Creek, California, Jane attended Walnut Acres Elementary School, Foothill Intermediate School, Ygnacio Valley High School (1973-1974) and was in the first graduating class of the newly built Northgate High School (1975 and 1976). Jane took piano lessons from Doris Marliave in Walnut Creek from age six through high school, and continued to apply her classical musical talents in college and later, playing the piano, conducting choirs and singing in church.

In 1976, Jane began studies in Psychology and Sociology at University of California Los Angeles (UCLA), where she also became a legacy member of the Chi Omega Sorority, Gamma Beta Chapter, in 1976. Jane was active in leadership roles over the next four years in Chi Omega, as the Song Chairman, Vice President and Rush Chairman. She received her Bachelor's Degree in Psychology from UCLA in 1982.

In 1981, Jane met Frederick Henry Keeve (b. August 29, 1954, San Francisco, California) and they were married on September 26, 1981 in Santa Monica, California.

Their first child, Alexander Leonard Keeve, was born naturally on April 9, 1982 in Santa Monica, California – a healthy, 9 lb. 2 oz. Their second child, Natalie Jane Keeve, was born on August 26, 1983 naturally at home in Sylmar, California – also a healthy 9 lbs. 2 oz. Soon thereafter, the family moved to Redding, California, where their third child, Anna Teresa Keeve, was born on October 2, 1985 – again, a healthy 9 lbs. 10 oz. baby, born naturally at home in Redding. After Fred obtained his Master's Degree in Business Administration, they decided to move to the east coast, where, after a time of rambling and exploring with the three children under the age of 4, they landed in Boston where Fred worked for the Jewish Community Center as the Performing Arts Director for a time. The family stayed in Charlestown, Massachusetts with loving and considerate family members, Fred's Aunt Sandra Jacobs (sister of mother Mary Ann) and her husband, Bill. During the cold winter months, Jane would bundle up the children and bring them across the street to the Charlestown Library, where they participated daily in the activities offered there. The children had no exposure to television until years later, growing up on reading, writing, crafts, and creative play during their developmental years.

Longing for the warmth of California, Fred and Jane brought the family back to Santa Monica in 1987 and laid down their Southern California roots once again. The family continued to move frequently, renting houses in Santa Monica, Pacific Palisades, and West Los Angeles. For a number of years, Jane worked as a Publications Supervisor for Omniplan Corporation in Santa Monica, handling government contracts and RFP submissions for local redevelopment projects. She then worked for Barry T. Hirsch, Ph.D., a Forensic Psychologist for close to eight years as a Case Administrator and Office Manager. Fred worked as a teacher and counselor with the Los Angeles Unified School District during these years.

In April 1992 during the upheaval of the infamous Los Angeles riots, Fred and Jane were able to purchase their first home in Culver City, California (4120 Jasmine Avenue) and the children finally had a sense of foundation and roots, attending the local elementary school, middle school, and high school. During that time, fourth child, Lillian Grace Keeve ("Lilli"), was born naturally and quickly in Santa Monica, California on July 4, 1996, with Lilli's godmother, actress and humanitarian, Lindsay Wagner, at Jane's side.

After years of unresolved discord, Fred and Jane separated in 1999 and an amicable divorce was finalized in October 2002. Jane continued to work in various administrative and organizational capacities, including at

LEFT: *Natalie, Jane, and Anna* RIGHT: *Lilli, Natalie and Anna. Christmas 2006*

Moonlite Limousine Company in West Los Angeles, where she met her "Handsome Hungarian," Nick (Miklos) Kottek (b. September 18, 1957), to whom she is engaged to be married. Nick was raised as an only child in a Budapest family (mother, Elvira Tauber Kottek; father, Miklos Kottek), raised in Socialist Hungary, and defected to the United States in 1983 prior to the dissolution of the iron curtain.

Jane was hired by the City of Culver City in March 2002, filling a temporary position for the Fire Department for a limited time, and was

Jane and Nick, 2008

transferred to the Transportation Department as a Management Analyst in July 2002, where she continues to build her career in Transit and Fleet Management, Air Quality Programs and Alternative Fuel Projects, securing $1.5 million in grants for alternative fuel vehicle purchases for the city. She has held the leadership role of President of the Culver City Management Group, which is the bargaining unit for all of the City's management positions, for two consecutive terms, and she continues to serve on the CCMG Board.

In addition to working full-time and raising the children, Jane was, and continues to be, in active leadership with Westside Unity Church in Culver City since 1992, serving on the Board of Trustees as President, Secretary and Member-at-large, and as the Youth Education Coordinator and Choir Director. She has also served in various school-based organizations, fostering fund raisers and special events to help the schools her children attended.

Jane loves to garden and entertain, and enjoys serving in leadership roles to influence positive change in the communities in which she lives. She loves and is very proud of her children, Alex, Natalie, Anna, and Lilli, whose biographies are also included in this book.

FREDERICK HENRY KEEVE FAMILY LINEAGE:

Father: Raymond Henry Keeve, born June 24, 1923, New York City, New York

(remarried to Deborah Greenberg Hordiner Keeve in 1985 – Ray & Deborah currently live in San Francisco, California)

Raymond's Father: Frank Lupu (name changed to Keeve upon entering the U.S.) (b. Romania; d. San Francisco, California)

Raymond's Mother: Lillian Zietler Keeve (b. February 4, 1901, New York, New York; d. San Francisco)

Mother Mary Ann Jacobs, born August 20, 1931, Springfield, Massachusetts

(remarried to Ron Webster in 1984 – Mary Ann and Ron currently live in Culver City, California)

Mary Ann's Father: Carl Jacobs (b. 1907; d. 1967)

Mary Ann's Mother: Lois Spengler Jacobs (b. Nov. 9 1908, Duluth, Minnesota; d. age 87)

Alexander Leonard Keeve

Alexander Leonard Keeve was born on April 9, 1982 in Santa Monica, California. He attended Culver High School, leaving early to attend Santa Monica College at the age of 17.

Alex then enlisted in the United States Marine Corps in the summer of 2000. He completed Boot Camp at MCRD (Marine Corps Recruit Depot) in January 2001 and was stationed at Camp Pendleton with Alpha Company, 1st Battalion, 4th Marines, 1st Marine Division. Shortly after 9/11, Alex was deployed to the Persian Gulf with Marine Expeditionary Unit (MEU 13) in support of Operation Enduring Freedom. In 2003, he was deployed to Iraq, on the "Road to Baghdad," and functioned as a Team Leader for his unit with Regimental Combat Team 1 during the early stages of Operation Iraqi Freedom. Alex turned 21 on April 9, 2003, the historic day that Baghdad fell, marking the official end of the offensive phase of combat in Iraq. In late 2003, Alex returned to Pendleton and served the rest of his time in active service playing a vital role in training Marine units in tactical urban combat - SASO (Stability and Support Operations). Alex was Honorably Discharged from active duty in August 2004 as a Sergeant.

His interests and activities in civilian life include mentoring in human development and community building, such as working with at-risk youth and families to expand their awareness of self-empowerment. His educational interests are geared toward alternative economic models of community development and environmental economics. With lessons with Louis Kabok, Alex has become an excellent string bass player. He also enjoys working in the outdoors on trails with his grandparents, Mary Ann and Ron Webster.

Alex in uniform

Alex with his grandmother upon his receipt of his scholarship.

Natalie Jane Keeve

Natalie Jane Keeve was born on August 26, 1983 at home in Sylmar, California. Natalie attended Culver City schools and graduated from Culver High School early to attend Santa Monica College at the age of 16. While she attended school to get college credits, Natalie worked full-time at pet stores and in various animal welfare capacities for the SPCA Los Angeles, the Bureau of Humane Law Enforcement, and Farm Sanctuary. Natalie has always been a rescuer of abandoned animals, once saving a kitten from a Los Angeles freeway and then raising $900 to cover the kitten's surgery. She has rescued numerous other endangered and abandoned animals, including an iguana. She continues her active volunteer involvement in animal protection non-profit organizations. After moving to Rocklin, California in 2006, Natalie attended Chapman University and will have earned her Bachelor's Degree in Organization Leadership in the spring of 2010.

Natalie currently works in sales and event coordination in Granite Bay, California.

Natalie married Nicholas Eugene Olsen (born November 9, 1981 in Hayward, California) on June 6, 2008 in Newcastle, Placer County, California.

Nick is a specialty welder, working on many large commercial and industrial developments in Northern California. Natalie and Nick currently live in Rocklin, California. Their first daughter, Clara Jane Olsen, was born on June 18, 2009 in Roseville, California. Clara smiles and chatters a lot, and is a very healthy, happy baby.

Clara Jane November 2009

NICHOLAS EUGENE OLSEN FAMILY LINEAGE::
Father: Richard Michael Olsen, born December 26, 1957, Oakland, Alameda County, California
Mother, Kim Marie Dorpinghaus, born June 7, 1958, Oakland, Alameda County, California
Kim's Mother: Marcia Kaye Dirks, born October 11, 1938, Iowa.

Anna Teresa Keeve

Anna Teresa Keeve was born on October 2, 1985 in Redding, California, in a home-based birthing center. She attended Culver City schools and graduated from Culver High School in 2004. She was active in drama productions in middle school, holding the lead roles in various musicals, and was a leading player on the Culver City High School Girls' Water Polo Team.

Anna attended Cal State University Northridge for one year, then obtained additional undergrad units at Santa Monica College, transferring to San Diego State University, from which she graduated in May 2008 with a Bachelor's Degree in Kinesiology – Fitness & Nutrition. Anna's interests include all outdoor activities, roller blading, and surfing. When she took her first steps at the age of 10 months old in the sands of the Massachusetts shore, we knew she'd be a beach girl from then on!

Anna, Alex, Natalie and Nick. May 2009

Anna is actively involved in the community, organizing philanthropic events, and participating in various charitable organizations. She currently works at a private city club in San Diego in membership development.

Lillian Grace Keeve

LEFT: *Anna, Natalie, and Lilli* RIGHT: *Lilli and John Snow*

Lillian Grace Keeve was born on July 4, 1996 in Santa Monica, California. Lilli attended Linwood E. Howe Elementary in Culver City, and is currently in the 8th grade at Culver Middle School. Lilli's interests include photography, film, writing, listening to music, and playing the piano. Lilli is an excellent poet, and has written lyrics to songs that she composes as well.

Conclusion

Compiling and writing this book has certainly been an adventure. For over four years, I have transcribed journals, researched, gathered and transcribed histories, gathered and worked on wonderful photos to make them book-ready (many old ones miraculously found), learned new programs that were completely foreign to me, talked to cousins I haven't seen or heard from for years, received inspiration for what came next, and enjoyed the ride. I would like to thank all the cousins, their spouses, and their children for the time they took to write their histories and share their photos. I apologize for any errors you might find, but please know that I have proofed this book three times. Sometimes, things just slip by. You need to know that we have wonderful and caring ancestors who obviously wanted this book written. Their companionship these past four-plus years has been obvious to me as they prodded me along in compiling their histories. Prayer is a powerful tool that has enabled me to be the instrument to put this book together. I pray that you may enjoy it as you learn more about your ancestors and your Murdoch cousins.

www.ingramcontent.com/pod-product-compliance
Lightning Source LLC
Chambersburg PA
CBHW082031230426
43670CB00016B/2629